WINGS

ALSO BY TOM D. CROUCH

The Bishop's Boys
A Dream of Wings

WINGS

A HISTORY OF AVIATION
FROM KITES TO THE SPACE AGE

TOM D. CROUCH

Smithsonian National Air and Space Museum, Washington, D.C.
in association with
W. W. Norton & Company
NEW YORK • LONDON

For information about permission to reproduce selections from this book, write to
Permissions, W. W. Norton & Company, Inc., 500 Fifth Avenue, New York, NY 10110

Manufacturing by The Haddon Craftsmen, Inc.
Book design by Brooke Koven
Production manager: Anna Oler

Library of Congress Cataloging-in-Publication Data

Crouch, Tom D.
Wings : a history of aviation from kites to the space age / Tom D. Crouch.—— 1st ed.
p. cm.
Includes bibliographical references and index.
ISBN 0-393-05767-4 (hardcover)
1. Aeronautics—History. I. Title.
TL515.C76 2003
629.13'009—dc22

2003016110

W. W. Norton & Company, Inc.
500 Fifth Avenue, New York, N.Y. 10110
www.wwnorton.com

W. W. Norton & Company Ltd.
Castle House, 75/76 Wells Street, London W1T 3QT

1 2 3 4 5 6 7 8 9 0

CONTENTS

ACKNOWLEDGMENTS

Thirty years in the making, this book reflects what I have learned from the work of a great many predecessors and colleagues. Not all of my debts to these people are adequately acknowledged in the notes and bibliography. Special appreciation for their assistance and insight over the years goes to John Anderson, Janet Bednarek, Roger Bilstein, R. Cargill Hall, Dik Daso, R. E. G. Davies, Deborah Douglas, C. H. Gibbs-Smith, Michael Gorn, Richard Hallion, Jim Hansen, Peter Jakab, Lee Kennett, Richard Kohn, Nick Komons, Roger Launius, William Leary, W. David Lewis, Marvin W. McFarland, John Morrow, Dom Pisano, Alex Roland, Richard K. Smith, Bill Trimble, Robert van der Linden, and Rick Young. I am particularly grateful to Howard Wolko, a world-class engineer and a friend of many years who has always had time to share his incredible command of the history of flight technology with those wise enough to ask.

My thanks to colleagues who took the time to read and comment on sections of the book: John Anderson, Roger Bilstein, Dorothy Cochrane, Martin Collins, Dik Daso, Von Hardesty, Jeremy Kinney, Roger Launius, Michael Neufeld, and Robert van der Linden. The book is far better for their comments. Much of what is right in the pages that follow I owe to friends and colleagues. The deficiencies are mine alone.

Like all scholars, I owe much to the librarians and archivists who have assisted me over the years. Leonard Bruno, of the Manuscript Division, Library of Congress, provided the material with which I open this book. I thank him and Dawne Dewey, of the Archives and

Special Collections Division, Wright State University, for their many years of friendship and assistance above and beyond the call of duty.

My debt to the members of the archives staff of the National Air and Space Museum is beyond reckoning: Dana Bell, Marilyn Graskowiak, Dan Hagedorn, Kate Igoe, Allan Janus, Kristine Kaske, Melissa Keiser, Brian Nicklas, Paul Silbermann, Tom Soapes, Mark Taylor, Barbara Wheitbrecht, Patti Williams, and Larry Wilson. The staff of the NASM Library has put up with me for three decades, for which I am extremely grateful: Bill Baxter, Elaine Cline, Phil Edwards, Carol Heard, Paul McCutcheon, Mary Pavlovich, Mimi Scharf, Kitty Scott, and Leah Smith.

I have been fortunate to make my professional home in the Smithsonian Institution's National Air and Space Museum, where I have worked with the finest set of colleagues any scholar could wish. For their friendship and support over the years, my most sincere thanks to Dorothy Cochrane, Roger Conner, Dik Daso, Ron Davies, Tom Dietz, Von Hardesty, Jeremy Kinney, Russ Lee, Suzanne Lewis, Rick Leyes, Joanne London, Don Lopez, Robert Mikesh, Chris Moore, Claudia Oakes, Alex Spencer, Jay Spencer, Robert van der Linden, Collette Williams, Tim Woodridge, Fritz Baetz, Jo Ann Bailey, Paul Ceruzzi, Martin Collins, Jim David, David DeVorkin, Gregg Herken, Roger Launius, Cathleen Lewis, Valerie Neal, Allan Needell, Michael Neufeld, Toni Thomas, Frank Winter, and Amanda Young.

Melissa Keiser went above and beyond the call of duty in selecting the photographs for this book. As always, her unerring eye chose illustrations that would illuminate and extend the text. Patricia Graboske negotiated the contract for this book. Special thanks to Dominick Pisano and Ted Maxwell, my immediate supervisors during the course of work on this book, for their encouragement and support.

Ed Barber of Norton has been my editor and friend for a quarter of a century. My debt to him has grown over the years and has never been greater than for this book. Thanks also to Norton's Deirdre O'Dwyer, who was always there to answer questions and put my mind at ease.

As always, my greatest appreciation is to my family, who have paid a considerable price for making a life with a husband and father obsessed with the past. This book is for Nancy, Christopher, Bruce,

Abigail, and Nathan—and for the newcomers, Emma, Alex, and John. Finally, all thanks to my mother and father. My dad spent his career in the Propulsion Laboratory at Wright-Patterson Air Force Base. Several years ago an engineer whom I had never met called me out of the blue to ask if I knew that my father is a national treasure. I don't need anyone to tell me that.

Tom D. Crouch
Fairfax, Virginia
November 17, 2002

WINGS

PROLOGUE:

"WELL NED, IT'S WONDERFUL"

Gutzon Borglum (1867–1941) had trouble falling asleep on the evening of September 10, 1908. After a late supper with friends, he returned to his room in high spirits, "as if charged with champagne from the excitement of the afternoon." He sat down at 11:35 P.M. to write a long letter to a friend. "Well, Hell's popping," he began, "the gasoline motor is in the air, and man with outspread sheets is astride of it." He assured his friend that this was neither a hoax nor an experiment. "Man has put, safely and forever, his shod heel into the blue heavens, and glides about as on ice." He had seen the wonder for himself.[1]

Borglum was the first son in a family of Mormon polygamists who had emigrated from Denmark to the wilds of Idaho. Decades before he accepted the challenge of carving Mt. Rushmore, he had begun to establish his reputation as a talented artist with a broad range of enthusiasms. "A man," he once remarked, "should do everything."[2] Following his own advice, he studied art in Paris, served as an official of the New York Boxing Commission, was active in the work of the American Numismatic Society and the Architectural League, and was currently serving as president of the American Association of Sculptors and Painters. It was his membership in the Aero Club of America, however, that drew him to Washington, D.C., on this occasion.

The newspapers that summer had been filled with aeronautical news. Glenn Hammond Curtiss had won the *Scientific American* Trophy on July 4, 1908, for a one-kilometer straight-line flight of his airplane *June Bug* at Hammondsport, New York. Just two days later, U.S. Army officials announced the establishment of the Signal Corps Aeronautical Board to supervise testing of the "dirigibles, balloons and airplanes" for which the government had issued contracts over the preceding months.

During the last week in July, Thomas Scott Baldwin and the now-famous Glenn Curtiss arrived at Fort Myer, Virginia, just across the Potomac from the nation's capital. They were soon chugging over the rooftops of Arlington, perched on the open framework of their hydrogen-filled airship, preparing for the official speed and endurance trials that would lead to the selection of their machine as the first powered aircraft to enter the U.S. Army arsenal.

During the second week in August, before the airship trials began, Washington newspapers reported on Wilbur Wright, the elder of the two mysterious brothers who claimed to have perfected a practical, heavier-than-air flying machine during the years 1903–1905. Wilbur made his first public flight at the Hunaudières racetrack, near Le Mans, France, on August 8. Flying tight, banked turns around the field, he proved beyond any doubt that the Wrights had achieved a mastery of the air far beyond any of their rivals.

"I have seen him! I have seen them! Yes!" enthused a reporter for the French newspaper *Le Figaro*. "I have today seen Wilbur Wright and his great white bird, the beautiful mechanical bird. . . . There is no doubt. Wilbur and Orville Wright have well and truly flown."[3] As the London *Times* noted, Wilbur's performance was proof that all of the Wrights' claims were true, and earned them "conclusively, the first place in the history of flying machines."[4]

Orville Wright arrived at Fort Myer with another airplane on August 20. While his brother was making international headlines in France, Orville would satisfy the terms of a contract for the sale of an airplane to the U.S. Army. He made his first flight on September 3, one and a half circles over the long narrow parade ground followed by a hard landing, which damaged the machine. He was back in the air for two more short flights on September 4 and 7. Growing accustomed to the machine and to the very tight quarters of the parade ground, he remained in the air for over ten minutes on September 8.

"The whole town is up in the air," Augustus Post, secretary of the Aero Club of America, assured a friend on the morning of September 9. "All the big guns are going to boom this afternoon and the great American Eagle is going to spread its wings." On his first flight of the day, Orville Wright flew fifty-two laps over the field in fifty-seven minutes and thirty seconds, shattering the world's record established by his brother in France just four days earlier. He immediately returned to the air and broke his new record, remaining aloft for sixty-two minutes, fifteen seconds.[5]

His third flight of the day also marked his first public flight with a passenger, Lt. Frank Lahm. "It was getting dark," Augustus Post remembered, "and the moon was rising over the trees of Arlington Cemetery, but it was quite still and the air was calm." The pair remained in the air for six minutes and twenty-four seconds, establishing a new world mark for duration of flight with a passenger. "All burst into loud hurrahs and waved their hats and caps and shouted in exaltation," Post concluded, "on account of the success of Orville Wright and the supremacy of American Genius."[6]

Gutzon Borglum boarded a traction car in Georgetown at 3:30 P.M. on September 10. He was accompanied by two influential friends, Augustus Post and Maj. George Owen Squier, the assistant chief signal officer of the army, who would command the nation's first aerial unit. The trio transferred to a car at the far side of the bridge that took them to Fort Myer. They walked through the historic front gate and out onto a parade ground that, until a few days ago, had been best known as the showcase for the U.S. cavalry. Strolling the length of the field, Borglum was "keyed to the breaking point in anticipation of . . . my first impression of this aircraft that had for years been the labor and the secret of two simple men from Ohio."

Arriving at the "aviary," a "simple barn like affair, built of flooring," the artist was puzzled and a bit disappointed by his first glimpse of an airplane. "I had conceived nothing like it," he explained. "There is nothing that met the layman's idea of a flying machine." It looked as if it had been "put together as casually as a boy would do it and could be duplicated for less than a thousand dollars."

The machine consisted of a "most unlikely, spiderlike frame, with twin cotton covered horizontal frames, one above the other, about six feet apart." The propellers resembled nothing more than "shaped fence boards stained green." Borglum remarked that if you were to find this thing abandoned in a field, there would be "nothing . . . [to] suggest . . . what it might do or that it was built for anything in particular."

With perhaps eight hundred spectators looking on, Orville Wright, whom Borglum described as "a light waited [*sic*] and not an overkeen looking man," orchestrated the troopers maneuvering the airplane out of the hangar and positioning it on the launch rail. "The wind from the propellers drove the hats from the spectators heads," Borglum reported. Then a sixteen-hundred-pound weight was released from the top of a derrick, catapulting airplane and pilot into the air. The plane skimmed above the ground for one hundred yards before rising into a tightly banked turn to the left and sweeping back down the field over the heads of the spectators. Borglum's doubts vanished at the first sight of the machine in the air. "He could fly as he wished," the artist admitted, and "move as he willed."

"The crowd stood open mouthed," he noted, "with murmurs of wonder and an occasional toot from [an] automobile horn; then as he passed over us everybody let go in an uproar of shouting and handclapping. The miracle had happened!" Around and around he flew, never passing out of sight. People around Borglum wondered why Orville did not fly "'to New York . . . to Philadelphia . . . Why fly continuously around?'" They were "mad . . . to see 'stunts,' " Borglum remarked. "Nothing seemed impossible."

Orville Wright flew fifty-nine circles around the field, breaking his own record once again with a flight of one hour, five minutes, and fifty-two seconds. "He flew 67 minutes in a 16 mile wind," Borglum reported, "handled his pair of planes like a chauffeur, and rode the air as deliberately as if he were passing over a solid macadam road. Nothing I have ever seen is comparable in action to this gliding bird. . . . There is no action of the wings, so you do not think of birds. It has life, power, . . . selects its course, [and] holds its position, so that it is unlike and unre-

The old army and the new

lated to the gas bag. It is so simple it annoys one. It is inconceivable, yet having seen it, it now seems the most natural thing in the air. One is amazed that human kind has not built it before."

Orville Wright landed at dusk, coming down "in long sweeps, settling rapidly, then turning upward and down again, on he slid over the tops of the woods, then stopping so gently—more gently than does the bird." The curious "rushed for Wright," Borglum reported, "the boisterous shouted and tooted their horns; officers [and] scientists drew together in groups. We had seen the most wonderful demonstration of heavier-than-air flight ever made. We had seen a simple little pair of planes driven against the air, rise to a height of sixty feet; a machine, weighing in all about nine hundred pounds, heavy as a horse, glide away, directed at will for an hour."

"The crowd broke," he continued, "everyone raced for the machine." Borglum paid special attention to the reaction of individuals in the crowd. He watched as one "quaint old lady, who had been left in a small buggy . . . whipped up her horse, drove straight to the aeronaut and begged for a shake of his hand." Then there was the old couple who watched the flight, then turned for home. "'Well,' said the old man, 'I'm ready to go now,' and his old mate drew nearer to him, smiled, and they disappeared into the night."

A reporter described a man in the crowd at Fort Myer who watched Orville fly and then wandered away into the crowd muttering, "My God! My God!"[7] It was a common reaction to the first sight of an airplane in the sky. Wilbur Wright noticed the "intensity of enjoyment" and "sense of exhilaration" on the faces of those who came to see him fly. "Never have I seen such a look of wonder in the face of the multitude," noted a Chicago commentator describing the crowd at an early airplane exhibition. "From the gray-haired man to the child, everyone seemed to feel that it was a new day."[8]

It was indeed a new day. And what did the future hold for a world in which humans had taken to the skies on wings of their own design? The inventors of the airplane were careful to restrain their enthusiasm. "No airship will ever fly from New York to Paris," Wilbur Wright would remark to an Illinois reporter in 1909. "That seems to me to be impossible." No engine, he explained, "can run at the requisite speed for four days without stopping." Nor did he hold out any great hope for improved carrying capacity. "The airship will always be a special messenger," he predicted, "never a load-carrier." His brother Orville agreed, explaining to a Dayton reporter that he did not "believe that the airplane will ever take the place of trains or steamships for the carrying of passengers."[9]

Some of the official observers at Fort Myer took a similarly conservative view of the military potential of the invention. "I can't see that these aeroplanes are going to be especially practical just yet," Secretary of War Luke E. Wright (no relation to the famous brothers) commented to the press. "They are remarkable in that they represent the actual conquest of the air, but until they are further developed, I do not think they will be of much service from a military standpoint."[10]

There were other points of view as well. In a novel published that year, *The War in the Air, Particularly How Mr. Bert Smallways Faired*

While It Lasted, Herbert G. Wells offered a much darker vision of an air age in which German aerial vessels would attack New York, spreading terror through indiscriminate bombing. "With the flying machine," Wells suggested, "war alters its character; . . . neither side remains immune from the gravest injuries; and while there is a vast increase in the destructiveness of war, there is also an increased indecisiveness."[11]

Still others preferred to look farther in the future and to take a more hopeful view. Borglum, for example, predicted that the airplane would "wipe out the borders of the world." The Wright brothers were even more optimistic. "When my brother and I built the first man-carrying flying machine," Orville commented in 1917, "we thought that we were introducing into the world an invention which would make further wars practically impossible."[12]

It was a dream that would not die. In 1945, at the end of a war in which the nations of the world had done their best to destroy one another from the sky, a professional educator hired by American Airlines unveiled an "air age globe." The surface of the globe was covered by a series of apparently random dots connected by lines. The message was clear. The air routes linking the cities of the world would become more important than national borders.

The flying machine would not wipe out international boundaries, and it certainly would not make war any less thinkable. Just two years after Charles Lindbergh flew from New York to Paris, Orville Wright admitted that "no one could have foreseen, and I myself never expected, the tremendous development of aviation at the present time."[13] Indeed, the airplane would profoundly shape the history of the twentieth century, and be shaped by it, in ways that those who saw Orville Wright fly at Fort Myer could scarcely have imagined.

WHEN CITIZENS OF the distant future look back on the twentieth century, they will surely remember it as the time when humans took to the sky. Images of flight already dominate our memory of the century past. In the fall of 1999, *USA Today* and the Newseum, a museum in Arlington, Virginia, devoted to the history of news gathering, announced the results of a year-long poll in which thirty-six thousand newspaper readers, and a substantial number of journalists, were asked to select the top one hundred news stories of the century. The atomic bombing of Japan led the public list, followed by the attack on Pearl Harbor, the landing on the Moon, and the invention of the airplane. The journalists chose precisely the same top four stories, although they thought the Moon landing more important than the attack on Pearl Harbor.

Was flight really so important in a century marked by war and revolution, hope and despair, and the rise and fall of nations, ideologies, and empires? Certainly the results of the poll did not surprise the professional historians who were consulted by the newspaper. Douglas Brinkley of the University of New Orleans commented that Hiroshima was the "correct choice" for the top story. Arthur M. Schlesinger Jr. countered that the moon walk is what people will remember in five hundred years. My personal response was to call attention to the fact that the first three events could not have occurred without the fourth.[14]

How are we to understand the impact of flight on the twentieth century, or the impact of the century on the history of flight? We can begin with a great truth. "Technology," historian Melvin Kranzberg explains, "is neither good nor bad; nor is it neutral."[15] The direct effects of aviation on society are easy enough to catalogue, but the deeper consequences of technological change are difficult to anticipate, frequently contradictory or ambiguous, and almost always impossible to evaluate outside a specific point of view.

Flight has affected us in some obvious ways. The frail contraption of wood, wire, and fabric flown at Fort Myer evolved into the definitive weapon of the century, a machine that redefined the way in which we fight our wars, and radically altered our traditional notions of what constitutes a battlefield and who qualifies as a combatant. While New York escaped attack from the sky, at least in the twentieth century, Shanghai, Coventry, London, Hamburg, Dresden, Tokyo, Hiroshima, and a hundred other places were far less fortunate. H. G. Wells's prophetic vision of war in the air proved much closer to the mark than that of the inventor of the airplane.

The airplane opened the distant corners of the globe to commerce, transformed common folk into globe-girdling air travelers, and created new industries catering to the needs of business travelers and tourists. Flight brought people together and made it possible for exotic viruses to spread with frightening rapidity. It facilitated commerce and encouraged the homogenization of diverse cultures. If aviation increased the level of global standardization and made the world a less interesting place, it also helped the peoples of the world to become more familiar with one another, and made it possible for international aid to reach areas plagued by famine, disease, or natural disaster at the earliest possible moment.

Aviation opened vast areas of the planet for study, settlement, and economic exploitation. It also played a critically important role in twentieth-century nation building. "Of all the inventions that have helped to unify China," Mme. Chiang Kai-shek commented, ". . . the airplane was the most outstanding."[16] Could the Soviets have held their vast and wildly diverse empire together without a state airline linking population centers west of the Urals with the most remote oasis in Kazakhstan and the smallest mining camp in Siberia? Modern leaders in Africa, Latin America, Asia, and the Pacific rely on the airplane to stitch their nations together, reducing travel time and closing the gaps in thin transportation networks.

But if the airplane was a tool for nation builders, it was also a boon to those with aspirations to rule an empire. "Aviation," Charles Lindbergh commented in 1939, "seems almost a gift from heaven to those Western nations who were already the leaders of their era, strengthening their leadership, their confidence, their dominance over other peoples."[17] Flight was a tool employed by empire builders of every stripe, enabling them to forge stronger links to the colonies, suppress revolts against imperial authority, and extend a "sphere of influence" over smaller nations in the immediate neighborhood.

Air travel has reshaped the more trivial aspects of our lives, and the most profound. The airplane allows families who have spread across the continent or around the world to maintain personal contact. It inaugurated a new era in athletic competition, increased the frequency and popularity of international fairs and trade shows, and made overseas business meetings, conferences, and conventions an everyday occurrence.

Flight facilitates centuries-old religious practices. By the mid-1990s half of all of the pilgrims making the hajj to Makkah, over one million people, passed through a special terminal at Jeddah's King Abdulaziz International Airport during a single six-day period each year. Small towns with special religious significance, from Lourdes, France, to Tirupati, India, boast busier airports than those of much larger cities.[18]

The airplane embodied our notions of modernity. It was the machine that would change things forever and carry us into the future. Modernist painters from Henri Rousseau to the artists of the futurist school explored aeronautical themes. The Cubists Georges Braque and Pablo Picasso visited the flying field at Issy-les-Moulineaux during the years before World War I. Picasso, who crafted model planes with his talented fingers, referred to his friend Braque as "Vilbour."

Flight shaped the look and style of the century. The airplane became the ultimate symbol of speed, efficiency, and all that was up-to-the-minute and headed toward tomorrow. From modernist architects like Le Corbusier (Charles-Édouard Jeanneret, 1887–1965) to the first generation of industrial designers, aviation inspired a style that reflected the sleek and streamlined elegance of wings, and applied it to everything from huge locomotives to automobiles, furnishings, and household appliances. We found our heroes in the sky as well, from the intrepid birdmen of World War I, through the legendary pilots of the 1920s and 1930s, to the postwar aviators and astronauts who defined the "right stuff."

The memorable events in the history of flight have become the yardstick of our lives, the moments when the trajectory of our daily routine intersects great events. If you are of a certain age, you will recall where you were and what you were doing when you heard that Lindbergh had landed in Paris, that the airship *Hindenburg* had burned, that the atomic bomb had been dropped, that the Soviets had launched *Sputnik I*, that humans had set foot on the Moon, that the Space Shuttle *Challenger* had exploded in flight.

Beyond its impact on war, commerce, society, and culture, the aerospace industry drove the juggernaut of twentieth-century technology. Lavish government spending on aviation and space flight fueled revolutionary change, from the development of new materials to the introduction of electronic computing, not to mention entirely new approaches to the management of complexity.

Who among those who witnessed the birth of the airplane could have imagined a time, less than half a century later, when the vast sums spent on aerial weaponry would create new relationships between government, business, and research. Because we fly, the support and management of technological change must be a primary goal for nations that are to prosper, or simply survive.

General Carl M. Spaatz, who began his career as a combat pilot during World War I and concluded it by serving as the first commander of the independent U.S. Air Force, underscored the importance of basic research in the air age. "Science is in the saddle," he remarked, "Science is the dictator, whether we like it or not. Science runs ahead of both politics and military affairs. Science evolves new conditions to which institutions must be adopted. Let us keep our science dry."[19]

Early in the air age, pioneers like Charles Lindbergh burned with a pure faith in the potential of the airplane to effect positive social change. "The development of transport aircraft," he noted late in life, "once seemed to me a wonderful way to increase human freedom and to bring the peoples of the world together in understanding and peace."

Lindergh's youthful faith soured as he noted the consequences of technological enthusiasm. "When I . . . assess the fundamental value of aeronautics and astronautics," he remarked near the end of his life, ". . . I am forced to the conclusion that mankind in general would be better off if we had never found a way to fly or to launch missiles through space." The most famous aviator of the century ended his life convinced that "the destructive effect of our flight sciences in war has been far greater than their constructive effect in peace."[20]

Whatever positive things the airplane had achieved, it had also encouraged a "dreadful standardization" and fearful environmental consequences, ranging from the loss of wilderness to the increasing pollution of the upper atmosphere that would result from the operation of a commercial supersonic airliner. "I have seen the science I worshipped, and the airplane I loved," Lindbergh explained, "destroying the civilization I expected them to serve."[21]

The inventor of the airplane took a more optimistic view. "I feel about the airplane much as I do in regard to fire," Orville Wright explained at the height of World War II. "That is, I regret all of the terrible damage caused by fire. But I think it is good for the human race that someone discovered how to start fires and that we have learned to put fire to thousands of important uses."[22]

While caution and concern regarding the long-term impact of technology were hallmarks of the late twentieth century, most citizens of the air age seem to have preserved their enthusiasm for flight and admiration for those who fly. I can be regarded as something of an authority on public attitudes toward the history of flight. For three decades, perilously close to half my lifetime, I have been employed at the most significant shrine of the air age.

In an average year, nine million people will walk through the doors of the National Air and Space Museum (NASM)—fourteen million in our best year. We welcome more visitors than the British Museum, the American Museum of Natural History, the Metropolitan Museum, or the Louvre. It is the most visited museum in the world. When NASM opened to the public on July 1, 1976, the staff was confident of success, but no one expected the enormous number of visitors who arrived that first summer, or the wave of media enthusiasm that washed over the building. President Gerald Ford commented that the museum was "our bicentennial birthday present to ourselves." In fact, those of us who planned the museum could take only limited credit for its success.

The quality of the NASM collection is a far more important factor. What other museum in the world, covering any subject, can offer such riches? Visitors to the NASM can see the world's first airplane; the world's first military airplane; the first airplane to fly around the world; the *Spirit of St. Louis*; the Lockheed Vega that Amelia Earhart flew across the Atlantic; Wiley Post's *Winnie Mae*; Howard Hughes's classic H-1 racing aircraft; the B-29 *Enola Gay*; the Bell X-1 that Capt. Charles Yeager, he of the right stuff, first flew faster than sound; the world's fastest airplane; the first airplane to fly around the world nonstop and unrefueled; the first balloon to circumnavigate the globe; the first helicopter to fly around the world; the world's oldest liquid-propellant rocket; the spacecraft that carried the first American into orbit; and the

Apollo 11 Command Module that brought home the first humans to walk on the surface of another world. And that is only the tip of the iceberg.

But the core of the museum's appeal runs even deeper than the opportunity to see the actual aircraft and spacecraft in which intrepid men and women wrote the history of the twentieth century in the sky. However one assesses the immediate consequences of aviation, flight remains one of the most stunning and magnificent of human achievements. People flock to the NASM from around the world because this museum makes them feel proud to be human.

The achievement of heavier-than-air flight had a profound psychological impact. It began with our deep and distant ancestral envy of birds and involved nothing more or less than the realization of the oldest and most potent of human symbols. To fly is to escape restraint, soar over obstacles, and achieve mastery and control of our fate.

The locomotive was portrayed as a relentless and inhuman force rushing across the nineteenth-century landscape. The airplane, by contrast, represented the liberating power of technology. Unconstrained by rails, the flying machine responded completely to the will and the skill of the pilot, who was always in command of the machine and of his own fate. The airplane not only conquered time and distance but also set us free and satisfied our deepest aspirations.

From the beginning, we placed our gods in the sky and made flight, the one gift we had been denied, an attribute of divinity. "The natural function of a wing," Plato explained, "is to carry that which is heavy up to the place where dwells the race of gods."

For most of human history, flight with artificial wings defined the impossible. "If God had intended for human beings to fly," it was said, "he would have given us wings." Instead, we crafted them with our clever brains and nimble hands. What was one to make of creatures who could accomplish such a wonder? If humans could fly, was there any limit to what they might accomplish?

Anthropologist Richard Potts, an authority on human origins, suggests that flight has altered our destiny as a species.[23] Historian Walter McDougall agrees. The early years of the space age, he argues, represented a saltation, a period of rapid evolutionary change equivalent to the era when the earliest amphibians crawled out of the water to take up residence on land.[24]

The notion is intriguing, but space travel is clearly an extension of flight within the atmosphere. The moment of profound change had occurred decades before, when a pair of brothers from Dayton, Ohio, made their first flights from a remote North Carolina beach.

THE BOOK THAT YOU hold in your hands is a narrative history of the airplane, offered on the occasion of the centennial of powered, controlled, heavier-than-air flight. The approach is interpretive, rather than comprehensive. Those in search of encyclopedic coverage of the subject will be sorely disappointed. I offer an aerial photograph of the forest, not a checklist of the individual trees.

Spaceflight is considered here only as a major factor in the evolution of the aerospace industry. Although the manufacture of spacecraft flowed directly from the research organizations and companies that conceived, designed, and built airplanes, the story of flight beyond the atmosphere deserves its own telling.

While this volume tells an international story, coverage of the last half of the century focuses heavily on events in the United States. Many of the fundamental breakthroughs in the history of flight, from all-metal construction to development of the jet engine and invention of the helicopter, originated in Europe. But if the Old World provided fertile ground for new ideas, America became the place where those innovations were transformed into products that have dominated the marketplace and the battlefield since the mid-1930s.

Americans put their stamp on the second half of the century of wings. Setting aside the Soviet bloc, which was artificially walled off from the international marketplace, U.S. manufacturers built perhaps 80 percent of the large commercial aircraft operated by the world's airlines since the introduction of the DC-2 in 1934. Before the 1980s Americans dominated the international market for general-aviation aircraft even more completely.

Aviation was peculiarly suited to the American way of war. Technological prowess became a defining characteristic of the nation, and aerospace weaponry the defining technology of the century. In spite of our occasional doubts, Americans have been masters of the sky since the Second World War. Superiority in the air and space provided us with a longer reach than the other fellow, the ability to project our national will to distant points on the globe. It is no accident that the American century coincided with the air age.

This study aims to trace the process of innovation by which the flying machine evolved from an artfully arranged bundle of sticks and string into a complex machine capable of traveling to other worlds. The history of flight technology is not entirely the story of rational decision making by professional engineers guided by scientific principles. Social and cultural forces have been as important in shaping the airplane as the laws of physics. Pure enthusiasm sometimes overwhelms the cool judgment of the technician. The notion that the airplane might replace the automobile as means of personal transportation, the dream of reviving the rigid airship, and the determination to achieve wings with perfect aerodynamic efficiency stand as cases in point.

Nor has the path from Kitty Hawk to the stars been a slow, steady walk up the steep slope of aeronautical progress. Rather, the history of flight technology is characterized by long periods of gradual improvement punctuated by brief interludes of rapid change, resulting in sudden leaps in performance and fundamental alterations in the appearance of the machine.

The basic pattern of the wood-framed, wired-braced, fabric-covered flying machine was in place by 1914. The next two decades produced a host of incremental improvements in propulsion, aerodynamics, and structures, but no fundamental shifts in the basic pattern. While an aerial veteran of World War I visiting a flying field of 1930 would certainly have noticed these changes, he would also have found much that seemed familiar.

A return visit to the same airfield just four or five years later would have taken his breath away. Engineers had integrated the many developments that had occurred since the end of the war into a fundamentally new pattern—a sleek, streamlined design that represented a sharp break from the old tradition and an entirely new point of departure for the future. The all-metal, cantilevered-wing, stressed-skin template would hold true through World War II, when the turbojet revolution brought another sudden leap in performance and redefined our notion of what an airplane should look and even sound like.

Why did these basic shifts occur where and when they did? What forces drove the process of innovation? How can technology be applied most effectively to achieve national goals? What is the impact of technological change on society and culture? The history of the twentieth century has hinged on the answers to these questions.

Most readers will probably approach this story with an unconscious sense of the inevitability of things. The history of flight seems to have followed a predestined trajectory from the sands of Kitty Hawk, across the Atlantic, around the world, through the sound barrier, and on to the Moon. I hope that this telling of the tale of the airplane carries with it a sense that events did not have to transpire as they did.

Because of the extent to which flight symbolizes the power of technology to realize ancient dreams, to overcome obstacles once regarded as insuperable, and perhaps even to alter human destiny, the story of aviation has the capacity to capture our imaginations. That does not mean that this is a linear tale of steady progress and unalloyed triumph, however.

Frustration, failure, and the futile exploration of blind alleys have been part of the price of technical progress. Moments of exaltation and transcendence have been tempered by bitter disappointments, scandals, and tragedies. While examples of heroism and brilliant achievement abound in these pages, there are also scoundrels and villains aplenty, and moments of stark terror and utter disaster. All of which is to say that the threads of this story can only be understood and appreciated when woven into the rich and complex tapestry that is the history of the twentieth century.

I

FOUNDATION STONES

THE ANCIENTS COULD HAVE FLOWN

Sir George Cayley (1773–1857) called his invention a "flying para-chute." The word *aeroplane* would not appear in print until 1871–1872, when a brilliant engineer, inventor, and adventurer named Francis Herbert Wenham used that term to describe the stiff wings of a beetle. Cayley's craft, a glider built in 1804, was the predecessor of all fixed-wing flying machines. It consisted of a horizontal pole, four feet long, with some surfaces attached. A kite, set at a six-degree angle to the horizon, served as the wing. A weight could be positioned to alter the center of gravity and maintain balance. A cruciform tail mounted on a universal joint served as both elevator and rudder. "It was very pretty to see it sail down a steep hill," Cayley remarked, "and it gave the idea that a larger instrument would be a better and a safer conveyance down the Alps than ever the surefooted mule."[1]

Why did it take so long to begin to realize the ancient dream of winged flight? "They could have done it, the Carthaginians. Or the Etruscans, or the Egyptians. Four thousand years ago, five thousand years ago, they could have flown." Aviation author Richard Bach argues that ancient peoples had access to all of the materials required to

Flying parachute, 1804

build gliders of the sort that flight pioneer Otto Lilienthal flew in the closing years of the nineteenth century. "It was possible all those years ago," he insists. "It could have been done."[2]

An interesting thought, but the availability of the materials and a moment of inspiration would never have done the trick. Simple as they seem, such gliders evolved from centuries of brilliant insights in physics and engineering, of data gathered with sophisticated instruments, of forays down countless blind alleys, and of a thousand difficult lessons learned. Could Pharaoh's craftsmen have short-circuited that long and difficult process? Could they have made an intellectual leap over the three millennia of knowledge and experience that separated them from Otto Lilienthal? Not likely.

There is another way in which the ancients could have flown, however. The secrets of the wing took centuries to fathom, but the balloon was quite another matter. The Greek philosopher Archimedes (287–212 B.C.) explained the very simple principle of buoyant flight. Ancient people knew that hot air rises, and many of them could produce the lightweight, tightly woven fabrics required for a balloon envelope.

Evidence that buoyant flight was within the grasp of our remote ancestors came in 1975, when a balloon constructed only of materials available to the Inca carried two researchers to an altitude of 380 feet over Peru's Nazca plain. The aircraft, *Condor I*, featured an eighty-thousand-cubic-foot envelope that was sealed with smoke and filled with superheated air from a specially prepared fire on the ground. With the two-man crew seated astride a reed "gondola," the balloon climbed rapidly to altitude and then sank back to earth as the air in the envelope cooled. While the experiment did not prove that ancient South Americans flew, it did prove that they could have done it had they but tried. Why didn't they try? It was a failure of the imagination. Birds and insects inspired the desire to fly with wings, but nature offered no examples of lighter-than-air flight, other than rising smoke.[3]

In the end, seventeenth- and eighteenth-century natural philosophers who studied the physics and chemistry of the atmosphere laid the foundation for the invention of the balloon. This extraordinary era of discovery began with the realization that the atmosphere could be pumped out of a closed vessel like any fluid, and proceeded through the statement of the physical laws explaining the behavior of "air," the only gas of which they were aware.

This early work had profound technological consequences, from the introduction of the barometer to the development of the steam engine. These new discoveries also inspired the earliest useful speculations on buoyant flight. In 1670, the Jesuit priest Francesco Lana de Terzi suggested that if air were pumped from a large, thin-walled copper sphere, the thing might then weigh less than the amount of air it displaced, and rise into the sky. Four such globes, each twenty feet in diameter, might carry a human being aloft. Theoretically, Lana was on the right track. In practical terms, however, it was not possible to construct globes sufficiently large, light, and strong.

The public debut of a more practical device came on August 8, 1709, when Father Bartolomeo Lourenço de Gusmão (1685–1724), a Jesuit priest from the Brazilian town of Santos, flew a small balloon in the presence of the King of Portugal at the Salla das Embaixadas in Lisbon. The burning spirits employed to heat the air inside the envelope, or "canopy," set fire to the wall hangings and carpets in the room. Lisbon was far from the intellectual center of eighteenth-century Europe, however, and the prints and stories of the Portuguese "flying man" became widely regarded as fanciful. A bit more intellectual conditioning was required before the technology of buoyant flight would fully take root.

If seventeenth-century studies of pneumatic physics had inspired the notion of buoyant flight, the eighteenth-century effort to analyze the constituent gases of the atmosphere led directly to the invention of the balloon. The Scottish chemist Joseph Black identified the first truly elemental gas, "fixed air," or nitrogen in 1765. A decade later Henry Cavendish announced the discovery of "phlogisticated" or "inflammable" air, a gas (from the German *geist*, meaning "spirit") that was much lighter than either nitrogen or atmospheric air. The balloon would be seven years old before Antoine-Laurent Lavoisier applied the name *hydrogen* to Cavendish's gas. The discovery of a new gas many times lighter than air inspired several pioneering chemists to explore just how much weight "inflammable air" might lift.

Joseph Montgolfier (1740–1810), like many curious Frenchmen, grew fascinated by the work of the English pneumatic chemists. The twelfth of sixteen children born to a family that had manufactured paper since the fourteenth century, Joseph was an absent-minded eccentric, quite unlike his younger brother Étienne, the fifteenth child and the best businessman of his generation of Montgolfiers. Yet Joseph would immortalize the family name.

Inspired by what he knew of the new science of the atmosphere, Joseph began to conduct his own experiments in the fall of 1782. Convinced that "heat" was a fluid related to the other new "airs," and that the combustion of organic materials would produce a "rarified air," he constructed a light wooden frame covered with finely woven taffeta and filled it with very hot air. It flew. "Get in a supply of taffeta and cordage, quickly," he wrote to Étienne, "and you will see one of the most astonishing sights in the world."[4]

On June 4, 1783, the Montgolfier brothers sent a thirty-five-foot balloon constructed of a sandwich of paper and fabric up from the public square of their hometown of Annonay, France. Intrigued by the first sketchy reports from provincial Annonay, Barthélemy Faujas de Saint-Fond (1741–1819), a geologist at the Muséum d'Histoiré Naturelle in the capital, sold tickets to the launch of a balloon that did not yet exist, and turned the money over to Jacques-Alexandre-César Charles, his choice to construct the first balloon to be flown in Paris.

Charles, one of the best-known scientific lecturers in Paris, had given up a budding career in government administration after reading Benjamin Franklin's treatise on electricity. The notion of "inflammable air" was very much on his mind. In mid-June 1783, Lavoisier had demonstrated that water was a compound of that very light gas and "dephlogisticated air," or oxygen, which Joseph Priestley had identified in 1774. It probably did not even occur to Charles that the Montgolfiers had filled their balloon with anything other than hydrogen.

With the assistance of the brothers A. and M. N. Robert, who had developed a process for coating fabric with natural rubber, Charles built a demonstration balloon and an apparatus for generating large quantities of hydrogen. On the afternoon of August 27, 1783, an enormous crowd of Parisians gathered near the Champ de Mars, the great parade ground in front of the École Militaire, to witness the first flight of a gas balloon, just as Faujas had promised. "It diminished in Apparent Magnitude as it rose," Benjamin Franklin reported, "till it entered the Clouds, when it seem'd to me scarce bigger than an Orange." At the conclusion of the demonstration, Franklin, the leader of the American diplomats living in Paris to negotiate an end to the American Revolution, overheard a spectator remark that the balloon was nothing more than a useless toy. "Of what use," the American responded, "is a new born babe?"[5]

Over the next three months, one balloon after another rose above the Paris skyline. The royal family was in attendance on September 19, when Étienne Montgolfier sent a sheep, a duck, and a rooster aloft from the palace at Versailles. Jean-François Pilâtre de Rozier, who lectured on science under the patronage of the Comte de Provence, and François Laurent, the Marquis d'Arlandes, became the first humans to make a free flight when they rose from the grounds of the Chateau de la Muette aboard a Montgolfier hot-air balloon on November 20. On December 1, Jacques-Alexandre-César Charles and M. N. Robert became the first humans to rise into the air aboard a hydrogen balloon. Two millennia after the basic materials required to build a balloon were in hand, the age of flight began at long last.

The invention of the balloon, a very simple technology well within the reach of ancient peoples, had to wait for the inspiration of early modern science. Just six months after the appearance of the first small balloon, Charles flew a craft sporting all of the major features that would define the technology for the next century. There would be a few improvements around the edges, but no fundamental changes.

Achieving winged flight would prove much more difficult and have far greater consequences. For millennia, the notion of building wings that would carry us into the sky had seemed so impious, arrogant, and outrageous as to be the very definition of the impossible. While the thing ultimately proved to be possible, it would take a great many brilliant and ingenious minds and clever pairs of hands a very long time to accomplish.

PRACTICAL AERODYNAMICS

Forget Icarus and Daedalus. The people who took the first serious steps toward the invention of the airplane were not mythic figures, but generations of anonymous craftsmen who developed a variety of flying toys, water wheels, and windmills. The wing of Cayley's "flying parachute" directly descended from the earliest plane-surface (essentially flat) kite, which appeared in China around 1000 B.C.E., then spread northeast to Japan and Korea and south into Asia and the Pacific Islands. The first flying objects crafted by human hands, kites were used for everything from fishing to signaling and served a variety of religious and ceremonial functions. They carried lights, noise makers, and pyrotechnics aloft at night to frighten enemy troops, and there is every reason to accept the validity of Chinese and Japanese tales, and the testimony of Marco Polo, suggesting that the first humans to venture aloft did so aboard large kites.[6]

Another influential aerodynamic device never left the ground. Simple vertical-post windmills were in use in Afghanistan by the tenth century. The classic horizontal-post windmill seems to have been a Western innovation. The earliest records of wind-driven mills in England and France date to approximately 1170. Over the next century windmills of various designs would sprout across northern Europe.

By the fourteenth and fifteenth centuries, water wheels and windmills powered a Medieval industrial revolution. Pumping, sawing, the

fulling of cloth, tanning, laundering, polishing, the grinding of everything from grain to pigments, the preparation of wood pulp for paper
and mash for beer, the crushing of everything from ore to olives, and
the operation of bellows and hammers—all depended on the power of
wind and water. The forgotten craftsmen who designed and built
water wheels and windmills had mastered practical lessons in fluid
dynamics. That knowledge, and the desire to improve the performance
of windmills, would play a critical role in the prehistory of the airplane.[7]

The spread of windmills inspired a new toy, the pinwheel or *petit
moulinet à vent*, which first appears in illustrations in thirteenth- and
fourteenth-century manuscripts. These "little windmills," in turn,
inspired the invention of the first powered flying machine, a helicopter
toy first seen in a Flemish manuscript dating to 1325. In its original
form, the toy consisted of a spindle with a vertical hole in which to
place a shaft topped with a horizontal pinwheel. The operator held the
spindle in one hand and pulled a string wrapped around the shaft with
the other, sending the shaft and blades twirling up into the air.

In a gigantic leap of the imagination. A long-forgotten genius had
reversed the normal process. Now the pinwheel blades originally spun
by the pressure of the wind became blades that were artificially spun to
generate enough lift to resist the pressure of air and send it bouncing
along the ceiling. Perhaps our craftsperson was a mother or father who
fixed a pinwheel blade horizontally to the top of a shaft, which could be
spun between two palms to produce the simplest form of a toy that
delights youngsters even today.[8]

The little rotary-wing toy appears in a number of early modern
portraits of children, and in paintings such as Pieter Brueghel's
Children's Games. A significant variant turns up in a fifteenth-century
manuscript. It is apparent that the secret of handcrafting various forms
of the flying toy passed from one generation to the next until 1784,
when the Frenchmen Launoy and Bienvenu introduced a new and
much improved version featuring a pair of two-bladed contra-rotating
propellers powered by a bowstring twisted around a shaft.[9]

This old toy literally changed the course of history a decade later,
when it fell into the hands of Sir George Cayley. In 1796, eight years

before he developed the "flying parachute," the twenty-three-year-old Englishman produced his own simplified version of the helicoper toy, which he called a Chinese Top. Apparently, Sir George had no notion of the toy's deep roots in the European past. "It was," the man who would become known as "the Father of Aerial Navigation" remarked, ". . . the first experiment I made upon this subject."[10] Appropriately enough, half a century later, at the end of a distinguished career in aeronautics, Cayley designed and constructed another version of the original string-pull device introduced over five centuries before.

Alphonse Pénaud, another important aeronautical contributor, transformed the old toy into a sophisticated flying model powered by twisted rubber strands. Dubbed a *hélicoptère* and introduced in about 1870, the little Pénaud model held the world's record for powered, propeller-driven flight, climbing to altitudes of up to fifty feet and remaining in the air for as long as twenty-six seconds. As the American engineer and historian of flight Octave Chanute noted, the little craft was "simple, cheap, efficacious, and not easily broken."[11]

In 1878, a Pénaud helicopter toy caught the eye of an American churchman, who bought one for his two youngest sons. "Our first interest began when we were children," Orville Wright explained. "Father brought home to us a small toy actuated by a rubber spring which would lift itself into the air." We do not know where Bishop Milton Wright found the helicopter, or what it cost. Its impact is clear, however. Eleven-year-old Wilbur and his seven-year-old brother Orville sent the little gadget aloft time after time. Rather than pouting and turning to something else when the fragile gadget inevitably broke, these youngsters built a new helicopter and began experimenting.

"We built a number of copies of this toy, which flew successfully," Wilbur explained. Miss Ida Palmer, Orville's second-grade teacher, discovered the boy assembling one of the helicopters instead of finishing an assignment. When asked what he was doing, Orville explained that he was building a model of the flying machine that might one day enable him to fly with his brother.[12]

The boys quickly discovered a problem, however. When they tried to build larger models, Wilbur explained, "They failed to work so well."[13] A marvelous flying toy had taught two bright young boys a lesson in weight management that they would never forget. A quarter of a century after their father surprised them with his gift, they were still handcrafting helicopters "out of bamboo, paper, corks, and rubber bands," as their nephew Milton recalled, "and allowing us [youngsters] to run after them when they flew them."[14]

Never underestimate the power of play to spark innovation. The little rotary-wing toy inspired generations of aeronautical experiments. The kite, the only aerodynamic device capable of remaining aloft for a significant time, enabled researchers to test aircraft structures, wing designs, and control systems. At the beginning of the nineteenth century the kite provided Sir George Cayley with his only model for the design of an artificial wing. Virtually all nineteenth-century flying-machine experimenters used kites in their research. In 1899, ninety-five years after Cayley flew his "flying parachute," Wilbur and Orville Wright inaugurated their own aeronautical experiments with a kite that was specially designed to test their control system. The brothers gathered their first trustworthy bits of aerodynamic data by flying their earliest full-scale machines as kites.

BASIC PRINCIPLES:
FROM LEONARDO TO CAYLEY

Leonardo da Vinci (1452–1519) seems to have been the first person to honestly believe that mechanical flight was possible and would be achieved through careful observation, the study of the basic physical principles underlying flight in nature, and a rational attempt to imagine artificial flying machines based on those principles. His drawings of an ornithopter, a parachute, and a helicopter propelled by a giant Archimedean screw are among the most familiar images of Renaissance technology. In the history of fluid dynamics he stands as a lone giant between the Greeks and the seventeenth-century precursors of the scientific revolution.

If ever there was a man ahead of his time, it was Leonardo. Unfortunately, he kept his most interesting ideas in a wide variety of fields entirely to himself. His notebooks, jealously guarded and frequently written in reverse script, were dispersed after his death. The ideas that would have qualified him as the founder of aerodynamics remained completely unknown until the nineteenth century.

As a result, several generations of brilliant thinkers who were not in the least interested in flight laid the foundation for aerodynamic theory. Researchers from Galileo Galilei (1564–1642) to Sir Isaac Newton (1642–1727) established the science of mechanics, complete with the laws of motion and some basic notions regarding fluid dynamics. Edme Mariotte (1620–1684) and Christiaan Huygens (1629–1695) each contributed to the discovery of a major principle of aerodynamics—the velocity square law, which suggests that the force operating on a surface varies as the square of the change in velocity.

Other pieces of the puzzle fell into place early in the eighteenth century. The Swiss physicist Daniel Bernoulli (1700–1782) first announced that pressure decreases with an increase in the velocity of fluid flow. Other significant figures, including Jean Le Rond d'Alembert (1717–1783), Leonhard Euler (1707–1783), Joseph-Louis Lagrange (1736–1813), and Pierre-Simon de Laplace (1749–1827), established fundamental physical and mathematical principles of fluid flow.

More important, the men who first defined the engineering profession put theory to work by solving problems in practical aerodynamics. In 1732, Henri Pitot (1695–1771) described the Pitot tube, an instrument designed to measure fluid velocity at any given point in a flow.

Convinced that "all the theories of [air] resistance hitherto published are extremely defective," Benjamin Robbins (1707–1751), an English mathematician and military engineer, developed the whirling arm, an instrument that enabled generations of engineers to measure the forces acting on a solid body immersed in a fluid stream.[15] It was far from perfect. Readings were subject to patterns of artificial circulation created as the horizontal arm swung the test surface around in a great circle. Until the invention of the wind tunnel, however, and for a few decades thereafter, the whirling arm remained the instrument of choice for gathering aerodynamic data.

Englishman John Smeaton (1724–1792) built his towering engineering reputation by raising the famous Eddystone lighthouse and similar large-scale construction projects. His studies of the efficiency of windmill and water-wheel blades revealed some basic aerodynamic principles. "When wind falls upon a concave surface," he reported in a 1759 paper to his colleagues of the Royal Society, "it is an advantage to the power of the whole."[16] In addition to providing the first statement of the superiority of cambered, or curved, surfaces to flat plates, Smeaton also employed a whirling arm to measure the resistance to a flat plate mounted perpendicular to the flow, and correlated the reading to the wind velocity at the time of the test.[17]

Some bits of misinformation entered the evolving science of fluid dynamics along with the intellectual treasure. By the late seventeenth century, for example, researchers knew that the forces acting on an object in a stream depended on the density of the fluid, the size and shape of the object, and the square of the velocity. One unresolved question involved the extent to which those forces varied with a change in the angle at which the object met the stream. An anonymous author, drawing on Newton's work, erroneously concluded that very little lift would be generated by a flat plate at low angles of attack. In practical terms, this meant that a successful flying machine either would have to sport very large wings to generate sufficient lift to fly or would have to operate at such a high angle of attack that the resulting air resistance, or drag, would be prohibitive. It was a discouraging prospect.

In similar fashion, Smeaton credited an associate, a Mr. Rouse, with creating a table of data published in his 1759 paper that showed the forces operating on a flat plate tested on the whirling arm. The result of this effort was a figure (.005) representing the density of air, as opposed to some other fluid. This number became known as Smeaton's coefficient, and in spite of the fact that the calculation was based only on his data, the erroneous figure would be employed to calculate the performance of experimental flying machines until it was finally corrected by both Samuel Pierpont Langley and the Wright brothers in the late nineteenth and early twentieth centuries.

With the exception of Leonardo, none of the contributors to aerodynamic theory before the end of the eighteenth century were interested in flight. That was soon to change, as the twin streams of craft tradition and engineering research finally came together in the mind of one of the most remarkable figures in the history of aeronautics.

THE FOUNDING FATHER

Born to a life of privilege in the England of King George III, George Cayley grew up in a bucolic landscape where rustic gentry and their sturdy yeomen tenants met the pioneering entrepreneurs and protesting Luddites of the industrial revolution. Cayley was already a baronet with his seat at Brompton Hall in Yorkshire when he conducted his first experiments with the helicopter toy. He bore little resemblance to the country squires in Jane Austin's novels, however.

His mother, a religious nonconformist, arranged for her talented son to receive a rational education that would prepare him for leadership in a society increasingly shaped by science and technology. She selected George Walker, a dissenting parson, to serve as his tutor. Described by a friend as "one of the most heretical ministers in the

Sir George Cayley

neighborhood," Walker was a fellow of the Royal Society who maintained his own machine shop. He was perhaps best known as president of the Literary and Philosophical Society of Manchester, whose members had included Joseph Priestley, the political, social, and religious radical who had discovered oxygen; his friend Benjamin Franklin; and John Dalton, the local man whose atomic theory would revolutionize chemistry. George Cayley married Walker's daughter, cementing his relationship to the radical parson who had encouraged his deep interest in science and technology.[18]

Unlike those who simply read about new developments, Cayley contributed to fields ranging from architecture and railroading to the design of lifeboats and prosthetics. He patented the design of a caterpillar tractor, experimented with caloric, or "hot-air" engines, and invented the tension, or bicycle, wheel.

His friends included Thomas Young, who described the modulus of elasticity and proposed the wave theory of light; the chemist Sir Humphry Davy; Charles Babbage, who had earned fame with his "calculating engine"; and the pioneer industrialists and railroad builders George and Robert Stephenson. Cayley was a founder of both the Yorkshire Philosophical Society and the influential British Association for the Advancement of Science.

He wrote poetry, fought hard for improved conditions for the poor in Yorkshire, supported William Wilberforce and the abolitionist cause, and actively participated in Whig politics, leading the powerful Whig Club of York and serving as a member of Parliament for Scarborough. Convinced that few things proved more important to society than the education of working men, he helped to found the Regent Street Polytechnic, now Westminster University.

The great passion of his life, however, remained the dream of "aerial navigation." Here was the most difficult technical challenge imaginable, the achievement of which would result in a great public good. "An uninterrupted ocean that comes to every man's door," Cayley believed, "ought not to be neglected as a source of human gratification and advantage."[19] He became convinced that the "noble art" of aeronautics would "soon be brought home to man's general convenience," and that "a new era in society will commence from the moment aerial navigation is familiarly realized."[20]

As a boy, George Cayley had been fascinated by balloons, but his experiments with the small helicopter toy in 1796 marked the beginning of his serious interest in heavier-than-air flight. The old toy illustrated his understanding of the central problem: "to make a surface support a given weight by the application of power to the resistance of air."[21]

Cayley's work in aeronautics was well underway by 1799, when he engraved his conception of a flying machine as a fixed-wing craft with separate systems for lift, propulsion, and control on one side of a small silver disk and a remarkable diagram of the forces acting on a wing on the other. The first researcher to bring the growing power of science and technology to bear on the problems of flight, he realized that a century and a half of work in fluid mechanics provided a starting point.

Cayley made good use of existing research instruments as well, conducting the first whirling-arm tests of wing surfaces at low angles of attack. The young baronet put his theoretical insights and hard-won knowledge to practical use in 1804, when he designed and built the "flying parachute," the world's first successful model glider and the ancestor of all modern fixed-wing aircraft. He built a larger version in the summer of 1809. "When any person ran forward in it, with his full speed," he explained, "taking advantage of a gentle breeze in front, it would bear upward so strongly as scarcely to allow him to touch the ground; and would frequently lift him up, and convey him several yards together."[22]

The inventor described these early experiments to Mrs. Susan Sibbald, whom he met at a tea party in 1810 or 1811. "He [Cayley] mentioned how he had from a boy fancied that some machine might be made to go through the air," she remarked, ". . . [and] that he had set to work and made an article in the shape of a large bird." Cayley explained that he had enlisted a lightweight stable boy as test pilot "after some persuasion and promise of reward." The boy succeeded in getting into the air, but only for a very short time. "Whether the boy got frightened, . . . or was too fat and heavier than the bird liked, . . . down the bird came plump on the ground." Bird and boy survived,

Mrs. Sibbald continued, "and the manner in which Sir George told of his experience . . . kept us in fits of laughter."[23]

In 1809, English newspapers reported that Jacob Degen, a Swiss clockmaker living in Vienna, had risen over fifty feet into the air by flapping the wings of his ornithopter. The stories failed to mention that the would-be airman and his machine dangled beneath a large balloon at the time. Worried that he might be upstaged, Cayley immediately published an account of his aeronautical work in three issues (1809–1813) of *A Journal of Natural Philosophy, Chemistry and the Arts*. These articles, titled "On Aerial Navigation," provided a solid foundation for future aeronautical research. The "triple paper"

- confirmed earlier suggestions that a curved, or cambered, wing produces greater lift than a flat plate set at low angle of attack;
- identified an area of low pressure on the upper surface of a cambered wing in flight and an area of high pressure on the underside;
- suggested that angling the tips of the wings above the centerline of the aircraft, creating a dihedral angle, which produces a measure of lateral stability;
- provided the earliest studies on the movement of the center of pressure on airplane wings during flight; and
- explained how to calculate the performance of an aircraft.

Cayley's technical judgments sometimes missed the mark. Although balloonists had been trying, and failing, to row themselves across the sky since 1784, Cayley had a lifelong preference for oars and paddles over propellers. Moreover, while he singlehandedly established the superiority of fixed wings, he also produced paper designs for other configurations, including ornithopters and a helicopter.

Cayley moved on to other activities during his middle years, entering his second great period of aeronautical creativity in 1849. Forty years after he had constructed his first successful flying models, he produced two new aircraft. The first was a much improved version of his 1809 monoplane glider in which the rudder sat directly on top of a horizontal elevator. This time the wing was a sixteen-square-foot rectangular sheet of fabric stretched between thin poles. The pressure of the air gave the wing a cambered appearance in flight.

The second aircraft featured triplane wings of equal span and chord (the straight-line distance from the leading edge to the trailing edge) set above a boatlike structure that housed the pilot, complete with wheels, paddles for propulsion, and a combination rudder and elevator for steering. "The balance and steerage was ascertained," Cayley reported, "and a boy of about ten years of age was floated off the ground for several yards on descending a hill, and also for about the same distance by some persons pulling the apparatus against a very slight breeze."[24]

Cayley continued to refine the design. In 1852 he published the drawing of an improved monoplane version of the 1849 "boy carrier," referring to it as a "governable parachute." Apparently intended to be launched from a balloon, the new craft was more sturdily rigged than its predecessor and featured a large (five-hundred-square-foot) kitelike overhead wing.

This period of renewed aeronautical activity culminated in 1853, when the baronet designed an improved model of the helicopter toy that had drawn him into aeronautics. He also built and flew his two most successful machines: the last in an evolutionary series of "flying-parachute" single-wing gliders (designed in 1804, 1849, and 1853), and the final and most fully developed version of his basic design (1849 and 1852) for a piloted glider.

The new monoplane glider featured a rectangular wing measuring over thirty-six square feet, more than twice the size of the 1849 model, and weighing some sixteen pounds. Cayley's description of the craft's flight indicates that he had achieved pitch stability by positioning the horizontal tail at a slight negative angle. It was one more in a long list of critically important insights.

Details of the "new flyer," as Cayley styled his final piloted design, are not completely clear. Since he referred to the triplane "boy carrier" of 1849 as the "old flyer," we may assume that the 1853 machine was of the same pattern. Given the amount of time and thought that went into the 1852 variation, however, the "new flyer" may have featured an overhead monoplane wing. If Cayley incorporated his own findings, the glider may have had wing dihedral and a horizontal tail to provide stability in roll and pitch.

Seven decades later, Mrs. George Thompson, Cayley's grand-daughter, remarked that she had seen "the said [new flyer] flown across the dale in 1852, when I was nine years old." Moreover, she was thoroughly familiar with family stories about the performance of the craft. "I remember in later times hearing of a large machine being started on the high side of the valley behind Brompton Hall where he lived, and the coachman being sent up in it, and it flew across the little valley, about 500 yards at most, and came down with a smash. . . . He [the coachman] struggled up and said, 'Please, Sir George, I wish to give notice. I was hired to drive and not to fly.'"[25] If the family tradition is not true, it should be.

Modern aviation begins with Sir George Cayley. He identified heavier-than-air flight as a problem amenable to solution through scientific and technological research; he established a significant number of basic principles in aerodynamics; and he functioned as the first aeronautical engineer, building and flying the first fixed-wing gliders capable of giving humans a taste of flight.

"Sir George Cayley was a remarkable man," Orville Wright commented in 1912. "He knew more of the principles of aeronautics than any of his predecessors, and as much as any that followed him up to the end of the nineteenth century. His published work is remarkably free from error and was a most important contribution to science." He was the giant on whose shoulders others, including Orville Wright and his remarkable brother, would stand.[26]

AFTER CAYLEY

The invention of the airplane began in earnest with Sir George Cayley and concluded in the 1890s, a decade that opened with the German aeronautical pioneer Otto Lilienthal and closed with Wilbur and Orville Wright. Between 1850 and 1890, European and American publications were filled with reports of flying machines, real and fanciful. Although none of the would-be aviators of the period could match the impact of the giants who opened the era and closed it, some of them did provide insights and scraps of information that contributed to the final success.

Take the case of John Stringfellow (1799–1883) and William Samuel Henson (1812–1888), inventors and mechanics involved in the lace-making industry in Somerset. As early as April 1843, Frederick Marriott, a local journalist and a founder of the *London Illustrated News*, published images of the Aerial Steam Carriage patented by Henson and Stringfellow. Attractive prints designed to impress enthusiastic investors showed the projected craft in full flight over the Taj Mahal and a variety of other scenic locations.

Stringfellow and Henson designed and built an unsuccessful steam-powered flying model in 1845–1847. Following Henson's emigration to the United States in 1848, Stringfellow continued to build models and the steam engines to power them, eventually settling on a braced triplane design. Marriott emigrated to California, where he turned his attention to lighter-than-air flight. In 1868, he flew the *Avitor*, an unmanned, steam-powered, helium-filled, cigar-shaped airship measuring twenty-eight feet long, near Shell Mound Park in the San Francisco Bay area. That was also the year in which Stringfellow won the grand prize at the Aeronautical Society of Great Britain's Crystal Palace exhibition for a small aeronautical steam engine, which survives in the collection of the National Air and Space Museum.

"Henson [Stringfellow and Marriott] made no contribution to the art or science of aviation worth mentioning," Orville Wright remarked in 1944. "Every feature of Henson's machine had been used or proposed previously. His mere assemblage of old elements certainly did not constitute invention."[27]

Octave Chanute, a historian of flight and confidant of the Wright brothers, offered a more generous assessment. The original design for the Aerial Steam Carriage, he noted, called for a very long wing of the sort that Newtonian theory predicted would be required for flight. The triplane design that Stringfellow unveiled in 1868 offered a practical means of increasing the amount of wing area while limiting span and maintaining a solid and rigidly braced structure. The sturdy biplane designs in which the early-twentieth-century pioneers first took to the air, Chanute argued, were rooted in the work of John Stringfellow.

THE PROFESSIONALIZATION OF A DREAM

Half a century after the publication of Cayley's triple paper, professional engineers began to take a serious interest in mechanical flight. They were new men, generalists trained to apply a broad understanding of scientific and technical principles to the solution of a wide range of practical problems. They built canals, iron bridges, railroads, steamships, and hundreds of new machines and procedures that generated revolutionary economic, social, and cultural change.

The airplane would be the product of engineers. Science had little to do with it. By the nineteenth century, physicists had achieved genuine breakthroughs in fluid dynamics, including the development of equations that enabled them to calculate complex aspects of flow. Unfortunately, the mathematical tools, theoretical insights, and even some of the experimental data on fluid dynamics proved of little value in solving the practical problems that barred the way to winged flight. The twin streams of fluid dynamics and practical aeronautical engineering would not fully converge until the early twentieth century, when the German university professor Ludwig Prandtl and others wove the disparate scientific threads into a coherent theory to explain the circulation of the air around a wing.

While the general public continued to regard mechanical flight as nothing more than a chimerical dream, a growing number of engineers became attracted to the field, intrigued by a fascinating set of problems that might be overcome by the application of their methodology. Engineers defined themselves as a distinct, self-governing profession like medicine or law, through membership in organizations such as the Society of Engineers (founded by John Smeaton in 1771), the Institution of Civil Engineers (1819), and the Institution of Mechanical Engineers (1848). Engineers interested in flight realized that they could enjoy the same benefits from a specialized professional organization that would honor achievement, encourage research, sponsor publication, and provide a forum for the discussion of key issues and problems.

Cayley had tried unsuccessfully to establish an aeronautical society in 1816, 1837, and 1840. The first such group, founded in Paris in 1852, emphasized lighter-than-air flight and had a little in common with professional engineering societies. Then came the Society to Encourage Aerial Navigation by Heavier-Than-Air Means, organized by the pioneer French photographer and balloonist Félix Tournachon ("Nadar") in 1863. Jules Verne, secretary of the society, patterned Michael Ardan, the hero of his novel *From the Earth to the Moon*, after Nadar. Several members of the group dreamed of a heavier-than-air machine that would rise straight up into the air. Vicomte de Ponton d'Amecourt constructed a small steam-powered rotary-wing model that did not fly, and a clockwork-powered rotary-wing craft that did, in 1863. He was the first to refer to such a craft as a *helicopter*. Gabrielle de la Landelle coined the term *aviation* in 1862 and published plans for a steam-powered multirotor helicopter in 1863 that inspired the aircraft flown by Verne's Robur the Conqueror (1886). In 1864 he founded *L'Aeronaute*, the world's first journal devoted to flight technology.

The men who founded the Aeronautical Society of Great Britain in 1866 patterned their organization after the older engineering societies. James Glaisher typified those solid, no-nonsense professionals. An astronomer and meteorologist, he was a fellow of the Royal Society, the Astronomical Society, and the British Photographic Society. A founder and fellow of the Meteorological Society, he became a leading member of the British Association for the Advancement of Science. His pursuit of knowledge had carried him far beyond the confines of the lecture hall and observatory, to balloon flights into the thin, frigid air seven miles above the surface of the earth. As a scientist with an impeccable reputation, his presence among the founders proved that the organization would not welcome cranks or eccentrics.

Glaisher enlisted the aid of Frederick William Brearey, a friend and neighbor whose father had known Sir George Cayley and witnessed some of his experiments. An unabashed enthusiast for heavier-than-air flight, Brearey was given to flapping his arms like a bird while lecturing, and took great delight in setting as many as thirty model gliders loose on an audience during a single talk.[28]

Brearey's own injuries suffered in the cause of flight were less amusing. On one occasion a propeller blade that he was testing broke loose, slicing off part of his nose and slashing his cheek to the bone. The nose was sewn back on, and an operation saved the sight in one eye.

The Aeronautical Society of Great Britain quickly attracted leading technicians, including fellows of the Royal Society and past presidents of the British Association for the Advancement of Science, the Institution of Civil Engineers, and the Society of Engineers. Charles Bright, planner of the Atlantic cable; Charles William Siemens, who pioneered the dynamo and the telegraph; and James Nasmyth, the inventor of the steam hammer, served on the council of the society and offered papers at early meetings. While the total membership numbered only sixty-five at the end of 1867, some of Britain's finest engineers were on board.

The leaders of the Aeronautical Society arranged lectures and technical meetings to attract young engineers. They established the *Annual Report of the Aeronautical Society* (1867), a journal by engineers for engineers seeking to extend professional standards into the new field.

The Aeronautical Society of Great Britain also popularized the subject among laymen. The promotion of the world's first public exhibition of flying apparatus, which opened for ten days at the Crystal Palace in Sydenham on June 25, 1868, was their most noteworthy public endeavor. The exhibition featured a hodgepodge of aircraft models, lightweight power plants, and other bits and pieces of aeronautical paraphernalia. As the promoters had hoped, the show drew attention to the serious prospect of winged flight.

The real business of the Aeronautical Society of Great Britain was to encourage progress toward powered flight. No member of the group contributed more to the achievement of that goal than Francis Herbert Wenham. A native of Kensington, born in 1824, he became a talented engineer with professional interests ranging from photography to microscopy, scientific instrument design, and the development of high-pressure steam and internal combustion engines. "When I was a little chap," Wenham remarked many years later, "I was fond of making kites and flying them."[29] His first aeronautical experiments, in 1859, involved propeller design. Over the next six years he progressed to flight tests with a full-scale manned glider featuring long, narrow, or high-aspect-ratio, venetian blind–style wings.

Wenham recognized that aircraft designers were operating in the dark. "A series of experiments is much needed," he explained, "to provide data for construction." In his first paper to the Aeronautical Society, he announced that he would "shortly . . . try a series of experiments by the aid of an artificial current of air of known strength, and to place the Society in possession of the results."[30]

The result was the wind tunnel, an invention that would play a critically important role in the history of flight. Designed by Wenham and constructed by John Browning with a grant from the Aeronautical Society, the world's first wind tunnel operated in Greenwich and London in 1870–1872. Through a hollow box, ten feet long and open at both ends, a fan moved a constant stream of air over a "balance," an instrument mounted in the tunnel which measured the forces generated by the model wing being tested.

Wenham's primitive balance was not sensitive enough to record measurements on a test surface operating at the relatively small angles of attack that an airplane would actually fly. As one of his few genuine discoveries, he found that the center of pressure on a flat plate moves toward the leading edge with a decrease in the angle of attack. Still, it was a beginning.

Horatio Phillips (1845–1912), a member of the Aeronautical Society who had attended Wenham's lectures, developed a much improved tunnel and balance in the 1880s, gathering lift and drag data on a series of six cambered airfoils, which he patented in 1884. By 1901, when Wilbur and Orville Wright built their first wind tunnel, at least ten such instruments had been employed in European and American laboratories.[31] Oddly, the new technology did not immediately drive the obsolete predecessor from the field. Whirling arms remained the instrument of choice for leading aeronautical figures, including Samuel Langley and Otto Lilienthal, until 1900.

FLYING MACHINES, 1875–1899

In the last quarter of the nineteenth century, three basic approaches to solving the flying-machine problem emerged. In a first approach, some experimenters moved directly from research to the construction of full-scale, powered and piloted aircraft.

Felix du Temple de la Croix (1823–1890), a distinguished French naval officer, working with his brother Louis, built and perhaps flew, in 1857–1858, a model originally propelled by a clockwork mechanism and then by a small steam engine. While stationed at Thiers, France, in 1871, he began work on a full-scale tractor monoplane featuring tricycle landing gear and powered by a hot-air power plant or a steam engine. In about 1874, du Temple launched his machine down a ski jump and into the air with a young sailor on board. The craft, incapable of either sustained or controlled flight, represented the first powered take-off of a heavier-than-air machine.

Alexander Fyodorovitch Mozhaiski (1825–1890), a Russian naval captain, designed a glider that horses towed into the air. A government commission that included the great Russian chemist D. I. Mendeleyev approved Mozhaiski's plans for a full-scale, steam-powered flying machine, apparently inspired by the work of John Stringfellow. Patented in 1881 and completed in 1883, the craft is said to have jumped as much as one hundred feet through the air after a run down a ski jump near St. Petersburg with a passenger, I. N. Golubev, on board. Mozhaiski's aeronautical experiments were almost completely unknown until Stalinist propagandists rediscovered them and falsely portrayed Mozhaiski as the inventor of the airplane.

Clément Ader (1841–1926) built his early reputation as an engineer and inventor involved with the expanding French railroad system, then turned his attention to communications. Between 1878 and 1885 he earned a total of eighty-four French and foreign patents covering telephones, microphones, and public address systems. Before entering aeronautics he was best known for Theatrephone, a system that carried the sound of live theatrical performances through electrical lines laid in Paris's sewers to coin-operated stereophonic receivers in hotels, cafes, and private homes.

Between 1882 and 1890, Ader designed and built a steam-powered, tailless monoplane named *Eole*, in honor of the god of the winds. The batlike craft made a powered hop of 160 feet through the air on October 9, 1890. Although *Eole* was incapable of either sustained or controlled flight, this represented the first occasion on which a powered aircraft carrying a human made a take-off from level ground. Claims for a second hop of over 300 feet in September 1891 are not generally accepted.

In 1892, the Ministry of War offered Ader the first installment of what would eventually become a 650,000-franc subsidy to construct a new flying machine. Ader abandoned the initial design, *Avion II*, before completion. He tested *Avion III* on a circular track at Sartory on October 12 and 14, 1897. An official report noted that the machine did not fly. The Ministry of War refused to fund further tests.

Nine years later, as the excitement over the first public heavier-than-air flights washed over Europe, Ader announced that he had actually flown *Avion III* over 980 feet on October 14, 1897. The event, he claimed, had been cloaked in military secrecy. Ader produced one surviving witness who now recalled that the machine lifted into the air, then crashed "almost immediately afterwards." While several historians have credited the flight, most agree with Charles Dolfuss, the leading French historian of aviation, and Charles H. Gibbs-Smith, his English counterpart, who rejected claims for flights in 1891 and 1897.

Hiram Stevens Maxim (1840–1916) a native of Sangerville, Maine, patented everything from mousetraps to gas appliances and electric lamps. Many years later he reported that while visiting Paris in 1881, he had encountered a man who advised him to "invent something that will enable these Europeans to cut each other's throats with greater facility."[32] He took the advice and in 1885 demonstrated the first portable, fully automatic machine gun to officials of the British army. Nine years later a thin red line of fifty troopers operating four Maxim guns handily repulsed five thousand Matabele warriors. Originally the weapon of choice for imperial powers, Maxim's wonder weapon would one day enable those same great nations to kill one another "with greater facility" than even Maxim had imagined.

Maxim launched his aeronautical career in 1887 with an enormous steam-powered whirling arm. Unlike more ambitious experimenters who sought to achieve a practical flying machine, Maxim announced that his craft would be nothing more than a test bed to provide aerodynamic data. Completed in 1893, the elephantine craft weighed eight thousand pounds (including the three-man crew), featured four thousand square feet of lifting surface, and was powered by a 180-horsepower steam engine driving an almost eighteen-foot propeller. It ran on a circular track, restrained by upper guard rails that prevented it from rising more than two feet into the air.

During the course of its third trial, the machine rose against the upper restraint and traveled off the ground for an undetermined distance prior to becoming tangled in the rails and grinding to a stop. Unwilling to invest additional funds in the work, Maxim brought his experiments to an end.

Neither Maxim nor any of the other full-scale builders had the slightest influence on the invention of the airplane. If none of them had entered the field, it is likely that Wilbur and Orville Wright would still have flown their first powered machine on the morning of December 17, 1903. Doubtless that statement would have enraged the outspoken French pioneer Gabriel Voisin (1880–1973), who identified Ader as the man who had inspired his own work. Whatever Ader's value as inspiration, the single, short, unsustained bounce of his *Eole* did not teach anyone anything.

It is important to recognize and applaud the vision and the courage demonstrated by virtually all of these pioneers. At the same time, a decent regard for the tiny handful of experimenters whose work did contribute to the final success requires that we distinguish them from others whose projects had the principal value of serving as case studies in how not to invent a flying machine, Ader, Maxim, du Temple, and Mozhaiski among them.

THE DESIGN AND TESTING of model aircraft offered a second approach to solving the problems of flight. Cayley began the tradition of conducting research with models. Stringfellow and Henson, and their countryman D. S. Brown (1873–1874), followed in his footsteps. Ponton d'Amecourt (1863 and 1866 models), Enrico Forlanini (1877 model), Emmanuel Dieuaide (1877), and P. Castel (1878)—an entire generation of helicopter enthusiasts—were model builders, as were a few ornithopterists, notably Gustav Trouvé (1870).

Alphonse Pénaud (1850–1880) was the best of the early modelers. The son of an admiral, Pénaud suffered from a crippled hip that precluded a naval career. On August 18, 1871, he flew his "planophore," an inherently stable model airplane powered by twisted rubber strands, in the Jardin des Tuileries. The little hand-launched aircraft featured wing dihedral for lateral stability and a combined horizontal and vertical tail surface that provided a measure of inherent stability in pitch and yaw. The model completed a circular flight of 130 feet, providing the first public demonstration of genuine stability in a powered heavier-than-air machine.

Pénaud also developed ornithopter and rotary-wing models of the sort that inspired Wilbur and Orville Wright. Eager to move toward the development of a full-scale machine, in 1876 he published an extraordinarily advanced design for a streamlined amphibious aircraft featuring externally braced monoplane wings, a glazed canopy, a fully enclosed engine, a wheeled undercarriage, and a sophisticated control system. Discouraged by his failure to attract financial support, and by public ridicule of his ideas, he took his own life.

A FEW EXPERIMENTERS recognized that the design and flight testing of piloted gliders offered the most direct approach to a powered flying machine. Cayley led the way here, as well. Count Ferdinand Charles Honore Phillipe d'Esterno (1806–1863) inspired future experimentation by suggesting that air currents might keep a glider aloft for extended periods of time.

At least five humans actually glided for short distances during the years 1849–1890. Cayley had flown a young boy (in 1849) and his coachman (in 1852). Jean-Marie Le Bris (1817–1872), a French sea captain, broke his leg while flying his *Albatross* glider near Trefeuntec, France, in 1857, and tested a second glider in 1868 with sand ballast aboard. Louis Mouillard (1834–1897), a French farmer and school teacher living in Algeria and Egypt, made at least one short flight with a hang glider in 1857 and was working on another machine at the time of his death.

John Joseph Montgomery (1858–1911), the first American to leave the ground on wings of his own design, made a single flight from Otay Mesa, south of San Diego, California, in 1884. He returned to the air in 1904–1905 with a tandem-wing glider design. Acrobat Daniel Maloney died in the crash of one of these gliders after it had been carried aloft beneath a balloon. Montgomery himself died of injuries sustained during a hard landing with a parasol-wing monoplane glider in 1911.

Gliding flight offered a direct approach to aeronautical problem solving, but it was also the most dangerous. "If you are looking for perfect safety, you will do well to sit on the fence and watch the birds," Wilbur Wright explained. "But if you really wish to learn, you must mount a machine and become acquainted with its tricks by actual practice."[33]

None of the experimenters who flew gliders before 1890 made more than one or two flights apiece. The experience of Louis Mouillard was typical:

> I strolled onto the prairie with my apparatus upon my shoulders. I ran against the wind and studied its sustaining power, but it was almost a dead calm. The wind had not yet risen, and I was waiting for it. Nearby there was a wagon road, raised some five feet above the plain. It had been raised with the dirt taken from ditches about ten feet wide dug on either side. Then came a little puff of wind, and it also came into my head to jump over that ditch . . . with my aeroplane; so I took a good run and jumped at the ditch. . . . But, Oh Horrors! Once across the ditch my feet did not come down to earth; I was gliding on the air and making vain efforts to land, for my aeroplane had set out on a cruise. I dangled only one foot above the soil, but do what I would, I could not reach it, and I was skimming along without any power to stop. At last my foot touched the earth. I fell forward on my hands, broke one of my wings, and all was over. But goodness! How frightened I had been![34]

Mouillard had flown 138 feet, a world record. He would never fly again. And so it was with others—one flight sent them back to the laboratory and the drawing board, where things were far safer and moved much more slowly. After millennia of dreams and a century of achievement, all of that was about to change, however.

1896: THE YEAR OF THE FLYING MACHINES

In the early spring of 1896, readers of American newspapers were bombarded with stories about flying machines. Victor Oches, a convict serving three to five years in the King's County jail in New York, announced plans to build an aircraft that would travel at speeds of up to 300 mph and "do away with battleships." He would begin work upon receipt of $25,000 cash, providing a full pardon was thrown into the bargain. Captain John W. Viern, "an old steamboat man and mechanic," planned to build a fish-shaped, paddle wheel–powered flying machine. Chicagoan Arthur de Baussett promised to construct a huge airship, as did Capt. Charles E. Smith of San Francisco, sole incorporator of the Atlantic and Pacific Aerial Navigation Company.

Cleveland inventor Rudolph Koesch developed a "spiral-winged aircraft," while Rev. B. Cannon of Pittsburgh, Texas, based his Ezekial Flying Machine on Biblical instructions. A New Yorker had to be restrained by police when he sought to fly his ornithopter from a lumber pile near the 155th Street Bridge. Charles Avery of Rutherford, New Jersey, was less fortunate. He fractured two ribs and was bleeding from the nose and mouth when he was rescued from the shattered remains of the flying machine in which he had hurled himself from a cliff. Avery attributed the catastrophe to a "poor start."

None of this would have led a sensible, hardworking, no-nonsense, feet-on-the-ground American to suspect that the age-old problem of winged flight was in any danger of being solved. By the end of the year, as a result of the success of two Americans and the death of a German, things would look very different indeed.

AFTER A DECADE of effort, Samuel Pierpont Langley (1834–1906), the unofficial chief scientist of the United States, tasted his first real success in the air on May 6, 1896, when he launched his Aerodrome No. 5, a steam-powered model aircraft with a wingspan of fifteen feet, on a flight of almost three-fourths of a mile over the Potomac River. A native of Roxbury, Massachusetts, Langley trained himself as an astronomer and developed a sterling reputation as an administrator of science and a pioneer of the "new" science of astrophysics. In 1886, after almost twenty years as director of Pittsburgh's Allegheny Observatory, he was named third secretary of the Smithsonian Institution. However impressive his scientific and administrative accomplishments, Secretary Langley was best known, then and now, for his work in aeronautics.

Samuel Pierpont Langley

Langley set out in 1884 to discover "how much horse-power was needed to sustain a surface of a given weight by means of its motion through the air."[35] First in Pittsburgh, then in Washington, D.C., he conducted a variety of tests with precision instruments mounted on whirling arms. "The most important general inference from these experiments," he announced in 1891, "is that . . . mechanical flight is possible with the engines we now possess."[36]

Langley's basic discoveries ranged from a critically important correction of Smeaton's coefficient, to a clear demonstration of the superiority of high-aspect-ratio wings. Had the Wright brothers and other subsequent experimenters paid more attention to his work, their own efforts might have gone more smoothly.

When colleagues questioned the accuracy of Langley's work, he resolved to provide a practical demonstration of powered flight that could not be doubted. Putting his study of the science of flight (aerodynamics) behind him, he turned his attention to *aerodromics*, his term for the business of building a flying machine. The long and difficult process, best described as "cut-and-try" empirical engineering, began in 1890 with lightweight models powered by rubber strands, and culminated six years later with the flight of May 6 and the successful trial of a second steam-propelled Aerodrome No. 6 on November 27. For the first time in history, relatively large powered models had unequivocally flown for significant distances.

On June 23, 1896, an enterprising Chicago newsman stumbled across a small camp pitched in the heart of the isolated Indiana dune country, some thirty miles southeast of Chicago at the southern tip of Lake Michigan. His report headlined "Men Fly in Midair" appeared in the *Chicago Tribune* the following day. Octave Chanute (1832–1910), sixty-five years old and one of the most distinguished engineers in the nation, had brought a party of five younger experimenters into the dunes at his own expense with one goal in mind. They had come to fly. For a total of forty-five days in the summer and fall of 1896, Chanute and his employee-associates camped in the dunes and did exactly that, testing four distinct glider designs.

Chanute and Augustus M. Herring, and engineer-experimenter who had also worked for Samuel Langley, developed the best of these craft, a trim little biplane hang glider with a cruciform tail. Clearly inspired by the box kite designed by Australian Lawrence Hargrave, "the two-surface machine" featured biplane wings securely trussed into a sturdy beam structure. This most successful design reflected Chanute's years of experience in bridge building. It was also the first modern aircraft structure, and the ancestor of the generations of externally braced biplanes that would follow.

A native of Paris, Chanute had immigrated to the United States at the age of six with his father, a university professor. Eleven years later, following a rather sheltered childhood, the young man signed on as the lowest-ranking member of a crew surveying a route for the new Hudson River Railroad. Like so many other nineteenth-century engineers, Chanute acquired his technical skills as he moved up the ladder to positions of greater responsibility.

Following the Civil War he served as chief engineer for a series of railroads that brought "civilization" to the Kansas frontier, built the first bridge over the Missouri River, and planned water and sanitation systems for cities that sprouted on the Great Plains. Virtually every cow driven north from Texas passed through the stockyards that he designed for Kansas City and Chicago. Chanute, and engineers like him, played as great a role in the opening of the West as any cowboy or cavalryman.

In the mid-1870s, the "flying bug" bit Chanute, after considering the aerodynamic problems he had encountered during his engineering career, from the air resistance of locomotives, to bridges that collapsed and roofs that lifted off in high winds. What began as a matter of professional interest, however, soon blossomed into a consuming passion.

Having served as president of the American Society of Civil Engineers, vice president of the engineering section of the American Association for the Advancement of Science, and president of the Western Society of Engineers, an important local group, Chanute appreciated the role of information sharing and cooperation in the process of technical problem solving. During the critical years 1885–1903, he emerged as the creator and focal point of an informal and critically important international community of flying-machine experimenters.

Chanute corresponded with virtually everybody active in the field, from aging pioneers like Francis Herbert Wenham to such promising newcomers as Wilbur and Orville Wright. He drew geographically isolated pioneers into an international dialogue, communicated the latest bits of news from leaders in the field, provided encouragement, and occasionally offered financial support for their experiments. Australian Lawrence Hargrave, Louis Mouillard, a resident of Algeria and Egypt, and Californian John Montgomery were but three of the far-flung experimenters whom Chanute introduced to the larger community of flying-machine builders.

He organized sessions for presenting aeronautical papers to professional engineering societies and attracted fresh talent and new ideas into the field through his lectures at universities. Samuel Langley was only one of the individuals whose interest in aeronautics was inspired by a presentation of papers on flight organized by Chanute. Finally, Chanute produced critically important publications that helped to establish a baseline of shared information. The publication of his classic, *Progress in Flying Machines* (1894), represented a milestone in the early history of aviation. Having accomplished all of that, Chanute decided to join the experimenters himself, inspired by admiration for a third great aeronautical figure who was making headlines in the summer of 1896.

BORN IN ANKLAM, Pomerania, Otto Lilienthal (1848–1896) studied mechanical engineering and established a small but successful machine shop and factory in Berlin. A tall barrel-chested man with red hair and a full beard and mustache, Lilienthal was as brilliant as he was daring.

Together with his brother Gustav, he had been fascinated by the flight of birds since childhood. At age thirteen he built an unsuccessful fixed-wing glider. By 1878, he was conducting whirling-arm tests aimed at uncovering some basic principles of wing design. "Formerly men sought to construct flying machines in a complete form," he commented, ". . . but gradually the conviction came that our physical and technical knowledge and our practical experience were by far insufficient to overcome a mechanical task of such magnitude without preliminaries."[37]

Lilienthal reported on his years of experimentation in the treatise *Der Vogelflug als Grundlage der Fleigkunst* (Birdflight as the Basis of Aviation) (1889). Here, at last, was practical information for those who

Otto Lilienthal in the air

wanted to fly. He even provided graphs charting the changing values of lift and drag generated by an airfoil with the peak of the arch at the center of the chord.

Written in German, the book sold poorly. It did not become available in English until 1911 and had little direct impact on other researchers. Rather, word spread through magazine and journal articles in which Lilienthal, Chanute, the German Hermann W. L. Moedebeck, and other writers summarized the information, complete with tables of data that could be used to calculate the wing area required to lift a machine into the air under specific conditions.

By 1890, Lilienthal had begun to put his principles into practice. "To invent an airplane," he said, "is nothing. To build one is something. To fly is everything."[38] Over the next six years he would make some two thousand flights in sixteen glider types. Most of these were simple monoplanes with stabilizing surfaces at the rear, although Lilienthal did experiment with biplane designs with an increased surface area. The ribs and most of the wooden portions of the craft were made of split willow and ash, covered with a cotton twill sealed airtight with a special colloidal solution.

All of Lilienthal's machines were hang gliders. The pilot hung suspended between the wings, with his legs and lower body dangling beneath the aircraft. He exercised control over the machine by shifting his torso to maintain the center of gravity over the center of pressure. If the glider nosed up, the pilot threw his feet toward the front. If the right wing was struck by a gust and rose, he shifted his weight to that side. It was a dangerous approach to flight control, one that led to injury and more.

Even so, the German engineer captured the world's imagination. Scientific and engineering journals, newspapers, and the new illustrated magazines around the globe published stories of "the flying man" who swept down hillsides on artificial wings. Dozens of dramatic photographs showed Lilienthal in the air. While the means to reproduce photos in printed media was not available, high-quality engravings gave readers an accurate notion of just what a human looked like flying through the air. No one who saw those illustrations could doubt that the age of flight was at hand.

Lilienthal inspired emulation. Experimenters in Great Britain, Russia, France, Rumania, and the United States purchased standard monoplane gliders directly from the German master. Others, like Augustus M. Herring and Charles H. Lamson, a pair of young American engineers, and the Englishman Percy Pilcher, built and flew their own Lilienthal pattern gliders. "Professor" William B. Felts transported his Lilienthal-style glider to the top of Colorado's Pikes Peak aboard a cog railway. Felts would have attempted a flying descent but for the onset of bad weather. By the summer of 1896, after five years of gliding, Lilienthal had become the most significant aeronautical figure since Sir George Cayley.[39]

On the morning of August 9, 1896, Lilienthal took his glider to the top of a hill above the village of Rhinow, some sixty-two miles northwest of Berlin. Launching into the air, he flew straight away from the summit, rather than sweeping down the slope and staying close to the ground as he preferred. Fifty feet in the air, his machine stalled and fell to earth. Lilienthal, his back broken, died the next day in a Berlin hospital.

A short time later, Wilbur Wright (1867–1912), the twenty-nine-year-old proprietor of a local bicycle shop, ran across a brief report of the tragedy in a newspaper that he was reading to his brother Orville (1871–1948), who lay desperately ill with typhoid fever in the family home on the west side of Dayton, Ohio. "My own active interest in aeronautical problems dates back to the death of Lilienthal in 1896," Wilbur explained in 1901. "The brief notice of his death which appeared in the telegraphic news aroused a passive interest which had existed since childhood."[40]

2

TAKING TO THE AIR

WILBUR AND ORVILLE

Wilbur and Orville were the third and sixth of seven children born to Milton and Susan Catherine Koerner Wright. Seventh-generation Americans on their father's side, they were direct descendants of Samuel Wright, a Puritan worthy who arrived in Massachusetts as early as 1637. Their mother, the daughter of a skilled mechanic and wheelwright who had fled Germany to escape conscription, represented another sort of American story.

Milton and Susan Wright were an extraordinary pair. As a girl, Susan had the run of her father's well-equipped workshop and learned to use tools at an early age. A very well-educated woman for her time and place, she met Milton Wright at Indiana's Hartsville College, a church institution where she was a student and he a young minister supervising instruction in the preparatory department.

Milton had begun his career as a circuit riding preacher in the service of the Church of the United Brethren in Christ. He had a will of iron and an unshakable faith in his own judgment. Determined to walk the narrow path of virtue, whatever the cost, he rose to the rank of bishop and took leadership of a "radical" church faction opposed to any change in traditional doctrines. A controversy with more liberal elements in the church waxed and waned for over a decade, finally resulting in a national schism in 1885, followed by protracted legal battles.

Together, Milton and Susan Wright created a home that was both a fortress to which the bishop could retreat from his church troubles and a bulwark against the temptations that beset honest men and women in the harsh world beyond the family doorstep. The Wrights were an insulated, tightly knit and loving family. Their parents cherished their children, taught them to think for themselves, to have confidence in their own opinions, and to trust in one another.

The oldest Wright boys, Reuchlin (1861–1920) and Lorin (1862–1939), were natives of Indiana, as was Wilbur, born on a farm near Milville on

Wilbur and Orville Wright

April 16, 1867. The growing family moved to Dayton, Ohio, in 1869, where Milton took up new duties as the editor of *the Religious Telescope*, the principal newspaper of the denomination, and where Susan gave birth to twins, Ida, who died at birth, and Otis, who lived less than two months. Orville was born thirty months later, on August 19, 1871, three years to the day before their sister, Katharine (1874–1929).

The family spent the years 1878–1884 living in Iowa and Indiana, as Milton moved from one church post to the next. They had just arrived in Cedar Rapids, Iowa, in 1878, when Milton Wright presented the Pénaud helicopter toy to eleven-year-old Wilbur and his seven-year-old brother Orville. Both boys exhibited a decided curiosity about the world around them and a capacity to solve problems through experimentation. "The other day I took a machine can and filled it with water . . . ," Orville explained to his absent father, "then I put it on the stove [and] I waited and the water came squirting out of the top about a foot."[1]

The three youngest Wright children were always careful to recognize their debt to a father who worked hard to spark his children's curiosity and to a patient and understanding mother who encouraged her son to conduct a messy experiment. Bishop Wright sought to mold his children's character. Their mother taught them the use of tools and crafted some of their toys, including a much beloved sled. "[We] . . . were lucky enough to grow up in an environment where there was always much encouragement to children to pursue intellectual interests; to investigate whatever aroused curiosity," Orville once explained. "In a different kind of environment our curiosity might have been nipped long before it could have borne fruit."[2]

"From the time we were little children," Wilbur explained, "my brother and myself lived together, played together, worked together and, in fact, thought together. We usually owned all of our toys in common, talked over our thoughts and aspirations so that nearly everything that was done in our lives has been the result of conversations, suggestions and discussions between us."[3] They were mechanically inclined as well, designing and building a machine to fold copies of the church newspaper and constructing a treadle-powered wood lathe.

The family returned home to Dayton for good in 1884, just a few weeks before Wilbur was scheduled to graduate from high school in Richmond, Indiana. Intending to enter Yale University to study for the ministry, he enrolled in special college preparation courses at Dayton's Central High School. Then, during the winter of 1885–1886, he was struck in the mouth by a stick while playing "shinny," a sort of free-form ice hockey. The injury seemed minor at first but led to complications and, apparently, depression. All thoughts of college vanished. Wilbur spent three years as a semi-invalid, caring for the house, reading in his father's extensive library, and nursing his mother, who was dying of tuberculosis.

Following her death in 1889, Orville, who had finished the eleventh grade that spring, decided to establish himself as a printer. He had pursued printing as a hobby since childhood and had worked in Dayton print shops during the past two summers. Wilbur emerged from his bout of depression just in time to enter into a partnership with his brother.

As Wright and Wright Printers, they produced everything from calling cards and letterhead stationery to religious tracts and advertising handbills. For a time in 1889–1890, they focused on the publication of two short-lived neighborhood newspapers. They also sold photographic supplies and assisted Orville's high school classmate, the black poet Paul Laurence Dunbar, in his attempt to launch a newspaper for the African-American community.

Locally, however, they were probably best known for their unique presses, constructed from tombstones, folding buggy tops, and other spare parts. After inspecting one such press, an out-of-town printer walked away impressed, commenting, "Well, it works, but I certainly don't see how it works."[4] Ten years before their serious involvement with the airplane, the Wright brothers were already demonstrating an ability to imagine a complex machine that had yet to be built, and to develop their own unique and effective solutions to technical problems.

Printing became a sideline after 1892, when the Wrights opened their first bicycle shop. The "merry wheel" had begun to capture America's imagination with the introduction of the safety bicycle in 1887. With its two wheels of equal size, sturdy triangular frame, trustworthy chain-drive system, and effective brakes, the safety introduced an entire nation to the freedom of the road.

The bicycle bridged the gap between horse and automobile. It was the point of convergence for technologies that would be crucial to automobile production: electrical welding, ball-bearing production, chain-and-shaft transmission systems, metal stamping, and rubber tires. Moreover, cyclists paved the way for the automobile by campaigning for improved roads. The millions of bicycles pouring out of American factories laid the foundation for a social revolution, an insatiable appetite for personal mobility that would characterize America in the twentieth century.

Enthusiastic cyclists, the Wright brothers soon earned a reputation among their friends as expert cycle repairmen. In addition to providing these services, Wilbur and Orville sold bicycles and accessories. Four years after they entered the trade, they began building their own bicycles for sale. Their shop never became more than a neighborhood operation, but they gained local fame for quality, particularly for their invention of a self-oiling wheel hub.

Had you known the Wright brothers in 1896, they would have seemed the most ordinary of young men. Bachelor brothers who still lived under their father's roof, neither would ever marry. They ran two small businesses, were well liked, and were generally recognized for their technical skills. Nothing suggested, however, that they were in any danger of "committing an immortality," as the poet Robert Frost would later suggest.[5]

But appearances deceive. Beneath the surface, they were restless and eager to make their mark on the world. Wilbur, in particular, seems to have been looking for a challenge against which to measure himself and through which to demonstrate his value to the world. He would find it in the airplane.

WHAT HAD BEEN an interest since their childhood encounter with a flying toy took a more serious turn in the summer of 1896. "From the date of the death of Lilienthal in 1896," Orville later remarked, "we were so interested [in aeronautics] that we discussed matters in this line almost daily."[6] Perhaps so, but it would be another three years before the spark of serious interest was fanned to a flame, apparently by something as simple as a chance reading of a book on birds. "Our own growing belief that men might . . . learn to fly," Wilbur explained, "was based on the idea that . . . thousands of creatures of the most dissimilar bodily structures, such as insects, fishes, reptiles, birds and mammals, were every day flying through the air at pleasure."[7]

Having decided to move beyond the limited resources of the local library, Wilbur wrote to the Smithsonian Institution on May 30, 1899, requesting "such papers as the Smithsonian Institution has published on this subject, and if possible a list of other works in print in the English language."[8] After digesting the Smithsonian materials and other publications recommended to them, the Wrights proceeded to demonstrate analytical abilities that set them far apart from their predecessors.

Their reading complete, they cut straight to the heart of the matter. A successful airplane, they reasoned, would require wings to lift it into the air, an engine powerful enough to propel the craft to flying speed, and a means of controlling the machine in the air. Lilienthal and others had built wings that seemed to work quite well, and automobile experimenters were developing lighter and more efficient internal combustion engines. That left the problem of control. "We reached the conclusion," Wilbur explained, "that . . . the problem of equilibrium had been the real stumbling block in all serious attempts to solve the problem of human flight, and that this problem of equilibrium in reality constituted the problem of flight itself."[9]

THE ABILITY TO apply lessons learned in one technology to a new situation gave the Wright brothers a big advantage in solving the problems of flight control. Several late-nineteenth-century commentators had recognized a potential link between bicycling and aviation. In June 1896, the editor of the *Binghamton Republican* in New York actually predicted that the airplane would be the work of bicycle makers. "The flying machine will not be in the same shape, or at all in the style of the numerous kinds of cycles," he explained, "but the study to produce a light, swift machine is likely to lead to an evolution in which wings will play a conspicuous part."[10]

James Howard Means, editor of the influential *Aeronautical Annual*, pointed to the most important connection between the bicycle and the flying machine. "To learn to wheel one must learn to balance," he noted. "To learn to fly one must learn to balance."[11] Lilienthal wrote from Germany to congratulate Means on his insight. "I think that your consideration on the development between the flying machine & the bicycle and the analogy between . . . [their] development, is excellent," he wrote. "I am sure the flying apparatus will have a similar development."[12]

Manufacturing bicycles had taught the Wrights a lot about precision crafting in wood and metal and the design and construction of lightweight structures. Ultimately, they would even incorporate some bicycle parts, including wheel hubs, chain, sprockets, spoke wire, and tubing into their early powered aircraft designs. But the most important lessons that the Wrights learned from cycling had to do with the control of unstable vehicles.

Most experimenters assumed that controlling an aircraft in flight would be very difficult. They aimed to develop inherently stable machines that would automatically fly straight and level until the pilot ordered a change in course or altitude. The Wrights, however, recognized that riding a bicycle also seems very difficult to a beginner, who is expected to simultaneously pedal, balance, and steer with the handle bars. They set out to develop a means of controlling an airplane with the precision and ease of a bicycle.

But how to achieve that goal? The most difficult task would be to exercise control in the roll axis, balancing the wing tips to maintain level flight or banking for a turn. Wilbur made the breakthrough. They would twist the wing across the span, so that one wing tip would generate more lift and the other less. The pilot of such an aircraft, provided with suitable controls, could balance the wings with ease or bank for a turn. Their friend Octave Chanute would dub the technique "wing-warping."

They designed their first real aircraft, a biplane kite with a five-foot wingspan, to test the principle. Flown from a hill a few blocks from the bicycle shop in late July 1899, the little craft climbed, dived, and banked in either direction, all under the complete control of the operator. Having demonstrated that their wing-warping control system worked in practice, the brothers began to plan a kite-glider large enough to carry one of them aloft.

On May 13, 1900, an energized Wilbur wrote to Chanute, the world's authority on the history of the flying machine. "For some years," he admitted, "I have been afflicted with the belief that flight is possible to man." It was the first of hundreds of letters, notes, and telegrams that would pass back and forth between them over the next decade, marking the course of a relationship that was both very close and at times very difficult.[13]

Neither of the Wrights had attended college or received any formal engineering training. That did not matter. They would prove themselves to be practical and intuitive engineers of genius. From the outset, they were determined to calculate the wing area required to lift a given weight at a given air speed. Chanute had published a table, based on the work of Otto Lilienthal, that provided precise mathematical values for the amount of lift and drag generated by a particular wing shape at varying angles of attack.

Plugged into a relatively simple equation, Lilienthal's data revealed that the only hope of getting into the air with a glider of reasonable size was to fly into a head wind of 15 to 20 mph. In addition to offering such strong and steady winds, the ideal test site ought to be isolated, with gently sloping sand dunes just right for long flights and soft landings. Dayton had none of those advantages. Kitty Hawk had them all.

They learned about Kitty Hawk, an isolated village on the Outer Banks of North Carolina, from a table of average wind speeds at each of 120 field stations maintained by the U.S. Weather Bureau. William J. Tate, a local notary and Currituck County commissioner, responded to a letter from the Wrights, assuring them that the area was perfect for kite flying, with wide flat beaches, tall sand hills, few trees, and strong, steady winds. "If you decide to try your machine here," he promised, ". . . you will find a hospitable people when you come among us."[14]

Wilbur would pioneer the route, with Orville to follow if things looked promising. Wilbur set off on their "scientific vacation" in early September 1900. He broke his train journey in Norfolk, Virginia, braving 100-degree temperatures to scour the city for lumber suitable for wing spars. Moving on to Elizabeth City, on the North Carolina coast, he could not find anyone who had even heard of Kitty Hawk. The journey culminated in an epic voyage aboard a leaky fishing schooner across the storm-tossed waters of Albermarle Sound and into Kitty Hawk Bay.

Wilbur had almost completed work on the kite-glider when Orville arrived three weeks later. When complete, the craft was a trussed biplane weighing just under fifty pounds. The wings were constructed of pine spars, two feet shorter than intended, that had been purchased in Norfolk and ash ribs that had been steam bent to shape in Dayton. The pilot would lay prone in a cut-out section on the lower wing, grasping the bar that flexed the rear edge of the forward elevator up or down to control the aircraft's pitch.

Applied diagonally on the wing, a tightly woven fabric was the key structural element holding the ribs and spars in place and distributing flight loads across the span. The result was a tough, flexible wing capable of absorbing punishment that would probably break a more rigid structure.

This first full-scale Wright aircraft had a career of less than two weeks, October 5–20, 1900. After testing the new machine as a kite for some time on the first day, Wilbur could no longer resist the urge to venture aloft. This first attempt to ride the machine was frightening and less than satisfactory. It became apparent that the wings developed far less lift than the calculations based on the Lilienthal data had predicted. After one or two tries, they abandoned the notion of testing the machine as a kite with a pilot on board.

Since the steady winds were almost never strong enough to lift the weight of a pilot, virtually all of the tests in 1900 involved flying the machine as an empty kite or with a load of sand or chain. The brothers turned the situation to their advantage, measuring the performance of their glider and collecting data that could be used to create accurate aerodynamic tables. They measured the total force on the machine with a grocer's scale, checked the wind speed with an anemometer, and recorded the angle of attack. With that information, they could calculate the actual lift and drag of the glider. "So far as we knew," Wilbur remarked, "this had never previously been done with any full scale machine."[15]

They invited Tom Tate, a lightweight local youngster, to take some thrilling rides on their kite, an activity that enabled them to calculate the resistance of an upright body on the machine. They also demonstrated the effectiveness of their control system by running separate lines from the plane to an operator on the ground. Satisfied that they had gathered as much data as possible, Wilbur made the first free glides with the machine from the closest elevated spot, a group of dunes known locally as the Kill Devil Hills, located some four miles south of Kitty Hawk. During the course of a single day of gliding in late October, he amassed less than two minutes' time in the air.

They returned to Dayton and the routine of the bicycle shop, but flight never wandered far from their minds. Their key to technical innovation involved learning from mistakes as well as successes and incorporating lessons learned with each machine into the next. They moved toward the development of a practical airplane through an evolutionary chain of seven aircraft: one kite (1899), three gliders (1900, 1901, 1902), and three powered machines (1903, 1904, 1905).

In an effort to improve the inadequate lift of the 1900 aircraft, they covered the wings of the new machine with a tightly woven muslin, increased the curvature of the wing, and enlarged the surface area from the 165 square feet used in 1900 to 290 square feet. Weighing in at ninety-eight pounds, it was the largest glider anyone had flown to date.

Back on the Outer Banks in the second week of July 1901, the Wrights constructed a wooden shed in which to assemble and store their new glider. They would live in a tent and share their spartan quarters with several guests. They invited Octave Chanute to spend some time in camp, along with Edward C. Huffaker and George Spratt, two young experimenters whom Chanute had hired to conduct aeronautical tests.

The Wrights made more than fifty free glides and kite tests with their new machine between July 27 and August 17. There were problems, however. On Wilbur's first attempt to glide, the machine nosed sharply into the sand after flying only a few yards. Trial after trial, the pilot moved farther back on the glider, until he completed "an undulating flight" of a little more than three hundred feet. Something was very wrong.

It was the wings. The brothers realized that the longer and far more flexible ribs allowed the wings to deform in flight. They reduced the camber, and the flexibility, by trussing down the ribs of both the upper and the lower wing. When testing resumed, flights in excess of 350 feet, lasting as long as seventeen seconds, became the order of the day. Clearly, however, the 1901 glider, like its predecessor, developed much less lift than had been predicted by performance calculations.

Moreover, the brothers now encountered a new and frightening problem with the control system. All too often, the positively warped side of the wing, the side on which the angle of attack and the lift had been increased, would slow and drop, rather than rising as expected. It was the first step in a frightening sequence of events that led to the aircraft spinning into the sand. "Well-digging," the Wrights called it. Critical problems remained to be solved, and the dangers were very real. "When we left Kitty Hawk at the end of 1901," Wilbur later recalled, ". . . we doubted that we would ever resume our experiments."[16]

But the picture was not entirely bleak. The Wrights had established new distance records for gliding. Chanute assured them that their results were the best ever obtained. Anxious to prepare a record of what they had achieved to date, Wilbur accepted Chanute's invitation to address the Western Society of Engineers in Chicago. His remarks, titled "Some Aeronautical Experiments," combined a brilliant statement of the problem of flight with an analysis of the current state of aeronautics and a careful summary of their own experiments. "A devilishly good paper which will be extensively quoted," Chanute assured the elder brother.[17]

But what of the disparity between their calculations and actual performance in the air? The brothers conducted two preliminary experiments to prove that the problem originated in the published aerodynamic data. Next, they designed and built a wind tunnel with which to gather accurate information. The tunnel itself was simple

The 1901 Wright glider

enough, a wooden box, six feet long and open at both ends. A fan moved a steady stream of air through the tunnel at a constant 25 mph.

The secret lay in the balances, delicate instruments constructed of spoke wire and hacksaw blades. Mounted in the tunnel, they measured the minute forces operating on small model wings. The genius of the brothers was never more apparent than in their ability to visualize the chain of forces cascading through a complex apparatus to produce precisely the bit of information required.

In a few short weeks during the late fall and early winter of 1901, the Wrights tested over forty model airfoil shapes through an entire range of angles of attack. Their tunnel yielded answers to critically important aerodynamic questions, including the ideal aspect ratio, the efficiency of different wing and wing-tip shapes, and the effect of changing the gap between the two wings of a biplane. Small enough to fit in a shoe box, the balances proved as important to the invention of the airplane as any of the gliders in which the brothers risked their lives.

The 1902 Wright glider represented two years of flight testing and a few weeks' worth of priceless wind tunnel data gathered in the back

The 1902 Wright glider

room of the bicycle shop. With a longer span and a narrower chord, the machine had far more elegant proportions than its predecessors. It was also the first Wright glider to sport a rudder, intended to solve the problem of well-digging caused by the increased drag on the positively warped side of a wing.

On August 25, 1902, the Wrights left Dayton for Kitty Hawk and their third experimental season. Once again, Chanute visited camp, along with two of his protégés. The brothers found George Spratt delightful and respected his aeronautical insight, but they had little regard for Augustus M. Herring. Herring had worked for both Chanute and Samuel Langley and claimed to have made a short hop with a powered hang glider of his own from a beach at St. Joseph, Michigan, in 1899. The glider he tested for Chanute at Kitty Hawk was a complete failure.

Wilbur and Orville completed over seven hundred glides with their new machine between September 19 and October 24, 1902. The new glider was a complete success and marked the end of their original quest for an efficient flying machine operating under the control of the pilot. It embodied their core invention, a complete system of flight control. However, the system needed refinement, and the brothers would have to continue learning to fly their machine. Still, the 1902 glider rep-resented a stunning breakthrough: control. When they patented their invention, the brothers described the central elements of their flight control system, but on a glider, not a powered flying machine.

SUCCESS

The Wrights were now ready to fly a powered airplane. When a letter outlining their requirements failed to elicit a response from experienced engine manufacturers, the brothers designed a power plant of their own and asked Charles Taylor, a machinist who helped out in the bicycle shop, to build it for them. The result was a water-cooled, four-cylinder internal combustion engine weighing some two hundred pounds, including fluids. When it had been running for a few minutes, it developed about 12.5 horsepower.

Obviously, the engine was an integral part of the world's first successful airplane. It is also true, however, that the Wrights kept the engine problem very much in perspective. They had calculated how much power they would require to fly and how much the engine could weigh. They produced an engine that met their requirements, but it was far from the most successful or efficient of the first-generation aeronautical power plants. Samuel Langley's team produced an engine that weighed the same as the Wright power plant but developed 52 horsepower. Never mind. The goal was to fly, not to build the world's most efficient aeronautical engine. The Wrights flew, and Langley crashed.

The design of effective propellers presented a far greater challenge. The Wrights knew precisely how much thrust would be required to get their flying machine into the air. They began to think of the propeller as a rotary wing. Knowing the number of rotations per minute, the brothers could calculate the speed of rotation at any point along the blade and select an appropriate airfoil from their wind tunnel. It sounds simple enough, Orville explained, "but on further consideration it is hard to find even a point from which to make a start, for nothing about a propeller, or the medium in which it acts, stands still for a moment."[18]

The Wrights arrived back on the Outer Banks with their new

machine on September 26, 1903, determined to stay until they had flown. Chanute and Spratt returned for a third season, although neither visitor could stay long enough to witness the flight tests of the powered machine. Engine tests started by early November, but repeated damage to the propeller shafts led to long delays and one trip back to Dayton to supervise repairs.

So far, the Wright brothers had completely escaped the attention of the press, but another aeronautical experimenter made front-page news from coast to coast. With the outbreak of the Spanish American War in 1898, the U.S. government had offered Samuel Langley $50,000 to design, build, and test a full-scale, piloted version of the steam-powered model aerodromes he had flown in 1896. Designed to be launched from a catapult mounted on the roof of a houseboat anchored in the Potomac, the Aerodrome was first tested on October 7. Structurally weak and virtually uncontrollable, the machine dropped straight into the water "like a handful of mortar," in the words of one Washington journalist.[19]

Charles Manly, the pilot, escaped injury and was ready for a second test of the repaired craft on December 8. On that occasion the rear wings of the machine began to fold before it reached the end of the launch rail. It nosed straight up into the air, flipped onto its back, and fell into the water. Manly was rescued from the icy river for a second time, but the aeronautical career of Samuel Langley was over.

The Wrights finally prepared to attempt their first powered flight on December 14. With some assistance from local residents, they carried the airplane to the head of a launch rail that had been laid down the lower slope of the big Kill Devil Hill. Wilbur won a coin toss for the honor of making the first attempt. During the launch he lifted the airplane from the rail at too sharp an angle and slammed immediately back to earth, damaging the forward elevator.

Conditions were perfect for a second trial on the morning of December 17. The wing blew at 20 to 27 mph, and the temperature was close to freezing, 34 degrees. The cold air, combined with the fact that they were operating at sea level, increased the effectiveness of the wings and the propellers. The opportunity to fly into the high winds that prevailed that morning was daunting but further increased their chances of success.

10:35 A.M., December 17, 1903

With the assistance of five local residents, the Wrights completed their preparations by 10:30 A.M. Orville set up a camera, aimed at the spot where he thought the airplane might rise into the air, and asked John Daniels, an employee of the U.S. Lifesaving Service, to squeeze the bulb if anything interesting happened. The propellers were pulled through to draw fuel into the cylinders, after which the dry battery coil box was carried on to the lower wing to start the engine. With Wilbur steadying the right wing tip, Orville climbed into the pilot's position and released the line holding the airplane in place. Clattering down the rail and into the air, the airplane flew 120 feet forward, touching the sand twelve seconds after take-off.

Wilbur took his position on the lower wing at 11:20 and made a flight of 195 feet. Twenty minutes later, Orville flew 200 feet in fifteen seconds. Just at noon Wilbur took his second turn, traveling 852 feet through the air in fifty-nine seconds. The flight ended in a hard landing that broke one of the forward-elevator supports.

After carrying the machine back to the starting point, the group was discussing the events of the morning when a gust of wind slowly tumbled the airplane backward. The cast aluminum feet that attached the engine to the airframe snapped. The crankcase shattered when it struck the sand, the chain guides and propeller supports twisted, and the ends of virtually all of the ribs snapped off. John Daniels, who held on too long, was carried right along with the machine. He would later comment that he not only had taken the first photograph of an airplane in the air but also had been the first victim of an accident with a powered flying machine!

THE ACTIVE CAREER of the 1903 Wright airplane was at an end. It had spent less than two minutes in the air. The brothers had expected more of their machine. "Speaking conservatively," Orville Wright remarked in 1923, "the 1903 machine in the hands of an experienced operator was capable of flights of up to twenty minutes, or more, and of reaching an altitude of more than a thousand feet. . . . Thirty miles an hour, however, was practically its limit in speed. In our inexperienced hands, the machine resembled something between a bucking broncho and a roller coaster. We intended to fly it at a uniform altitude of about six feet from the ground, which we thought would be safest, but in some of its antics, in spite of all our efforts to keep it down, it made its altitude record of fifteen feet."[20]

Still, the world's first airplane had traveled far enough to demonstrate that it could stay aloft under its own power and under the control of the pilot. On a lonely Carolina beach, before a handful of spectators, men had flown.

After lunch, the brothers walked four miles up the beach to Kitty Hawk, where they visited friends and telegraphed their father: "Success four flights Thursday morning all against twenty-one mile wind started from level with engine power alone average speed through the air thirty-one miles longest 57 [sic] seconds Inform press home Christmas."[21]

THE ROOTS OF GOVERNMENT INTEREST

Long before the invention of the airplane, several governments had made modest investments in aeronautics. The U.S. Army had sunk

$50,000 into the Langley project. France had entered the field much earlier, supporting efforts to develop a powered airship, or dirigible. As early as 1844, a Dr. Le Berrier had flown a steam-powered airship model in Paris. Two years later, Pierre Jullien flew a clockwork-powered model airship at the Paris Hippodrome. Henri Giffard, an engineer who had assisted Le Berrier, built and flew the world's first successful full-scale, steam-powered airship from the Hippodrome to Trappes and back on September 24, 1852, averaging a blistering 5 mph over the seventeen-mile trip.

During the Franco-Prussian War (1870–1871), France became the first nation to commission a powered flying machine. Constructed by a mechanical engineer named S.C.H.L. Dupuy de Lôme in 1870, the craft was even less practical than Giffard's underpowered machine. Thirteen years later, on October 8, 1883, Albert and Gaston Tissandier, brothers who were among the best-known balloon heroes of the Franco-Prussian War, flew their electrically powered airship over the Paris suburbs for one hour and fifteen minutes.

The decision to launch an official aeronautics program came in the wake of the Franco-Prussian War. Balloonists had carried messages out of besieged Paris and operated with the armies in the field, enabling the French to salvage some shred of pride from the disaster. As a result, the government created a balloon section following the defeat of 1871 and placed Col. Charles Renard (1847–1905) in command.

A graduate of the École Polytechnique, twenty-three-year-old Renard won the Legion of Honor during the Franco-Prussian War. Intrigued by the military potential of flight, he worked with Alphonse Pénaud before beginning his own experiments with unmanned gliders. Renard initially established the government balloon group in the upper story of the Hôtel des Invalides, but quickly shifted operations to more spacious quarters at a Paris park, Chalais Meudon, a government-owned estate that was being refitted to serve as an astrophysical observatory.

With the assistance of Léon Gambetta, chairman of the Budget Committee of the Chamber of Deputies, who owed much of his own political popularity to his flight from Paris aboard a balloon at the height of the siege, Renard transformed a portion of Meudon into the world's first military aeronautical laboratory. The organization devel-

oped the balloons and related equipment used by French military aeronautical units operating in such far-flung places as Indochina,
Morocco, Madagascar, and China.

Renard and his assistant, Lt. Arthur Krebs, also became heavily
involved in experiments with aeronautical power plants and the construction of dirigible balloons. *La France*, the first dirigible airship produced at Chalais Meudon, made its maiden flight on August 9, 1884.
Powered by an electric motor driven by batteries, the 165-foot-long airship made seven flights in 1884–1885, including a five-mile circle.

The old fear of death from the sky, coupled with these early French
airship experiments, inspired a new generation of novelists to look into
the future. Jules Verne (1828–1905) described the power and influence
exercised by an obsessed tyrant armed with a flying machine in *Clipper
of the Clouds* (1887) and its sequel, *Master of the Universe* (1904). Albert
Robida (1848–1926), an artist and writer who was a countryman and
contemporary of Verne's, described his vision of aerial warfare in *La
guerre au vingtiéme siécle* (War in the Twentieth Century) (1887).

Research drove the work at Chalais Meudon. In 1891 Renard constructed the first French wind tunnel, with which he studied airship
hull resistance and propeller design. It was the largest tunnel built to
date and the first to be constructed at national expense to serve military needs. Chalais Meudon also came to represent a source of long-
term aeronautical experience of enormous value to the nation.
Lieutenant J. B. E. Dorand is but one case in point. Assigned to the
facility in 1894, he rose to head French aeronautical procurement during World War I.

Renard was naturally disposed to support the work of first-generation heavier-than-air experimenters after 1903. But the times turned
against him. Antimilitarist socialist politicians controlled the government. Scandals, including the Dreyfus Affair, rocked the general staff,
leading to declining military budgets between 1895 and 1910. As might
be expected, Renard's research budget was an early casualty of
retrenchment. Discouraged by falling allocations and humiliated by his
failure to win election to the Academy of Sciences, Renard took his
own life on April 13, 1905, just as French interest in heavier-than-air
flight was building.

• • •

RENARD'S WORK had given the Germans much food for thought. Count Ferdinand Adolf August Heinrich von Zeppelin (1838–1917) paid particularly close attention. A serving officer in the Army of Wurttemberg since age fifteen, he made his first balloon flight at St. Paul, Minnesota, in 1863, immediately after completing his tour of duty as a military observer with the Army of the Potomac during the American Civil War. Zeppelin's thoughts returned to aeronautics a decade later, following his forced retirement from the army, when he became concerned about French experiments with powered dirigible airships.

He was not alone. The minister of war, encouraged by Kaiser Wilhelm I, created a balloon section of the army in 1883. The following spring the Prussian government created an Experimental Section for Captive Balloons, renamed the Airship Detachment in 1887. While most of the section's work concerned the development of improved captive observation balloons, officers attached to the unit were involved in various airship projects proliferating in Germany.

Count Ferdinand von Zeppelin

Zeppelin had studied the work of Dr. Karl Wolfert, who built his first airship in 1879 and died in the fiery crash of his final machine at Berlin Tempelhof on the evening of June 12, 1897. He also knew of Austrian engineer David Schwarz's plan for a rigid airship featuring an envelope constructed of thin aluminum sheets. Work on the craft began in 1895 and ended with a catastrophic crash in the fall of 1897.

As early as 1894, the German government had impaneled a prestigious aeronautical commission chaired by physicist Hermann Helmholtz to consider potential funding for various airship proposals. The panel rejected Zeppelin's initial plans, which called for a sort of aerial railroad train, in favor of a rival scheme. Undeterred, Zeppelin asked the advice of a member of the commission, Professor Müller-Breslau. With that advice in hand, the count and his team, chief engineer Theodore Kober and Ludwig Dürr (1878–1956), developed the basic design of the classic rigid airship by 1898.

When complete, LZ 1 (Luftschiffbau Zeppelin) measured 420 feet long and was operated by a crew of five. First flown on July 2, 1900, the behemoth was so underpowered and impossible to control that it was immediately abandoned. The original company collapsed. Undeterred, Zeppelin and Dürr, who quickly emerged as the greatest of all airship designers, went to work on LZ 2, which was destroyed on its second flight.

The persistent count finally tasted limited success with LZ 3, which completed two flights of two hours each on October 9–10, 1906. The Kaiser's government took notice. In the fall of 1906, a new Motor Airship Research Committee awarded the lion's share of the available funding to the rival nonrigid airship scheme of Major August von Parseval and provided Zeppelin with a smaller grant of 500,000 deutsche marks to repair his airship hanger. In 1907, Zeppelin received an additional 400,000 deutsche marks toward the cost of a new airship.

LZ 4 was lost during a storm in 1908 while completing trials that would lead to its purchase by the army. After more than a decade of effort, the count seemed finished. But in an extraordinary outburst of enthusiasm, unsolicited money, in large amounts and small, poured in from every corner of the Reich. The German people had adopted

Zeppelin and his airships as a suitable icon for the power of the nation. By 1913, a small fleet of Zeppelin airships conveyed sightseers over German cities.

Count Zeppelin had transformed the airship from a frail experimental craft with a top speed of less than 15 mph, into something approaching a practical weapons system. An attack from the air was no longer difficult to imagine, and the fanciful nineteenth-century dreams of Jules Verne gave way to the much darker and far more prophetic vision of aerial devastation provided by H. G. Wells (1866–1946), author of *The War in the Air* (1908) and *The World Set Free* (1914). Here at last was an aerial prophecy that would be realized.

THE ENGLISH GOVERNMENT could not ignore a subject so fascinating to France and Germany. In 1878 the War Office ordered Capt. James Lethbridge Brooke Templer, an experienced amateur aeronaut, to establish a balloon school for the aeronautical instruction of officers and men at the Woolwich arsenal. Nine years later the same wealthy young officer established the Balloon Factory at Aldershot. He survived administrative tribulations for the next decade, continuing to serve as chief balloon instructor to the Royal Engineers and chief balloon builder to His Majesty's forces.

Thanks entirely to Templer, the British balloonists who boarded ship for the Boer War in 1899 comprised the best-equipped and -prepared military aeronautical unit in the world. France and Germany had given more encouragement to technological advance, but the English were far better prepared to operate traditional observation balloons in the field. "When the war ended," one authority commented, "public opinion, impressed by one of the few bright spots in a dismal and disappointing expedition, demanded a re-appraisal of military ballooning."[22]

The favorable testimony relating the success of the balloons in the South African campaign guaranteed increased government interest and support. By 1902, the pressure of French and German airship programs led the War Office to appropriate funds for an English dirigible. Aldershot wouldn't do. It was far too small, so the Balloon Factory moved from Aldershot to an area on the Farnborough Plain, a mile or so north of the old site. Success with the observation balloon, already a battlefield anachronism, paved the way for the world's leading aeronautical facility, the Royal Aeronautical Establishment.

A NEW AGE NOW BEGINS

A new century called for a new technology. The nations of Europe had begun to invest in flight research aimed at developing dirigible airships. Interest in heavier-than-air flight, on the other hand, was at an ebb in Europe.

Percy Pilcher (1866–1899), one of Octave Chanute's English correspondents, had died from injuries suffered in a glider crash on September 30, 1899, underscoring the danger of following in the footsteps of the great Lilienthal. In October 1901, Wilhelm Kress (1836–1913), an Austrian who had been experimenting with rubber-powered models since the 1870s, tested a tandem-wing flying boat powered by a thirty-horsepower Daimler engine. The machine capsized before it left the water. In August 1903, Karl Jatho managed to bounce a short distance through the air near Hanover, Germany, accomplishing nothing more than the dead-end goal that Clément Ader had achieved before he gave up attempting to fly.

The work of Ader and Maxim, both government-supported experimenters, had ground to a halt far short of success. Langley's effort, lavishly supported by both the War Department and the coffers of the Smithsonian Institution, had come to an even more catastrophic end, with two crashes in the Potomac in October and December 1903. The prospect of winged flight, so bright in 1896, had dimmed considerably.

All of that began to change in Paris on the evening of April 2, 1903. The occasion was a speech given by Octave Chanute at a dinner conference for members of the Aéro-Club de France, during which he introduced the work of two American bicycle makers to an audience well qualified to appreciate what they were hearing.

THE HOMELAND OF THE MONTGOLFIER

Founded in 1898, the Aéro-Club de France was a favorite gathering place of the balloonists, one of the wealthiest and most fashionable social circles in fin de siècle Paris. Ballooning, for over a century the province of aerial showmen, soldiers, and scientists, had attracted a host of wealthy dilettantes. A short voyage aloft, dangling beneath a gaily decorated bag of hydrogen, proved just the ticket for a jaded young man with time on his hands, money in his pocket, and a taste for adventure. Stories of romantic flights over the countryside aboard balloons laden with picnic baskets and bottles of champagne filled the society pages.

At the turn of the century, a small band of influential enthusiasts began to edge the Aéro-Club de France toward new aeronautical technologies. Initially, they focused on the airship, a field France had dominated throughout the nineteenth century. On October 19, 1901, Alberto Santos-Dumont, a Brazilian living in Paris, piloted his one-man airship, No. 6, from his stripped tent-hangar at the Aéro-Club Parc d' Aérostation in the Paris suburb of St.-Cloud to the Eiffel Tower and back in just under half an hour.

Awarded a 100,000-franc prize by Henri Deutsche de la Meurthe, a leader of the Aéro-Club and a pioneer of the French petroleum industry, Santos-Dumont promptly donated 75,000 francs to the poor people of Paris and divided the remaining 25,000 francs among members of his crew. The adulation of the City of Lights, La Belle France, and the world he reserved for himself.

In the entire history of flight there is no one quite like him. He stood only five feet, five inches tall in his shiny patent-leather boots fitted with lifts. Dark hair, parted in the center and held in place with pomade, capped a cadaverous face dominated by large protruding eyes. Those who knew him well assure us that a cool patrician manner more than offset his faintly comic appearance.

Alberto Santos-Dumont aloft in his airship No. 9

The son of one of the wealthiest coffee planters in Brazil, twenty-three-year-old Santos-Dumont arrived in Paris in 1897 to study engineering. He acquired his first balloon the following year, but he disliked being at the mercy of the winds and built the first of the seven one-man airships that would follow over the next three years. The sight of the bold little Brazilian chugging slowly across the rooftops of Paris epitomized the spirit of Belle Epoque.

There were, of course, larger airships in the air. Count Zeppelin had already taken to the air in his first aircraft. Inspired by the German count and the work of Renard and Krebs, the brothers Pierre and Paul Lebaudy, sugar refiners from Nantes, launched the first in a series of large nonrigid airships for which they would become famous. Following his Deutsch prize flight, however, *le petite* Santos lost his enthusiasm for lighter-than-air flight. "To propel a dirigible balloon through the air," he announced, was something akin to "pushing a candle through a brick wall."[23]

Santos-Dumont's growing enthusiasm for heavier-than-air flight was shared by his colleagues of the Aéro-Club de France, who dined at the club on the evening of April 2, 1903. While Chanute's discussion of Wright technology was fuzzy and inaccurate, he had no trouble communicating the fact that the brothers had moved far beyond any potential rivals and were rapidly moving toward a powered flying machine.

European enthusiasts were aware of the Wright brothers. Wilbur Wright had published two articles in well-known European journals in the summer of 1901.[24] In addition, Chanute had spread word of their achievements through his network of European correspondents. As a result, the brothers had acquired their earliest European admirer, Capt. Ferdinand Ferber.

Ferber was a near-sighted and overweight artillery officer who walked with a slouch. Having corresponded with both Lilienthal and Ader, he had built and flown a series of unsuccessful gliders. In 1902, inspired by Chanute and a careful reading of Wilbur's 1901 talk, Ferber built and attempted to fly a frail and uncontrollable version of a Wright glider. Unsatisfactory as the experience may have been, Ferber had at least succeeded in calling the attention of his colleagues to the work of the Wright brothers.

Another of Chanute's correspondents, Maj. Baden Fletcher Smyth Baden-Powell, president of the Royal Aeronautical Society, had informed the membership of the "wonderful progress" made by the Americans. Surely there was no reason to doubt that "such experts, having attained proficiency in the delicate art of balancing themselves . . . should not be able to soar away on the wings of the wind and remain indefinitely in the air."[25]

SEVENTY-ONE YEARS OLD, Octave Chanute delivered the most important speech of his career and his life on the evening of April 2, 1903, but he was delivering unwelcome news. The Comte de la Vaulx, one of the founders of the Aèro-Club, explained that the talk came as a "disagreeable revelation" to French enthusiasts who had been "resting on the laurels of their predecessors too long," awakening them to the fact that "it was time to get seriously to work if they did not want to be left behind."[26]

"Will the homeland of the Montgolfier suffer the shame of allowing . . . the greatest scientific revolution since the beginning of the world . . . to be realized abroad," asked Ernest Archdeacon, a wealthy lawyer, balloonist, and automotive pioneer. "Gentlemen scholars to your compasses! You Maecenases; and you too, of the Government, put your hands in your pockets—else we are beaten!"[27]

HUFFMAN PRAIRIE

The Wrights knew that the wind and sand of Kitty Hawk had been essential to their success. Nevertheless, they decided to carry on in the Dayton area, where they could live at home, keep an eye on the bicycle shop, and fly from the early spring to late fall at minimum expense. They selected Huffman Prairie, a one-hundred-acre pasture eight miles east of Dayton, as their new flying field. Although conveniently located near a stop on an interurban railroad line, the field was several miles from the nearest village and as isolated a spot as one could find in the area. Just as important, the owner, Dayton banker Torence Huffman, allowed the brothers to use the field for free, asking only that they chase the livestock pastured there into the safety of a fenced area before they attempted any flying.

The Wrights unveiled their new airplane, a close copy of their first powered machine, on May 23, 1904. Rather than hiding from the press, they invited everyone to come watch them fly. Some forty spectators were on hand, including a dozen or so newsmen. The wind refused to blow, however, and Wilbur ran the machine off the end of the launch rail without rising into the air. After three days of driving rain, a handful of spectators came back to watch as Orville kept the machine in the air for all twenty-five feet. Unimpressed, reporters went away convinced that there was no story here.

Struggling to achieve flying speed in the light Ohio breezes, the Wrights used launch rails as long as 240 feet, but they did not exceed the best of the four flights of 1903 until August 13, 1904. Their propeller design had improved, and they were experimenting with the balance of their machine, adding weight to the front. Their first real breakthrough, however, came only after they began catapulting the machine into the air through the use of a sixteen-hundred-pound weight dropped from the top of a large derrick.

Comfortable with the catapult, Wilbur flew the world's first circle with a heavier-than-air machine on September 20 and set new time and distance records in the process: 4,080 feet in just over ninety-five seconds. Fortunately for history, an articulate visitor, Amos I. Root, of Medina, Ohio, witnessed the flight. The proprietor of an apiary supply house, Root had heard rumors that the Wrights were flying near Dayton and came to see for himself. Readers of his journal, *Gleanings in Bee Culture*, were, for a time at least, better informed with regard to one of the great news stories of the century than subscribers to the *New York Times*: "When it turned that circle, and came near the starting-point, I was right in front of it, and . . . it was . . . the grandest sight of my life. Imagine a . . . locomotive with wings that spread 20 feet each way, coming right toward you with a tremendous flap of propellers, and you have something like what I saw. . . . I tell you friends, the sensation that one feels in such a crisis is something hard to describe."[28]

Wilbur and Orville continued to fly until December 9, 1904, and resumed testing at Huffman Prairie in the spring of 1905 with a third powered airplane. The wings of this craft were the same as its predecessors. It was also longer and taller, however, with a larger elevator and improved propellers. For the first time, the rudder was disconnected from the wing-warping system and operated with a separate hand control.

Growing experience in the air led to the final breakthrough late in the summer of 1905. By early September, flights of two to five minutes had become commonplace. On September 26, Wilbur remained aloft for over eighteen minutes. By the first week in October, the record had climbed to over thirty-three minutes in the air. The best flight of the season, almost twenty-five miles in just over thirty-nine minutes, came on October 5. The Wright brothers had transformed the marginal success of 1903 into the first practical flying machine.

Passengers on the interurban now had a good view of the airplane in flight. Crowds began to gather along the fence line to watch, and newsmen returned to the prairie. Worried that rivals would copy their machine before they had patent protection or contracts for the sale of an airplane, the brothers simply stopped flying after Wilbur flew a single circuit of the field on October 16, 1905. They would not fly again for the next thirty-one months.

SHIFTING GEARS

The brothers filed their original patent on March 23, 1903, and were promptly rejected by an official who advised them to "employ an attorney skilled in patent proceedings." It was good advice. Henry A. Toulmin, a patent attorney with offices in nearby Springfield, Ohio, transformed the brothers' achievement into the masterfully crafted application. Patent No. 821,393 was granted on May 22, 1906.

The Wrights had begun the difficult business of attempting to sell their invention long before they received a patent. Their challenge was to convince potential buyers that they could supply a practical flying machine while at the same time protecting their invention by restricting the release of photographs or other information that might enable rivals to copy their technology. In a way, the brothers had succeeded too well in masking the details of their achievement from the press. It didn't help that they refused to fly until a customer signed on the dotted line.

In January 1905 the brothers approached officials in the War Department through their local congressman. It soon became apparent, however, that the U.S. Army had little interest. These military officers have become stock figures of derision over the years, portrayed as stodgy military conservatives unwilling to seize the future. But this was simply not the case.

Official interest in the military potential of aviation can be seen in lavish U.S. Army support for the Langley project of 1898–1903. That very public and embarrassing failure triggered congressional investigations and accusations that the Army's Board of Ordnance and Fortification had wasted precious resources on a pipe dream. Is it so surprising that officers and administrators in Washington should dismiss the claims of two bicycle makers from Dayton, Ohio? Where were the photos? Where were the demonstration flights?

To be sure, the Wrights did not expect any payment until they demonstrated the performance of their airplane. It never occurred to them that a badly burned officer would follow bureaucracy's first rule: avoid embarrassment above all else. The brothers were attempting to do business with the governments of the world as if they were merchants in West Dayton. At the moment, U.S. Army officials felt justified in asking for a bit more proof.

The governments of Europe were more interested in the Wrights than was the U.S. Army. Colonel John E. Capper, the officer most responsible for aeronautics in the British army, corresponded with the brothers and actually visited them in Dayton in 1904. While he fairly represented the Wrights in reports to His Majesty's government, Capper believed that Britain should develop its own aeronautical talent.

The French government took an even stronger interest in the Wrights, dispatching a military commission to Dayton to investigate the matter and negotiate with the brothers in 1905. In the end, these contacts also came to nothing. No government would sign a contract without a demonstration flight.

Having failed to conclude a sale on their own, the Wrights accepted an offer of assistance from Charles Flint & Company, a firm specializing in the sale of arms and new technology to the governments of the world. Flint representatives arranged for the Wrights to visit Europe in 1907, where they met with military and political authorities but failed to strike an immediate bargain.

Quite suddenly, their luck changed. In January 1908, the U.S. Army developed performance specifications for an airplane and accepted a bid from the Wright brothers. Two months later, the brothers signed a second contract, for the sale of an airplane to a French syndicate that would also have the right to produce and sell Wright aircraft under license.

It was time for the Wrights to brush up their flying skills in preparation for the demonstration flights that would be required to complete both sales. They refurbished their 1905 machine, installing seats for the pilot and a passenger and a new upright control system, then shipped the aircraft to Kitty Hawk in early April, where they could fly in relative secrecy. They made twenty-two flights between May 6 and 14, including their first with a passenger, mechanic Charles Furnas. Wilbur left for France without returning to Dayton. Orville went home by way of Fort Myer, Virginia, where he was scheduled to demonstrate a second airplane for U.S. Army officials in a few months.

Knowledgeable opinion on the Wrights was divided. Some important journals, including *Scientific American* and *Cosmopolitan Magazine*, supported their claims of repeated flights between 1903 and 1905; so did the Aero Club of America. Others, including most of the leading French aeronautical experimenters, doubted the Wright claims. Time alone would tell.

3

THE WORLD TAKES WING,
1904‒1909

LES AVIATEURS MILITANTE

By the spring of 1904 the seeds planted by Octave Chanute's Paris lecture had begun to blossom. With Capt. Ferdinand Ferber and Ernest Archdeacon, a wealthy lawyer and aeronautics enthusiast, leading the charge, a small band of enthusiasts, popularly identified as *"les aviateurs militante,"* set off in pursuit of what the mysterious brothers had achieved in faraway Ohio.

The French failed to appreciate the Wrights' emphasis on control or the details of the wing-warping system, but they were universally impressed by Chanute's account of the 1902 glider. Access to the (inaccurate) drawings of the aircraft published in the Aéro-Club journal, *l'Aérophile*, had not been much help though. Ferber's *"type de Wright"* glider was "crudely constructed by a common carpenter." The glider *"de type Wright 1902"* that Col. Charles Renard and the workmen at Chalais Meudon produced for Ernest Archdeacon in January 1904 was only two-thirds the size of the original, weighed forty pounds less, and did not feature wing-warping.

Archdeacon chose an extraordinary individual to test-fly his glider. Gabriel Voisin (1880–1973), the son of a provincial engineer, was born

Gabriel (left) and Charles Voisin

in Belleville, France, on the banks of the river Saône. Trained as a draftsman and architect at the École de Beaux-arts in Lyon, he was a handsome fellow with flowing hair, a full mustache, and dark penetrating eyes. Voisin spent his early years balancing an interest in boats, automobiles, and kites with the pursuit and seduction of a long string of housekeepers, shop girls, seamstresses, dental assistants, postmistresses, landladies, prostitutes, and errant wives. "My life," he recalled, "was full, and I never knew boredom."[1]

An admirer of Clément Ader and a family acquaintance of Col. Renard, who had introduced him to Archdeacon, Voisin took to the air aboard the new glider on Easter Sunday, 1904, from the dunes at Merlimont, on the Channel coast. Over the next two weeks, the young novice and his older rival, Captain Ferber, flew up to eighty feet through the air. Enormously pleased, Archdeacon predicted that his group would soon be able to surpass the Wright brothers.

Work was soon underway on other variants of the 1902 Wright glider. Stefan Drzewiecki, a Polish pioneer aerodynamicist and propeller theorist who had been elected vice president of the Aerial Navigation branch of the Tsarist Russian Technical Association in St.

Petersburg in 1882, produced a Wright-type glider, "a little different from that of M. Archdeacon," at Chalais Meudon.

Skeptical about reports of success in America, Robert Esnault-Pelterie, a nineteen-year-old graduate of the Sorbonne with a degree in general science, set out to "make a repeat experiment." He flew his own "exact copy" of the Wright machine near Paris in May 1904, with what he regarded as disappointing results. Wing-warping, the "twisting of the surfaces," he reported, "magnified tensions on the wires," causing him to fear "breakages in the air."[2]

Wilbur and Orville Wright remained distant and mysterious figures to the French, but their work had sparked a renaissance of interest in heavier-than-air flight. No one quite understood the Wrights' control technology, but the 1902 Wright glider provided a universal starting point for new experimenters entering the field and established the pattern of a successful airplane as a biplane propelled by pusher propellers and featuring a "canard" (*canard* means "duck") elevator forward of the wings.

By October 1904, members of the Aéro-Club had established rich prizes to reward aeronautical achievement and lure newcomers into the field. A silver trophy, the Coupe Ernest Archdeacon, would go to the first pilot to fly 25 meters (82 feet). The Aéro-Club would present 100 francs and a silver medal to the first ten pilots to fly 60 meters, and 1,500 francs for the first flight of 100 meters (330 feet). The 50,000-franc Grand Prix d'Aviation Deutsch-Archdeacon would honor the first circular powered flight of one kilometer. The club also hosted a model competition in the spring of 1905 that attracted talented newcomers into the field, including Hubert Latham, José Weis, and Louis Paulhan. Each would emerge as a leading aviator.

With Gabriel Voisin as their chief engineer, Archdeacon and three other investors launched the aerospace industry in the spring of 1905, establishing Syndicate d'Aviation, the first company founded to manufacture airplanes. The initial product of the new firm, a two-bay biplane inspired by Hargrave's box kite, broke apart in the air while being tested as an unmanned kite. Voisin rebuilt the craft, outfitted it with floats, and allowed himself to be towed into the air by a speed boat on June 8, 1905.

Early the next morning one of the spectators paid a call on Voisin. Louis Blériot (1872–1936) had come to buy a flying machine. Thirty-three years old, Blériot was a striking man with a sweeping moustache, clear, deep-set brown eyes, and high cheek bones. Frederick Collin, his mechanic, called attention to his "patron's" prominent nose, suggesting that such a birdlike profile must be evidence of predestination.

A native of the northern industrial town of Cambrai with an engineering degree from the École Centrale des Arts et Manufactures, he founded the Société des Phares Blériot, a firm specializing in the production of acetylene headlamps and accessories for automobiles. Married to Alice Vendene, with the first of their six children about to arrive, Blériot seemed to be settling into the position of a prosperous small industrialist.

But the young businessman had caught the flying bug. He had been interested in heavier-than-air flight while still a student, but kept his enthusiasm in check, for fear of looking foolish. Now, earning some 60,000 francs a year from the sale of his headlamps, he could finance his own aeronautical experiments and was naturally drawn into the Ferber-Archdeacon-Voisin circle.

Only five weeks after gliding above the Seine, Voisin returned to the river to retest the original machine and try out the craft he had built for Blériot. The Syndicate glider was damaged during the take-off run, and the Blériot machine proved so wildly unstable that Voisin barely escaped drowning. Far from discouraged, Blériot offered to partner with Voisin, who accepted immediately, eager to leave the ranks of the hired mechanics and launch his own business.

THEN THERE WAS Alberto Santos-Dumont. Disenchanted with dirigible balloons and fascinated by the activity of *les aviateurs militante*, he built an unsuccessful glider (No. 11) in 1905. In January 1906 he was rumored to be working on the design for a helicopter. The aircraft that finally rolled out of his workshop in July 1906, however, appeared very different. Originally intended to be test-flown while dangling beneath

Santos-Dumont's airship No. 14, the craft was officially named *14-bis* (No. 14, second version). Newsmen preferred the more dramatic *Bird of Prey.*

To a modern eye, *14-bis* appears as awkward and ungainly a machine as ever took to the skies. But looks can be deceiving. The design reflected an interesting reinterpretation of the Wrights' configuration. It combined elements of Hargrave's box kite in the biplane cellular wing and canard elevator. Beyond that, however, much of the machine was pure Santos-Dumont. Who else would have arranged for the pilot to control his machine while standing up in a wicker balloon basket?

Like other Europeans, Santos-Dumont installed a forward elevator and a rear rudder but relied on wing dihedral for inherent lateral stability. After the initial tests, however, he added large center-pivoted elevon surfaces mounted in the outer wing bays.

Perhaps his wisest decision was to select an Antoinette engine. These light, powerful engines were originally developed by the engineer Léon Levavaseur (1863–1922) to power racing boats. A native of Cherbourg, Levavaseur named his creation in honor of Antoinette Gastambide, the daughter of his employer. The Antoinette, initially offered in twenty-four- and fifty-horsepower versions, literally propelled Europe into the air age and launched an industry as well. Levavaseur and Louis Blériot, who would serve as vice president of the firm with the same name as the engine, incorporated Antoinette in 1906 as the first corporation dedicated to the manufacture of aircraft engines.

Late in June 1906, Santos-Dumont decided to enter his new craft in the competition for some of the new prizes. Following initial tests and a few false starts, *14-bis* left the ground under its own power for a hop of four to seven meters on September 13. He took to the air once again on the afternoon of October 23, covering fifty meters at an altitude of three to four meters, capturing the first half of the Coupe Ernest Archdeacon for a flight of over twenty-five meters.

Santos-Dumont next flew from Bagatelle, a Paris polo field and exercise area for race horses near the Bois de Boulogne, on November 12, covering 222 meters (720 feet) through the air in twenty-one and a half seconds. Just one hundred feet and thirty-eight seconds short of the Wrights' best flight of December 17, 1903, it was as far and as long as *14-bis* would ever fly.

All of France knew that the Wrights claimed to have flown up to twenty-four miles the year before. No newspapers had covered the long flights, however, and the French were suspicious of the American brothers who refused to fly in public and wouldn't show photographs of their powered aircraft in the air. The Aéro-Club members, having watched Santos-Dumont fly, now hailed the Brazilian as the "Triumphant One."³ He was feted at banquets and lionized in the newspapers. Archdeacon puffed up his chest to announce that Santos-Dumont had "assuredly gained the greatest glories to which a man can aspire. . . . He has just achieved, not in secret or before hypothetical and obliging witnesses, a superb flight . . . a decisive step in the history of aviation."⁴

Nor was the excitement limited to France. Even American newspapers lauded the flights of *14-bis* as "The First Important Demonstration . . . of an Aeroplane Made in Public."⁵ However, Alexander Graham Bell quickly pointed out that the Wright brothers deserved "the credit of solving the great problems of aeronautics," suggesting that "Santos-Dumont has borrowed their ideas."⁶

VOISIN AND BLÉRIOT were among the more dispirited members of the crowd gathered at Bagatelle to watch Santos-Dumont fly on November 12. Their latest machine (Blériot III), an elliptically winged craft on floats powered by a twenty-four-horsepower Antoinette, had repeatedly refused to leave the water. Rebuilt with wheels and a second engine, the craft ran along the field until it hit a stone, bounced across a shallow ditch, and came to rest nose down, with the elevator crushed and the propellers smashed. Discouraged, the pair dissolved their business arrangement.

Voisin quickly forged a new, and much more successful, partnership with his brother Charles. The Voisin Frères immediately set to work on the three new pusher, canard, biplanes with which they would earn their reputations in 1907–1908. The first of these aircraft, sold to automobile enthusiast Henry Kampferer, refused to leave the ground.

Léon Delagrange (1873–1910), a well-known sculptor and a contemporary of Gabriel Voisin at the École des Beaux-Arts, bought the second aircraft, which Charles Voisin flew for the first time on March 30, 1907. By the fall, Delagrange himself had completed several hops, covering up to five hundred meters through the air.

The Voisins progressed with each aircraft they completed. They sold their third machine to Henry Edgar Mumford Farman (1874–1958) in the summer of 1907. The second of three sons born to an English news correspondent living in Paris, Farman attended school in France, spoke English with a thick accent, and eventually became a French citizen. He had taken up aviation while recovering from injuries suffered in the 1905 James Gordon Bennett Automobile Race. Having tried his hand with a homemade Chanute-Herring glider, Farman approached Voisin Frères in search of a powered machine.

He made a 30-meter flight with his new machine on September 30, 1907, from an open area in the Paris neighborhood of Issy-les-Moulineax, soon to become the most famous flying field in the world. He stretched his distance to 285 meters on October 15, and eleven days later made four flights of 363, 403, 350, and 771 meters. The last of these—2,350 feet in fifty-two and three-fifths seconds—won the Archdeacon Cup. Farman capped the season with a circular flight of some 1,500 meters on November 18 but failed to win the Deutsche-Archdeacon prize because one wheel had touched the ground.

As his confidence grew, Farman modified his machine, then flew two circles at Issy on January 13, 1908, the first ever flown by a non-Wright machine. Two days later he won the 50,000-franc Deutsch-Archdeacon prize for an officially witnessed circular flight of one kilometer (actually 1,500 meters in one minute, twenty-eight seconds).

Henry Farman had electrified France. One could write off Santos-Dumont's performance of the previous year as a hop, but a 1,500-meter circle was undeniably a flight. "The famous Wright brothers may today claim all they wish," Archdeacon crowed. "The first *authentic* experiments in powered aviation have taken place in France; they will progress in France; and the famous fifty kilometers announced by the Wrights will . . . be beaten by us as well before they will have decided to show their phantom machine."[7]

What compelled the French to underrate their debt to the Wrights? The Europeans had stumbled into the air in machines with ineffective control systems. They had applied a thin veneer of their own design notions over the basic Wright configuration of a pusher biplane with a canard elevator. Finally, they simply could not believe that successful aviators would remain on the ground while newcomers were beginning to take to the sky.

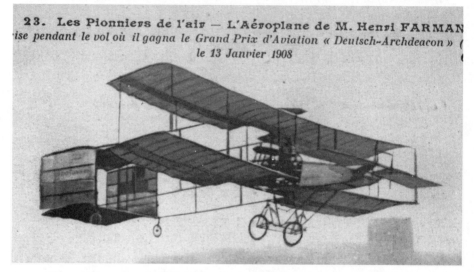

23. Les Pionniers de l'air — L'Aéroplane de M. Henri FARMAN
ise pendant le vol où il gagna le Grand Prix d'Aviation « Deutsch-Archdeacon » (
le 13 Janvier 1908

Henry Farman earns the Deutsch-Archdeacon prize, January 13, 1908

Farman was back in the air on March 21, 1908, raising his own record distance to 4,500 meters and his time aloft to three minutes, twenty-nine seconds. He ended the day by carrying the world's first passenger aloft, Léon Delagrange. Late that month Farman temporarily transferred operations to Ghent, where he gave Archdeacon his first airplane ride. He was now covering distances that would have seemed incredible two months before. On July 6, 1908, he won the 10,000-franc Armengaud prize for the first flight by a Frenchman of over fifteen minutes, covering 20.4 kilometers in twenty minutes.

By the summer of 1908, Santos-Dumont and Farman no longer had European skies to themselves. Ferdinand Ferber had finally left the ground, completing eight hops between July 22 and September 19,

1908. Delagrange, who had failed to get airborne in his first Voisin, bought a second aircraft incorporating the improvements developed with the Farman machine, and completed some forty flights between March 14 and the end of July 1908, including the first flights in Italy at Rome, Milan, and Turin.

Robert Esnault-Pelterie, already universally known as "REP," Louis Blériot, and Alberto Santos-Dumont were breaking new ground, having abandoned the Wright and Hargrave-inspired biplane configuration in favor of the monoplane. Rumanian-born Trajan Vuia and the Danish engineer Jacob C. Ellehammer had pioneered the monoplane in Europe, coaxing single-wing aircraft into the air for short hops or tethered circular flights in 1906 and 1907.

As early as November and December 1907, REP was making flights of six hundred meters in the first truly successful monoplane, powered by an engine of his own design. Santos-Dumont made three flights with his first monoplane in November 1907. After a string of failures, Louis Blériot finally left the ground in the fall of 1907 and tasted real success when he flew his first circle and remained in the air for up to eight minutes in July 1908. Both Blériot and REP were pursuing patents covering the use of stick-and-rudder pedal controls.

The brothers Ernest and Paul Zens and Réné Gasnier also succeeded in coaxing biplanes aloft in 1907–1908. Alfred von Pischoff not only introduced the classic tractor biplane configuration that would emerge fully after 1910, but also introduced two key figures to the world of aeronautics, propeller maker Lucien Chauviere and bicycle-racer-turned-engine-builder Alessandro Anzani. Experiments were also underway with far less conventional craft. In November 1907 French experimenter Paul Cornu made the first significant vertical take-off with a large twin-rotor helicopter powered by a twenty-four-horsepower Antoinette engine.

ACROSS THE CHANNEL

The world might have been watching Paris, but other nations were also taking to the air. Inspired by the Wright brothers, John E. Capper, superintendent of the Government Balloon Factory (predecessor of the Royal Aircraft Establishment), was determined to encourage home-grown aeronautical talent.

He offered significant financial support to both Samuel Franklin Cody (1861–1913) and John William Dunne (1875–1949). Cody (née Franklin Samuel Cowdrey), an American actor, was touring England with a barnstorming theatrical troop when he became interested in the man-lifting kite experiments of Baden Fletcher Smyth Baden-Powell. Cody patented his own design for a man-lifting kite system in 1901, and by 1904 was conducting powered airplane experiments under Capper's auspices.

Dunne, another Capper protégé, built and flew a swept-wing glider, in 1907. Attempts to transform the craft into a powered machine the following year were unsuccessful. Cody, on the other hand, completed work on his British Army Aeroplane No. 1 in the spring of 1908 and made the first powered heavier-than-air flight in Great Britain with this machine on October 16, 1908.

The Short brothers, Eustace, Horace, and Oswald, official balloon builders to the Aero Club of Great Britain, were drawn into the heavier-than-air field by John Theodore Cuthburt Moore-Brabazon late in 1907. Only twenty-two years old at the time, the wealthy young man was an experienced balloonist who had flown as ballast during Baden-Powell's kite experiments. Returning from a trip to France, where he had seen men leave the ground in winged machines, he commissioned the Shorts to build a typically inaccurate variant of the 1902 Wright glider. It was the first product of what was destined to become a great name in the aviation industry.

The management of the Brooklands Race Track, where Moore-Brabazon stored his glider in a hastily constructed shed, offered a money prize of 2,500 pounds to the first aviator to fly a circle around the track before the end of 1907. Edwin Alliott Verdon Roe (1877–1958) was first on the scene, erecting a hanger with the hopeful legend "AVROPLANE" emblazoned over the door. A marine engineer who had served as secretary of the Aero Club of Great Britain and won a major model competition, Roe made some short hops following a downhill run in 1907 but would not make a sustained and controlled powered flight until 1909. Moore-Brabazon would precede him, becoming the first Britain to fly from British soil aboard the Voisin that he had named *Bird of Passage*, in April and May 1909.

THE STARS AND STRIPES FOREVER
(. . . AND THE MAPLE LEAF, TOO)

On September 30, 1907, a group of five individuals were ushered into the office of the American consul in Halifax, Nova Scotia, where they signed articles of agreement establishing an Aerial Experiment Association (AEA). The leader of the group, Alexander Graham Bell, was no newcomer to aeronautics. The inventor of the telephone had conducted flying-machine experiments as early as 1891 at his newly acquired estate, Beinn Breagh (Ben Vrēah—Gaelic for "beautiful mountain"), near Baddeck on Cape Breton Island, Nova Scotia. A member of the Smithsonian Board of Regents and a close friend of Samuel Langley, he had contributed $5,000 to the aerodrome experiments, attended a great many of the flight trials in 1896–1903, and remained one of the secretary's most loyal supporters in the face of ridicule and controversy.

Bell sought to achieve inherent stability in the air, using the kite as his research tool of choice. By 1902 he had produced the first of his famous tetrahedral kites. The giant *Frost King* of 1905, with 1,300 individual pyramid-shaped cells arranged in twelve layers, could lift a man thirty feet into the air, and remain steady as a rock. Bell then turned his attention to potential power plants and the use of hydrofoils for a take-off from water.

By the spring of 1906 Bell had decided to create a team of professional technicians in order to push his work forward. His first recruits included a pair of young friends: John Alexander Douglas McCurdy, a student at the University of Toronto and the son of a Bell employee, and Frederick Walker (Casey) Baldwin, a senior at the same school.

Thomas Etholen Selfridge (1882–1908) joined the group next. A West Point graduate (class of 1903), he had served with artillery regiments and distinguished himself as a troop commander during the San

Francisco earthquake. His decision to pursue aeronautics was a carefully calculated career move. The young officer's notion, Bell later explained, was "that sometime or other the U.S. government would require flying machines in the army and . . . when that time came, the services of an officer who had made an expert study of the subject would be in demand, and he would be sure of promotion into a field of great usefulness."[8]

Impressed, Bell wrote to President Theodore Roosevelt requesting that the young officer be detailed to Baddeck. Selfridge reported for duty at Beinn Breagh in August and was a full-fledged member of the team by December, having ascended to an altitude of 168 feet during a seven-minute flight aboard a new kite, the *Cygnet*.

The final, and most important, founding member of the AEA arrived at Baddeck in July 1907. Glenn Hammond Curtiss (1878–1930) came from a very different mold than the group of well-educated professional technicians already on the scene. He was born and raised in Hammondsport, New York, on the shores of Lake Keuka in the Finger Lakes wine country, and left school at age fifteen to accept a job as a bicycle delivery boy for Western Union. It was the beginning of a career devoted to speed.

Curtiss earned an early reputation as a bicycle racer, then moved on to motorcycles. In 1900 he established his own shop where he designed and built motorcycles and engines. Within four years the G.H. Curtiss Manufacturing Co. was a going concern with a stock issue of $40,000. By 1907 he was producing five hundred motorcycles a year and operating a chain of cycle shops. Curtiss continued to race and win, spreading the fame of his product from coast to coast. He made national headlines in 1907 when he set a new world speed record of 136.3 mph with a Curtiss motorcycle at Ormond Beach, Florida. But it was the engines, not the motorcycles, that would bring him real fame.

Captain Thomas Scott Baldwin, an ex-circus performer turned balloonist, drew Curtiss into aeronautics. Inspired by the small one-man airships flown by Santos-Dumont, Baldwin had designed his own airship, the *California Arrow*, in 1904 and set out in search of a suitable power plant. Aware of the reputation of Curtiss engines for reliability, he wrote to Curtiss in Hammondsport outlining his needs but did not receive a reply. Visiting Curtiss in person, he discovered a no-nonsense young man who demanded cash in advance and was not at all eager to become involved with the flying-machine crowd.

Baldwin persevered, became a steady customer, and ultimately transferred his entire operation to Hammondsport. Bell was so impressed by the Baldwin engine, which he saw at a New York air show, that he placed an order for a motor to propel the hydroplane test bed then in the planning stages. Curtiss, recognizing that it might, after all, be worth pursuing the small market for flying-machine engines, began to offer his services to aeronautical experimenters whose names appeared in the newspapers. On May 16, 1906, for example, he wrote Wilbur and Orville Wright.

Curtiss met the Wrights in the fall of 1906, when he traveled to Dayton to repair the engine of an airship that Baldwin was operating at the local fairgrounds. The visitors found the brothers to be very friendly, exhibiting "the frankness of schoolboys in it all," Curtiss recalled, and having "a rare confidence in us." Shown photographs of

Glenn Hammond Curtiss

the 1903, 1904, and 1905 machines in the air, Curtiss asked one question after another and had to be cautioned by Baldwin not to appear too anxious and inquisitive.[9]

As Curtiss grew more intrigued with aeronautics, Bell became more interested in Curtiss. He ordered a second engine and invited him to visit Baddeck that summer to deliver the power plant and instruct Bell's engineers in its operation. Arriving at Beinn Breagh in July 1907, Curtiss became immediately intrigued and agreed to join the team and return for an extended visit that fall.

Glenn Curtiss was the quintessential Yankee, with a rugged face and hard lines etched across his forehead by years of concentration. A bristling mustache completely hid his upper lip, so that he always appeared to be frowning into the camera recording his image. In fact, those who knew him well found it difficult to remember the last time they had seen him smile. Frivolity was simply not in his nature. Neither was he given to idle chatter, hard drink, or profanity, although he was known to use harsh language for effect. Of medium height, his lanky build and aloof manner led a surprising number of casual acquaintances to remember him as having been tall.

With Curtiss on the scene, Bell decided to transform his little band of enthusiasts into a formal organization, the Aerial Experiment Association. Mabel Bell, his loving and supportive wife, and wealthy in her own right, funded the effort. Bell and Selfridge worked without salary, while McCurdy and Baldwin received $1,000 per year. Curtiss earned a salary of $5,000 for his services as director of experiments.

Loyalty to Bell ensured that the first AEA effort would be the completion and testing of the tetrahedral aerodrome *Cygnet*. With this project complete, the younger members of the group insisted that the construction of a powered aircraft based on contemporary American and European practice would be far more valuable than further work with Dr. Bell's kites.

Like the Europeans, the members of the AEA began their own work on the foundation provided by the Wright brothers. Curtiss wrote to the Wrights on December 30, 1907, bringing them up-to-date on AEA activities and offering "gratis" a fifty-horsepower Curtiss engine for their own experiments. Selfridge followed up with a second letter to the Wrights on January 15, 1908. His questions to the brothers were straightforward and practical. What had been their experience with the travel of the center of pressure on wings? What was "a good efficient method" of constructing light, strong ribs that would maintain their camber? How should the fabric be applied? Could the Wrights offer any general structural advice?

The Wrights provided specific answers to these questions and directed the newcomers to their patents and published papers for additional details. Why were the Wrights so careful in their dealings with the Europeans and yet so apparently open in these early contacts with the AEA? The brothers almost certainly assumed that the new organization would not pose a threat for a very long time. Moreover, they admired Bell, who had come to their defense at the time of Santos-Dumont's flights on *14-bis*.

The AEA members shifted their operations to Hammondsport in the early months of 1908, where Curtiss workmen built a variant of the Chanute-Herring glider, which allowed them to sample the thrill of skimming rapidly through the air. Selfridge, who had been among those pushing the hardest for a retreat from the tetrahedrons to more conventional aircraft, was credited with the design of the first AEA powered machine, *Red Wing*.

The new machine, which derived its name from some leftover fabric that they used to cover its wings, displayed all of the now standard external Wright characteristics so familiar on French aircraft. And like the French, the members of the AEA seem to have paid little attention to the most important lessons that the Wrights had to teach with regard to control in the air. Selfridge had returned to active duty in Washington by the time *Red Wing* rolled out of the Curtiss workshops. Baldwin ran the aircraft across the frozen surface of Lake Keuka on March 12, 1908, flew a short distance through the air, and returned to earth with a crash landing.

Casey Baldwin was responsible for the basic design of the next aircraft, *White Wing*, which featured two small ailerons mounted at the tips of the upper wing surfaces. Bell suggested the innovation following the crash of the original AEA craft. It is not clear whether Bell came up with the notion independently, or borrowed the idea from

Esnault-Pelterie, Santos-Dumont, Blériot, or Cody, each of whom had made earlier use of these movable tabs on or between the wings for lateral control.

The aileron was simply an alternative to wing-warping and, particularly in the case of early monoplanes, not necessarily a superior one. In later years Glenn Curtiss himself would remark that if the Wrights had thought of ailerons, they would have incorporated them into their basic patent. As Curtiss was fully aware, they had done precisely that. Not only had they explained the operation of wing-warping in precise detail in their patent, they had described alternative mechanical systems that would provide the same effect, one of which was the aileron. A complete description of these devices had been available for all to see since the publication of the Wright patent in 1906.

Casey Baldwin and Selfridge completed three flights of 100 to 285 feet with *White Wing* on May 17 and 18, 1908, at the Stony Brook racetrack near Hammondsport. Curtiss flew for the first time on May 21, covering 1,017 feet and demonstrating that the skills honed in racing bicycles and motorcycles were immediately transferable to controlling aircraft. McCurdy followed with a very creditable 720-foot performance later that day, but wrecked the machine in landing.

The third powered machine constructed by the AEA flew into history as the *June Bug*, a name supplied by Bell to commemorate the plague of small insects infesting Hammondsport when the aircraft was completed on June 19, 1908. With its double-bowed wings, canard, rear rudder assembly, and tricycle landing gear, the craft represented a natural step in the evolution of AEA airplanes.

Curtiss flew the airplane for the first time on June 21 and within four days was covering distances of up to 725 yards. After upping his record to 1,040 yards on June 27, he informed the Aero Club of America that he would try for the *Scientific American* Trophy on July 4.

Founded in New York in the summer of 1905, the Aero Club of America was both inspired by and patterned after Aéro-Club de France. The founders, wealthy sport balloonists, became convinced that "the aeronaut is made of the kind of stuff out of which they make the most perfect specimens of American humanity." As had been the case in France, however, the more venturesome members of the Aero Club of America soon began to turn their attention to the far more interesting problems of heavier-than-air flight.[10]

It was only natural, therefore, that the editors of *Scientific American* should ask the leaders of the Aero Club of America to supervise the competition for a new trophy to be awarded annually for some significant achievement in the field of mechanical flight. Officials of the club announced that the initial award would be made to the first individual to complete a straight-line flight of one kilometer in the presence of designated witnesses. Requirements for the subsequent award of the trophy would be devised as needed to keep pace with the advancement of aeronautics. The first individual to win the trophy three times would gain permanent possession.

When Charles Munn, the publisher of *Scientific American,* learned of the AEA bid for the trophy, he immediately contacted the Wrights, offering to postpone Curtiss's trial if the brothers would agree to take part in the competition. The Wrights refused. They could easily have won the trophy, just as they could have won all of the European prizes, but they had a number of concerns. First, premature disclosure of the details of their machine might invite patent infringement and the loss of significant revenue. The fact that potential French, English, and now American rivals had succeeded in leaving the ground on the basis of even an incomplete understanding of the Wright technology served only to strengthen their resolve in this regard.

In addition, the Wrights did not want to compete against newcomers. They knew that their machine performed vastly better than any other aircraft. Why should they join hands with those who were copying their technology to provide circus entertainment for the masses? Finally, the Wrights would have been required to alter their launch system in order to participate in the *Scientific American* competition. The fine print of the competition rules called for an unassisted take-off. The Wrights could very easily have added wheels to their basic machine and abandoned their derrick-and-track launch mechanism, but did not regard the effort as worthwhile. Curtiss and the AEA would have no competition for the trophy.

July 4, 1908, proved a day of triumph for the AEA. Twenty-two members of the Aero Club, including President Allan Hawley and such aeronautical pioneers as Charles Manly and Augustus Herring, made the trip to Hammondsport, accompanied by a small army of newspapermen and a newsreel camera crew. High winds and rain prevented any preparations for take-off until six o'clock that evening. After an initial abortive try, Curtiss took off once again. Trailing a thick plume of exhaust smoke, he flew 5,360 feet in one minute and forty seconds, winning the prize with ease. Glenn Curtiss had joined Santos-Dumont, Gabriel Voisin, and Henry Farman in the world headlines. Telegrams of congratulation poured in from all quarters.

Wilbur and Orville Wright, now less than a month from the public unveiling of their machine in France, did not share the general enthusiasm. Writing to Curtiss on July 20, Orville called attention to the assistance that he and his brother had afforded the members of the AEA, and noted the fact that all of the key elements of the *June Bug* were covered by the Wright patent. His letter closed with an ominous warning: "We did not intend, of course, to give permission to use the patented features of our machines for exhibitions or in a commercial way."[11]

The *June Bug* made eighteen flights during the course of an active career lasting just nineteen days, from June 21 to July 10, 1908. That of

The June Bug *in the air, July 4, 1908*

July 4 was the longest, in terms of both distance and duration. Three additional AEA machines followed: the *Loon*, a nonflying hydrofoil test bed; the *Silver Dart*, in which McCurdy made the first flights in Canada on February 23, 1909; and the fantastic *Cygnet II*, based on Bell's tetrahedral kite principle.

The activities of the AEA officially terminated on March 31, 1909. The life span of the organization had been short, only eighteen months, yet its impact on the future of aeronautics had been incalculable. Each of its members would go on to earn genuine fame in his own right. Curtiss was to become the most successful of all first-generation American aircraft manufacturers. Bell would remain an honored spokesman on aeronautical subjects. Selfridge was to become the first man to die in an aircraft accident. Baldwin would enjoy a distinguished career as an engineer, sportsman, and politician. McCurdy rose even higher, capping his long career in government and industry by serving as lieutenant governor of Nova Scotia until 1952.

Santos-Dumont, Voisin, Esnault-Pelterie, Blériot, and Farman in France; Cody, Dunne, Roe, and others in Great Britain; the members of the AEA in North America—all of these pioneers had left the ground and flown into the world's headlines by midsummer 1908. The future of the airplane remained uncertain, even to the handful of individuals who had hazarded their lives in the air. That there would be a future for the flying machine could no longer be in doubt, however. Whatever one believed about the accomplishments and claims of Wilbur and Orville Wright, it was clear that the age of flight had arrived.

"WE ARE AS CHILDREN ..."

Arriving in France as the excitement over recent French aeronautical triumphs was approaching a peak, Wilbur reported to Orville, "I found our affairs here about like Peter Cartwright found religion to be on one of his circuits, 'looking upward'—in other words, flat on its back." Their initial supporters in France seemed to be "about scared out," losing their enthusiasm "as a result of the excitement over recent flights of Farman and Delagrange." "We would," Wilbur concluded, "have been as well or better off without a contract."[12]

But the time for business maneuvering was long past. Wilbur had no choice but to prepare for his first demonstration flight with all possible dispatch. The problems were daunting. Wilbur had to supervise the work of Bariquand et Marre, the Paris firm that was producing the Wright engines to power his aircraft. Then he started off on the first of a quick series of trips to inspect possible flying fields. He finally settled on the Hunaudières race course near Le Mans, where Léon Bollée, a local automobile manufacturer, agreed to allow Wilbur to use his factory area to assemble and store his machine.

By mid-June, pressures were mounting and Wilbur was stretched to the limit. Unexpected difficulties with the airframe compounded continuing problems with the engines. Opening the crates in which the machine that he intended to fly had been shipped to Europe the year before, he discovered a tangled mass of wood, wire, and fabric, the result of poor repacking following a customs inspection. Pain made the situation even worse when, early in July, Wilbur was scalded on the chest and arm by a loose radiator hose.

Finally, on Monday, August 8, 1908, Wilbur made two rounds over the track at Le Mans. It was the first of over a hundred flights he would make at Hunaudières and at a larger artillery testing field at nearby Camp d'Auvors, where he flew from August 21 to January 24, 1909. During this period, he spent over twenty-six hours in the air and flew a full eight hours carrying some sixty passengers. On six occasions Wilbur remained in the air for more than an hour, with the longest flights lasting more than two hours.

The public reaction was immediate and overwhelming. As the London *Times* reported, "These experiments . . . proved over and over again that Wilbur and Orville Wright have long mastered the art of artificial flight. They are the public justification of the performances which the American aviators announced in 1904 and 1905, and they give them, conclusively, the first place in the history of flying machines, that rightly belongs to them."[13]

Even the French press, so long doubtful of the Wrights' claims, found it impossible to contain their enthusiasm. "I've seen him! I've

seen them!" gushed a reporter for *Le Figaro*. "Yes! I have today seen
Wilbur Wright and his great white bird, the beautiful mechanical bird
which, for eight years, in the solitude of Virginia [*sic*] and Carolina, has
accomplished so many prodigious exploits that, in the course of time,
one has ended by believing that it was only a 'canard.'" All of that was in
the past, he explained, "There is no doubt! Wilbur and Orville Wright
have well and truly flown. . . . Without wishing in any way to diminish
the value of what our aviators—Blériot, Farman, Delagrange, Esnault-
Pelterie, Zens, Mangin, Gastambide and others—have done in France,
one is obliged to recognize that there is a whole world of difference
between their machines and the Wrights'."[14]

The French aviators were forced to agree with the reporter.
Compared to the Wright aircraft, their machines seemed "rudimen-
tary." Five years of doubt were laid to rest by the flights at
Hunaudières. As *l'Aérophile* reported, "Not one of the former detrac-
tors of the Wrights would dare question, today, the previous experiments of the men who were truly the first to fly."[15]

The aviators themselves echoed this praise. "Who can doubt that
the Wrights have done all that they claim," asked Réné Gasnier. "My
enthusiasm is unbounded."[16] Paul Zens commented that "Mr. Wright
has us all in his hands. What he does not know is not worth knowing."[17] M. Surcouf, the airship designer, remarked on Wilbur's "titanic
genius,"[18] while Delagrange was forced to admit, simply, "We are
beaten."[19]

Once the initial shock had washed over them, however, some of the
French aviators would reconsider. Farman, in a *Le matin* interview
published on August 26, objected that "our machines are as good as
his."[20] Blériot, who had initially been quoted as praising the Wrights'
accomplishment, soon expressed the view that while the brothers from
Dayton might have forged ahead of the French, it was only a "momentary superiority."[21] Charles and Gabriel Voisin refused to credit the
Wrights with even that much. "Where was aviation born?" they asked
in a joint letter to *Le matin*, "IN FRANCE."[22]

For the most part, everyone realized that the reaction of the Voisin
brothers was little more than sour grapes. Less-biased observers concluded that all of the Wrights' claims to priority were in fact true, that

contemporary French aircraft were rooted in the Wrights' technology, and that in the summer of 1908, the Wrights' airplane remained far superior to those made by their European rivals.

By September 3, Orville had joined his brother in the air. He had arrived at Fort Myer, Virginia, with the disassembled parts of a new airplane and engine, and with mechanics Charley Taylor and Charles Furnas to assist in its assembly, on August 20. As Orville and his crew went to work each day in the old balloon shed chosen for the assembly of their flyer, they could hear Glenn Curtiss and Thomas Scott Baldwin chugging along overhead aboard the SC-1, the two-man airship that would be the first powered flying machine to enter the U.S. inventory.

Orville made his first test flight, one and one-half circles around the artillery field at Fort Myer in one minute and eleven seconds. On September 9 he was making flights of up to eleven minutes in duration with Lt. Frank Lahm as a passenger. Orville had joined his brother in the headlines of the world's newspapers.

But tragedy was to mar the triumph at Fort Myer. Flying at an altitude of 125 feet with Tom Selfridge on September 17, Orville heard a sudden thumping coming from the rear of the machine. One of the two pusher propellers had split, cutting a guy wire and causing the collapse of the rudder. Wright and Selfridge crashed to earth in view of hundreds of horrified spectators. Wright survived the crash, although he would carry the pain of the injuries received that day for the rest of his life. Selfridge, who suffered a fractured skull, died a few days after the crash. Tom Selfridge, who had already earned a place of honor in the annals of flight as a result of his work with the AEA, merited one final, though unwanted, distinction. He was the first man to die in the crash of a powered airplane.

TOGETHER AGAIN

Wilbur Wright arrived at Pau in Southwestern France, where he would base his winter flying operations, on January 14, 1909. Katharine and Orville, who was recuperating from the accident, joined their older brother two days later. Wilbur would complete approximately sixty-four more flights by March 20, when the Wrights moved to Centocelle, a new flying field near Rome.

In addition to fulfilling the terms of the contract with the French syndicate, Wilbur taught a small number of European aviators to fly. Everywhere the three Wrights went, kings, queens, presidents, prime ministers, and millionaires applauded them. Alphonso XIII of Spain came with his camera, anxious to snap his own photos of the three Americans. King Edward VII of England watched two flights, including one on which Katharine flew as a passenger. Some of the most distinguished members of European society lined up for the honor of helping to pull the 1,600-pound launch weight back up to the top of the tower for the next flight.

The Wrights were showered with honors and awards and deluged with invitations to banquets and luncheons when they returned to America in May 1909. President William Howard Taft presented them with special gold medals in a White House ceremony. They received a congressional gold medal from General James Allen, chief signal officer of the army; a state gold medal from Ohio Governor Judson Harmon; and a city of Dayton medal from Mayor Burkhardt at the great Wright Brothers Home Days celebration held in Dayton on June 18, 1909. It was just nine years and eleven months since Wilbur had flown their original wing-warping kite.

"NO LONGER AN ISLAND"

Clément-Armand Fallières, eighth president of the Third Republic of France, opened the First Annual Paris Aeronautical Salon in the Grand Palais at 1 P.M. on December 24, 1908. It was an historic event, the first large-scale display of aircraft, both practical and impractical, ever held. A full-scale model of the Wright airplane was the star of the show. Wilbur Wright created a sensation when he paid a personal visit to the salon on December 29. During the course of the exhibition, the French syndicate selling Wright aircraft claimed to have received deposits on twenty-six machines.

Virtually all of the emerging French aircraft builders were present as well. Monoplanes, biplanes, and helicopters produced by Léon Levavaseur, Alberto Santos-Dumont, Robert Esnault-Pelterie, Gabriel and Charles Voisin, Louis Breguet, the Clement-Bayard company, Alfred von Pischoff, and Raoul Vendôme were on display.

Louis Blériot exhibited three aircraft in his pavilion, only one of which would ever fly. Officially known as the Blériot XI, it was initially identified as "the short span monoplane," because of its narrow wingspan and surface area of only twelve square meters.

Raymond Saulnier, who would soon emerge as a leading manufacturer in his own right, designed the Blériot XI. However, that Blériot himself had a good deal to do with engineering the new machine, which incorporated many of the elements that had evolved through his earlier models, including the three-wheel undercarriage, with the front wheels mounted on a shock-absorbing bedstead; the pylon supports for the wings; the rectangular "trellis" fuselage, uncovered at the rear; the small rudder and pivoting elevators; and the now standard Blériot stick-and-rudder-pedal arrangement of cockpit controls.

Moreover, the all-important choice of wing-warping for lateral control was Blériot's idea. He had witnessed Wilbur Wright's first European flights and had been quoted as saying that "I consider that for us in France, and everywhere, a new era in mechanical flight has commenced."[23] Ross Browne, an American who had witnessed the scene, remarked that "Blériot was all excited; he looked over the machine . . . he tested the wings, and Mr. Wright showed how the warping was done . . . how it worked."[24] Blériot could scarcely be contained. "I'm going to use a warped wing," he announced to his entourage. "To hell with the aileron." He was, Browne recalled, "just like a young boy."[25]

Blériot flew the little machine for the first time on January 23, 1909, after which he increased the wing area to fourteen square meters and, by the end of May, added a lightweight, three-cylinder, twenty-five-horsepower Anzani power plant. Alessandro Anzani, who had designed and built the engine, was an Italian bicycle racer with a feisty temper and the manners and vocabulary of a trooper. He had entered the aviation market after adding a third cylinder to his standard motorcycle engine.

Compared with the craftsmanship of the beautiful fuel-injected Antoinette engines, the Anzani certainly didn't look very impressive. Its three iron cylinders were rough castings, with seventeen holes drilled in the base to exhaust spent gases. In later years a Blériot mechanic recalled that the Anzani "rattled and spat oil out of the holes at the end of every stroke, covering the pilot with a greasy film, so that one had to be heroic and long suffering to keep flying with these miserable engines."[26] Yet the Anzani had one great virtue—it ran for up to an hour without missing a beat.

All of the pieces were now in place. On July 14, 1909, Blériot flew his machine from Étampes to Orleans, capturing a 14,000-franc prize offered by Aéro-Club de France for the first straight-line flight of over forty kilometers. Looking for his next challenge, Blériot decided to fly the English Channel.

Alfred Harmsworth, Lord Northcliffe, engineered the enormous excitement that surrounded the Channel flight. Publisher of the English newspaper the *Daily Mail*, Harmsworth had become alarmed at the rapid aeronautical progress being made in the United States and France while Britain remained inert. In an effort to rouse British interest in flight, he established a number of major aeronautical prizes for distance flights, races, and model competitions in the years prior to 1914.

Northcliffe issued his most important challenge on October 5, 1906, when he offered 500 pounds ($1,250—later doubled to $2,500) to "the first person who shall succeed in flying across the Channel from a point on English soil to a point on French soil, or vice versa." The flight had to be made in a heavier-than-air machine that could cover the distance between sunrise and sunset without intermediate landings in the water.[27]

Recognizing Wilbur and Orville Wright as the only aviators capable of flying the Channel, Lord Northcliffe offered them an additional $7,500, three times the original prize money. But the Wrights refused this challenge as they had all others, preferring to concentrate all their energies on demonstrations directly linked to negotiations for the sale of their machines.

In June 1909 Hubert Latham (1883–1912) announced his intention

to try for the prize. In an era dominated by eccentric and individualis-
tic pilots, Latham exceeded the most colorful of the lot. A native
Parisian, he was born to an extraordinarily wealthy family that main-
tained English citizenship in spite of the fact that they had lived in
France for three generations. Latham had spent fifteen months at
Oxford's Balliol College, long enough to pass his law examinations,
before beginning his two years of required service as a private in the
French army stationed at St.-Cloud.

Unable to settle into business following his military service,
Latham became a world traveler and adventurer, leading safaris to
Africa, racing automobiles and motor boats, and ballooning across the
Channel with his cousin, Jacques Faure. Several years later, when
President Fallières asked Latham what his profession was, he replied,
"Monsieur le President, je suis un homme du monde."[28]

Latham had been drawn into aeronautics in February 1909, when
his neighbor, Jules Gastambide and his chief engineer, Léon Leva-

Hubert Latham and Antoinette Gastambide

vaseur, invited him to learn to fly their Antoinette aircraft. On June 5, 1909, no longer a novice, Latham kept the Antoinette IV in the air for one hour, seven minutes, and thirty-seven seconds, establishing a new French duration record and a world record for monoplanes. The following day he flew six kilometers in four minutes, thirteen seconds to capture the Goupy prize. On June 12 he demonstrated the Antoinette before government officials, covering a distance of forty kilometers in thirty-nine minutes. Almost overnight Latham became one of the most popular pilots in Europe. With his natty attire topped off by an ever-present checkered cap and cigarette holder poised at a rakish angle, he was the very image of the intrepid aviator.

His first attempt to fly across the Channel from Sangatte, near Calais, France, to Dover, England, on July 13, 1909, ended in a rough landing from which he escaped without injury. During the course of a second attempt on July 19, Latham's engine stopped and he glided down to a landing at sea close to the French warship that had been assigned to assist him in the event of just such an emergency. Latham and Levavaseur accepted their initial failures with grace and humor. Latham had the faulty distributor component made into a stickpin, while Levavaseur remarked that his machine "can go on land, in the water, or in the air. It runs, it flies, it swims. C'est un triomphe!"[29]

While the Antoinette was being repaired and Latham waited for good weather, Blériot saw an opportunity and seized it. The Blériot XI arrived in Calais on July 22, the same day as Latham's new engine. Newsmen accustomed to the gossamer elegance of the Antoinette expressed disappointment with the Blériot XI. "It is a monoplane less than half the size of Mr. Latham's," one reporter noted. "It is not beautiful, being dirty and weather-beaten, but it looks very businesslike."[30]

After several days of waiting for improved weather, Blériot arranged to be awakened early on the morning of Sunday, July 25. Latham overslept. By the time he was up and about, the wind was too high for him to take off in Blériot's wake. He did get off the ground two days later, but wound up in the water once again, this time suffering facial injuries when his head struck the aircraft. He remained one of the most popular pilots in Europe and America for several years, a familiar sight at meets and competitions. He died on June 7, 1912, not

in a crash, as one might expect, but gored to death by a wounded buffalo while on a hunting expedition near the Chari River in the French
Sudan.

Louis Blériot, on the other hand, flew into history. Traveling at just
over 40 mph and flying at an altitude of 250 feet, he covered the
twenty-three miles separating Calais from Dover in a little over thirty-
six minutes. Approaching the White Cliffs of Dover, he saw French

Louis Blériot and the Blériot XI

journalist Charles Fontaine waving a huge tricolor back and forth to
guide him through a gap that led to a suitable landing spot at North
Foreland Meadow. England, Lord Northcliff proclaimed, was "no
longer an island."[31]

By flying across the narrow sleeve of water that had halted the
troops of Napoleon, man and machine had become immortal. A number of pilots, including Blériot himself, had flown greater distances,
and they would most certainly fly higher, faster, and farther in the years

to come. Not until Charles Lindbergh soloed the Atlantic in 1927, however, would another flight have such a profound impact on the public consciousness. The reasons for that are easy enough to identify.

As the *Pall Mall Gazette* observed, Blériot had created "a revolution in human affairs" in less than half an hour. He had "brought home to the minds of the people of all nations the possibilities of the flying machine in the future."[32] No nation could afford to ignore a new machine capable of soaring over traditional barriers and borders. The flight, pioneer aviator Allan Cobham noted, "marked the end of our insular safety, and the beginning of a time when Britain must seek another form of defense beside its ships."[33]

Lord Northcliffe's fundamental message rang clear. In the process of restoring French confidence and pride, Blériot had underscored England's backward position in aeronautics. H. G. Wells spoke to this point in the pages of the *Daily Mail*:

> What does it mean for us? One meaning, I think, stands out plainly enough, unpalatable enough, to our national pride. This thing from first to last was made abroad. . . . Gliding began abroad when our young men of courage were braving the dangers of the cricket ball. The motor car and its engine were worked out over there. . . . Over there where the prosperous classes have some regard for education . . . where people discuss all sorts of things fearlessly and have a respect for science. . . . It means that the world cannot wait for the English. It is not the first warning we have had. It has been raining warnings on us—never was a slacking, dull people so liberally served with warnings of what is in store for them.

"Either we are a people essentially and incurably inferior," Wells suggested, "or there is something wrong in our training, something benumbing in our atmosphere and circumstances."[34] For a people who were already giving considerable thought to the possibility of German Zeppelins crossing the North Sea, the image of French airplanes streaming across the Channel was indeed unsettling.

LA GRANDE SEMAINE D'AVIATION DE CHAMPAGNE

The excitement engendered by the emergence of the airplane in Europe in 1907–1909, capped by Wilbur Wright's incredible performances and Blériot's crossing of the English Channel, set the stage for the first great aerial spectacular—a full week of flying activity that attracted many of the world's aviators to the Plains of Bethany, just north of the cathedral city of Reims. The great Reims meet, which ran from Sunday, August 22, to Sunday, August 29, 1909, was conceived and funded by leading champagne producers of the region. A blue ribbon organizing committee headed by the Marquis de Polignac, with the patronage of the president of the Republic, established seven rich prizes totaling 167,000 francs for the distance, speed, altitude, and passenger-carrying competitions to be held during the course of the week.

From the outset, the Reims meet was hailed as an unofficial debut that would introduce the airmen and their machines to a wondering public. For months news accounts had chronicled the coming of the age of flight, but scarcely anyone had actually had an opportunity to see an airplane in the air. The local committee planning the meet was certain that the chance to see not one, but many airplanes in the sky at once would draw thousands of visitors into the city. No expense would be spared to ensure that this would be the greatest in a long string of Reims spectaculars that had begun with the coronation of Clovis I in A.D. 45.

The citizens of Reims began to prepare for the anticipated deluge of visitors months before the event. Ten miles of fencing enclosed a small, hastily constructed city on the Plains of Bethany. Within this enclosure workmen had laid out a rectangular flying course some six miles in circumference with a pylon at each corner. Two enormous, ornate, gingerbread grandstands ran along one end of the course. The sheds and tents housing the aircraft dotted an area fronting the smaller and more exclusive of these two grandstands, where "grand tribune boxes" would rent for $50 to $200 for the week. Forty thousand less-affluent spectators would pay one franc for admission to the remaining seats. Visitors could dine at one of several restaurants constructed on the site, and wash their meals down with champagne dispensed at ten cents per tumblerful from booths behind the grandstands.

By opening day, thousands of spectators had swarmed into the ancient cathedral town. Three full infantry regiments, two regiments of dragoons, three hundred mounted gendarmes, a company of military bicyclists, the entire Reims police force, and a field ambulance unit handled security problems, unsnarled traffic, and were responsible for the safety of both visitors and participants.

As those planning the event had hoped, the aviators also turned out in force. Prior to December 31, 1908, a grand total of seven humans had made flights longer than one minute. At Reims, only eight months later, twenty-two airmen coaxed twenty-five airplanes into the air for a grand total of over 120 take-offs, 67 of which resulted in flights of more than three miles.

While Wright aircraft would be flown by pilots like Paul Tissandier, whom Wilbur had taught to fly, the brothers themselves, as usual, refused to participate. They realized that it did not make good business sense to compete with latecomers who were infringing on their patents.

During the two weeks prior to the beginning of the meet, the aviators arrived at the newly created airfield looking like a corps of walking wounded emerging from the smoke of battle. Blériot still hobbled about on a foot that had been injured prior to the Channel flight. Farman had been scalded in the face by a broken radiator hose early in August. Robert Esnault-Pelterie nursed an injured hand. And the press avidly awaited news from the physician treating the American Glenn Curtiss for a recent foot injury.

The pilots covered the spectrum of experience from veterans like Farman and Blériot to newcomers, including Étienne Bunau-Varilla, who had received his airplane as a high school graduation present just a few weeks before, and Eugene Ruchonnet, who had learned to fly during the course of a long weekend immediately prior to the meet. The jaunty Latham, undaunted by his Channel defeat, emerged as one of the stars of the meet. "You shall find him coming along the straight in front of the grand stand," one reporter noted, "and letting go his wheels while he lifts his cap well above his head, and replaces it more comfortably."[35]

Voisin, prepared for any mechanical difficulty, arrived on the scene with seven airplanes, a small army of mechanics, and three tons of supplies, including a full field kitchen. Esnault-Pelterie and Farman were not afraid of getting their hands dirty and could usually be found working with their mechanics. Other aviators, including Blériot, seemed to pay scant attention to their aircraft, trusting the machines in which they would risk their lives to the hands of the mechanics.

The aviators who braved the skies at Reims flew a variety of aircraft. The Voisin brothers led the pack, with nine machines entered into the competition. Six Wright aircraft were registered, but only four of them flew. One of the Wright pilots, Eugene Lefebvre, whom Wilbur Wright had taught to fly, would become the first pilot to die in the crash of a powered machine (on September 7, 1909).

There were four Antoinettes, four Farmans, and three Blériots on the program. Two of the remaining aircraft, a Fernandez and a Kluytmans, failed to leave the ground. Two others, the single Curtiss machine and a biplane entered by Louis Breguet, were only the first in a long and distinguished line of aircraft bearing those names.

The meet offered the first opportunity to make direct comparisons of the advantages and disadvantages of the various designs. The airplanes entered in the meet covered the spectrum of possible control systems, take-off procedures, configurations, and structures. Wright aircraft obviously performed far better in the turns, while the Antoinettes seemed to offer the advantage of superior pitch stability. The Farman machines were exceptionally sturdy.

The engines that powered these pioneer aircraft proved to be as critical to success as the wings that lifted them into the sky. Wright, Antoinette, Anzani, and REP engines, the leading aeronautical power plants developed over the past four years, were all represented. Two of the power plants originated from new firms that would emerge as giants of the industry, Curtiss and Renault. The most revolutionary bit of propulsion technology to appear at Reims, however, were the three, lightweight, fifty-horsepower Gnôme rotary engines that powered two of the Farman aircraft and one Voisin.

The tens of thousands of ticket holders who entered the ornate grandstands had no cause for complaint. Reims was as much an emotional experience as it was a demonstration of technology. A French correspondent writing for an English journal recalled "that one thrilling moment" when he saw a tier of three machines rounding a pylon, one above the other. "Of course, we have had to wait for the Reims meeting to behold these spectacles," he concluded.[36]

A great many records were set and broken that week, but the real excitement centered on the various speed runs aimed at capturing the James Gordon Bennett Trophy, the climactic event of the meet. If ever there was a larger-than-life figure, it was Bennett (1841–1918), the legendary American publisher of both the New York *Herald* and the Paris *Herald* and cofounder of Associated Press.

As a young man, his outrageous behavior included a drunken episode at a New Year's Eve party in 1877, when he urinated into a fireplace in the presence of his future father- and mother-in-law. As a publisher he made his own news, dispatching Henry Morton Stanley to darkest Africa and sponsoring the disastrous *Jeanette* expedition to the Arctic, during the course of which twenty crew members lost their lives.

Bennett was a sportsman as well, having introduced polo to the United States and established a James Gordon Bennett Trophy for yacht racing. The first James Gordon Bennett Road Racing Trial for automobiles was run in 1904, followed by the James Gordon Bennett Trophy for balloons in 1906. The next natural step was to award a prize for the highest speed attained by the airplane. The Coup Gordon Bennett, a solid silver trophy and a $10,000 purse, would go to the aviator with the fastest time for two circuits around the great ten-kilometer course at Reims.

When the Wright brothers refused to participate, the Aero Club of America asked Glenn Curtiss to represent his nation at Reims. Following the dissolution of the AEA on March 31, 1909, he had entered into what proved to be an ill-advised partnership with Augustus M. Herring, who had worked for both Langley and

Chanute, and visited the Wright brothers at Kitty Hawk. As chief executive of the Herring-Curtiss Company, he was officially in the airplane business now, having just completed the first sale of an airplane in America.

The machine that Curtiss brought to Reims had a larger engine and less surface area than the *Golden Flyer*, the airplane that he had delivered to the Aeronautical Society of New York just a month before. With only a single machine, a tiny crew, and virtually no spare parts, Curtiss had little choice but to avoid unnecessary risk and focus on his major goal, victory in the Gordon Bennett race. The strategy succeeded. Curtiss won the trophy, averaging 46.5 mph over a distance of thirty-two miles. It was the peak moment of an extraordinary week that marked the transition between the era of the invention of the airplane and the birth of the aviation industry.

4

FROM EXPERIMENT TO INDUSTRY, 1909–1914

SHOWING OFF

La Grande Semaine d'Aviation set the stage for five years of incredible achievement in the air before catastrophe descended on Europe. The airplane was the wonder of the age, and people everywhere flocked to see it for themselves. Air meets and aerial competitions popped up all across Europe. In America, aviators earned their keep by attracting crowds of paying spectators with feats of derring-do over the local fairground or racetrack.

Just nine weeks after the conclusion of the event at Reims, nine European cities hosted major meets: Johannisthal, Cologne, and Frankfort in Germany; Paris and Anvers in France; Doncaster and Blackpool in England; Brescia in Italy; and Spa in Belgium. The following year saw over thirty meets, from Heliopolis, St. Petersburg, and Budapest in the east, to Boston, Baltimore, and Los Angeles in the west.

Once again, Lord Northcliffe made his own headlines by sponsoring an aerial race from London to Manchester in April 1910. Pitting the victorious English aviator Claude Grahame-White against a valiant French rival, Louis Paulhan, the competition made front-page news around the world. Other city-to-city contests followed in 1911: Paris to Rome to

Turin; St. Petersburg to Moscow; Angers to Saumur; Paris to Madrid. The years 1911–1913 were dominated by the great circuit races: Les Circuits . . . de l'Est, . . . Brescia, . . . de Saxe, . . . du Haute, . . . Européen, . . . d'Allemand, . . . d'Angleterre, . . . d'Anjou, . . . Belgique, . . . Wurtemburg.

Consider the activity at a single flying field. Between May 1910 and October 1913, Berlin Johannisthal hosted *seven* Flugwoche (Flying Weeks), offering 312,900 Deutsche marks in prize money. In addition, the field served as either the starting point or an important stop on a number of long-distance contests, including the Circuit of Germany (June 12–July 10, 1910), the Berlin to Vienna Race (June 9, 1912), and the Circuit of Berlin (August 31–September 1, 1912).

The competition for the James Gordon Bennett Trophy remained a premiere international speed event. Following victories by Americans Glenn Curtiss (in 1909) and Charles Weyman (1911) and Englishman Claude Grahame-White (1910), French aviators Jules Védrines (1912) and Marcel Prévost (1913) won the last two prewar events. Each flew a sleek Deperdussin monoplane. France won its third victory and retired the trophy in 1920, when Joseph Sadi-Lecointe won the first postwar race.

During the years after 1909, *les aviateurs militante* stood triumphant. The French pioneers swept past the Americans and everyone else to establish La Belle France as the world's dominant aeronautical power. The French language shaped the lexicon of the air, contributing words like *aviation, aileron, fuselage, empennage, longeron, helicopter, and monocoque.* As early as 1910, France boasted 387 licensed or otherwise well-known French aviators, three times the number in Great Britain. The same count listed 46 German, 38 Italian, 37 Russian, 31 American, and 4 Japanese aviators.[1]

French aviators had amassed an impressive number of firsts. Mme. la Barrone Raymonde de la Roche, who would die in an airplane crash in 1919, became the world's first certified woman pilot in 1910. Within twelve months seven other French women joined her. French pilots made the first flights in Sweden and Denmark. Henri Fabre made the first take-off from the water (on March 28, 1910), and Emile Aubrun flew at night (March 10, 1910).

Marcel Prévost became the first victor of what would become a classic race flying a Deperdussin on floats at Monaco in 1913. Jacques Schneider, a French industrialist, had established the event. A balloonist and licensed pilot who once held the world's altitude record (33,074 feet), he noticed that seaplane technology seemed to be lagging behind that of other aircraft. His answer was to establish the Coupe d'Aviation Maritime Jacques Schneider. Known as both the Schneider Trophy and the Schneider Cup, the prize was to be awarded annually. The aero club to capture it three out of five years would retire the trophy. In years to come, the race would become one of the great international competitions, with national prestige at stake.

French aviators flying French aircraft powered by French engines won the major European races of 1911. But 1913 would be remembered as "la glorieuse année." French aviators and machines flew higher, faster, and farther than those of any other nation. On June 17, 1913, Prévost set a new speed mark of almost 125 mph, two and one-half times faster than Glenn Curtiss had flown in 1909. Edmond Perreyon, Blériot's chief test pilot, climbed to an altitude of 19,281 feet over the company aerodrome at Buc, France, on March 11, 1913. In September 1913, just four years after Blériot had struggled to cover the twenty-three miles from Calais to Dover, Roland Garros, an athlete turned aviator, flew his Morane-Saulnier monoplane nonstop across the Mediterranean.

Hélène Dutrieu, "the girl hawk," was awarded the Legion of Honor for her accomplishments in 1913. Lieutenant Petyr Nesterov of the Imperial Russian Air Service completed the first-ever loop, flying a French-built Nieuport on August 20. One month later, Adolphe Pégoud climbed to three thousand feet over Buc and flew the world's first aerobatic exhibition, complete with loops, inverted flight, and the "spit S" maneuver that would become his trademark. Within a few weeks he was attracting crowds of two hundred thousand spectators to witness his aerial performances.

NEW SKIES!

Like everyone else, the artists and intellectuals got caught up in the excitement of flight. Leading men of letters—Anatole France, Maurice

Maeterlinck, Pierre Loti, Edmond Rostand, and Henri Bergson— joined the thousands who swarmed to Issy-les-Moulineaux to watch the flying.

The cubist painters Pablo Picasso and Georges Braque attended as well. The two of them put their talented fingers to work building model airplanes. The aviators at the flying field nicknamed the enthusiastic Braque, "Vilbour." Picasso thought that his friend's paper sculptures resembled the wings of a biplane. In 1912, Picasso produced "Still Life: Our Future Is in the Air," a commentary on the importance of aviation to the defense of the nation.

Nor was the excitement limited to France. In September 1909, Franz Kafka, a twenty-six-year-old Austrian with literary aspirations, traveled to Brescia, where the heroes of Reims were competing for more rich prizes. The sight of the great Blériot in flight took Kafka's breath away. "What is happening," he asked. "Here above us, there is a man twenty meters above the earth, imprisoned in a wooden frame, defending himself against an invisible danger which he has taken on of his own free will. But we are standing below, pushed away, without existence, and looking at this man."[2]

In addition to the aviators, Kafka also caught a glimpse of the Italian poet and novelist Gabriele D'Annunzio. As well known for his pursuit of women as his literary pursuits, D'Annunzio flew with both Glenn Curtiss and Mario Calderara at Brescia. Flying was a "divine thing," he told reporters. "Divine and at the moment inexpressible." Aviation, he was certain, would transform the world. "A new civilization, a new life, new skies," he enthused. "Where is the poet who will be capable of singing this new epic?"[3]

Filippo Tommaso Marinetti, a wealthy Italian poet captivated by new technologies that shattered old perceptions of time and space, was eager to try. Among the most potent symbols of modernity, he wrote, was "the flight of airplanes, whose propellers whirl through the air like flags and attract the applause of the enthusiastic crowds." He was the prophet of a new artistic movement—Futurism. Words, he taught, were now far less important than deeds. Artists should participate in technologies that will shape the future.[4]

The Russian writer Vasily Vasilyevich Kamensky followed his

lead. "What are poems and novels," he asked. "The airplane—that is the truest achievement of our time." He moved to Paris, bought a Blériot monoplane, and learned to fly. He entered competitions in Russia and elsewhere in Europe before being seriously injured in a 1912 crash. Together with David Burlyuk and Valdimir Mayakovsky, Kamensky began lecturing on airplanes and Futurist poetry.[5]

Kamensky and his friends commissioned the artist Kazimir Malevich to prepare the stage sets for "Victory over the Sun," an incoherent mix of Futurist prose, poetry, and song staged in St. Petersburg in 1913. The best known of the Futurist artists, Malevich would incorporate aeronautical themes in his art for another quarter-century. Flight also played an important role in the work of avant garde French painter Robert Delaunay, who rejected any link to Futurism.

But the real impact of flight was on popular culture. Tin Pan Alley rode the coattails of the flying-machine craze with dozens of tunes, from classics like "Come Josephine in My Flying Machine" to such forgettable offerings as "My Little Loving Aero Man" and "Take Me Down to Squantum, I Want to See Them Fly." George M. Cohan premiered *The Aviator* at Boston's Tremont Theater in September 1910. The hero of the piece, who falsely claims to be a pilot, has to prove himself in the air or lose his girl. At a critical moment in the plot, they wheeled a real Blériot XI onstage and started the engine.

Clocks, fans, pencil boxes, cigarette cases, pitchers, plates, and ginger jars were a few of the items emblazoned with images of airplanes in flight. Children played with model aircraft, aviator dolls, and a wide variety of aeronautical games and puzzles. Aeronautical postcards became enormously popular, and for a time it seemed that images of aviators and airplanes could be used to sell anything.

Parents who had grown up reading dime-novel tales of Deadeye Dick and Buffalo Bill shook their heads in wonder as their own children devoured pulp-magazine yarns in which Frank Reade, Motor Matt, Tom Swift, or some other adolescent hero performed feats of derring-do in an airship, balloon, or airplane. Sinclair Lewis wrote his first novel, *Hike and the Airplane*, during a three-week vacation in Provincetown, Massachusetts, in 1911. Lewis later claimed that Glenn Curtiss, John Alexander Douglas McCurdy, and army aviator Paul

Beck had read and approved the manuscript, a straightforward adventure yarn of the Tom Swift variety. A decade later, Maj. Henry H. "Hap" Arnold would supplement his meager government pay with the royalties from his Bill Bruce aviation novels for young people.

THE SCIENCE OF WINGS

The men who invented the airplane and pioneered its earliest development could not fully explain how the thing worked. They were engineers of genius, researchers who precisely measured the forces operating on an airfoil, then applied that information to the design of more efficient aircraft. They were far less interested in scientific theory or the fundamental physical principles underlying flight.

Just as the first airplanes were taking to the sky, a handful of other researchers were laying the foundation for aerodynamics—the science of wings. The process began in 1878, when the English physicist John William Strutt, Lord Rayleigh (1842–1919), pointed out that a cylinder placed in a fluid stream experiences only resistance, or drag. When the cylinder is spun in a clockwise direction, however, it generates a lifting force.

The question of why this is so can still inspire a lively debate among engineers. One theory suggests that the spinning object imparts a downward motion to the molecules flowing off the backside of the cylinder. As Sir Isaac Newton's third law of motion explains, such action produces an equal and opposite lifting force. Another explanation notes that the spinning cylinder speeds the motion of molecules moving over the top of the object and slows the speed of those passing beneath it. Daniel Bernoulli, an eighteenth-century Swiss physicist, discovered that the pressure in the faster-moving stream would be relatively lower than that in the slower-moving stream, resulting in an upward force. In the end, both explanations are correct and contribute to lift.

Whatever the physical explanation, two pioneering aerodynamicists, working independently, developed a means of calculating the amount of lift generated by the spinning cylinder. Inspired by Otto

Lilienthal's gliding experiments, Wilhelm Kutta, a German mathematician, presented a key paper on the subject in 1902. Russian scientist Nikolai E. Joukowski published his work between 1902 and 1909. Between them, they established the mathematical foundation for the circulation theory of lift.

Two other researchers took the next step, explaining how the circulation of air around a cambered, or curved, wing could generate lift. Frederick Lanchester (1868–1946), an English engineer and amateur mathematician, built his early reputation as an automotive pioneer. He began experimenting with model aircraft in 1891 and presented his first paper on flight theory in 1894. Lanchester published his most important book, *Aerial Flight*, in two volumes, *Aerodynamics* (1907) and *Aerodonetics* (1908).

Lanchester had a difficult time expressing his ideas in clear mathematical terms. Ludwig Prandtl (1875–1953) had no such problem. Born in Freising, Germany, he earned a doctorate in engineering and became interested in fluid dynamics while studying the flow of air through industrial vacuum systems. In 1904, he presented an eight-page document that one authority considers "one of the most important fluid dynamics papers ever written."[6]

Prandtl had discovered the boundary layer. He theorized that friction held a very thin layer of fluid motionless on the surface of the wing. Beyond this boundary layer, the flow was scarcely affected by surface friction. This notion served as the cornerstone of a circulation theory of lift presented in elegant mathematical form. It was only the beginning. The complex elements of wing theory fell into place over the next decade and a half. A professor of applied mechanics at historic Göttingen University since 1904, Prandtl supervised the development of a wind tunnel and laboratory facilities second to none. His reputation as the world leader of aerodynamic research attracted talented graduate students, including a young Hungarian named Theodor von Kármán, who would extend Prandtl's work and spread it around the globe, altering the way in which engineers were trained and aircraft designed. The twin streams of theoretical science and practical engineering had merged at last.

THE BUSINESS OF WINGS

Inevitably, the French pioneers transformed their experimental work-shops into factories. The aircraft industry in France grew steadily. A modern study that seems far too conservative reports that French builders produced 1,023 airplanes between 1909 and 1913 (732 domestic sales and 291 exports).[7] Actual production figures were probably much higher. *L'Aéro-manuel*, a trustworthy contemporary reference guide to the international aircraft industry, notes that a single firm, Blériot Aéronautique, produced over eight hundred aircraft in 1909–1914. That figure was widely reported in Blériot promotional materials and in standard accounts of the industry.[8]

Louis Blériot, the conqueror of the Channel, ruled the roost. His career as an exhibition pilot ended in Istanbul in December 1909, when he fractured several ribs and suffered internal injuries in a crash. He continued to give lessons, test factory aircraft, and go aloft for the occasional joyride until 1912, when he grounded himself for good. After 1909, business consumed him.

As early as September 1909, Blériot had orders in hand for 101 copies of his famous type XI aircraft and was seriously worried about his ability to meet delivery dates. Factory space posed a problem. The original workshop in the Paris district of Neuilly, scarcely more than a shed, was supplemented by a building devoted to production of the Blériot model XII high-wing monoplane. Late in 1910, the firm moved into new quarters on the Route de la Révolte in the suburb of Levallois. By the end of 1911, when the five-hundredth Blériot airplane was wheeled through the doors, more than 150 engineers and workmen were employed at the new plant.

Between 1909 and 1914 Blériot produced forty-five distinct types of aircraft, ranging from canards reminiscent of his earliest machines, to flying buses capable of carrying eight passengers. Most were experimental machines.

Throughout this period, variants of the classic Blériot XI remained the firm's most successful product. Frequently altered and updated, the classic monoplanes served as trainers, sport or touring models, military aircraft, and racing or exhibition machines. In 1911 a standard type XI cost some $2,350.

Flight instruction comprised an important part of the company's business. When the first two Blériot XI's were sold to Alfred Leblanc and Leon Delagrange, the familiar Issy flying field had sufficed for flight instruction. By 1910, Blériot had new flying fields suitable for summer and winter operations, as well as a training school at Hendon, near London. As early as 1912, some two hundred civilian aviators from seventeen nations and over seventy French and foreign military officers had learned to fly at Pau or Étampes.

Earl Ovington, an American student at Pau, would never forget his first solo.

The grease-covered mechanics wheeled out one of the patched-up machines kept especially for "taxi-drivers" like myself, and I clambered into the cockpit. The cane-bottom seat was not ten inches wide and its back consisted of a strip of three-ply veneer, three inches wide and a quarter of an inch thick. To make it still lighter, it was bored full of holes. The French certainly do peel down their machines to make them light. I had been told to steer for a pylon at the other end of the field, and as my little monoplane bumped unevenly over the ground, I must have concentrated too much on the pylon and not enough on what I was doing. I pressed my feet so heavily on the rudder cross bar that the back of the seat gave way, and I slipped over onto the bottom of the fuselage, pulling the elevator control to me as I went. Not realizing in the least what had happened, I scrambled back into position as quickly as I could. Instead of being on the ground as I supposed, I was three hundred feet in the air and still rising. Between wiggling the rudder with my feet, working the wings to keep the horizon where it belonged, and pushing and pulling the elevator to stop the earth from jumping up and down, I had a busy sixty seconds.[9]

But Blériot Aéronautique had competition. By 1913, thirty-three French companies were actively involved in airframe production.[10] A 1912 study revealed that 158 of 770 aviators who had flown since 1906 preferred Blériot aircraft, while 135 reported a preference for the sturdy biplanes produced by Henry Farman. Voisin aircraft remained the choice of 59 aviators. The already obsolete Antoinette designs had attracted the loyalty of 47 pilots.

With the exception of a handful of current U.S. military aviators, most of the thirty-nine pilots who had flown Wright aircraft had done so prior to 1912. Glenn Curtiss was the only other American manufacturer included on the list. Up-and-coming firms included Bristol, Aviatik, Etrich, Nieuport, Hanriot, and Morane, names that would become familiar to young boys around the world after 1914.

The ultimate airplane of the prewar era was, not surprisingly, French. The story begins with Armand Deperdussin (1870–1924), a Belgian cabaret singer who had worked as a barker luring customers into motion-picture theaters operated by the famed Lumière brothers. Determined to make his fortune, Deperdussin entered the silk trade, wholesaling bolts of fabric to French department stores. In the fall of 1909 he agreed to supply the Bon Marché of Paris with an airplane for display in the store at Christmastime.

Fascinated by aviation, but knowing little of the subject, Deperdussin approached a new firm, the Société de Construction d'Appareils Aériens, where Louis Bechereau, a brilliant thirty-two-year-old graduate of the École des Arts et Metiers d'Angers, was chief engineer. Impressed with the canard aircraft produced for the Bon Marché, Deperdussin took over the firm in 1910 and renamed it the Société de Production des Appareils Deperdussin (SPAD).

Over the next two years, Bechereau turned out a string of sleek designs that dominated the racing circuit. His most revolutionary achievement was a streamlined, externally braced monoplane with a monocoque ("single shell") fuselage. Eugene Ruchonnet, shop foreman of the Antoinette factory, originally devised the strong, lightweight monocoque design, but Bechereau was the first engineer to fully realize the idea. Thin strips of tulip, a wood favored by cabinetmakers, were criss-crossed and glued together in three thin layers inside a mold, and then covered, inside and out, with varnished fabric. The resulting shell, a lightweight masterpiece of the woodworker's art, would carry heavy stresses without the need for internal bracing.

The 1912 Deperdussin airplane looked as if it had just flown in from the future. Sleak, lightweight, and powered by a powerful Gnôme rotary engine, nothing in the sky could keep up with it. The Deperdussin immediately became the mount of choice for the premiere racing pilots of the day, Jules Védrines and Marcel Prévost.

Jules Charles Toussant Védrines (1881–1919), nicknamed "Julot," was a confirmed socialist known for profanity and a good-natured truculence. A native of working-class St. Denis, he entered aeronautics as a mechanic and earned fame for his incredible skill in the air. He won the Paris-to-Madrid race in 1911 and became the first human to fly faster than 100 mph a year later. He traveled to Chicago to win the 1912 James Gordon Bennett race with an average speed of 105.5 mph, edging out his Deperdussin team mate, Marcel Prévost, who finished second.

Born in Reims, Prévost graduated from École Pratique de Comerce et d'Industrie but gave up a career in business to take up flying. Following a series of important aerial victories and world records, he was named chief instructor at the Deperdussin flying school. He piloted the most powerful Deperdussin available to a record breaking win in the 1913 Gordon Bennett competition, becoming the first pilot to exceed 125 mph.

Just as Armand Deperdussin's triumph seemed complete, his empire crumbled. In 1913, at the peak of his success, Deperdussin was convicted of financial chicanery and imprisoned. Unwilling to allow the firm producing the finest aircraft in the world to collapse into bankruptcy on the eve of a war, Louis Blériot stepped in and reorganized it as the Société Pour l'Aviation et ses Dérives (SPAD). Planes carrying the name of the new company would carry some of France's most famous warriors into aerial combat.

Blériot remained a towering figure in French aviation until his death in 1936. Deperdussin was less fortunate. Released from prison, he was unable to lift himself out of poverty for a second time and ended his life with a pistol shot in 1924. "Julot" Védrines survived gallant ser-

Jules Védrines in his Deperdussin racer, June/July 1911

vice in World War I only to die in a 1919 crash. Prévost outlived them all, surviving until 1952, when he died as an honored hero of France.

As FRENCH AIRFRAMES went, so went French engines. The Gnôme factory alone produced 3,638 engines between 1908 and 1913.[11] One study suggested that French engine production increased fifteen-fold from the 95 engines (45 domestic, 50 export) sold in 1909 to peak production of 1,580 units (580 domestic, 1,000 export) in 1913. Exports exceeded domestic sales in every year except 1910.[12]

In a normal reciprocating engine, the pistons turn a crankshaft on which the propeller is mounted. In a rotary engine, the body of the engine, with the propeller bolted to it, spins around a fixed crankshaft. An engine that is spinning away at 1,200 rotations per minute presents some obvious difficulties, but also offers some distinct advantages. Since the engine itself is turning, there is no need for a radiator, pumps, or water supply for cooling. Moreover, since the rotary features a much shorter crankcase and crankshaft than an in-line design, it weighs much less.

The virtues of the rotary engine were obvious to aeronautical pioneers like the Australian Lawrence Hargrave (1887), who designed a compressed air rotary engine to power a model aircraft. Both the De Dion Bouton firm (1889) in France and the Adams Company (1898) of Dubuque, Iowa, manufactured rotary internal combustion engines for automobiles. New York engineer Stephan Balzer produced a rotary engine for the Langley Aerodrome (1903), although Charles Manley rebuilt the power plant as a fifty-two-horsepower, water-cooled radial before attempting a flight.

Laurent Séguin (1863–1944), who designed the Gnôme rotary, and his half-brother Louis (1869–1918), who supervised production, came from a family with deep roots in the history of French technology. Their great-grandfather, Marc Séguin, a nephew of the Montgolfier brothers, invented both the horizontal fire-tube boiler for railroad locomotives and the iron-cable suspension bridges that carried them across rivers. Late in 1907, the Séguin brothers made a conscious decision to advance aviation by building a new sort of lightweight power plant.

Henry Farman introduced the engine, capturing the Grand Prix at Reims with a Gnôme-powered biplane. The rotary also propelled the first airplane to rise from water, the canard floatplane, designed, built,

A Deperdussin workman carries a lightweight monocoque fuselage

and flown by Henri Fabre, another Séguin relative. Within months it had become the power plant of choice for designers all across Europe.

A masterpiece of precision engineering, the Gnôme featured components manufactured from solid, drop-forged blocks of steel, with every spare ounce of metal being trimmed away. The piston walls were machined so thin that they could be crushed by hand. A rough crankshaft weighing 100 pounds when it emerged from the forge was trimmed down to 13.5 pounds for installation in the engine. The Gnôme factory, it was said, produced more metal shavings than engines. The engine exemplified the degree to which the latest and best in American machine-tool technology could be combined with the older French tradition of handcrafted excellence in the metal trades.[13]

When World War I broke out in 1914, the Gnôme factory employed 650 to 800 workers. They would produce twenty thousand Gnômes of various models, power ratings, and designs by 1918. Thousands more copies were manufactured, with or without license, by firms like La Rhone and Clerget in France, Bentley in England, and Oberussel in Germany.

Leading European automobile manufacturers—Rolls-Royce, Renault, Bentley, Mercedes—also turned to the manufacture of aircraft engines. Eventually, in-line and radial engine designs would outlast the rotary. In its time, however, it had powered the first revolutionary increase in aircraft performance.

THE ABILITY TO FLY higher, faster, and farther came at a price. On September 7, 1909, Eugene Lefebvre, whom Wilbur Wright had taught to fly, became the first aviator to die while flying a powered airplane. Ferdinand Ferber, who dreamed of flight longer than any of them, died less than three weeks later. By the end of 1910, the death toll had climbed to thirty-four since the loss of Tom Selfridge. Eighty-four aviators lost their lives in flying accidents in 1911. Eugene Ruchonnet, the inventor of monocoque construction, was the first of 143 pilots to die in 1912.[14]

Aircraft were often underpowered, control systems less than perfectly reliable, and the principles of aerodynamics poorly understood.

Loss came with the territory. By 1912, however, an increase in monoplane crashes in which the wings had simply folded raised a new concern.

Given the wood, wire, and fabric technology of the period, the ideal aircraft had a pair of wings trussed one above the other, creating a single beam supporting the fuselage and other elements. Such biplane structures were stronger, lighter, and more rigid than a monoplane.

In contrast, the key element of the monoplane was the fuselage, with the wings guyed precariously in place. To stiffen and strengthen the thin and flexible wings of monoplanes like the Antoinette and Blériot, designers added extra material and weight. But to decrease drag and increase flight speed, they had to pay the price of reduced wing area, higher wing loadings, and faster landing speeds. Speed meant publicity. Publicity meant increased sales and government contracts. All of these changes produced a few more miles per hour of speed, which might spell the difference between victory and defeat.

By 1912, however, the list of fallen monoplane pilots was growing longer. Granville Bradshaw of England's Royal Aircraft Factory commented that there was "a feeling amongst us all that monoplanes as at present constructed are not everything to be desired from a mechanically sound point of view. Indeed, the more one investigates the loading on wing wires and main spars the more does one feel concerned about machines of this type that are flying."[15]

British military authorities fretted. Twenty-one of the fifty-six aircraft in the inventory that spring were monoplanes, a mix of Blériots, Nieuports, Bristols, Deperdussins, Shorts, and Etrichs. For a time, authorities considered grounding those machines and banning further purchase of single-wing aircraft. The French government did temporarily ground all monoplanes in their inventory while they studied the problem.

Louis Blériot strengthened the wing spars and brace wires of his company's products, then provided spectacular proof of monoplane safety. In 1913, Adolphe Pégoud, his most experienced test pilot, provided the earliest demonstrations of aerobatic prowess with a Blériot XI over the company aerodrome at Buc, France. The situation eased, although doubts remained.

We know now that the most important cause of wing collapse on a monoplane was beam-column failure, which occurred when the structure was placed in compression, as when an aircraft pulled out of a high-speed dive. The final solution to the old problem came with the advent of thick cantilevered wings capable of housing a strong supporting structure.

INVESTING IN THE FUTURE:
GOVERNMENT INVESTMENT IN FLIGHT

French dominance left the rest of Europe with little choice but to invest in flight technology. The military potential of the airplane remained unclear, but it would not do to allow a potential enemy to forge too far ahead.

A 1913 congressional study revealed that the nations of the world had spent a total of $86,750,000 on aviation between 1908 and 1913. Even before the start of World War I, Germany had overtaken France in total spending.

Total Government Expenditures on Aviation, 1908–1913 (All figures in U.S. dollars, 1913)[16]

Germany	$28,000,000
France	$22,000,000
Russia	$12,000,000
Italy	$8,000,000
Austria	$5,000,000
England	$3,000,000
Belgium	$2,000,000
Japan	$1,500,000
Chile	$700,000
Bulgaria	$600,000
Greece	$660,000
Spain	$550,000
Brazil	$500,000

United States	$435,000
Denmark	$300,000
Sweden	$250,000
China	$225,000
Rumania	$200,000
Holland	$150,000
Serbia	$125,000
Norway	$100,000
Turkey	$90,000
Mexico	$80,000
Argentina	$75,000
Cuba	$50,000
Montenegro	$40,000

In addition to official appropriations, several leading aeronautical powers had also established national subscriptions that provided an additional $7,100,000 in financial support for their aeronautical industries. Once again, Germany led the way with $3,500,000 in private funds, followed by France ($2,500,000), Italy ($1,000,000), and Russia ($100,000). According to official U.S. government estimates, the nations of the world had spent a total of $93,620,000 in public and private funds on aviation in the years 1908–1913. How was this money spent?[17]

Long before the first airplane flew, European leaders had chosen to invest relatively small sums in aeronautical research and development. The French General Staff, the British War Office, and the Kaiser's government had created aeronautical research, development, and construction facilities before 1900 and increased funding after 1909.[18]

In France, private philanthropy played an important role. Industrialist Henri Deutsch de la Meurthe founded the Institut Aérotechnique de St. Cyr and presented the facility to the University of Paris, where Basil Zaharoff, the munitions maker who would earn dubious postwar fame as the "merchant of death," also established the first chair in aeronautics.[19]

Gustave Eiffel began to conduct serious aeronautical research high on his famous tower in the 1890s. By 1905, he had created an aerodynamic laboratory at the foot of the Eiffel Tower, complete with perhaps the finest wind tunnel in the world. In 1912, the eighty-year-old engineer opened another facility, and an even larger wind tunnel, at Autiel. Eiffel tested a wide range of model airfoils and developed an accurate coefficient of enlargement that led to full-scale values. The achievement proved enormously valuable to aircraft designers.[20]

In addition to the work at the Balloon Factory (1889) at Farnborough on Laffon's Plain, in Hampshire, Col. John E. Capper drew Britain's National Physical Laboratory into aeronautics by 1902. Capper knew that Col. Charles Renard of Chalais Meudon employed wind tunnel testing to develop efficient airship hull forms, and asked Dr. G. E. Stanton of the National Physical Laboratory Teddington to begin similar work in England. Impressed by the results, Capper designed and built an experimental wind tunnel for Farnborough.

In 1911, Prime Minister Herbert Asquith's Committee on Imperial Defense asked Lord Rayleigh, a Nobel laureate and Britain's leading physicist, and Dr. Richard Glazebrook, director of the National Physical Laboratory, to suggest ways that science could support the military. This led to the Advisory Committee for Aeronautics, headed by Lord Rayleigh and including seven other members of the Royal Society. Charged with coordinating aeronautical research in Great Britain, this distinguished panel was proof that officials at the highest level of British government appreciated the potential of aviation.[21]

Major changes were afoot at the Balloon Factory as well. Rayleigh and another committee member, Master General of Ordnance Sir Charles Haydon, arranged in 1909 for Mervyn O'Gorman to replace Capper as director of the facility. An Irish engineer with long experience in the design of internal combustion engines, O'Gorman was a brilliant and colorful administrator famed for his monocle, ivory cigarette holder, bushy mustache, and dapper wardrobe.

Capper, for all of his contributions, had outlived his usefulness; he left behind a facility that was little more than a simple workshop. O'Gorman reorganized the operation, creating the first technical and scientific departments. Renamed HM Aircraft Factory in 1911 (the Royal Aircraft Factory in 1912, and finally the Royal Aircraft Establishment in 1918), the facility conducted world-class basic research in a variety of fields, as well as designing and building airplanes.[22]

O'Gorman also helped give birth to professional flight testing. Edward "Teddy" Busk, whom he had hired as an assistant engineer/physicist in 1912, became the model test pilot. Having earned an honors degree from Cambridge, Busk had studied aerodynamics at the National Physical Laboratory and took flying lessons with Geoffrey De Havilland. By 1913, O'Gorman and Busk had codified scientific test-flight procedures, using De Havilland's R.E 1 and B.E. 2 machines as test vehicles. Busk, the first of a legendary breed, died in November 1914, when his B.E. 2 caught fire and crashed while De Havilland looked on in horror.[23]

By 1914, the German universities of Göttingen, Aachen, and Berlin had taken the lead in aerodynamics. In addition to university research facilities, a government agency, the Deutsche Versuchsanstalt fur Luftfahrt, established a laboratory at Aldershof. Pioneering German aircraft manufacturers also pursued research. The Zeppelin company, for example, hired leading graduate engineers like Claudius Dornier and funded work in fields ranging from aerodynamics to materials in support of the design of both the rigid airships and the large multi-engine airplanes the firm produced. As a result of these initiatives, Germany remained the leader of world aviation, even as the nation spiraled down to defeat.

Russia rivaled Germany as a center for research in theoretical and experimental fluid dynamics. Nikolai E. Joukowski had begun operating a relatively small wind tunnel at the University of Moscow as early as 1891. His work led to the founding of the Aerodynamic Research Facility at Koutchino. Joukowski's work with the German Wilhelm Kutta resulted in a mathematical transformation of major importance to theoretical aerodynamics, as already noted.[24]

WHILE CONSIDERABLE AMOUNTS of public money supported state-sponsored research, far larger sums were spent on buying airplanes and instruction of military aviators. As usual, the French led the way, with 260 aircraft in service in August 1913. An official U.S. government source estimated that Imperial Russia was in second place, with 100 aircraft in its inventory, followed by Germany (48), England (29), Italy (26), Japan (14), and the United States (6).

The French War Ministry centered its earliest aeronautical activity in the Engineering Directorate under the command of General Pierre August Roques, the chief engineer, who purchased a pair each of Wright and Farman aircraft and a Blériot machine shortly after the Reims meet. The artillery command established its own aviation unit in 1909, complete with five aircraft. The following year, the minister of war resolved the issue, placing all aviation activities under a new Inspectorate of Aeronautics within the Engineering Directorate.

Army planners and procurement officers used their purchasing power to ensure that France would lead Europe in the air. As early as August 1912, the army inspector of aeronautics operated 238 aircraft, 137 of them suitable for frontline service. French officials used their appropriations to shape a strong national aviation industry. At least occasionally they offered special support to troubled firms, as when they bought thirty-five aircraft from Voisin Fréres in April 1910, to shore the firm up after a flood had devastated the company factory.[25]

The result was a strong and growing French aircraft industry. By 1914, the Farman company, which produced aircraft designed by the brothers Henry and Maurice Farman, employed one thousand workers in plants scattered around Paris.[26] The firm's best-known product was the relatively large, slow, and stable reconnaissance biplane popular with the military. Known as "bird cages"—no bird, it was said, could escape the maze of wires trussing the wings together—the Farman flying machines would remain in service well into World War I.

French aircraft outsold those of other nations. France was also the international center for military flight training. Officers of the Russian, Swedish, Serbian, and Rumanian armies enrolled at the Blériot and Farman schools. The Greek government sent six officers to the Farman school in 1912 and invited twelve French officers to advise the government on air policy. In 1913, at the height of the Mexican Revolution, President Victoriano Huerta ordered thirty officers to France for flight training.[27]

By 1914, however, Germany rivaled France for leadership in the air. Count Ferdinand von Zeppelin, the great public hero of the age, headed an umbrella of companies that produced airships, airship engines, aluminum, hangers, the huge gas cells made of goldbeater's skin, and multiengine bombers that attacked Allied targets during World War I.[28]

The German General Staff valued winged aircraft for reconnaissance, communication, and artillery spotting duties. As early as July 1910, the government contracted with the Albatros Company for two aircraft and pilot training for ten officers. The National Aviation Fund, organized by government and industry officials in 1912 and headed by Prince Heinrich of Prussia, encouraged and funded aircraft purchases. As already noted, Germany led the world in aviation investment by 1914.

As in France, the government sought to shape and strengthen a native airframe and engine industry. Officials followed a generally conservative course, encouraging the production of slow, stable machines, like the Austrian-designed Etrich Taube monoplane. Limited support went to newcomers like the Dutch designer Anthony Fokker, who would emerge as one of the great designers and manufacturers of World War I aircraft. By 1914, the Rupler firm had a payroll of 400 workers, while the Albatross Company employed 745.

In Great Britain, Prime Minister Herbert Asquith's government found itself on the receiving end of vocal press campaigns calling for preparedness in the air. The Air Battalion was organized in 1911 as a unit of the Royal Engineers. The embryonic reconnaissance force fielded five airplanes (a Blériot XI, a Wright A, a Farman, a De Havilland FE-1, and a Paulhan) and less than a dozen aviators. The following year, War Office officials, on the recommendations of the Committee on Imperial Defense, established the Royal Flying Corps (RFC), complete with military and naval wings, a central flying school, and a research establishment.

Commanded by the redoubtable Mervyn O'Gorman, that research establishment, the Royal Aircraft Factory, not only probed the secrets of flight but also designed and built aircraft. Geoffrey De Havilland (1882–1965), born the son of a clergyman at High Wycombe, was O'Gorman's best designer. His B.E. 2, the standard RFC machine at the outset of the war, went through five design revisions and remained in service until 1917, long after it had become fatally obsolete.

British critics attacked a procurement policy that seemed to favor aircraft designed and built by the government factory over those manufactured by private builders, who struggled to create an aviation industry in Great Britain. While the facility at Farnborough would continue to build aircraft in moderately large numbers through the war, the government ameliorated the situation by contracting private industry to produce the experimental machines developed at the factory and by recognizing the importance of using procurement funds to encourage and support hard-pressed aircraft builders.

Vickers, for example, a traditional armaments firm, got the contract for the design and production of the *Mayfly*, an unsuccessful Naval airship, as well as orders for B.E. 2 and B.E. 2a aircraft from the Royal Aircraft Factory. Frederick Handley Page, who founded his company in 1909, also received contracts for B.E. 2s. Thomas Octave Murdoch Sopwith entered the business in 1912, with Harry G. Hawker as his test pilot, and soon had a contract from the Royal Naval Air Service for ship-based floatplanes. Alliott Verdon Roe, the first Britain to fly from British soil, had contracts for military versions of his Avro 504, introduced in 1913. With a top speed of 80 mph and the ability to reach fifteen thousand feet, the Avro 504 entered the war as a frontline aircraft and remained in service as a trainer after 1918.[29]

Other nations also sought a place in the air. Russian aviators tended to earn their wings on machines of foreign designs, but there was no more imaginative aeronautical engineer in Europe than Igor Ivan Sikorsky, who had produced the *Bolshoi* (1913), the first successful multiengine aircraft in history. Another Sikorsky machine, *Il'ya Muromets*, was the first of an entire fleet of large aircraft that would be operated by the Imperial Russian Air Service on the Eastern Front. By August 1914, the Imperial government had spent lavishly on aviation, building an air force that, in terms of sheer size, rivaled the French.[30]

Vienna emerged as a European aeronautical center before 1914, and Austro-Hungarian aviators were second only to their French brethren in terms of the number of records held. Imperial officials failed to establish an effective national aviation policy, however. The

Etrich Taube, an Austro-Hungarian design, was the standard machine in Central Powers service at the outset of hostilities, yet most of these machines were built under license by Rumpler, a German firm.

In Italy, the Army Brigata Specialisti began studies for a military airship in 1904. The following year, the government invested in the *Italia I*, the first civilian dirigible constructed in Italy. The first Italian military airship, the SCA 1-bis, took to the air in 1908.

Early Italian aviators also learned to fly on foreign machines. The first Italian aviation factory was established in 1912 to build French designs under license. Giulio Douhet and a few other officers sought support for the talented Italian designers like Giovanni Caproni, who had produced his first trimotored bomber in 1913. Nevertheless, the Italian air arm entered World War I operating Blériot, Nieuport, and Farman aircraft.

THE SITUATION IN AMERICA

The U.S. aircraft industry was born in 1907, when the Wright brothers shipped seven Model A airplanes to Europe. These aircraft, soon to be flown in France and Italy, were the first multiple copies of a single aircraft type ever constructed. Each Model A was a hand-built original, however, and most would be powered by French engines.

The Wright Company was incorporated under the laws of the State of New York on November 22, 1909. Wilbur served as president of the firm, and Orville as vice president. The board of directors included August Belmont, Cornelius Vanderbilt, Robert Collier, and other leading figures in American business and finance. Corporate offices would be in New York, but the heart of the operation, the factory and flying school, stayed in Dayton, where the brothers could retain personal control.

The new factory began production in November 1910, turning out Wright Model B aircraft. Powered by a forty-horsepower engine, the new airplane was fitted with wheels and no longer required a catapult launch. When operating at full capacity, the workmen could push two airplanes a month out the factory door.

The company produced twelve distinct aircraft designs prior to 1915, when Orville Wright sold his interest in the firm. While precise figures are not available, the Model B and Model C were produced in the largest numbers. Other models included the EX, which Calbreath Perry Rodgers flew from coast to coast in 1911; the Model R, designed for air racing; and the Model G flying boat. Orville Wright estimated the total production at the Dayton factory in the years 1910–1915 at 100 airplanes.

By 1910, the familiar sights and sounds of airplanes once again filled the air over Huffman Prairie, where the Wrights taught the art of flying. Graduates of the Wright school would include Henry H. "Hap" Arnold, who would command the U.S. Army Air Forces in World War II, and pioneer naval aviator John Rodgers.

Glenn Curtiss and Augustus Herring incorporated the Herring-Curtiss Company on March 3, 1909. The relationship proved to be disastrous for Curtiss, ending in bitter accusations and lawsuits. At the time, an American market for airplanes scarcely existed. Curtiss sold one machine to the New York Aeronautical Society and a handful of others to individuals. Then the market dried up.

The Wright brothers had no better luck. Reluctantly, in January 1910, they began planning for an exhibition team of pilots who would earn money for the company by thrilling millions of ticket holders at flying meets across the nation.

Wilbur earned $15,000 and made national headlines in November 1909 when he flew from Governor's Island around the Statue of Liberty and to Grant's Tomb and back as part of the Hudson-Fulton celebration. The victory tasted especially sweet, as Glenn Curtiss, also scheduled to fly as part of the festivities, was grounded by bad weather.

The European enthusiasm for exhibition flying had invaded America, and at least one European pilot with it. Louis Paulhan, fresh from a sterling performance at Reims, participated in a great ten-day air meet that opened at Dominguez Field, Los Angeles, on January 10, 1910. It was the first great "flying carnival" ever held in America. Curtiss flew his *Golden Flyer*. Two aviators whom he had trained, Charles Willard and Charles Hamilton, flew other Curtiss machines at the event. Glenn Luther Martin, an Iowa native transplanted to

California, also made his public debut in Los Angeles, in his own version of the classic Wright/Curtiss-pattern biplane.

The Los Angeles meet launched the era of the great American air meets and touring exhibition flyers. Two months later, Orville Wright took an airplane, two mechanics, and five student pilots who would make up the original exhibition team to Montgomery, Alabama, where they would train until the weather improved in Ohio. Returning to Dayton in May, Orville made over one hundred training flights from Huffman Prairie before the end of the month. The original Wright aviators—Walter Brookins, Arthur Welsh, Duval La Chapelle, Frank Coffyn, Ralph Johnstone, and Arch Hoxsey—flew in public for the first time at an Indianapolis, Indiana, meet on June 13–18, 1910.

The Wright exhibition team would face stiff competition. Glenn Curtiss, already locked in the opening stages of a patent battle with the brothers, organized the Curtiss Exhibition Company in September 1910. The Moisant International Aviators put some of the leading European and American fliers on the exhibition circuit. John Moisant was the star of the troupe, along with his sister Mathilde and her friend Harriet Quimby, the first licensed American woman pilot and the first woman to fly the English Channel. Lincoln Beachey and other famous aviators operated as independents.

Boston, Philadelphia, Chicago, St. Louis, San Antonio, Indianapolis, and dozens of other cities and towns across the nation witnessed pilots racing one another across the sky. It was a daring time and a dangerous business. Beachey, famed for looping his airplane, died in a 1915 crash in San Francisco. John Moisant, the first American to fly the English Channel, was killed at a New Orleans meet. Harriet Quimby lost her life in a Boston crash. The Wright brothers retired from exhibition flying in November 1911, after losing two of their pilots, Ralph Johnstone and Arch Hoxsey, in accidents.

It was an era of heroic flights. Calbreath Perry Rodgers, a graduate of the Wright school at Huffman Prairie, took off from a field in Sheepshead Bay, New York, on September 17, 1911, intent on capturing a $50,000 prize offered by William Randolph Hearst for the first flight coast to coast in thirty days or less. Robert Fowler, another recent graduate of Huffman Prairie, had taken off from California six days before, intent on taking the prize with a flight from west to east.

Rodgers won the race but lost the prize when he rolled the tires of his Wright EX *Vin Fiz*, named for a grape drink marketed by his sponsor, into the surf at Long Beach, California, on December 10. He had survived five major crashes, each requiring substantial repairs to the aircraft; innumerable hard landings; aborted take-offs; broken fuel lines; blown valves; and engine failures. He finished the flight with crutches tied to the wings. He had broken his ankle landing in Pasadena and spent a month in bed before flying the short final leg to the Pacific.

Fowler, who finally arrived in Jacksonville, Florida, 112 days after his departure, missed the prize as well. Five months later, Cal Rodgers flew into a flock of gulls over Long Beach. He crashed into the surf and died of a broken neck near the spot where he had landed in triumph.

But aerial skills were growing, and pilots were putting the airplane to work in new ways. On November 7, 1910, Phil Parmalee, a member of the Wright exhibition team, carried ten bolts of silk from Dayton to Columbus, Ohio, for delivery to the Moorehouse-Martens department store. The air freight business had been born.

One week later, Eugene B. Ely lifted a standard Curtiss biplane off an eighty-three-foot-long platform built over the bow of the light cruiser USS *Birmingham*, about to get underway in Hampton Roads, Virginia, and landed at Willoughby Spit, 2.5 miles away. Two months later, and on the other side of the continent, Ely took off from a field near San Francisco and landed on a 119-foot-long platform built on the stern of the armored cruiser USS *Pennsylvania*. He took off again after lunch and returned to the city. It was, remarked the captain of the *Pennsylvania*, "the most important landing of a bird since the dove returned to the ark."[31]

Glenn Curtiss saw a big future for aircraft in naval operations. As early as the fall of 1908, long before Henri Fabre made the first take-off from water, Curtiss conducted unsuccessful experiments with a version of his *June Bug* mounted on a float. Two years later, he began serious work on water take-offs and landings with a standard Curtiss machine mounted on a canoe. Success came the following year at Lake Keuka. Curtiss's first successful flying boat, the Model E, took to the sky in 1912.

The event marked the beginning of his prosperity, earned from marketing flying boats to the U.S. Navy, private individuals, and European governments. By 1914, he had developed a twin-engine flying boat with an enclosed cockpit, the *America*. He would have dared the Atlantic with this craft had war not intervened.

Other American aircraft builders, notably Thomas Benoist, followed suit, building and selling their own Curtiss-style flying boats. In January 1914, pilot Anthony Jannus began the world's first regular passenger air service, shuttling a Benoist flying boat back and forth between Tampa and St. Petersburg, Florida. The service operated for four months.

BLAMING WILBUR AND ORVILLE

Then there were the patent suits. "Probably no single phase of aviation is as little known by those who should be well-informed on the subject," engineer Charles B. Hayward remarked in 1911, "as the actual status of aviation where the Wright patent is concerned. . . . The move on the part of the Wright brothers to establish the standing of their patents by having them adjudicated and, as this is an extremely lengthy process, to restrain infringers in the meantime, has lead to a perfect flood of criticism—even abuse and vilification—all of which has been misguided to say the least."[32]

The era of the patent suits began on August 18–19, 1909, when the Wrights filed a bill of complaint enjoining Glenn Curtiss and the Herring-Curtiss Company from making, selling, or exhibiting airplanes that infringed on the Wright patents. The following day, they filed suit prohibiting the Aeronautic Society of New York from exhibiting a Curtiss airplane.

That was only the beginning. Within a few months, the Wrights sought injunctions restraining visiting aviators Louis Paulhan and Claude Grahame-White from operating aircraft that infringed on the patent. In 1910, the Wrights and their licensee, the Compagnie Generale de Navigation Aerienne (CGNA), sued six rival French aircraft manufacturers (Blériot, Farman, Esnault-Pelterie, Clement-

Bayard, Antoinette, and Santos-Dumont) for infringing on the Wright's French patents. The following year, a consortium of five German aircraft builders, in turn, sued the German Wright Company in an effort to overturn the Wright patents in that nation.

The Wrights simply rolled over independents like Paulhan and Grahame-White. The cases involving the Herring-Curtiss Company and European firms proved more difficult, expensive, and time-consuming, however, and seldom produced a clear-cut resolution. Courts invalidated the Wright's German patent, arguing that prior disclosure, the publication of information on basic elements of the Wright airplane before patent approval, had compromised their claims. The French suit was complicated by the peculiarities of the legal system. Lacking a spirited prosecution by the CGNA, the case remained unresolved until the Wrights' French patents expired in 1917.

The situation in the United States was just as complex. As early as January 3, 1910, Judge John R. Hazel of the U.S. Circuit Court in Buffalo, New York, had enjoined Glenn Curtiss from the manufacture or sale of aircraft. Curtiss posted a $10,000 bond and appealed. He could legally continue flying until the appellate court reached a decision, but he took a terrible risk in doing so. If Curtiss lost, financial ruin would follow.

On January 13, 1914, the Court of Appeals ruled for the Wrights. Rather than clobber their principal rival, Wright Company management sensed the opportunity for monopolistic profits. They announced a schedule of rates that they would charge anyone who wished to exhibit an airplane in the United States. Curtiss, represented by the best lawyers that money could buy, announced that he would immediately alter his control system so that it no longer infringed on the Wright patent. Few aviation people believed that to be possible, but it was enough to muddy the waters and set the legal process in motion once again.

Ultimately, Orville did profit from the patent suits. He sold his interest in the company to a group of New York financiers in 1915, at a time when a Wright monopoly still seemed possible, a perfect moment to sell. The amount of the sale was reputed to be $1.5 million, enough to enable Orville to live comfortably for the rest of his life. Two years later, the federal government approved the creation of a patent pool composed of leading manufacturers who would purchase the rights to all aeronautical patents and share access with other members of the group.

The patent suits consumed Wilbur and Orville between 1910 and 1912. Family members believed that the tension and exhaustion of the patent battles weakened Wilbur and increased his vulnerability to the typhoid that took his life on May 30, 1912. Nor could they mistake the fact that the patent wars were joined, not only before the bar of justice but also in the court of public opinion.

THE PUBLIC ASSUMED that the patent suits had retarded the growth of American aeronautics, and many in government and industry agreed. One federal official bluntly summed up the matter in 1917, explaining that the Wright patent suits had "caused the United States to fall from first place to last of all the great nations in the air."[33]

America certainly lost its early role of aeronautical leadership. In August 1913, the United States boasted a grand total of six serviceable military airplanes, 260 less than France and 8 less than Japan. The situation had improved a bit by the end of 1914, when sixteen corporations had produced 145 aircraft with a total value of less than $800,000. It is interesting to note that 34 of those aircraft were exported, at an average value of $5,557 each. By 1916 the export number had risen to 269, with an average value of $8,025 each. Virtually all of the machines exported during these years must have been Curtiss flying boats.

While some American companies were able to remain afloat during this period, and even turn a modest profit, the gulf increased as the pressure of combat and wartime spending spurred aeronautical development in Europe. Ironically, the Wright Company proved to be the big loser in the patent suit. Between 1909 and 1917 the firm sold only twenty-six aircraft to the U.S. Army, its largest customer. Twelve of those were built and sold after Orville Wright left the firm for good.[34]

In truth, the Wrights had been reluctant to abandon the pusher design in favor of a tractor configuration that pointed to the future. After a series of accidents with Wright C and other pusher aircraft, Signal Corps officials grounded all such machines. Curtiss, already developing new tractor aircraft designs, remained the major supplier to the army. Orville Wright and the army would not do business again.

During the years 1909–1917, Glenn Curtiss sold 232 aircraft to the U.S. Army, almost half of the total number of aircraft purchased by the service and nearly ten times the number of Wright aircraft purchased. Moreover, most Curtiss sales involved tractor biplanes like the Model R scout machines and, especially, the J, JN, and legendary JN-4 "Jenny" training aircraft designed by the English engineer B. Douglas Thomas.[35]

Glenn Luther Martin, who paid a negotiated fee to the Wrights, sold forty-two machines to the army, including seventeen TT training machines, replacing all of the earlier Wright and Curtiss pusher training aircraft. The Standard, Burgess, Sturtevant, Burgess-Dunne, Aeromarine, Thomas, and L.W.F. Companies were awarded smaller contracts for the sale of aircraft to the army prior to 1917.

The navy followed suit, buying twenty of its first twenty-seven aircraft from Curtiss. The Wright brothers sold only three machines to the navy. After 1913, Curtiss sales to the navy skyrocketed, as did his production of flying boats for the Allies. When the patent suits ended in 1917, Glenn Curtiss ruled the industry of which the Wright brothers were no longer a part.[36]

It is an important lesson. The long journey from Kitty Hawk to the edge of the solar system was fueled by billions of dollars, francs, pounds, deutsch marks, rubles, lira, and yen expended for a series of ever improving winged weapons systems. Government funding led to aircraft with sufficient range and carrying capacity to be commercially viable. From that day to this, the complex interplay between commercial and military imperatives has driven technology.

THE ROOTS OF AIR POWER:
MILITARY AVIATION

Knowledge is power, and knowledge of the whereabouts and strength of one's enemy is especially powerful. Pioneer airmen in France and Britain began to explore the potential of aerial reconnaissance as early as 1910, during the course of their respective army maneuvers in

Picardy and on the Salisbury Plain. Austro-Hungarian officials followed suit the next year, as did the Italians, who provided their "red" and "blue" forces with five airplanes each. The commanding general and King Victor Emmanuel III observed the mock conflict from the gondola of an airship. An observer who witnessed the use of aircraft during the 1912 U.S. Army field exercises noted that intelligence delivered by the airmen was "much more accurate and full than that gathered by the cavalry patrols on either side."[37]

Aircraft performed well on maneuvers. The question of what would happen in combat remained unresolved until the fall of 1911, when Italy included two airships, a pair of tethered observation balloons, nine airplanes, and eleven pilots in an expeditionary force intended to wrest Libya from the Ottoman Empire. The officers of the Italian Engineers Brigade had entered aeronautics in 1908–1909, constructing two dirigible airships and contracting Wilbur Wright to provide demonstration flights and flight instruction for two officers. The following year, the brigade ordered ten Italian-built airships and ten airplanes from French manufacturers.

The Italian invasion of Libya was a response to the Ottoman determination to drive foreigners out of its North African provinces. Less than a month after the declaration of war, Capt. Carlo Piazza flew the world's first combat mission, a reconnaissance patrol along a road connecting Tripoli and Aziza. Piazza also took the first aerial photographs of enemy positions from his Blériot. Before it was over, Italian aviators were the first to bomb ground positions.

The airships proved valuable as well, completing 127 observation and bombing sorties. Guglielmo Marconi himself traveled to North Africa to supervise experiments with airborne wireless communication. The Turks achieved some antiaircraft firsts of their own, wounding a civilian volunteer aviator and bringing down an airplane with ground fire for the first time.

The French sent aircraft into combat against Moroccan rebels in 1912. The airmen played a critically important role in the campaign, locating native encampments, discovering a French column cut off from the main force, and maintaining communication between headquarters and troops in the field.

Both the Mexican government and rebel forces hired itinerant aviators from across the border to look around, attack, and harass one another during the Mexican Revolution. Two American mercenaries, Dean Lamb and Phil Rader, may well have been the first aviators to trade shots while flying for opposite sides.

The Balkan Wars offered a final pre-1914 testing ground for air power. Throughout 1912, Greece, Serbia, Bulgaria, and Montenegro allied themselves to regain control of Ottoman lands in Europe. Declaring war on Turkey in October, they captured Macedonia, Thrace, and Albania within a few weeks. Both sides used air power as the war flowed back and forth. The Turks had struggled through the Libyan campaign without a single flying machine. By the outbreak of the First Balkan War, they boasted twenty foreign-built aircraft and a complement of eight competent Turkish flying officers.

The Bulgarian aviation corps operated twenty-five aircraft, most of them obsolete machines obtained thirdhand from the Russians. Ten officers just out of flight training abroad and nine hired aviators from Germany, France, Russia, and Austria would fill the cockpits. Most of these mercenaries refused to do more than fly reconnaissance or scatter leaflets from the air. The Turks, after all, had announced that they would summarily execute any aviators who fell into their hands.

Opinion was divided as to the performance of the airplane during the course of the maneuvers and little wars that preceded the crisis of August 1914. Commenting on the use of aircraft in the Balkans, the French designer and manufacturer Etienne Borel remarked that "war has not been revolutionized." Giulio Douhet (1869–1930), an Italian officer who had already begun to emerge as a pioneering air strategist, disagreed. "A new weapon has come forth," he pronounced. "The sky has become a new battlefield."[38]

5

INTO THE FIGHT: THE AIRPLANE AT WAR, 1914–1918

MEN WITH WINGS AT WAR

"Aviation is fine as sport," Gen. Ferdinand Foch remarked in March 1913, ". . . as a weapon of war, it is worthless."[1] Conservative officers like Foch could not imagine a military role for the airplane. Others disagreed. Colonel Pierre August Roques (1856–1920), chief of the Engineers Directorate and commander of the French army's first aeronautical unit, was certain that the airplane would be "as indispensable to armies as cannons or rifles."[2]

In the four short, terrible years, General Roques and his colleagues would demonstrate just how wrong General Foch had been. The First World War was the seminal event of the twentieth century. The unimagined horror of the conflict set the stage for the birth of the Soviet Union and Nazi Germany. The United States entered the war late and emerged as a great world power, while Great Britain and France would never regain the status that they enjoyed in 1914. The forces set in motion by the war continued to play themselves out into the last decades of the century, when the collapse of communism in Eastern Europe finally seemed to mark the beginning of a new era. The evolution of the airplane from the frail powered box kite of 1914 into a powerful weapon of war was by no means the least of the changes wrought by the great catastrophe of the century.

Much had been learned in the months and years preceding the war. Two-place (two-person) machines made the best reconnaissance aircraft. The vulnerability of low-flying observation machines to ground fire led designers to give serious thought to armored aircraft. Anxious to transform their product into an effective weapon, French and British manufacturers considered arming their machines with a cannon or providing the observer, who often outranked the pilot, with a light machine gun. Beginning in 1912, the Michelin firm established an annual bombing competition.

From 1910 to 1914, French officials poured money into their own airframe and engine manufacturers, building a considerable air service called l'Aviation Militaire. France flew into the Great War in August 1914 with twenty-three frontline squadrons operating 141 aircraft, with an additional 126 machines in reserve and 50 more assigned to flight training. A total of 220 trained aviators wore the French uniform. Russia was prepared to commit 190 serviceable aircraft to combat, including the Il'ya Muromets, the first of what would eventually become 40 four-engine bombers.

The Royal Flying Corps (RFC) initially dispatched four squadrons and sixty-three aircraft to France, manned by 105 pilots and observers and maintained by 755 ground personnel. Many of the 95 support vehicles had been commandeered from the streets of London, with product advertisements still in place. Each airman flew to France equipped with a revolver, a small stove, and packets of chocolate, bouillon, and meat. Their orders required them to ram any Zeppelins encountered on their aerial voyage to the continent. Perhaps seventy-five RFC aircraft, most of them training machines, remained in England, along with some fifty aircraft assigned to the Royal Navy Air Service.

In terms of sheer numbers and the quality of its equipment, Germany rivaled France as the world's leading air power by the high summer of 1914. The Kaiser's air units had a roster of over 250 pilots and more than 270 trained observers. The air service had over 230 aircraft suitable for frontline service, almost all of them up-to-date two-place observation machines. Like their counterparts in France,

German procurement officials sought to strengthen German firms, including Albatros and Rumpler.

Initially, all of the belligerent powers saw the airplane as a vehicle to supplement the cavalry's role as the long-range eyes and ears of the army. Before the war was two months old, the airmen had put the cavalry out of business. On August 23, RFC Capt. Phillip Joubert de la Ferté spotted the German II Corps attempting to sweep around the British flank. Joubert, who would end his career as air chief marshal of the RAF, carried the news back to base with one hand on the control stick and one finger of the other hand plugging a bullet hole in his gas tank. British troops soon put an end to the German maneuver.

Over the next several weeks, aviation starred on two fronts. German aviators detected the Russian advance at the Battle of Tannenburg (August 26–31, 1914). French and British airmen spotted German troops moving toward a confrontation on the Marne River (September 5–10, 1914). Stopped in their tracks after the fighting along the Marne, the Germans began to dig in. Unable to move through or around the entrenched enemy, the Allies began digging in as well. By the spring of 1915 a thick band of trenches snaked across the French landscape from Ypres, Belgium, to the Swiss border. The war of movement on the Western Front was at an end, thanks in no small measure to aviation.

Commanders on both sides quickly integrated the airplane into their thinking. "Almost every day," Sir John French, commander of British troops in France, remarked, "new methods for employing [aircraft] . . . , both strategically and tactically, are discovered and put into practice."[3] Most of the military roles that the airplane would play over the next four years—reconnaissance, artillery direction, ground attack, and bombing—had been conceived before the war. Oddly, no one had thought of a single-seat *avion de chasse* with a fixed machine gun firing forward, an airplane that would enable a pilot to shoot down enemy aircraft simply by aiming his own machine at the target and pulling the trigger.

Prior to the spring of 1915, there was no easy way to attack another machine in the air. Aviators of every nation flew off to war armed with everything from rifles, pistols, and hand grenades to ropes and grappling hooks with which to snag the wings of an opposing aircraft. James McCudden (fifty-eight "victories") described a Bristol Scout aircraft operating with No. 3 Squadron RFC that flew with rifles attached to each side of the fuselage, angled out so that the bullets would clear the propeller arc.[4]

On October 5, 1914, Pilot Sgt. Joseph Franz and his observer, Quenault, of l'Aviation Militaire, brought down a German Taube with a forward-firing machine gun mounted on their Voisin pusher, scoring the first aerial victory in history. Later that month, Lt. Louis Strange, of No. 5 Squadron RFC, provided his observer with a lightweight Lewis gun mounted on a cockpit rail and a safety harness so that he could stand up in the rear cockpit and sweep the sky with fire. For all of these experiments in aerial gunnery, aviators still had more to fear from ground fire and the frailties of their own machines than from enemy airmen. All of that began to change in the spring of 1915.

DURING THE FIRST eighteen days of April 1915, Roland Garros brought down at least three enemy aircraft while flying a Moraine-Saulnier L monoplane fitted with a machine gun that could fire straight through the arc of the propeller. Already the best-known aviator on either side of the lines as a result of his prewar aeronautical achievements, Garros had fitted the propeller with steel wedges designed to deflect away from the machine any bullets striking the blade. Brought down by ground fire on April 19, he was captured and sent to prison camp. Finally escaping in January 1918, the first great aerial hero of the war returned to combat and died in a burning aircraft just a month before the Armistice.

Those three weeks when Garros ruled the air demonstrated the enormous potential of a high-performance single-seat machine designed only to shoot other airplanes out of the sky. Initially, it was known as a scout, then as a pursuit machine, and finally, and most appropriately, as a fighter plane.

German authorities shipped Garros's downed airplane to Anthony Herman Gerard Fokker at his factory in Schwerin. A Dutch aviator and engineer who had pioneered aviation in prewar Berlin, Fokker received his first contract for military aircraft in 1913. Two years later, he was manufacturing Oberursel rotary engines and completing work on a light, sturdy monoplane, the Fokker E (*eindecker*).

Ordered to adapt the Garros system to his new aircraft, Fokker was aghast at the possibility of a deflected bullet striking the pilot or a vital part of the machine. He set three trusted associates, including Reinhold Platz, a welder who had pioneered the welded steel-tube fuselage that was the company's signature, to work on a synchronizing gear that would enable a machine gun to fire between the blades of a spinning propeller. They were aware of earlier systems developed in France, Austria, and Germany. In point of fact, Fokker's synchronizer—he claimed they had produced it in only forty-eight hours—looked identical to that patented by Franz Schneider of the LVG Company.

A handful of armed Fokker E aircraft began to reach the front during June and July 1915. At first, the imperfect synchronizer system was given to occasional catastrophic failure. By midfall, however, the "Fokker scourge" was underway. The five hundred or so Fokker E.I,

Fokker E.III

E.II, and E.III machines were the first effective aerial weapons, airplanes that enabled a handful of aviators to emerge as the first great heroes of the war.

NO WONDER YOUNG MEN flocked to enlist in the first air war. The war on the ground was fought by mass armies composed of millions of men mired in the filth, misery, and terror of the trenches. "Here was I in mud up to my knees," infantryman turned aviator E. M. Roberts explained, ". . . [while those] other fellows were sailing around in the clean air."[5]

The soldiers on the ground who had scarcely glimpsed the enemy faced an anonymous, impersonal death from disease, a random artillery round, or a sniper's bullet. If he escaped the mechanized slaughter of the machine gun, he might fall victim to the latest scientific marvel, poison gas. Notions of honor, glory, and personal achievement had vanished. During four long years, very few great public heroes emerged from the sheer horror of the trenches.

The aviator, on the other hand, was like a Medieval knight, boldly carrying the national standard into combat with a champion from the other side. Such a man would live or die on the basis of his own skill and courage, in a battle fought in the clear blue sky. Small wonder that their exploits were celebrated and their names remembered.

The cult of the heroic airman began as a natural extension of the adulation lavished on the aeronautical heroes of the prewar era. The French had hailed their great racing and exhibition pilots as national champions, men who risked life and limb to achieve victory and honor for the homeland. How much more heroic and worthy of celebration were these same men when they donned the uniform of France and flew off to defend the nation itself.

Roland Garros was the first of the breed. The war was less than ten days old when the editor of *Flight*, the English-language journal of record for aviation, reported that he had been "regaled with a story of how Garros had sacrificed himself for France by flinging himself and his machine straight at a German airship, involving the enemy and himself in an inevitable common ruin." It mattered little that the story was not true; the French needed heroes.[6]

Adolphe Pégoud, the famous prewar aerobatic pilot, became the first aviator to earn the title of ace. He followed Garros's lead, flying a Morane-Saulnier N fitted with the bullet-deflecting wedges on the propeller. "About every sixth shot hits the propeller and bounces back at me," he remarked. "Often I hear it whistle past my ear. Sometimes I fear I am more apt to shoot myself down than I am to shoot down my intended victim."[7] With six kills to his credit, a French newspaper referred to him as "l'as de nôtre aviation."[8] Other nations began to apply the title to their "high-scoring" pilots, five kills generally being accepted as the requisite number. Pégoud died in August 1915 while pursuing his seventh victory.

Max Immelman (1890–1916) and Oswald Boelcke (1891–1916) emerged as the first German aerial heroes of the war as they swept Allied airmen from the skies with their Fokker E.III aircraft. In the process, they discovered some basic truths governing air combat that would guide generations of fighter pilots yet unborn. Known as "the Eagle of Lille" because of his success in that sector, Immelmann (fifteen victories) mastered aerial tactics, and his name would survive in the aerobatic maneuver known as the Immelmann turn. His death in a dogfight in June 1916 marked the unofficial end of the Fokker scourge.

Oswald Boelcke claimed the first victory with a Fokker monoplane. A shrewd analyst of aerial combat, he devised a series of rules that would enable his young charges to survive:

- Whenever possible, attack from above and from the rear.
- Try to attack from out of the Sun.
- Do not fire until you have closed with the enemy and have him squarely in your sights.
- Attack when the enemy least expects it, or when he is preoccupied with other tasks.
- Never run from an attack, but turn and meet it head on.
- Keep your eye on the enemy and do not be deceived. If an aircraft appears to be fatally damaged, follow it to the ground to be certain.
- Foolish acts of bravery lead to death. Always obey the signals of the leader.

With forty victories to his credit, Boelcke summed up his philosophy in a discussion with his most talented pupil, Manfred von Richthofen. "I fly close to my man," Boelcke explained, "aim carefully, fire, and then, of course, he falls down."[9]

The pattern was set. Aviators would emerge as the most celebrated heroes of the war. And they would not be forgotten. Take the case of Georges Guynemer (1894–1917).

CAPTAIN GEORGES-MARIE LUDOVIC Jules Guynemer took off at 8:25 on the morning of September 11, 1917, flying a new SPAD XIII, accompanied by his wingman, Lieutenant Bozon-Verduaz. Flying at twelve thousand feet over the village of Poelcapelle, near Ypres, they saw a two-place German observation machine below them in the distance. Noticing a group of Albatross fighters rising toward them, Bozon-Verduaz broke off pursuit and turned away from the newcomers, assuming his leader would follow. He did not. Guynemer seemed simply to have vanished.

On the day of his disappearance, Georges Guynemer was three

Georges M. Guynemer

months' short of his twenty-third birthday. A native of Paris, and the son of a retired officer, he belonged to a family that had supplied France with warriors for almost a thousand years. Short, thin, and frail, he looked decidedly unheroic. His parents feared that he suffered from tuberculosis, but his teachers found him active enough. He may have been inattentive, disruptive, and disorganized in class, but he was also a master roller skater, a skilled fencer, and a crack marksman. Treated to an airplane ride at the age of seventeen, he determined to become an aircraft designer but had to withdraw from the École Polytechnique because of continued ill health.

Rejected for pilot training five times after the declaration of war, Guynemer finally enlisted as an apprentice aviation mechanic and worked his way into flight school. He graduated in June 1915 and was posted to Escadrille MS3, equipped with a Morane-Saulnier Type L two-seat monoplane. Guynemer initially flew an airplane that Charles Bonnard had flown and named *Vieux Charles*, "Old Charles." The budding ace kept the name and applied it to most of the aircraft that he flew subsequently.

Guynemer shot down his first enemy aircraft on July 16, 1915. Over the next twenty-seven months he would be wounded twice, earn most of the honors that his nation could offer, and raise his victory score to 53 enemy aircraft. The war went on for thirteen months following Guynemer's death, yet, when the guns fell silent, he still ranked as the second-best French ace and tied for tenth overall. "He will remain the model hero," remarked President Georges Clemenceau, "a living legend, the greatest in all history."[10]

A month after Guynemer's disappearance, German officials informed the French that he had fallen victim to Lt. Kurt Wisseman, who had become an ace in the process. A German medical team soon reached the scene where Guynemer crashed, and determined that he had died from a bullet to the head. An artillery barrage drove the team away, however, and destroyed the aircraft, the body, and all identification. Lieutenant Wisseman died seventeen days later in a melee with No. 56 Squadron RFC.

It was entirely too grisly an end for this frail young demigod so close to the French heart. His admirers preferred to imagine that he had simply flown off into the clouds that morning and never returned. The apotheosis, the exaltation of mortals to the rank of gods, had long been a feature of Western art. George Washington, Benjamin Franklin, Napoleon, and Abraham Lincoln had all been portrayed being carried aloft by angels. Now Guynemer joined them, gracing walls across France.

Nor would he be forgotten. He remains today one of the greatest of all French heroes. A monument to him stands in front of 26 Avenue Victoire in Paris, the headquarters of the Armée de l'Air, which was created in 1933. His surviving SPAD VII was suspended in the crypt of the Pantheon at Les Invalides for sixty-four years, before being reverently restored and transferred to an honored place in the Musée de l'Air. A marble plaque on the wall of the crypt still bears Guynemer's name, the insignia of the Legion of Honor, and an inscription:

> Fallen in the field of honor, at Poelkapelle, on September 11, 1917— a legendary hero, fallen in glory from the sky after three years of fierce struggle. He will remain the purest symbol of the qualities of his race, indomitable tenacity, ferocious energy, sublime courage; animated by the most resolute faith in victory he bequeaths to the French soldier an imperishable memory which will exalt the spirit of sacrifice.

Every September 11, wherever they are stationed, officers and men of the Armée de l'Air assemble for a reading of that inscription. It is the most honored tradition of French military aviation.

Guynemer has plenty of company. In spite of books, television programs, and stage plays calling into question the single most famous episode in his career as a World War I fighter pilot, William "Billy" Bishop (seventy-two victories) remains the most famous Canadian war hero of the twentieth century. A generation later, in the middle of a worldwide conflagration in which dozens of young men were pilling up many more victories in the air than he had achieved a quarter-century before, Capt. Eddie Rickenbacker (twenty-six victories) remained the American ace of aces.

Ask any bright high school graduate to name the leading ace of the

*Pilots of Jasta 11: (left to right) Sebastian Festner, Karl Emil Schäfner,
Manfred von Richthofen, Lothar von Richthofen, Kurt Wolff*

Second World War. Few of them will have heard of Erich Hartmann
(at 352 victories), the all-time international ace of aces. You will surely
have better luck if you ask for the top-scoring airman of the First
World War, particularly if you give full credit for Manfred Albrecht
Freiherr von Richthofen's (eighty victories) nom de guerre, the Red
Baron or the Red Knight.

Eighty years after he died in combat, the name and image of the
Red Knight of Germany have been pressed into the service of popular
culture and commerce. Snoopy, America's favorite beagle, cursed the
Red Baron while piloting his doghouse across newspaper funny pages
for more than two decades. Check the *Yellow Pages*. There are Red
Baron travel agencies, express companies, casinos, and restaurants. In
the closing decades of the twentieth century, shoppers could purchase
Red Baron oranges and wash down slices of Red Baron frozen pizza
with glasses of Blue Max wine, named for the medal (Pour Le Merit)
that von Richthofen wore at his throat.

Warring governments hailed their leading aviators in order to boost morale on the home front; it is equally true that most of these pioneering aerial warriors achieved distinction on the basis of their own skill and daring. Ironically, however, the fighter pilots had far less impact on the outcome of the conflict than the airmen who manned the reconnaissance aircraft, bombers, and flying boats that patrolled for submarines.

THERE IS NO ACCURATE COUNT of the number of airmen who flew in World War I. RFC and Royal Air Force records indicate that Britain trained almost 22,000 aviators during the conflict. French flying schools graduated 16,648 pilots and 2,000 observers, during 1914–1919.[11] German personnel records were largely destroyed, but the air units of that nation included 5,000 active airmen at the time of the armistice, and were receiving 750 replacements a month at the front.[12]

Flight training varied from nation to nation. The French continued to start student pilots out on the "rollers" or "penguins," clipped-wing airplanes which trained them to taxi with the use of the rudder. A hopeful single-seat pilot *de chasse* moved on to an obsolete Blériot XI, gradually learning to leave the ground on his own. "Certain it is," remarked one airman, "that men have greater confidence when they learn to fly alone from the beginning." The Blériot, he explained, "which requires the most delicate and sensitive handling, offers excellent preliminary schooling for the Nieuport and SPAD, the fast and high-powered biplanes which are the *avions de chasse* above the French lines."[13]

Perhaps so, but René Fonck, France's leading ace (seventy-five victories), who originally trained as an observation pilot, counted himself fortunate to have received dual instruction in a Caudron G-4. Following his solo flight, Fonck was required to make a dead stick landing and to complete two more flights over an hour long, during which he had to demonstrate his ability to navigate. Finally, he had to pass a written examination.[14]

British aviator Cecil Lewis was only seventeen when he enlisted in the RFC. He spent six weeks in primary flight training at Brooklands airfield, a converted race course near London where Alliott Verdon Roe, Thomas O. M. Sopwith, and other pioneers of British aviation had built their first hangars. He earned his "ticket" on a "museum piece," a Maurice Farman Longhorn, soloing after one and a half hours of dual instruction.[15]

Leonard Bridgeman was another RFC pilot who soloed a Maurice Farman after less than two hours of "instruction." "The pupil sat behind and above the instructor," he recalled, "leaning forward and around him" to place his hands on the controls. The student was expected to master the use of the rudder pedals as rapidly as possible during the first few moments of his solo flight.[16]

Willy Coppens, a Belgian ace (thirty-four victories) who learned to fly at RFC Hendon, would never forget his introductory flight in a Caudron fitted with dual controls but no windshield. "I found the draught most offensive," he recalled. "The wind, driven back obliquely by the airscrew, drove in one side of my face and sucked out the other! To make matters worse, we flew without goggles, and until our eyes grew accustomed to the rush of air . . . we flew in tears."[17]

Canadian Billy Bishop began his career as a pilot in the summer of 1916 at an RFC school of instruction, "a ground school where the theory of flying and the mechanical side of aviation are expounded to you." Then he took his turn on the Maurice Farman. His solo, he recalled, was something like "the first time you started downhill on an old-fashioned bicycle." Next he took to the air in "more warlike machines" and began training as a night fighter pilot who would join the hunt for the Zeppelins cruising over England.[18]

A teenaged Ernst Udet (sixty-two victories), Germany's highest-ranking ace to survive the war, signed up for private flying lessons because he was too young to enlist in the air service. Like many leading pursuit pilots, Manfred von Richthofen began as an aerial observer. His pilot, Lieutenant Zeumer, taught him to fly. Richthofen showed little promise as a student, requiring twenty-five flights before his first solo, which ended in a crash. True to form, he failed his initial test for pilot certification. Never the best pilot in the air, Richthofen is proof of the importance of other factors in the making of a successful fighter pilot, including a hunter's aggressive instincts, an awareness of the constantly changing positions of all participants in an aerial combat, a determination to persevere, and absolute self-confidence.

With the passage of time, those who directed the air war bemoaned the fact that the need for more pilots had radically curtailed the training provided to novice aviators. "Fourteen hours! It's absolutely disgraceful to send pilots overseas with so little flying," Cecil Lewis complained. "My God. It's murder."[19] Across the lines, Franz Schlenstedt, an instructor pilot with combat experience, agreed, noting that the needs of the units at the front controlled the amount of training provided to budding aviators.

THE PATTERN AND SCALE of the air war changed over time, but the goal of tactical air operations remained the same. Each side attempted to control the air over a critical section of the front, enabling pilots to conduct aerial reconnaissance, attack opposing ground positions, and deny those advantages to the enemy.

Beginning with the Verdun offensive early in 1916, senior commanders on both sides of the lines integrated air operations into their plans for action on the ground. As the Germans prepared for a massive push, one designed to end the stalemate in the trenches, they tried to create a *Luftsperre*, or aerial blockade. The plan was for Fokker E.III aircraft, masters of the air over the front since the previous summer, to fly up and down the lines, intercepting Allied reconnaissance flights.

A fine idea, but it was foiled by the introduction of the first generation of Allied fighters, like the British D.H. 2 and the French Nieuport 11 Bébé. These machines proved more than a match for the suddenly obsolete German monoplanes. French aerial tacticians, with a superior weapon in hand, gathered groups of squadrons, or escadrille, into larger units and deployed them en masse. German aircraft fell during this onslaught just as the French and British had fallen in the preceding months.

That fall, British commanders seeking to break through German lines along the Somme River sent waves of aircraft over the front. Their mission was to identify enemy artillery positions that could be shelled and destroyed prior to the attack, and to clear the air of German fighters and observation machines that might reveal the British buildup. This extraordinary aggressive aerial push was as disastrous for the British airmen as the fighting on the ground was for their countrymen in the trenches. A new generation of German fighters had come up to meet them. Once again technology had foiled obsolete tactics.

As the war progressed, nations deployed airplanes in ever larger units, from the individual squadrons and escadrille of 1916 to the aerial armada of 1,471 French, British, and American aircraft under the command of U.S. Gen. William "Billy" Mitchell that captured and held control of the air during the Allied advance against German positions in the St.-Mihiel salient in 1918. German aviators were grouped into larger operational units as well, the famous "circuses" that fought up and down the lines as needed. By 1917, all facets of the air war were stretched to the limit—pilots, planes, factories, and training units.

The nation for which a pilot fought could literally be a matter of life and death. Consider the statistics. The French kept the best records. From 1914 to 1918, l'Aviation Militaire trained 16,458 pilots and 2,000 observers; 5,533 (29 percent) of them died in combat or flying accidents.[20] The number of casualties (dead, wounded, or captured) for French air crewmen totaled 7,255, or roughly 39 percent of flying personnel.

General Ernst von Hoeppner, commanding general of the Luftstreitkräte (Imperial German Air Force), provided a figure of 7,780 killed in combat or flying accidents for the years 1914–1918. While no record for the total number of German air crew who served has survived, we may assume that the number of German airmen, and therefore the percentage of dead and wounded, was a bit larger than that for the French.[21]

The total number of air crew members serving with the RFC, Royal Naval Air Service, and Royal Air Force is unknown, but records indicate that the nation trained 22,000 pilots during the war. If the ratio of observers to pilots in Britain was close to that in France, then the total number of flying personnel would be close to 24,600, of whom 9,378 (38 percent) died in combat. Given a total casualty figure of 16,623, we can assume something close to an astounding 68 percent total casualty rate among British airmen![22]

How are we to explain such a horrific loss rate among the British? French historians Charles Christienne and Pierre Lissarague begin by pointing to "the general and long-lasting—until the middle of 1917—inferiority of English fighter planes."[23] Aircraft like the Vickers F.B. (Fighting Biplane) 5 were easy prey for a Fokker E.III in the hands of a good pilot. Moreover, while replacement aircraft like the British Airco D.H. 2 pusher helped tame the Fokker scourge, they remained in service with some squadrons well into 1917, long after they had been badly outclassed by early models of the German Albatross.

The B.E. 2C, which also remained at the front into 1917, is another case in point. Originally designed for the Royal Aircraft Factory by Geoffrey De Havilland in 1912, a B.E. 2 had been the first British airplane to land in France at the beginning of the war. "The most urgently and frequently reviled of all war-time aeroplanes," one veteran pilot recalled, ". . . in combat it was utterly incapable, the most defenseless thing in the sky."[24]

And there were other factors. While Oswald Boelcke's dicta called for caution by German fliers, British air leaders like Gen. Hugh "Boom" Trenchard, who had been named general officer commanding of the RFC in August 1915, expected British airmen to take the offensive, engaging the enemy at every opportunity. Royal Air Force pilot Cecil Lewis thought this approach suited the spirit of his fellow airmen, whom he characterized as the "adventurous, the devil-may-care young bloods of England, the fast livers, the furious drivers . . . [who were] not happy unless they were taking risks."[25]

The results are not difficult to imagine. Lewis estimated the average life span of a British pilot in France in the summer of 1916 to be three weeks. As historian John Morrow notes, the RFC entered the Battle of the Somme in July 1916 with 426 pilots and 410 aircraft. By November 1916, they had lost 592 aircraft and 499 aircrew were dead, wounded, or missing. In five short months the RFC lost more men and machines than it had taken into battle. Even if the German figure of 3,128 total aircraft lost in combat for the period 1914–1918 is far too low, it still seems clear that the number of British losses exceeded the number of victories.[26]

In addition to the danger they posed to one another, the airmen of every nation shared the most daunting hazards. They flew open-cockpit aircraft, behind roaring engines, in subzero temperatures, with the frigid slipstream blasting past them. Rotary engines blew a mist of light-weight castor-oil lubricant out the exhaust valves and over the pilot. Oxygen systems were largely ineffective, and usable seat-type parachutes were unavailable, except for German aviators in the last months of the conflict. Take-offs and landings proved especially dangerous, particularly for planes with rotary engines. Their torque could flip an aircraft handled by an unwary pilot onto its back at the worst possible moment. Most novice pilots found it daunting simply to control an airplane in the hostile environment of the sky, let alone stay alert enough to spot the enemy and to fight.

BUILDING AIRPLANES: AN INDUSTRY AT WAR

And what of the aircraft they flew? During the war, France developed only thirty-eight production aircraft types from the 264 prototypes that were built and tested. Britain developed seventy-three service aircraft from 309 prototypes. The German ratio of seventy-two service aircraft from 610 prototypes was even higher. These figures underscore the French emphasis on standardization and centralized control of production and the extent to which Britain, and especially Germany, pursued research programs.

In 1914, serious engineering was rare in the international aircraft industry. "It was a constant gamble," English designer Thomas O. M. Sopwith remarked of the prewar years, when structural analysis had been a matter of judgment, not mathematical calculation. "Some of us were lucky," he opined, "and some of us were not."[27]

The earliest warplanes were sturdy enough when not required to perform aggressive or evasive maneuvers. The aerodynamic stresses of combat, however, revealed a great many structural problems. First-generation pursuit machines like the Nieuport 11 Bébé were fatally prone to shedding wing fabric. The lower wings of the classic Albatros fighters of 1916–1917 were given to failure in torsion. The advanced parasol monoplane Fokker D.VIII of 1918 was infamous for its wing failures.

Despite these very real problems, aeronautical engineering began to mature during the First World War. The German aircraft industry valued research. Firms from Fokker to Zeppelin emphasized engineering standards and paid careful attention to research underway at universities like Göttingen and Aachen. Ludwig Prandtl, his colleagues, and graduate students were putting the finishing touches on aspects of the circulation theory of lift during the war years.

The superior performance of the thick-winged Fokker aircraft testifies to the impact of engineering research on aircraft design. Some of Europe's finest engineers, men with solid university backgrounds, performed computational analyses of complex structures like rigid airship frameworks. After the war, German aerodynamic theory spread across Europe and around the world, revolutionizing the practice of aeronautical engineering.

Research gave Germany a technological edge. The battle for control of the air over sections of the front seesawed back and forth as new generations of aircraft were introduced. A new fighter that offered even a slight improvement in speed, rate of climb, or maneuverability could, for a time, tip the balance. In general terms, however, the Germans maintained the advantage. The Fokker D.VII is regarded as the finest fighter aircraft of the war. An American pilot commented that aviators flying the Sopwith Camel, England's most agile and maneuverable fighter, "had to shoot down every German airplane in the sky as a Camel could neither outclimb nor outrun a Fokker."[28]

The Germans pioneered the use of new materials and innovative aircraft design. The Fokker M5, a prewar monoplane designed by Rheinhold Platz, introduced the wire-braced, welded steel-tube fuselage, which became the standard structural pattern for the first generation of postwar aircraft.

A CLIMATE THAT rewarded experimentation and innovation soon produced a genuine revolution—the all-metal airplane—courtesy of Hugo Junkers (1859–1935), a central figure in the early history of aviation. He had been an outsider, combining a career manufacturing hot-water heaters with an engineering professorship at an Aachen technical school. He and his colleague, Hans Reissner, had produced the *Ente* (Duck), an unsuccessful 1909 design featuring monoplane wings covered with sheets of corrugated aluminum. They patented the very advanced design for a very large, all-metal flying wing with internal bracing.

In pursuit of the all-metal airplane, Junkers gave up teaching early in 1915 and built a laboratory and workshop in his Dessau factory. Under government contract, he produced the J 1, a monoplane prototype for an armored ground-attack aircraft. It had thick cantilevered wings skinned with "supporting covers," thin sheets of iron backed by sheets of corrugated metal. Junkers had perfected this technique while manufacturing hot-water heaters. It represented a breakthrough, the first cantilevered, stressed-skin wings that could carry an aerodynamic load. Flight-tested in December 1916, the J 1 proved to be heavy and underpowered, resulting in a very slow rate of climb. It was a start, but only that.

Junkers J 1

Junker turned from using iron to duralumin, a lightweight, high-strength aluminum alloy. The most common metallic element in the earth's crust, aluminum is not found in its elemental state because of its affinity for oxygen. The Danish physicist Hans Christian Oersted isolated metallic aluminum in 1825, but it was not until 1866 that the American Charles Martin Hall and the French experimenter Paul Héroult simultaneously developed a practical means of producing the metal in commercial quantities. Aluminum was difficult to cast and exhibited no apparently useful properties. Consequently, it remained so rare that, as late as 1884, a single ounce cost as much as an ounce of silver.

The answer lay in alloys. In 1909, German metallurgist Alfred Wilm patented a product in which a hot aluminum-copper-manganese alloy was quenched under precise conditions after heat treatment. Mysteriously, the casting would continue to grow stronger and harder over the next four days before finally stabilizing.

The new metal had the qualities of mild steel at one-third the weight. It was produced under the trademark Duralumin, a contraction of the company name (Dürner Metalwerke) and the word *aluminum*. Once the properties of the new metal became apparent, companies in other nations developed their own versions of duralumin. In America, Alcoa had their product, 17S aluminum, on the market by 1916.

Often in the history of technology, products like duralumin flow from a process that is little understood. Duralumin's nature was a puzzle until 1919, a full decade after it went on the market. Once it was understood that duralumin changed character because constituent metals continued to precipitate out during the first few days after annealing, the process became known as precipitation hardening. Despite a serious corrosion problem, duralumin's value to aviation was apparent.[29]

Count Ferdinand von Zeppelin spun the spidery frameworks of his earliest airships with an aluminum-zinc alloy recommended by Carl Berg, a manufacturer who donated the metal in the hope of encouraging a market. So important was aluminum to the operation that when the Luftschiffbau Zeppelin Company was founded in 1908, Berg's son-in-law, Alfred Colsman, was named general manager. Under his leadership, the company pioneered the use of duralumin in aircraft construction beginning in 1914.

A first-rate manager, Colsman conceived and organized the

DELAG (Deutsche Luftschiffahrts-Aktein-Gesellschaft) Zeppelin passenger-carrying operation just before World War I. Colsman's appointment says much about the importance of the aluminum industry to the operation and exemplifies the count's business strategy, the creation of interlocking networks of companies involved in airship production.

Hugo Junkers made his first duralumin airplane in 1916. The Junkers J 4, a biplane designed for low-level observation and ground attack, was the first all-metal airplane to enter production. Its relatively poor altitude and speed performance was less critical for its purposes than the metal construction, which was thought to make the plane less vulnerable to ground fire.

The German authorities who ordered the Junkers machine into production were nervous about the designer's lack of manufacturing experience. They forced Junkers to team with Fokker, which led to a breakthrough for the young Dutch manufacturer. Junkers had developed a thick wing to contain his cantilevered structure. Recognizing the aerodynamic and structural advantages of the design, Fokker began to provide his own aircraft with thick cantilevered wings.

The advantages of dural, as duralumin was finally called, came at a price. The metal lost strength when heated, so riveting had to be substituted for welding. Also, dural corroded into a white powder when it was exposed to oxygen, and did so at top speed when it was exposed to salt air. However, the life expectancy of a warplane was short anyway, and industry would get by for another few years before it solved the corrosion problem.

Claudius Dornier (1884–1969) gained experience with duralumin while working for the Zeppelin Company, designing and building large flying boats with externally braced wings. By 1918 he had his own firm and was producing the D1, a fighter with a dural structure partially covered with fabric—another expansive German leap and a good example of a national industrial strategy that rewarded innovation.[30]

NOT THAT THE BRITISH were idle. The flight facilities at the National Physical Laboratory, Teddington and at Farnborough were among the best in the world. More important, the quality of the work conducted at these facilities was second only to the fundamental aerodynamic research underway in the German universities.

The Royal Aircraft Establishment (as Royal Aircraft Factory was renamed in July 1918) remained an important and controversial feature of the British aeronautical scene during the war. By mid-1915 approximately five thousand employees worked for the organization. Between 1914 and 1918, engineers designed some thirty aircraft types. The factory rolled out perhaps five hundred airplanes. The common practice, however, was to turn a promising government design over to private firms for serial production.

Even so, Britain lacked Germany's innovative spirit. Government authorities placed a ban on the use of duralumin in aircraft structures, for example, following the loss of the first British airship, the *Mayfly*. While Britain achieved occasional air superiority, as in early 1916 with the introduction of the D.H. 2, German aircraft retained the edge for most of the war—even in 1918, when first-class British aircraft like the S.E. 5, the Bristol Fighter, and the Sopwith Dolphin entered service.

The French, so innovative before 1914, now focused on practical reality. The nation's only wind tunnel dated to 1910. Large expenditures on research or radical innovations, officials reasoned, represented a foolish waste of effort at a moment of national crisis. Rather, French success keyed on a firm determination to produce large numbers of a few combat-worthy aircraft and engines. France produced only thirty types of aircraft in 1918, far fewer than either Germany or Britain.

In the end, a nation's productive capacity proved as important as the quality of its aircraft. Almost 235,000 airplanes and 225,000 engines were produced worldwide during the conflict. Great Britain (55,092 airframes) and France (51,700 airframes) each produced more than one-fourth of the total. Germany rated a distant third, with an estimated 38,000 aircraft. The rest of the world made roughly 89,400 machines. France may have built as much as two-fifths (92,067 units) of the world's aircraft engines.[31]

French industrial planning for the air war had been remarkably successful. The Aeronautical Manufactures Service (S.F.A.), established in the Directorate of Military Aeronautics at historic Chalais

Meudon in 1914, provided "general direction" to the private firms manufacturing airplane, engines, and aeronautical equipment. By 1918, the S.F.A. was monitoring contracts at three thousand factories.

The aircraft produced in the largest numbers during the war was the SPAD XIII (7,300 aircraft), a sturdy, well-designed machine that French and American airmen regarded as a near match for the Fokker D. VII. The Nieuport XI Bébé (7,200 units), the Breguet XIV (3,500), the SPAD VII (3,500), and the Salmson A 2 (3,200) were also manufactured in very large numbers. British production figures indicate both the enormous numbers of aircraft rolling out of the factories in 1917–1918 and the large production runs of some models that had appeared relatively early in the war: 5,500 Sopwith Camels, 5,200 S.E. 5s, 4,077 R.E. 8s, 3,600 B.E. 2s, and 3,200 D.H. 9s.

The contrast with German production figures is stunning. The Albatros CV, a two-seat observation machine was produced in the greatest numbers (2,800 units), with Pfalz D III and Fokker D.VII fighters close behind (2,100). Focused attempts to increase production proved less than fully successful. The Amerikaprogramm of 1917, designed to increase fighter production and maintain air superiority prior to the expected waves of American aircraft, was disappointing. By the time the Albatros DV aircraft selected for extended production reached the front, they were already outmatched by the Sopwith Camel and the SPAD.

While Germany held the technological edge in the spring of 1918, the nation's industrial capacity was strained to the breaking point. Occasionally this stymied innovation. Government planners frowned on the development of improved engines, for example, because it might slow current production. A rubber shortage resulted in new combat aircraft flying to the front with wooden tires.

Just as often, a failing economy and shortages encouraged fresh approaches. A lack of aircraft-quality lumber, and the ease with which unskilled workers could be taught to weld, favored steel-tube construction. Other innovations, including the imaginative use of plywood in the construction of semimonocoque fuselages and load-bearing wings, represented major technological advances.

THE BIRTH OF STRATEGIC AIR POWER

The German airship had been Europe's bête noir since the fall of 1906. Until then Ferdinand von Zeppelin could have been called either an unrealistic eccentric or a brilliant visionary. Underpowered and uncontrollable, Luftschiffbau (airship) Zeppelin (LZ) 1 (first flown in 1900) was broken up after only three short flights. The much improved LZ 2 (1905) was destroyed in a storm before it could return to the hanger following its second flight.

LZ 3 represented the turning point. On its maiden flight on October 6, 1906, the airship flew sixty miles in two hours and repeated the feat the next day. In September 1907 it set a record for time aloft—over eight hours. Rebuilt, LZ 3 was purchased by the German army in 1909 and used as a training ship until a fire destroyed it in 1913.

As early as July 1908, the *Daily Mail* claimed that LZ 3 could carry fifty soldiers from Calais to Dover. Zeppelins said to be on the drawing board would soon be able to transport double that number a far greater distance.[32] That fall, the newspaper reported a Berlin meeting in which a city official described plans for an invasion of England by a fleet of airships carrying soldiers who would "capture the sleeping Britons before they could realize what was taking place."[33]

The possibility of an attack from the sky spawned a series of apocalyptic novels by the Frenchmen Albert Robida and Emile Driant, the Englishman George Griffith, and the German Rudolph Martin.[34] It was H. G. Wells, however, who provided the master narrative of the genre, an account of an attack by German Zeppelins on New York City entitled *The War in the Air* (1908): "There is no place where a woman and her daughter can hide and be at peace. The war comes through the air. The bombs drop in the night. Quiet people go out in the morning and see air-fleets passing overhead—dripping death—dripping death!"[35]

The members of England's ruling elite worried about the reaction of the working class to the hardships of war, including the possibility of bombing. Major Stewart L. Murray, in a 1913 lecture to the Royal United Services Institution, expressed particular concern about the "volcanic" social forces bubbling away beneath the surface. "Unless steps are taken to prevent the hardships of war pressing intolerably upon the new working classes," he warned, "the whole organized power of labour may be used to demand the cessation of the war, even at the price of submission to our enemies."[36]

The French, like the English, were far more concerned about Germany's airships than its airplanes. "The French nation believes that the 'fifth arm' [French military aviation] protects it from the German aerial invasion as nothing else can," aviator-author Jacques Mortane remarked, certain that ". . . the aerial forces of [France] would meet the mighty Zeppelins . . . ere they cross the frontier and defeat them."[37]

The Germans, however, faced serious problems with their wonder weapons. The Naval Airship Division had lost its commanding officer and most of the crew of the airship L 1 in a crash in the fall of 1913. Shortly after, a fire had destroyed the L 2 along with its designer and most of the twenty-eight crewmembers. Army officials remained enthusiastic, although some skeptical German officers suggested that antiaircraft fire might be something of a problem for a 450-foot-long, hydrogen-filled aerial behemoth. The events of the days and weeks following the German invasion of Belgium and the beginning of the war on the night of August 3–4, 1914, supported both views.

Initially, German strategists ignored the notion of long-range attacks on the enemy homeland; they put the Zeppelins to work supporting army operations at or very near the front. On April 6, 1915, the crew of the LZ 21 (Z IV) dropped five hundred pounds of bombs on the military fortress at Liége, Belgium. Damaged by antiaircraft fire on its return flight, the airship crash-landed near Bonn. Less than three weeks later, on August 23, LZ 23 (Z VIII) was brought down by fire from seventy-five-millimeter French field guns, while the LZ 22 (Z VII) fell victim to ground fire on the Eastern Front. Except for the captain, who died of wounds, the entire crew surrendered to the Russian troops they had just bombed.

Three days later, on August 26, the LZ 17, commanded by Capt. Ernst Lehmann dropped eighteen-hundred pounds of high-explosive bombs on the besieged city of Antwerp. The airship, constructed in 1913 as the *Sachsen*, had been a passenger ship before the war, carrying hundreds of passengers over German cities for DELAG, the German airship transportation company established in Frankfurt in 1909. Lehmann would become the most successful of all Zeppelin commanders, only to die in 1937 as a result of injuries suffered in the crash of the *Hindenburg* at Lakehurst, New Jersey.

The LZ 25 (Z IX), just completed by the Zeppelin factory at Friedrichshafen, joined *Sachsen* at Düsseldorf, home base for the attacks on Belgian cities. Together, the two airships continued to raid Antwerp. "All told," Lehmann reported, "we must have dropped ten thousand pounds of bombs on the fortifications, a bit of military strategy, which, if it did no appreciable damage to the enemy, accomplished a greater purpose. For we succeeded in restoring the confidence of the high command in airships."[38]

The month that had begun with bombing attacks conducted by airships concluded with the first bombing of a major city by airplane. Just after noon on August 30, 1915, Lt. Von Hindelsen piloted his Taube over Paris and dropped bombs that took the life of one woman.

The Allies did their best to strike back. On October 8, 1914, following one failed attempt to bomb the Zeppelin sheds at Düsseldorf, Flight Lt. R. L. G. Marix and Squadron Cmdr. Spencer Grey of the Eastchurch Squadron of the Royal Naval Air Service, flying Sopwith Tabloids armed with two 20-pound bombs apiece, attacked the railway station at Cologne. They killed three civilians and destroyed the LZ 25 (Z IX) in its hanger.

But it would be the German navy, its capital ships bottled up in port, that would launch the first genuine strategic bombing campaign. Captain Peter Strasser, who would command the German Naval Airship Division, was frustrated by the futile attempts to use the huge Zeppelins as tactical weapons. For all of its fear of the Zeppelin, England remained defenseless against attack from the sky in 1914–1915. Airplanes could not yet climb as high as an airship, and in any case were not yet armed. Antiaircraft guns scarcely existed.

In January 1915, the Kaiser, anxious to break the deadlock at the front, lifted his own order forbidding air attacks on Great Britain. The first small-scale raids that month underscored problems inherent in the enterprise—mechanical failures, navigational difficulties, the near impossibility of hitting a specific target on the ground. Still, the first bombs dropped on the coastal town of Yarmouth on January 13, 1915, killed four people and marked the beginning of the first strategic bombing campaign in history. Over three years, German airships would attack Allied cities from Belgium and France to Russia, but Britain would remain the primary target.

During 1913–1918, the German navy operated seventy-three rigid airships, and the army fifty-eight. The largest of the wartime Zeppelins was almost 694 feet long and over 78 feet in diameter. With a crew of thirty, the behemoths could fly more than twenty thousand feet above the earth at speeds of over 80 mph with a range of 7,500 miles.

Two companies made them. Luftschiffbau Schütte-Lanz, a firm founded by Johann Schütte (1873–1940), a professor of shipbuilding at a Danzig technical school, built 19 airships, distinguished by their rigid frameworks of wooden girders. The various organizations controlled by Count von Zeppelin and his chief assistant, Hugo Eckner, built the other 112.

By mid-1917, the Zeppelin empire employed 17,075 workers. Corporate headquarters and the main construction facility were at Friedrichshafen on Lake Constance. The Staaken Company, a subsidiary, produced the large multiengine bombers that would replace the Zeppelins in attacks on England in 1918.

Ballon-Hüllen Gesselschaft, located at Berlin Templehoff, manufactured the large cells that contained the hydrogen gas inside each airship's frame. Butchers all over Germany shipped tons of cleaned animal intestines to the firm, for use in the manufacture of the gas-tight goldbeater's skin that lined the huge linen hydrogen cells.

Karl Maybach, son of automotive pioneer Wilhelm Maybach, ran Luftfahrzeug Motorenbau Gesselschaft, the associated firm that built airship engines. Ultimately, there was even a subsidiary corporation to build the sheds that housed these huge machines.

Between January 1915 and August 1918, German airships conducted fifty-one raids on Great Britain, dropping 196 tons of bombs that took 557 British lives and injured an additional 1,358. But the campaign took an even heavier toll in German lives. In June 1915, RFC Sublieutenant Reginald A. J. Warneford, flying a Morane-Saulnier, encountered LZ 37 crossing over Belgium at a relatively low altitude on its way to London. Climbing above the airship, he dropped a bomb on it, earning credit for the first destruction of a Zeppelin in air-to-air combat.

During the weeks and months that followed, improved antiaircraft guns and more-advanced pursuit aircraft brought down the airships in ever increasing numbers. The Naval Airship Division lost fifty-three of its seventy-three Zeppelins in combat or to accidents. Twenty-six of the fifty-eight army airships would never return. An incredible 40 percent of wartime Zeppelin crewmen lost their lives. The Zeppelin raids took far more German lives in the air than English lives on the ground. Among the dead was Capt. Peter Strasser. He had died in the flames of LZ 70, three miles high in the sky, on the very last Zeppelin raid against England.

While Zeppelins were attacking in the west, Imperial Russia put four-engine bombers in service. Igor Ivan Sikorsky had build and flown the first such craft, the *Bolshoi Baltinski* (Great Baltic), in 1913. It was followed by the even larger Il'ya Muromets which could stay aloft for up to five hours with sixteen passengers aboard.

The Russian government ordered the machines into production and created the Eskadra Vozdushnykh Korablei (Squadron of Flying Ships) of forty aircraft to conduct bombing missions on the Eastern Front. The first bombing raid occurred in February 1915, with operations still underway when the Bolshevik Revolution brought an end to Russia's participation in the war. Many of the big bomber missions were tactical, aimed at railroad junctions rather than population centers.

By January 1915, the Fluzeugbau Frierichshafen, German specialists in the design and construction of flying boats, had finished the first *Grossflugzeug*, or large flying machine. Within a year Gotha Wagonfabrik A.G. turned out twin-engine bombers under license and proceeded to design a series of Gothas, G.II to G.V. Powered by 220- to 260-horsepower Mercedes engines, the Gothas had a crew of three and carried three machine guns for defensive fire.

The G.IV, the first production model, was also the first to be used for air raids on England. Operating from an airfield at Nieuwmunster, near Ostend, on the Belgian coast, the twenty-three Gothas of the England squadron crossed the Channel for the first time on May 25, 1917, striking Folkestone and taking 95 lives and injuring another 195. The "wong-wongs," as the British civilians came to call the raiders, because of the discordant beat of their unsynchronized engines, reached London for the first time on June 13, killing 162 and injuring 432 more.

During the course of the war, several German manufacturers built Riesenflugzeug (giant aircraft). The most successful of these machines were the Zeppelin Staaken R types. While single aircraft in the series served both on the Eastern Front and in raids on England, the only type to enter production was the four-engine R.IV, with Zeppelin company, Aviatik, Schütte-Lanz, and O.A.W. building eighteen of them. By September 1917 these planes joined the Gotha in raids on French and English cities.

In all, the Gotha (383 aircraft) and Riesenflugzeug (30) would return to England 52 times. They took 1,414 lives and injured 3,416. Sixty-two German aircraft were lost to combat or accidents. The campaign would have a much greater impact than the numbers suggest.[39]

WORRIED ABOUT THE IMPACT of the bombing on civilian morale, and the potential for public unrest and the disruption of production following the second daylight raid in July 1917, David Lloyd George created the Prime Minister's Committee on Air Organization and Home Defense against Air Raids and placed South Africa's General Jan Christian Smuts in charge. Less than twenty years before, Smuts had been a Boer commander and one of Britain's most dedicated foes. Now he would be responsible for creating the world's first independent air force.

Smuts's report called for the creation of a web of antiaircraft gun emplacements and barrage balloons throughout London; the establishment of an early warning system that would detect the approach of German bombers; a means of warning Londoners of the approach of a raid; the identification of subway stations and other facilities that were to serve as shelters; and the recall of squadrons from France to defend London. That fall, after the appearance of the first Riesenflugzeug over the capital of the Empire, the government announced that it would reorganize British air units, creating the Air Ministry and merging the Royal Naval Air Service and the RFC into a Royal Air Force (RAF).

But the world's first independent air force would not simply defend London and continue the struggle in France. Armed with bombers of their own, the RAF would carry the war to the enemy. As early as December 1914, the Royal Naval Air Service had placed an order with the Handley Page Company for "a bloody paralyser of an aeroplane" with which to attack Germany. It turned out to be the twin-engine Handley Page O/100, flown for the first time at the end of 1915. The O/100, and the O/400 that followed, were used for tactical bombing on the Western Front.

By the spring of 1917, the Handley Pages were attacking submarine bases, railroad junctions, marshalling yards, and factories. Two of the aircraft served with British forces in the Arab Revolt and the Palestine Campaign. Another, based in the Aegean Sea, bombed Constantinople and German warships in the area.

In Italy, Count Giovanni Battista Caproni had built his first large aircraft in 1913. Throughout the war, the firm would continue to produce advanced twin-engine and trimotor bombers, Models Ca 1 to Ca 5. The Italian Corpo Aeronautica Militaire launched bombing raids against Austro-Hungarian targets beginning in the spring of 1915 and continuing to the end of the war. In France, Breguet, Caudron, and Farman produced tactical bombers that were occasionally used in strategic attacks. In addition, French manufacturers like Esnault-Pelterie produced the superior Caproni designs under license for service with l'Aviation Militaire. Through 1918, French and British squadrons, some of them flying Italian aircraft, bombed railroad stations and junction points used by trains transporting iron ore and other raw materials into Germany.

Had the war continued into 1919, England's Independent Force, armed with the new four-engine Handley Page V/1500, the Vickers Vimy IV, and the latest Caproni designs, would have struck German cities. The American Martin Company was producing an advanced twin-engine bomber. Other American projects included experimental flying bombs and balloon bombs that would have been launched in a terror campaign against German civilian and military targets. All of that would have to wait for the next war.

Bomb damage fell far short of dire prewar expectations. As a dress rehearsal for something far more horrific in the not-too-distant future, however, it would do. None realized that better than the men who had commanded the bombers.

Each had come late to aviation. Thirty-nine-year-old Hugh "Boom" Trenchard, who had made his reputation both as an officer and as a polo player during the Boer War, had graduated from Central Flying School just weeks before age would have made him ineligible to fly. William "Billy" Mitchell enlisted in the U.S. Army five years before the invention of the airplane. Giulio Douhet, who came from a family of soldiers, had only seen three airplanes and had never flown when he wrote his first article on the revolutionary potential of air power. All of them would be heard from in the decade to come.

AMERICAN EAGLES:
ORGANIZING A NEW INDUSTRY

While French firms like Blériot and Farman had produced up to eight hundred airplanes apiece before 1914, the Wrights output stood at some one hundred machines between 1909 and 1915. A limited market, difficult legal environment, and government apathy combined to slow U.S. development.

Things began to improve after 1914. The pioneers, intuitive engineers and self-taught entrepreneurs like the Wrights, Glenn Curtiss, and Glenn Luther Martin, began the process of change by luring professional engineers into the embryonic industry. Grover Loening (1888–1976) was one of the first.

Born in Bremen, Germany, the son of the U.S. counsel-general, Loening held three degrees from Columbia University, earned from 1908 to 1911, including the first degree in aeronautics (M.A., 1910) ever granted by an American university. Following graduation, he served as chief engineer for the Queen Company, owned by Chicagoan Willis McCormick (1911–1913); engineer and assistant to Orville Wright and manager of the Wright Company factory (1913–1914); and chief aeronautical engineer in the U.S. Army Signal Corps (1914–1917).

Jerome Clarke Hunsaker (1886–1984) deserves full credit for establishing the profession of aeronautical engineering in the United States. A native of Creston, Iowa, Hunsaker graduated from the U.S. Naval Academy at the head of the class of 1908 and spent a year aboard the cruiser USS *California* before pursuing a master's degree in naval architecture at the Massachusetts Institute of Technology (MIT).

Hunsaker's thesis described the hydrodynamic forces that affect the rudder of a high-speed destroyer. He became interested in aeronautics when he and his wife translated Gustave Eiffel's classic treatise on airfoils. Professor Richard Maclaurin, who moved to MIT after supervising Loening's aeronautical studies, arranged for Hunsaker to visit Richard Glazebrook, director of England's National Physical Laboratory, and to spend time with the engineers at the Eiffel laboratory.

Together with Albert Francis Zahm, an associate of Octave Chanute who had built the first wind tunnel at Catholic University in America, Hunsaker concluded his grand tour of aeronautical laboratories with a visit to Germany, where he was treated to a flight aboard a Zeppelin. The young naval officer returned to the United States early in 1914 and quickly became the American authority on the current state of flight research. His report on the trip and his long articles on the work of European laboratories argued for a similar large-scale research effort in America.

Hunsaker would personally lead the way. Under his direction, the MIT program became a national center for aeronautical research and a principal source of engineers. He constructed an important wind tunnel at MIT and, in October 1914, established the first graduate program in aeronautical engineering in the United States.

He was assisted by Donald Wills Douglas (1892–1981), a Brooklyn native who had arrived at MIT in 1912. As a teenage visitor to Washington, D.C., Douglas had watched Orville Wright fly at Fort Myer in September 1908. The following year he saw Glenn Curtiss pilot the *Golden Flyer* around a racetrack at Morris Park, New Jersey.

Douglas followed his older brother Harold into the U.S. Naval Academy in the fall of 1909 but dropped out in 1912. "I never had any trouble, scholastically or . . . in any way," he later explained. "I just didn't like the idea of discipline over me. I thought there wasn't enough freedom."[40] Determined to pursue his own dreams, Douglas sought employment with both the Curtiss and Wright Companies. Rebuffed, he enrolled at MIT in 1912 and completed a four-year degree program in mechanical engineering in only two years.

Broke and with no prospect of a job, Douglas accepted a temporary position as Hunsaker's assistant. He helped to install and operate the wind tunnel, assisted in developing the first course in aeronautical engineering, and handled consultations with the Connecticut Aircraft Company, the inimitable "Captain" Thomas Scott Baldwin, and other would-be entrepreneurs of the air who came in search of advice.

"Nobody persuaded me to go into aeronautical engineering," Douglas recalled late in life. "The only person I really talked to about it was Jerry Hunsaker, and he tried to dissuade me from it."[41] While he may have thought that it was not in the best interest of his assistant and friend, Hunsaker recommended Douglas when Glenn Luther Martin asked for the name of a young man whom he might hire as a chief engineer.

Glenn Martin would remain at the helm of a major aircraft firm longer than anybody else, and he would nurture a great many other future leaders of American aviation. Like Douglas, Lawrence Bell and James Smith McDonnell cut their professional teeth at Martin. So did James H. "Dutch" Kindelberger, who headed North American Aviation during World War II; his contemporary, C. A. Van Deusen, who headed the Brewster Aircraft Company; and Leroy Randle Grumman. Douglas, the first in that long and distinguished line of Martin alumni, was hired to replace Clarence Day, who left to be chief engineer with Standard Aircraft, and Charles Willard, a pioneer Curtiss aviator who would become one of the founders of the L.W.F. (Lowe, Willard and Fowler) Company.

Martin's early success lay in his ability to identify talented engineers and managers. He assisted William E. Boeing (1881–1956) as well. A graduate of Yale's Sheffield Scientific School, Boeing had established

Glenn Luther Martin

himself in the timber business before becoming interested in flight. Martin taught him to fly in 1910 and sold him his first airplane. Six years later, Boeing established his own company, having watched Glenn Martin do business, and valued solid engineering. Right away, he hired two engineering graduates of the University of Washington who would shape the future of his company, Phillip Johnson and Clair Egtvedt.

When Donald Douglas arrived at the Martin factory in Los Angeles, however, his employer still had much to learn. Up to this time, empiricism, the rule of thumb, and educated judgment had substituted for professional analysis. No detailed drawings were prepared. Structural testing consisted of placing an airplane on wooden supports, climbing aboard, and "jouncing around." Douglas was appalled. At MIT, he had learned to calculate the precise stresses that an aircraft would encounter in flight.

Douglas spent most of the year 1916 designing airplanes for Glenn Martin, before falling victim to corporate politics. The problems began in August, when the financiers who controlled the Wright Company talked Martin into a merger. The resulting Wright-Martin Company seemed poised for success, especially when it acquired the Simplex Automobile Company, with its large manufacturing capacity and experience with engines. Soon the new company landed juicy foreign contracts for engine production. But bad business decisions offset all of that.

One mistake occurred in December 1916, when the new corporate president ordered Vice President Martin to replace the company's young chief engineer. Undaunted, Douglas immediately went to work for the Aeronautical Division of the Signal Corps in Washington, D.C., headed by Virginius "Ginny" Evans Clark, a West Point graduate and MIT classmate, the most talented aeronautical engineer in American uniform.

THE NATIONAL ADVISORY COMMITTEE FOR AERONAUTICS

American universities emerged as centers of research and a source of trained engineers. It became clear to Progressives, however, that the government should also play a role in supporting a research-based technology that was critical to national defense. Inspired by the success of flight research programs in England, France, Germany, and Russia, American enthusiasts yearned for a national aeronautical laboratory. Captain Washington Irving Chambers, who had run naval aviation since 1910, spoke for many when he argued that it was time to replace "the crude efforts of the pioneer inventors" with "the methods of scientific engineers."[42]

Early proposals called for a program based at the Smithsonian Institution, the National Bureau of Standards, or a naval research organization. Others disagreed. Captain David W. Taylor, head of hydrodynamics and fluid research for the navy, argued that flight was the business of the military. Richard Maclaurin, now the president of MIT, argued for the German model of university laboratories. Professor William F. Durand, a Stanford University authority on fluid dynamics, agreed. William S. Stratton, head of the National Bureau of Standards, wanted aeronautical research for his outfit. In September 1912,

Chambers and Albert Francis Zahm, a professor of physics at Catholic University, favored establishing the laboratory under the auspices of the Smithsonian Institution.

In 1913, Charles Doolittle Walcott, secretary of the Smithsonian, took matters into his own hands, setting up the Langley Aerodynamical Laboratory with internal funds and the approval of President Woodrow Wilson and his own Board of Regents. He intended for his laboratory to cast a wide net, undertaking research for government agencies as well as pursuing projects funded by private individuals or corporations.

Zahm would direct the laboratory, under the supervision of a governing board of eleven leaders drawn from government, universities, and industry. Plans were going well until someone pointed out the illegality of the governing board. Federal employees could not sit on such a panel without congressional approval. Walcott reluctantly dissolved the Langley laboratory in May 1914.

That December, Walcott offered a new and very different proposal for an American version of the British Advisory Committee for Aeronautics, which was a free-standing organization created in 1909 to coordinate English aeronautical work. Composed of government employees and knowledgeable citizens, the American committee would "supervise and direct the scientific study of the problems of flight with a view to their practical solution, and to determine the problems of flight which should be experimentally attacked and to discuss their solution and their application to practical questions."[43]

Congress approved legislation creating the Advisory Committee for Aeronautics (later the National Advisory Committee for Aeronautics, or NACA) on March 3, 1915. President Wilson signed the bill that day. Chaired by Secretary Walcott, NACA first surveyed 112 universities, 22 Aero Clubs, 10 manufacturers, and 8 government organizations to determine what they were doing in aviation.

After considerable political maneuvering, Congress appropriated funds for the long-sought national aeronautical laboratory under the auspices of NACA on August 29, 1916. Walcott would have his Langley Memorial Aeronautical Laboratory after all. The facility opened its doors in Hampton, Virginia, the following year. NACA would grow and mature over the next fifty-three years, earning, in the words of a leading historian of the organization, a well-deserved reputation as "arguably the most important and productive aeronautical research establishment in the world."[44]

The military services were in the research business as well. Glenn Curtiss had made use of U.S. Navy hydrodynamic facilities at Annapolis, Maryland, to perfect his flying-boat hulls. A wind tunnel would join the test tanks at the Washington Navy Yard, and additional facilities would be provided at the Philadelphia Navy Yard. The U.S. Army Air Service Engineering Division Facility at McCook Field, Dayton, Ohio (which opened in 1917), would become a center of both theoretical work and empirical testing of airframes, engines, and aeronautical equipment of every description.

BUYING AND SELLING AIRCRAFT

The new aviation industry would thrive on military contracts. Between 1909 and the American entry into World War I on April 6, 1917, the U.S. Army purchased 478 airplanes from a total of eleven manufacturers: Wright (sold 14 aircraft); Curtiss (332); Burgess/Burgess-Dunne (17); Martin (25); Standard (32); Sturtevant (11); L.W.F. (23); Thomas (2); Aeromarine (6); Gallaudet (4); and Wright-Martin (12). Almost 85 percent of those machines were purchased in 1916–1917, and most were trainers.[45]

The American aircraft industry had also begun to tap the rich foreign market. Official records indicate that U.S. industry produced 411 airplanes in 1916, 269 of which were sold abroad. The 110,000-square-foot Curtiss Company factory constructed in Buffalo, New York, in 1915 unofficially became known as the "Churchill plant," in honor of one of the company's best customers, Winston Churchill, First Lord of the Admiralty. Hundreds of Curtiss flying boats (Models A-2, F, H-4, H-12, H-12b, HS-2L) were built under license in Europe and exported in large numbers to England, Italy, and Russia during the years 1911–1917. They were the only products of the American aircraft industry regarded as suitable for active service by the warring nations of Europe.

Curtiss, whom Grover Loening regarded as "a promoter and not an engineer or even his own designer, excepting in a vague way," followed Wright-Martin Company officials and hired a professional engineer to oversee aircraft design and analysis.[46] He met B. Douglas Thomas, chief engineer with the Sopwith Aviation Company, during a trip to England and convinced him to design the Curtiss J tractor biplane to be powered by the new Curtiss OX-5 engine. Having completed the design, analysis, and working drawings in England, Thomas came to America and held lead engineering positions at Curtiss, Thomas-Morse, and Consolidated Aircraft before retiring in the 1930s.

Under the direction of B. Douglas Thomas, the new airplane evolved into the JN-4 "Jenny," the great commercial success of the U.S. aircraft industry in World War I and one of the classic American airplane designs of the century. So good was the Jenny's design that Curtiss captured the Canadian market as well, establishing a subsidiary firm, Canadian Aeroplanes, that delivered twelve hundred "Canuck" variants by November 1918.

No American aircraft engine could yet meet European standards. The Wright Company, now allied with the Simplex Automobile Company, acquired the rights to manufacture the famous Hispano-Suiza engine, designed by Swiss engineer Marc Bergket. With a contract for the sale of 450 of the engines to France, Wright officials negotiated a merger with the Martin Company (1916) in an effort to increase productive capacity. However weak the embryonic American industry might have appeared, it had begun to attract foreign investment. As early as 1916 the Japanese Mitsui Company had acquired a controlling interest in Standard Aircraft.[47]

There was hope for the future. When the United States entered World War I in the spring of 1917, the Allied nations called on American industry to produce 25,000 airplanes, an increase of more than 600 percent over the 1916 total of 411. A joint Army Navy Technical Aircraft Board established the precise quotas: 8,075 training aircraft; 12,400 frontline pursuit, bombing, and observation machines; and 41,810 engines. That would cost a great deal of money, and Congress provided it—appropriating some $1,250,000,000 before it was all over.[48]

THE TASK AT HAND was huge. Entire federal bureaucracies were established to acquire the millions of board feet of straight-grained spruce, miles of aircraft fabric, and thousands of tons of castor beans required for lubrication. A host of complex manufactured items, aircraft instruments, for example, would have to be obtained. And such an enormous increase in aircraft and engine production would have to be organized. The decision as to which airplanes to build, at least, had been resolved. A commission dispatched to Europe in the spring of 1917 recommended the production of proven European aircraft types, rather than developing untried American designs.

The Council of National Defense, a cabinet-level committee charged with coordinating resource management and war production, called attention to one untapped resource—the automobile industry—famed for its mastery of assembly-line mass production. Indeed, automobile moguls had taken a serious interest in aviation from the outset. Detroit interests played a key role in organizing the Wright Company. Wright-Martin was teamed with Simplex, while Willys Motors owned much of Curtiss. Clement M. Keys, a Willys executive, would eventually replace Glenn Curtiss.

Resolution of the Wright patent suits in the spring of 1917 through the creation of a federally approved patent pool, the Manufacturers Aircraft Association, made the new industry even more attractive to automobile men, who now led the drive for American strength in the air. The *New York Times* identified one Detroit executive, Howard E. Coffin, vice president of the Hudson Motor Car Company, as "the man who converted the War Department to the importance of an air fleet, won the public to his view, and obtained from Congress the appropriation of $645,000,000 for this purpose, all within six weeks in 1917."[49]

In April 1917, after consultation with NACA, the Council of National Defense created the Aircraft Production Board. Its members would organize aeronautical production and distribute contracts for the waves of aircraft and engines that would darken skies over the Western Front. The board included the two senior officers responsible for aviation in the two military services, a banker, and three automobile executives.

Howard Coffin, the appointed chairman, was joined by Sidney D. Waldon, a one-time Packard vice president and a senior executive at Cadillac, and Ohioan Edward A. Deeds. A former vice president of the National Cash Register Company, Deeds had organized a group of associates who developed the electric starter for automobiles (in 1909) and founded the Dayton Engineering Laboratories Company (Delco) to make and market the starter to automakers. As one of the four founders of the Dayton Wright Company in 1916, with Orville Wright as consulting engineer, Deeds was the only member of the board with any connection to aircraft manufacture.

Deeds emerged as the most influential member of the Aircraft Production Board. In August 1917, less than five months after coming to Washington, he was commissioned a colonel in the regular army, appointed chief of the Equipment Division of the Signal Corps, and then promoted to industrial executive in the Office of the Chief Signal Officer.

From that perch, Deeds and Coffin served as czars of wartime aeronautical production in the United States. The Aircraft Production Board distributed contracts, bought land for their contractors, built new factories, hired workers, arranged resources and subcontracted parts, and supervised production. By the end of the war, the board employed the services of 2,064 officers, 31,307 enlisted personnel, and 8,969 civilians.

The board had agreed that U.S. factories would turn out battle-tested European designs. But why copy the many in-line, rotary and radial engines that powered those airplanes? Would it not be better, Jesse G. Vincent suggested to Deeds, Coffin, and Waldon on May 27, 1917, to lean on U.S. automobile industry for standardized power plants that could be mass-produced with interchangeable parts?

An Arkansas native who had learned engineering via a correspondence course, Vincent had served as superintendent of inventions with the Burroughs Adding Machine Company, joined the Hudson Motor Car Company as chief engineer in 1910, and then stepped up to become vice president of engineering at Packard in 1912. Deeds asked Vincent to cooperate with Elbert John Hall, of the Hall Scott Motor Car Company, in designing a family of engines. This they did, working in a suite at Washington's Willard Hotel to produce layout drawings for a water-cooled, eight-cylinder, 270-horsepower Liberty engine in less than a week. The first engine was flight-tested on August 29, 1917.

Buick produced only fifteen L-8 engines before turning back to the tried-and-true 300-horsepower Hispano-Suiza power plant. But the 410-horsepower Liberty 12-A was quite another matter. This engine was heavy, too heavy to power single-seat aircraft, but quite suitable for larger machines and more than a match for contemporary European power plants in the same class.

Some thirteen thousand engines had been manufactured by the time of the armistice, although only five thousand had actually been delivered, most of them mounted on American-built DH-4 light bombers. In addition, over twenty thousand Liberty engines had rolled off the assembly lines at Packard, Ford, Lincoln, Buick, Cadillac, and Marmon. The Liberty would continue to make history in the postwar era, powering the Curtiss NC-4 flying boat that completed the first transatlantic flight (in 1919); the Fokker T-2 that made the first non-stop flight from coast to coast (in 1923); and the Douglas World Cruisers that first flew around the globe (in 1924).

The record of airframe production was quite another matter. One vociferous postwar critic of the program quipped that the enormous U.S. industrial effort had amounted to "196 planes for one billion dollars."[50] In fact, over five hundred American-built airplanes had reached France as early as June 1918. Still, the gap between bright promise and sobering reality was undeniable. Worse, as American newspapers trumpeted, all of the aircraft delivered to France were DH-4 light bombers produced by the Dayton Wright Company, machines that had been dubbed "flaming coffins" by their crews.

Ex-President Theodore Roosevelt's aviator son Quentin would die in combat while serving with the American 95th Aero Squadron. He had remarked that while not completely satisfied with the Nieuport 28 that he was flying, "I'd be much more comfortable in it than in a Liberty [powered DH-4] if I had to cross the lines."[51]

"None of us in France could understand what prevented our great nation from furnishing machines equal to the best in the world," Capt. Eddie Rickenbacker, the American ace of aces, remarked. "Many a gallant life was lost to American aviation during those early months of 1918, the responsibility for which must lie heavily on some guilty consciences."[52]

And there were charges of corruption. During the last six months of the war, Gutzon Borglum, the sculptor who had watched Orville Wright circle the parade ground at Fort Myer only ten years before, charged the "Detroit-Dayton group" who dominated the Aircraft Production Board with corruption. Senator Charles Thomas launched a committee investigation of the program, while President Wilson, deploring the "baseless optimism" of the board, asked Charles Evans Hughes to look into the situation.

Just before the war's end, Deeds and Waldon were removed from duty and ordered to cooperate with the Hughes Committee. Accused of profiting from lucrative contracts awarded to his old colleagues at Dayton Wright and for having perjured himself to congressional investigators, Deeds was recommended for court-martial. An Army Board of Review declined to bring charges. The committee further recommended that Vincent face criminal charges for having shown favoritism to Packard. While never prosecuted, he was pardoned by President Wilson.

Despite the problems, an embryonic U.S. aviation industry emerged from the conflict poised to hold its own and ultimately surpass foreign competitors. The maturation of aviation would be marked by an evolving relationship between government, universities, and manufacturers. That web of relationships, and the infrastructure that would support the growth of the aerospace enterprise, was rooted in the war years.

Manufacturers hit their stride by the fall of 1918. While the Aircraft Production Board missed its deadlines, an industry composed of three hundred plants employing 175,000 workers had produced 13,894 aircraft and 41,953 engines between April 1917 and November 1918.

And while the Aircraft Production Board certainly favored automobile manufacturers, a few pioneers prospered. Curtiss was producing JN-4D trainers for the army and navy and selling flying boats to the navy, not to mention having designed the large multiengine NC flying boats. B. Douglas Thomas had left Curtiss for a partnership in the Thomas Morse Company and designed the MB-3 Scout, a fighter plane destined for the front in 1919.

Discouraged, Glenn Martin withdrew from active leadership of the Wright-Martin Company to organize a new Martin Company in Cleveland, Ohio, in September 1917. Donald Douglas also moved on, resigning his government job to sign on with Martin once again, leading the engineering team that developed the MB-1 bomber. Had the war continued, the Kettering "Bug," a flying bomb developed by Dayton Wright engineers, would have been launched against targets in Germany. In twenty short months, American industry had almost closed the gap with European aircraft manufacturers.

THE FIRST GREAT WAR IN THE AIR:
ASSESSING THE IMPACT

Defense spending fueled aeronautical development in the twentieth century. But what was the impact of combat on technological change? The development of aviation in World War I offers an ideal case study. In general terms, the war did not produce revolutionary advances. High-performance aircraft in service in 1914 flew almost as fast, high, and far as did aircraft in 1918. Important wartime innovations—steel-tube construction, the introduction of duralumin, and the production of all-metal aircraft, multiengine bombers, and flying boats capable of crossing the Atlantic—were rooted in the prewar era.

Yet war did have a profound impact on flight technology. What had been a record-setting performance for a few machines in 1914 was substandard for the great fleets of warplanes in 1918. Experimental metal aircraft that had been constructed before the war were in combat by 1918. In a few cases, notably American experiments with unpiloted flying bombs, brand new ideas that would bear fruit in the decades to come were explored for the first time.

And aircraft production boomed. France made 1,000 machines or so in 1914 and 44,563 airplanes in four war years. In every belligerent nation, what had been an embryonic industry in 1914 matured by the end of the conflict. Even in defeated Germany, innovative manufacturers like Junkers, Dornier, and Zeppelin emerged as technological leaders of the new civil aviation industry.

Military aviation had added new and revolutionary dimensions to warfare. Early on, European nations had only general-purpose aircraft that could be used for reconnaissance, dropping bombs, liaison, or any other task within the machine's limited capability. By 1918, a range of specialized aircraft flew into battle. High-performance fighter aircraft roamed the sky in search of the heavily armed photo reconnaissance machines sure to reveal preparations for a buildup or an advance. Armored ground-attack machines made life in the trenches that much deadlier. Giant multiengine bombers struck at the enemy's centers of production and terrorized civilians. Huge flying boats capable of crossing the oceans conducted long-range antisubmarine patrols.

If the air war did not dominate the conflict on the ground, the experience convinced air leaders, and the general public, that the airplane was the weapon of the future. The prophets of air power—Giulio Douhet, Billy Mitchell, and "Boom" Trenchard—wondered aloud if aviation had not made land and naval warfare obsolete. That debate, and a sometimes fearful, sometimes enthusiastic discussion of the efficacy and morality of strategic bombing, would echo down the corridors of power for the two decades between the wars.

6

LAYING THE FOUNDATION,
1919–1927

1919: A YEAR OF TRIAL, TRIUMPH,
AND NEW BEGINNINGS

Not all of the guns fell silent on the eleventh hour of the eleventh day of the eleventh month of 1918. In Russia, counterrevolutionary forces waged a bitter civil war that lasted into 1921, in an unsuccessful effort to wrest control of the nation from the Bolshevik government. The victorious Allies sent expeditionary forces numbering up to two hundred thousand men into an unsuccessful fight against the Soviets. Józef Pilsudski, head of the newly constituted Polish state, sought to take advantage of the situation and push the border of his own nation east by attacking the Ukraine in 1920–1921. The Soviets emerged bruised but victorious from their civil war, and achieved a negotiated settlement with the Poles that preserved most of the Ukraine as a Soviet republic.

The Poles had fielded a small air force of volunteer airmen and mercenaries who had "cut their teeth" in combat above the trenches. A tiny Soviet air force struggled to rise from the shambles of war and revolution. The obstacles were overwhelming. Factories were deserted; many pilots had fled the country or enlisted in the White armies; men with technical training were scarce. Initially, the Red Air Fleet seemed scarcely a match for the veterans arrayed against them.

Lenin and his comrades defined themselves as the wave of the future, however, and they wanted to ensure that others saw them in the same way. Support for a cutting-edge technology like aviation proved useful to the new state and sent a signal to a watching world. At the moment, a modest air force was critical to survival. The application of available air power, especially with Il'ya Muromets four-engine bombers, played a role in the Bolshevik victory.

During the next two decades, the new regime invested considerable sums in aviation. Factories, flying schools, and technical centers flourished. Aeronautical spectacles, ranging from the flight of the eight-engine giant *Maxim Gorky* to record-setting balloon voyages, helped to present a positive image to the world. But if flight served propaganda purposes, Soviet enthusiasm was nevertheless real, and their vision often reached very far into the future.

Lenin himself attended a lecture on space flight in 1920. The world's first exhibition on the prospect of interplanetary space travel, reminiscent of the aeronautical exhibition at the Crystal Palace in 1868, was staged in Moscow in 1924. State publishers issued entire series of books on the future of flight, film makers offered their visions of the future in the sky, and government-sponsored engineering societies conducted pioneering rocket research. The seeds of *Sputnik* were planted early and deep in the revolutionary soil of the Soviet Union.[1]

Elsewhere in the world, demobilization remained the order of the day. The strength of the U.S. Army Air Service fell from a total of 190,000 officers and enlisted men in November 1918 to a roster of 27,000 six months later. Some $100,000,000 in contracts for airframes, engines, and accessories were canceled with no warning. Total annual aircraft production fell from the wartime peak of 14,000 in 1918, to a record low of 263 in 1922. Ninety percent of the factory space devoted to aviation during the war had been redeployed by the end of 1919.

All war industries suffered, but aviation manufacturers were unique in having no civilian market to which they could return. A handful of companies, including Martin and Curtiss, with contracts that continued on a limited basis, remained afloat solely as aircraft producers. William

Boeing and his company were less fortunate. With its contracts canceled and no prospects for aeronautical work in sight, the Seattle manufacturer put its crews to work building wooden furniture until 1921, when a fresh army contract put it back in the airplane business.[2]

Other nations preserved at least some of their wartime aerial strength. French officials sent 20 percent of their air units to occupation duty in Germany and another 20 percent to their colonies in North Africa and Asia. As a result, the strength of l'Aviation Militaire only fell from a wartime peak of 90,000 officers and men to just under 40,000 personnel at the end of 1920.

Rather than abruptly canceling contracts, the French government continued to accept thousands of additional engines and aircraft through 1919, phasing out wartime production gradually. As an additional subsidy, the government sold the surplus material at cut-rate prices, kept 60 percent of the money for the state, and returned 40 percent to the manufacturers. Finally, the government continued to order new equipment and directly subsidized commercial aviation.

Even so, the number of active aeronautical manufacturers in France fell from 50 in 1918 to 10 two years later. Hispano-Suiza, Salmson, and Renault all returned to automobile manufacturing. At the same time, the number of commercial air carriers grew from four, operating 46 aircraft in 1919, to twelve with 185 airplanes by the end of 1920.

The Royal Air Force remained engaged on several fronts as well. Britain sent over 275 aircraft and 400 volunteer officers, including the great ace Raymond Collishaw, to serve with the White Russian forces. Other units were dispatched to the Indian-Afghan border country, to Somalia, and to other distant corners of the Empire.

As in France, Britain's Ministry of Munitions allowed selected wartime contracts for aircraft and engines to run into the summer of 1919. Then hard times settled over the industry. Airco, which had built Geoffrey De Havilland's D.H. 2, dispatched a delegation to Detroit to study the mass production of automobiles, while Thomas Sopwith's enterprise considered building motorcycles. Ultimately, neither company survived, but their demise would plant the seed of two new firms founded by their chief engineers, De Havilland and Harry Hawker. By the early 1920s, fearful that the industry would collapse altogether, the government finally supported six competing companies that had weathered the storm. This decision would pay enormous dividends in less than two decades.

The Allies intended to strip Germany of its capability to make war. The Treaty of Versailles, signed on June 23, 1919, forbade the production or importation of aircraft in Germany for the next six months. Anthony Fokker fled to Holland at the end of the war, accompanied by six trains filled with aircraft, engines, and parts. Other firms turned to the production of nonaeronautical goods or simply collapsed. By 1921, in the face of economic hard times and Allied strictures, only five German companies survived: Junkers, Dornier, Heinkel, Albatros, and Zeppelin.

Hugo Junkers continued to deliver metal aircraft to the military after hostilities ceased in 1918. He had also built the first J 13 (F 13), an all-metal, low-wing, cantilevered monoplane that represented the absolute cutting edge of commercial-aviation technology in the years immediately after the war. Even Junkers, with his genius for technology, needed help, accepting an offer from the Weimar government to operate a covert aircraft and engine factory and pilot-training center in the Soviet Union.

But if 1919 brought economic hard times to the industry, it was also a banner year that would demonstrate how far aviation had come in the sixteen short years since Kitty Hawk. The spring and summer would be a time remembered for heroic aviators and spectacular flights over the Atlantic.

THE NOTION OF FLYING across the Atlantic Ocean had begun with nineteenth-century American aeronauts like John Wise, James Allen, and Washington H. Donaldson. They had dreamed of crossing the ocean in huge balloons, a feat not accomplished until the flight of *Double Eagle II* in 1978.

In 1913, just four years after he had rewarded Louis Blériot for flying the English Channel, Lord Northcliffe announced a prize of 10,000 pounds sterling for the first flight across the Atlantic. He did not insist on a nonstop voyage. Aviators could hopscotch across the Atlantic, flying the shortest route from Newfoundland to the Azores and on to Lisbon. If operating flying boats, they could set down on water and even be towed into port, so long as they began again from the spot where they had landed. Glenn Curtiss had planned to try for the prize in 1913 with the *America*, his first large, closed-cabin, multiengine flying boat, but the war in Europe intervened.

By 1918, aircraft had become larger, and the odds in favor of a transatlantic flight much improved. The success of antisubmarine patrols in combating German U-boats led the U.S. Navy in the fall of 1917 to contract with Curtiss for the construction of four of the largest aircraft built in America. Designated NC (for Navy Curtiss), the big flying boats had a wingspan of 126 feet and were initially powered by three 400-horsepower Liberty engines.

NC-1 flew before the armistice, carrying fifty-one people aloft on one flight. Even so, judging the craft to be underpowered, engineers added a fourth engine to each of the aircraft. An experimental engine installation on NC-2 proved unsatisfactory, and after being battered by a storm, the aircraft was sacrificed to provide spare parts for the other three "Nancies," as they became known.

In the fall of 1918, Lt. John Towers (1885–1966), the third person to become a naval aviator and the officer who established the flight training operation at Pensacola, Florida, suggested flying the four big NC flying boats to Europe. Lt. Richard Evelyn Byrd (1888–1955), a naval aviator who had invented a special bubble sextant and a drift indicator for aerial navigation, was assigned to develop a seaplane base at Halifax, Nova Scotia. From there, the aircraft would begin their flight across the Atlantic. With the end of the war, aviation enthusiasts in the navy decided to press ahead with plans for the mass flight as a means of underscoring their growing capability and publicizing the role of naval aviation.

The effort to span the Atlantic was a masterpiece of logistical planning. A picket line of forty-one destroyers stretched across the Atlantic to the Azores, where the aircraft would refuel before pressing on to Lisbon. With John Towers in command aboard NC-3, the three aircraft took off together from Trepassey Bay, Newfoundland, on the

Curtiss NC-4

evening of May 16, 1919. When bad weather set in the following morning, they were forced to separate within 350 miles of their first stop. NC-4, with Lt. Comdr. Albert C. "Putty" Read and Lt. Walter Hinton at the controls, landed safely at Horta, in the Azores, after more than fifteen hours in the air.

Lost and low on fuel, however, NC-1 and NC-3 landed at sea. The six-man crew of NC-1, including aircraft commander Patrick Bellinger and pilot Marc Mitscher, both of whom would earn fame as naval commanders during World War II, were rescued by a Greek freighter. Sadly, their aircraft capsized and sank during the attempt to tow it to port. John Tower and the crew of the NC-3 had an even more adventurous time of it, riding out a storm at sea for over sixty hours and then literally taxiing their airplane into port. Towers took command of NC-4, which completed the trip with a hop to Lisbon on May 27 and a final flight to Plymouth, England, on May 31.

The NC-4 was first across, but the U.S. Navy had announced that it would not accept the *Daily Mail* prize. (The first abortive attempts to win the prize occurred in the spring of 1919, prior to the flight of the NC boats, so the money was still there to be claimed.) Supplemented by additional funds from a private businessman and a tobacco company, the first-qualifying aviator now stood to win 13,000 pounds sterling.

First to try were a pair of British entrants going west to east, starting from Newfoundland with the wind at their backs. Frederick Raynham and his navigator, Capt. C. W. Fairfax Morgan, would fly the *Raymor*, a single-engine Martinsyde aircraft. Harry Hawker, the renowned Australian aviator and engineer whom Raynham had taught to fly before World War I, would pilot the single-engine Sopwith biplane *Atlantic*, with Lt. Comdr. Kenneth Mackenzie Grieve flying as his navigator.

Hawker and Grieve took off at 3:40 P.M. on May 18, circled over the *Raymor*, and headed out to sea. Two hours later, convinced that he could overtake his old student, Raynham bounced into the air only to fall back to earth, shearing the undercarriage off the big Martinsyde. Both crew members survived, although Morgan lost an eye in the accident.

For a week, the fate of the *Atlantic's* crew was in doubt. Four hours after take-off, their radio had failed, and soon Hawker and Grieve found themselves caught in deteriorating weather with their engine temperature climbing and their fuel consumption much higher than expected. Dropping out of the clouds, Hawker spotted a Danish tramp steamer, the *Mary*, and set the *Atlantic* down in a trough between the waves. The world would assume that the aviators were lost, until the ship reached the Hebrides six days later.

Two more teams had arrived in Newfoundland during the week before Hawker and Grieve's departure. Anxious to prove their most advanced wartime product in dramatic fashion, Handley Page shipped a V/1500 bomber to Harbor Grace, Newfoundland. Three houses, a farm building, and a line of stone walls had to be removed in order to construct a runway for the huge aircraft. Test flights revealed engine problems, however, temporarily grounding fifty-five-year-old Adm. Mark Kerr and his crew.

Then along came Capt. John Alcock (1892–1919) and Lt. Arthur Whitten Brown (1886–1948), the last of the competitors to arrive in Newfoundland. An extraordinary airman, Alcock had taught himself to fly in 1912. He had bombed Constantinople as a Royal Naval Air Service aviator, was captured by the Turks, and landed a job as chief

Alcock and Brown take off from Newfoundland, June 14, 1919

test pilot for Vickers after his release from the prisoner-of-war camp. By the end of May 1919, a crew of Vickers workmen had begun to assemble the twin-engine Vimy bomber, Alcock and Brown's chariot to challenge the North Atlantic.

Clad in a mix of uniform parts, inflatable waistcoats, and heated flying suits, and carrying their good-luck charms, a pair of stuffed cats named "Lucky Jim" and "Twinkletoe," Alcock and Brown lifted off from a meadow near St. Johns on June 14. For over sixteen hours they would struggle with mechanical problems, balky instruments, disorientation, ice, clouds, and wind, ending their epic journey of 1,890 miles with a nose-down but safe landing in an Irish bog.

The U.S. Navy had regarded the flight of the NC flying boats as a well-planned expedition involving three aircraft, a chain of surface ships along the route, and the provision of fueling opportunities at intermediate points. Such a venture demonstrated a new military capability to the public, the Congress, and even navy traditionalists.

Alcock and Brown, on the other hand, had bridged the ocean in one heroic leap, adding their names next to that of Louis Blériot in the book of fame. Knighted immediately following the flight, Sir John Alcock had little enough time to enjoy his celebrity. He died just seven months later while delivering an amphibian to a French customer.

Clearly, the airplane could cross the Atlantic, if only barely and with heroic effort. Three weeks after Alcock and Brown landed in Ireland, thirty-two officers and men of the Royal Airship Service, one stowaway, and a cat named "Woopsie" flew across the Atlantic and back again in relative safety and comfort aboard His Majesty's airship R 34. Built by Beardmore Motors, at Inchinin on the Clyde, the design of the R 34 was based on the L 33, a German Zeppelin forced down over Little Wigborough, England, in the fall of 1916, and the L 49, a Zeppelin "height climber" captured in France a year later.

The R 34 was powered by five 250-horsepower Sunbeam Maori engines and had a top speed of roughly 60 mph, some 10 mph slower than the German original. Departing its base at East Fortune, England, on July 2 under the command of Maj. George Herbert Scott, the airship reached Mineola, New York, 108 hours and 12 minutes later with enough fuel left to fly two more hours. "We couldn't have cut it much finer," Maj. Scott commented, "and are lucky indeed to get through." The return trip, with the wind at their backs, went considerably faster. This double crossing of the Atlantic demonstrated the dirigible's commercial potential and launched the golden age of the rigid airship.[3]

The performance of the airship as compared to the airplanes of the period was no surprise to Rudyard Kipling, who commented that he had "always fancied the dirigible against the aeroplane for the overhead haulage in years to come." In his novella, *With the Night Mail* (1904), Kipling had prophesied that lighter-than-air craft would completely supercede the airplane by the year 2000. Like so many airship enthusiasts over the years, he was wrong. The dirigible was a transitional technology, filling an important commercial niche in a less-than-perfect way while a more practical technology matured.[4]

The year that had opened with preparations for a race across the Atlantic closed with another race to capture a 10,000-pound-sterling prize meant for the first Australian to fly from England to the southern continent. Five aircraft entered the competition, most of them wartime bombers. Four of the flights ended in crashes far short of the goal, but the brothers Ross and Keith Smith, highly decorated wartime airmen, accompanied by two mechanics, won the prize with a twenty-eight-day (November 12–December 10) aerial journey from Hounslow, England, to Darwin, Australia, in a Vickers Vimy. For this, the brothers were knighted. Ross Smith died testing another aircraft in 1922.

In addition to being a year of epic flights and records, 1919 marked the beginnings of world civil aviation. Representatives of twenty-seven nations, including the United States, signed the International Convention on Air Navigation at Paris on October 13. The treaty recognized the right of all nations to control their own airspace; it declared that all nations observing the tenets of the convention should be allowed free access to airspace; and it created the Commission for Aerial Navigation under the League of Nations to adjudicate disputes.

IN THE UNITED STATES, the National Advisory Committee for Aeronautics (NACA) recommended that the federal government take responsibility for licensing pilots, inspecting and certifying aircraft, and establishing and maintaining airports. The U.S. Congress was not ready to go that far, but it did increase funding to the U.S. Weather Service for meteorological support for aviation.

In fact, a meteorological revolution was underway. As a boy, Norwegian Vilhelm Bjerknes (1862–1951) had helped his father, a mathematician, check theoretical predictions based on his research in hydrodynamics. He had earned degrees from the University of Kristiania, pursued doctoral studies in Paris and Bonn, and then taught applied mechanics and mathematical physics at the University of Stockholm.

By 1897, Bjerknes realized that mathematical theorems describing circulation patterns in hydrodynamics and thermodynamics might apply to the atmosphere and the oceans. Given very accurate and detailed information on current conditions, it should be possible to predict future weather patterns. The calculations required were so complex, however, that the mathematical prediction of weather would remain impractical until the advent of the electronic computer. Still, Bjerknes remained convinced that the analysis of large-scale air masses could improve weather forecasting, and that this should be the primary goal of meteorology.

Bjerknes accepted the Chair of Geophysics and the directorship of the Geophysical Institute of the University of Leipzig in 1912 and then moved on to the University of Bergen in 1917. He attracted a new generation of students and colleagues, including his son Jacob. With the data gathered from weather stations established across Norway, the group developed what became known as the "polar front theory," which suggested that weather activity occurs in the narrow boundaries, or fronts, between masses of warm and cold air.

Dr. Walter Georgii was a leader in the application of new meteorological ideas to aviation. A physicist and mathematician who had earned his doctorate before the war and worked as a scientific assistant with the Prussian Meteorological Institute, Georgii made use of weather data from stations in Iceland and Norway to guide the German attack on Verdun. Eventually, he was transferred to the "England Squadron" at Ostend, Belgium, where he became known as the "weather frog" by the men who carried out the bombing attacks on England in 1917 and 1918. Georgii would remain an important figure in aviation and meteorology during the years between the wars.

With the return of peace, Bjerknes and his colleagues continued to build a new meteorology in which mathematical analysis and numerical forecasting replaced empirical guesswork. The publication of Bjerknes's classic, *On the Dynamics of the Circular Vortex with Applications to the Atmosphere and Atmospheric Vortex and Wave Motion* (1921), capped his early creative years and was as important to the future of aviation as any of the great flights that captured the popular imagination during the decades to come.

As historian R. E. G. Davies noted, 1919 was also "the first year of air transport."[5] The short-lived commercial ventures with heavier-than-air craft undertaken before the war comprised nothing more than interesting experiments. The DELAG Zeppelin operation that had carried thousands of tourists on sightseeing jaunts was the one genuinely impressive commercial achievement of the prewar era.

During the war, France, England, Germany, Austria, Italy, and the United States had established military or civilian airmail service and, in some cases, military passenger routes. The availability of high-quality war-surplus aircraft and experienced airmen provided a foundation for commercial aviation.

Ironically, Germany, the defeated nation, established the world's first sustained scheduled airline passenger service. The Deutsche Luft Reederei (DLR), organized by such industrial giants as the electrical combine A.E.G. (Allgemeinen Electrizitäts Gesselschaft), the Zeppelin company, and the Hamburg-Amerika shipping line, inaugurated the first postwar scheduled civil air passenger service on February 5, 1919, using war-surplus aircraft to link Berlin, Leipzig, and Weimar.

By September, DLR and a handful of other carriers flew scheduled air routes extending from Vienna in the south to the Baltic and North Sea coasts, and from Frankfurt in the west to Danzig and Konigsburg in the east. Between August and December of 1919, when French authorities seized their equipment, a reconstituted DELAG company made 103 flights with the Zeppelin *Bodensee*, carrying 2,400 passengers and 30,000 kilograms of freight between Freidrichshafen and Berlin, with one flight to Stockholm.

Pilot Lucien Bossoutrot, flying a Farman F.60 Goliath, made the earliest cross-Channel commercial flight on February 8, 1919, and opened the route between Paris and Brussels two days later. He was a key figure in the pioneer firm Lignes Aériennes Farman. The Compagnie Général Transaériennes (CGNA), chartered as early as 1919, had conducted its first experiments with flying boats and airships. CGNA began offering London-to-Paris service with war-surplus Breguet bombers in August. Other companies, often organized by syndicates of aircraft manufacturers, opened service to various French and Belgian cities that year.

As in France, aircraft manufacturers in Great Britain ran some of the first commercial air operations. The A.V. Roe Company opened service over a fifty-mile route between Manchester and Blackpool in

September 1919. Aircraft Transport and Travel, with Sir Sefton Brancker as managing director, operated war-surplus D.H. 9 aircraft between various British cities and the continent. By fall, three British air services vied with the French for the fares of businessmen eager to reach the continent in a hurry or the adventurous Londoner off for a romantic weekend in the City of Lights.

In the United States, commercial air transportation began with a handful of visionaries at the U.S. Post Office. On September 1, 1915, Postmaster General Albert Sidney Burleson appointed newsman Otto Praeger to be second assistant postmaster. Asked to consider airmail service for Alaska and remote sections of New England, Praeger countered with the notion of a national airmail service and, with the assistance of NACA, persuaded Congress to fund the idea. The first step involved contracting with an aircraft manufacturer willing to operate an experimental demonstration route between Washington and New York. At the last moment, in the spring of 1918, Edward A. Deeds, of the Aircraft Production Board, offered the U.S. Army Air Service.

The army placed Maj. Reuben Hollis Fleet (1887–1975) in command of the operation. A native of Monsanto, Washington, Fleet had dabbled in real estate and local politics before being called to active duty in 1917. He earned his wings as army aviator No. 74 at San Diego, California, and was then assigned to Air Service headquarters, where he planned and supervised all air crew training.

Fleet and his command (six additional pilots and six JN-4Ds) went into business with considerable fanfare on May 15, 1919, flying between Washington and New York. President Woodrow Wilson and a host of dignitaries watched as Lt. George Boyle took off from Washington, D.C., only to become confused and fly south instead of north. He landed twenty-five miles south of Washington, clipped his propeller, and wound up with the airplane on its back. Fortunately, the southbound mail run from New York went smoothly, as did operations over the following weeks.

The army operation was important but short-lived. By August 1918, the U.S. Post Office had, in effect, established its own air force, the U.S. Air Mail Service. Maj. Fleet was placed in command of business operations at the Air Service Engineering Division headquarters

President Woodrow Wilson and Maj. Reuben Hollis Fleet
confer before a mail flight, May 15, 1918

at McCook Field in Dayton, Ohio. He would leave the Air Service in 1923 to establish his own company, Consolidated Aircraft.

As previously noted, pilot Anthony Jannus had operated the world's first regularly scheduled passenger air service with daily flights from Tampa to St. Petersburg from January to April 1914. The next passenger air service in the Western Hemisphere came five years later, on November 1, 1919, when Aeromarine West Indies Airways opened passenger, freight, and mail service from Key West, Florida, to Havana, Cuba. The 150-mile aerial voyage took up to two hours in adverse winds, and cost $50, more than twice the cost of a steamer ticket.

Entrepreneur Inglis Uppercu, who had constructed large flying boats during World War I, merged two small operations, Aero Limited and West Indies Airways, to form the new corporation, which won the first U.S. contract for overseas airmail in 1920. Beginning in the spring of 1921, Uppercu moved his three flying boats north to link New York and Atlantic City by air during the summer months. Between June and October of that year, he operated twice-daily service across Lake Erie, between Cleveland and Detroit. Returning south again in the winter of 1921–1922, he added to his fleet of Aeromarine flying boats and expanded his routes to include flights from Miami to Nassau, Bahamas. Operations ceased completely in 1924, when both the United States and Cuba withdrew their postal subsidies.

COMMERCIAL AVIATION IN EUROPE, 1920–1932

The pioneering postwar airline ventures in England, France, and Germany enjoyed some early successes. British and French air services carried sixty-five hundred passengers between London and Paris in 1920, with the three British operations carrying perhaps three times as many passengers as their French counterparts. At the same time, actual revenues amounted to only 17 percent of total costs.[6]

These figures presented a fatal difficulty for the English pioneers of 1919–1920, who did not receive any form of government subsidy. As Winston Churchill explained to Parliament in 1919, it was not "the business of government to carry civil aviation forward by means of great expenditure of public money." Official support of aviation through research and the provision of air routes and airport improvements was one thing, he argued, but when it came to the actual business of air commerce, His Majesty's government was well advised to "keep out of the way."[7]

The consequences of that thinking soon became apparent. The British firms, operating at an 83 percent loss, ceased operations for a time in 1921. The government quickly reversed its policy and joined France in subsidizing domestic carriers offering overseas service. In 1924, the British government negotiated the merger of four private airlines into a single new "chosen instrument." Imperial Airways would carry the Union Jack overseas and receive an annual subsidy of 1,000,000 pounds sterling.

Imperial Airways was not the first officially sponsored and subsidized government airline. Business and financial leaders headed by Alfred Plessman had organized KLM (Koninklijke Luchtvaart Maatschappij Voor Nederland an Kolonien) in October 1919. Anointed "the

Royal Dutch Airline" by Queen Wilhelmina, it functioned as an instrument of national economic, colonial, and foreign policy. SABENA (Societe Anonyme Belge d'Exploitation de la Navigation Aerienne) became the Belgian national air carrier in May 1923.

French and British airline operators continued to share the busiest air route in the world. Ten years after the inauguration of regularly scheduled air service between London and Paris, 48,000 people a year (an average of 138 passengers a day, and as many as 500 a day during the summer rush) were flying between the two capitals.

By 1930, the five independent French commercial air carriers were enjoying the world's largest government subsidy. Rather than linking the cities of Metropolitan France, however, the French extended air routes south through Lyons to the Mediterranean coast; east and south into Poland and the Balkans; and west and south to Algeria and Morocco.

One of the five subsidized airlines, the legendary Aéropostale, came to represent the danger, adventure, and romance of early air commerce. The company (originally Latécoère) began in 1919, offering mail service along a route running east from Toulouse past the Bay of Biscay and south across Gibraltar to Tangier, Rabat, and Casablanca. In 1924, Marcel Bouilloux-Lafont, a banker with business connections in Argentina, began to acquire the airline. The following year Aéropostale pushed its routes across the Sahara and down the coast to Dakar, from which point the pilots would leap across the South Atlantic to Natal, Brazil, and a connection with their existing South American routes.

As early as 1925, German airline operators had also been attracted to the potentially lucrative South American market. By 1930, Aéropostale routes stretched south from Natal to Montevideo, Uruguay. On May 11, 1930, pilot Jean Mermoz connected the two halves of the Aéropostale empire when he flew a Latécoère 28 flying boat from Dakar to Natal, Brazil. Mermoz and his crew were rescued when they landed in the water five hundred miles short of the African coast on the return flight.

In France, Mermoz rivaled Charles Lindbergh as a hero of the air. One of his colleagues, the aviator and author Antoine de Saint-

Exupéry (1900–1944), recorded Mermoz's exploits and those of the other aviators of Aéropostale in the pages of three great novels of the air age: *Southern Mail* (1929), *Night Flight* (1931), and *Wind, Sand and Stars* (1939).

Mermoz, he explained, was one of the "handful of pilots . . . [who] surveyed the Casablanca-Dakar line across the territory inhabited by the refractory tribes of the Sahara." Forced down in the desert by an engine failure, he was taken captive by nomads, who, "unable to make up their minds to kill him, kept him captive a fortnight." They finally ransomed him back to Aéropostale, where he "continued to fly over the same territory."[8]

"When the South American line was opened," Saint-Exupéry continued, the man "who had flung a bridge over the Sahara" was asked to pioneer a route through the Andes. Flying an aircraft with an absolute ceiling of sixteen thousand feet through a mountain chain with peaks rising over twenty thousand feet, Mermoz had to establish air routes through passes "whose surfaces are bleached white in the storms, whose blustering gusts sweep through the narrow walls of their rocky corridors and force the pilot to a sort of hand-to-hand combat."[9]

On one of those flights, the intrepid aviator became "a prisoner of the Andes" as surely as he had been captive of the desert tribesmen. Forced down onto a bit of tableland twelve thousand feet up with a sheer drop on every side, Mermoz and his mechanic waited two days for rescue, meanwhile attempting some make-shift repairs. Finally, they strapped themselves into the airplane and rolled down the incline and over the edge. Fortunately, the machine responded to the controls, enabling Mermoz to maneuver down through a pass and out over the Chilean plain. "And the next day," Saint-Exupéry concluded, "he was at it again."[10]

He remained "at it," building his legend, until December 7, 1936, when he disappeared on yet another flight across the South Atlantic. At the time of his death, Mermoz was an employee of Air France, which had been created three years before when four powerful airlines forced Aéropostale to merge. The resulting national airline would receive the largest subsidy offered by any European government. Bouilloux-Lafont, who had forged an aerial empire stretching from Madagascar to Buenos Aires, fell victim to the government policies and political machinations that led to the creation of Air France.[11]

In Germany, the Versailles Treaty ended virtually all of the promising air commerce ventures initiated in 1919. No aircraft could be produced or imported for six months after the signing. When the initial restrictions were lifted, production was limited to light aircraft. Struggling aircraft manufacturers like Fokker, Dornier, and Junkers had no choice; they moved to facilities outside Germany and tapped foreign markets. For a decade after the war, German firms built aircraft in the Soviet Union, Holland, Italy, Sweden, Switzerland, and the United States.

A handful of air carriers had survived the confusion and chaos of 1920–1921. Now they entered into a series of consolidations, culminating in the final merger of Deutsche Aero Loyd and Junkers Luftverkher AG into a single state-supported corporation, Deutsche Luft Hansa, on January 6, 1926—Lufthansa after January 1, 1934.

Meanwhile, British and French air planners built aerial links to colonial markets in Africa, Asia, and South America. German commercial air operators provided stiff competition in some of those remote markets, but Luft Hansa initially concentrated on developing a compact route structure linking the cities of Europe. Busier and more successful than its foreign rivals, and one of the most heavily subsidized airlines in Europe, it played an especially important role in the life of a nation recovering from defeat and forbidden to maintain a military air force.

National Subsidies Expressed in French Francs for Commercial Air Transportation, 1930–1933[12]

NATION	1930	1931	1932
France	119,800,000	133,444,115	124,829,625
Germany	96,960,000	96,380,000	86,010,000
Italy	95,750,030	95,058,920	94,552,630
United Kingdom	27,861,750	19,750,800	17,334,400
Belgium	16,263,410	17,350,835	11,516,200
Poland	13,035,310	13,812,120	15,171,070

USSR	9,780,995	9,747,365	11,293,510
Netherlands	8,859,425	6,636,885	6,431,170
Spain	7,935,000	7,841,850	7,196,700
Austria	7,622,100	7,513,200	5,508,000
Switzerland	5,748,750	7,541,663	7,250,135
Czechoslovakia	5,128,995	7,811,375	6,270,265
	4,944,340	5,186,140	4,136,075
Sweden	4,084,820	3,729,395	5,638,846
Yugoslavia	2,957,755	3,389,235	2,824,455
Denmark	2,381,750	1,955,450	1,672,550
Finland	1,322,350	1,043,150	723,140
Greece	*No traffic*	2,713,420	5,976,000
Hungary	890,000	890,000	890,000
Norway	68,050	56,080	43,710
Rumania	*No traffic*	*No traffic*	1,297,090

THE EUROPEAN AIRLINER, 1919–1926

Germany had emerged from World War I at the cutting edge of flight technology. The Allies insistence on the destruction of the nation's war-surplus air fleet set the stage for Germany's leap forward into the next generation of civil aircraft. British and French manufacturers faced a bleak postwar environment marked by decreased military spending and a market well supplied with converted wartime bombers.

Germany had to build anew. Anthony Fokker had scarcely caught his breath before establishing a new firm in Holland, the Dutch Aviation Company, and reasserted control over the old factory at Schwerin from a distance. As early as 1919, with the financial support of the founders of the embryonic German airlines that would combine to form Luft Hansa in 1926, Fokker had developed the F.2, his first commercial aircraft, a high-wing cantilevered (no external bracing) monoplane with a characteristically thick airfoil. The F.2 and its fol-low-on, F.3, equipped the early airlines that linked German cities to Austria, the Baltic, Scandinavia, and Russia.

Back on his feet, Fokker visited the United States in 1920–1921, starting up the Netherlands Aircraft Manufacturing Company, which was nothing more than a sales agency for aircraft manufactured in Holland. Three years later he moved to America and reorganized the venture as a manufacturing organization, the Atlantic Aircraft Corporation (later renamed the Fokker Aircraft Corporation). By the late 1920s, Fokker had two factories in New Jersey and one in West Virginia and had become one of the leading aircraft manufacturers in the United States as well as Europe. The Fokker F.VII (1924) and F.VIIA (1925) Super Universal, a seven-passenger single-engine aircraft that pioneered the route from the Netherlands to the Dutch East Indies, were popular with airlines in other parts of the world.

But Anthony Fokker was not the only phoenix to rise from the ashes of German defeat. The Allies had almost nipped Claudius Dornier's postwar career in the bud. During the war, the leadership of the Zeppelin Company had placed the young engineer in charge of the design and construction of flying boats at Lindau on Lake Constance. By 1918, the facility had been spun off into an independent firm, in true Zeppelin fashion. After the Treaty of Versailles, Dornier was forced to stop development of the Gs-1, a six-passenger flying boat aimed at the civilian market. He then developed a smaller flying boat, the Delphin, which transformed into the land-based four-seat Dornier Komet.

The improved Komet III (1924) and the six-person Dornier Merkur, fitted with a more powerful Bavarian Motor Works (BMW) VI engine, equipped German airlines and were exported in considerable numbers to areas as distant as Japan and South America. In addition to these workhorse aircraft, the Dornier name became known around the world during the years between the wars through its development of large flying boats, from the Dornier Do J Wal series (Do J II, Do R2, Do R4) to the famous twelve engine Do X (1929).

But it was Hugo Junkers, the third surviving German pioneer, who would develop the best first-generation airliner. The Junkers F 13 was an all-metal, low-wing monoplane seating four passengers. Legend has it that Hugo Junkers had ordered his chief engineer, Otto Reuter, to begin design of a civilian airliner on Armistice Day. First flown on June 25, 1919, the F 13, like earlier Junkers aircraft, featured a well-designed metal-tube framework with a cantilevered wing, covered with a corrugated duralumin skin. In an effort to escape the treaty restrictions, Junkers began producing water heaters at his factory in Dessau, Germany, and manufactured airplanes in Sweden.

Fokker and Dornier had interlocking business agreements with pioneering German airline builders. Without that advantage, Junkers had to reach farther afield to market his aircraft. He established the Junkers-Larsen Company in America, which sold F 13s to the U.S. Post Office, Army, and Navy, and to the Soviet Union. The firm participated in the establishment of the first Persian airline, and inaugurated the age of commercial air transportation in Japan, China, Africa, and Australia. The F 13 became one of the most familiar aircraft in South and Central America. By 1924, Junkers controlled or heavily influenced thirty airlines around the globe. After the merger of smaller German airlines to form Deutsche Luft Hansa in 1926, the F 13 continued to carry up to 40 percent of the traffic for the first few years.

Official records indicate that some 322 F 13s were manufactured in series, an extraordinary number considering the price of the machine, the poor economic conditions, the availability of war-surplus airplanes, and competition from Fokker and Dornier. The airlines of thirty-four nations operated the F 13, a rugged and long-lived aircraft. Many remained in service for as long as twenty years.

But the F 13 could be improved. Junkers built some two hundred W 33 aircraft, a freight-carrying version of the basic design. One of them, the *Bremen,* carried Guenther Von Huenefeld, Hermann Koehl, and James Fitzmaurice on the first east-to-west crossing of the Atlantic in 1928. The original all-metal, trimotor, nine-passenger G 23 (1924) and the more powerful G 24 (1926) set records for distance and duration and saw service in Asia and South America. A handful of special variant G 31s set records for tonnage hauled by air when they were employed to supply gold field operations in the remote mountains of New Guinea during the 1930s. The G 24 remained in service until the appearance of the ultimate descendant of the F 13, the famous Junkers Ju 52/3m, in 1932.

Technological treasure seemed to pour out of postwar Germany. Like Claudius Dornier, Dr. Adolf Rohrbach had begun his career with the Zeppelin company, where he designed E.4/20, a four-engine bomber with a 120-foot wingspan. The huge semicantilevered wing was constructed around a revolutionary box spar, stronger and lighter than the separate front and rear spars of normal wings. Rohrbach established his own firm in 1922, locating the initial production facilities in Copenhagen. By 1926, he had delivered the prototype Rohrbach Roland, a ten-passenger airliner with a box-spar wing, to Luft Hansa.

The prodigy Wilhelm "Willy" Emil Messerschmitt (1898–1978) designed, built, and flew his first glider at the age of seventeen. Between 1921 and 1926, while studying engineering at a Munich technical college, the young enthusiast and a friend constructed a glider, three sailplanes, two motor gliders, and a light aircraft. Following graduation in 1926, he served as chief designer and engineer of the Bayerische Flugzeupwerke at Augsburg (to be renamed Messerschmitt in 1938). Two years after joining the firm, Messerschmitt introduced the Me 20, a high-wing monoplane seating ten that remained in service well into World War II.

Focke-Wulf Flugzeug GmbH, a Bremen firm founded in January 1924 by Professor Heinrich Focke, Georg Wulf, and Dr. Werner Neumann, established itself with the A 16, a light transport with a high thick wing. Real success eluded the firm until a merger with Albatros and the arrival of the legendary designer Kurt Tank in 1931.

COMMERCIAL AVIATION IN THE UNITED STATES, 1920–1925

American industry had not produced a large supply of multiengine military aircraft that could be converted into airliners. Moreover, air travel was far less appealing in the absence of large bodies of water and international borders of the sort that complicated rail service in Europe.

There were exceptions. Alfred W. Lawson had made a reputation in baseball, but was committed to aviation. He established his own aeronautical journal and operated a small aircraft factory in Wisconsin during World War I. With the help of his chief engineer, the talented Vincent Burnelli, Lawson designed and built the C-2, a twin-engine airliner that could carry twenty-six passengers on flights of up to four hundred miles. A larger airliner, the L-4, came complete with sleeping accommodations. Unfortunately, it crashed on its first take-off.

Most American airmen preferred the life of a freelance aerial entrepreneur and showman. If the U.S. military did not release large aircraft suitable for carrying passengers, they did swamp the market with surplus training aircraft and Liberty engines, just what returning aviators needed to remain in the air at a reasonable cost.

Lester Durand Gardner, editor of *Aviation* magazine, commented on the situation in October 1919. "One of the most interesting phases of present aviation activities," he noted, "is the great number of small companies engaged in exhibition flights and in passenger flights of short duration." While "such work" had not yet achieved the "dignity" of the commercial air transport ventures sprouting in Europe, Gardner noted, the aerial gypsies now criss-crossing the nation were nevertheless "educating" the public about aviation.

An MIT graduate, Gardner would spend a long and active career advancing the "cause" of aviation with the fervor of an evangelist. He warned the aviators who were "barnstorming" across America that "stunting should be avoided." "Even if the passenger should ask for stunting, he will not enjoy it. He will come down congratulating himself on being a brave man but with the feeling he has had a very serious experience. The passenger should come down feeling as though he has had a perfectly safe and normal experience which he would like to repeat."[13]

Not many aviators took Gardner's advice. "It was true that aviation was dangerous," Charles A. Lindbergh (1902–1974) remarked of his own barnstorming days.[14] Twenty years old, he paid $500 for flight training at the Nebraska Standard Aircraft Corporation in Lincoln. During his first week as a student, he saw two men die when the wings of their aircraft failed during a loop. In addition to learning to fly, he received instruction in engine mechanics and aspects of aircraft repair. Since Ray Page, the proprietor of the company, also operated Page's Aerial Pageant, Lindbergh's professional education included some experience with wing walking and parachute jumping.

In the spring of 1923, Lindbergh traveled to Americus, Georgia, and paid another $500 for a war surplus JN-4D, in which he would "barnstorm" through the South and Midwest for the next year. His experience was typical: flying from place to place, offering rides at a dollar a minute, signing on with a flying circus for a time. "I managed to make a living," Lindbergh recalled, "and even put away a little money each month."[15]

BESSIE COLEMAN (1892–1926) dreamed of organizing her own group of touring aviators. As the first African-American to earn an official pilot's license from the Fédération Aéronautique Internationale (FAI), however, she scarcely represented the typical barnstormer. A native of Atlanta, Texas, Coleman escaped the rural poverty of her youth by migrating to Chicago in 1915, where she trained as a beautician. Apparently inspired by stories of French women aviators, she became determined to fly.

Through her own efforts and with the assistance of supporters, including Robert Abbott, the founder of the influential *Chicago Defender*, Bessie Coleman crossed the Atlantic and enrolled in a flying

Bessie Coleman

school operated by Gaston and René Caudron in the war-ravaged Somme valley. Living in a foreign country, and learning French as she went, Coleman persevered and graduated after ten months of effort in June 1921.

Returning to the United States after spending time in Holland and Germany, she began flying in public, often in borrowed airplanes, clad in a stylish semimilitary uniform that included a short jacket, Sam Brown belt, and jodhpurs. Occasionally she appeared with Hubert Fauntleroy Julian, a flamboyant Jamaica-born aviator and parachutist who billed himself as "The Black Eagle of Harlem."

African-American newspapers soon advertised appearances by "Queen Bess, the Daredevil Aviatrix." Little known in the white press, Coleman was famous in the black community. Struggling with accidents and financial woes, she eked out a living giving exhibition flights and lecturing on aviation. And she died as she lived, preparing for an exhibition at Jacksonville, Florida, on April 29, 1926, when she and her mechanic were killed in the crash of her JN-4.[16]

AFTER A YEAR as a gypsy flyer, Charles Lindbergh tired of his under-powered Jenny and in 1925 enlisted in the U.S. Army as an aviation cadet. Other U.S. airmen were also settling down. A 1920 survey conducted by the Aeronautical Chamber of Commerce listed 87 commercial flying services operating a total of 425 aircraft carrying 41,390 pounds of freight from airports across the nation. Two years later, the survey counted 129 flying services based at 107 airports in thirty-one states. By 1926, 357 commercial air operators flew 710 aircraft over 8,417,517 miles.[17]

In addition to normal air taxi and freight service, these embryonic commercial air operations took on virtually any task that they could perform from the cockpit. Aerial surveying and mapping operations began in 1919, when the U.S. Coast and Geodetic Survey mapped Atlantic City from the air. Sherman Mills Fairchild (1896–1971), a wealthy young man fascinated by aerial photography, founded the Fairchild Aerial Camera Corporation in 1920, Fairchild Aerial Surveys in 1921, and Fairchild Airplane Manufacturing in 1925. By the end of that year, Fairchild, and at least sixty other U.S. firms that offered aerial photographic services, reported annual earnings of $1,000,0000.

Aviation could play a role in agriculture as well. Crop dusting was born in August 1921, when Lt. John Macready of McCook Field treated a grove of catalpa trees near Troy, Ohio. This initial demonstration, sponsored by the Ohio Department of Agriculture, was a complete success and led B. R. Choad of the U.S. Department of Agriculture's Delta Laboratory at Tallulah, Louisiana, to conduct further tests in 1922. By 1923, the U.S. Army Air Service was dusting sixty-five hundred acres of cotton and attacking gypsy moths in New England and locusts in the Philippines.

Like aerial photography, crop dusting became a viable business. The Huff-Daland Manufacturing Company of Ogdensburg, New York, cooperating with the Delta Laboratory on the initial experiments, began commercial dusting operations in 1924 with a fleet of eighteen specialized aircraft based at nine flying fields across the South. The service became so popular and successful that insurance companies offered to insure cotton crops that had been dusted.

By the mid-1920s, hundreds of local flying services demonstrated the commercial value of aviation in a variety of ways. Aircraft participated in political campaigning and skywriting. They transported payrolls, film, and perishables. Airplanes conducted oil and timber surveys, herded sheep and cattle, and provided emergency medical services. They scouted for schools of fish, patrolled borders, facilitated police work, delivered newspapers, bombed ice jams, and prepared real-estate surveys.

Some of the companies started by these local aeronautical pioneers would become important players in commercial aviation. Fairchild became a major aircraft manufacturer, while Huff-Dalland evolved into Delta Airlines. In terms of long-range, scheduled operations, however, the U.S. Air Mail Service *was* commercial aviation in the United States from the high summer of 1918 until its last official flight on September 1, 1927.

THE U.S. AIR MAIL SERVICE began with four pilots and six specially built Standard JR-1B biplanes for the route between Washington,

D.C., and New York. These were soon replaced by the larger De Havilland DH 4; the service took over 250 of them as surplus from the army between May 1918 and January 1925, along with one thousand Liberty engines. Ultimately, the service would acquire some larger machines, including a dozen Liberty-powered Handley Page O/400s and twelve more specialized versions of the Glenn Martin bomber. By the end of operations, Air Mail Service pilots would be flying some more up-to-date aircraft, including the Liberty-powered Douglas M-4 and the Curtiss Carrier Pigeon.

The aging DH 4s remained the standard of the service to the end, however. Some DH 4 aircraft were updated with steel-tube fuselages and Liberty engines. Most of the older aircraft were rebuilt at the Air Mail Service Repair Depot at Maywood, Illinois. The fabric covering the fuselage was replaced with wood veneer, and the "infamous" gasoline tank mounted between the two cockpits of the "flaming coffin" was placed directly behind the engine. The forward cockpit was enclosed to serve as a mail compartment.

The goal was to create a twenty-six-hundred-mile national airmail route linking the coasts. The Air Mail Service operated from New York to Cleveland and Chicago by May 1919, and pushed on through Omaha to Sacramento by the fall of 1920. Shorter routes linking Minneapolis and St. Louis into the system were eventually abandoned in order to concentrate on coast-to-coast service. There was much cause for celebration on February 22, 1921, when a load of mail that had started in San Francisco reached its destination in New York thirty-three hours and twenty minutes later.

In an effort to increase delivery speed, the service moved toward twenty-four-hour operations. This required experience with instrument flying and establishing lighted beacons of various sorts. The engineers at McCook Field had begun this process, creating a model airway linking New York and San Antonio with special navigational aids by 1922–1924. The Air Mail Service inaugurated night-flying operations in August 1923, lighting the airports between Chicago and Cheyenne, Wyoming. By 1926, the entire route was lit. Once the service hit its stride, an eastbound letter traveled from take-off in San Francisco to a safe landing in New York in an average twenty-nine hours and fifteen minutes.

The Air Mail Service was an undeniably heroic operation. In January 1925, close to its peak, the post office employed forty-six pilots, with an average age of twenty-nine. One of them had flown the mail for over six years. Others were veterans of five to six years. Thirty-two pilots lost their lives in the line of duty with the Air Mail Service. In addition to providing coast-to-coast commercial air service over a sustained period, the airmail pilots pioneered routes that airlines would follow. They flew nights and in bad weather. The effort achieved all that Otto Praeger and other visionaries had hoped for.

Flying with outmoded airplanes and engines, however, the Air Mail Service had done little to develop the U.S. aircraft industry, which lay moribund in the early and mid-1920s. Moreover, probusiness Republican politicians were not pleased with a national air commerce system owned and operated by the U. S. government. Finally, there was a general sense that serious problems continued to plague American aviation. As it had in 1918, Congress turned its attention to these issues.

MILITARY AVIATION, 1920–1925

The decade following the end of the war represented a period of crisis and stagnation for military aviation around the globe. When postwar cost cutting threatened the Royal Air Force (RAF), Gen. Hugh "Boom" Trenchard (1873–1959), chief of the Air Staff, invented the role of "air control," the use of air power to police the Imperial domain. "Even in the benign British Empire," the acerbic journalist C. G. Grey noted, "we have had to do a certain amount of bombing."[18]

Trenchard was a veteran of service in that empire, having enlisted in the British army in 1893 and served in South Africa and West Africa. He graduated from the Central Flying School in 1913, only weeks before age would have disqualified him from flying. During the war he rose to command the Royal Flying Corps in the field and then became chief of the Air Staff at the time of the creation of the RAF. By the end of the war, he was commanding a strategic bombing campaign that would have struck a blow deep into the industrial heart of Germany had hostilities continued.

With the return of peace, Trenchard had to defend his creation, the world's first independent air force. His effort to demonstrate the continuing value of the RAF began in January 1920, with a bombing campaign against the forces of Mohammed Abdullah Hasan, who had all but driven the British army out of Somalia during World War I. In three short weeks of bombing and strafing, the RAF, in turn, drove the "Mad Mullah," as he was known in the British press, out of the country. One cabinet official congratulated Trenchard on having won "the cheapest war in history."[19]

The next trouble spot centered on India's Northwest Frontier, where, for over a century, Pathan peoples had attempted to spill over into the fertile valley of the Ganges. When bombing villages failed to remedy the situation, the RAF bombed the villages' irrigation reservoirs, which washed the topsoil off the terraced fields. Starvation and capitulation followed.

Over the next decade, RAF airmen attacked recalcitrant tribes in Iraq, Afghanistan, and Aden. "Aircraft skillfully used without causing serious loss," Trenchard insisted, "can produced a maximum of discomfort and weariness."[20] When questioned about the morality of the campaign, the air chief marshall resorted to dark and tasteless humor. C. G. Grey reminded his readers that Trenchard had joked "about the peculiar affinity which bombs have for women and children." It almost seemed, the air chief marshall remarked to the House of Lords, "that women and children were fitted with special magnets to attract bombs."[21] Worse, while Trenchard believed that air control was appropriate for African and Asian rebels, he rejected the notion that aircraft might also be used to police Ireland or Palestine.

The RAF survived as an independent force, but it did not prosper. As a means of limiting defense expenditures, Prime Minister David Lloyd George had instituted a "Ten Year Rule" in 1919, indicating that government would feel justified in cutting military budgets so long as it did not envision a major European war in the next decade. The rule was renewed each year until 1932. As a result, one authority noted, "the equipment of the Royal Air Force in 1929 . . . was not very different from what it had been ten years earlier."[22]

In 1922, France could still boast roughly twice the air strength of any other nation. The French conducted their own highly publicized air operations against unruly colonials. Rejecting the British euphemism, the French called it what it was: "colonial bombing." The specialized "Type Coloniale" aircraft developed for such duty provided a seat for a rear-facing gunner beneath the fuselage, so that, an English wag noted, "he could sit in the shade, with plenty of traverse for his gun, and shoot at the indigenes in comfort." In this way, "any odd Syrians and Moroccans and Senegalese and Gaboonese and French Equatorial Africans and Indo-Chinese who happened to object to French rule were kept in order."[23]

Ultimately, however, like their English counterparts, French military airmen had to make do with reduced budgets and aging, obsolescent equipment. Wartime mainstays like the Breguet 14 remained in service until 1928. Replacement aircraft, from the Spad XX, Morane-Saulnier 128, and Nieuport-Delage 29 to the Farman Goliath, were more closely tied to the past than indicative of the future.

WHILE THE FRENCH and British air planners justified their continued existence by policing the colonies, U.S. airmen sought to dazzle Congress and the public with their prowess in the air. The era began with the U.S. Navy's transatlantic triumph. Army airmen were just as anxious to capture headlines. During the summer and fall of 1919, Lt. Col. R. L. Hartz and Lt. Ernest E. Harmon completed a much publicized 9,823-mile flight "around the rim" of the United States in a new Martin bomber.

Curtiss test pilot Roland Rohlfs and Maj. Rudolph W. "Shorty" Schroeder, a test pilot at the Air Service Engineering Division headquarters at McCook Field, Dayton, Ohio, battled back and forth for the world's altitude record. In February of 1920 Schroeder captured the "icicle crown," as he called it, by coaxing his Liberty engine–powered Le Pere LUSAC 11 biplane to 33,313 feet. When Schroeder left the service later that year, Lt. John Macready took up the challenge and rose to 34,508 feet on September 28, 1921.

In May 1923, Lts. John Macready and Oakley Kelly made the first nonstop flight across the continent in a Fokker T-2. Thirteen months later, on June 23, 1924, Lt. Russell Maughan made the same trip between dawn and dusk. Between April 6 and September 28, 1924, U.S. Army airmen circumnavigated the globe in Douglas World Cruisers.

In June 1925, Lt. James "Jimmy" Doolittle (1896–1993) reported to the Naval Air Station in Washington, D.C., for special training in flying high-speed seaplanes. Already a well-known army test pilot, Doolittle entered MIT in October 1922, where he earned his master's degree in 1924 and a doctorate in engineering the following year. He flew a Curtiss R3C2 floatplane to victory in the 1925 Schneider Trophy Race, at an average speed of 232 mph.

Those colorful and well-known young airmen stood in the shadow of their commander. William "Billy" Mitchell (1879–1936) was born in Nice, France, to American parents vacationing in Europe. He was the son of U.S. Senator John Lendrum Mitchell and the grandson of a Milwaukee railroad baron. Billy Mitchell withdrew from Columbian College (now George Washington University) in 1898 in order to enlist in the 1st Wisconsin Infantry. He earned a commission in the Signal Corps, served in Cuba and the Philippines, and then distinguished himself in 1901–1902 by establishing a network of telegraph lines in the Alaskan wilderness.

"How handsome and fascinating all the girls found him," a friend once told his mother. "He seems the perfect type of the ideal American soldier."[24] His superiors agreed. Having graduated from the School of the Line and the Staff College at Fort Leavenworth, Kansas, Mitchell became the youngest officer assigned to the General Staff, in 1912.

Long fascinated by the military implications of new technology, the thirty-eight-year-old major paid for his own flight instruction at the Curtiss facility in Norfolk, Virginia. For the rest of his career, Mitchell would command airmen, and he made it a point to prove that he was one of them. On October 18, 1922, he flew a Curtiss R-6 racer to a record speed of over 222 mph. Lester Maitland, a leading Air Service test pilot, remarked that Mitchell "could fly anything with wings, and fly it well."[25]

Named deputy chief of the Signal Corps Aviation Section in 1916,

William "Billy" Mitchell

Mitchell was already in Europe when the United States entered the war. He earned his Junior Military Aviator rating and was promoted from major through lieutenant colonel to colonel in four months. With his outgoing personality and command of the French language, Mitchell seemed to be everywhere, meeting everyone with knowledge and experience of the war in the air.

Mitchell had developed an especially warm relationship with Trenchard and other Allied leaders, but he found it considerably harder to get along with his fellow Americans. He waged a running battle with Benjamin Delahauf Foulois, who took over as chief of the Air Service, First Army, when Mitchell assumed command of American air units in combat. To be sure, many regarded Mitchell as a flamboyant prima donna. His success in commanding Allied air operations against the German salient at St.-Mihiel in 1918 swept all such thoughts aside.

Returning from Europe in triumph, Mitchell was assigned to oversee Air Service training and operations under Gen. Charles T. Menoher, a nonaviator. Mitchell would never rise higher than brigadier general and deputy commander of the Air Service, but neither would he behave like anyone's second in command. He seldom hesitated to speak out and quickly emerged as the most vocal proponent of air power.

Mitchell had been eleven years old in 1890, when Alfred Thayer Mahan, a professor at the Naval War College in Portsmouth, Rhode Island, published his classic treatise on *The Influence of Sea Power upon History, 1660–1783*. He was attending Staff College two decades later, when a young Italian officer began to argue that the airplane, still a frail and experimental device, would replace navies of the world as the ultimate strategic weapon.

Born into a family with a tradition of military service to the House of Savoy, Giulio Douhet (1869–1930) had become interested in flight while serving as commander (1905–1912) of the Bersaglieri, a motorized battalion of the Italian army. While he was apparently never a pilot, and had little direct experience with aircraft, he commanded the Aviation Section for a short time in 1913–1914. Even so, his abrasive manner and early articles on aviation, with their implied criticism of government policy, led to his transfer to the infantry.

When a memo outlining the failures of Italian military planning became public not long after the nation entered World War I, Douhet was court-martialed and imprisoned for a year. Released, and partially exonerated when the Italian line collapsed at Caporetto, Douhet returned to duty with the air service for a time in 1918, and then retired. Four years later he accepted Benito Mussolini's offer of a government aeronautical post, but quickly returned to private life.

Douhet published his first articles on aviation before 1910. A novel, *How the Great War Ended—The Winged Victory*, appeared in 1918, followed by his classic *Command of the Air* in 1921. In the beginning he argued specific questions, such as the superiority of the airplane over the airship. Nor did he have any doubt that aviation would become an equal partner of land and naval forces. By 1921, he had moved well beyond that. "Because of its independence of surface limitations and its superior speed—superior to any other known means of transportation," he wrote in 1921, "the airplane is the offensive weapon par excellence."[26]

He favored "relentless" long-range aerial bombing attacks on the enemy homeland "making no distinction between military and non-military objectives." Targets would include the "peacetime industrial and commercial establishment; important buildings, private and public; transportation arteries and centers; and . . . civilian population as well." Douhet argued for the use of three types of bombs. "The explosives will demolish the target, the incendiaries set fire to it, and the poison-gas bombs prevent fire fighters from extinguishing the fires."[27]

Douhet was not a particularly deep thinker. His vision reflected a perfect world where the weather was always good, every bomber got through, and all bombs fell on target. Unrestricted bombing would destroy a nation's industrial capacity and break the will of the civilian population, he argued. "Humanity and civilization may avert their eyes," he admitted, "but this is the way it will be, inevitably."[28]

At the time of his death, Douhet and his ideas of aerial warfare were widely known and quite controversial in fascist Italy. Some scholars speak of the Douhet "myth" and argue that his work was little known and had no impact outside Italy. The French, German, and Russian translations of *Command of the Air* did not appear until the mid-1930s. It is noteworthy, however, that the earliest-known English-language translation of the book was prepared for the U.S. Air Corps Tactical School in 1932. This school provided virtually all of the senior U.S. air commanders of World War II with their notions of how to apply air power.[29]

THE ARGUMENT, in any case, is pointless. Officers like Hugh Trenchard and Billy Mitchell, who had actually commanded bombers in combat and who would have led even deeper strikes into Germany had the war continued, did not need the Italian theorist to point them toward the future.

Mitchell sensibly favored a balanced force. Pursuit aircraft would control the air, while ground-attack and observation machines would supply tactical information to ground forces. He recognized, however, that long-range strategic bombing was a unique mission that would revolutionize warfare and justify a strong independent air force. "The advent of the air power which can go to the vital centers and entirely neutralize or destroy them has put a completely new complexion on the old system of war," he explained in 1930. "It is now realized that the hostile main army in the field is not the objective and the real objectives are the vital centers. The old theory that victory meant the destruction of the hostile army is untenable. Armies themselves can be disregarded by air power if a rapid strike is made against the opposing centers."[30]

As early as 1919, Mitchell suggested that the distinction between combatants and noncombatants had little meaning in the air age. Given the isolationist sentiment that followed the armistice, however, Mitchell considered it impolitic to argue the need for an offensive bomber force designed to carry the war to the enemy. Instead, he sponsored the long-distance, high-speed, high-altitude flights that kept the men of the U.S. Air Service in the public eye, and suggested that his bomber crews should be entrusted with the defense of the American coast. Airplanes could not only destroy factories, he insisted. They could also sink battleships.

Already regarded as one of the most controversial officers in the upper ranks of the army, Mitchell now prepared to take on the U.S. Navy. Many high-ranking naval officers did tend to dismiss aviation. Admiral Charles Benson, chief of naval operations, commented in 1920 that he could not "conceive of any use that the fleet will ever have for aircraft."[31]

Even in the face of such conservatism, some leaders of naval aviation supported Mitchell's notion that airplanes offered the best defense against an attacking fleet. Admiral William Fullam, a naval strategist from the generation following Mahan, agreed that "sea power will be . . . subordinated to . . . air power."[32] The most farsighted of the naval officers, however, parted company with Mitchell on the matter of how air power could best be applied at sea. Admiral William S. Sims, commandant of the Naval War College and hero of World War I, remarked that he would prefer to spend the taxpayers' precious dollars on "airplane carriers and the development of airplanes" designed to meet the special needs of naval aviation.[33]

Mitchell had spoken of the vulnerability of surface ships to aerial attack during congressional testimony in 1921. "It seems to me," remarked Congressman Bascom Slemp of Virginia, "that the principal problem is to demonstrate the certainty of your conclusions."[34] Mitchell saw an opportunity to do just that—he would bomb a small fleet that included some obsolete American ships and four wartime German vessels (the submarine U-117, the destroyer G-102, the cruiser *Frankfurt*, and the battleship *Ostfriesland*) acquired by the U.S. Navy for gunnery practice. Over vigorous protests from the Navy Department, Senator William E. Borah of Idaho and his colleagues insisted that the airmen be allowed an opportunity to demonstrate what they could do.

Mitchell approached the bombing tests with great care. He gathered men and planes from Air Service bases across the nation to gather at Langley Field in Hampton, Virginia. Major Thomas DeWitt Milling organized them into a temporary unit, the 1st Provisional Air Brigade. The planes were Handley Page, Martin, and Caproni bombers, and DH 4s. Some airmen had practiced before their departure for Virginia, bombing battleships that had been outlined on the ground. Once at Langley, they received instruction in the use of bombsights, bombs, bomb racks, armament, and radio. They made use of bombing simulators and attacked targets on Mulberry Island in the James River.

The trials began with attacks by naval aircraft on the obsolete battleship *Iowa*. The navy pilots were outfitted with dummy bombs, to avoid "excessive damage" to the target. Mitchell had refused to take part in such an empty charade. His turn came on July 13, when his airmen attacked and sank the destroyer G-102, anchored off the Virginia Capes. Three days later, they sent the cruiser *Frankfurt* to the bottom. On July 21, army and navy aircraft under Mitchell's command sank the *Ostfriesland*, while General Pershing, the secretary of war, and the secretary of the navy watched from the safety of a nearby ship.

Following the trials, Mitchell's airmen underscored their success by conducting mock bombing attacks on New York, Philadelphia, Wilmington, Baltimore, and the U.S. Naval Academy at Annapolis. In September 1921, the 1st Provisional Air Brigade proved themselves once again, sending the old battleship *Alabama* to the bottom. In September 1923, flying aircraft based near Cape Hatteras, North Carolina, sank the battleships USS *New Jersey* and *Virginia*, scheduled to be scrapped under the provisions of the Washington Disarmament Conference.

Now far better known than his superior, Chief of the Air Service Gen. Mason F. Patrick, Mitchell set out in pursuit of his ultimate goal—an independent air force that would be the equal of the army and navy. His views, freely expressed in news interviews and testimony before Congress, antagonized military leaders and politicians alike. Finally, in March 1925, Secretary of War John W. Weeks refused to renew Mitchell's appointment as deputy chief of the Air Service. He reverted to his permanent rank of colonel and took up new duties as air officer of the Eighth Corps Area, at Fort Sam Houston in Texas.

But Mitchell could not be silenced. Six months after he had gone into exile, a navy flying boat disappeared on a flight from California to Hawaii. Although the crew was eventually rescued, worse news soon came. During the early-morning hours of September 3, 1925, the pride of the navy, the *Shenandoah*, the first U.S.-built rigid airship, was destroyed in a storm over eastern Ohio while on a publicity tour of the Midwest. Unable to contain himself, Mitchell reported to newsmen that "these terrible accidents are the direct result of incompetency, criminal negligence, and almost treasonable administration of the national defense by the War and Navy Departments."[35]

Charged with insubordination and making statements contrary to good order and discipline, Mitchell was ordered to Washington, D.C., for a court-martial, which began on October 28, 1925, and lasted for seven long weeks. The airman and his supporters and admirers used the trial as an opportunity to present their case for increased attention to air power. Found guilty and suspended without rank or pay for five years, Mitchell resigned his commission and carried on his fight as a civilian. Portrayed as a martyr for the cause, he remained a very visible public figure, prophesying the danger facing an America that ignored the need to build an air force second to none. Even today, Mitchell remains one of the most controversial American military leaders of the century.

The court-martial of Billy Mitchell underscored deep-seated concerns over the state of air power and aviation in America. As early as the spring of 1923, Secretary of War Weeks had asked Gen. William Lassiter, the assistant chief of staff of the army, to chair a committee to study General Patrick's own ambitious plans for expansion. The Lassiter committee reported that the Air Service was "in an unfortunate and critical situation," and urged the War Department to approve additional funding, which it did not do.

Why, Representative Florian Lampert asked, had the War Department ignored the Lassiter Report? Noting that an air force was critical to national defense, Lampert launched a well-publicized congressional investigation of the state of American military aviation early in 1924.

THERE WAS CONCERN about American civil aviation as well. Republicans objected to the domination of commercial aviation by an air force owned and operated by the U.S. Post Office. Newly elected President Warren Harding had announced that he intended to eliminate the government airmail operation once he took office. The success and popularity of the program changed his mind. By 1926, however, it had become apparent that while the U.S. Air Mail Service had accomplished a great many things, it had not done much to support the American airframe and engine industry, or to encourage the development of civil aviation as a competitive business.

Moreover, European experience and the failure of American ventures such as Aeromarine Airways demonstrated the importance of government support if private companies were to be drawn into the field. Finally, there were now repeated calls for the regulation of aeronautics. If the business of aviation was to grow and prosper, Secretary of Commerce Herbert Hoover commented, the public had to feel safe in the air.

By 1925, most European nations had created civil ministries to oversee air commerce. Great Britain, Germany, Japan, Italy, Norway, New Zealand, Austria, Switzerland, Spain, Czechoslovakia, the USSR, and even Venezuela required aircraft licensing and certification before the United States did. "No financial backing and consequently no real development can be hoped for [in the United States]," the British air attache to Washington commented in 1922, "until civil aviation receives legalized status and protective regulation through Federal Legislation."[36]

The Air Mail Act, which President Calvin Coolidge signed into law on February 2, 1925, represented an important first step in the right direction. Drafted by Representatives M. Clyde Kelly and William C. Ramseyer, the bill marked the end of the Post Office operation and turned the carriage of airmail over to private contractors, who would be paid up to four-fifths of the actual revenue realized from all airmail and any first-class mail that the Post Office consigned to them.

Post Office officials realized that they were laying the foundation for commercial aviation in the United States, and announced that contracts would not be awarded as the result of "a bargain basement competition." The notion was to select and support sound and well-managed companies that not only would offer reliable mail service but also hold the promise of growing into airlines that would one day make a profit carrying freight and passengers across the country.[37]

President Coolidge took another important step toward the solution of the nation's aviation problems on September 12, 1925, when he asked Dwight Morrow to chair yet another committee to study the status of military aviation in the United States. The two men had known one another since their undergraduate years at Amherst College. Coolidge had entered politics. Morrow pursued a career in finance, eventually rising high in the ranks of J.P. Morgan and Company.

Now the president called on his old friend for assistance. Coolidge suspected, with good reason, that Congressman Lampert's committee, which had not yet issued its report, might support Billy Mitchell's attacks on administration policies and recommend the creation of an independent air force and an air ministry after the British model. The

Morrow Board, filled with Coolidge supporters, would retrace the steps of the Lampert Committee as rapidly as possible and issue its own report.

The quick succession of events taking place during a few weeks in the fall of 1925 would shape the course of American aviation. The Morrow Board completed its hearings on October 15, one month and three days after Morrow had been appointed. The Mitchell court-martial opened ten days later. The president released the Morrow Board report on December 2. Congress convened five days later, and the Lampert Committee released its report one week after that. Billy Mitchell was convicted ten days later, on December 17.

The Morrow Board rejected the notion of a unified air force and a single air ministry governing both military and civil aviation. Instead, they recommended the creation of a bureau of aeronautics within the Department of Commerce, headed by an assistant secretary. They had heard the lamentations of the military airmen as well. The board recommended that the Air Service be organized as an Air Corps, complete with an assistant secretary of war for aeronautics, and that a significant amount of money be spent on expansion and improved equipment. They made similar recommendations on behalf of naval aviation. Ironically, while the Lampert Committee recommended the creation of an independent air force and a department of defense, its report on civil aviation sounded a lot like that from the Morrow Board.

With the direction so clearly mapped by two very different committees, Congress took quick action. Senator Hiram Bingham, a big supporter of aviation, introduced Senate Resolution 41 on December 8, 1925. Initially, the bill split the legislative responsibility for aviation, assigning the direction of interstate commerce to the federal government and allowing the states to regulate aerial activities occurring strictly within their borders. The House of Representatives would produce quite a different product.

William P. MacCracken, Jr., a young Chicago lawyer who had learned to fly with the army during World War I, played a major role in shaping the final legislation and the organization that it created. Linking his profession with his love of flying, he became chairman of both the American Bar Association's Committee on the Law of Aeronautics and the Aviation Law Committee of the National Conference of Commissioners on Uniform State Laws.

In 1922, at the invitation of Harold E. Hartney, a fellow lawyer and wartime pilot, MacCracken became counsel and head of the legislative committee of the National Aeronautic Association (NAA). The new group had been organized by Howard E. Coffin, with encouragement from Secretary of Commerce Hoover. It would replace the old Aero Club of America as the collective voice of American aviation and serve as U.S. representative to the Fédération Aéronautique Internationale (FAI), the international record-keeping organization.

MacCracken worked with members of the congressional conference committee to produce the Air Commerce Act of 1926, and Coolidge signed it into law on May 20, 1926. One important change set it apart from the original legislation—expanded federal responsibility for aircraft certification and registration, pilot licensing, the establishment of national air traffic regulations, and the provision of uniform aides to aerial navigation. Federal responsibility for airport planning and construction was removed from the final legislation. Local governments would have to develop and pay for their own airports. MacCracken was Hoover's choice for assistant secretary of commerce for aeronautics. It was a wise and critically important appointment.

Acting on the recommendation of the Morrow Board, the Congress also passed the Naval Aviation Expansion Act and the Air Corps Act in late June 1926. The legislation changed the name of the Air Service to the Air Corps, created an assistant secretary of war for aeronautics (F. Trubee Davison) and an assistant secretary of the navy for air (Edward P. Warner), and authorized five-year aviation expansion programs for both services. The plan called for the new Air Corps to acquire 1,800 airplanes, 1,650 officers, and 15,000 enlisted men in regular increments over a five-year period. The number of first-line naval aircraft in service would be increased to 1,000. Although never fully funded, the programs nevertheless reinvigorated U.S. military air power and pumped much-needed money into the aviation industry.

In large measure, the aeronautical legislation of 1925–1926

reflected the ideas of Herbert Hoover. An orphaned Iowa farm boy who worked his way through Stanford University, Hoover earned a fortune as a mining engineer, invested his money wisely, and emerged as a multimillionaire determined to contribute to the public good. He earned international fame as director of the Food Administration under President Woodrow Wilson and then served as an extraordinarily successful secretary of commerce under Presidents Harding and Coolidge before being elected president himself in 1928.

Hoover was guided by his vision of an "associative state" in which progress and economic prosperity would flow from voluntary cooperation between business and government. The Air Mail Act and the Air Commerce Act fit his model.

IF GOVERNMENT LAID a foundation for commercial aviation, however, philanthropy also played an important role. The philanthropist in question, Daniel Guggenheim, would never leave the ground in an airplane. A talented entrepreneur, he had built his family's mining empire into one of the world's great fortunes, then turned his attention from making money to performing good works.

Earlier generations of wealthy Americans built public libraries, endowed museums, supported the arts, sought to improve education, and promoted world peace. Members of the Guggenheim family would do all of those things. In addition, Daniel would join the ranks of Gustave Eiffel, Henri Deutsch de la Meurthe, and Lord Northcliffe, whose philanthropic purpose had been to advance the state of flight technology. It would be money very well spent.

Daniel's son, Harry Frank Guggenheim, a graduate of Yale and Oxford, had served as a naval aviator during World War I. As a sportsman pilot on Long Island following the war, Guggenheim met Alexander Klemin, a British graduate of Jerome Hunsaker's program who was organizing a new aeronautical engineering department at New York University.

Early in 1925, officials at New York University announced plans to launch a campaign to fund an aeronautical laboratory and an expanded teaching program in the field. Harry Guggenheim warned that the public might not see the value of such a project. Instead, he offered to raise the issue with his father and uncles. Daniel Guggenheim liked the idea and announced that he would give $500,000 to fund and endow a Guggenheim School of Aeronautics at New York University.

Daniel Guggenheim began to discuss the possibility of expanding his involvement, spending several million dollars on the creation of a fund that would support civil aviation. Father and son, the Guggenheims discussed the idea with everyone from Orville Wright to Secretary of Commerce Hoover and President Coolidge. The decision to forge ahead had been made by January 1926.

The Daniel Guggenheim Fund for the Promotion of Aeronautics would support aeronautical education; fund research in "aviation science"; promote the development of commercial aircraft and equipment; and "further the application of aircraft in business, industry and other economic and social activities of the nation." Running it would be a blue-ribbon panel of leading figures from aviation, business, finance, and science, including the inventor of the airplane and a Nobel laureate in physics.[38]

In addition to the school at New York University, the fund created six more Guggenheim schools of aeronautics at major universities across the nation: California Institute of Technology, Stanford University, University of Michigan, University of Washington, MIT, and Georgia School (later Institute) of Technology. Later, the fund would also offer assistance to Northwestern, Syracuse, Harvard, and the University of Akron. The impact of the Guggenheim schools on the history of American aviation is simply incalculable, both in the work of the graduates of those programs and in the research sponsored and conducted at these institutions.

Beyond their emphasis on education, the Guggenheim trustees focused on air safety. Their Full Flight Laboratory at Mitchel Field, Long Island, worked on improved radio navigation systems and cockpit instruments that would enable an aviator to fly "blind," in bad weather and at night. The fund supported pioneers like Elmer Sperry, who developed gyroscopically controlled cockpit instruments, and Paul Kollsman, who invented a sensitive pressure altimeter.

Lieutenant "Jimmy" Doolittle, an army test pilot with a Ph.D.

from MIT, conducted dozens of flights, testing new techniques and establishing the basic procedures for flying "blind." On September 24, 1929, with fellow army aviator Lt. Benjamin Kelsey riding as his safety pilot, Doolittle took off, flew, and landed using instruments alone, without being able to see outside the cockpit. It was the beginning of the end for seat-of-the-pants flying.

The Guggenheim Fund also sponsored a "safe aircraft" competition in 1927. Its aim was to identify and reward aircraft designs that were exceptionally stable and capable of low-speed operation and short-distance take-offs and landings. The well-publicized effort attracted twenty-seven competitors from the United States and Europe. While none of the aircraft proved especially noteworthy, including the victorious Handley Page HP 39 Gugnunc, they did underscore the importance of wing flaps and slats, devices intended to increase the efficiency of the wing at very low speeds.

The Daniel Guggenheim Fund for the Promotion of Aeronautics would achieve a great many other things before it closed down on February 1, 1930. Some of those achievements will be considered in the next chapter. But the Guggenheims continued to do what they could to support the cause of flight. During the 1930s, at the urging of Harry Guggenheim and Charles Lindbergh, the Daniel and Florence Guggenheim Foundation offered liberal support to Robert Hutchings Goddard, a Clark University physicist who pioneered the development of liquid-propellant rockets.

In its four short and very active years, the Guggenheim fund promoting aeronautics had fulfilled it purpose. "With commercial aircraft companies assured of public support and aeronautical science equally assured of continued research," the senior Guggenheim noted, "the further development of aviation in this country can best be fulfilled in the typically American manner of private business enterprise." Well, perhaps the government would have something to do with it as well.[39]

7

BIG BUSINESS,
1927-1935

MR. FORD, MR. FOKKER, AND
MR. RENTSCHLER

C. G. Grey, the editor of the English aeronautical journal *Flight*, arrived in New York in January 1925 to gauge the state of aeronautics in the United States. "The general atmosphere of aviation in America," he remarked, "impressed one as being in a state when something is about to happen. Not so much the calm before the storm, but rather the slump before the boom."[1]

It was an astute observation. Since the foundation of the Wright Company, aviation had attracted some major investors. Clearly, however, no one was getting rich in the airplane business.

The federal legislation of 1925–1926 had a big impact on Wall Street's view of the industry. The government was now offering financial incentives to private companies flying the mail; providing both the army and the navy with funding for the purchase of new equipment; and ensuring the safety of airmen and aircraft. The great names in American industry now began to appear on the letterhead of aeronautical firms, and there was no greater name in American business than Henry Ford.

In April 1925 Ford set out to establish regular air service between Detroit and Chicago. The operation would demonstrate the potential of commercial aviation, introduce the new Stout 2-AT high-wing monoplane, and serve the business needs of the Ford Motor Company, founded just five months before the Wrights flew at Kitty Hawk.

Ford and his son Edsel had followed the work of Detroit-based aircraft builder William Bushnell Stout. A veteran automotive engineer who yearned for wings, Stout had worked for Packard and helped design the Liberty engine. He also advised the Aircraft Board and the Bureau of Aircraft Production. Backed by prominent Detroit businessmen, he founded the Stout Metal Aircraft Company in 1923 and turned out the Stout Air Sedan, a four-seat monoplane powered by a war-surplus, Wright-Martin–built, 150-horsepower Hispano-Suiza. Impressed, Edsel Ford joined Stout's growing list of investors late that year.

Recognizing that Stout might offer a shortcut into a new and promising industry, Henry Ford bought the company and established it in a new factory at a new model airport in Dearborn, Michigan. Equipped with a dirigible mooring mast, radio facility, weather station, well-equipped hangars, restaurant, hotel, and good connections to ground transportation, Ford's airport set a new standard. It also gained national recognition as the start and finish point of the annual Ford Reliability Tour.

Reliability tours had helped to establish the automobile in America, demonstrating that the horseless carriage was reliable and had come of age. Ford was sure that an aerial tour would do the same thing for air commerce. Seventeen entries took off from Ford Airport on September 28, 1925. Six days later, the original Fokker trimotor was among the first to cross the finish line. Anthony Fokker, a familiar name from the last war, was back in the headlines.

A NONSMOKING TEETOTALER with a cleft chin and an impish smile, Fokker was a controversial figure in postwar Europe. The display of his first commercial aircraft at the 1921 Paris aeronautical salon occasioned a near riot in which René Fonck, the highest-ranking surviving French ace, now a member of the Chamber of Deputies, was involved.

Policemen shadowed Fokker as he went about the City of Lights. Clearly, wartime animosities were still running strong. Sensing fresh opportunities across the Atlantic, Fokker established a sales operation in the United States in 1920–1921 and enjoyed some success marketing his aircraft to the military.

With a manufacturing operation in America by 1925, Fokker recognized the Ford tour as a ground-floor entryway into the promising U.S. commercial aircraft market. He ordered his engineers to mount two additional engines beneath the wings of one of his single-engine monoplanes, creating the first of the modern trimotor aircraft. The trimotor F.VIIA-3m and longer-span F.VIIB-3m (introduced in 1925) were produced in Holland and America and were built under license in seven other nations. They served as standard equipment on fifty-four airlines. In 1930, KLM placed the Fokker trimotor into regular service on its flights from Holland to the East Indies, the longest scheduled air route in the world.

Fokker aircraft, with their range and reliability, dominated the headlines through the 1920s:

- 1923—U.S. Army Air Service aviators Oakley Kelly and John Macready complete the first nonstop, coast-to-coast flight in a Fokker F.IV (U.S. designation T-2).
- 1925—Anthony Fokker unveils the first Fokker F.VIIA-3m in the Ford Reliability Tour.
- 1926—Lt. Comdr. Richard Evelyn Byrd and Floyd Bennett challenge the North Pole in the Fokker *Josephine Ford*.
- 1927—Richard Byrd and his crew fly the Atlantic in the *America*.
- 1927—Lt. Albert Hegenberger and Lester Maitland fly the *Bird of Paradise* from California to Hawaii.
- 1928—Australian Charles Kingsford-Smith flies the *Southern Cross* from Australia to San Francisco.
- 1928—Amelia Earhart became the first woman to fly the Atlantic, making the trip with pilots Wilmer Stultz and Louis Gordon aboard the Fokker *Friendship*.
- 1929—Carl "Tooey" Spaatz, Ira Eaker, and Elwood R.

"Pete" Quesada, each of whom would rise to the rank of general officer in the U.S. Army Air Forces of World War II, demonstrated the potential of aerial refueling with the *Question Mark*.

Like their predecessors in the company lineage, the various models of the Fokker F.VII-3m featured standard steel-tube fuselages and wooden wings skinned with veneer. It marked the first of a series of trimotored aircraft produced by companies like Ford, Sikorsky, and Stinson that would dominate U.S. air transportation in the late 1920s. However, the new airplane proved far less revolutionary than its three radial engines.

THE AMERICAN RADIAL-ENGINE story begins with Charles L. Lawrance, a naval officer assigned to an engine-development program during World War I. While rotary engines had remained in service on some fighter aircraft to the end of the war, they were approaching their maximum size and power and were being supplanted by more advanced and powerful water-cooled in-line engines in which the cylinders were arranged in a V shape.

As early as 1917, British firms like Armstrong-Siddeley and Bristol had begun to produce promising lines of air-cooled radial engines. With the cylinders arranged in a circle around the crankshaft, the radial design offered a shorter, and therefore lighter, engine block and crankshaft than the in-line engine. Moreover, as an air-cooled engine, the design dispensed with the weight of the radiator, pumps, pipes, and fluid required for a water-cooled power plant. While overheating remained a serious problem, Sam D. Heron, an English engineer and expert on radial-engine design, introduced specially designed cylinder heads as the first step toward a solution.

Lawrance paid close attention to the developments in Europe. He knew that radial engines would be especially attractive to the U.S. Navy. The first American carrier, a collier refitted with a flight deck and christened the USS *Langley*, was launched in 1922. Smaller, lighter, and easier-to-maintain engines would have a special appeal to engineers planning carrier-based aircraft.

When the Wright-Martin, Curtiss, and Packard companies ignored the new designs, Lawrance set up his own small firm, Lawrance Aero-Engine Corporation, to produce the R-1 and the improved R-2, the first reasonably powerful U.S. radial engines. The navy bought five of these power plants and were impressed with their performance, but it recognized that Lawrance did not have the capacity to produce them in quantity.

Given the postwar slump and the widespread availability of inexpensive Liberty and other wartime engines, the owners of Wright-Martin sold their factory to Mack Truck. However, they invested in the creation of a new and smaller firm, the Wright Aeronautical Company, which, under the leadership of Frederick Brant Rentschler, would continue production of the improved Hispano-Suiza.

Frederick Rentschler and his brother Gordon hailed from Hamilton, Ohio. After graduating from Princeton, Frederick worked

Frederick Brant Rentschler

in the family foundry and then enlisted in the aviation section of the Signal Corps. Given family connections with members of the Dayton-Detroit faction on the Aircraft Production Board, he was assigned to oversee aircraft engine-manufacturing operations at Wright-Martin.

Recognizing that Wright Aeronautical might solve their problem, navy officials pressured Rentschler to buy the Lawrance Aero-Engine Corporation in 1923. Charles Lawrance, hired as vice president and chief engineer, brought his newest engine, the J-5, with him. Sam Heron, who was consulting at the Air Service Engineering facility at McCook Field in Dayton, solved the formidable challenge of cylinder cooling. Ultimately, Heron would achieve a genuine breakthrough with the development of a valve filled with liquid sodium that dispersed heat. By 1924–1925, all of this work resulted in the Wright J-5C "Whirlwind," the foundation for many radial engines that would power American aircraft through World War II and beyond.

The J-5C, a nine-cylinder power plant with an empty weight of 510 pounds, could generate 220 horsepower at 1800 rotations per minute. The only real drawback to the design was the relatively large frontal area, which created considerable drag. To solve this problem, H. L. Townend of the British National Physical Laboratory developed a narrow ring, called the Townend ring, that circled the cylinders of the engine and reduced drag without retarding the cooling effect of the air flowing over the cylinders.

In 1926 officials of the U.S. Navy Bureau of Aeronautics asked the staff of NACA Langley if they could improve on the Townend ring. Working under the leadership of Fred E. Weick (1899–1993), a University of Illinois graduate who had worked for the Air Mail Service before joining NACA, the Langley engineers put their new propeller-research wind tunnel to work and achieved a great breakthrough, the NACA cowling, which was actually two structures in one. The cowling itself functioned as an airfoil, reducing the drag of the radial engine. It also housed an inner structure designed to direct the flow of air around the cylinders to maximize the cooling effect.

The new device was so efficient that when the famous Frank Hawks flew a Curtiss Hawk AT-5A biplane fitted with the NACA cowling, the speed improved from 118 to 137 mph. In 1929, Fred Weick and his team won the first Collier Trophy, honoring the greatest aeronautical achievement of the year. For the next fifteen years, radial engines grew from the relatively simple, nine-cylinder Wright J-5C to the 2,200-horsepower, eighteen cylinder R-3350 Cyclone that powered the B-29 bomber of World War II. The steady redesign of the complex inner structure of radial-engine cowlings in an effort to speed the flow of cooling air across the twin and triple banks of cylinders became an ongoing, bread-and-butter task for NACA and industry engineers.

Rentschler and his colleagues selected Guiseppe Bellanca to design and build an advanced aircraft to demonstrate their power plant. A Sicilian immigrant who made his home with his brother in Brooklyn, New York, Bellanca had a reputation for advanced aerodynamic thinking. His Wright-Bellanca WB-2 was responsible for some memorable aeronautical moments, including the flight of the *Columbia*, which carried Clarence Chamberlin and Charles Levine from New York to Germany in June 1927.

That flight was not, of course, the first time a J-5C Whirlwind had been used to fly a plane across the Atlantic. Just two weeks before, on May 20–21, 1927, a J-5C had propelled a twenty-four-year-old pilot named Charles Lindbergh from New York to Paris. In fact, virtually every American airplane attempting to fly the Atlantic that year was powered by a Whirlwind.

WRIGHT AERONAUTICAL RODE the crest of a wave, but Frederick Rentschler refused to rest on his laurels. Looking toward the future, he discussed with Chance Milton Vought (1890–1930) the propulsion requirements for the advanced carrier-based fighters that were then on the drawing board. A talented student, Chance Vought had abandoned his engineering studies at the University of Pennsylvania in 1910 to work for Harold McCormick, an aviation enthusiast and president of McCormick Reapers. Vought edited the journal *Aero and Hydro*, learned to fly a Wright aircraft at Chicago's Max Lille School of Aviation (in 1912), and designed and built several aircraft of his own during these years. He worked for Curtiss (in 1915) and Wright-Martin (in 1916) before establishing the Lewis and Vought Corporation (in 1917) to produce training aircraft.

Eight years later, Vought explained to Rentschler that the next generation of naval aircraft would require radial engines developing up to 350 horsepower and weighing no more than six hundred pounds. These specifications were a long jump up from the 220-horsepower Whirlwind. Confident in the future of the business, but unable to convince other corporate officers that they should reinvest a substantial portion of company profits into research and the development of new products, Rentschler resigned as president of Wright Aeronautical.

Edward Deeds, leader of the old Dayton-Detroit group and a friend of Rentschler's father, chaired the executive board of the Niles-Bement-Pond Corporation, parent company of Pratt & Whitney, a nineteenth-century machine-tool company with machinery and factory floor space. The firm was slowly collapsing. With the assistance of his brother Gordon, a director of the National City Bank, Rentschler acquired control and became its president. He then set two engineers, George Mead and Andrew Willgoos, to work on a new engine. When finished, the 425-horsepower Wasp, as it was called, far outclassed the competing engine produced by Wright Aeronautical.

Together, Wright Aeronautical and Pratt & Whitney would dominate the U.S. engine market for years to come. Their rise illuminates several key points. First, the support of the government, in this case, NACA and the U.S. Navy, was central to aeronautical progress. Next, with some elements of infrastructure and market incentives in place, bankers and businessmen could regard aviation as a business in which they could make money. Finally, a breakthrough in engine technology would both reinvigorate a design tradition and prepare the way for a period of revolutionary change.

Everyone recognized that the Whirlwind power plants had allowed Fokker's trimotor to steal the show during the Ford Reliability Tour. Stories to the effect that the F.VIIA-3m, with its wooden wings, had inspired the all-metal Ford Tri-motor, however, are simply not true. Bill Stout, the designer in whom Henry Ford had placed his trust, above all things, believed in metal aircraft.

His first aircraft for Ford, the 2-AT Air Pullman, a high-wing, all-metal monoplane powered by a Liberty engine, interested the engineers at McCook Field and the Naval Aircraft Factory. Most civilian buyers, however, judged it to be substandard. Corliss C. Moseley, a former test pilot and a founder of Western Air Express (WAE), agreed to consider buying the machine if Ford would finance the new West Coast airmail operation. After flying the 2-AT, however, Moseley pronounced it to be "actually pitiful." An airplane requiring a one-mile take-off run at sea level, he explained to his backers, "couldn't possibly operate at the altitude of Salt Lake City with a load."[2]

Stout's next venture, the 3-AT, was an open-cockpit trimotor plane powered by a Wright Whirlwind mounted on the blunt nose and two more bolted to the leading edge of the wing. Stout's high hopes for this decidedly ugly aircraft were dashed when the first test flight revealed that the pug-nosed 3-AT could barely stay aloft long enough to circle the field for a landing. "My advice," remarked test pilot and McCook Field veteran Rudolph "Shorty" Schroeder, "is to forget this plane."[3]

Henry Ford had announced to the world that the 3-AT would revolutionize air commerce. Now outraged, he ordered Stout removed from all engineering duties and placed Tom Towle, a Stout-trained engineer, in charge of the project, assisted by three young MIT graduates: James Smith McDonnell (of whom much was to be heard), Otto Koppen, and John Lee. A mysterious fire destroyed the 3-AT and several 2-ATs, and the Stout Metal Aircraft Division was immediately renamed the Airplane Manufacturing Division of the Ford Motor Company.

Ford's reaction may seem a bit extreme. As much as anyone, Stout had pioneered metal aircraft construction in the United States. Even so, he had presented the short-tempered Mr. Ford with an airplane that did not fly, whereas the four younger engineers who took his place would produce the Ford 4-AT, the famed Ford Tri-motor.

The notion that the Ford team had slavishly copied important features of the Fokker trimotor are simply not true. Beyond general configuration, the two aircraft had little in common. The airfoil of the 4-AT, for example, was a standard NACA design, very different from that of the Fokker wing. In addition, the 4-AT was one of the first airplanes built of Alclad to prevent corrosion. That fact alone marked the 4-AT as the wave of the future and distinguished it from the traditional wooden structure of the Fokker.

The first version of the classic Ford Tri-motor, the 4-AT, featured a seventy-four-foot wingspan and three 220-horsepower J-4 engines. The final 5-AT model featured a longer wing and 450-horsepower Pratt & Whitney Wasp engines. Fitted with wicker seats for twelve

Ford 5-AT Tri-motor City of Columbus

passengers, the final version of the 5-AT carried a maximum gross weight of 13,500 pounds for a distance of 560 miles at 115 mph. Between 1926 and 1932, the basic airplane would be produced in at least eleven variants, 196 airplanes in all.

The Ford Tri-motor was the first American airplane truly designed to carry passengers, although the brave souls who clambered aboard faced a rough ride. The wise passenger accepted the wad of cotton offered to muffle the roar of the engines. There were no seatbelts even though the airplane was prey to turbulence when flying low over the countryside. A queasy passenger visiting the lavatory might have been shocked to see the commode installed over a hole in the floor.

Nor was the airplane easy to fly, even by the standards of the day. "Even in smooth air flying a Ford became a chore, if only because it was so difficult to keep in trim," remarked aviator and author Ernest K. Gann. "Even a normal bank in a Ford was an experiment in muscular coordination mixed with a practiced eye for anticipation, since whatever physical input was directed to the control a relatively long time passed before anything happened." Under the best conditions, he continued, flying a Tri-motor was a "workout." In bad weather, "the pilot sometimes wondered who was in charge of affairs."[4]

Despite all its faults, the Tri-motor, nicknamed the "Tin Goose," proved rugged and dependable. In 1931, famed Notre Dame coach Knute Rockne died in the crash of a Fokker F.10, blamed on the failure of its wooden main wing spar. All Fokkers were temporarily grounded and inspected. The company never recovered from the Rockne crash, which seemed to underscore the importance of all-metal construction.

Henry Ford saw the opening and mounted a major advertising campaign. Articles in leading American magazines extolled the virtues of air travel in general, and his all-metal airplane in particular. For millions of Americans, the name *Ford* meant efficiency and all that was modern. "Now you know," Will Rogers remarked, "that Ford wouldn't leave the ground and take to the air unless things looked pretty good to him up there."[5]

AMERICA: CLEARED FOR TAKE-OFF

Henry Ford pioneered in air commerce, as well as aircraft manufacture. The Air Mail Service would continue to operate the main intercontinental route from coast to coast through 1926. Initially, the Post Office advertised for bids to carry airmail over half-a-dozen regional air routes feeding into the national trunk line. The response was extraordinary. In the two months following the passage of the Air Mail Act of 1925, the Post Master General received two thousand inquiries from aspiring airline builders.

On February 15, 1926, Ford Air Transport became the first civilian contractor to fly mail under the provisions of the Air Mail Act, covering the two routes linking Cleveland, Detroit, and Chicago. Operating with Ford Tri-motors, naturally enough, the company also carried passengers. During their three years of operation, Ford Air Transport and its successor, Stout Air Services, suffered no fatalities.

Ultimately, the Great Depression ended Henry Ford's short career as a major figure in American aviation. United Aircraft and Transport Corporation took over the Ford airmail routes in 1929, the year in which a corporate executive calculated that the auto builder could satisfy the next five years of American demand for commercial aircraft in just six months of production. Henry Ford's interest in aviation faded along with the prospect of profits. The Ford Airplane Manufacturing Division closed for good in 1933.

While Ford's big Tri-motors no longer represented the cutting edge of technology, the aging aircraft seemed to fly on forever. Phased out by American airlines, they migrated into Central and South America, where they ferried passengers and freight in and out of remote areas. As late as the 1980s, a Ford Tri-motor hauled tourists and commuters to and from islands in Lake Erie. Henry Ford may have faded from American aviation, but he left his mark.

OTHER SUCCESSFUL BIDDERS for feeder routes included Colonial Air Lines (Boston–New York), Robertson Aircraft Corporation (St. Louis–Chicago), National Air Transport (Chicago–Dallas–Ft. Worth), WAE (Los Angeles–Salt Lake City), Varney Speed Lines (Elko, Nevada–Pasco, Washington), Pacific Air Transport (Seattle–San Francisco), Charles Dickenson (Chicago–Minneapolis–St. Paul), Florida Airways Corporation (Atlanta–Jacksonville), and Clifford Ball (Cleveland–Pittsburgh).

Some were already in the aviation business. The St. Louis–based Robertson Aircraft Company had refurbished 450 surplus Standard biplanes, which they sold to buyers all over the country. On winning the St. Louis–Chicago mail contract, they hired three pilots, headed by twenty-five-year-old Charles Lindbergh, and outfitted them with the DH 4s that the Air Mail Service had been operating.

Robertson was a local company supported by public-spirited St. Louis bankers, newspapermen, and business leaders. In contrast, Colonial Air Lines (later Colonial Air Transport, or CAT), which flew the mail between Boston and New York, had national aspirations. Initial investors included William Rockefeller and Cornelius Vanderbilt Whitney. John H. Trumbull, ex-governor of Connecticut, chaired the board, while W. Irving Bullard, vice president of the Boston Chamber of Commerce, served as company president. Other corporate officers included Sherman M. Fairchild, an important name on Wall Street and a figure of increasing importance in aviation; Juan Terry Trippe, an aviator who would rise to the pinnacle of success in the air transport business; and Harris Whitmore, of Connecticut Bond and Share.

Western Air Express was among a few first-generation airmail contractors to turn a small profit. Organized in the summer of 1925 by a veteran race-car driver, Harris M. "Pop" Hanshue, funding for the venture came from William May Garland, a wealthy real-estate promoter, and Harry Chandler, owner and publisher of the *Los Angeles Times*. WAE began carrying the mail in April 1926, and a month later, became the first contractor under the Air Mail Act to offer regularly scheduled passenger service. Company pilots carried 125,000 pounds of mail and 325 passengers during their first year of operation, and canceled only 9 of 735 scheduled flights.

Officials of the Guggenheim Fund were not interested in making a profit or in giving competitive advantage to a commercial firm. At the same time, Daniel Guggenheim wanted to show what a well-equipped airline, one determined to carry passengers in relative comfort and safety, could achieve. Such a "model airline" would include a weather-forecasting facility, improved radio equipment, and the finest aircraft.

Oddly, the emerging airlines did not rush to seek grants from Guggenheim. Most felt fortunate to deliver the mail on time, without the burden of carrying passengers. Not so for WAE officials, who wanted to carry passengers, even if only two at a time, aboard Douglas M-2 and M-4 mail planes. In June 1927, the Guggenheim board approved a grant not to exceed $400,000 to fund improvements in the WAE passenger operation. WAE's ground and communication facilities became state-of-the-art. Now corporate officials considered using a new airliner proposed by the consortium of Boeing, Douglas, Keystone, and Sikorsky. In the end, however, they selected the Fokker F.10, a trimotor plane fitted with the new 425-horsepower Pratt & Whitney Wasp.

THE MOST INTERESTING ASPECT of the "model airline" operation remained on the ground. Anxious to demonstrate the value of meteorology, Guggenheim officials hired Carl-Gustaf Rossby, a Swedish student of Vilhelm Bjerknes, the founder of modern meteorology, to establish a weather-reporting system for WAE. Emigrating to the

United States in 1926, Rossby had struggled to convince U.S. Weather Bureau officials of the value of forecasts based on the Bjerknes air-mass analysis system. The Guggenheim grant gave him the opportunity to reduce theory to practice.

Working with Jerome Hunsaker, who had left the government to work for Bell Telephone Laboratories, Rossby established weather observation posts at every airport on the WAE line and at critical intermediary points. Meteorologists prepared and radioed forecasts to the individual stations and to aircraft in the air. The army and navy loaned equipment to the project and made use of the forecasts.

The commander of the Army Air Corps base at Crissy Field, San Francisco, liked what he saw. "Formerly," he remarked, "a pilot did not know what was ahead; now he knows and is prepared." Carl Rossby would eventually join the MIT faculty, and the U.S. Weather Bureau would inherit the experimental system and spread it across the nation, just as the airlines themselves were merging and stretching across the continent.[6]

With mail flowing into Los Angeles, Chicago, and New York aboard aircraft operated by companies like Ford, Robertson, CAT, and WAE, the Post Office turned over the main East-West line to private contractors in 1927. Boeing Air Transport won the contract to carry the mail over the 1,918-mile route from San Francisco to Chicago.

BY 1927 BOEING had recovered from the postwar slump, principally owing to its contracts with the army and navy. Guided by Chairman of the Board William E. Boeing, President Phillip Johnson, and First Vice President and Chief Engineer Clair Egtvedt, the company set out to explore the civil market. Moreover, Boeing officials felt that they had just the airplane for the job. The Boeing Model 40A, powered by a Pratt & Whitney Wasp, represented a real improvement over older aircraft like the Douglas M-2 with its aging Liberty engine. When sales proved slower than expected, the company decided to bid on the long mail route, earning money and demonstrating the superiority of its product at the same time.

National Air Transport (NAT), an original feeder-route contractor, won the New York–Chicago half of the intercontinental route.

The quality of its backers demonstrated just how attractive aviation had become to major business interests: Phillip Wrigley, Lester Armour, William Rockefeller, Marshall Field, Robert Lamont, and Jeremiah Millbank, president of the Allis-Chalmers Corporation, were among investors who contributed to the $10,500,000 capitalization of NAT. William P. MacCracken Jr. handled the incorporation and served as its first corporate counsel. Howard E. Coffin resigned as vice president of Hudson Motor Car to run the company. Clement M. Keys, the Wall Street veteran now at the helm of Curtiss, assembled the investors and was named head of the advisory board. Charles Lawrance of Wright Aeronautical and Charles Kettering, a member of the Dayton-Detroit group who was heading the General Motors Research Laboratory, also played a role in managing NAT.

Paul Henderson, organizer of night operations for the Air Mail Service, left the Post Office to manage NAT. His equipment would include ten Curtiss Carrier Pigeons and a Travel Air "Aerial Mercury," a brand new aircraft designed specifically to carry the mail, as well as a Ford Tri-motor and a single obsolete Liberty-powered DH 4. After a bitter 1930 proxy battle, Boeing Air Transport acquired NAT, which eventually was folded into United Air Lines.

FROM SAN DIEGO TO PARIS

At 10:22 P.M. on the evening of May 21, 1927, an extraordinary young American landed a small silver monoplane on the great grassy circle that was Le Bourget Air Field in Paris, France. He had taken off from a prepared runway at Roosevelt Field, New York, 3,614 miles and 33 hours, 30 minutes, and 29.5 seconds earlier. His life, and the world, would never be the same.

Nothing since has matched the American response to the shy, tousle-haired, twenty-five-year-old Charles Lindbergh. It was the Jazz Age, and the celebrity was king. "Babe" Ruth, "Red" Grange, Rudolph Valentino, Charlie Chaplin, and Mary Pickford achieved a fame once reserved for victorious generals or heads of state. Here was a young man who had demonstrated his value, not on a playing field or the silver screen, but by an act of incalculable skill and courage.

"It isn't Lindbergh the person who inspires them, so much as it is Lindbergh as an ideal," aviator Margery Brown explained to the readers of *Popular Aviation*. "They recognize in him qualities they would like to possess—courage, quiet confidence, modesty, and spiritual freedom."[7]

By the spring of 1929, the copyright office in the Library of Congress had registered almost three hundred songs about Lindbergh. They ran the gamut from forgettable Tin Pan Alley ditties to a Lindbergh-inspired cantata written by Kurt Weil, Bertolt Brecht, and Paul Hindemith that was performed in Baden-Baden and Berlin before Leopold Stokowski conducted the American premiere in a 1931 nationwide broadcast.[8]

He was never the man they thought he was. Far from the boy next door, he was a child of privilege. His mother was the daughter of a wealthy Detroit dentist; his father, a U.S. congressman. An only child, he grew up on a farm near Little Falls, Minnesota, at his grandparent's home in Detroit, and in Washington, D.C. He was a lonely boy in a dysfunctional family who had a lifelong need to be in control of himself and the world around him. His command of hurtling machinery—motorcycles, automobiles, and airplanes—allowed that control.

Lindbergh learned to fly with a barnstormer and practiced that trade himself before joining the army to fly faster and more powerful machines. When he signed on as an airmail pilot with the Robertson brothers, Lindbergh was a seasoned professional who had logged 1,100 hours flying thirty-five different types of aircraft. He spent a little over a year flying the mail and became the first American to parachute to safety four times.

But he was restless and looking for a new challenge. He wrote to the National Geographic Society. Did they know of any upcoming expeditions in need of pilots? He read of Richard Byrd's plan to fly to the North Pole and applied to go along. Then, during a night flight to Chicago, he began to ponder the challenge of flying from New York to Paris.

On May 22, 1919, Raymond Orteig, a native of France who had earned his fortune as a restaurateur and owner of New York's Brevoort and Lafayette Hotels, offered a $25,000 prize for the first nonstop flight from New York to Paris, or vice versa. Six years passed before anyone announced an intention to try for the prize. Moreover, the first attempts ended in tragedy.

Charles A. Lindbergh and the Spirit of St. Louis

On September 26, 1926, René Fonck, the French ace of aces, crashed the Sikorsky trimotor S-35, *New York-to-Paris*, during a take-off run. Fonck and his copilot escaped without injury. Two other crewmen died in the subsequent fire.

In April 1927 Richard Byrd and three crew members were badly injured when Anthony Fokker flipped their trimotor *Atlantic* onto its back while landing from a test flight. Two less fortunate contenders,

Lt. Comdr. Noel Davis and Lt. Stanton Hall Wooster, lost their lives on April 26, 1927. Their trimotor Keystone Pathfinder, *American Legion*, buried its nose and its crew in the mud following a failed take-off attempt from Langley Field in Virginia.

Two weeks later, on May 6, Charles Nungessor, a hero of the air war, and Francois Coli, a one-eyed veteran, took off from Paris in *l'Oiseau Blanc*, a large, single-engine biplane. They dropped their landing gear after take-off, intending to set their machine down in New York Harbor. They were never seen again.

Some of the world's most famous airmen were waiting in New York, also poised to try for Paris, when Lindbergh flew the *Spirit of St. Louis* into Curtiss Field on May 12. Clarence Chamberlin had been selected to fly the Wright-Bellanca *Columbia* across the Atlantic. He couldn't go at the moment, however, because of legal complications relating to his choice of a copilot. Byrd and his crew had mended, or been replaced, and the *Atlantic* was repaired and ready to go for another attempt. Lindbergh and his single-engine airplane were clear underdogs, which only added to their appeal.

Lindbergh had rejected the big trimotors selected by other Atlantic challengers. Recognizing that the Wright-Bellanca was the ideal machine, he had traveled to New York to discuss the purchase of the *Columbia*. Unfortunately, while the airplane was for sale, the company would insist on selecting the pilot. Far from discouraged, the young pilot began to query companies producing aircraft that had done well on the mail routes.

His first choice was the Travel Air Manufacturing Company of Wichita, Kansas. The key figure at Travel Air, Walter Herschel Beech (1891–1950), had been an army flight instructor during the war, then toured the Midwest as a barnstormer. He settled in Wichita in 1921, where he quickly rose to general manager of the E. M. Laird Company, which made a three-place biplane called the Swallow.

Anxious to pursue his own ideas, Beech founded Travel Air in 1924 with talented associates who would make Wichita world famous in the aircraft manufacturing industry. Clyde Cessna was vice president and Lloyd Stearman the new firm's chief engineer. The office secretary, Olive Ann Mellor, whom Beech quickly married, became one of the most talented corporate executives in aviation history.

A 1925 Travel Air cabin model did well in the first Ford Reliability Tour. NAT began flying the mail aboard Travel Air 5000 airplanes the next year. When Lindbergh asked for a price on a Travel Air equipped with a Wright Whirlwind engine early in 1927, Beech declined to bid.

Lindbergh had also heard good things about the Hispano-Suiza–powered Ryan M-2 that Pacific Air Transport operated on its airmail route. The founder of the company, Kansas-born Tubal Clyde Ryan, had learned to fly in the army and then worked with the U.S. Army-Forest Service for a time. In 1922, he bought a war-surplus JN-4D and started the Ryan Flying Company in San Diego, California. The enterprising Ryan sold rides and offered any sort of flying service that a customer might want. He also purchased six war-surplus J-1 Standards and rebuilt them into "mini-airliners" with a closed forward cabin seating four passengers.

Benjamin Franklin Mahoney approached Ryan in 1925, offering to partner with the newly formed Ryan Airlines in a flying service operating between San Diego and Los Angeles. In the process, they made the acquaintance of other young aircraft builders putting down roots in southern California. In 1925, for example, they bought the Cloudster, a machine developed by the Davis-Douglas Company of Los Angeles. With it, they intended to make the first coast-to-coast nonstop flight. When Lts. Oakley Kelly and John Macready achieved that goal with the Fokker T-2, Ryan Airlines purchased the Cloudster for use on its San Diego–Los Angeles route. It was the beginning of a long business relationship.

Donald Wills Douglas had left Cleveland, and the Glenn Martin Company, in 1920, determined to launch his own firm. He returned to Los Angeles, drawn by his pleasant memories of a short stay there with the original Martin Company, the promise of nearly ideal flying weather, and low labor costs in the antiunion atmosphere of southern California. His original partnership with sportsman David R. Davis produced the Cloudster, then collapsed.

After reincorporating the firm on his own, Douglas designed the DT-1, a folding-wing torpedo plane. While navy officials agreed to purchase three of the aircraft, they would not advance all of the construction money required. At this critical juncture, Harry Chandler stepped forward to guarantee a $15,000 loan. Further, he introduced Douglas to a group of local investors who would back the new company.

Donald Wills Douglas

Chandler's decision to support Douglas was completely in character. Standing larger than life at a full six feet, two inches tall, he presided over the *Los Angeles Times*, served on more than fifty corporate boards, and wielded unrivaled power in the City of Angels. Chandler had been central to breaking the back of labor unions in southern California. He had also built the Santa Anita Race Track, the Biltmore Hotel, and the first radio station in Los Angeles. A key figure in the organization of WAE, he saw his city as a world center of aviation, and was as important as the weather in guaranteeing that it would be so.

"I'm interested in the growth of Los Angeles," Chandler explained to Douglas. "We need people like you and new plants, so I'm going to help you." Douglas was now able to complete the first three DT-1s and capture a contract for thirty-eight more. The following year, Douglas's firm won an army contract for the airplanes that would complete the first aerial circumnavigation of the globe in 1924.

By January 1925, Douglas had 112 employees on the payroll at his plant in the Los Angeles suburb of Santa Monica. Over the next several years, the company would earn an enviable reputation for well-engineered aircraft designed by men like James Howard "Dutch" Kindelberger, John Knudsen "Jack" Northrop, Gerard F. "Jerry" Vultee, Arthur Raymond, John Leland "Lee" Atwood, and Edward H. Heinemann. Some of them would remain with Douglas. Most would break away to found their own companies. These men would compete and cross-pollinate for decades to come, writing the history of aviation in the clear blue skies of Los Angeles. Harry Chandler had spent his money wisely.

JACK NORTHROP (1895–1981), a native of Newark, New Jersey, bounced west through Chicago and Lincoln, Nebraska, before finally putting down roots in Santa Barbara. His father, Charles Northrop, initially settled his family into a large tent with a wooden floor erected near the beach and gradually established himself as a contractor participating in the southern California boom.

Their father paid for the college education of Jack's two elder half-brothers. In spite of his obvious gift for mathematics, the youngest Northrop went to work as an architectural draftsman in 1913, straight out of high school. While still in school he had worked in an automobile repair shop that shared a building with a pair of brothers, Allan and Malcolm Loughead, who were building an airplane with the assistance of a Czechoslovakian-born mechanic named Anthony Stadlman. Bored with his work in the architectural office, and noting that the Lougheads were building their machine "by guess and by golly" without mechanical drawings, Northrop offered his services. He would also sweep the floors.

Going to work for the Lougheads in 1916, the budding engineer began to teach himself the fine points of stress analysis, strength of materials, aerodynamics, and structural design. The design of that first machine ratified his on-the-job training, he later remarked, pointing out that "at least the wings didn't fall off." Drafted into the army in World War I, Northrop was transferred to the Air Service, then ordered to report back to Loughead to assist the firm in producing Curtiss HS2L flying boats. Out of uniform and back on the payroll following the armistice, he took the lead in designing the next project, the Loughead S-1 Sportsplane. Unable to sell even a single airplane, however, the little team soon tired of struggling to stay afloat and closed their doors in 1920.[9]

Northrop then went to work as a draftsman with his father's construction firm, marking time until he could reenter aviation. The opportunity came in 1923, when Donald Douglas snapped him up to work on the globe-girdling army planes.

Douglas, the Annapolis- and MIT-trained engineer, turned the technical work over to Northrop and other subordinates. "He was a master salesman and a fine engineer," Northrop recalled many years later, "but his primary job was to contact the military or other potential customers and try to get additional work for the company." The boss had a tough job. At one point during this period, things looked so bleak that Douglas laid off four or five engineers, keeping only Northrop and Al Mankey, a draftsman, on the payroll.[10]

Northrop earned a bit of extra money moonlighting for other manufacturers. In 1926, he traveled to San Diego on the weekends to work with the staff of Ryan Airlines. Ryan was refining the high-wing M-1 mail monoplane into the M-2, which would be fitted with a Wright J-4 engine. He helped to rework both the fuselage and the main spar of the wing. The next year, a longer version of that wing would be fitted to a new Ryan machine being sold to a young airmail pilot and his St. Louis backers. Having put his mark on the first airplane to circle the globe, Northrop now contributed to the *Spirit of St. Louis*. And his career had scarcely begun.

Northrop's contribution had been important, but Donald Hall, Ryan's chief engineer, deserves credit for the design of the *Spirit of St. Louis*. By this time, Benjamin Franklin Mahoney was in charge of Ryan Airlines, having bought T. Clyde Ryan's shares in November 1926. He continued to operate the airline and the factory, which was situated in an abandoned fish-packing plant. When Lindbergh's telegram inquiring about an airplane capable of flying the Atlantic landed on Hall's desk, he assumed that a modified M-2 could fly the Atlantic. However, when Lindbergh arrived in San Diego and laid out his specific requirements—a single-seat monoplane powered by a Wright J-5C engine carrying more than 400 gallons of gasoline—Hall realized that he needed a new airplane, a big brother of the M-2.

In the end, there was nothing radical or cutting edge about the *Spirit of St. Louis*. The fuselage was two feet longer than that of the M-2. The wing was longer and stronger. The airfoil was the same, a famous design known as the Clark Y, introduced by Virginius "Ginny" Evans Clark, an engineer and aerodynamicist at McCook Field. Given the aircraft's extraordinary take-off weight, the landing gear was beefed up.

The engine was the latest in power plants, but the *Spirit of St. Louis* was scarcely the first airplane to be propelled by a Whirlwind. The earth inductor compass mounted in the cockpit also received considerable attention. Drs. Lyman Briggs and Paul Heyl of the National Bureau of Standards had developed the instrument, which indicated the precise direction of magnetic North, to meet the special needs of aerial navigators. Richard Byrd had used it on his polar flight the year before.

Nor did the *Spirit of St. Louis* offer superior flying qualities. "I found . . . that it takes Charles Atlas-like strength to handle the ailerons," Frank Tallman, who flew a replica of the airplane, explained. "Rudder and elevator are adequate but must be used constantly, and they were enlarged considerably on the later Ryan B5s [that were based on the *Spirit of St. Louis*]." Lindbergh had thought that the airplane flew beautifully.[11]

For all of that, the airplane did precisely what was asked of it. When Lindbergh took off from San Diego on May 10, bound for New York with a stop over in St. Louis, he knew that Nungessor and Coli were over the Atlantic and expected to succeed. When he landed in St. Louis, he learned that the Frenchmen were missing. When Lindbergh landed at Curtiss Field at 5:33 p.m. on May 12, he became a favorite with the reporters, a curse and a blessing that dogged him for the rest of his life.

Lindbergh and his airplane returned home from Paris aboard the USS *Memphis*. Wildly enthusiastic receptions greeted him everywhere he went. Determined to use his celebrity on behalf of aviation, he spent three months (July 20–October 23, 1927) on a national tour to boost air-mindedness and to encourage the construction of local airports. He flew the *Spirit of St. Louis* 22,350 miles, visiting eighty-two cities and

towns and landing at least once in every state. On December 13 he flew
from Bolling Field, Washington, D.C., to Mexico City on the first leg
of a Latin American tour that would carry him to thirteen countries in
sixty-two days.

The Latin American tour was as much a personal turning point as
the flight to Paris. While visiting Mexico, he met U.S. Ambassador
Dwight Morrow's daughter, Anne. He proposed to her on their fourth
meeting. For the next decade, the Lindberghs would be America's
favorite couple. Newspaper photographers always seemed to catch them
landing from one flight or taking off on another. Anne learned to fly and
qualified as a licensed radio operator, so that she could "crew" on their
epic aerial journeys. They flew across the arctic north and down the
Siberian coast to China and Japan (in 1931), and around the rim of the
Atlantic (in 1933), surveying potential routes for the airliners that were
sure to follow. Anne took up writing and chronicled their great flights in
two best-selling books: *North to the Orient* and *Listen! The Wind.*

Lindbergh used his fame to boost commercial aviation. He helped
to create two great airlines: Transcontinental Air Transport (TAT, later
TWA), also known as "the Lindbergh Line," and Pan American
World Airways. He played a highly visible role in launching TAT's air-
ground transcontinental passenger service (in 1929), surveyed Pan Am
routes, and served as a technical consultant for both companies. And he
looked to the future, introducing American rocket pioneer Robert H.
Goddard to Harry Guggenheim.

Americans were as fascinated by the tragedies of the Lindberghs as
by their triumphs. The kidnapping and murder of their first child and
the arrest, trial, and execution of Bruno Richard Hauptmann in 1936
riveted public attention for months. Hounded by the press, and determined to protect their second son, Jon, the Lindberghs fled to Europe,
where they would remain until 1939. Impressed by what he had seen
during his travels in Germany, he expressed doubt as to the ability of
the British to prevail against the might of the Luftwaffe.

When he brought his family home to the United States, Lindbergh
emerged as a major spokesman for America First, a strong voice
against U.S. intervention in the European war. His repeated doubts
regarding the ability of the Allies to triumph over Germany, his attacks
on the Roosevelt administration, the fact that he had accepted an award

from the Nazis, and his identification of Jews as being among the "war agitators" attempting to draw America into the conflict all combined to damage Lindbergh's popularity. In the wake of a particularly disastrous speech at Des Moines, Iowa, newspapers proclaimed, "LINDBERGH ATTACKS JEWS."

It has been said that Lindbergh's anti-Semitism was what one would have encountered in any restricted country club or hotel in the United States. In fact, the strain of racism ran very deep in him during the years before World War II. Aviation, he remarked to the readers of the *Reader's Digest*, "is a tool specially shaped for Western hands, a scientific art which others only copy in a mediocre fashion, another barrier between the teeming millions of Asia and the Grecian inheritance of Europe—one of those priceless possessions which permit the white race to live at all in a pressing sea of Yellow, Black, and Brown."[12]

The man who had inspired hundreds of admiring songs now found himself the target of Woody Guthrie, who parodied the Lindberghs as native fascists aiming for high political office. Barred by President Franklin D. Roosevelt from military service during World War II, Lindbergh worked as a consultant and test pilot with the Ford Motor Company and the United Aircraft Corporation. Visiting the South Pacific in that capacity, he flew fifty combat missions as a civilian, in the process teaching combat pilots half his age how to conserve fuel and extend their range. He remained an important public figure following the war, serving on important committees planning for the future of the air force and helping to select the site for the new Air Force Academy.

Few Americans have been held in such high esteem, only to fall so very far from favor. Charles Lindbergh was perhaps the best-known aviator of the twentieth century. He exhibited the attributes that have made fliers heroic figures since the years before World War I: courage, confidence, the ability to function under pressure, and a rare ability in the cockpit.

But if he was the personification of the hero, he was also seen as deeply flawed. It was not simply a matter of his racism or his lifelong enthusiasm for eugenics. Lindbergh seems to have been convinced that a lifetime spent watching the world from a godlike perch on high had endowed him with special insight. Moreover, he felt obligated, even compelled, to share his thoughts with the public, whether the subject was aviation, politics, international affairs, or the environment. Whatever the public response to his actions or point of view, he never apologized.

That is not to say, however, that he did not change his mind. His growing concern about the human impact on the natural world led him to question the most basic assumptions of his youth. Lindbergh had once applauded aviation as a tool for defending Western Civilization against the black, brown, and yellow peoples of the world. Late in life, he became fascinated by those distant cultures.

Concerned about damage to the upper atmosphere, he spoke out against the development of an American supersonic transport jet. At the end of his life, he admitted that he had "seen the science I worshipped, and the airplane I loved, destroying the civilization I expected them to serve."

Ultimately, Charles Lindbergh's youthful faith in technology was transformed, rather than shattered. As early as 1928 he had taken an interest in Goddard's work on rockets and helped to convince Harry Guggenheim to support "upper-atmosphere" research. "When I see a rocket rising from the pad," Lindbergh remarked in 1974, "I think of how the most fantastic dreams come true, of how dreams have formed into matter, and matter into dreams. Then I see Robert Goddard standing by my side, his human physical substance now ethereal, his dream substantive. When I watched the fantastic launching of Apollo 8 carrying its three astronauts on man's first voyage to the moon, I thought about how the launching of a dream is more fantastic still, for the material products of dreams are limited in a way that dreams are not. What sunbound astronaut's experience can equal that of Robert Goddard, whose body stayed on earth while he voyaged through the galaxies."[13]

The same can be said of Lindbergh.

BOOM AND BUST

Capital began to flow into aviation with the legislation of 1925–1926. The Lindbergh ballyhoo helped to build enthusiasm for flight, but the business boom in aviation was already underway.

Even during the doldrums of 1920–1924, the army had spent $246 million on aviation and the navy $187 million. Aviation stock prices had been rising. Between 1923 and 1925, the price of Wright Aeronautical stock rocketed from 8¼ to 32⅜ and Curtiss stock from 5 to 26½. But the aviation business soared even higher with the passage of the military aviation expansion acts for both services, the inauguration of commercial airmail service, and government regulation and support for civil aviation.[14]

Inevitably, the entry of Wall Street investors into the aviation business led to a restructuring of the industry. "There were three hundred aircraft factories," Dutch Kindelberger recalled, "including those where you had to shove the cow outside to see the airplane." The men who regarded aviation as a business like any other saw opportunities for merger, consolidation, and profitable vertical combinations.[15]

THE ERA OF CONSOLIDATION and expansion began in 1927, when industry veteran William Boeing established a subsidiary company to carry the mail between San Francisco and Chicago aboard Boeing Model 40A aircraft. Two years later, he chartered the Boeing Aircraft and Transport Corporation, renamed United Aircraft and Transport in 1929.

Frederick Rentschler manufactured the Pratt & Whitney Wasp that powered the Boeing Model 40A. He saw the possibilities of a holding company that combined aircraft and engine manufacturers with an airline operating their equipment. Brother Gordon Rentschler, president of National City Bank, provided the money that linked the Boeing combine with Pratt & Whitney and Chance Vought, another leading consumer of Wasp engines. Boeing became chairman of the board of United Aircraft. Frederick Rentschler served as president.

Next, United Aircraft acquired the manufacturers of the metal propellers driven by Rentschler's engines mounted on Boeing's planes. Propellers posed a special technical problem. As early as the end of World War I, the tips of the blades mounted on the powerful engines were moving close to the speed of sound and encountering enormous stress. The Standard Propeller Company, founded in 1919 by Thomas Dicks and James Lutterll, had a license to build the strong, light-alloy-metal propellers patented by Dr. Sylvanus Reed. The outer half of the blades of these propellers were solid and could withstand the stress. United also acquired a second manufacturer of metal propellers, Hamilton Aero Products, and merged the two firms to create Hamilton Standard.

Ultimately, United would acquire four other firms founded by leading engineer-manufacturers: Stearman, founded by Lloyd Stearman in 1927 when he left Travel Air; Jack Northrop's Avion Corporation; Chance Vought; and the Sikorsky Aviation Corporation, founded by the émigré Russian genius who had pioneered multiengine aircraft. Finally, Boeing and Rentschler gained control of three other airlines: Stout Air Services, Varney Air Lines, and NAT.

Clement Keys was hot on the heels of Rentschler and Boeing. A Canadian-born banker, he had edited the *Wall Street Journal* and Walter Hines Page's magazine, the *World's Work*. Having acquired American citizenship, Keys started his own brokerage firm in 1911. Five years later, John Willys, the automobile pioneer who had taken control of the Curtiss Aeroplane and Motor Company, offered Keys the vice presidency in exchange for marketing securities and managing the enormous wartime expansion of the company.

In 1920, Curtiss was driven close to bankruptcy during the postwar decline. Keys purchased control of the company from John Willys for a bargain basement price of $650,000. It was the end of an era. Glenn Curtiss would remain on the payroll as a technical consultant, but his active years in aviation were at an end.

Keys next incorporated his holding company, North American Aviation, in December 1928. His serious efforts to build an industrial combine began the following July, when he merged a dozen or so companies (including Travel Air, Curtiss-Robertson, Curtiss-Caproni, Keystone, Moth, and Loening) with Wright Aeronautical and his own Curtiss Aeroplane and Motor Company to form Curtiss-Wright. Between 1929 and 1933, North American owned or controlled a majority interest in a wide range of companies: Sperry Gyroscope, Ford Instrument Company, Berliner-Joyce Aircraft, and General Aviation Manufacturing. For short periods of time, North American also held substantial minority interest in Douglas Aircraft, TAT, and WAE.

Clearly, however, North American was never as well integrated or managed as United Aircraft. Beyond the creation of Curtiss-Wright, the combine was plagued by financial difficulties, which ultimately led to a nervous breakdown for Keys. Companies were brought and sold at a confusing rate. Eventually, Curtiss-Wright left the North American group, which General Motors subsequently acquired, although the manifold corporate shifts meant that it was the same company in name only.

The third giant, AVCO (Aviation Corporation), was principally the creation of Sherman Mills Fairchild, the only son of George Fairchild. The senior Fairchild was a remarkable American business leader who had financed the production of an early rotary printing press, helped to found IBM, and served a dozen years in Congress. The younger Fairchild, a handsome man, entered Harvard in 1915 and continued his studies at the University of Arizona and Columbia. A tennis player, a gourmet cook, and something of a playboy, he was also fascinated by photography. With his father's financial support, he founded a company near the end of World War I to produce aerial cameras, and then a second company in 1922 to conduct aerial survey work. Dissatisfied with the standard biplanes used for aerial photography, he founded two new companies in 1925: Fairchild Airplane Manufacturing Company and Fairchild Engine Corporation. In addition to serving as photographic platforms, this distinguished line of cabin monoplanes would go on great exploratory journeys and earn a reputation as the most rugged and successful bush airplanes of their generation. Fairchild monoplanes also served as corporate aircraft and small airliners.

Fairchild followed his father onto the board of IBM and maintained Wall Street connections. Underwritten by W. Averill Harriman and Lehman brothers, AVCO was originally intended to finance a Cincinnati-based air service that sold and operated Fairchild aircraft. Along the way, the firm acquired a handful of small airlines, as well as the Kreider-Reisner Company, an aircraft producer. All were folded into Fairchild. Juan Terry Trippe, founder of Colonial Airlines, was also associated with AVCO. Like North American, the new combination went through a confusing series of alterations. At one point or another, the holding company controlled the Lycoming Manufacturing

Company, Lockheed, and the firm headed by Vultee. The entry of the E. L. Cord Company into the combine in 1932 marked the end of Fairchild's leadership.

NOT EVERY COMPANY took the merger route. Martin and Consolidated (founded by Rueben Fleet in 1923) traveled alone, and Douglas stayed essentially independent. Some newcomers to the field also remained aloof. Clyde Cessna went into business in 1927 when he left Travel Air. Guiseppe Bellanca, the Italian engineer who had built the cabin monoplane for Wright Aeronautical, set up on his own. Leroy Grumman, a graduate of MIT and Cornell who had worked as a naval aircraft constructor, and served as a factory manager for Grover Loening, set up shop on Long Island in 1929.

Business was booming. Aircraft sales rose from $21 million in 1927 to $71 million in 1929. Aviation stocks soared as well. Between March 1928 and December 1929, aviation securities valued at a billion dollars changed hands on the New York Stock Exchange. As Elsbeth Freudenthal, the first historian of the industry, pointed out, aviation ranked fourth among new issues traded during that period. Yet the total value of equipment produced in 1929 was only $90 million. The corset industry was bigger.

Prior to 1933, while a handful of companies like Lockheed and Travel Air concentrated on commercial aircraft, most manufacturers relied on military sales.

Sales to the Military Services as a Percentage of Total sales, 1927–1933[16]

Glenn L. Martin	100%
Douglas Aircraft Company	91%
Consolidated Company	79%
Curtiss Aeroplane and Motor Company	76%
Chance Vought Company	75%
Grumman Aircraft Engineering Corp.	75%
Great Lakes Aircraft Company	73%

Keystone Aircraft Corp.	72%
Pratt & Whitney Aircraft Company	64%
Boeing Airplane Company	59%
Wright Aeronautical Company	58%

American aircraft exports were growing too. Between 1925 and 1934, Latin American purchases of U.S. aircraft, engines, and parts totaled $26,912,000. European nations imported $16,411,000 worth of U.S. aeronautical products. Another $15,208,000 of equipment went to Asia, over half of that to China.

Then, along came the stock market collapse of 1929. Its effect is apparent in the following table:

Total U.S. Aircraft Production, 1924-1933[17]

Year	Military	Civil	Total
1924	317	60	377
1925	447	342	789
1926	532	654	1,186
1927	621	1,374	1,995
1928	1,219	3,127	4,346
1929	677	5,516	6,193
1930	747	2,690	3,437
1931	812	1,988	2,800
1932	593	803	1,396
1933	466	858	1,324

AIR COMMERCE IN THE UNITED STATES, 1929–1933

Before July 7, 1929, it took seventy-two hours to cross the American continent by rail. That evening, the Airway Limited pulled out of Pennsylvania Station and headed west with sixteen passengers on board, including Amelia Earhart, who would present the greetings of New York Mayor Jimmy Walker to the mayor of Los Angeles. A continent away, two Ford Tri-motors took off from Los Angeles and headed east. Charles Lindbergh, now a technical consultant to TAT, piloted one of those machines.

Safe night passenger flights still lay in the future. But Paul Henderson, the veteran Air Mail Service administrator now managing TAT for Clement Keys, had worked out a new kind of coast-to-coast service with the Pennsylvania and Atchison, Topeka, and Santa Fe Railroads. While Lindbergh and his passengers flew east, Earhart and her fellow travelers spent a comfortable night in Pullman cars, arriving in Columbus, Ohio, the next morning. They continued their journey west during the day aboard two Tri-motors. Earhart and company then transferred to a train again that evening at Waynoka, Oklahoma, and awoke the next morning in Clovis, New Mexico. Then it was on to Los Angeles by air, arriving forty-eight hours after departing Pennsylvania Station. The price: $345.

The New York Central and the Universal Aviation Corporation, eventually to become a part of American Airlines, had inaugurated the first train-plain service a month before, using Fokker trimotors to whisk passengers across the nation in sixty hours. With the introduction of the TAT service, the New York Central announced a new route that would cut travel time to the coast to forty-six hours. While the new ventures captured headlines aplenty, they lost enormous amounts of money. One authority estimated that the TAT–Pennsylvania Railroad initiative lost $2,750,000 in eighteen months of operation.

For the first four years of private airmail carriage, 1926–1930, air passenger traffic was negligible. WAE, Ford, and Boeing Air Transport had established demonstration passenger routes, but they remained highly visible experiments rather than money-making operations. With these coast-to-coast ventures of 1929, investors sought to increase profits by emphasizing passenger traffic.

As early as 1930, thirty airlines carried 385,910 passengers over fifty thousand air miles. New names like Eastern Air Transport (founded by Harold Pitcairn, in 1926), Braniff (founded by Tom and Paul Braniff, in 1927), and Northwest Airlines entered the marketplace. New twin-engine passenger airliners like the Boeing Model 80 and the Curtiss Condor, the last of the big commercial biplanes, joined the

Ford, Fokker, and Stinson trimotors already in service. As late as 1933, however, the Post Office still contributed almost 75 percent of corporate revenues through the airmail contracts.[18]

It was enough to keep the airlines profitable, and more so with the passage of time. In the three years following passage of the Air Mail Act, two amendments generally favored the contractors. William P. MacCracken Jr., who had left the Department of Commerce to become chief counsel of WAE, admitted that WAE would still turn a profit if the postal contract fee was cut to less than half the current fee of $3.00 a pound.

By shifting the means of calculating payment from a pound of mail carried per mile to the amount of space provided for mail and the distance carried, the McNary-Watres Act of 1930 encouraged the budding airlines to operate larger aircraft over longer routes where the airmail traffic was light. Postmaster Walter Folger Brown (1869–1961) was clearly aiming to achieve more than the expeditious transportation of mail. He would use the power of airmail contracts to shape a rational network of air routes binding the nation.

A native of Massillon, Ohio, Brown was an old-time Republican politician and one-time political boss of Toledo. In 1921, President Warren G. Harding appointed his old political crony to head the Committee on the Reorganization of the Executive Departments. President Coolidge appointed him assistant secretary of commerce under Herbert Hoover, the man whom Brown most admired. Hoover named him postmaster general.

From the outset, Brown pursued his larger goal, stretching federal contracting regulations to the breaking point. He was determined to weed out "shoe string operations" and strengthen the strongest and most efficient airlines. "Well," he explained to a congressional committee, "competitive bidding in the air mail business is of doubtful value and is more or less of a myth."

In May 1930, postmaster General Brown invited the leaders of the large air transport firms to a conference, chaired by MacCracken. At the meeting, the contractors agreed to the allocation of seven major routes among themselves. Brown distributed five other routes aimed at filling in the gaps in his national system.[19]

Smaller carriers without airmail contracts, those who had struggled in vain to turn a profit carrying passengers, were cut out of "the Spoils Conference." They howled, and so did industry leaders like Harris Hanshue, founder of the healthy WAE. Hanshue testified that Post Office officials had pressured him to merge with TAT to form Transcontinental and Western Airlines (TWA). One airline executive who had emerged from the conference a big winner later testified that he thought at the time the meeting was a joke: "It seemed so ridiculous to me that anything as important as the creation of a large number of new air-mail routes could be determined in this offhand manner."[20]

Charges against Brown and his Spoils Conference would echo in the halls of power and on the pages of American newspapers until, in 1933, the Roosevelt administration finally took action. But if there were political clouds on the horizon, three Republican administrations, 1920–1932, could take real pride in what had been achieved. America's major cities were linked by a network of air routes that would serve it well in the future.

THE NEW DEAL AND CIVIL AVIATION

By 1931, five major airlines linked the nation. Transcontinental and Western Airlines (TWA) connected New York and San Francisco via Chicago, St. Louis, Kansas City, Oklahoma City, Los Angeles, and points in between. United Air Lines cut a swath across the middle of the nation. Its branch lines ran south to Texas and north and south along the Pacific Coast. American Airways linked the Northeast, Midwest, and South to Los Angeles. Northwest Airlines ran across the northern tier of states, from Chicago to Seattle. Eastern Air Transport controlled the East Coast, from New England to Florida.

All of these were part of the system of holding companies that dominated American aeronautics. Some of them, TWA and Eastern, for example, operated over noncompetitive routes under the same corporate umbrella. If no carrier was getting rich, they weren't losing great sums of money either—the U.S. Post Office saw to that. Even so, rumors of the Spoils Conference would not die.

As early as 1931, Fulton Lewis, a Hearst newspaper columnist and radio commentator, had been poking into the airmail contracts. Most of the complaints came from small companies who had underbid larger operators on very short routes. Brown, determined to build a strong network of air routes for the nation, freely admitted accepting higher bids from contractors who would carry the mail over longer routes. The larger operators were willing to invest in newer and larger aircraft, and offered passenger service over their longer routes. Brown was happy to pay a premium for that.

As the Hoover administration spiraled down to its painful conclusion, members of the incoming Roosevelt team and Democratic legislators examined the situation. Senator Hugo Black (D-Alabama) and the other members of his Special Committee on the Investigation of Air Mail and Ocean Mail Contracts led the way.

The Black Committee opened hearings in the fall of 1933, leaning on information supplied by Fulton Lewis. William MacCracken, pioneer of air commerce legislation, had been the first head of the Aeronautics Branch of the Department of Commerce. In that post he had helped to organize the airline industry during the Hoover years. Now he became an early target of the committee. Industry leaders like Frederick Rentschler were branded as profiteers. The process of distributing airmail contracts to the large carriers was castigated as "graft," "collusion," and "waste."

Details of the unfolding "Air Mail Scandal" spilled across the front pages of American newspapers. Riding the crest of a political wave, investigators happily exposed the perceived misdeeds of Hoover's administration while burnishing Roosevelt's reputation for reform. With the benefit of hindsight, it would become apparent that the establishment of a well-considered and effective civil aviation policy represented one of the most significant achievements of the Harding, Coolidge, and Hoover administrations. For the moment, however, political perceptions overshadowed rational analysis.

On February 9, 1934, President Franklin Roosevelt issued Executive Order 6591, canceling all airmail contracts as recommended by Postmaster General James Farley. The chief of the Air Corps, Gen. Benjamin Delahauf Foulois, whom Wilbur Wright had taught to fly, agreed that the army would once again fly the mail beginning on February 19.

Army officials took ten days to plan their operation, identify resources, deploy personnel and equipment, and conduct test flights over essential routes, roughly one-half the distance then covered by the airlines. When three pilots lost their lives to accidents on February 16, Foulois ordered all commanders to remind their crews that safety was "the first policy of the Air Corps."[21] Bad weather marked the beginning of operations, leading to three more accidents, one of them fatal, on February 22. By March 9, three more officers had lost their lives.

President Roosevelt recognized a looming disaster when he saw one. He ordered the army to stop carrying the mail except under the safest possible conditions. After standing down for a week, the Air Corps resumed operations on March 19 under new rules—flying only in daylight and good weather. By April 1, twelve more airmen had crashed and sixty-six had made forced landings.

What had gone wrong? It was a matter of training and equipment. Army aviators were trained in aerial maneuvering and formation flying. Airline pilots, on the other hand, were used to their routes and had been trained to fly on instruments at night and in poor weather. In addition, army aircraft did not measure up to the newer and larger commercial aircraft, planes that could carry even more mail than was available, and passengers as well.

Most of the commercial carriers faced disaster when they lost their airmail contracts. TWA, which had been growing stronger under the Brown regime, immediately furloughed its employees and desperately set to work on plans to carry passengers over a much restricted route structure.

The Army Air Corps disaster offered a golden opportunity for the airlines to make their case. Charles Lindbergh spoke for them. Defending Brown's efforts to strengthen civil aviation in the United States, he urged Roosevelt to stop risking the lives of army airmen on airmail duty. The president was furious when a telegram from Lindbergh appeared in the newspapers before it reached the White House. Bitter feelings between the most famous men in America peaked during the America First campaign of 1940 and continued until Roosevelt's death in 1945.

Determined to resolve the crisis on his own terms, the president outlined his thoughts on new airmail legislation to Senator Black and the chairmen of the Post Office Committees on March 7, 1934. New three-year contracts should be put out to bid on the basis of absolutely free competition. Any carrier that had operated under the old system would be barred from bidding, as would any airline linked to one of the large holding companies.

Lindbergh lost no time in renouncing "one of the most unjust acts I have ever seen in American legislation." Eddie Rickenbacker, America's ace of aces and vice president of Eastern Air Transport, opined that Roosevelt's bill would ban every man with any experience from the airline industry. Others described the president's plan as a "bill of attainder," an act "the smacks of Medieval law."[22]

The airmail crisis was a watershed of sorts. It marked the end of General Foulois's long career, along with that of a dozen or so key airline executives. At a corporate level, however, things were not all that bad. In the end, a small change in the name of an airline that had carried the mail under the old regime was sufficient to qualify the firm to bid on a new contract. Moreover, membership in a holding company had worked against some airlines. United, for example, had been locked into continued use of Boeing 247 aircraft long after the competing Douglas airplanes had demonstrated their superiority.

The Air Mail Act of 1934, which closely reflected White House thinking, did little to ease the situation. The Department of Commerce retained authority over infrastructure and safety issues, and the Post Office continued to create and distribute airmail routes. A new organization, the Interstate Commerce Commission, was given responsibility for fixing lower postal rates. With the all-important postal subsidy reduced, the airlines struggle to remain afloat.

IN ADDITION to the economic woes of the airlines, public concern for air safety was on the rise. In 1932, the air passenger fatality rate was 4.8 per hundred million miles flown. By 1936, that figure had more than doubled to a catastrophic 10.1 deaths per hundred million passenger miles. One pilot calculated that during the years 1930–1935, one airman had died in a crash every twenty-eight days. "We are nowhere near the safety record of railroads or even steamships or buses or private automobiles," Cy Caldwell, a pilot and aviation journalist, commented, "and we probably won't be for some time."[23]

The Aeronautics Branch of the Department of Commerce was supposed to increase air safety, but it hadn't prospered under the New Deal. Eugene L. Vidal, director of the Aeronautics Branch—renamed the Bureau of Air Commerce in 1934—had lost the battle for funds. Consequently, he was short of inspectors and unable to make improvements. The last Hoover budget (in 1932) allocated $1.4 million for the regulation and inspection of airmen and aircraft. By fiscal 1936, the sum requested for that purpose had fallen to $644,000.

As funds shrank, requirements increased. Senator Bronson M. Cutting (R-New Mexico) and four other people died in the crash of a TWA flight near Kansas City, Missouri, on May 6, 1935, underscoring the crisis—America needed better ground-to-air communications and an air traffic control system. Vidal, who in 1934 had encouraged the airlines to set up the first three air traffic control centers, accepted federal responsibility for the effort in 1936 and began to expand it across the nation.

But Vidal's days, and those of the Bureau of Air Commerce, were numbered. Clearly, aviation had grown beyond the regulatory capacity of a small branch of the Department of Commerce. The time had come for fundamental change. The Civil Aeronautics Act of 1938 replaced the Bureau of Air Commerce with an independent agency, the Civil Aeronautics Authority (CAA). The new agency took over the duties of the predecessor agency and also assumed the regulation of airlines fares and routes, items that had previously been the business of the Post Office and Interstate Commerce Commission.

Two years later, President Roosevelt split the CAA in half. The new Civil Aviation Administration would manage the air traffic control system, licensing, and registration; enforce safety regulations; and see to airway development. A new Civil Aeronautics Board would establish safety regulations, investigate accidents, and regulate air fares. The long and difficult pioneering era of the federal regulation of U.S. domestic air commerce was at an end.

8

THE ROAR OF THE CROWD,
1927–1939

HIGHER, FARTHER, . . .

Sigismund Levanevsky, Jimmy Mattern, Louise Thaden, James Weddell, Clarence Chamberlin, James Mollison, Art Goebel, Bert Hinkler, Bert Acosta, Bernt Balchen, Beryl Markham, Ruth Elder, Roscoe Turner, Clyde Pangborn, Dieudonné Costes, Walter Hinchliffe, George Haldeman, Doug Davis, Elsie Mackay, Maurice Bellonte, Ruth Nichols, "Mattie" Laird, Hubert Wilkins, Lincoln Ellsworth, Valery Chkalov, Frank Hawks, Charles "Speed" Holman—all were names to conjure with in the twenties and thirties.

They crossed oceans, flew over the poles, and set records for speed, altitude, and duration aloft. They were as well known as movie stars and sports heroes. Some of the names still strike a familiar cord. Most have been forgotten by all but those who cherish memories of the golden age of aviation.

Theirs was a dangerous craft. Between May 1927 and March 1928, nine aviators and passengers lost their lives attempting to follow in Lindbergh's wake across the Atlantic. In June 1928, Lts. Albert Hegenberger and Lester Maitland became the first to fly from San Francisco to Honolulu. Two months later, aviators gathered in Oakland,

California, determined to win the $45,000 prize for the first three to arrive in Honolulu in pineapple king James Dole's derby.

Thirteen aircraft and crews entered the race. Accidents before the start led to the withdrawal of three of them. Department of Commerce officials refused to certify two more for so long a flight. Two of the remaining aircraft were unable to get off the runway. The pilots in two airplanes wisely turned back after take-off. Four airplanes did get into the air and headed for Hawaii. Art Goebel and Bill Davis were the first to arrive in Honolulu in the Travel Air *Woolaroc*, followed two hours later by Martin Jensen and Paul Schluter in the Breese monoplane *Aloha*. Jack Frost and Gordon Scott, flying the *Golden Eagle*, the very first Lockheed Vega, and the three crew members of *Miss Doran*, including Mildred Doran, "the flying schoolmarm," were never seen again.

Aviators became heroic exemplars for their nations. Captains Gago Coutinho and Arturo Sacadura da Cabral of the Portuguese navy were lionized for conquering the South Atlantic in 1922. The achievement stood, even though the aircraft they started in came apart in landing at St. Paul Rocks in the middle of the ocean. Coutinho and Sacadura da Cabral finished in another plane, taking off from their crash point.

All Australia celebrated Charles E. Kingsford-Smith, Charles Ulm, and their two crewmen, who flew the Fokker trimotor *Southern Cross* from Oakland to Sydney in 1928. Amy Johnson, a university graduate working as a London secretary, had scrimped and saved to pay for flying lessons. She won the hearts of all Britons when she flew *Jason*, her little De Havilland Gypsy Moth biplane, from England to Australia in 1930. The first flights linking New York and the capitals of Hungary, Poland, Rumania, Lithuania, and other European nations were regularly accorded full attention in the *New York Times*.

The tyrants of the age promoted aviation feats meant to demonstrate their national strength and technological prowess. Benito Mussolini dispatched Umberto Nobile and the crew of the airship *Italia* on an expedition to the North Pole in 1928. The dirigible was forced down on the ice, and an international search-and-rescue mission retrieved the crew. Seventeen people died in the airship crash and the accidents befalling the rescuers, including Roald Amundsen, the first man to reach the South Pole.

Mussolini had a dashing airman to command his air force, the flamboyant Gen. Italo Balbo. Balbo led a flight of twelve Savoia-Marchetti S-55 flying boats across the South Atlantic in 1931, an enormous success in spite of the loss of one crew in a crash. Just two years later he led eighty men manning twenty-four big twin-hull S-55 torpedo bombers on a 6,100-mile flight from Orbatello, Italy, to Chicago for a goodwill visit to the 1933 world's fair, the Century of Progress Exhibition.

But it was Joseph Stalin who was most enamored of flight spectaculars. By 1929, Stalin, the Man of Steel, had dealt with his rivals and kept a firm grip on the reins of power. Having launched his first modernization program, he was determined to use aviation to increase morale and impress the rest of the world.

The Soviets began with an attempt to capture the world's altitude record. On May 27, 1931, the Swiss physicist Auguste Piccard became the first man to climb into the stratosphere aboard a balloon with a pressurized cabin. Officials of the Aviation Branch of Stalin's Ministry of War and the Scientific Investigation Institute for the Rubber Industry set out to top Piccard's record with the *USSR*, the largest balloon in history. Standing 118 feet tall when fully inflated, the craft featured a gondola made of riveted aluminum sheets. On September 30, 1933, George Prokofiev and two additional crew members rose to a record altitude of 60,695 feet.

The following year, when a pair of American airmen climbed to 61,237 feet aboard the balloon *Century of Progress*, the Soviets prepared to raise the mark with a new balloon, *Osaviakhim I*. The three crew members were selected in a national search. Their rigorous training included time in a simulator. On January 10, 1934, the balloon rose over Moscow to a new record altitude of 72,178 feet. Low on both ballast and gas, everything seemed to go wrong on the way down. The gondola broke loose from the balloon and smashed to earth, killing the crew. Stalin and Marshall Kliment Yefremovich Voroshilov, the head of the Soviet military, presided as the ashes of the heroes were buried in the Kremlin wall.

But the Soviets were moving forward on other fronts. In 1932 Stalin set one of the nation's greatest aeronautical engineers, Andrei

Tupolev (1888–1972), to work on the world's largest airplane. The *Maxim Gorky* featured eight engines and a wingspan longer than that of a Boeing 747. It was literally a flying billboard, with a lighted sign on the underside of its wings flashing propaganda messages to the world below. The airplane flew with a crew of twenty-three, most of them stewards to serve the forty passengers, a mix of party officials and workers who were being rewarded for performance. While flying a typical publicity junket on May 18, 1935, the airplane was struck by a smaller one flying in formation with it. Forty-nine people died in the crash.

Even so, the Soviets earned their share of records and headlines. By 1938 they held more than sixty altitude and distance marks. The era of the great Russian long-distance flights began in 1936, when Valery Chkalov, "the Russian Lindbergh," and the brothers Georgii and Alexander Baidukov, flew six thousand miles from Moscow across the USSR to Kamchatka on the Pacific in an ANT-25, a specially designed long-distance aircraft. That same year Sigismund Levanevsky and Victor Levchenko flew twelve thousand miles from Los Angeles over Alaska and Siberia and on to Moscow.

In June 1937, three airmen, Chkalov, Baidukov, and navigator Alexander Belyakov flew an ANT-25 from Moscow across the North Pole 5,288 miles to Vancouver, British Columbia. The following month, Stalin dispatched an ANT-25 with another crew of three on a world-record flight from Moscow to San Jacinto, California. The Soviet press announced plans for regular mail service between the United States and the USSR via flights over the pole. On August 12, 1937, Levanesvsky and a five-man crew took off from Moscow with a new four-engine aircraft, bound for California. They disappeared somewhere in the Alaskan wilderness. No trace was ever found.

AMERICANS SELDOM focused on the foreign aviators. Heaven knows, they had plenty of their own. Lindbergh had set the stage for a generation of American pilots, men and women, who quickly joined him in the headlines.

In just nine short years, Amelia Mary Earhart (1897–1937) became

Amelia Earhart

as famous as Lindbergh. A native of Atchison, Kansas, she was the eldest of two daughters born into a loving, if dysfunctional, family, and a fearless risk taker from her earliest years. After attending a series of finishing schools and universities, and working for a time as a nurse, Earhart took flying lessons from California pilot Neta Snook and soloed in 1921. Over the next few years she flew when she could, while working as a social worker in a Boston settlement house. The turning point came in 1928, when Mrs. Amy Guest, a wealthy aviation enthusiast, and publisher George Palmer Putnam selected her to join aviators Louis Gordon and Wilmer Stultz for a flight across the Atlantic on June 17.

Earhart was basically a passenger aboard the Fokker trimotor *Friendship*. But that didn't matter. The public was as drawn to the tall young woman with the tousled hair as they had been to Lindbergh. Using her fame well, she helped to organize the first Women's Air Derby in 1929.

Nineteen contestants would race from Los Angeles to Cleveland. One of them was eighteen-year-old Elinor Smith, already an experienced pilot with a transport license. In a burst of high spirits, she had once flown under four East River bridges. The feat earned Smith a fifteen-day suspension of her license and the title "Flying Flapper." Florence "Pancho" Barnes, the granddaughter of Civil War balloonist T. S. C. Lowe, was a one-time socialite turned rough-edged movie-stunt pilot. Marvel Crosson had flown in the Alaskan bush; Alabama-born Ruth Elder earned her living as an actress. Other contestants hailed from points as distant as Germany and Australia.

Amelia Earhart did not win what Will Rogers dubbed "the powder puff derby." That honor went to Louise Thaden, a mother of three who demonstrated Travel Air and Beech airplanes. Seven years later, she and her copilot Blanche Noyes became the first women to win the cross-country Bendix Trophy, flying a Beech C 17R Staggerwing.

Whatever other women might achieve in the sky, Amelia Earhart remained the favorite. She set a series of women's records in 1930, and, with the assistance of George Putnam, whom she married in 1931, acquired a candy apple–colored Vega that she dubbed her "little red bus." In this airplane she became the first woman (and second human) to solo the Atlantic and the first woman to fly coast to coast nonstop, accomplishing both feats in 1932.

In 1935 she made the first flight from Honolulu to Oakland in another Vega. Two years later, she and her navigator, a Pan American Airways veteran named Fred Noonan, disappeared somewhere between Lae, New Guinea, and Howland Island in the Pacific while attempting to circumnavigate the globe in a twin-engine Lockheed 10E. She had celebrated her fortieth birthday just five days before. A tireless worker for the right of women to pursue their dreams, Earhart remains one of most famous and admired women of the twentieth century.

Then there was Wiley Post (1899–1935), a Texas roustabout who had spent time in a reformatory for armed robbery and bought his first airplane, a Canuck, with disability payments he received after losing an eye in an oil field accident. He would earn fame flying *Winnie Mae of Oklahoma*, a lovely blue and white Vega that oilman F. C. Hall had bought as a business airplane and named after his daughter. With Hall's permission (and funding), in 1931 Post flew *Winnie Mae* around the globe with navigator Harold Gatty. In 1933 he did it a second time by himself, and in 1934–1935 went on to probe the substratosphere clad in a pressure suit of his own design. He died later in 1935, with humorist Will Rogers, in the crash of a hybrid Lockheed Orion at Point Barrow, Alaska.

In 1932 a young Texan, Jimmy Mattern, flying with Bennett Griffin, attempted to beat Post and Gatty's time around the world, only to wind up with their Vega, *Century of Progress*, upside-down in a Siberian bog. Mattern's 1933 solo attempt ended with engine failure and another crash landing in Siberia. In spite of a broken ankle, Mattern made his way to a native settlement, and from there to civilization.

Not long after leaving the Army Air Corps, Mattern had done some stunt flying for another young Texan, Howard Robard Hughes Jr. (1905–1976), who spared no expense to capture stunning images of mock aerial combat for his film *Hell's Angels* (1930). Nine years later, Hughes would end fifteen years of around-the-world flights by circumnavigating the earth in the twin-engine Lockheed Super Electra named *New York World's Fair 1939.*

Heir to an enormous fortune based on a patented oil drilling bit, "Sonny" Hughes was seventeen years old and stood six feet, three inches tall when his mother died. He attended seven schools and graduated from none. His father died when Hughes was nineteen years old and studying at Rice Institute. The young man stormed Hollywood and then sought to make his mark on aviation. Having taken flying lessons as a teenager, he signed on as a Transcontinental and Western Airline copilot under an assumed name in 1932 and remained on the job for two months.

Over the next few years, Hughes bought several airplanes and modified them. Working with a young Caltech engineer named Richard Palmer, he designed his masterpiece, the Hughes H-1. Unveiled in 1935, the sleek monoplane with the huge radial engine and counter-sunk rivets looked like a stainless-steel sculpture. That year he set a new world speed record of 352.338 mph. Two years later Hughes established a new transcontinental record, averaging 327.148 mph in the H-1 and won the Harman Trophy as outstanding airman of the year. Hughes's best efforts to market his airplane to the military came to naught, although he did demonstrate the potential of radical streamlining and attention to aerodynamic detail. Clearly, the Hughes H-1 should be close to the top of any list of most beautiful and efficient airplanes of the era.

Hughes's around-the-world flight in 1938 symbolized an achievement of a very different sort. He did it in a Lockheed 14 Super Electra, perhaps the fastest airliner in the world at the time of its introduction in 1937. Designed by Hal Hibbard and the legendary Clarence Leonard "Kelly" Johnson, it was intended to compete with the Douglas DC-3 and DST (Douglas Sleeper Transport) aircraft that were dominating the world's airways. The Super Electra seated only fourteen passengers, or ten with a galley and flight attendant. While smaller and less cost-effective than the DC-3, the Super Electra, with its exceptional cruising speed, was widely used on long-distance foreign air routes with lighter traffic.

Howard Hughes's Super Electra Model 14N was fitted with extra fuel tanks in the fuselage and wings, as well as flotation gear and the most up-to-date radio and navigation equipment. The crew of five took off from New York's Floyd Bennett Field on July 10, 1938, and returned on July 14, having touched down at Paris, Moscow, Omsk, Yakutsk, Fairbanks, and Minneapolis. They covered 14,672 miles in just ninety-one hours and fourteen minutes of flying time. Hughes set an around-the-world record in a modern airliner. That was his point. It was the most appropriate way in which to end the era of long-distance flights, by pointing to the day when millions of airline passengers would fly trails in the sky blazed by the pioneers.

. . . AND FASTER

For most of the twentieth century, speed defined the cutting edge of flight technology. On September 17, 1920, the Italian naval aviator Luigi Bologna won the first postwar Schneider Trophy race with a speed of 105.971 mph. Fourteen years later, on October 23, 1934, another Italian military pilot flew the Macchi-Castoldi 72, the last of the great floatplanes designed to win the Schneider Trophy, to a speed of over 440 mph. That record, at least 100 mph faster than the best land plane of the day, would stand for over four years, until an early model of a new generation of fighter aircraft would break it. Even so, the Macchi-Castoldi 72 remains today the fastest piston-powered seaplane ever flown.

During the period 1920–1934, the official world speed mark was raised thirty-five times. Schneider Trophy racers or variants of machines that entered the race set thirty of those records. The trophy itself, a lovely silver concoction topped by a winged fairy dipping to kiss figures rising from breaking waves, was known as "the Flying Flirt." It went to the victor of a great annual tournament where nations vied for prestige. The competition was a serious matter, one on which the United States, Great Britain, and Italy would expend considerable sums and establish special handpicked units, such as the Royal Air Force (RAF) High Speed Flight.

The United States won it twice (1923, 1925) during the postwar years. Italy emerged victorious on three occasions (1920, 1921, 1926), and Great Britain won four races (1922, 1927, 1929, 1931). So great was the sense of national pride in the Schneider Trophy that when the British government decided that it could not afford to defend its title in the 1931 competition, Lady Lucy Houston donated $453,000 to the cause. "Every Briton would rather sell his last shirt," she remarked, "than admit that England cannot afford to defend herself."[1]

Flight Lieutenant John Boothman's victory that year marked the third consecutive British win, and the retirement of the trophy. Lady Houston's money had been well spent. The Italians would continue to build a few very-high-performance floatplanes of the Schneider type, but an era had ended.

The Schneider Trophy, and a handful of other international competitions involving specially designed high-speed military aircraft, had a considerable impact on flight technology. Aircraft entered in the competitions were the ultimate airplanes of their generation, powered by the ultimate engines.

The in-line Curtiss D-12 engine, with its small frontal area and extraordinary power-to-weight ratio, established an entirely new design tradition. Introduced by engineer Dr. Arthur Nutt to power the Curtiss R-6 at the 1922 Pulitzer Race, it was the critical first step in a long line of high-compression water-cooled engines that would power some of the finest Allied aircraft of World War II.

Since World War I, almost without exception, the British had preferred air-cooled rotary or radial engines for their fighters. The example of the D-12, and the experience of the Schneider Trophy, would change all of that. In the mid-1920s, the Fairey Aviation Company purchased the right to build the D-12 under license. Sir Henry Royce studied the American design and produced the Kestrel, the starting point of a critically important family of engines.

The Rolls-Royce R series engines powered the Schneider Trophy–winning S.6 produced by Supermarine Aviation Works. Forty years after he produced the D-12, Dr. Nutt was placed in charge of producing the Rolls-Royce–designed Merlin engine at Packard. The grandson of his original D-12, or the grandnephew at least, it was the engine that would power the Hurricane, Spitfire, and P-51 Mustang as well as the Whitworth and Lancaster bombers.

The impact of the Schneider Trophy on basic aircraft design was nowhere more apparent than in the work of Englishman Reginald Joseph Mitchell. Like Jack Northrop and a handful of others, Mitchell had no formal engineering training. Rather, he was the son of a printer who served his apprenticeship at a locomotive works. Noel Pemberton-Billing, the controversial head of Supermarine, hired the young man as his personal assistant. By 1920, at age twenty-five, Mitchell had risen to the position of chief engineer. Over the next three years the company produced twelve new types of flying boats.

Mitchell had produced the Sea Lion I, II, and III flying boats as entries in the 1919, 1922, and 1923 Schneider races. Sea Lion II won the 1922 contest. Stunned by the 1923 victory of a Curtiss floatplane, Mitchell broke Supermarine tradition and designed the revolutionary S.4 to compete in the 1925 race. Mounted on floats, the beautiful new monoplane had clean lines and a completely cantilevered wing. The S.4 set a new world speed mark during flight testing but crashed prior to the race. Better things were to come. The S.5 did win the trophy (in 1927), as did the S.6 (in 1929), and the S.6B (in 1931).

Just five years after final victory in the Schneider Trophy, on March 5, 1936, the prototype Spitfire took to the sky for the first time. It was Mitchell's masterpiece and the ultimate demonstration of the value of high-profile international air racing during the years between the wars.

SEPTEMBER CHAMPIONS

A very different sort of civilian air racing captured headlines in America during the 1930s. Each fall, aviation enthusiasts turned to Cleveland, Ohio, and the National Air Races, Clifford Henderson's annual spectacle. Shortly after returning from wartime service in France, and determined to become involved in aviation, Henderson purchased three surplus Jennies, traded one for flying lessons, and offered anyone who purchased an automobile from his dealership a free airplane ride.

The National Aeronautic Association had begun to organize National Air Races around the annual Pulitzer Race for high-performance military aircraft in 1923. With the cancellation of the Pulitzer Race in 1925, however, the public lost interest in the annual event. Having managed to rekindle interest when they hosted the event in Los Angeles in 1928, promoter Clifford Henderson and his businessman brother Phillip were invited to plan the 1929 races in Cleveland.

Henderson, a born promoter, set out to attract the best-known aviators and aircraft to the National Air Races. He arranged for the first Women's Air Derby to end in Cleveland during the races. Both the U.S. Navy "High Hats" and the Canadian exhibition team provided daily thrills. Charles "Speed" Holman, of Northwest Airlines, looped and rolled a Ford Tri-motor while the great airship *Los Angeles* and the ZMC-2, a Navy airship with an envelope made of thin sheets of aluminum, cruised overhead.

The races climaxed on the final day with a new closed-course contest that the Henderson brothers hoped would replace the defunct Pulitzer Race. Victory went to Doug Davis, flying the *Mystery Ship*, a red and black monoplane produced by Walter Beech's Travel Air Company. The National Air Races proved such a success that the

Henderson brothers would continue to promote the event for the next decade.

Convinced that an annual competition would guarantee the success of the National Air Races, the Henderson brothers persuaded Charles Thompson, president of Thompson Aviation Corporation, to fund a Thompson Trophy (1930–1939), which would go to the winner of an annual fifty-mile closed-course free-for-all scramble around a set of pylons standing fifty feet tall. The following year, Vincent Bendix, an automotive and aeronautical parts manufacturer, established a new Bendix Trophy (1931–1939) to be awarded to the winner of an annual race from the West Coast to the National Air Races in Cleveland.

To be sure, a closed-course racer and an aircraft intended to fly across the continent at top speed would be quite different machines. Even so, both contests would be the preserve of a little band of small-scale aircraft designers and builders. Airplanes built by James Weddell, a one-eyed Texan, captured two Thompson (1933, 1934) and three Bendix Trophies (1932, 1933, 1934). Emil M. "Mattie" Laird, who had been flying before World War I, did almost as well. His airplanes captured three Thompson Trophies (1930, 1938, 1939) and won one Bendix race (1931).

Although the legendary Gee Bee racers, built by New Hampshire–born Zantford D. "Granny" Granville and his brothers, couldn't fly across the country, they did earn two Thompson Trophy victories (1931, 1932). And Benny Howard did well, taking the 1935 Bendix in his *Mister Mulligan*, the same airplane in which Harold Neumann captured that year's Thompson Trophy.

Danger played a big part in the race excitement. Captain Arthur Page, a Marine flying a highly modified Curtiss Hawk, died of injuries sustained in the 1930 Thompson race. Charles Holman won that race in the Laird Solution, and Lowell Bayles won the 1931 race in a Gee Bee; both died in racing accidents within a few months after their Thompson Trophy victories. Jimmy Weddell, the 1933 winner, lost his life the following year.

The men and women who flew those airplanes emerged as some of the best-known figures of their generation. Roscoe Turner was the most winning aviator of the era. Flamboyant and larger than life, with a sweeping mustache, winning smile, and military uniform of his own design, he captured one Bendix Trophy (1934) and three Thompson Trophies (1934, 1938, 1939). Jimmy Doolittle and Doug Davis each won one closed-course race and one Bendix Trophy. Doolittle was the only pilot to win the triple crown of air racing—the Schneider, Bendix, and Thompson Trophies.

Louise Thaden's 1936 Bendix victory flying a stock Beech C17R marked the beginning of the end for the golden age of air racing in America. The final three prewar Bendix races would be won by a prototype fighter, the Seversky SEV-S2. Two of those victories went to Frank Fuller (1937, 1939) and one to Jacqueline Cochran (1939). Production airplanes were now flying faster than specialized racing aircraft.

The Schneider Trophy's founder envisioned an international competition that would foster the advance of technology—and he got it. The Thompson and Bendix races, on the other hand, provided almost pure entertainment. True, they created a new generation of American heroes. Just as surely, many industry leaders feared that the Thompson Trophy race had given aviation a bad name.

Both the Bendix and the Thompson Trophy classics were resuscitated after World War II, but the races had changed. Postwar entries included either refurbished wartime fighters or contemporary military aircraft bent on setting new records and generating headlines. While closed-course air racing remains a popular spectator sport in the early years of the twenty-first century, it can scarcely be distinguished from aerial stock-car racing.

GIANTS IN THE SKY

The rigid airship emerged from World War I with a mixed record. These long, thin structures had always been a compromise between minimum weight and sufficient strength. Early in World War I, when the Zeppelins proved vulnerable to antiaircraft fire and fighters, German designers began to pare down both the structural weight and the strength of their airships so that they could climb to higher altitudes. As a result, the most advanced German airships, the aircraft that served as the models for postwar Allied designs, were structurally much weaker than the original Zeppelins, with tragic consequences.

The L 72, turned over to the French as war reparations and renamed the *Dixmunde*, suffered a catastrophic structural failure on December 21, 1923, and fell burning into the Mediterranean, killing all fifty crew members. The British airship R 38, based on the wartime L 70 class and destined for transfer to the U.S. Navy, broke up in the air and fell into the Humber River on August 21, 1921. Forty-four of its forty-nine crew members died. Her Majesty's Airship R 80, designed by Vickers engineer Barnes N. Wallis, suffered a near-catastrophic structural failure during her first flight, on September 21, 1921.

ZR-1 *Shenandoah*, the first rigid airship commissioned by the U.S. Navy, was heavily influenced by the design of Germany's L 49. Constructed at the Philadelphia Navy Yard under the supervision of Jerome Hunsaker, *Shenandoah* was principally employed in testing mooring equipment and the development of operational procedures. It also served as a gigantic recruiting poster in the sky. Early on the morning of September 3, 1925, however, a violent storm literally tore it in half while on its way to a publicity appearance. It fell to earth in Noble County, Ohio. Commander Zachary Lansdowne died along with fourteen of his forty-three crew members.

If there were disasters aplenty, the airship still offered the only practical means of moving freight and passengers through the air over intercontinental distances. Or so it seemed to British officials eager to forge aerial links to the far corners of the Empire. In May 1924, Ramsay MacDonald's Labor Government rejected plans to contract with Vickers to build and operate airships over routes to India and Australia. Instead, the prime minister created a unique public-private experiment.

Vickers represented private industry; the government owned and operated the Royal Airship Works at Cardington. Each would design and build one rigid airship. The performance of the two airships might point toward the future of the society and the economy.

The Imperial Airship program was enormously ambitious and fraught with technical challenges. The two airships would be huge, far larger than their German contemporary, *Graf Zeppelin*. The government airship, R 101, first flown two years behind schedule on October 14, 1929, was 731 feet, 3 inches long and had a maximum diameter of 131 feet, 6 inches. Built primarily of steel (accounting for 60 percent of the frame), the airship had a distinctive streamlined shape. Pride in the product of British technology led to extravagant claims as to the range and carrying capacity of the R 101.

On October 4, 1930, after only a single seventeen-hour test flight in her final configuration, the R 101 set out on a highly publicized aerial journey to India. This feat, it was hoped, would mark the inauguration of a new era in intercontinental transportation. The passenger list included Lord Thomson, head of the Air Ministry; Sir Sefton Brancker, director of civil aviation; R. B. B. Colmore, government director of airship development; and Vincent C. Richmond, chief designer. A few hours later, early on the morning of October 5, they and forty-four others died when the airship struck a hillside near Beauvais, France, and burned. No definitive cause was ever established for the disaster, although bad weather was certainly a factor.

The Vickers airship, R 100, first flown two days after R 101, was a far better aircraft. The chief designer, Barnes Wallis, the most experienced airship designer outside Germany, headed a talented engineering team that included the novelist-engineer Nevil Shute Norway. The airship completed a fully successful round-trip flight to Canada in July–August 1930, only to be grounded and broken up following the disaster of the R 101. So ended the British airship program of 1924, a victim of politics quite as much as technical shortcomings.

From the beginning to the end, the Germans mastered the rigid airship. At the end of World War I, the various Zeppelin companies employed 22,800 workers at five major factories. The Treaty of Versailles banned construction of military airships, but Dr. Hugo Eckner, who replaced Alfred Colsman as principal director of the company, ordered the completion of two examples of two new-generation civilian Zeppelins. Ultimately, the Allies insisted that Germany turn those two airships over to France and Italy as reparations.

With the company facing disaster, Eckner approached U.S. Navy officials who wanted to gain experience with lighter-than-air craft.

The result, LZ 126, first flew on August 27, 1924. The sale of the new airship, renamed USS *Los Angeles*, saved the Zeppelin company from financial ruin. It also became one of the most successful of all lighter-than-air craft, outliving any other rigid airship. *Los Angeles* enabled naval aviators to gain experience in handling and operating a big rigid airship and to explore the military role of such an aircraft. The airship would log some 4,180 hours during her fifteen-year career, and was finally broken up in October 1939.

Advocates extolled the virtues of the big rigid airships for fleet reconnaissance, but how could the largest, slowest, most vulnerable aircraft in the sky dodge in and out of the clouds while searching for the enemy? The answer, enthusiasts suggested, might lie in a special "trapeze bar" fitted to the *Los Angeles*, enabling an airplane to be launched and retrieved in flight. Naval planners began to consider the rigid airship as a "flying aircraft carrier," that could remain hidden from the enemy while the faster and more agile fighter airplanes could be launched, conduct scouting or attack missions, and come back aboard the airship.

William A. Moffett

Early aerial hook-on experiments conducted with *Los Angeles* worked well and led to initial plans to build two larger airships that would launch and retrieve Curtiss F9C-2 Sparrowhawk fighters specifically designed to operate from a flying aircraft carrier. Following the purchase of the LZ 126, the Goodyear company partnered with the Zeppelin firm, creating the Goodyear-Zeppelin Corporation, head-quartered in Akron, Ohio. Dr. Karl Arnstein, who had joined Luftschiffbau Zeppelin in 1915, emigrated to the United States in 1924 to head the Goodyear-Zeppelin design team.

In October 1928, the new firm contracted with the U.S. Navy for the design and construction of two new airships: USS *Akron* (ZRS 4) and USS *Macon* (ZRS 5). Capable of flying at 83 mph, they were the fastest rigid airships ever built. *Akron*, first flown on September 25, 1931, went down at sea during a storm off the coast of New Jersey on April 4, 1933, killing all but three of the seventy-six souls aboard. The dead included Adm. William A. Moffett, three-time chief of the Bureau of Aeronautics, the architect of naval aviation, and the navy's most important supporter of the rigid airship.

The USS *Macon* flew for the first time on April 21, 1933, just two and one-half weeks after her sister ship's demise. She was destroyed, in

LZ 127 Graf Zeppelin

turn, by severe turbulence off the California coast on February 12, 1935. Fortunately, only two of the eighty-three crewmen died in the accident. While nonrigid pressure airships would continue in service with the U.S. Navy until 1962, performing antisubmarine patrols and electronic surveillance, the age of the American rigid airship was at an end.

The sale of LZ 126 and the partnership with Goodyear breathed new life into the Zeppelin Company. Things looked even brighter after 1925, when the Treaty of Lucarno lifted Allied restrictions on airship production. Hugo Eckner immediately launched a public subscription to fund a new commercial airship. Between depression-era public contributions and German government funding, work began on LZ 127, *Graf Zeppelin*, early in 1927. The finished product measured 775 feet in length and 100 feet in diameter. It was unique among rigid airships. The five Maybach engines propelling the craft burned *blaugas*, a mixture of combustible gases only slightly heavier than air and far lighter than gasoline or diesel fuel.

Over a nine-year career, this most successful of all Zeppelins would spend 17,178 hours in the air during almost six hundred flights. In the summer of 1929, *Graf Zeppelin* flew around the world in twenty-one days, seven hours, and thirty-four minutes, including a nonstop flight across Siberia. The airship flew the North Atlantic on several occasions and offered regularly scheduled passenger service across the South Atlantic between 1932 and 1937.

LZ 128 was to have been a slightly larger version of the *Graf*, but the destruction of the British R 101 in 1930 led Eckner and his colleagues to scrap their plans. Instead, they began work on an even larger airship that would be inflated with helium, rather than inflammable hydrogen, and powered by diesel engines, which burned fuel oil, far safer than either gasoline or *blaugas*. At the time, the United States had a monopoly on the world's supply of helium, produced by a handful of wells in the American Southwest. All U.S. airships had flown with helium. They had crashed, but they had not burned.

Fearing that the United States would reject a request for the sale of helium, however, the German government did not raise the issue. The new airship, *Hindenburg* (LZ 129), would fly with hydrogen. The most luxurious aerial vehicle of the era, *Hindenburg* was designed to convey forty crew members and seventy-two paying passengers across the Atlantic in style. With a speed to match the American *Akron* and *Macon*, LZ 129 offered regular service across both the North and the South Atlantic during the 1936 season.

In one of the century's great aerial catastrophes, *Hindenburg* caught fire and burned while approaching the mooring mast at U.S. Naval Air Station Lakehurst in New Jersey on the evening of May 6, 1937, just one year and two days after her first flight. Of the ninety-seven people on board, thirty-five, including thirteen paying passengers, lost their lives. Captain Ernst Lehmann, who had survived the Zeppelin campaign of World War I, would succumb to his injuries. One member of the ground crew also lost his life.

Why did the *Hindenburg* burn? There is little evidence to support the rumors of sabotage. Given the fact that the craft carried 232,000 kilograms of hydrogen, no detailed explanation seems necessary. A slightly torn gas cell coupled with some form of simple static discharge would have been sufficient. The *Hindenburg*'s fabric had been treated with a new and more combustible dope than what had been employed on earlier airships. It could have been the ignition source.

The Zeppelin Company built one more rigid airship—*Graf Zeppelin II* (LZ 130)—in 1938. It probed British radar defenses during the early months of World War II and was broken up in May 1940. The story of the rigid airship illustrates the role of transitional technologies that flourish until more appropriate means of performing a task reach fruition. It was no accident that the era of the airship closed just as large flying boats proved capable of linking the continents.

And there is no better example of the role of enthusiasm in the history of technology. The Zeppelins inspired deep affection and loyalty among those who built and flew these ships of the sky, and a sense of awe and enthusiasm among the public. The sight of aircraft seven football fields long cruising majestically across the sky at an altitude of a thousand feet and a speed of less than 100 mph was never to be forgotten. At the end of the twentieth century, the desire to find an economic niche that would justify the construction of a new generation of rigid airships remained very much alive.

AN AIRPLANE FOR EVERYONE

Between the wars, the airplane began to fill a number of new economic niches. As the barnstormers of 1919 became the fixed-base flying services of 1927, farsighted American businessmen began to see aviation as good for business. That year, thirty-four nonaeronautical corporations reported employing airplanes for business purposes. Aircraft operated by the top-fifteen companies logged 197,858 miles of flying, carrying 560 company executives and guests.

The A.W. Shaw Company of Chicago, for example, bought a six-place Stinson cabin monoplane in 1926 to ferry its executives about. During its first year of operation, the Shaw airplane logged over twelve thousand miles. The Continental Motor Company's Ford Tri-motor traveled over ten thousand miles shuttling personnel and parts between company facilities in Detroit and Muskegon, Michigan. Standard Oil of Indiana executives were airborne in 1926, as were the leaders of Phillips Petroleum. Ford entered aeronautics by establishing a company airline. During 1928, Ford Company airplanes completed an astounding 1,009 flights, covering 278,949 air miles between various company facilities. Company freight carried on these flights totaled 1,663,120 pounds.

The Richfield Oil Company operated Fokker, Stearman, and Waco aircraft as executive transports. These airplanes were also placed at the disposal of the governors of California, Washington, and Oregon for the entertainment of distinguished guests. Some forty-two firms owned airplanes by 1928, including B.F. Goodrich, Parker Pen, Anheuser-Busch, Continental Motors, Firestone Tire and Rubber, Jell-O, Pittsburgh Plate Glass, Remington, Royal Typewriter, Walgreen Drug Stores, Cleveland Pneumatic Tool Company, and National Lead Battery Company.

During 1929 the number of business firms known to own at least one airplane climbed sharply to 148. One-third of the airplanes built in

America that year were sold for business use. A 1930 survey uncovered three hundred business firms operating airplanes. Oil companies led the field.[2]

Clearly, this boom in business flying represented a major market for aircraft manufacturers. Seeking to increase these sales, aircraft advertising emphasized safety, comfort, and speed, factors that would appeal to potential business flyers. Companies like Mahoney-Ryan, Travel Air, Stearman, Fairchild, and Advance Aircraft established franchises and distributorships. While many of these distributors also functioned as fixed-base operators, offering a variety of flying services, a substantial portion of their income resulted from aircraft sales to local businesses.

The Great Depression and the growth of the airlines slowed the initial boom in business aircraft sales, but the market remained an important one. At least thirty-eight of the four hundred Beech Model GB 17 Staggerwing airplanes produced between 1932 and 1939 were sold as business airplanes. The twin-engine Beech 18, which remained in production for thirty-three years, longer than any other airplane, became one of the most popular business aircraft ever produced.

PRIVATE FLYING also was on the rise around the globe following World War I. In England, established aeronautical firms, including De Havilland, Shorts, Parnall, Hawker, and Avro, marketed one- and two-place machines powered by converted motorcycle engines or specially developed lightweight power plants like the thirty-two-horsepower Bristol Cherub.

Flying clubs offered inexpensive flight instruction while sharing the cost of airplane ownership and maintenance. Amy Johnson, the British heroine of the air during these years, was a graduate of the club movement. His Majesty's government, sensing the value of the movement to aircraft manufacturers, and recognizing the importance of building a reserve of potential military pilots, encouraged the growth of private flying.

Sport aviation in Germany, where the manufacture of large aircraft was forbidden, followed a similar course. The first aircraft designed by

Willy Messerschmitt was a light sport airplane. The soaring movement provided Germans with a way to escape the restrictions of the Treaty of Versailles. The generation of pilots who would make up the Luftwaffe earned their wings flying gliders designed by men like Alexander M. Lippisch, who would pioneer the pattern for the swept-wing rocket- and jet-propelled aircraft that marked a new era in aviation.

The first great season-long glider meet took place near Mt. Wasser-kuppe in the Rhön Mountains of central Germany, July–September 1920. Wolfgang Klemperer set the record that year, covering 1.3 miles in two minutes, twenty-two seconds. Not until September 1921 did a glider pilot stay aloft for over twelve minutes, finally beating the record of nine minutes, forty-five seconds set by Orville Wright, the pilot who invented soaring in 1911. By 1931, though, the pioneers of soaring had discovered rising columns of air known as *thermals*. Immediately, they extended their time in the air to hours, rather than minutes.

By the mid-1920s, the soaring movement had spread across Europe. The value of the sport as a means of training pilots and inspir- ing new work in aerodynamics was apparent. "Forced to design within arbitrary limits," remarked the editor of the American *Aircraft Yearbook* in 1923, "the [Germans] have, in the opinion of some, been aided rather than handicapped."[3]

Soaring came to America in 1928 when three German pilots demonstrated their gliders from Corn Hill, near Provincetown, Massachusetts. Companies like Fairchild, Bellanca, and Stout quickly supported the new activity. Hawley Bowlus, who, as an employee of Ryan, had helped to build the *Spirit of St. Louis*, pioneered soaring on the West Coast. Wolfgang Klemperer emigrated to the United States to work with Goodyear-Zeppelin and helped to establish a glider launch site on the top of Harris Hill, overlooking Elmira, New York, which he pronounced "the Wasserkuppe of America."

If soaring thrived—and continues to thrive—the European flying- club movement never took root in the United States. The expense of learning to fly and the cost of owning an airplane limited the growth of private flying. Consequently, the image of the private pilot was that of a wealthy man who could afford to pursue flying as a sport. The aerial country-club movement, organized in 1929, supported such a view.

Clubhouse facilities would cater to the very rich; flying would replace golf, tennis, and polo.

The few airplane manufacturers who did hope for private sales during the 1920s aimed their advertising at this group. In 1929 the editors of *Country Life*, seeking to attract advertising from aircraft manufacturers, provided a "Portrait of a Prospect for a Private Plane."

This hypothetical customer, naturally a reader of *Country Life*, owned a Park Avenue penthouse, a summer place in the Berkshires, and a ranch in Wyoming. He "goes South" after Christmas, slips off to his gun club on the Eastern Shore in the fall, and takes a party "north of Rangely" for trout fishing every spring. His eldest son, now in his last year at Yale, is eager to purchase "a sport amphibian for the jolly crowd he travels with." This is the fellow, argued the editors, who would purchase a private plane to supplement his yacht and three cars. Obviously, the market for private airplanes would remain tiny until it could include less affluent customers.[4]

With the disappearance of inexpensive war-surplus aircraft by 1925, home-built airplanes seemed to offer an alternative for the pilot with an average income. Plans and kits for airplanes that could be powered by converted automobile or motorcycle engines were on the market. By 1930 scores of amateur-built Heath Parasols (the original Heathkit), Swallow Sports, and Pietenpol Air Campers took to the skies over small airports across the nation.

Often based very loosely on the original drawings, many of these home-built airplanes were dangerous and very difficult to fly. Consider the Pou du Ciel, or Flying Flea, a design imported from France in 1935. Hailed by its promoters as a "foolproof" airplane, simple to build, and easy to fly, the Flea actually proved to be a poorly engineered craft that carried many novice pilots in England and America to their deaths.

The Great Depression dashed the hopes of many manufacturers who dreamed of an enormous post-Lindbergh market for private aircraft. Even so, a number of firms continued to believe in a lightweight, easy-to-fly airplane for the general public. The Aeronautical Corporation of America (Aeronca) opened the field with its C-2, first marketed in 1929. Priced at $1,495, the C-2 was a single-seat ultralight plane powered by an Aeronca-built motor generating twenty-six to twenty-nine horsepower. The new firm had built and sold 164 airplanes by the end of 1931.

Encouraged by Aeronca's success, other firms began offering light planes at under $2,000 after 1930. American Eagle, Alexander, Curtiss-Wright, Welch, Rearwin, Porterfield, Taylorcraft, Piper, and others all sought a share of the limited market. By September 1939, the Civil Aeronautics Authority (CAA) listed 7,412 airplanes seating five persons or less being flown in the United States. Thirteen manufacturers were in the business of producing such planes:[5]

Aeronca	853
Beech	163
Cessna	114
Stinson	779
Curtiss-Wright	741
Fairchild	567
Fleet	191
Luscombe	61
Piper	1,658
Rearwin	170
Taylorcraft	623
Monocoupe	293
Waco	1,050
Total	**7,412**

Moreover, CAA officials indicated that 80 percent of these airplanes were two-place, closed-cabin, high-wing monoplanes powered by a single engine producing from fifty to one hundred horsepower. These figures indicate the enormous growth of that segment of the general-aviation industry devoted to the production of light airplanes during the decade following the introduction of the Aeronca C-2.

The small private airplanes of the 1930s were remarkably similar. Typically, a light plane of the period featured a thirty-five-foot wingspan and weighed from 1,100 to 1,300 pounds. It could cruise at 50 to 80 mph and a ceiling of 12,000 to 16,000 feet. Almost all aircraft in this class were priced in the $1,500 to $2,500 range.

The Piper Aircraft Company of Lock Haven, Pennsylvania, led the pack by 1939. William Piper, founder of the firm, was originally drawn into aircraft manufacturing by C. Gilbert Taylor in 1929. Taylor at that time was producing the E-2 "Cub." Dissatisfied with the arrangement, Piper dissolved the relationship and founded the Piper Aircraft Company in 1937. The fully developed Piper J-3 Cub, which first appeared in 1937, became one of the most popular airplanes ever produced.

Like other manufacturers, Piper struggled through the lean years of the mid-1930s by selling to private pilots and flying schools. As early as 1937 Piper claimed to have built 31.8 percent of all American commercial aircraft produced that year. A major market expansion followed establishment of the government Civilian Pilot Training Program in 1939. Between 1939 and 1941, the firm constructed 8,020 airplanes, most of them Cub variants used to train fledgling military pilots. By the beginning of World War II, when production of private aircraft was halted, the light-plane industry could look back on a decade of growth and forward to the return of thousands of veterans eager to continue flying as civilians.

New light aircraft had come a long way, but flying remained an expensive enterprise for the private pilot. With $1,500 price tag, it soared above that of a yacht. Maintenance costs might run $8 an hour for a Piper Cub flown 150 hours a year. Such expense discouraged airplane ownership. A 1941 CAA survey revealed that fifteen thousand airplane owners had registered with the agency between 1931 and 1936. Interestingly, in that period only five thousand new airplanes were produced. One-third of those surveyed had been forced to sell their airplanes within the first year of ownership and did not purchase another. Eighty-three percent abandoned ownership within two and one-half years.

While most industry leaders expressed satisfaction with the growth of private flying, some enthusiasts were convinced that light aircraft could ultimately be mass-produced and marketed on a scale comparable to that of the automobile. They dreamed of a very light, cheap machine that could be flown with absolute safety after minimum instruction. Such a craft, priced at current automobile levels of $500 to $1,000, would guarantee "an airplane in every garage."

Eugene L. Vidal, a West Point football hero and friend of Amelia Earhart, was the most vocal public advocate for a radically new type of safe and inexpensive airplane. Appointed director of the Aeronautics Branch of the Department of Commerce in September 1933, Vidal served as President Roosevelt's ambassador to the aeronautical community. He proposed a "New Deal for Aviation." In his view, the government should assist the recovery of the aviation industry by subsidizing the development of the "Poor Man's Airplane."

First Vidal had to demonstrate that a market did exist. In November 1933 he mailed questionnaires to thirty-four thousand pilots, mechanics, and student flyers. Would they be willing to purchase a hypothetical low-wing, all-metal monoplane with a maximum speed of 100 mph, a landing speed of 25 mph, and a retail price between $700 and $1,000? At the same time he queried airplane manufacturers. Could they produce such a machine given automotive-style mass-production techniques and a guaranteed market for ten thousand airplanes.

Working with the White House, Vidal gained approval for a Public Works Administration grant of $500,000 to assist manufacturers willing to develop the new machine. The plan sparked immediate discussion in aeronautical journals, where Vidal's proposed machine was dubbed the "$700 airplane."

Some eighteen thousand respondents returned the questionnaires by February 1934. Thirteen thousand of them indicated a willingness to purchase the airplane described. The industry reacted very differently, however. Most firms expressed no interest or open hostility to the program. Aircraft manufacturers saw the Vidal plan as an attempt by inexperienced bureaucrats to circumvent the normal operation of the market. The "Poor Man's Airplane," they believed, was an impossible pipe dream.

The craft Vidal envisioned would require an impossibly low landing speed and a means of preventing stalls and spins in the hands of a novice. These requirements would price the airplane far above the $700 range. Moreover, manufacturers feared that talk of a $700 "dream ship" by federal officials would encourage prospective buyers of standard light planes to postpone their purchase until prices dropped. The resulting controversy convinced Harold Ickes, head of the Public Works Administration, to withdraw the $500,000 grant in March 1934.

Undeterred, Vidal unveiled a new plan to encourage development of an extraordinarily safe, mass-produced light aircraft. In July 1934, he announced a competition for the purchase of twenty-five new airplanes to be used by Bureau of Aeronautics inspectors. Entries were to be two-place, all-metal aircraft with a cruising speed of at least 110 mph and a stalling speed no lower than 35 mph. In order to qualify, a machine had to take off in eight hundred feet, land in half that distance, and demonstrate a range of three hundred miles.

The Department of Commerce eventually purchased four machines. The first, and most significant, of these was the W-1, designed and built by Fred E. Weick, a senior aeronautical engineer at NACA Langley. In 1931, Weick and nine Langley Laboratory associates had launched an informal study aimed at developing a safe airplane for private pilots. The result was the W-1, completed early in 1934. A high-wing, pusher monoplane, the W-1 featured tricycle gear for ease in landing and control on the ground and fixed-wing slats to increase stability and reduce the distance required for take-off and landing.

When Department of Commerce officials learned of the W-1 in January 1934, they sought to encourage Weick's efforts by requesting that NACA conduct wind tunnel studies and flight testing of the aircraft. The 1934 competition requirements were partially based on the outcome of those tests. An engine failure during a W-1 flight test in 1934 led to a forced landing and some damage to the airplane, but under Weick's direction the Fairchild Company rebuilt it. Renamed the W-1A, the craft was purchased by the bureau and returned to NACA for further testing. It was not entered in the competition because there were no plans for producing the aircraft for commercial sale.

The W-1A differed in significant respects from its predecessor. The earlier wing slats were replaced by flaps and midwing slot lip ailerons. A two-control system was also introduced to counter the tendency of student pilots to cross-control the rudder and ailerons. In 1936, Weick resigned his NACA post to accept a position with a firm willing to develop a production model based on the advantages demonstrated in the W-1A. The resulting Ercoupe, introduced in 1940, became an extremely popular airplane. Some six thousand of them were produced before and after World War II.

The three additional aircraft acquired by the Department of Commerce as part of the safe airplane competition clearly indicated a desire to promote a revolutionary flying machine that might rival the automobile as a means of mass transportation. One of the new machines, the Waterman Arrowbile, was a tailless pusher monoplane with swept-back wings, tricycle landing gear, and a two-control system similar to that of the W-1A. Waldo Waterman, designer of the Arrowbile, intended the craft to serve as the first step toward a "road-able airplane," capable of being flown as a plane or driven as a car on the highway. The Department of Commerce paid $12,500 for its Arrowbile but only flew it on special occasions because of its dangerous tendency to stall and spin.

The department also purchased a roadable autogiro. Delivering it in 1937, the pilot landed in a park adjacent to the Commerce building, folded the rotors, disconnected the propeller, and drove to the main entrance. Later he drove the craft to the Mall, where he took off for a short flight to Bolling Field. Though underpowered, the roadable autogiro performed well as a one-man machine. When oil ran low during a flight to Charleston, South Carolina, the pilot was able to land on a highway and drive to a filling station.

The third aircraft purchased was a more conventional Hammond-Stearman Model Y pusher, featuring tricycle landing gear. When it won the competition, the department ordered fifteen of them, although only one was ever delivered. This two-control airplane, in which the operation of the rudder was linked to lateral control, proved easy to fly. Its speed and rate of climb were so low, however, that department officials asked that it be reengineered before purchase.

The Department of Commerce's $700 airplane and competitive purchase programs had little impact on the general-aviation industry, which continued to produce the standard types on the market by 1935. By encouraging experimentation and publicizing new aircraft types, however, Vidal's plans had helped to shape the general public's view of the future of aeronautics, for better or worse.

From the mid-1930s through the early years of the Cold War, the *Popular Mechanics* fantasy of a bright future in which all of us would take to the sky flourished. Sometimes it was a "roadable automobile," sometimes the autogiro, the helicopter, or a radically new design that could be flown by anyone who could drive an automobile. The notion of the airplane in every garage, of flight made so simple and easy that everyone could do it, has been the ultimate dream of the air age. At the beginning of the second century of flight, it remains unrealized.

THE LOOK OF WINGS

Everyone but his wife called him "Bucky." As much as anyone else, Richard Buckminster Fuller (1895–1983) can be seen as proof that the old tradition of Yankee ingenuity continued to flourish in the twentieth century. A grandnephew of the transcendentalist Margaret Fuller, he apprenticed with the Armour Company before World War I and climbed the ladder of corporate success until the mid-1920s, when he became interested in the power of technology to transform daily life.

One of Fuller's first design projects included an automobile with wings, an example, he remarked, of "omni-directional transport." While he would never build the flying car, aircraft technology would play an extraordinarily important role in his thinking over the next half-century. From the teardrop-shaped autos that would drive along his future streets, to aluminum-clad Dymaxion (dynamic maximum efficiency) houses, Fuller envisioned a world constructed of aircraft materials, using techniques developed in the manufacture of aircraft, and shaped by the streamlined principles of efficiency and energy that characterized the air age.

Bucky Fuller was not alone in believing that the values of aeronautical technology would provide a firm foundation for a rational future. Charles-Édouard Jeanneret, Le Corbusier (1887–1965), an iconoclastic Swiss architect who sought to rationalize art and design, saw the airplane as an ideal metaphor for a sensible world in which form expressed function. "The airplane," he wrote, "embodies the purest expression of the human scale and a miraculous exploitation of materials."[6]

Like the shiny aluminum, glass, and rubber of a modern aircraft, Le Corbusier's architecture displayed clean lines and simple structures that reveled in the qualities of his preferred building materials—concrete, metal, and glass. Awarded the contract for the design of the new Brazilian capital of Brasília, two of his disciples developed a city plan roughly shaped like an airplane.

The influence of aviation, however, was not confined to the esoteric realms of the avant-garde. By the mid-1920s the notion that the airplane symbolized honest values for a machine age—speed, efficiency, simplicity of line, and a form that perfectly expressed its function—became embedded in popular culture.

Streamlining had actually begun with W. R. McKeen Jr., who developed a prototype streamlined train for the Union Pacific in 1905. By 1913, sleek vehicles were the order of the day, from airplanes like the Deperdussin monoplane to racing automobiles. The Austro-Hungarian engineer Paul Jaray had begun testing automobile bodies in a wind tunnel as early as 1921. Advertisers quickly took advantage of the link between flying and the automobile. As early as 1929, the Franklin company suggested that the "AIRPLANE FEEL of the Franklin opens the road to new motoring thrills."[7]

Streamlining, however, would not fully emerge as a critically important element of a *style moderne* until the 1933 Century of Progress Exhibition. The great Chicago fair provided a spectacular backdrop for a series of great aeronautical events. Hugo Eckner brought the *Graf Zeppelin* on a much-publicized visit to the Windy City. The arrival of Italo Balbo with a fleet of Savoia-Marchetti flying boats made headlines across the nation. The launch of the *Century of Progress*, the first great American stratosphere balloon, from Soldier's Field was, quite literally, the high point of the exposition.

A new generation of vehicles flowed out of the aeronautical excitement of the world's fair. One of Buckminster Fuller's early model Dymaxion automobiles was on view, along with E. M. Bud's streamlined masterpiece, the *Burlington Zephyr*, the most famous locomotive of the decade.

The Dutch designer John Tjaarda (pronounced "charda") introduced the Briggs Dream Car at the Fair. Tjaarda had trained as an aeronautical engineer and served in the Dutch Air Force before emigrating to the United States in 1923. He worked under the leadership of the famed auto designer Harley Earl at Duesenberg before accepting a post as chief designer for the Briggs Company, Ford's chief body supplier.

Chrysler, which had begun aerodynamic testing as early as 1927, introduced the Chrysler Airflow in 1934. While that streamlined model failed to attract depression-era buyers, the Lincoln Zephyr (1936), an outgrowth of Tjaarda's dream car, proved far more successful, properly launching a new design tradition in automobile styling.

But locomotives and automobiles inspired by the sleek shapes of airplanes and airships were only the beginning. Given the abysmal economic conditions in the nation, manufacturers turned to industrial designers to craft products and packaging that would appeal to consumers. These new professionals were drawn from neighboring fields. French-born Raymond F. Loewy was a top fashion designer, while Walter Dorwin Teague had worked as an advertising illustrator, and both Norman Bel Geddes and Henry Dreyfuss were theatrical designers.

Geddes referred to their work as "utilitarian art." They redesigned items ranging from locomotives and automobiles to radios, cameras, telephones, pencil sharpeners, ballpoint pens, bathroom scales, and product packages. The creation of the Coca-Cola bottle represented but one example of how much the designers gave a flowing, aerodynamic look and feel to the entire era. It was a means of attaching the sense of efficiency, power, and rational design represented by the airplane to consumer goods.

FIGHTING FOR WINGS

Aerodynamics sold because the airplane had come to symbolize the highest values of the machine age. Groups formerly excluded from full participation in society yearned to take to the sky as a means of demonstrating their worthiness to take part in a bright future shaped by science and technology. Surely a mastery of flight would banish the notion that some were less capable than the white males who had dominated the new technology.

The sense of liberation provided by flight particularly appealed to many whose lives had been circumscribed by society. Feminist Margery Brown explained the attraction of flight to women:

> From conversations I have had with women I have come to the conclusion that flying, to them, is more symbolical than to men. To many men it is merely mechanical; to women it seems to signify rising above their environment in one way or another. If anything bespeaks freedom from limitation, flying certainly does. I believe it symbolizes, to women, freedom from the irking limitations that have hedged them about for so many centuries. [8]

Women had taken to the air almost from the beginning. In the early days, however, male aviators doubted that it was a good idea. Claude Grahame-White, the British aviation pioneer, believed that women were not "temperamentally suited" to handle the controls of an airplane. Were "calamity" to "overtake" women whom he had taught to fly, he remarked, "I shall feel in a way responsible for their sudden decease."[9]

When Grahame-White made his silly remark, women had already more than demonstrated their perfect suitability for the cockpit. They were always outnumbered by male aviators. Throughout the 1930s their number never climbed much above five hundred, perhaps accounting for one-thirtieth of the country's licensed aviators. Their visibility belied their numbers, however. Nations around the globe could point to well-known women aviators: England, Germany, Australia, Turkey, and China. Nowhere were they better known than in the United States.

Amelia Earhart was arguably the second-most recognizable aviator in America. And she was not alone.

The 1936 Bendix race underscored how women had reached equality with men at the highest level of aeronautical competition. The popular favorites, pilots like Roscoe Turner and Benny Howard, dropped out of the race because of mechanical problems. Louise Thaden and Blanche Noyes captured first place flying a lovely, blue Beech C 17R Staggerwing with white stripping. With a top speed of

210 mph, this sleek, off-the-shelf, top-of-the-line biplane aimed at a corporate market could outrun contemporary fighter aircraft. Laura Ingalls finished second, followed by male aviators in third and fourth place. Amelia Earhart and Helen Richey finished fifth, still in the money, flying the twin-engine Lockheed 10E "Flying Laboratory" in which Earhart and Fred Noonan would disappear the following year.

The women came from a wide variety of backgrounds. Louise Thaden, an Arkansas farm girl, had worked as a clerk for a Wichita coal company before learning to fly; Laura Ingalls had attended a posh private school. Jacqueline Cochran, who won the Bendix race in 1939, lifted herself from deep poverty as the daughter of a sharecropper to leadership of a cosmetics firm and world fame as an aviator.

Many of them earned their living in the air. Louise Thaden worked in aircraft sales. Helen Richey was an airline pilot until the all-male pilots union forced her out of the cockpit. She then joined Blanche Noyes as a pilot with the U.S. Department of Commerce. Prior to taking a government job, Noyes had been a corporate pilot with Standard Oil of Ohio.

As historian Joseph Corn has argued, the prejudice that dogged pilots ultimately worked in their favor. "Nothing impresses the safety of aviation on the public quite so much as to see a woman flying an airplane," Louise Thaden remarked. If a woman can handle the controls, she continued, "the public thinks it must be duck soup for men."[10]

Helen Richey's experience had shown that some flying jobs were still denied to women. Most airplane manufacturers of light or corporate airplanes regarded women as perfect salespeople, however. In 1932, the government listed 143 male pilots who earned their living in the air, but only 15 women professional aviators, one-third of them involved in aircraft sales and demonstration. As one writer put it in 1930, a woman pilot "was the greatest sales argument that can be presented" to the potential buyer of an airplane.[11]

IF WOMEN HAD a difficult time demonstrating that they were the equals of men in the air, black Americans struggled against far greater obstacles. Eugene Bullard, a native of Columbus, Georgia, had flown with the French air force during World War I and may well have been the first black American to pilot an airplane. As noted earlier, Bessie Coleman was the first to earn a pilot's license.

"Negroes will never ride as free men and women below the Mason-Dixon Line . . . ," William J. Powell remarked in 1934, "until they ride in airplanes owned and operated by Negroes."[12] Powell, a native of Kentucky, had been a combat officer in France and graduated from the University of Illinois in 1922 with a degree in electrical engineering. Over the next five years he established a chain of automobile service stations in Illinois.

Powell had what historian Von Hardesty describes as an "encounter with the future" in August 1927. While attending a veterans convention in Paris, he visited Le Bourget and took his first airplane ride, an aerial tour over the City of Lights. An immediate convert to the future of aviation, he believed it was a field in which black Americans should have a role. "The automobile, the radio, the motion pictures . . . have produced thousands of millionaires and millions of good paying jobs," he noted, "all of which have passed the Negro by." Participation in aviation, he was sure, would demonstrate what African-Americans could do, and provide the economic power that would help to break the strangle hold of Jim Crow segregation.[13]

Returning to the United States, Powell relocated to Los Angeles and founded a school that would teach him to fly. He organized a Bessie Coleman Aero Club and sponsored an all-black air meet in 1931 that attracted as many as fifteen thousand spectators. Powell convinced James Herman Banning (1900–1933) to migrate to Los Angeles. With two years of education at the University of Iowa under his belt in 1927, Banning had talked an ex-army aviator into teaching him to fly. He had barnstormed in the Midwest, amassing some seven hundred flying hours and earning a reputation as the most experienced black pilot in the United States.

In 1932, Banning and Thomas C. Allen, an aircraft mechanic, borrowed an Alexander Eaglerock biplane from a local black businessman-pilot and set out to fly from Los Angeles east across the continent, gathering publicity as they went. With $25 in cash between them, "the flying hobos" traversed the American Southwest, selling their watches and other personal items to buy gasoline. Churches held potluck suppers to raise money for the young aviators. When their engine failed short of St. Louis, students at a white trade school helped them to rebuild the power plant with parts salvaged from a local junkyard. Flying over Pennsylvania they dropped fifteen thousand campaign leaflets for Franklin Roosevelt.

They hopscotched across the nation to a landing at a Long Island airport twenty-two days after they started their trip. Only forty-four hours, less than two days of their total travel time, was actually spent in the air. They had attracted considerable attention in the black press but were generally ignored by the mainstream media. Informed of their feat, Mayor Jimmy Walker presented them with the key to New York City. While flying home to California, they suffered one last crash and were forced to finish the round-trip by bus. Banning died the following year in an airplane flown by another pilot.

C. Alfred "Chief" Anderson and Dr. Albert E. Forsythe would continue the work that Banning and Allen had begun, making a series of long-distance flights. In 1933 they flew a Fairchild 24 christened the *Spirit of Atlantic City*, from the East Coast to Los Angeles and back, the first such round-trip for black aviators. The following year they flew to Canada and back, and undertook a Pan-American goodwill tour with their Lambert monoplane, the *Spirit of Booker T. Washington*.

William Powell continued his efforts in Los Angeles. He published a book, *Black Wings* (1934), produced a film designed to attract young blacks into aviation, and organized an educational group, Craftsmen of Black Wings, complete with a newspaper, the *Craftsmen Aero-News* (1937–1938). He dreamed of a vast interlocking empire of black-owned aviation businesses that would provide jobs for air-minded youngsters and reshape American society. While it failed to materialize, Powell proved that enthusiasm for aviation was color-blind. He also underscored the extent to which millions of Americans regarded aviation as a social movement, quite as much as a technology.

Black Americans wanted to fly. "Chief" Anderson would become an important figure in the organization of the Tuskegee Airmen during World War II, but he had to purchase an airplane before anyone would teach him to fly. Cornelius R. Coffey entered the field in 1931 as a member of the first all-black class of aircraft and engine mechanics at Chicago's Curtiss-Wright School of Aeronautics. He learned to fly and established the Coffey School of Aeronautics.

John C. Robinson, a colleague of Coffey's, founded the Challenger Air Pilot's Association in Chicago in 1931. Because blacks were excluded from Chicago's local airports, Robinson built his own flying field in a black township. By the mid-1930s, Robinson and Coffey had become the focal point for a growing community of enthusiasts. Robinson traveled to Ethiopia in 1935, where he served as aviation advisor to Emperor Haile Selassie, narrowly escaping back to Chicago as Italy swept across that nation.

Black involvement in aviation in the 1920s and 1930s did not bring fundamental social change. The achievements of the era remained virtually unknown to white newspaper readers. A foundation had been laid, however. The black Americans who had struggled to fly during the difficult years of the Great Depression had prepared the way for a great experiment in the decade to come.[14]

"INTO THE AIR JUNIOR BIRDMEN . . ."

Between the wars, aviation became a dominant theme in popular culture. Beginning with the release of director William Wellman's *Wings* (1927) and the Howard Hughes classic *Hell's Angels* (1930), aviation-related films rivaled Westerns in number and popularity. Films portraying the First World War in the air were especially popular. *Flight Commander* (1930), *The Lost Squadron* (1932), *The Eagle and the Hawk* (1933), *Ace of Aces* (1933), *Suzy* (1936), *The Dawn Patrol* (1938), and *The Story of Vernon and Irene Castle* (1939) all helped to establish the legend of the Knights of the Air.

Hollywood was quick to demonstrate that civil aviation could be just as adventurous a pastime as military flying. Lindbergh's flight inspired one of the best known of all interwar aviation films, the Mickey Mouse classic *Plane Crazy* (1928). Shirley Temple danced in the aisle of an airliner, while Cary Grant, Clark Gable, Fred McMurray, James Cagney, and a host of other stars appeared in films like *Test Pilot*

(1938), *Only Angels Have Wings* (1939), *Men with Wings* (1938), and *Captains of the Clouds* (1942). Buck Rogers and Flash Gordon, those ultimate flyboys of the future, put in an appearance at the Saturday matinee.

With the coming of radio, aviators came into the family living room each evening. The half-million members of the "Jimmy Allen Club" could be counted on to tune in for their hero's latest adventure, courtesy of the Richfield Oil Company. Youngsters could see Jimmy in at least one movie as well—*Sky Parade*. Rival Pure Oil Company brought "Jimmy Mattern's Diary" to listeners young and old and offered them a nicely illustrated set of three books on Mattern's flight training and barnstorming career, his years as a movie stunt pilot, and his attempts to circle the globe in a red and white Lockheed Vega.

"All of the 'name' oil companies were hiring well-known pilots at that time. The pilots represented their oil products at air races, set records and otherwise presenting their respective companies . . . in a favorable way," Jimmy Doolittle recalled. Doolittle himself flew for Shell, while Frank Hawks represented Texaco; Roscoe Turner, Gilmore; Edwin Arnold, Standard Oil; and Billy Parker, Phillips Petroleum.[15]

Aviation comic strips were all the rage in the 1930s. Glen Chaffin launched the genre in the spring of 1928, with "Tailspin Tommy." "Scorchy Smith," which followed in 1930, recounted the adventures of a vagabond aviator, a blonde temptress named Mickey Lafarge, and "Heinie" Himmelstross, a World War I German aviator who realized the error of his ways and became Scorchy's sidekick. Milton Caniff's "Terry and the Pirates" debuted in October 1934. Zack Mosely's "Smilin' Jack" followed in June 1936 and ran for forty years. Captain Eddie Rickenbacker and aviation artist Clayton Knight began producing "Ace Drummond" in 1935. The strip also inspired a title in the Big Little Book series published by the Whitman Company and came to life on the silver screen as a Saturday afternoon serial.

Clubs for air-minded youths abounded. The best known, if only for its theme song, was the Junior Birdmen of America, sponsored by Hearst newspapers. Far from seeking to take financial advantage of the youngsters, William Randolph Hearst insisted, the organization was a "permanent youth movement devoted to the boys and girls of America who are interested in aviation."[16] The Boy Scouts of America introduced the aviation merit badge and then subdivided it into several aviation-related badges. A full-fledged Air Scout program was instituted in 1942, lasting until 1949.

In Nazi Germany, the Hitler Youth could participate in a fully developed glider training program aimed at creating a pool of potential military aviators. American youth groups, in contrast, preferred building model airplanes. The history of flying model aircraft as a youth activity began in the first decade of the century. Leading aviation magazines, notably the English journal *Flight*, published regular columns on flying models. Modeling also attracted serious young engineers who entered competitions sponsored by major aeronautical organizations. Alliott Verdon Roe was only one of the major figures who entered aviation through aircraft modeling.

Following World War I, modeling was redefined as an activity aimed at young people. Moreover, particularly in the United States, it was seen as a means of attracting bright youngsters into careers in aeronautics. The Cleveland Model Company advertised one testimonial from a veteran of the hobby who claimed that the experience of modeling had been as valuable to him as a year in college studying aircraft design.

The Guillow Company was an industry leader. Paul K. Guillow, a U.S. Navy veteran, marketed his first kits for static shelf models of twelve World War I aircraft in 1926. Priced at ten cents, each kit contained a three-view drawing, a sheet of balsa wood, cement, a strip of bamboo for the wing struts and landing gear, and two bottles of colored dope for the tissue paper. Guillow began to produce kits for stick-and-tissue paper flying models in the early 1930s and was soon marketing miniature versions of the most popular airplanes in the sky.

Regarded as a wholesome, even patriotic activity that would produce a generation of pilots, engineers, and scientists, aircraft modeling quickly became an officially approved pursuit carried out under adult supervision. Playground associations, scouting groups, specialized organizations like the Jimmy Allen Flying Clubs, and even schools sanctioned modeling and model competitions. The Academy of Model

Aeronautics, founded in 1936, became the official sanctioning body for the activity.

The death of aviator Frank Hawks, who had taken a special interest in youth, inspired the formation of the Air Youth of America in the fall of 1938. The planning committee, with headquarters at 30 Rockefeller Plaza, was chaired by Winthrop Rockefeller and included such aviation luminaries as Edwin A. Aldrin, Jacqueline Cochran, Lester Gardner, and Grover Loening. Within a year, the organization claimed to have assisted nine hundred youth groups and touched the lives of a quarter of a million youngsters. The founders explained that their purpose was "to encourage youth activities in aviation, and to teach a citizen's understanding of our national aviation program." Unlike the dictators of Europe, they noted, the Air Youth of America was a voluntary and entirely civilian organization. "The enthusiasm of the youth of this country has needed no forcing or compulsory instruction."[17]

All of this culminated in a movement for "Air Age Education," launched during the early years of American participation in World War II and continuing into the twenty-first century. The notion was simple enough. Children were thought to be so fascinated by aviation that virtually any subject, from science and mathematics to geography and English, could be taught more effectively if only couched in terms of the air age.

While enthusiasm for this approach to teaching began to decline in the early postwar years, the National Aeronautics and Space Administration and the Federal Aviation Agency continue to spend handsomely on the production of "aerospace age" teaching materials, the operation of specialized educational television networks, and regular programs of teacher training. The desire to foster interest in flight among the young citizens of the next generation is still with us.

9

REVOLUTIONS IN THE SKY,
1926–1941

THE NEW AIRPLANES OF 1933

In 1933, Arthur Herbert Roy Fedden was one of the best-known and highest-paid engineers working in the British aircraft industry. As chief designer of the Bristol Aeroplane Company's engine division, he had designed the successful Jupiter series of radial engines that enabled Britain to capture the world altitude record and to send the first aerial expedition winging over the top of Mt. Everest.[1]

Far from being a narrow specialist, however, Fedden had a breadth of vision rare in British aviation. His colleagues regarded him as eccentric because of his close contacts with U.S. industry and, especially, his appreciation for American aeronautical advances. He returned home from a visit to California in 1933 with photos of the DC-1, then under construction at the Douglas plant. Colleagues refused to believe that this sleek aircraft was anything other than a prop for a Hollywood science-fiction film.[2]

Roy Fedden's friends failed to appreciate developments in America, where an aeronautical revolution was well underway. The Boeing 247, the first of the "new American airplanes," had been flight-tested in February 1933. The Douglas DC-1 made its first flight just five months later. The Sikorsky S-42 flying boat first flew in March 1934, the year the Boeing 247 and Douglas DC-2 entered service.

And that was only the beginning. British engineers would find it hard to believe that the Martin M-130 flying boat, a passenger airliner that took to the air in 1934, could lift a load heavier than its own weight. The Douglas DC-3, one of the most remarkable airplanes in the history of aviation, first flew on December 17, 1935, thirty-two years to the day after the Wright brothers took off at Kitty Hawk. Within two years it had captured the world's market for land-based airliners.

These aircraft represented a revolutionary leap in performance. They were not the result of a single breakthrough, nor had their development been entirely unexpected. Rather, they represented the full convergence of a series of critically important technologies that had begun to coalesce in the fertile mind of John "Jack" Northrop.

IT'S A LOCKHEED!

New companies were popping up in southern California, and Jack Northrop played a key role in the most important of them. He had remained at Douglas through 1926, when James "Dutch" Kindelberger came west from Baltimore, the city to which Glenn Martin had relocated in 1929. With Kindelberger as head of the Douglas engineering department, Northrop was reduced to performing stress calculations under the leadership of another newcomer, John "Lee" Atwood.

Eager to pursue his own half-developed design for a high-wing cabin monoplane, Northrop approached Allan Loughead, who was anxious to return to aircraft manufacturing. Impressed with Northrop's design, he established the Lockheed Aircraft Manufacturing Company. Malcolm Loughead, his brother, who was now producing hydraulic brakes in Detroit, had taken to writing his name "Lockheed," to suggest the correct pronunciation. Allan followed suit.

The new company was up and running by the end of 1926, with Northrop as chief engineer and his old friend Anthony Stadlman as shop foreman. The firm's first product, the Vega, was one of the great

airplanes of the century. A sleek, all-wooden craft, it featured a fuselage constructed of two pressure-molded spruce-veneer halves fitted to
an internal framework and a thick cantilevered wing. Wright J-5C
Whirlwind engines powered the early Vegas, and Pratt & Whitney
Wasp power plants, the later models.[3]

Jack Northrop cranked up the engine on the first Vega on July 4,
1927. Over the next seven years, the factory would turn out just 128 of
the high-wing monoplanes, in six models: the Vega 1, 2, 2A, 5, 5A, and
5B. Ten of the aircraft, designated model DL, were constructed of
duralumin. Some of the most famous pilots of the era flew Vegas across
continents, over oceans, and around the world. Jack Northrop's masterpiece seemed two generations ahead of everything else in the sky.

By 1929, a standard Vega (priced at $14,750 with a Whirlwind
engine and seating for four passengers) included an electric self-starter;

*The team that created the Lockheed Vega. Leaning against the top of the fuse-
lage are (left) Anthony Stadlman and Ben Hunter; Gerard Vultee is in the fuselage; (front row left to right) Jack Northrop, Ken Jay, Allan Loughead*

a steel propeller; a cabin heater; a standard complement of instruments; dash, cabin, and navigation lights; and a first-aid kit. The Executive model ($19,250 with a Wasp engine) was outfitted with a folding desk, a portable typewriter, a lavatory complete with a chemical toilet, and extra baggage space.

Northrop remained at Lockheed until June 1928, when W. Kenneth Jay, Lockheed's treasurer, formed the Avion Corporation. Northrop became chief engineer of the firm, which would eventually become the Northrop Division of United Aircraft, then the Northrop Division of Douglas.

Lockheed would go on without its most famous designer. Gerard "Jerry" Vultee had worked with Northrop at Douglas and served as his assistant at Lockheed. Now he stepped into the chief engineer's role. Vultee, who had studied aeronautical engineering at Caltech, applied the NACA cowling to a production airplane for the first time, the high-wing, open-cockpit Lockheed Air Express. He then finished work on the Explorer and the Sirius, an airplane at least partially shaped by the ideas of Charles Lindbergh.

The Lindberghs would fly their black and orange Sirius on their long exploratory flights of 1931–1933. During a stopover in Greenland, Anne Lindbergh was standing with a group of Inuit while her husband circled overhead. When the people around her began pointing at the airplane in the sky and murmuring, "Tingmissartoq," she asked what the word meant. "Great Bird in the Sky," was the response. That became the name of Lindbergh's second most famous aircraft.

When Vultee left Lockheed in 1930 to help found what would become Vultee Aircraft, his assistant, Richard A. Von Hake, stepped up to the position of chief engineer and took responsibility for the design of the Orion, the last of the single-engine Lockheeds. A handful of Swissair Orions, painted a deep crimson, became known throughout Europe as the speedy "roten [red] Lockheeds."

No firm in the business could challenge Lockheed's engineering staff and the quality of the company's product. While Lockheed airplanes soared, however, corporate management crashed and burned. Allan Loughead, a self-trained engineer and mechanic who regarded himself as primarily a technical person, left the company when it was acquired by a Detroit consortium in 1929. Under the new leadership of men like Carl Squier, a veteran airman and salesman, the company continued to produce world-beating aircraft, but ended in receivership in 1931–1932.

The turning point in Lockheed's business history came in June 1932, when investment banker Robert E. Gross arranged for the capital required to incorporate under the familiar name Lockheed Aircraft Company. Two years later, Gross replaced Lloyd Stearman as president, a post that he would hold for the next twenty-five years.

The new management continued the Lockheed tradition of excellence in engineering. Hal Hibbard, vice president and chief engineer, hired Clarence "Kelly" Johnson, a young graduate of the aeronautical engineering program at the University of Michigan, who went to work designing the classic twin-engine Lockheed Electra, an aircraft that maintained the firm's sterling reputation.

In 1928, however, all of that lay ahead. Jack Northrop had left Douglas in 1926 to pursue his own ideas. Now he departed Lockheed, determined to try his hand at the design of all-metal airplanes. The first product of his new firm, the all-metal Northrop Alpha, would set the stage for revolutionary change.

ALL-METAL AIRPLANES

Metal aircraft were nothing new. Hans Reissner and Hugo Junkers had built and flown the Ente (Duck), a monoplane with wings covered in corrugated sheets of aluminum, before World War I. Metal aircraft had been flown in combat during the war, and pioneered postwar civil aviation. Most designers had simply substituted metal for wood, without taking full advantage of the new material. The German Adolf Karl Rohrbach was the exception. His box-spar, stressed-skin wings—light and strong, and without ribs—had intrigued American engineers throughout the 1920s. The central structure was a rigid, internally braced, metal box spar, to which separate leading and trailing edges were attached.

Why are modern airplanes built of metal instead of wood? Wood

Adolf Karl Rohrbach

would remain an acceptable material for airplane construction for decades to come. Classic aircraft from the Lockheed Vega to the Vickers Wellington and De Havilland Mosquito of World War II prove what talented engineers and workmen could achieve with an all-wooden structure. At least one historian has argued that the rapid transition from wood to metal resulted, in some measure, from a "cultural prejudice" in favor of the material that seemed most appropriate for the technology of the future.[4]

While cultural prejudices certainly influence technology, things were a good deal more complex than that. In considering the future of his industry in 1931, Glenn Martin carefully analyzed wood and metal construction using a variety of criteria: strength-weight characteristics, suitability for machining and forming, adaptability for fastening and connecting, reaction to moisture and temperature, uniformity and the presence or absence of defects, cost, and ease of inspection. "It will be seen," Martin concluded, "that wood fails to adequately satisfy several of the above conditions." As Martin and other manufacturers considered the matter, they saw metal as a uniform material, ideal for the sort of standardized, large-scale production that they hoped to achieve. Moreover, aluminum seemed to be the ideal metal for aircraft construction. There were problems, however.[5]

As discussed earlier, duralumin the tough, light alloy of aluminum used in most aircraft applications since World War I, was subject to intercrystalline corrosion that slowly turned the metal into a white powder. When the U.S. Navy airship *Shenandoah* crashed near Ada, Ohio, in September 1925, U.S. Bureau of Standards investigators found extensive corrosion in the two-year old duralumin framework. The damage hadn't caused the disaster, but the problem could not be ignored.

Corrosion was the single biggest factor retarding the development of all-metal aircraft. In Britain, metallurgists at the National Physical Laboratory developed a process of anodizing an aluminum alloy with a protective coating. By 1927, researchers at Alcoa, NACA, and the U.S. Bureau of Standards announced a new product, Alclad. A very thin layer of soft but corrosion-resistant pure aluminum was bonded to either side of a sheet of duralumin. By the late 1920s standard sheets of wrought aluminum alloys (17S for the Boeing 247; 24ST in Douglas aircraft), treated with the Alclad process, became readily available for use in aircraft manufacture.

To take full advantage of the new material required an entirely new set of manufacturing procedures, machines, and techniques. Sheets of Alclad-treated metal had to be handled with great care to avoid damaging the thin coating of pure aluminum. Moreover, unlike iron and steel, welding damaged aluminum. To avoid this damage, early manufacturers, notably the Zeppelin company, bolted their aluminum frames together, a labor-intensive and time-consuming process.

Charles Ward Hall (1877–1936), a Cornell University graduate who established the Hall Aluminum Aircraft Corporation in Buffalo, New York, in the late 1920s, pioneered new manufacturing procedures, including the riveting of aircraft structures. In riveting, a series of holes are driven through the two pieces of aluminum to be fastened. Each hole is then permanently filled with a metal pin called a *rivet*, which is then flattened on the underside with a special tool. Driven while hot and allowed to cool in place, the rivet hardens over three or four days. Hall's first riveted aircraft was the XF-H1 (1929), a navy fighter.

Quickly recognized as the most cost-efficient means of producing a sound aluminum aircraft structure, riveting changed everything—procedures on the factory floor, training for the workforce, and specialized tools and equipment. Tooling evolved over a decade. Hall acquired or developed the presses and machine tools that transformed sheet aluminum into tubes, flanges, angles, and other pieces that made up the airframe. His first "semiportable" rivet gun weighed 136 pounds!

Hall took the next step as well. A 1933 report from the NACA Langley Laboratory focused on the importance of streamlining and drag reduction. The presence of exposed rivet heads on the wings and fuselage would significantly reduce the speed of an otherwise smooth and streamlined aircraft. Hall took the lead in developing a flush riveted structure in which the rivet heads did not protrude above the surface. The Hall PH-1 flying boat may have been the first flush-riveted aircraft. By the time of his death in an aircraft accident, Hall had pioneered the aluminum manufacturing procedures and tools for those that followed. The coming revolution in design would bring with it a revolution in building airplanes.[6]

THE DESIGN REVOLUTION

The Zeppelin-Staaken E.4250, developed by Adolf Rohrbach at the end of World War I, was the first all-metal, four-engine, stressed-skin airliner. Dr. Herbert Wagner, who had worked with both Rohrbach and Junkers, published his diagonal-tension field-beam theory in 1928 to explain the behavior of large sheets of thin metal held by the edges. Northrop was not aware of Wagner's work when he built his first stressed-skin aircraft. He devised his own method of building relatively lightweight, stressed-skin structures that were stronger than if theory had been applied.

No one had paid closer attention to metal aircraft design and construction than Jack Northrop. He had left Lockheed in 1928 to join the Avion Corporation, in Inglewood, California. He would always regard his first product, the Alpha, as one of his most important contributions to aviation. A sleek, low-winged, all-metal monoplane with a monocoque fuselage and stressed-skin, cantilevered wings, it could carry up to six passengers and over four hundred pounds of mail.

Northrop Alpha 3

The Alpha was a mix of old and new. An open-cockpit airplane with fixed landing gear, it featured an innovative wing. Beneath the smooth skin, a series of longitudinal spars intersected with the ribs, creating multiple "cells" that gave the wing its strength. The unique wing structure led to the retention of fixed landing gear, however, underscoring the complexity of design decisions in an era of rapid change.

A World War I–era aircraft had high-drag characteristics. The increased air resistance of a fixed undercarriage was negligible. However, when the aircraft was streamlined, such as in the low-drag Northrop machine, the fixed landing gear represented a significant fraction of total drag. Northrop didn't want to weaken the wing structure by breaking into the boxes to make room for retracted wheels. Instead, he conducted extensive wind tunnel testing to develop fairings to reduce drag on the fixed landing gear.[7]

Boeing Company officials, impressed by Northrop's approach, and eager to begin metal production themselves, acquired the Avion Corporation, whose chief engineer, Northrop, had now produced his second all-metal design, the Beta. Then, in association with Donald Douglas, he founded the Northrop Company (1932–1938) and produced the Gamma and Delta. The Gamma featured a multicellular wing and empennage, with the center section of the wing blended with the fuselage, and representing a step away from the Alpha toward the

Boeing Model 200 Monomail

DC-1. In the hands of pilots like Frank Hawks and Howard Hughes, Gammas set repeated transcontinental records. The aircraft was also selected for the first attempt to fly across Antarctica.

Boeing's first entry into the all-metal field was the Model 200 Monomail, in 1930. The Monomail featured semiretractable landing gear and a unique wing structure. Technical reports by U.S. Army Air Corps engineers at Wright Field contributed significantly to the wing design. Boeing constructed only one Model 200 and a single follow-on, Model 221, but the products convinced the company to forge ahead with metal aircraft design.

The Boeing B-9, produced in 1931, was the first operational military aircraft embodying key elements of the new technology. Heavily influenced by the Monomail, the new bomber featured an internally trussed wing and semiretractable landing gear. For the first time, the engines, a pair of fully cowled Pratt & Whitney Hornets, were faired directly into the leading edge of the wing. Fred E. Weick and his colleagues at NACA Langley had discovered that such an arrangement would increase lift and efficiency to such an extent that a third engine mounted on the nose, as in the classic trimotor design, was not necessary.

At the time of the introduction of the B-9 in 1931, the standard U.S. heavy bomber, the fabric-covered, biplane Keystone B-4A, cruised at 100 mph, just 15 mph faster than the Martin MB-2 of 1919. The B-9, with its slim fuselage and low drag, bettered that, cruising at 165 mph with a top speed of 188 mph, as fast as any fighter in the sky. Right away, Boeing provided the army with its first all-metal fighter airplane, the flush-riveted P-26, first flown in 1932.

Boeing's next step—a big one—involved applying the lessons learned with the Alpha, Monomail, and B-9 to the design and construction of an all-metal airliner. By 1931, U.S. airlines were replacing their aging Ford and Stinson trimotors with newer aircraft, including the Boeing Model 80 and the Curtiss Condor. Fabric-covered, externally braced biplanes, they could carry fifteen to eighteen passengers, three crew members, and up to eight hundred pounds of mail as far as 460 miles, but at very slow speeds.

The twin-engine Condor cruised at 105 mph and topped out at 129 mph. With its huge wing area, light wing loading, and slow speed, the

Curtiss Condor T-32 (Condor II)

airplane dipped and swayed its way through the air. The motions caused such air sickness in some travelers that Boeing Air Transport company officials hired registered nurses as female flight attendants. They served aboard the ten Boeing Model 80A aircraft that entered service in 1929–1930.

United Air Lines corporate officials disagreed about the basic design of a replacement for the obsolete Model 80. Some went along with Igor

Sikorsky, who had built the first multiengine aircraft in history, and George Mead of Pratt & Whitney. They argued for a giant leap into the future with an airliner that would carry as many as fifty passengers. Boeing chief engineer C. N. Montieth, a graduate of Washington University and MIT who had learned his trade at McCook Field, preferred to design a smaller aircraft. Frederick Collins, Boeing's sales manager and an experienced United pilot, marshaled powerful economic arguments in support of Montieth's position.

Phillip Johnson, the thirty-one-year-old engineer who had been named president of Boeing upon the retirement of the founder, and Clair Egtvedt, vice president for production, recommended that a twin-engine airliner with seating for eight passengers would be a logical step beyond the Monomail and the B-9. While such an aircraft was not expected to fully replace the larger airliners in service, it would at least serve as an intermediate step toward a larger machine. Frederick Rentschler, the ultimate decision maker at United Aircraft, concurred.

But the new plane, the Boeing 247, wouldn't stay small. It grew larger as it moved through design and production. Controlling the weight of the finished airplane remained a constant concern. The use of lightweight magnesium in noncritical areas of the structure saved

Boeing Model 247D

just under a hundred pounds. Boeing engineers saved additional weight by foregoing paint—the airplanes arrived at United Air Lines, Boeing's partner in United Aircraft, in the natural gray finish of the anodized aluminum skin. A system of running water was rejected in favor of a thermos of cold water mounted on the wall of the lavatory.

The airplane that first flew on February 8, 1933, could carry ten passengers, three crew members, and four hundred pounds of mail—for about 500 miles at 180 mph. United bought fifty-one aircraft to replace, not just its smaller aircraft, but its entire fleet. Boeing increased its workforce to 2,200 employees as it completed the order.

This new airplane was less than a passenger's dream, however. The main wing spar passed directly through the passenger cabin. More important, the Boeing 247 failed to take full advantage of the new technology. That fact became clear when the new airliner turned in a very disappointing performance during United Air Lines acceptance trials over the Rocky Mountains in February 1933.

The Hamilton Standard Corporation, another member of the United Aircraft family, had marketed the answer to the problem a year earlier. The variable-pitch propeller would be almost universally described as "a gear shift of the air." As the Boeing engineers were to learn, it was one of the integral technologies required to fully realize the aeronautical design revolution that was underway.

The variable-pitch propeller story begins and ends with Frank Walker Caldwell (1889–1974). During his active years as a propeller specialist, he was responsible for the most important achievements in the field: a metal propeller with separate hub and blades; the ground-adjustable pitch propeller; hydraulically controlled two-position model; and the constant-speed propeller.

A son of the mayor of Chattanooga, Tennessee, Caldwell attended the University of Virginia before earning a degree in mechanical engineering from MIT. After serving as foreman of the propeller division at Curtiss Aeroplane and Motor Company (1912–1917), he became chief engineer with the Propeller Department of the Air Service Engineering Division at newly established McCook Field in Dayton, Ohio.

Caldwell invented the modern system of whirl testing propellers to destruction on an electrically driven test stand, and instituted the testing of propellers manufactured of different materials. Together with Thomas Dicks, of Standard Steel Propeller, an Air Service contractor, Caldwell developed standardized, drop-forged metal propellers with separate blades and hubs.

The pitch, or angle, of the blades could be adjusted on the ground to suit varying conditions. If take-off was to be made from a high-altitude field, say, Denver or Cheyenne, the pitch would be set to take a big "bite" of the air. On other occasions, a propeller could be set for a less-than-optimum take-off, but a fuel-efficient cruising speed. The navy purchased its first metal, ground-adjustable propellers for use on carrier-based aircraft in the mid-1920s.

Caldwell had begun work on variable-pitch propellers that could be operated in flight at McCook Field during World War I. So long as airplanes with relatively large wing areas flew at low speeds, however, there was no reason to place a very high priority on such effort. While other teams focused on the development of mechanical systems, Caldwell left his position with the Air Service in 1928 and went to work on a trustworthy hydraulic system for Standard Steel Propeller. Frederick Rentschler merged Standard and another propeller manufacturer, the Hamilton Aero Manufacturing Company, in November 1929 to form Hamilton Standard, the new giant in the field.

Caldwell introduced his two-position, variable-pitch propeller in 1930 and spent the next two years testing and perfecting it. The device operated on the basis of the engine oil system and centrifugal weights and enabled a pilot to change the propeller-blade position, or "shift" from "low" gear at take-off into "high" gear for cruising. When the poor high-altitude performance of the Boeing 247 became apparent, Caldwell traveled to Cheyenne, Wyoming, to demonstrate the value of his new propeller. The device shortened the take-off run of the airplane by 20 percent, increased the rate of climb by 22 percent, and increased the cruising speed as well.

Boeing immediately placed the first order for controllable-pitch propellers and set out to fit them to every single one of the Boeing 247 and advanced 247D aircraft. Douglas engineers, who had included fixed-pitch propellers on the DC-1, moved to variable-pitch propellers as a key factor increasing the performance of the DC-2. Hamilton-Standard sold the one-thousandth variable-pitch propeller in 1934 and had negotiated rights to their design to manufacturers in Britain, France, and Germany. President Franklin Roosevelt presented Caldwell with the Collier Trophy for the most important aeronautical achievement of 1933.

Frank Caldwell was not done yet. By 1935, he had developed a constant-speed propeller that automatically adjusted its pitch to meet changes in engine speed under altered flight conditions. His improved "Hydromatic" propeller, introduced in 1938, would be a critically important feature of the aircraft that fought and won World War II in the air. Caldwell would spend the rest of his career (1940–1955) as director of research for United Aircraft.[8]

The final version of Boeing's 247 aircraft, the 247D, sported an improved cowling and Caldwell's variable-pitch propellers. But the euphoria in Seattle would be short-lived. The fact that Boeing had broken new ground did little more than to set the stage for the ultimate triumph of the Douglas Company.

THE DECISION TO PURCHASE the entire first year's production of Boeing 247 aircraft guaranteed that United Air Lines would have a huge advantage over its competition. One competitor, Jack Frye, vice president for operations with Transcontinental and Western Airlines (TWA), faced some special problems. Most of the TWA fleet had been temporarily grounded following the death of legendary Notre Dame football coach Knute Rockne and eight others in the crash of a TWA Fokker F.10A on March 31, 1931. The incident seemed to underscore the problems of wooden aircraft and the advantages of all-metal structures.

Fearful of falling even farther behind the competition, Frye wrote to five aircraft manufacturers on August 2, 1932, requesting bids for the design and construction of a trimotor capable of operating on one engine in an emergency and carrying twelve passengers for 1,080 miles at a cruising speed of 150 mph. Donald Douglas seized this opportunity to take a leap into the future.

Unconstrained by corporate partners, the Douglas design team (Harry Wetzel, vice president and general manager; Dutch Kindelberger, chief engineer; Arthur Raymond, assistant chief engineer; Fred W. Herman, Lee Atwood, Ed Burton, and Fred Stineman) decided to build their airplane around the most powerful radial engine on the market, the seven-hundred-horsepower Wright Cyclone, fitted with a supercharger. With that power plant, they could meet the TWA requirements with a twin-engine airplane.

The Douglas design incorporated all of the advanced features offered on the Boeing 247D and more. Having grown restive at United Aircraft, Jack Northrop had returned to an association with Douglas. The multicellular wing that had been a feature of his aircraft since the Alpha would prove a technical key to the success of the new machine. Using a series of spars to break the wing structure up into sturdy boxes, the design permitted a much higher wing loading than that of the Boeing 247D.

One way to increase the speed of an airplane is to decrease drag by reducing wing area. This fact was obvious in the transition from biplane airliners like the Boeing Model 80 and the Curtiss Condor to the Douglas DC series. A smaller wing area translated into high wing loading, which is the wing area divided by the weight of the machine. An airplane with higher wing loading has to increase its speed to maintain lift. Flaps and other high-lift devices that can be deployed to increase lift at the critical moments of take-off and landing became a critical feature of this revolutionary new generation of metal aircraft.

The Boeing Model 80A, a very large biplane, had a wing loading of fourteen pounds per square foot. Engineers took a cautious approach to the design of the Boeing 247D, listening to the reservations of United pilots with regard to high landing speeds. With a wing loading of only sixteen pounds per square foot, the plane did not require wing flaps. But Douglas took a much bolder approach, designing a relatively small wing for such a heavy airplane. They accepted a high wing loading of 24.3 pounds per square foot, and the need for flaps, as the price they paid for a faster airplane.

The fuselage of the new airplane, to be called the DC-1 (Douglas Commercial) would ride on top of Jack Northrop's wing, so that the passenger compartment would be free of the impediments that marred the Boeing 247. The DC-1 featured a host of other touches, including a trim tab on the rudder for use in engine-out situations, and cowl flaps to alter the flow of air around the cylinders as required.

Wetzel and Raymond were dispatched to TWA headquarters in New York with plans for the revolutionary aircraft. After some initial nervousness about the safety of twin-engine design, as opposed to the trimotor that had been requested, the airline offered Douglas a contract for a single prototype DC-1, to be followed by the purchase of as many as sixty production machines.

Boeing officials were initially convinced that the Douglas airplane would be too large and underpowered. Montieth, who saw the DC-1 under construction in Santa Monica in February 1933, remarked that it would be a "huge affair, about the size of our 80-A." The shiny aluminum skin would certainly "give it a pleasing appearance," but he was sure that the Northrop wing structure was entirely too heavy.[9]

For once, Montieth totally missed the mark. From the first flight of the DC-1 on July 1, 1933, just five months after the acceptance trials for the Boeing 247, the new airplane moved from one triumph to another. Certification was achieved, and minor problems were discovered and corrected. On February 19, 1934, Jack Frye and Eddie Rickenbacker, an executive of Eastern Air Lines, raced a storm front across the continent in the DC-1, carrying the last load of airmail before the Roosevelt administration shut down the airmail service, to a safe landing at Newark, New Jersey, just thirteen hours and two minutes after taking off from Glendale, California. It was a perfectly timed demonstration that delighted the industry and enraged the administration.

This aircraft, one of the most influential in history, would suffer through a long and not very distinguished career. TWA loaned the DC-1 to the National Aeronautic Association in 1935, so that it could be altered and used to establish new speed records. In January 1936, with production DC-2 aircraft entering service, TWA sold the DC-1 to Howard Hughes, who was planning another around-the-world flight. By the spring of 1938, Hughes had given up his plan and sold the machine to an Englishman. It passed into the hands of the Loyalist government in Spain, where it saw service in the Civil War before crashing and being abandoned while serving as an airliner in 1940.

Except for being two feet longer and sporting some other alterations under the skin, the DC-2 was the production version of the DC-1. Douglas produced a total of 193 DC-2 variants between May 1934 and July 1936. While most aircraft went to the world's airlines, the company did enjoy significant military sales. The production of fifty-four C-33/C-39 cargo variants for the U.S. Army ultimately kept the production line in operation until September 1939. Aircraft built under license abroad, or produced with parts shipped overseas, raised the production total to 198.

This new generation of American airplanes roared into international public consciousness with the conclusion of the England-to-Australia MacRobertson Air Race on October 26, 1934. Businessman Sir William MacPherson Robertson offered a $10,000 prize to the winner in a race intended to celebrate the centennial of the state of Victoria, Australia. Sixty-four teams signed up, but only twenty of them took off on a race that would cover over eleven thousand miles.

The smart money was on three D.H. 88 Comets the De Havilland firm had designed and built especially for the race. One of those experimental beauties, flown by Charles Scott and Tom Campbell Black, won the race. The next airplane to touch down was a stock KLM Douglas DC-2, which normally operated on the Amsterdam-Jakarta route. Three hours after that, Roscoe Turner and Clyde Pangborne, both veterans of the barnstorming and air-racing era, landed their stock Boeing 247D in Melbourne. A second Comet came in fourth place.

That two of the new American airliners had finished ahead of all but one of the specially built racing machines was nothing short of stunning. The *London Morning Post* captured the essence of the moment:

> The results of the England-Australia Race have fallen like a bomb in the midst of British every-day commercial and military aviation. Preconceived ideas of the maximum speed limitations of standard commercial aeroplanes have been blown sky-high. It had suddenly and vividly been brought home that, while the race has been a triumph for the British de Havilland "Comet," British standard aero-

plane development, both commercial and military, has been standing still, while America has been growing ahead. It has been realized with astonishment that America now has in hundreds standard commercial aeroplanes with a higher top speed than the fastest aeroplanes in regular service in any squadron in the whole of the Royal Air Force.[10]

CYRUS R. SMITH, president of American Airlines, was as responsible for the DC-3 as anyone at Douglas. He wanted to replace the Curtiss Condors that American operated as sleeper aircraft on longer routes. Rather than designing an entirely new machine, it seemed to him far more sensible to enlarge the narrow fuselage of the Douglas DC-2.

However, Douglas corporate officials were initially reluctant to move so far beyond their very successful model. Production facilities at Douglas were barely able to keep up with the orders for DC-2s. Company engineers were preparing to pursue what they hoped would be a series of lucrative military orders. The notion of redesigning the most successful machine in the history of U.S. aviation to date held little appeal for them.

But Smith persevered, placing a historic telephone call to Donald Douglas late in 1934. American Airlines engineers, he pointed out, had already done most of the required calculation and prepared a preliminary redesign that stretched the length of the DC-2 by two and a half feet and its width by two feet, two inches. Such an airplane would carry fourteen passengers in seats that folded into sleeping berths, or twenty-one passengers in the nonsleeper version.

Smith assured Douglas that he could obtain a $4.5 million federal loan to cover the cost of research, design, and initial production. Finally, he promised that while Douglas would not be required to sell the new aircraft only to American, the airline would purchase ten sleeper models, which would be dubbed DST (Douglas Skysleeper Transport), and ten of the twenty-one-passenger DC-3s.

Agreement in hand, Douglas placed Arthur Raymond in charge of the redesign. The first DC-3 took to the air on December 17, 1935, a little more than a year after Smith's telephone call and just thirty-two

Douglas DC-3, with flight attendant Margaret Nesmith

years after Wilbur and Orville Wright had flown at Kill Devil Hills. It quickly emerged as one of the two or three most significant commercial airplanes of the century.

And no one expressed more pleasure with the new airplane than Smith, who explained to anyone who would listen that the DC-3 was the first airplane with which an airline could make money without a government subsidy. The new machine's potential was immediately apparent. American inaugurated service between New York and Chicago with the DST in July 1936. By the end of 1938, DC-3s made up an incredible 80 percent of the entire U.S. airline fleet and had become standard equipment for two-dozen airlines around the globe.[11]

From 1935 until the end of production in the postwar years, Douglas produced 803 commercial DC-3s. The number of C-47s, the famous military transport version of the aircraft introduced in 1940, would rise to 10,123 before the end of production. The Japanese produced some five hundred copies of the airplane. The Soviets turned out three thousand of their Li-2 version. For U.S. civil and military service from 1935 to 1975, the DC-3/C-47 would be produced or modified in seventy-seven variants identified by distinct model numbers.

The DC-3 marked a new era in aviation and became the symbol of all that was modern. Few airplanes have had so great an impact on the world. With it, the age of air transportation arrived on the doorstep of a world already falling into the abyss of war.

DEFINING THE DESIGN REVOLUTION

The appearance of the new American airplanes in 1931–1935 marked an unmistakable shift from one design tradition to another. At the simplest level, airplanes suddenly looked different. Compared to the fabric-covered, trimotor biplane airliners like the Curtiss Condor and Boeing Model 80A, the DC-3 looked like a Brancuşi sculpture. Of course, it was not a work of art, but a complex machine performing a function that only four decades before had been generally regarded as impossible.

The form of the DC-3 directly reflected its function. The successful aircraft designer must exercise solid technical judgment in making an endless series of difficult trade-off decisions, all the while struggling to control the plane's weight. The aesthetic quality of the design is literally the last matter to which the engineer turns his attention.

"If you cannot measure that of which you speak," Lord Kelvin remarked, ". . . your knowledge is unsatisfactory."[12] Engineer-historian Dr. John Anderson showed that it is possible to move beyond appearances and find a quantitative measure of performance that can identify moments of revolutionary change in flight technology. He compared the zero lift–drag coefficient (the drag of an aircraft flying at an angle of attack at which it generates no lift to its size, shape, speed, and altitude) of fifteen aircraft, from World War I fighters to modern jets. When this coefficient is plotted against time, the airplanes fall into three distinct periods: the age of wood, wire, and fabric biplanes; the era of the streamline monoplane; and the jet age. When the maximum lift–drag ratios of the same aircraft are plotted against time, the same three groupings are readily apparent.[13]

For those watching from outside the field of aviation, the fundamental change in flight technology seemed to occur in a short period of time. Knowledgeable insiders knew better. The drafting tables at Lockheed, Boeing, Douglas, Sikorsky, and Martin were the convergence points for a wide range of innovations that occurred over a period of at least fifteen years.

The multifaceted process of change began with the first metal aircraft prior to World War I, continued with the introduction of duralumin, and culminated with the Alclad process and the appearance of new machine tools and production techniques. Variable-speed and constant-pitch propellers enabled the new aircraft to make full use of powerful radial engines shrouded in drag-reducing cowlings. Stressed-skin cantilevered wings, streamlining, the retractable landing gear, and flush riveting reduced drag, while high-lift devices enabled the new all-metal, high-performance monoplanes with their high wing loading to take off and land safely.

Each innovation was significant in its own right. When engineers combined the technologies to create the American airplanes of 1933–1935, they added up to a revolution in aircraft design and performance.

It was an international revolution. Streamlining, monocoque construction, and other structural innovations appeared in France before 1914. Metallurgical developments, experience in metal aircraft design, and Wagner's diagonal-tension field-beam theory flowed from Germany to other parts of Europe and America. English engineers took the early lead in radial-engine design, as well as such associated breakthroughs as the sodium-cooled valve and the Townend ring. A Handley Page airplane won the Guggenheim Fund's Safe Airplane Prize by demonstrating the use of slats and flaps for short take-offs and landings.

Why then did these technologies coverage in the American aircraft industry during 1929–1935? Why had the center of innovation in aeronautics shifted across the Atlantic? In part the answer is in timing and opportunity. Germany, and to as lesser degree England, had emerged as wartime technological leaders, but the aviation industry in both nations struggled with postwar economic conditions and political limitations. An environment of vastly reduced defense spending in which pioneer commercial aviators could earn government subsidies with war-surplus aircraft was scarcely designed to encourage technological innovation.

Not that encouragement for research, development, or innovative thinking in U.S. aeronautics was abundant during the immediate postwar years. With the passage of critically important pieces of legislation supporting civil and military aviation in 1925–1926, however, the picture began to change. The sharp rise in investment that followed, and the economic benefits enjoyed by some firms during the era of consolidation, did encourage the development of new technology and up-to-date equipment.

U.S. government support cannot be underestimated. The U.S. Post Office kept civil aviation afloat with escalating payments for the carriage of mail, while the Bureau of Air Commerce worked to regulate and create an infrastructure to support commercial air operations.

Across the spectrum of research, from basic airfoil studies, through metallurgical discoveries, to the development of cowls and propellers, the NACA, the U.S. Army Air Service Engineering Division, and the U.S. Navy Bureau of Aeronautics laid a solid foundation for American aircraft designers and manufacturers. The work of the Guggenheim Fund for the Promotion of Aeronautics and the rise of aeronautical engineering research and education in American universities also played a role in pushing the United States to the center of world aeronautical innovation.

Ultimately, the revolutionary airplanes of 1933–1935 were the product of brilliant engineering minds. While a talent for aeronautical engineering seems well distributed around the globe, conditions in some nations limited opportunities for the expression of that talent. Prior to the collapse of England's ten-year rule, for example, Reginald Joseph Mitchell's best-known aircraft, the Supermarine S.6B, was of so little interest to a parsimonious government that it was purchased by a private philanthropist and presented as a gift to RAF High Speed Flight. The Spitfire came at the very end of his career, when the threat of war opened new opportunities.

Things were easier in America, where economic conditions had attracted European engineers like Anthony Fokker and Sam Heron. At the same time, the ability and readiness of talented engineers to move from company to company uniquely characterized American industry. Jack Northrop spent the critically important decade of the 1930s moving from Lockheed to Douglas, Ryan, Lockheed, Douglas, Boeing, and back to Douglas. Along the way, he explored his own ideas in revolutionary designs ranging from the all-wood Vega to the all-metal Alpha. Just as important, he played a critically important role in the design of other people's airplanes, from the wing that carried Donald Hall's *Spirit of St. Louis* across the Atlantic to Arthur Raymond's DC-3. Cross-pollination of that sort was not something to be found in other nations.

Competition also came into play in the United States. While European governments subsidized their national air carriers, competition between rival U.S. airlines clearly fueled a demand for new and improved aircraft. The story of the Boeing 247 and the Douglas transports is a case in point. So, as we will see, was the evolution of the large flying boat in America.

The aeronautical revolution broke out in America for several reasons. The U.S. government helped to create an environment in which the business of building and operating airplanes could enjoy modest and structured growth. Competition stimulated progress, as did the ability of talented individuals to move from one country and one firm to another. Military officials and business leaders could afford to encourage engineers to stretch their imaginations to the fullest and produce a new generation of airplanes that took full advantage of the available technology. Three decades after Kitty Hawk, the American aviation industry had once again emerged as the world leader, and not a moment too soon.

PROFESSIONALIZING AVIATION

By 1939, a new generation of commercial airliners dominated the international skyways, with a new generation of pilots at the controls.

The 1910 census had counted "aeronauts"—the operators of balloons, airships, and airplanes—under the category of "showmen," right along with the other circus folk. The image of the airman as a daredevil and risk taker had continued through the war years and into the 1920s and 1930s. Lindbergh and Amelia Earhart epitomized the intrepid aviator, willing and able to perform feats of skill, courage, and daring that seemed quite beyond the experience of ordinary mortals.

The notion of a devil-may-care barnstormer at the controls of an airliner was not, however, calculated to sell tickets. Passengers wanted a calm, absolutely competent pilot whose first concern was their safety. Federal requirements for pilot licensing entered the books in 1926. By 1932, commercial pilots were required to hold a special air transport license. Airlines like Pan American and Boeing Air Transport established special training programs to instruct their employees in the fine points of instrument flying, aerial navigation, and radio operation.

As the use of radios became universal with airlines, control of take-offs and landings shifted from the pilot to air traffic control personnel on the ground. Cleveland opened the first control tower in 1931, quickly followed by other cities. The Civil Aeronautics Authority assumed responsibility for operating the air traffic control system in 1938. By then, the agency had also established minimum visibility and weather conditions for flying. Pilots were also losing control on the ground. Airline dispatchers became responsible for schedules, personnel, maintenance, and other business issues.

Western Air Express, the pioneer of passenger service on the West Coast, introduced stewards and box lunches in 1928. Boeing Air Transport followed suit the next year. United hired their first eight flight hostesses in 1930. Within six years, United had 164 air hostesses on the payroll. That year an article in Literary Digest suggested that the marriage of pilots and hostesses might produce "a race of superior Americans."[14]

Surely it was the dawn of a new era when pilots, the supreme individualists, began to organize. Shrinking authority and the threat of pay reductions led a group of aviators to create the Air Line Pilots Association (ALPA) in 1931 and undertake their first successful action against an airline the following year. ALPA would affiliate with the

American Federation of Labor (AFL), while the airlines created their own organization, the Air Transport Association, in 1936.

Just as pilots and airline operators were organizing, aeronautical engineers were creating a very different sort of professional association. The earliest attempt to organize American aeronautical engineers came in 1915, when Howard E. Coffin, founder of the Society of Automotive Engineers (SAE), established an American Society of Aeronautic Engineers (ASAE).

It seemed to Jerome Hunsaker, Grover Loening, and other pioneers, however, that automotive leaders like Coffin were attempting to hijack American aviation. That became even clearer the following year, when the ASAE became a part of the SAE. The SAE nevertheless continued to attract aeronautical engineers in search of a professional forum during the 1920s, as did the American Society of Mechanical Engineers (ASME), which began publishing a special aeronautical issue of its *Transactions* in 1928.

The founders of aeronautical engineering in America continued to dream of an organization all their own. Hunsaker, now serving as a vice president of Goodyear-Zeppelin, and his old MIT colleague Lester Gardner, who had been named president of the Aeronautical Chamber of Commerce, admired the Royal Aeronautical Society, an organization that provided a prestigious forum for its members, while representing the profession to the nation. The two men drew many of their old colleagues, including Jimmy Doolittle, with his newly minted doctorate from MIT, into their planning process. One hundred thirty-two leaders of American aviation met at Columbia University on January 26, 1932, to organize the Institute of Aeronautical Sciences (IAS). The founders created a new kind of technical society, open not just to engineering specialists, but to professionals of all sorts who were involved in aviation. The IAS's *Journal of the Aeronautical Sciences* quickly emerged as one of the nation's leading engineering publications.

Lester Gardner provided continuity and leadership for the organization over the next two decades and gave the IAS a unique cultural spin as well. The Skyport, high up in New York's Rockefeller Center, not only served as IAS headquarters during the early years but also housed a world-class library and museum of aeronautics. The IAS kept members abreast of the latest in technology and provided opportunities for them to meet and share ideas with their peers. Gardner, who thought big, wanted the IAS to impress aeronautical professionals with the deep historical roots of flight and to serve as a focal point for public inquiries on the subject.

And the IAS did become a major force in American aviation. With the retirement of Lester Gardner following World War II, and the enormous expansion of the industry, the organization focused on its central purpose: "to advance the arts and sciences of aeronautics, and to promote the professionalism of those engaged in these pursuits." The IAS merged with the American Rocket Society in 1963 to form the American Institute of Aeronautics and Astronautics, a leading engineering society.

THE AGE OF THE CLIPPER, 1919–1939

The *China Clipper* symbolizes one of the most romantic ventures in the history of American aviation. The name conjures up visions of iron men and wooden ships sailing the vast Pacific to reach the untold riches of a fabled orient. Now Juan Terry Trippe, who surely qualifies as one of the greatest swashbucklers of the air age, sought to cross the oceans with great flying boats.

Like rigid airships, the large flying boats represented a bridge technology, capable of covering intercontinental distances at a time when faster and more efficient land-based aircraft did not yet have the range or carrying capacity for the task. The era of the great flying boats began with the first flight across the Atlantic by the U.S. Navy NC-4. Introduced in 1923, the Dornier DO J Wal was the most successful of the early postwar models. As a result of restrictions on German aircraft production, Claudius Dornier arranged for the Wal to be manufactured in Italy (117 aircraft), Spain, the Netherlands, and Japan until 1932, when production finally began in Germany. In all, Dornier produced twenty distinct models of his masterpiece.

Explorers flew the twin-engine Wal, the trimotor Rohrbach Romar, and the four-engine Do R4 Super Wal II (1926) over the Arctic and to the far corners of the globe. Deutsche Luft Hansa operated these aircraft over the Baltic. They also saw extensive service in Scandinavia, over Mediterranean routes, in South America, and in Japan. Two ships stationed in the middle of the South Atlantic (*Westfalen* and *Schwabenland*) could retrieve, refuel, and catapult a Wal back into the air, allowing mail service between Africa and South America.

Dornier's ultimate flying boat, the twelve-engine Do X, first took to the air on July 25, 1929. That fall, the huge airplane carried 169 people into the air: 10 crewmen, 150 passengers, and 6 stowaways. For more normal operations, the Do X was designed to carry up to a hundred passengers on reasonably short flights. In spite of its size, the big Dornier could carry only enough fuel for a thousand miles, had difficulty climbing above an altitude of two hundred feet, and suffered severe engine-cooling problems. The ambitious Do X came before its time, doomed to impracticality by the limitations of contemporary technology.

LIKE THE GERMANS, the French sought to link Europe, Africa, and the Americas with an aerial bridge across the South Atlantic. The legendary Compagnie Général Aéropostale pilot Jean Mermoz made a first transatlantic mail flight in May 1930 with the single-engine Latécoère 28 flying boat, *Comte de la Vaulx*, named in honor of the patron of pioneer aviation. While engine failure cut the return flight short, the effort demonstrated the importance of multiengine aircraft for transoceanic operations.

New Aéropostale requirements led to the development of the extraordinary Latécoère 300 (production models would be identified as Laté 301). With its huge wing area and four engines turning fixed-pitch propellers, the big Latécoère cruised at slightly less than 100 mph. But the ultimate measure of success for a transport aircraft is how much of a useful load it can carry over long distances. With an empty weight of 25,000 pounds, the new French flying boat could lift an astounding 23,000 pounds of fuel and 2,200 pounds of mail. In those terms, the Latécoère 300 series were among the great aeronautical achievements of their generation.[15]

With the merger of Aéropostale and four other airlines to form Air France in 1933, the Latécoère flying boats continued regular service across the South Atlantic. Mermoz disappeared in December 1936 while flying an aircraft that had made the trip twenty-three times. "Slowly the truth was borne in upon us that our comrades . . . were sleeping in that South Atlantic whose skies they had so often ploughed," Antoine de Saint-Exupéry remarked. "Mermoz had . . . slipped away to rest, like a gleaner who, having carefully bound his sheaf, lies down in the field to sleep."[16]

Air France employed medium-range flying boats on its Mediterranean, African, and Middle Eastern routes. The dream of offering passenger service across the Atlantic led to the development of the six-engine Latécoère 521, which first flew in January 1935. Capable of carrying thirty passengers across the Atlantic, or seventy on shorter trips around the Mediterranean, the airplane set records for altitude, distance, and load carrying. By 1939, the Latécoère 521 offered passenger and mail service across both the South and North Atlantic routes. The performance of these aircraft was ultimately limited by erratic engines and propellers, however. In any case, war brought an end to the heroic French effort to link the old world and the new by air.

By 1939, Juan Terry Trippe (1899–1981) had achieved the goal of bridging the two continents and built an empire in the process. He was the most hard-nosed and determined of businessmen with the most romantic and compelling of visions. A native of Sea Bright, New Jersey, he saw his first airplane in 1909, when his father took him to see Wilbur Wright fly at the Hudson-Fulton celebration. A member of the freshman football squad at Yale University when the United States entered World War I, Trippe enlisted in the navy and became an ensign and a flying-boat pilot preparing to embark for Europe when the armistice was signed.

Returning to civilian life, he graduated from Yale in three years and worked for a brokerage house before establishing Long Island Airways with seven war-surplus Aeromarine 39-B flying boats. Having mastered the airline business on a small scale by 1924, Trippe became involved in the organization of Colonial Air Transport. When his expansive vision alarmed more conservative colleagues, Trippe and several wealthy backers became principals in the organization of the Aviation Corporation of America (AVCO).

Responsible for the operation of an airline being planned by AVCO, Trippe decided to pursue a pending Post Office contract for the airmail route from Key West to Havana. He would be in potential competition with Pan American Airways, an embryonic airline organized by U.S. Army Air Corps officers Henry H. "Hap" Arnold and Carl M. "Tooey" Spaatz. The pair had intended to retire from the military and operate Pan American as a counter to SCADTA (Sociedad Colomba-Alemana de Transportes), a German-owned airline operating in Central America. The Billy Mitchell controversy and the prospect of improved funding led them to abandon the plan, which was taken up by John Montgomery, an ex-naval aviator with ties to Wall Street.

True to form, the Post Office promoted a merger between AVCO, Pan American, and a third group anxious to capture the overseas mail contract. After considerable corporate maneuvering, Trippe emerged as head of Pan American Airways with the dream of extending his routes through Central and South America. In that regard, he would have to face competition from yet another airline supported by the U.S. military.

The NYRBA (New York, Rio and Buenos Aires Air Line) was the creation of yet another American swashbuckler, Ralph A. O'Neill. In 1928, O'Neill, a World War I ace, began fundraising for an airline that would link sixteen nations in the Americas with a web of relatively short routes between cities. James Rand, of Remington Rand, and Adm. William A. Moffett, head of the U.S. Navy's Bureau of Aeronautics, quickly emerged as O'Neill's most influential backers. With investors falling into place, Moffett introduced the airline executive to Rueben Hollis Fleet, who ultimately took a position on the board of NYRBA and agreed to deliver six of his new Commodore flying boats.

Rueben Fleet had resigned his commission and his management position with the Engineering Division at McCook Field in 1922, and accepted a post as general manager of the Gallaudet Aircraft Corporation. When other corporate executives opposed a decision to produce a primary trainer designed by his old McCook Field colleague, Virginius "Ginny" Evans Clarke, Fleet resigned and established the Consolidated Aircraft Company to build the very successful PT-1 Trusty in an old Curtiss plant in Buffalo, New York.

Business problems balanced the successes at Consolidated. When Air Service Chief Mason Patrick accused him of profiteering, Fleet chose to turn fifty PT-3s over to the army at a dollar a piece in order to preserve his relationship with the government. Admiral Moffett refused to follow suit, arguing that navy contracts were negotiated with care and the manufacturer deserved any resulting profits. Things improved for Consolidated in 1928, when the company won a navy design competition for flying boats with its XPY-1 Admiral. Unfortunately, the production contract for nine of the aircraft went not to Consolidated, but to Glenn Martin. Fleet recouped the situation when he struck a bargain with Ralph O'Neill for six civilian versions of the XPY-1, the Model 16 Commodore.

By 1930, O'Neill was operating what one author described as "the most efficient, longest and safest air line in the world."[17] Unfortunately, he was also losing money at a rapid rate and facing Juan Trippe, a rival who was as adept at maneuvering through the halls of national power as he was at business. Recognizing Trippe's unassailable support in both the Post Office and the State Department, the NYRBA board voted to accept an offer to merge with Pan American.

It was good business for Rueben Fleet as well. Having inherited the six Commodores already in service with NYRBA, Trippe purchased eight more of the big flying boats and another twenty land-based aircraft from Consolidated. Commercial sales more than offset the financial losses resulting from the army controversy and the loss of the navy production contracts for the XPY-1. For the first time in the history of American aviation, the commercial market offered the possibility of profits equal to those available in the military markets. In this case, as in so many others, however, military funding had paid the research and development costs.

The big Commodores would remain in service in Latin America

and Asia through World War II. Consolidated was not the only company that Trippe supported. Anxious to acquire a twin-engine amphibian suitable for use on the shorter routes in Central and South America, he built a relationship with Igor Sikorsky.

Having pioneered the construction of multiengine aircraft in Russia, Igor Sikorsky fled the Revolution and arrived in New York on March 30, 1919. After four years of teaching and saving, he convinced other Russian emigrants to invest in the Sikorsky Aero Engineering Company, with composer Sergey Rachmaninoff as vice president. The early models produced by the firm, including the initial S-29A, which was destroyed in a crash, and the S-35, which René Fonck had hoped to fly across the Atlantic, had little appeal to embryonic airline entrepreneurs.

Sikorsky turned an important corner with his decision to develop a smaller, twin-engine amphibian. The ten-seat S-38, introduced in 1928, filled a niche in both the military and the civil market. As in the case of the Commodores, Admiral Moffett stood aside and allowed Ralph O'Neill to purchase the first ten S-38s, which were to have gone to the navy. Trippe was impressed with the aircraft and continued purchasing the lovely biplanes.

Charles Lindbergh, a major Pan American advisor, opened the company's route to Panama in 1929, flying an S-38. Osa and Martin Johnson, the producers of exotic travelogues, were among the highly visible explorers who flew the amphibians. Ten airlines, including Pan American, operated S-38s, as did the U.S. Army and Navy.

With money flowing into the company, the Russian engineer reorganized his firm as the Sikorsky Aviation Corporation in 1929 and relocated to larger and more modern quarters in Stratford, Connecticut, with access to Long Island Sound, an essential feature for a company producing flying boats. Sikorsky Aviation became a subsidiary of United Aircraft that year. On December 20, Juan Trippe contacted Igor Sikorsky, asking if he would be interested in building a four-engine flying boat with record range and carrying capacity.

The new aircraft, the Sikorsky S-40, seated forty, but it disappointed Lindbergh, who had hoped for a clean, streamlined aircraft with cantilevered wings. Sikorsky, the master of large-aircraft construction, believed that a traditional approach to construction would enable him to maintain better control over weight. Trippe's chief engineer, Andre Priester, agreed with Sikorsky.

One of the major factors in Pan American's success, Priester had learned the essentials of the airline business under the tutelage of Dr. Alfred Plessman, the legendary head of KLM. Emigrating to the United States in 1925, Priester had worked for Fokker and Ford before accepting a position with Pan American. If Juan Trippe was the public face of the airline, Priester was the chief of operations, the man most responsible for equipment, crews, and procedures. His stamp of approval guaranteed Sikorsky's position with Trippe.

Charles Lindbergh, Sikorsky, and Basil Rowe, a legendary Pan Am flying-boat skipper, flew the first S-40, christened the *American Clipper*, from Miami to the Canal Zone. During the course of the trip, Lindbergh and Sikorsky became fast friends and spent time discussing the next step, a more advanced flying boat. That airplane, the S-42, would become a Pan American workhorse, carrying mail and as many as thirty-two passengers between the cities of North and South America.

While the big Sikorsky might have carried mail across the Atlantic, like the Latécoère 300, it could not fulfill Trippe's dream of transoceanic passenger service. To achieve that goal, Trippe partnered with one of the nation's veteran aircraft builders, Glenn Martin. Martin had prospered during World War I and earned a reputation around Cleveland as a rather odd fellow. A snappy dresser who drove a Stutz touring car with snakeskin upholstery, he was generally recognized as one of the city's leading bachelors. For all of that, he would never marry and lived with his mother until her death.[18]

The immediate postwar years proved difficult for Martin. The number of employees in his company had dropped from a wartime peak of nine hundred to only ninety by 1922. The navy offered four contracts for experimental aircraft in order to preserve the firm. In truth, Martin survived by underbidding Curtiss for the production of observation floatplanes for the navy. The experimental contracts did allow him to explore new technologies, however. The most interesting of the new airplanes, the MO-1, was an all-metal seaplane scout. With little experience in metal construction, Martin did what he had always

Charles Lindbergh and Juan Terry Trippe, August 9, 1929

done—hired a good engineer. In this case, he imported George Madelung, a veteran of Junkers, to head the project.

By 1928 Martin's company had outgrown its Cleveland factory, and city officials did not offer financial incentives to persuade him to stay. In cooperation with Louis Chevrolet, he refinanced and reorganized his company in Maryland, where he acquired land for a new factory at Middle River, near Baltimore, close to the Chesapeake Bay, an ideal location for testing the new PM-1 flying boats that he had contracted to build for the navy.

The move and the new factory had been expensive, and business was slow during the depression. Martin and his mother continued to live well, however, maintaining a lavishly appointed apartment in

Washington, D.C., as well as a residence in Baltimore and a twenty-two-room "shack" in Hollywood, California, where he spent two months of the year "resting and recuperating." He kept the company afloat on the basis of ongoing contracts with the navy, sales to foreign, especially South American, governments, and the production of the B-10, a new army bomber.

For Martin, the design and production of the three M-130 flying boats for Pan American would bring more prestige and visibility than profit. In negotiations with Pan Am, Martin chose to overrule his own corporate officers and enter a low bid in order to win a contract that he hoped would lead to the sale of additional production aircraft. He would lose money on the project, but burnish his own reputation.

The *China Clipper* became the best known of the three M-130s. Completed in 1935, it was designed to carry over forty passengers across the world's oceans in stages. This extraordinary machine could lift more than its own empty weight into the air, an achievement in which both Martin and Andre Priester could take real pride.

First flown in 1934–1935, the Martin M-130s had been designed to carry mail and passengers between the United States and Europe. Any route over the North or South Atlantic, however, would require landing rights in Newfoundland, Bermuda, or some other part of the British Commonwealth. Imperial Airways, Britain's official carrier, could not match the performance of the Pan American Clippers. It was unlikely that His Majesty's government would negotiate landing rights until British industry could produce an airplane capable of crossing the Atlantic.

Undeterred, Juan Trippe turned his eyes toward the Pacific. It would not be easy. The airline would have to make use of stepping stones to cross the vast ocean—Hawaii, Midway, Wake, and Guam—and build facilities for refueling, servicing, and perhaps repairing the aircraft en route. His ultimate goal would be China, where Trippe had acquired an interest in the China National Aviation Corporation in the hope of securing rights to operate Pan American aircraft there. Ultimately, he would negotiate landing rights in the Crown Colony of Hong Kong. For the moment, however, the transpacific flights would end at the Philippines.

Not all of the problems would be aeronautical. Trippe's dream could not be realized without the assistance of the U.S. government. Fortunately, his interests coincided with those of the nation.

Anxious to encourage an American commercial presence in an area of potential interest to Imperial Japan, the U.S. government in December 1934 began to issue a series of decisions supporting Pan American's effort. President Roosevelt ordered that key Pacific islands controlled by other branches of the government be turned over to the navy. The Navy Department granted permission for Pan American to use government facilities in San Diego, Hawaii, Midway, Guam, and across the Pacific to the Philippines. Over the eight years remaining before the attack on Pearl Harbor, the level of cooperation between Pan American Airways and the U.S. government continued to grow. It was a unique and symbiotic public-private partnership in which Pan American emerged as what has aptly been called "the chosen instrument" of American foreign and military policy.

In the spring of 1935, the SS *North Haven* sailed from San Francisco. Chartered by Pan American, it carried provisions, construction equipment, and a crew of 118 who would carve support bases out of the rock and coral of the islands and atolls. When Glenn Martin informed Priester and Trippe that the first M-130 would not be delivered on time, Pan American officials decided to begin test operations in the Pacific using the *American Clipper*, an S-42 that had been stripped of all nonessentials and fitted with extra tanks.

On the afternoon of April 16, 1935, Capt. Edwin C. Musick, navigator Fred Noonan, and a crew of four took off from San Francisco Bay on a record-breaking round-trip to Honolulu. Several months later, Musick made the first trip to the new facility at Midway and back. In mid-October, the S-42 made the first round-trip flight to the new Wake Island base.

Finally, on November 22, 1935, Musick and his crew taxied the *China Clipper* away from the Alameda dock to the accompaniment of bands and the applause of twenty-five thousand spectators. President Roosevelt sent best wishes and Postmaster General James Farley addressed the crowd. The welcome-to-Manila celebration seven days later was even more boisterous, with a hundred thousand people on hand to greet the *China Clipper*. The trip had been scripted to the minute. When it was discovered that a Pan Am publicist had miscalculated the timing as a result of the international dateline, the crew spent an extra day at Guam rather than force a rescheduling of the arrival ceremony.

Ed Musick, the most quiet and laconic of men, became a hero in spite of himself. He joined Charles Lindbergh and Wiley Post as a winner of the prestigious Harmon Trophy for the most significant aeronautical achievement of the year, and found himself on the cover of *Time* magazine. Frank "Spig" Wead, himself an ex-naval aviator, scripted a Warner Brothers film, *China Clipper*, in which Humphrey Bogart played a scarcely disguised "Ed Musick" type, while Pat O'Brien was cast as the gruff, outspoken airline boss.

Musick had earned his status as a hero of the air age. Trailblazing air routes to remote areas of the earth was a dangerous business. On January 11, 1938, while on a survey flight out of Pago Pago, Musick and his crew were lost in the midair explosion of the *Samoan Clipper*. Ed Musick and Jean Mermoz, arguably the two most celebrated airline pilots of the interwar years, both died in the line of duty.

THE AMERICAN FLYING BOATS had stunned the British engineering community. They simply refused to believe the claims made for the Martin flying boats. Robert Mayo, chief technical advisor to Imperial Airways, charged that the reported performance of the M-130 "could not possibly be achieved." While admitting that American engineers had succeeded in reducing structural weight, the editors of *Flight*, the English journal of record for aeronautics, found it "difficult to believe that the saving can be anything like as great as these figures indicate."[19]

In 1934, in an effort to encourage English aircraft builders to develop long-range flying boats in a league with those produced in the United States and France, postal officials offered lucrative subsidies for airmail carriage to the far corners of the Empire. Mayo issued an Imperial Airways call for bids to design and build a large flying boat capable of carrying more than twenty passengers for a distance of seven hundred miles. The result was the Shorts S.23 Empire Flying Boat. By the end of production, a total of forty-one of the big Shorts boats would be constructed, a much larger run than that enjoyed by Martin or Boeing.

By 1937, Imperial Airways was at last prepared to negotiate transatlantic service with Pan American. On July 5, an S.23 left the Imperial Airways Atlantic seaplane base at Foines, Ireland, and headed west, while a Pan American S-42B took off from Newfoundland and headed for Ireland. In terms of carrying capacity and general suitability for the task at hand, the Sikorsky was far superior to the Shorts aircraft. During the remaining few years before the outbreak of war, Shorts would introduce larger flying boats, but they were never able to match Pan American's machines. Great Britain could at least demonstrate that it was in the game, however, and that was enough to overcome the political difficulties.

EVEN TRIPPE, with his S-42 and M-130 flying boats, remained dependent on mail subsidies. If Pan American were to mature into an intercontinental carrier, it would have to acquire a new generation of aircraft. In February 1936, Trippe invited bids on a large flying boat capable of carrying fifty passengers and eight thousand pounds of cargo for distances of up to 4,800 miles. Glenn Martin hoped to make up the losses suffered on the production of the three M-130s through the sale of a larger variant of his original design. Igor Sikorsky and his engineers moved in the opposite direction, submitting a design for a very large and luxurious flying boat that represented a radical departure from current practice.

A bid from Boeing, not a traditional builder of flying boats, came as something of a surprise. It had been something of a surprise to Boeing as well. Engineer Wellwood Beall realized that the wing and tail elements of the Boeing Model 294 (XB-15) might serve as the basis for a flying boat that would meet the Pan American requirements. Boeing President Clair Egtvedt approved the project. Convinced that the Martin proposal was too conservative and the Sikorsky design too much of a stretch, Juan Trippe signed a contract with Boeing.

When Boeing's legendary test pilot Eddie Allen first flew the

Boeing 314 on June 7, 1938, he discovered that the tail surfaces were too small. Wrestling the big flying boat down to a safe landing on Lake Washington, he compared the eighteen-minute flight to "trying to

Boeing 314 Capetown Clipper

herd a reluctant buffalo."[20] Additional wind tunnel testing led to the design of the final triple-vertical-stabilizer design that became the signature of the airplane.

In its final form, the Boeing 314 had seating for seventy-four passengers, or thirty-four in an aircraft configured with sleeping berths. At best, the Model 314 could carry a load 40 to 41 percent of the empty structural weight of the airplane. Considering its size, this meant that the big Boeing boat could lift a greater weight into the sky than any of its contemporaries and still boast an air range of three thousand miles.

Boeing eventually sold a dozen of the Model 314 flying boats to Pan American. Trippe, in turn, would sell three of those aircraft to British Overseas Airways. By December 18, 1939, the Boeing 314s had completed a hundred Atlantic crossings. They would provide valuable service during World War II. The Shorts Empire Flying Boats that had fared so poorly against their American competition performed valiantly in the antisubmarine and transport roles. Following the war, British Oversea Airways and Air France reinstated flying-boat service for a time. It was perfectly clear, however, that the day of commercial airplanes that operated off the water was over.

As engineer Laurence Loftin demonstrated, the aerodynamic performance of large flying boats, measured in terms of maximum lift over drag, had steadily improved over the period 1930–1942. They had not come close to the efficiency of land planes, however.[21]

On August 10, 1938, a Lufthansa Focke-Wulf Condor (Fw 200 S1), a lovely, slim, four-engine, land-based airliner that looked very much like the wave of the future, took off from Berlin and flew twenty-one hours nonstop to a safe landing in New York. The product of a design staff headed by Prof. Kurt Tank, Focke-Wulf's technical director, the Fw 200 could carry twenty-one passengers over distances of a thousand miles, cruising at 12,000 feet and 229 mph. No flying boat could match that.

The Douglas DC-4E flew for the first time in 1938, as did the four-engine Boeing Model 307 Stratoliner. With a pressurized passenger cabin based on development work conducted with the Lockheed XC-35 at the Army Air Corps engineering facility at Wright Field, the Stratoliner began flying passengers in 1940.

Lockheed had begun work on the L-049 Constellation in 1939. On April 17, 1944, Howard Hughes and Jack Frye flew the new four-engine, triple-tail Constellation from California to New York in a record six hours, fifty-eight minutes. TWA signed over its rights to the army for the duration, but it did not take a crystal ball to see that this airplane would make its mark on the postwar world.

The great flying boats that had winged across the Atlantic and to the fabled Orient during the years between the wars were the stuff of legend. Celebrities, journalists, movie stars, and diplomats, perhaps even a spy or two, crossed the oceans on the big flying boats. Modern air travel may be faster, safer, less expensive, and more convenient, but it is also commonplace. The sense of adventure offered by an aerial voyage aboard a Clipper is gone forever.

10

SETTING THE STAGE,
1929–1939

FEAR OF FLYING

"I wish for many reasons that flying had never been invented," Prime Minister Stanley Baldwin once remarked. Aerial attacks on civilian targets, he thought, would spell the end of civilization. "I think it is well for the man on the street to realize that there is no power on earth that can prevent him from being bombed," Baldwin announced in Parliament on November 10, 1932. "Whatever people may tell him, the bomber will always get through." The only defense, he concluded, was offense, "which means you have to kill more women and children than the enemy if you wish to save yourselves."[1]

Baldwin had aligned himself with a tradition as old as Christianity. Saint John Chrysostom (347–407), a church father who specialized in vicious anti-Semitic attacks, regarded wings as the symbol of inescapable divine judgment. Juan Caramuel y Lobkowitz (1606–1682), a Spanish theologian, explained that "God denied men the faculty of flight so that they might lead a quiet and tranquil life." Noel André (1728–1808), l'Abbé Pluche, agreed that "the art of flying would be the greatest calamity that could befall society," while the English natural philosopher William Derham (1657–1735) believed that flight would "give ill men greater Opportunities to do Mischief," and prove inconsistent with "the Peace of the World." The German experimenter Johann Daniel Major (1634–1693) suggested that flight would make "the world seem a thousandfold hateful and more ruinous" than the discovery of gunpowder. "Towns and castles, whole provinces and kingdoms, would . . . soon be obliged to fill the air . . . by means of frequent firing of cannon or by stirring up rising smoke; or else to protect themselves thoroughly with large iron gratings, used as nets, and to arm themselves . . . against the frequent throwing of fire and stones by the flying army, which, like . . . birds of prey . . . would otherwise raze everything to the ground."[2]

As was so often the case, author Samuel Johnson (1709–1784) summed the matter up: "If men were all virtuous . . . I should with alacrity teach them all to fly. But what would be the security of the good, if the bad could at pleasure invade them from the sky?" Clearly, Stanley Baldwin and Samuel Johnson were men who would have understood one another.[3]

THE FUTURE OF AERIAL WARFARE was on a great many minds in the two decades after 1918. The admirers of Douhet, Mitchell, and Trenchard were confident that air power would be a decisive factor in future conflicts. A new generation of Englishmen who shared Stanley Baldwin's fearful vision of an aerial Armageddon, on the other hand, had their own radical solutions to the problem.

Classicist Gilbert Murray advised a 1932 Anglo-French student conference on disarmament that the "first step to material security is the prohibition of military aviation, and the internationalization of commercial aircraft companies."[4] Accessing the lessons of the world war, Winston Churchill suggested that military aviation be banned, with the exception of an air force operated by the League of Nations.[5] A surprising number of British public figures supported the notion of a single international air force.

Of course, this peculiarly English pacifist approach was never a serious possibility. Far less radical attempts to place humanitarian limitations on the application of military aviation were unsuccessful. The draft "Rules of Aerial Warfare" developed by a six-nation commission of jurists at the Hague in 1922–1923, which would have outlawed attacks on most civilian targets, had still not been ratified when World War II began in 1939.

SETTING THE STAGE: THE PACIFIC POWERS

By 1932, the warnings of the old prophets of aerial doom seemed to be coming true. The Japanese conquest of Manchuria in 1931–1932 had inflamed nationalist sentiment in China. In January 1932, in an incident probably staged by the Japanese, a Chinese mob attacked five Buddhist priests on the streets of Shanghai. It provided an excuse for Japanese intervention. Rear Admiral Koishi Shiosawa arrived late that month, with fifteen hundred marines and eleven ships, including the aircraft carrier *Kaga*. A *Time* magazine correspondent described the ship as "the newest type of marine terror, . . . nestling 60 airplanes on her vast weird deck, [with] smoke snorting out from her strange horizontal funnel."[6]

On Friday, January 29, following the repulse of Japanese troops operating in the city, Admiral Shiosawa ordered the Nakajima A1N fighters and Mitsubishi B1M bombers of the *Kaga* air group to attack the densely populated Chapei section of the city. The airmen pursued the attacks "incessantly and indiscriminately," British officials informed the Foreign Office, killing "countless civilians."[7]

"Every twenty minutes," the *Time* correspondent reported, "a Japanese squadron swooped over, dove down on the unprotected roofs . . . and dropped a dozen whistling bombs. With each explosion towers of dust and smoke shot 150 feet into the air. The sky grew dark. It was a wonderful sight. Not for hours did the spectators realize what it meant. Under those roofs were women and children, coolies and their old fathers, being blown to bits. Flames began to leap from a dozen roofs. Chapei was on fire. . . . Now the flames of the burning native city . . . filled the sky. Into the international settlement poured streams of terrified Chinese. Wretched, many wailing piteously, they huddled their children and baskets and stumbled on in the darkness."[8]

The *New York Times* headline read "Planes Constantly Terrorize City." "Japanese airplanes constantly circled the Chapei area," correspondent Hallett Abend noted, "affording to astounded witnesses the unexampled spectacle of a lethal aerial bombardment of a densely populated and unfortified metropolitan area."[9]

The first Shanghai incident is rarely mentioned even in very complete histories of World War II. In fact, it began the long slide toward the Pacific war. "Shanghai," Stanley Baldwin remarked, "was a nightmare."[10] The conquest of Manchuria had seemed very far indeed from the immediate concern of the Western powers. An attack from the sky on innocent civilians, the heroic peasants of *The Good Earth* and *Oil for the Lamps of China*, was quite another matter, however. When an international report identified the Japanese as the aggressors, they withdrew from the League of Nations. It marked the beginning of a rift that would not heal.

The attack on Shanghai also demonstrated the fundamental role of an aircraft carrier: the projection of force in support of national policy in an area where land-based air power is unavailable. Just nine years later, *Kaga* would carry its aircraft into a far more memorable strike halfway across the Pacific. The ship that had been involved in the earliest events leading toward war ended its career at the bottom of the Pacific just six months after the attack on Pearl Harbor, the victim of dive-bombers launched by yet another aircraft carrier.

WHILE THE AMERICAN Eugene Ely made the first landing and takeoff from platforms mounted on the decks of cruisers, the British conducted the first operational experiments with ship-launched aircraft. During World War I, they added short decks to the front and rear of the aging cruiser HMS *Furious*. Early flight tests were so frightening, however, that deck landings were never attempted after the *Furious* began its operational cruises. The ship launched seven Sopwith Camels against the Zeppelin sheds at Tondern, Germany, in 1918. The only aircraft to return had to ditch in the ocean next to the ship.

Royal Navy officials remained intrigued by the notion of a ship that could launch and retrieve aircraft at sea, however. HMS *Argus*, launched in 1918, was a half-completed ocean liner redesigned as a true flattop with a single flight deck from stem to stern. The bridge from which the ship was controlled was constructed on an elevator and literally retracted into the hull during flight operations.

The Japanese followed the British lead. The Imperial Navy laid the keel of the first ship ever to be designed as an aircraft carrier, *Hosho*, or "Swooping Dragon," in 1919. As a result of the Washington Naval Treaty of 1921, Japan converted two warships then under construction into large carriers, *Kaga* and *Akagi*, each of which could put to sea with a complement of over sixty aircraft. The British remained in the game by converting two much smaller cruisers into the carriers *Glorious* and *Courageous*, capable of carrying just over forty aircraft.

Commissioned in 1922, the USS *Langley* (CV-1), the first American aircraft carrier, closely resembled the *Argus*, with smokestacks that tipped out of the way when aircraft were taking off or landing. Ungainly as she appeared, "the covered wagon," as she was affectionately known, remained one of the most important ships in the history of the twentieth-century navy.

The system of arresting gear developed for the *Langley*—cables stretched across the deck to capture the tail hooks on the airplanes— became standard equipment on the aircraft carriers of the world. Kenneth Whiting, an early naval aviator who served as the first captain of the *Langley*, developed some of the pioneering procedures and traditions that would mark life aboard this new class of ships.

It was Capt. (later Admiral) Joseph Mason Reeves, commander of all airplanes serving with the fleet, however, who developed the effective onboard operational procedures for aircraft carriers. His initial experiments in stowing, handling, and launching aircraft enabled him to speed flight operations and increase the number of airplanes carried aboard. Like the Japanese and the British, the U.S. Navy converted two of the seven cruisers that they were required to destroy under the terms of the Washington Naval Treaty into a pair of next-generation aircraft carriers, *Lexington* (CV-2) and *Saratoga* (CV-3).

With three carriers in the fleet, Captain Reeves, an Annapolis graduate (class of 1894) who had lectured at the Naval War College and qualified as an aerial observer at the age of fifty-three, developed a doc-

Rear Admiral Joseph Mason Reeves

trine to guide the use of these new ships. While a carrier air group could conduct reconnaissance and provide air cover for the fleet, Reeves insisted that force projection, the ability to attack the enemy from the sky, was the central purpose of an aircraft carrier.

Rather than tying the carriers to the speed of the slowest ship in the entire fleet, Reeves argued that a "fast carrier," like the *Saratoga*, could be operated more effectively as an independent unit capable of striking an enemy when and where it was least expected. He demonstrated the value of this approach during a fleet exercise in 1929. Referees agreed that aircraft from the *Saratoga* had destroyed the Panama Canal in what the admiral commanding the maneuvers described as "the most brilliantly conceived and most effectively executed naval operation in our history."[11]

Captain Reeves, Adm. William A. Moffett, the director of the Navy's Bureau of Aeronautics, and others were also considering the types of aircraft appropriate for carrier operations. Lightweight fighters would serve as scouts and provide air cover for the fleet. Torpedo planes were also an obvious choice.

The accurate delivery of bombs on targets would be a major problem. A bomber capable of dropping a significant load on an enemy fleet from any considerable altitude would be too large to operate from a carrier. An airplane small enough to operate from a flight deck would have to have a means of placing a smaller bomb load precisely on target.

Reeves favored dive-bombing. The origin of this radical approach to bomb delivery is unclear. Some pilots had experimented with the technique during World War I. Marine Corps aviators had dive-bombed bandits in Haiti (1919) and guerillas in Nicaragua (1927). It was the rise of the American aircraft carrier, however, that helped define the tactical role of dive-bombing.

The U.S. Navy conducted its first dive-bombing experiments in 1926, using sturdy Vought 02U Corsair biplanes. The following year, carrier-based 02U pilots honed their skills by attacking moving targets towed by destroyers. In order to prevent damage to the propeller or some other part of the aircraft, special mechanisms were introduced to lift the bomb away from the fuselage prior to release.

The Navy launched its first ship designed to be a carrier, *Ranger* (CV 4), in 1933. The next year, the Bureau of Aeronautics released a call for bids on four new types of aircraft: a single-seat fighter; a two-place light scout bomber; a two-seat dive-bomber; and a torpedo plane with a three-man crew that could do double duty as a high-level bomber. The airplanes were to be low-wing, all-metal monoplanes with retractable landing gear. The dive-bomber would also sport some form of dive brake, to slow it during descent and enable the pilot to improve his aim.

The Boeing F4B series, introduced in 1928, served as the standard U.S. Navy carrier-based fighter until the early 1930s, when a new firm, the Grumman Aeronautical Engineering Company, entered the field. Leroy Randle Grumman (1894–1982), a Long Island native, had earned his engineering degree at Cornell (in 1916), won his wings as a naval aviator, and completed his engineering education at MIT.

By 1924, Grumman was working as an engineer with the Loening Aeronautical Engineering Company. Keystone Aircraft Company acquired Loening in 1929 and transferred the operation to Bristol, Pennsylvania. Grumman and a colleague, Leon A. "Jake" Swirbul, remained behind and established their own firm in an abandoned

Leroy Randle Grumman

Long Island garage. While Grumman worked on a retractable landing gear system for carrier aircraft, his workmen kept busy producing aluminum truck bodies.

Grumman's first Navy fighter, the FF-1, first flew in 1931. The Grumman F2F (1933) had poor spin characteristics, but the follow-on F3F (1936) became the last biplane to serve as the standard carrier-based fighter with the U.S. Navy. The biplane XF4F-1, Grumman's response to the navy's request for an all-metal fighter, lost out to the Brewster F2A Buffalo. The Buffalo, the first monoplane fighter in service with the U.S. Navy, proved generally unsatisfactory as a shipboard airplane, although it gave good service in the hands of Finnish pilots battling Soviet airmen in 1940. Given a reprieve, Grumman came back to the navy with the XF4F-3 Wildcat, a stocky, midwing monoplane delivered to the fleet in 1940.

Donald Douglas, whose first contract had been for navy torpedo planes, turned the XTBD-1 Devastator over to the navy for testing in 1935. The first modern, low-wing, all-metal, carrier-based torpedo bomber in the navy's inventory, it was regarded as a radical airplane when it entered service in 1937. With a top speed of 206 mph, however, it would be no match for the standard Japanese fighter of 1940, which clocked in at 325 mph.

Jack Northrop's XBT-1 (1935), designed by engineer Ed Heinemann, beat out the competing Brewster XSBA-1 and Vought SB2U Vindicator as the navy's first all-metal monoplane dive-bomber. With its slow speed and poor lateral stability, however, the BT-1 was not fully satisfactory. In 1938, when Douglas acquired Northrop and its El Segundo, California, plant, Heinemann redesigned the airplane, equipping it with a new engine, split and slotted dive flaps, and fully retractable landing gear. Redesignated the SBD-1 (Scout Bomber Douglas), the Dauntless was first sent to Marine air units, and began to reach the fleet in March 1941.

The new generation of U.S. naval aircraft would be operating from new flight decks. With 55,000 tons of warship construction still allowed under the Washington Treaty, the U.S. Navy planned for two new carriers in 1933. *Yorktown* (CV 5) and *Enterprise* (CV 6) were constructed with Public Works Administration funds. The Japanese formally withdrew from the Washington naval agreements in 1936 and began work on five more purpose-built carriers for the Imperial Navy: *Ryujo, Hiryu, Soryu, Shokaku,* and *Zuikaku.* The United States followed suit with one more flat top, *Hornet* (CV 7), in 1939.

While U.S. officials scarcely noticed, Japan was also developing a new generation of carrier aircraft. The quality of the *Kaga* and the aircraft that it launched against Shanghai in 1932 was a testament to the success of Japanese modernization. The nation had been only too willing to learn from the West and to purchase European technology. In 1919, a large French delegation arrived in Japan to shape army aviation. Two years later, Capt. Sir William Francis Sempill and a group of British naval aviators arrived at Kasumigaura to advise the Imperial Navy on aviation matters.

Japan also drew on the finest European research talent. In 1927 Theodor von Kármán, who was eclipsing his own professor, Ludwig Prandtl, as the world's most influential aerodynamicist, paid an extended visit to Japan, where he not only lectured but also was involved in the development of a major wind tunnel. The following year he relocated permanently to the United States and took command of the aerodynamic research effort at the California Institute of Technology.

Just as the Japanese army and navy were rivals for power and influence, so were their air services. General Ikutaro Inuoe, a hero of the Russo-Japanese War, commanded army aviation from 1919 to 1933. Japanese naval aviation lacked a single high-ranking advocate to match Adm. Moffett or Reeves. During the early years, the navy air arm was in the hands of influential midlevel officers like Lt. Comdr. Hideo Sawai of the Navy Bureau of Aeronautics.

Japan offered lavish support for military aviation. While the government operated aircraft manufacturing plants, a number of private firms dominated the industry. Lieutenant Chikuhei Nakajima, one of Japan's first naval aviators, established the nation's first large-scale aircraft manufacturing firm in 1917. Mitsubishi and Kawasaki, heavy industrial firms and arms producers that had operated shipyards during World War I, launched aircraft manufacturing subsidiaries in 1918–1919. Aichi, a manufacturer of watches and electrical equipment, entered aviation in 1920. Kawanishi began building flying boats the next year.

Although the government imported aircraft, the preference was to purchase license-built foreign designs from local manufacturers. As early as 1922 Mitsubishi and Kawasaki produced 97 Nieuports and 145 Hanriots. From 1919 to 1923, Nakajima and Aichi received orders for a total of 570 copies of German and British aircraft. By the mid-1920s, Kawasaki was building the Dornier Komet under license.

The next step in Japan's conscious effort to stimulate the aviation industry was to hire European engineers to develop new designs for Japanese manufacturers. Herbert Smith, the designer of the Sopwith Camel, Pup, Triplane, and Snipe, arrived at Mitsubishi in 1921 with a small group of colleagues. His Mitsubishi B1M3 (Navy Type 13), a carrier attack aircraft introduced in 1924, spearheaded the attack on Shanghai in 1932.

The Mitsubishi 1MF1 (Type 10) navy fighter, designed by the Smith team in 1921, had been replaced by the Nakajima A1N2 (Navy Type 3) by the time of the Shanghai incident. Essentially an English Gloster Gamecock, specially modified to meet the requirements of carrier operations, three A1N2 aircraft from the *Kaga* air group scored the first aerial victory ever achieved by Japanese military aviators on

February 22, 1932, shooting down a Boeing P-12 flown by the American aviator Robert Shore.

The era dominated by foreign design teams was short-lived. The airplanes that attacked Shanghai were indistinguishable from the externally braced, open-cockpit biplanes produced in Europe and America. A new generation of Japanese designers would shatter tradition, producing airplanes that would enable Japan to push the Allies back across the Pacific.

The call for the design of an entirely new set of 7-shi (the seventh year of the reign of the Emperor Hirohito, 1932) carrier-based fighter, bomber, and attack aircraft resulted in such poor entries that none left the experimental stage. Two years later, Lt. Comdr. Sawai announced a 9-shi competition. Convinced that there had been too much government interference in 1932, Sawai now insisted on allowing Japanese engineers a freer hand.

Jiro Horikoshi emerged as a leader of the new generation of aeronautical engineers. As a grade-school student during World War I, Horikoshi had devoured the articles on air warfare that appeared in the children's magazines of the day. "In particular," he recalled a lifetime later, "the names of the famous airplanes—Nieuport, Spad, Fokker, and Sopwith . . . —excited my young blood."[12]

After entering the University of Tokyo in 1923, Horikoshi studied engineering in the newly formed Department of Aeronautics. He graduated three years later and immediately joined the Nagoya Aircraft Manufacturing Plant of the Mitsubishi Internal Combustion Engine Company, soon to be renamed Mitsubishi Heavy Industries. In 1932, he took command of the engineering team that would produce Japan's first modern fighter airplane.

The A5M (Type 96) was a low-wing, all-metal fighter with flush-riveting and stressed-skin construction. Like the smaller and lighter Boeing P-26, which had flown a year before, the Claude, as it would be identified by the Allies, was a transitional machine, with an open cockpit and fixed landing gear in a drag-reducing fairing. Fitted with wing flaps, it remained the standard Japanese naval air force land- and carrier-based fighter until the introduction of Horikoshi's masterpiece in 1940.

An 8-shi (1933) requirement called for a twin-engine, land-based navy reconnaissance/bomber. Horikoshi's colleague Sueo Hondo and the members of a small Mitsubishi design team produced the G3M Chukoh, or Nell, as Allied airmen would come to know it. Both the A5M and G3M proved themselves in the skies over China.

Unwilling to launch a full-scale war in China, Japan withdrew from Shanghai at the end of May 1932. Over the next four years, militarists consolidated their power over a nation that was sinking into the depths of the Great Depression. In February 1936, army extremists assassinated the finance minister, the lord keeper of the privy seal, and the army inspector general, all political moderates. The prime minister narrowly escaped with his life. The uprising was suppressed, but the incident underscored the power of the militarists and the fragility of the political process in Japan.

In July 1937, army leaders arranged an excuse to cross the Manchurian border and invade China. On August 14, 1937, thirty-eight G3M aircraft flew twenty-five hundred miles from Japan to bomb targets on the mainland and return home. No other bomber in the world could match that performance. But the extraordinary range and speed had been purchased at the cost of self-sealing gasoline tanks, protective armor, and other refinements that were regarded as essential on Allied aircraft. In years to come, Japanese airmen would pay a terrible price for the decision to trade safety for weight.

Japanese army aviation planners learned from the experience of the navy. A new generation of fighters like the Kawasaki Ki-61 and the Nakajima Ki-84, first-rate machines of heavier construction, more powerful armament, and some safety features, entered army service by 1944. Unfortunately for Imperial Japan, the national aircraft industry, starved for raw materials and skilled workmen, was unable to produce these advanced aircraft in anything close to the required numbers.

During the years 1937–1941, however, Japanese airmen ruled the skies over China and the Pacific. Widely regarded in the West as a nation of myopic copycats, Japan had created the most experienced and best-equipped naval air force in the world.

The all important 11- and 12-shi generations, the world's finest naval aircraft, joined the carrier air groups in 1940. Although somewhat underpowered and lightly armed, Jiro Horikoshi's masterpiece, the Mitsubishi A6M Reisen (Zero), flew at 330 mph and had a range of 1,930 miles with an auxiliary tank. The Nakajima B5N (Kate) was a torpedo bomber second to none. The Aichi D3A (Val) dive-bomber sank more Allied ships during the first ten months of 1942 than any other airplane in the entire Axis inventory.

By 1935, the men who would lead the sailors and airmen of their nations into the first great carrier battles were rising to command. In Japan, naval aviation had become the province of Adm. Isoroku Yamamoto (1884–1943), one of the great naval leaders of the twentieth century. As a young ensign in 1905, he lost a finger at the Battle of Tsushima Strait. Following World War I, he spent considerable time in the United States, studying at Harvard and serving as a naval attaché during Admiral Reeves's mock attack on the Panama Canal.

He linked his career to aeronautics soon thereafter, when he was named assistant commander of the Kasumigaura naval air training center, and learned to fly. Yamamoto pursued a unique approach to naval aviation, developing land-based bomber, fighter, and attack units, as well as those operating from carriers.

In the United States, some critically important senior officers also turned to naval aviation in midcareer. William Frederick Halsey Jr. (1882–1959) was a thirty-one-year veteran of battleships and destroyers when he learned to fly in 1935. It had become clear to him, as it had to Yamamoto, that the aircraft carrier would decide the next war at sea. In 1943, Halsey dispatched the long-range Lockheed P-38 fighters that would intercept the airplane in which Yamamoto was flying, and shoot it down in flames.

The war in China had led to a spiraling deterioration of relations between Japan and the United States. Determined to limit Japan's aggression, the Roosevelt administration threatened to cut off Japan's access to oil and other essentials. The militarists surrounding the emperor were determined to complete the conquest of China and expand their empire to include a greater East Asia co-prosperity sphere. Most Japanese leaders came to believe that conflict was inevitable, either with the Russians north of the Manchurian border or with the Western democracies that controlled Southeast Asia and the

Pacific. While not in full agreement with the decision to go to war, Admiral Yamamoto began to consider how best to wield the weapon that he had forged.

SETTING THE STAGE: THE EUROPEAN DICTATORS TAKE TO THE AIR

A single Heinkel He 111 twin-engine German bomber swept over the Spanish town of Guernica, near the French border, at 4:30 on the afternoon of April 26, 1937. It was the first step in an air attack that would sear itself into the conscience of a generation and inspire the most famous painting of the century.

Nine months before, on July 16, 1936, military officers in Spanish Morocco and garrison towns in Spain had launched a coordinated revolt against their government, initiating a bitter civil war. The years following the loss of her American and Asian colonies in 1898 had been difficult for Spain. Violent strikes, political assassinations, and protracted struggles between the forces of tradition and change had preceded the creation of the Spanish Republic in 1931.

For the next five years, power passed back and forth between left-wing reformers and conservative groups representing the Catholic Church, the military, and right-wing Falangists, most of whom admired the rising fascist parties in Italy and Germany. Finally, in February 1936, the Popular Front, a leftist coalition, won a key election and began to consolidate its power. Right-wing leaders, convinced that communist elements in the new government would move the nation into the Soviet orbit, backed a military uprising. Their leader, Gen. Francisco Franco, struck a bargain with the Germans.

Junkers Ju-52 transports ferried Spanish troops from Spanish Morocco to key points in Spain. The Spanish Civil War, which began with the first successful operational airlift, would provide a highly visible testing ground for the machines, men, and tactics that the Luftwaffe would take into World War II.

While the Treaty of Versailles had not destroyed the German aircraft industry, it had made things very difficult. Hugo Junkers, who had grown weary of war, watched his first F 13 transport take to the air on January 7, 1920. Three days later, the treaty was signed, officially outlawing the manufacture and sale of aircraft and engines in Germany.

Junkers was to become one of the most admired figures in German aviation, but he was not a seasoned aircraft manufacturer. The government had forced him to partner with the far more experienced Anthony Fokker in 1917 in order to undertake serial production of the all-metal J 4.

In order to remain in business after the war, Junkers transferred his aircraft manufacturing operation to Sweden, began marketing to other nations, and established or controlled thirty airlines worldwide, all of which flew F 13s. In spite of his own antimilitarist views, Junkers also

Hugo Junkers

cooperated with officials of the much-reduced German army (Reichswehr), establishing an aircraft factory and flying school at the Russian town of Fili.

The operation began in 1921, a full year before the Treaty of Rapallo, which established diplomatic relations between the former enemies, was signed. The project allowed Germany to build a secret air arm and train military aviators, while providing the Soviets an opportunity to tap German expertise and gain experience in aircraft manufacture. All told, the German government paid Junkers a total of almost eight million gold deutsche marks to support the operation at Fili.

The project represented a quiet turning point in the political evolution of postwar Germany. The nation had lurched toward chaos in the months following the armistice. A new National Assembly, which met in Weimar, was controlled by a weak coalition dominated by Social Democrats. Berlin suffered through a left-wing uprising in January 1919, followed by a right-wing putsch in March 1920. Militant communists and ultraconservative Freikorps troops faced off in streets and city squares across the country.

By August, Soviet troops threatened the nation that included both "Red Saxony" and right-wing Bavaria. The assassination of political figures on the right, left, and center no longer seemed surprising. Unemployment and runaway inflation became unpleasant facts of life. In such an atmosphere, fringe parties offering radical solutions to the growing problems attracted support. In November 1923, one of the most important of these groups, the National Socialist German Workers Party, under the leadership of an ex-army corporal named Adolf Hitler, launched an unsuccessful putsch against the government.

As chancellor, and, after 1923, foreign minister of the Weimar Republic, Gustav Stresemann reduced tensions. He allayed Allied concerns by continuing reparation payments; brought order to Saxony and Thuringia; and worked to restore German power and pride. In 1920, he named Gen. Hans von Seeckt, who had served on the prewar general staff and earned his nation's highest award for valor, to command the Reichswehr, the surviving core of the German military establishment. A confirmed believer in air power, von Seeckt supported civil aviation and aircraft manufacturers in order to prepare for the day when a German air force would once again take to the sky.

General von Seeckt was a key figure in arranging for Hugo Junkers to establish the operation at Fili (1921–1926). In addition, the government established another covert Soviet base at Lipetsk, where between 1926 and 1932 as many as 120 carefully selected young Germans learned to fly.

Like Junkers, Claudius Dornier and Adolf Rohrbach managed to remain in business. Up to 1932, Dornier manufactured his aircraft in other European nations and in Japan. Hans Klemm and other builders of light aircraft began to operate freely after 1922, when the restrictions on sport aircraft were lifted. Heinrich Focke and Georg Wulf, Ernst Heinkel, and Willy Messerschmitt all established themselves as aircraft manufacturers before 1930.

Von Seeckt also gained control of German airlines and used these operations as a means of acquiring aircraft and training personnel. As in other nations, the Germans used subsidies to shape civil aviation. Junkers, who sought to build an airline that would serve the needs of a Europe at peace, was swimming against the tide. By 1925, the government pressured the old professor to sell his domestic airline holdings to the Civil Aviation Ministry, which formed Deutsche Luft Hansa in 1926.

Junkers continued to manufacture aircraft for a few more years, introducing the Ju 52, which would remain the standard Luftwaffe transport throughout World War II. Soon after Adolf Hitler became chancellor, however, he lost control of his company and was placed under house arrest, accused of spending Reichswehr funds intended to support the operation at Fili on other company ventures. The seventy-six-year-old pioneer died at his home in 1935, the year in which Hitler finally announced that Germany would no long abide by the military provisions of the Treaty of Versailles.

New commanders rose to power under the Nazi regime. As Hitler's leading supporter and head of the Air Ministry, responsible for all military and civil aviation, Hermann Goering, a World War I ace who had been badly wounded during the 1923 putsch, became chief architect of aerial rearmament. Erhard Milch, the one-time Junkers aide who had led Luft Hansa to a position of strength, would handle industrial planning, as secretary of state in the Air Ministry.

Ernst Udet, another World War I ace, was charged with acquiring the finest aircraft for the new Luftwaffe. His own enthusiasm for the U.S. Navy's Curtiss dive-bombers led him to issue a requirement for a German Stuka (*Sturtzkampfflugzeug*—Plunge Battle Plane). Udet crashed while testing the Heinkel entry, and selected the Ju 87 Stuka for production. He proved to be a poor manager, though. Drinking heavily and depressed by the outcome of the Battle of Britain, the man who had been known as "Hitler's test pilot" committed suicide in 1941.

By the mid-1930s, German aviation was transformed. The Deutschen Luftsport Verband, the oldest German sport aviation organization, took the lead in the government-engineered gliding craze that swept Germany in the 1920s. Model clubs sprang up all over the nation. By 1925, the restrictions on light-aircraft construction and operation had been lifted, and fully one-half of the total budget for army aviation was spent on the civilian flying clubs that would train a generation of German airmen.

And they would have a new generation of aircraft to fly. The Treaty of Paris in May 1926 lifted all of the technical limitations on the production of civil aircraft in Germany. Although restrictions on military aviation remained in effect, there was no way to enforce them once the Allied Control Commission was dissolved in 1927.

Unlike their British counterparts, German engineers rushed to catch the Americans. Ernst Heinkel, for example, was determined to match the performance of the Lockheed Orion, introduced in 1931. Powered by a Wright Cyclone engine, the sleek, low-wing aircraft could carry four passengers and a load of mail at a speed of over 230 mph.

Speed was the goal. Flying a Nieuport-Delage racer on September 26, 1921, the French pilot Sadi Lacointe became the first human to travel faster than 200 mph (he went 210 mph). By 1936, most of the standard single-seat fighter aircraft in service with European air forces had a top speed of over 200 mph: Heinkel He 51 (206 mph); Arado 68E-1 (208 mph); Fiat C.R.32 219 (219 mph); Hawker Fury (210 mph); Polikarpov I-15 (228 mph). Each of them was an open-cockpit, externally braced biplane with fixed landing gear, and none of them could catch a Lockheed Orion, a production airliner that carried passengers and mail through the sky at a top speed of 235 mph.

Heinkel and Junkers both produced designs aimed at matching the Orion, and fell considerably short. Heinkel abandoned the He 65, with its fixed landing gear, and moved on to the He 70. A single-engine, fast mail carrier with some passenger seating, it still failed to match the performance of the Orion, let alone that of the newer Vultee V-1. It was, however, a step toward the He 111, one of the longest-lived aircraft in the history of military aviation.

In July 1932, the Inspection Department of the Army Ordnance

Office of the Weimar Republic asked German industry to develop an all-metal, low-wing, twin-engine aircraft that could serve as a fast airliner but would also be suitable as a bomber. Given the fact of German remilitarization, the He 111, Dornier Do 17, and Junkers Ju 86, all of which first flew in 1934, made much better bombers than they did airliners. Variants of those machines would still be serving as standard

Heinkel He 111

Luftwaffe equipment at the end of World War II. Spanish-built He 111Es would continue in active service until the 1950s.

A new generation of fighter aircraft also entered the scene. The first Luftwaffe fighter, the He 51, was an open-cockpit biplane with fixed landing gear. Then came a giant leap to the Bf 109. The product of the fertile brain of the brilliant, irascible, temperamental Willy Messerschmitt, who operated the Bayerische Flugzeugwerke, the little aircraft with very thin wings was originally thought to be too frail for a fighter. First flown in May 1935, the Bf 109 saw combat in Spain in the spring of 1937, where it proved to be not only very sturdy but also the most effective fighter in the sky. The Junkers Ju 88 Stuka, He 111, and Dornier Do 17 bombers also saw combat in Spain.

A new generation of pilots cut their teeth flying these machines. Major Werner Moelders, a man of serious demeanor who was nicknamed "Vati," or "Daddy," became the first German ace since 1918, flying the Bf 109 in Spain. Adolf Galland, who would rival Moelder's score during the Battle of Britain, fought a very different war in Spain. Assigned to He 51s, he had to avoid contact with the superior Soviet fighters. Focusing on the ground-support role, he helped to pioneer the tactical approach that enabled Germany to roll across the face of Western Europe.

The Germans developed other techniques that would prove useful in the not-too-distant future. Wolfram von Richthofen, chief of staff of the German Condor Legion, experimented with radio control of air units, while "Vati" Moelders developed the standard aerial formations of the Rotte (two aircraft) and Schwarm (four aircraft).

The Italians fought beside the Germans in Spain. The Italian air force had built a solid reputation during the 1930s. Italo Balbo, the

Adolf Galland (left) and Werner "Vati" Moelders
shake hands during World War II

commander of the Regia Aeronautica, made international headlines when he led a mass flight of flying boats from Italy to the Chicago World's Fair in 1933. Fighters like the Fiat C.R. 32 were up to the European standard and were used in Spain in considerable numbers. Like the Ju 52, the trimotor Savoia-Marchetti SM.81 (1935) became a standard transport aircraft during World War II.

Nazi and Italian airmen supported the Nationalist advance on Madrid. The Soviets (for Spanish gold) provided the republic with men and equipment, as well as leadership for the International Brigades composed of volunteers from Europe and America.

THE SOVIETS HAD WORKED hard to built their strength in the air. Just a year after the revolution, Andrei Tupolev, a young engineer, and Nikolai Joukowski, his seventy-year-old professor, called on Lenin. They argued persuasively for government support of aviation. The need for aerial defense of a regime that was under attack from every side was self-evident, as was the potential of the airplane to bind a nation that stretched from Europe to the Pacific, from the Arctic to South Asia.

With the full support of the regime, Joukowski and Tupolev established TsAGI, the Central Aerodynamics and Hydrodynamics Research Institute, a research organization like the National Physical Laboratory or the NACA Langley Laboratory. Osoavaviakhim, a paramilitary organization linking aviation enthusiasts across the nation, purchased aircraft for the military and established flying schools, airports, and glider training programs as a means of building Soviet air power. The regime also took advantage of the Weimar government's struggle to escape the limitations of the Treaty of Versailles, arranging for the establishment of German aircraft manufacturing plants, flying schools, and other aviation facilities in the Soviet Union.

A native aircraft industry put down roots. Tupolev himself produced his first airplane, the ANT-1, in 1922, the same year in which Nikolai Polikarpov produced the first postwar Soviet fighter at the Central Design Facility (TsKB). For much of this period, Soviet designers drew inspiration, and sometimes a bit more, from European and especially American aircraft. Polikarpov's last prewar design, the I-15 biplane, was often identified as a "Curtiss" machine, while his low-wing, all-metal I-16 was known as "the Boeing."

Soviet fighter aircraft had dominated the obsolete Heinkel He 51s, but the introduction of the Bf 109 sent them scurrying. The need for a new generation of engines and aircraft, especially fighters and ground-attack machines, and the importance of coordination between ground and air forces were among the lessons the Soviets learned in Spain. The Stalinist emphasis on huge aircraft as public relations tools gave way to a requirement for sturdy, heavily armored, ground-attack machines and medium bombers that could be sent against strategic or tactical targets.

During the early 1930s, Col. Walther Wever, chief of staff of the Luftwaffe, had supported the development of the four-engine Junkers Ju 89 and plans for a large Dornier bomber. His death in a 1936 crash brought an effective end to those programs. The Spanish experience had convinced Hermann Goering and others that strategic bombing could be conducted with twin-engine machines of limited range and carrying capacity. Without the need to accompany long bombing missions, range was not a major requirement for fighters like the Me 109.

The Spanish Civil War raged for three years, taking over half a million lives before the final Nationalist victory in March 1939. Beginning with aerial attacks on Madrid in November 1936, this was a bombing war. Republican aviators flew Tupolev S.B.2 bombers against Nationalist targets. The attention of the world, however, was focused on the attacks of Heinkel He 111 and Savoia-Marchetti SM.79 aircraft against the civilian population. Colorful Republican posters showed formations of menacing aircraft dropping bombs on defenseless children and grieving mothers. They remain today as masterpieces of the propagandist's art.

Guernica, located near the French border, was the center of Basque nationalism. In April 1937, Nationalist troops were approaching the city, while Republican forces retreated toward a bridge over the Mundaca River. General Wolfram von Richthofen, commanding German air units in the area, later claimed that he ordered the bombing to disrupt the retreat and destroy the bridge and a local small-arms factory. Republican sources portrayed the incident as a terrorizing bombing attack on civilians aimed at destroying Basque morale and support for the Republican cause.

Waves of bombers swept over Guernica late on the afternoon of April 26, 1937. In addition to high-explosive bombs, incendiaries rained down on the wooden houses. He 51 fighters attacked people fleeing the city. The raid continued for over two hours, completely destroying the local hospital, along with hotels and most of the residential sections of the city. George L. Steer, the London *Times* correspondent who arrived early the next morning, remarked that "the town . . . was a horrible sight, flaming from end to end."[13]

Estimates of the dead and wounded vary wildly. A standard popular history suggests that as many as 1,600 died, with an additional 900 wounded. German apologist David Irving insists that the number of dead was less than one hundred. The truth was somewhere in between. Forty-three German aircraft had dropped fifty tons of bombs on the town, taking perhaps 300 lives. Whatever the toll, the attack would have been forgotten had it not been for Pablo Picasso. Invited to paint a mural for the Spanish pavilion at a 1937 Paris exposition, the most famous artist of the twentieth century produced one of the most famous paintings of the century, *Guernica*. Whatever one thinks of modern art, the symbolic power of Picasso's masterpiece is undeniable.[14]

The artist vowed that the painting would never travel to his native Spain so long as the Franco regime remained in power. As a result, it was perhaps the most traveled painting of the century, moving almost constantly from museum to museum on three continents until 1957–1958, when it was placed on extended loan to the Museum of Modern Art (MoMA) in New York. During the Vietnam War, American artists repeatedly used the imagery of *Guernica* to express their own antiwar messages. One American arts organization asked Picasso to retrieve the painting from the MoMA, arguing that the nation attempting to bomb Vietnam "back to the stone age" was not a suitable home for *Guernica*. The painting finally found a permanent home in a democratic Spain in 1981. Thanks in large measure to a work of art, the attack on Guernica came to symbolize the horror of total war.

SETTING THE STAGE: BRITAIN AND FRANCE

At the close of World War I, France was Europe's aeronautical power-house. Two decades later, the France trailed Great Britain, Germany, and the United States in the air. What had happened? The French market was soft. After the creation of Air France, 98 percent of all French aircraft were purchased by the government. This might be regarded as an advantage for a nation blessed with a farsighted planning effort. Unfortunately, that cannot be said of France during the years in question.[15]

In 1935, the general staff of the Armée de l'Air called for a "miracle" aircraft type, a reconnaissance machine that could double as a light bomber and be so well armed that it could defend itself. The result was an airplane ill-equipped to perform any of the manifold tasks for which it was designed. The partial nationalization of the aeronautical industry, begun in 1936, created additional problems. Initially, manufacturers would continue to operate as private companies, but the government would be the principal shareholder. Eventually, the industry reorganized into six large companies scattered in various parts of the country to spread the jobs and economic benefits. Oddly, only one French engine builder was involved in the program. Four others, including all of those dominated by automobile manufacturers, remained independent.

Nationalization succeeded in reducing the level of chaos and led to a sharp rise in government expenditures and production in 1938 and 1939. But it was too little, too late. Many of the aircraft produced in the last two years before World War II were built from designs dating to the early 1930s. When war came, the number of French aircraft that met the world standard was very small.

ENGLAND BARELY ESCAPED a different trap. General Hugh "Boom" Trenchard had kept the Royal Air Force (RAF) alive in the immediate postwar years by arguing that air power provided the cheapest way to police the far ends of the empire. Taking Trenchard at his word, these were years of *radical* economy for the RAF. "One of the most serious failures was that over the period 1919–1934 the quality of the fighting equipment of the Royal Air Force steadily deteriorated," one authority commented. "The equipment in 1929 when Trenchard departed was not very different from what it had been ten years earlier."[16]

From 1920 into the early 1930s, the RAF maintained a very high public profile. The annual air shows at Hendon, outside London, drew hundreds of thousands of spectators. The newspapers were filled with images of British aircraft and airmen winging over exotic locations. But the best public relations could not disguise the extent to which the United States and Germany had swept past Britain.

It was apparent to any ten-year-old boy worth his salt that the Vickers Virginia, a night bomber which continued to fly at Hendon until 1937, was an updated version of the Vickers Vimy, introduced in 1918. As late as 1935, *Jane's All the World's Aircraft*, the bible of the international industry, listed the Vickers Valentia, yet another modification of the Vimy sporting new engines, as the standard RAF troop transport in the Middle East. The Handley Page Hyderabad, Hinaldi, and Heyford, the Westland Waipiti, the Boulton Paul Overstrand, the Gloster Gamecock, and even the Hawker Hart, introduced as late as 1931, were far more closely related to their World War I predecessors than to the aircraft in combat over Spain.

As the only nation that had experienced a strategic bombing campaign, England was obsessed with the notion of death from the sky. If the fear of bombing rang clear in the words of national leaders like Stanley Baldwin, and in the widespread British pacifist sentiment opposed to bombing, enthusiasm for strategic aerial attacks remained a basic principle of RAF planning in the Trenchard years.

Bombing had an additional appeal for British leaders. The depression years were marked by strikes and social unrest. Would the angry and disaffected workers of the 1930s be willing to go "over the top" in the event of another war? The bomber, it seemed to those close to the center of British power, offered a means of avoiding the mass slaughter of the Western Front.

Before 1934, the RAF air staff echoed Stanley Baldwin's assurance

that the bomber would always get through. They did not regard interceptor aircraft as a wise investment and thought civil defense measures
to be ultimately futile. The only rational defense, therefore, was to field
a fleet of bombers that would deter the enemy from striking in the first
place. That view would be moderated after 1934, but by no means
eliminated. A determined aerial offensive against the heartland of an
enemy nation remained at the center of British military planning
throughout the interwar years.

History celebrates the great wartime commanders of the RAF. Sir
Edward Ellington, marshal of the Royal Air Force and chief of the Air
Staff in 1934–1937, has been largely forgotten. Yet it was Ellington and
his staff who laid the foundation for victory. Consider the accomplishments of his few short years in command[17]:

> 1934—The Air Ministry specification (F.5/34) that produced
> both the Hawker Hurricane and the Supermarine Spitfire
> 1934—Origins of the RAF cipher system
> 1934—Initiation of the first RAF expansion scheme leading
> to preparedness for war
> 1935—Creation of the Committee for the Scientific Survey
> of Air Defense, headed by Sir Henry Tizard
> 1935—The construction of new airfields and redeployment
> of operational units
> 1936—The Air Ministry specification (B.12/36 and B.13/36)
> that produced the four-engine Shorts Sterling bomber, the
> Handley Page Halifax, and the Avro Manchester, which
> led to the Lancaster
> 1936—The creation of shadow factories to increase produc-
> tion
> 1936—New RAF purchasing policies that streamlined the
> development process
> 1936—Ordering American aircraft
> 1937— RAF reorganization

And so, at the last possible moment, Britain began to prepare for war.
Blessed with wise leadership and a generation of brilliant engineers and
scientists, the nation closed the technology gap with little time to spare.

The airplanes that would win the Battle of Britain and carry the war to the German heartland took shape in these years. The Air Ministry ordered the Hawker Hurricane in 1934. It flew for the first time on November 6, 1935, with designer Sidney Camm looking on. Work began on the Supermarine Spitfire, Reginald Mitchell's masterpiece, in 1934, with a first flight on March 6, 1936.

Sir Barnes N. Wallis, the brilliant Vickers engineer who had designed the airship R 100, began to lay out the Wellington in 1931. A twin-engine bomber with a unique geodesic structure, it flew in 1935 and entered squadron service in 1937. Work on the four-engine bombers that would pound Germany without mercy began in 1936. The Shorts Sterling would be the first large bomber in RAF service; the Handley Page Halifax would be the first to attack Germany. The Avro Manchester, an initial disappointment, led to the Avro Lancaster, one of the most successful bombers of the war. Engines were as important as airframes, and no engine of the war was more important than the Rolls-Royce Merlin, which powered everything from the Lancaster and Spitfire to the North American P-51 Mustang.

By 1937–1938, one European crisis followed another. Many in England recognized the Munich Agreement as a postponement of the inevitable that provided an opportunity to put aircraft and engine production into high gear. When that appeared inadequate, both Britain and France began to purchase weapons from American industry.

But victory would require more than aircraft. A. P. Rowe of the Air Ministry Directorate of Scientific Research, had become convinced that the offensive emphasis of the RAF would spell disaster in the event of war. He recommended the creation of a scientific committee to study the problems of air defense. Up and running by the end of 1934, the group was chaired by Henry Tizard, who had pioneered flight testing in World War I, and included two Nobel laureates in physics.

Tizard was willing to consider ideas that others regarded as absurd. He asked Robert Alexander Watson-Watt, head of the Radio Department of the National Physical Laboratory, for example, to look into the question of "death rays." Watson-Watt and his colleagues dismissed the idea but became intrigued by the possibility of using radio waves to locate aircraft in flight.

Radio began in 1887, when Heinrich Hertz used a spark to generate an electrical wave. Ten years later, the Italian Guglielmo Marconi used those waves to broadcast a radio message. That discovery revolutionized aerial combat by enabling ground-to-air and air-to-air communication. Beyond that, it now occurred to scientists that radio waves might also be used to detect distant objects.

The U.S. Signal Corps launched its experiments with radio detection systems in the 1930s. Two Navy researchers, F. R. Furth and S. M. Taylor, actually provided the official acronym, *radar*, for *radio detection and ranging*. In Germany, Dr. Rudolph Kühnhold used a radar system to detect ships at a distance of seven miles in 1934 and accidentally discovered that he could detect aircraft in flight as well.

The impact of radar on the Battle of Britain (1940) has obscured the fact that the Germans had superior radar systems in use at the outset of the war. The Seetakt equipment installed on German warships was used for determining the range to targets, while Freya, demonstrated in July 1938, was a long-range detection system installed on North Sea islands over which aircraft approaching from England would pass. A year later, the Wurzburg-A radar was sufficiently accurate to be used in conjunction with antiaircraft batteries. Together, these two systems were primarily responsible for the disastrous losses suffered by RAF bombers during their early air attacks on Germany.

Robert Watson-Watt and his colleagues demonstrated their radar equipment for members of the air defense committee in 1935. The government funded the effort and urged Watson-Watt's team to move forward with the utmost secrecy. In addition to developing the technology, Watson-Watt explored what he called "Operational Research." The ability to detect the enemy at a distance would be useless unless that information could be used to direct fighters to the target. That would require information management centers, complete with plotting boards, a decision-making apparatus, and the ability to communicate directly with the fighter pilots. The British would face the German assault with an air defense system.

The world expected, and feared, a war in which bombing would

Robert Alexander Watson-Watt

play a major role. No one envisioned an air war in which a battle between electronic detection and navigation systems, and the technical measures devised to counter them, would spell the difference between victory and defeat. In this war, scientists and engineers would play a more critical role than the soldiers and airmen in combat. It was the beginning of a new era during which the systems on board an aircraft would be as important as the airframe or engine. It was even more difficult to imagine the extent to which these new systems would enable humans to manage complex machines. The information they produced would reshape business, government, and society itself.

As the new aircraft entered service, and the tall towers of the Chain Home radar stations rose along the south coast, the RAF continued to expand and reorganize. The old service that had been described as something akin to a gentleman's flying club, gave way to a no-nonsense organization that included support services and a series of operational units: Training Command, Bomber Command, Fighter Command, and Coastal Command. The RAF would be ready when war came—barely.

THE U.S. ARMY AIR CORPS PREPARES

What was the business of an air force? Following World War I, the U.S. War Department ruled that the proper role of air power was to support ground operations. As late as 1931, the General Staff continued to define the Air Corps as "a highly mobile and powerful combat element which . . . conducts operations required to carry out Army missions."[18]

In 1934, President Roosevelt asked former Secretary of War Newton D. Baker to head a committee to review the need for an independent air force. "The idea that aviation, acting alone, can control sea lanes, or defend the coast, or produce decisive results in any other general mission contemplated under our policy are all visionary," the Baker Board reported, "as is the idea that a very large and independent air force is necessary to defend our country against attack."[19]

The airmen begged to differ. Whatever others might think, they quietly fleshed out their own vision of the next war in the hallways and classrooms of the Air Corps Tactical School (ACTS). Founded at Langley Field in Virginia in 1922, the school moved to Maxwell Field in Alabama in 1931. The highest educational establishment in the air arm, the tactical school trained officers and, like the Naval War College, crafted the doctrine that would guide the application of air power. The roster of faculty, staff, and students at ACTS constitutes a who's who of U.S. Army Air Force (USAAF) commanders in World War II.

The curriculum at ACTS covered the entire range of Air Corps missions, from observation and ground support to pursuit aviation. Basic doctrine called for a well-rounded force. Some instructors, notably Capt. Claire Lee Chennault (class of 1930–1931, faculty in 1931–1936), swam against the current by arguing the importance of pursuit aviation.

In their heart of hearts, most of the airmen saw strategic bombing as the mission that would revolutionize war and justify their independence. In Britain and France, bombing was an article of faith. At ACTS, they worked out the details. Unwilling to advocate terror attacks on civilian populations, and naturally inclined to accuracy and efficiency in all things, Air Corps planners called for precision attacks on vital systems—communications, transportation, power generation and transmission. "Surgical" strikes on key industries—petroleum production, machine tool factories, ball bearing plants—would destroy an enemy's capacity to make war with the loss of fewer civilian lives.

What began at ACTS continued in Washington, D.C. General Henry H. "Hap" Arnold, chief of the Air Corps, created an air intelligence sec-

Henry H. "Hap" Arnold standing in the cockpit
of a Martin B-10, July 18, 1934

tion to gather potential target information on foreign industry, power production, and communication and transportation systems. In 1941, the information gathered to date was folded into an Air War Plan (AWPD-I) that would guide the actions of the USAAF in the case of war. The leaders of the USAAF were committed to pursuing their own vision of strategic air warfare and were in the process of obtaining tools for the job.

Fortunately, another group of U.S. air planners was hard at work acquiring the weapons for an air force capable of executing the war plan. During the 1930s, the Materiel Division of the Air Corps, headquartered at Wright Field in Dayton, Ohio, was the center of all army flight research, testing, procurement, and supply. By 1935, the entire operation involved less than one hundred officers and a thousand civilian engineers and technicians.

That number included the men who would create the air force that would win the first global air war. The Materiel Division included a series of all-important project offices for pursuit aircraft, bombers, transport machines, and so on. In the mid-1930s, the bomber project office included a single project officer, a civilian engineer, and a stenographer. This was the office that watched over the birth of the B-17, B-24, B-25, B-26, and B-29, and saw each of these machines through the process of development, testing, and production.

As chief engineer and assistant chief of the Materiel Division from 1934 to 1940, Col. (later Major General) Oliver Patton Echols supervised the entire operation. He moved to Washington in 1940, where he had full responsibility for the procurement, development, distribution, and support of every airplane in the army inventory. Benjamin Kelsey,

Major General Oliver Patton Echols

who served as pursuit project officer under Echols, regarded him as "the man who won World War II."[20]

The close personal relationship between the procurement officers and the leaders of the aircraft industry proved key to success. As the project officer in charge of fighter development, Ben Kelsey had direct access to both the chief of the Air Corps and the president of Lockheed. It was an advantage that would be denied the Pentagon bureaucrats and armies of corporate executives who controlled the industry after the enormous expansion of World War II.

THE ACHIEVEMENTS OF Wright Field were not limited to the procurement of aircraft and engines. In 1935, the year in which the prototype B-17 first flew, Assistant Chief of the Air Corps Oscar Westover announced that the development of high-octane aviation gasoline "contributed more to aeronautical development in the world than any other single accomplishment in the past eight years."[21] The accomplishment was the result of Air Corps leadership and industrial research.

Leonard Hobbs, an authority on the history of aeronautical power plants, estimated that 75 percent of the 400-mile increase in the speed of fighter aircraft between the two world wars was the result of improvements in engine performance.[22] But those more powerful engines developed hotter interior temperatures, and a new problem. Normally, the spark plug ignites a mixture of fuel and air inside the cylinder, increasing the pressure and pushing the piston. When the temperature inside the cylinder becomes too high, however, the mixture can ignite spontaneously, a situation that can reduce power and eventually destroy the engine.

Engine knock had become a problem for automobiles before World War I. Thomas Midgley, a researcher at the Dayton Engineering Laboratories (Delco), began to study the problem when the firm's electrical ignition system was unfairly blamed for it. By 1922, he had discovered that lead, a noncombustible fuel additive, reduced knocking, although he did not understand why. Testing at nearby McCook Field, home of the U.S. Army Air Service Engineering Division, played a key role in solving additional problems that led to the introduction of leaded gasoline for automobile engines.

Knocking remained a problem, however, for powerful high-compression aircraft engines. The development of more effective aviation fuels that would eliminate it remained a high priority at the new Army Air Corps power plant laboratory at Wright Field, opened in the Dayton suburbs to replace McCook Field in 1927. Graham Edgar of the Ethyl Gasoline Corporation took a step forward in 1926, when he synthesized isooctane, a hydrocarbon that was very effective in reducing knock in high-compression engines. Isooctane was too expensive to burn as a fuel. It could, however, be used as an additive. The "octane rating," the percentage of isooctane that had to be mixed with a regular fuel to eliminate knocking, provided a critically important measure of fuel performance. The goal was to achieve 100 octane fuel, which would prevent knocking in the most powerful engines.

Few terms in automotive technology are so misunderstood. A fuel with a higher octane rating is not more powerful than a lower-rated compound. Whatever the octane, all gasoline produces between 17,000 and 20,000 BTUs (British thermal units) of power.[23] Increases in power are the result of improvements in engine design, such as increasing the compression or adding a supercharger to increase the pressure of the air flowing into the cylinders. The octane rating simply describes the resistance of a fuel to knocking, a condition that prevented the development of higher-compression engines.

Sam D. Heron, who had pioneered sodium-cooled valves, discovered the relationship between internal temperature and knocking while working at Wright Field. By the early 1930s, both the U.S. Navy and the Air Corps relied on the power plant laboratory to provide leadership in the drive to produce improved fuels. Shell Oil, anxious to move into a new market, hired aviator and engineer Jimmy Doolittle to head the program. A research breakthrough enabled the firm to begin production of 100 octane gasoline in 1934.

The airlines and the navy initially resisted the use of 100 octane fuel because of its higher cost. Air Corps officials persevered, however, and with increased production, costs began to drop. While it seldom received the credit that it deserved, the development of high-octane aviation fuel was one of the keys to the Allied victory in the air during World War II. Oscar Westover's 1935 judgment was well founded.

THE MODERN BOMBER emerged from the design revolution of the 1930s. The Boeing B-9 (1931), with its pencil-thin fuselage, open cockpits, light bomb load, and limited defensive armament, was not acquired in quantity, but it was a significant step toward the Boeing 247. The Martin B-10 (1933) was the first modern, all-metal monoplane bomber to enter service. It cruised at 200 mph, 45 mph faster than the B-9, and offered completely enclosed cockpits, a rotating gun turret, and an internal bomb bay. Boeing would eventually sell two hundred B-10s to the United States and to foreign air forces.

The B-10 demonstrated just how advanced the products of the American aviation industry were. The French Amiot 143, a frontline bomber sent against the Germans in 1940, flew at a top speed that was 10 mph slower than that of the B-10. Contemporary English bombers such as the Handley Page Heyford, a wood and fabric biplane with open cockpits and fixed landing gear, looked prehistoric when compared to the all-metal monoplane from Baltimore.

The earliest models of the legendary Norden bombsight were tested aboard the B-10. A precision bombsight, Air Corps planners believed, was as important as the airplane that carried it. In 1934, Gen. Benjamin Delahauf Foulois, chief of the Air Corps, remarked that the Norden bombsight was the most important of the Air Corps's secret military projects. It came to symbolize the American way of war, the efficient delivery of destruction in a clean, precise fashion. That, at least, was the theory.

The Norden bombsight actually became the best-known American "secret" of World War II. Films, newspapers, and popular magazines celebrated the importance of this single device to the war effort. But the innards of the gadget remained so secret that bombardiers were sworn to protect the bombsight with their lives.

Carl Lukas Norden began work on his bombsight in 1920. A Dutch citizen living in Brooklyn, he had developed gyroscopic stabilization systems for the Sperry Company. The Navy Bureau of

Ordnance asked him to put that experience to work improving the accuracy of their standard Mark III bombsight. His advice was to abandon the old sight and begin work on a new and much more accurate device.

Norden delivered the first hand-built test articles in 1923 and began manufacturing sights under a navy contract in 1928. The navy, however, had lost faith in the accuracy of horizontal bombing and turned to dive-bombing and torpedo attacks. By 1933, the navy had spent as much as $40,000 on the development of Norden's Mark XV bombsight. The Army Air Corps was more than willing to pick up the project. Technology and doctrine had converged.[24]

ACQUIRING THE IDEAL BOMBER in which to mount the Norden bombsight came next. In 1934 the Materiel Division announced a requirement for a multiengine aircraft capable of carrying a ton of bombs for a distance of two thousand miles at a speed of 200 mph. Most firms suggested twin-engine designs. Boeing won the development contract with engineer Ed Wells's more ambitious proposal for the four-engine Project 294, the only model of which flew in 1937 as the XB-15.

The largest U.S. military aircraft flown to date, the XB-15 was underpowered. As early as 1934, Wells and his team started work on a smaller four-engine aircraft identified as Project 299. Flown for the first time in July 1935, the 299 was dispatched to Wright Field for evaluation, where it crashed on take-off as a result of pilot error. In spite of the accident, the army ordered sixteen of the follow-on YB-17s.

It would be a uniquely American weapons system: a large, all-metal, multiengine airplane of the sort that the world had come to expect from U.S. industry, propelled by the most powerful radial aircraft engines in the world, fitted with a bombsight that promised unprecedented accuracy. The Air Corps fleet of B-17s would grow very slowly during the years before Pearl Harbor, but their promise was clear.

In 1939, with Boeing production facilities operating at full capacity, the Air Corps offered Rueben Fleet and Consolidated Aircraft a contract to built additional B-17s. Instead, the San Diego firm offered to design an even better four-engine bomber. Whether it was a better airplane or not would be argued by flight crews for years to come. In any case, the Consolidated Model 32, the prototype B-24 Liberator, first flew in December 1939.

That was the year in which North American Aviation rolled out the ancestor of all subsequent twin-engine B-25 medium bombers. Dutch Kindelberger, who had moved from Martin to Douglas, was at the helm of the reinvigorated firm that had begun a decade earlier as a holding company. The Martin Model 179, the prototype B-26, was completed at the Middle River, Maryland, factory in the fall of 1939.

Eager to acquire a fighter able to at least keep up with modern bombers, the army purchased over one hundred of the all-metal Boeing P-26s (1932). The little "pea shooter," with its open cockpit, fixed landing gear, and lightweight armament, however, seemed at least half a generation behind the bomber that it was designed to protect.

The Seversky P-35 (1937) was the first all-metal, closed-cockpit fighter with retractable landing gear procured by the Air Corps. Alexander de Seversky had lost his leg while flying with the Czarist Naval Air Service during World War I. He was visiting aircraft manufacturers in the United States on behalf of the Czarist government when the Bolsheviks came to power. He went to work as a test pilot and technical consultant to the Air Service and became a personal assistant to Billy Mitchell.

Seversky received over 350 patents, including one for an early bombsight, and founded the Seversky Aero Corporation, which folded in the stockmarket crash of 1929. Two years later he was elected president of the newly organized Seversky Aircraft Corporation. He hired several fellow Russian émigrés, most notably the engineer Alexander Kartveli. Their first product, the SEV-3, was a low-wing monoplane constructed by the Edo Float Company; Seversky did not yet have a factory. The breakthrough came with the sale of seventy-six P-35 fighters to the U.S. Army. The airplane also sold well to the Japanese navy (it was the only U.S. aircraft operated by the Japanese in World War II) and to Sweden.

The P-35 and the Curtiss Hawk 75 couldn't compare to the Bf 109,

Spitfire, or Hurricane, each of which made its appearance within a year of the Seversky. Alexander Kartveli's XP-41 lost a 1939 army design competition to the Curtiss XP-40. By 1938, the export versions of the P-35 were obsolete and no longer selling. That year, the company lost over half a million dollars.

In the spring of 1939, the board of Seversky Aircraft selected a new president. By the fall, the company had reorganized as Republic Aviation, and Alexander de Seversky was out of the aircraft manufacturing business. Kartveli and Republic would forge ahead to produce the final descendant of the P-35, and one of the masterpieces of U.S. aircraft design, the P-47 Thunderbolt (1941).

The U.S. Army Air Corps would fly into battle with the Bell P-39 Airacobra (1938) and the Curtiss-Wright P-40 Warhawk (1940), a pair of fighters that were obsolete by both European and Japanese standards before they entered production. Curtiss was the oldest aircraft company in Buffalo, New York. Bell was the newest.

As a young man, Lawrence Dale Bell attended the 1910 Dominguez Field air meet and worked with his brother Grover, an exhibition pilot who died in a 1913 crash. After graduating from Santa Monica Polytechnic, Bell got a job with Martin, and eventually became a vice president. Donald Douglas left Martin in 1919 following a dispute with Bell, who resigned in 1925 following a disagreement with Glenn Martin.

Rueben Fleet lured Bell back into aviation in 1928. When Fleet decided to move Consolidated from Buffalo to San Diego in 1935, Bell remained behind and founded his own firm in the old plant. Fleet promised to send subcontracting his way. Indeed, one of Bell's first contracts involved producing wing panels for the Consolidated PBY. Bell's early entries in the competition for military contracts were unsuccessful. However, the Bell P-39 put the company, and chief engineer Robert Wood's design team, on the map.

The P-39, and the P-40, the product of Curtiss-Wright's chief engineer, Don Berlin, were produced in very large numbers because they were the best products available to the army. Neither machine could match the performance of Messerschmitt's Bf 109 or Mitsubishi's Zero. In the hands of an experienced pilot, however, both airplanes gave a good account of themselves. The P-39 would prove itself with the USAAF in New Guinea and in the skies over the Eastern Front, while the members of the American Volunteer Group, the famous Flying Tigers, earned immortality with the P-40.

For the moment, these planes would have to do. Fortunately, however, the finest piston-engine, propeller-driven fighter aircraft that the world had ever seen were already taking shape on American drawing boards.

II

BATTLES IN THE SKY,
1939–1945

OPENING GUNS

Hitler's original plan for the invasion of Poland called for a massive air attack on military objectives in and around Warsaw. Hermann Goering hoped to quickly break the spirit of the Poles and introduce the rest of Europe to the might of German air power. The weather around Warsaw, however, forced postponement of the attack until September 13.

Instead, at 4:34 A.M. on September 1, 1939, three Ju 87 Stukas roared over the bridge crossing the Vistula River at the Polish village of Dirschau. Their mission was to disable electrical cables critical to destroying the bridge in the event of an invasion from nearby East Prussia. Eleven minutes after the raid, the vanguard of forty-four divisions, one and a half million troops, began pouring across the border under the protective umbrella of German air power.

It was not a walkover. Effective antiaircraft fire and the efforts of valiant Poles flying obsolete machines took a toll on German airmen. The defenses were soon overwhelmed, however. When the Soviet Union invaded from the east on September 17, the fate of Poland was sealed.

The conquest of Poland previewed things to come. Air superiority drove the Blitzkrieg of 1939–1940. Control of the air made all else possible, from strategic bombing to reconnaissance and ground support.

FLIGHTS OF JU 87s and He 111s based in East Prussia struck sixty-six Soviet forward airfields in southern Rumania at 3:15 on the morning of June 22, 1941. Air strikes continued through the morning, with German long-range artillery battering the airfields along the border. Operation Barbarosa, the invasion of Russia, was underway. The Soviets lost two hundred airplanes that day, two-thirds of them on the ground. The handful of open-cockpit fighters that managed to get into the air were no match for a Bf 109.

There had been warnings aplenty. For nine months Col. Theodor Rowhel had been sending single reconnaissance aircraft across the border to identify and photograph Soviet airfields. The Soviets made no attempt to stop them. Stalin refused to recognized that the Germans were preparing to invade, and would do nothing to provoke them. On two occasions when engine problems forced reconnaissance aircraft down on the wrong side of the border, a diplomatic note of apology sufficed to smooth matters over. But now it was too late. The Nazi ground-air juggernaut began to roll across the Motherland.

THE FIRST WAVE swept across the harbor at 7:55 A.M., on the morning of December 7, 1941: forty-nine bombers, forty torpedo bombers, fifty-one dive-bombers, and forty-three fighters. Below them lay the bulk of the U.S. Pacific Fleet, seventy warships in all, including eight battleships. Fortunately, the bulk of the cruisers and all of the aircraft carriers were at sea. This would be remembered as the day of infamy, a surprise attack like no other in American history. Yet there had been warnings.

At 3:45 A.M, the minesweeper USS *Condor* had spotted a midget submarine entering the harbor in front of a barge towed by the USS *Antares*. A Consolidated PBY patrol bomber confirmed the sighting. The *Condor*, not equipped to attack a submarine, signaled a nearby destroyer, the USS *Ward*, which reported at 6:53 A.M. that it had sunk the sub. At 7:25 A.M. authorities ordered the USS *Monaghan* to investigate the reported submarine sinking. She had just gotten underway when the air attack began.

A few minutes before, at about 6:45 A.M. a mobile radar unit at Opana Point detected a single aircraft approaching from the north. It was a Japanese floatplane scouting the way for the main force, which the radar operators detected shortly after 7 A.M. The radar sightings were assumed to be a flight of B-17s scheduled to arrive from the mainland that morning.

In 1821, Englishman Peter Corney described the harbor on the south coast of Oahu, noting "the many divers employed . . . diving for pearl oysters which are found in great plenty." Pearl Harbor it would be. Four years later, Andrew Bloxam, the ship's naturalist aboard the HMS *Blonde*, a man of more practical turn of mind, noted that it was "a most excellent harbor, as inside there is plenty of water to float the largest ship and room enough for the whole Navy of England."[1]

The U.S. Navy established itself in Pearl Harbor in 1898. Between 1900 and 1908 a dredging project produced port facilities that could handle the largest warships. Another round of improvements in 1939 prepared the way for the transfer of the Pacific Fleet from California to Hawaii in 1940. The intention was to signal the Japanese that America would defend its Pacific interests. The signal was received and understood.

After five years of air battles over China, the Japanese boasted the most experienced and best-equipped naval air force in the world. Having been ordered to develop a plan to begin a war in the Pacific, Adm. Isoroku Yamamoto chose the most audacious option: Japanese airmen would strike targets all over Asia and the Pacific. The key to success, however, would be a strike far to the West against the U.S. fleet in Pearl Harbor.

In addition to its distance from Japanese bases, U.S. officials had taken comfort in the fact that Pearl Harbor was thought to be too shallow for aerial torpedoes. Admiral Yamamoto, however, had paid close attention to a smaller-scale but very effective 1940 British attack on the Italian naval base at Taranto, a very shallow harbor. Twenty-one Fairey

Isoroku Yamamoto

Swordfish from HMS *Illustrious*—the "stringbags," as the aircrew called these obsolete fabric-covered biplanes—sank three battleships and a cruiser, forcing the Italian fleet to beat a hasty retreat to ports in western Italy, where they were less of a threat to British convoys.

Yamamoto recognized that Japan could never win a head-to-head confrontation with the United States. By December 1941, however, conditions seemed as favorable as they were likely to get. Germany had conquered Europe, had the Soviets on the run, and was threatening Cairo. A breakthrough might yet lead to a link between the Axis nations in South Asia. A strike at the U.S. fleet anchorage at Pearl Harbor, coupled with the seizure of Wake Island, the Philippines, Hong Kong, and all the remaining Allied possessions in Asia and the Pacific west of Hawaii, might at least buy Japan six months in which to consolidate its gains and prepare to resist an American advance.

The attack was to be carefully coordinated with diplomatic efforts. The United States was to be informed of impending hostilities immediately before the strike. Unlike the attack on Taranto, this would be a full-scale blow delivered by a far larger task force, operating the finest naval aircraft in the world. Admiral Chuichi Nagumo would command six aircraft carriers, two battleships, a cruiser, a screen of destroyers, and eight support ships. They would cross the North Pacific, outside the shipping lanes, and maintain strict radio silence. In spite of some U.S. success in reading Japanese radio traffic, the attack came as a complete surprise.

The first priority was to seize control of the air, striking the U.S. Army, Navy, and Marine Corps airfields at Ford Island, Ewa, Hickam, Wheeler, Bellows, and Kaneohe. The dive and torpedo bombers focused on "battleship row," along Ford Island. The USS *Arizona, Nevada, Oklahoma,* and *West Virginia* were sunk or badly damaged. There was a lull, but not a cessation of attacks from 8:30 A.M. until roughly 8:40, when thirty horizontal bombers and twenty dive-bombers arrived on the scene. Bombing and strafing attacks were also underway against ground and harbor facilities.

By 9:45, when the last of the attackers was on its way back to the carriers, the U.S. fleet had lost eighteen vessels, sunk or badly damaged, and 188 aircraft (96 from the navy and marines and 92 from the army). The number of dead American seamen, soldiers, and airmen totaled 2,251, almost half of them from the *Arizona.* There were 1,119 wounded survivors, with 22 missing in action.[2]

It could have been worse. Had the Japanese caught the American carrier force in port. . . . Had they struck the fuel oil storage and gasoline tanks that would fuel ships and planes in the weeks to come. . . . Had they destroyed the dockyard and port facilities that would put the damaged ships back in commission. . . . Even so, the attack ultimately became a Pyrrhic victory for Japan. As Admiral Yamamoto recognized, they had awakened a sleeping tiger. Americans would not forget Pearl Harbor. Armed with righteous anger, they would commit their awesome industrial might to the achievement of total victory. The leaders of Germany and Japan had no conception of the wave of destruction that would wash over their nations in a few short years.

THE AIR WAR

World War I set the twentieth century into terrible motion. World War II was its central tragedy. The defeat of fascism in Germany and Italy and militarism in Japan cost an estimated 60 million lives. As many as 25 million of those unfortunate souls were Russian. Perhaps two-thirds of them were civilians. One authority sets the number of Chinese dead for the years 1937–1945 at 15 million. The traditional estimate of 6 million Jewish victims of the Holocaust now appears to be low. Poland lost 6 million citizens, Germany 4 million, and Japan 2 million. Four hundred thousand Britons and three hundred thousand Americans lost their lives.[3]

The war brought an end to the Age of Empire and created a "Third World" of nations free of colonial bonds. It was billed as a war for democracy, but a tyranny as great as anything that had been defeated emerged as one of the two genuine victors. A second-rate power at the outset, the USSR had borne the awful brunt of the struggle against Nazi Germany and emerged with a sphere of influence that stretched from the Rhine to the Pacific, from the Adriatic to the Arctic, from the Black Sea to the Sea of Japan. The war to end fascism and militarism gave way to a new war, both hot and cold, for the hearts and minds of the world.

The global air conflict of World War II began with a series of strikes from the sky and concluded with the destruction of two cities by two bombers carrying two bombs. If air power did not win the war, as its pre-war adherents had hoped, it had shaped the nature and character of the conflict. The airplane had given birth to the awful reality of total war.

The airplane had created a global war and had been transformed by it. Flying across oceans and continents, once the stuff of heroes and head-lines, became a wartime commonplace. Land-based military planes flew scheduled intercontinental service across the Atlantic and Pacific. The air war laid the foundation for the age of international air commerce.

The Second World War produced the ultimate in piston-engine aircraft. The pressures of war pushed existing technology to its limits. The Dornier Do 335 still holds the world speed record for propeller-driven aircraft. Standard airplanes introduced during the war, including the P-51, F4U, and B-29, remained in active service into the next decade. Refurbished and heavily modified veterans of World War II continued to dominate the air race circuit in the United States until the end of the century.

The war had opened the door to the future. Highly experimental technologies, from jet and rocket propulsion to ground-based and onboard electronic systems, came of age during the conflict. Nuclear weapons and the first practical computers moved from pure theory to revolutionary practice during the war. The new airplanes and the weapons that they carried would redefine the very meaning of war and peace.

CONTROL OF THE AIR

Air control over the battlefield ruled every theater, on land and sea. The Nazi juggernaut had rolled across continental Europe in two years under the cover of the Luftwaffe. German aircraft facilitated the Blitzkrieg, as Nazi troops and armor swept through Belgium, France, Holland, and Denmark. Paratroopers, a new kind of army that dropped out of the sky, led the assault on Norway.

The importance of controlling the air over the battlefield was never more clearly demonstrated than during the Battle of Britain (July–September 1940). The air campaign against England began with attacks on shipping in the Channel and proceeded to strikes on RAF Fighter Command bases and the radar system that guided the young fighter pilots to their targets. The aim was to wrest control of the air over England from the RAF as a means of forcing a negotiated peace or clearing the way for a cross-Channel invasion.

Britain could not have won the war in 1940, but she could have lost it. Had Britain surrendered or negotiated a peace, the lights would have gone out all over Europe. Without a foothold in England, and with the Pacific in Japanese hands, American support for a beleaguered

Soviet Union would have been impossible. U.S. victory would have waited for the development of nuclear weapons, assuming that the more favorable military situation would not have encouraged a German nuclear program.

Fortunately, history turned on a dictator's pique. Angered by a small-scale RAF attack on Berlin, Hitler directed the Luftwaffe to attack London and other urban targets. While Londoners suffered through the Blitz, the RAF was able to catch its breath and explore the tactics that would enable the young heroes flying Hawker Hurricanes and Supermarine Spitfires to bring the German bombers down in ever increasing numbers.

Messerschmitt Bf 109E

The German were no more successful at reducing Moscow from the air than they had been in breaking the will of Londoners. When the German advance slowed on the road to Moscow in July 1941, the Luftwaffe launched a short-lived terror bombing campaign against the capital. General Mikhail Gromadin's Moscow Air Defense District fielded over 575 fighter aircraft, half of which could hold their own, and over a thousand antiaircraft guns. While the Nazi juggernaut would continue to roll toward the heart of Eurasia, the Soviets first tasted victory in the air over Moscow.

Control of the air was a key to the success or failure of strategic bombing campaigns. No significant Luftwaffe presence turned up over the Normandy beaches on June 6, 1944, or over the battlefields of France, Belgium, and Germany in the months that followed. The aerial defense of the Fatherland against around-the-clock bomber raids took precedence. The bombing campaign kept the German fighter force away from the battlefield, and chewed it up.

Air power on the Eastern Front was linked to bitter fighting on the ground. The Junkers Ju 87 Stuka, armed with a tank-busting thirty-seven-millimeter cannon; and the Ilyushin IL-2, a heavily armed and armored ground-attack aircraft, or "Shturmovik," became the workhorses of this war. The Americans did not know or care much about the Eastern Front, in spite of the fact that U.S. aircraft and equipment, provided through the Lend-Lease program, played a role in the final Russian victory. Nor would many of the Western Allies be willing to admit that the war in Europe was ultimately won there.

The most experienced fighter pilots of all time struggled for control of the air over the battle lines of Russia. The leading ace of the century, the German Erich Hartmann, destroyed an incredible 352 enemy aircraft. Gerhard Barkhorn (301 victories) and Gunther Rall (275) followed close behind. In all, fifteen German aces, most of them veterans of the Eastern Front, scored over 200 victories apiece!

A total of 119 Luftwaffe pilots ran up higher victory totals than Hiroyoshi Nishizawa (87 victories), a Japanese fighter pilot who emerged as the top-scoring non-German ace of the war. Ivan Kozhedub, the leading Russian ace, destroyed 62 enemy aircraft. Marmaduke "Pat" Pattlle (51 victories) was the top RAF scorer, while Richard Bong (40) led the list of American aces.

The incredible German victory tallies resulted from several factors. The Luftwaffe boasted the most-experienced pilots in the world. Other nations established tours of duty for their aviators, but a German pilot flew until he was killed or injured. Moreover, Germany maintained a technical edge under difficult conditions. Even as the nation crumbled into defeat, her pilots operated the finest fighter airplane in the world, the Me 262, powered by twin Junkers Jumo turbojet engines. One Luftwaffe pilot, Kurt Welter, scored over twenty aerial victories in the Me 262. At the end of the century, he remained the highest-ranking jet ace in history!

As the Allies began to attack the edges of the Axis empire in 1941–1944, they made the battle for air control the first order of business. The skies over occupied Europe became free of German planes long before the first soldier stormed ashore at Normandy. An aerial attack by the enemy was one of the few things the Allied soldiers did not have to worry about. German troops, on the other hand, lived in constant fear of roaming P-47 Thunderbolts, or "Jabos" (from the German *jaeger*, or "bomber"). Nothing could so cheer embattled American troops, or terrify their German opponents, as the sight of a flight of fighters peeling off for an attack.

While the North American P-51 and twin-engine Lockheed P-38 made their reputations escorting the B-17s and B-24s to their targets, the barrel-shaped Thunderbolt earned the affection of both the men and who flew it and the infantrymen whom they protected. Explaining his preference for the P-47 over the elegant P-51 Mustang, one veteran pilot commented that "when flying the Jug, I always felt as if I was in my Mother's arms."[4]

On the other side of the world, the war began with the Japanese controlling the air. The Imperial Army and Navy had destroyed Allied air power in the Philippines and had made the conquest of Southeast Asia a primary goal in the days following the attack on Pearl Harbor. Billy Mitchell's warning to the world's navies was realized on December 10, 1941, when an attack from the sky sent HMS *Prince of Wales* and *Repulse*, the pride of the Royal Navy's Indian Ocean fleet, to the bottom with 840 officers and men.

For a time, the American Volunteer Group, a handful of U.S. airmen fighting for Nationalist China, provided the most visible aerial opposition to the Japanese rampage across the subcontinent. The Flying Tigers, as they were better known, were commanded by rough-hewn Claire Lee Chennault, who had fought so hard for a hearing at the Air Corps Tactical School a decade before. During the critical weeks and months before the vanguard of the U.S. Army Air Forces (USAAF) arrived, the Tigers comprised the thin line of defense protecting the Burma Road, China's all-important lifeline, from the Japanese onslaught.

Land-based aircraft played a significant role in the air war over both the Atlantic and Pacific. Fighters and bombers operating from island bases crossed the vast Pacific to strike enemy airfields and convoys.

The large flying boats were also critical in the battle for air control at sea. The Consolidated PBY Catalina and Shorts Sunderlanda searched for submarines, rescued downed aviators, and conducted long-range reconnaissance patrols. An RAF Catalina discovered the German battleship *Bismark*, bringing on the last act in one of the great naval confrontations of the Atlantic war. A U.S. Navy PBY discovered the Japanese carriers steaming toward Midway, setting the stage for the pivotal battle of the Pacific war. From the Aleutians to New Guinea, from Hawaii to Japan, victory required command of the air.

CARRIER WAR

As noted earlier, Great Britain, Japan, and the United States were the only nations to employ aircraft carriers before and during World War II. Both Germany and Italy began to convert other vessels into carriers, but neither nation launched a completed vessel. As a result, carriers played a very different role in the Atlantic and the Pacific.

The U.S. Navy operated a total of 113 carriers in 1939–1945. The Royal Navy operated 68 flattops, and Japan 14. These statistics are a bit misleading, however. The United States was the only one of those nations to wage a full-scale naval war in both the Atlantic and the Pacific. Moreover, more than half of the U.S. (76) and British (44) vessels were small escort carriers (CVE in the U.S. designation system), or jeep carriers, bearing some thirty airplanes apiece. These smaller craft played a critical role in winning the Battle of the Atlantic, while the big *Essex-* and *Midway*-class carriers were employed exclusively in the Pacific.

Some notion of the ferocity of the war at sea is apparent in the fact that the U.S. Navy lost eleven carriers (9 percent) in action, while the Royal Navy lost eight (12 percent). By August 1945, Japan had lost all but three (87 percent) of its carriers. The only one of those three that had not been damaged was the obsolete little *Hosho* (completed in 1919), the first ship designed to be an aircraft carrier.

Early attempts to use carriers in antisubmarine operations ended in September 1939, when a U-boat sank the HMS *Courageous*. Carriers did play an important role in several early Royal Navy Atlantic operations, including the Norway campaign in 1940 and the pursuit and destruction of the battleship *Bismarck* in 1941. It was not until the introduction of the small CVEs in 1943, however, that the true potential of the aircraft carrier for antisubmarine operations was realized. When used in conjunction with new electronic searching systems, carrier-based airpower became the critical factor in breaking the back of the U-boats.

In the Pacific, the aircraft carrier emerged as one of the two principal naval weapon systems of the twentieth century. Five great, long-distance, carrier-to-carrier confrontations between the U.S. Navy and the Imperial Japanese fleet (in the Coral Sea, at Midway, in the Eastern Solomon Islands, at Santa Cruz, and in the Philippine Sea) shaped the very nature of the island-hopping campaign across the Central Pacific.

With hindsight, it is possible to see that the crucial early battles of Coral Sea (March 3–8, 1942) and Midway (June 3–7, 1942) marked the turning point of the Pacific war. Never again would the Japanese fleet threaten U.S. island bases in the western Pacific. For the first time, two fleets over a hundred miles apart fought a naval engagement. A relative handful of aircraft on both sides attacked and sank the most valuable capital ships in the enemy fleet.

If Midway was a critical American victory, however, the confrontations in the Eastern Solomon Islands during the Guadalcanal campaign (August 23–25, October 6, 1942) reduced the U.S. fleet, for a time, to a single active and undamaged carrier (*Hornet*) in the entire

Douglas SBD Dauntless flies over Wake Island, December 1943

theater of war. The ability of the United States to replace lost and damaged vessels, to produce an entirely new generation of naval aircraft, and to train an apparently endless stream of pilots spelled overwhelming defeat for Japan at the Battle of the Philippine Sea (June 19–20, 1944). With the defeat of Germany in the spring of 1945, British carriers, which had spent most of the war cruising the Indian Ocean, joined the U.S. fleet for the final air battles of the Pacific campaign.

At the deepest level, the needs of land-based air power drove American strategy in the Pacific. From Guadalcanal (1942) to Okinawa (1945), American troops stormed one beach after another, capturing the air bases that would enable them to carry the war closer to the enemy's homeland. The capture of Tinian, Saipan, and Guam finally put the B-29 bombers in range of Japan. Iwo Jima (1945) provided damaged bombers returning from the three-thousand-mile round-trip to Japan a safe refuge exactly halfway home.

THE BOMBING OF EUROPE

No aspect of the Allied war effort proved more controversial than strategic bombing. The worst fears of the Church Fathers, the apocalyptic novelists, and political leaders like Stanley Baldwin materialized. Battles on the ground and at sea came and went, but the bombing went on, by day and night, with little respite, from 1939 to 1945. Old definitions of what constituted a battlefield and who qualified as a noncombatant lost their meaning, as any possibility of restraining the escalating tide of destruction vanished.

At the outset lay an illusion that all of this could be avoided. President Franklin Roosevelt spoke out against aerial attacks on civilians. "The American government and the American people," he announced in 1939, "have for some time pursued a policy of wholeheartedly condemning the unprovoked bombing and machine-gunning of civilians." He had complained of the Japanese air campaign in China. On the day that the Second World War began, he urged the belligerents not to bomb civilians or unfortified cities.[5]

Talk was cheap. When the time came, whatever his public stance, President Roosevelt urged an unrelenting, around-the-clock, strategic air assault on the enemy's homeland as a keystone of Allied policy. Prime Minister Winston Churchill saw no other option. "There is one thing that will . . . bring [Germany] down," he explained, "and that is an absolutely devastating, exterminating attack by very heavy bombers from this country upon the Nazi homeland."[6]

Sir Charles Webster and Noble Frankland, official historians of the RAF campaign against Germany, defined this brand of aerial warfare as "a . . . direct attack on the enemy state with the object of depriving it of the means or the will to continue the war."[7] This vision of air power had been nurtured in the upper echelons of the U.S. Army Air Corps and the RAF, by dedicated officers who had also struggled to acquire the weapons that would transform theory into practice.

Ironically, Germany, Japan, and the Soviet Union, the nations that had horrified the world with their bombing attacks on Shanghai, Madrid, and Helsinki, did not prepare to undertake a sustained strategic air campaign. They entered the war with twin-engine medium bombers of relatively modest performance, airplanes that were well suited for a tactical role. They introduced improved versions of those standard types during the course of the conflict, but produced very few genuinely new bomber designs in significant numbers. None of them would operate four-engine heavy bombers in squadron service. The closest approach to such a machine, the Heinkel He 177, with its twin linked engines sharing twin nacelles, proved to be a failure.

German planners, who employed air power in support of ground operations, argued that cities like Warsaw (bombed on September 13–17, 1939) and Rotterdam (attacked in May 1940) comprised legitimate targets, well-defended fortresses blocking the advance of the German army. That point was lost on those who watched the two cities being devoured by flames in the newsreels at the local theater.

The earliest RAF raids on German cities delivered nothing more deadly than propaganda leaflets. In addition, RAF Bomber Command and the Luftwaffe traded relatively small-scale bombing attacks on shipping, naval installations, and other military targets on either side of the North Sea during the "phoney war" (of October 1939–May 1940).

The abilities to navigate and bomb accurately were abysmal on both sides. Unaccustomed to flying over water, the aviators strayed up to fifty miles off course in crossing the North Sea. On May 10, 1940, German units dispatched to bomb the French town of Dijon struck Freiburg instead. The Ministry of Propaganda promptly blamed the Allies.

Like the Germans, the British entered the war with twin-engine bombers of limited performance that were generally ill-equipped for the rigors of combat. Even the best of those machines, like the Vickers Wellington, designed by Barnes Wallis of R 100 fame, were poorly armed, underpowered, and lacked self-sealing gas tanks. The British quickly discovered that they had overestimated the ability of a group of bombers to defend themselves.

The leaders of Bomber Command based some critical decisions on this early experience. Between September 3, 1939, and April 9, 1940,

Bomber Command lost sixty-two airplanes during the course of 1,527 sorties. While the overall loss rate of 4 percent seemed acceptable, they were struck by the fact that almost twice as many aircraft had been lost on daytime attacks as in night raids. Effective German radar systems, combined with effective antiaircraft fire and superior fighter aircraft, had taken a fearful toll.

Some raids had been nothing short of catastrophic. Two attacks on December 14 and 18, 1939, resulted in losses of 50 and 55 percent of the Wellingtons involved. By February 1940, RAF leaders were transforming their day bomber force into an organization that would operate almost exclusively at night. Attempts to bomb well-defined military and economic targets gave way to less precise attacks on relatively large areas in the Ruhr, Germany's industrial heartland.

The airmen insisted that their proper function was to attack Germany. French military leaders protested, insisting that Bomber Command should undertake tactical strikes on the Panzer units pouring into France and on railroads and highway junctions critical to the German advance. RAF leaders attempted to support hard-pressed ground commanders without completely abandoning their continuing efforts to bomb Germany at night.

The tension between the need to support a ground campaign and the conviction of air commanders that they could best employ their forces in strategic air attacks against the enemy homeland would continue throughout the war. In April 1944, during the months leading up to the Normandy landings, Gen. Dwight D. Eisenhower demanded and received command of the Allied air forces, and redirected much of the bombing effort to the French transportation network and other targets that would have an impact on the invasion.

The German air campaign entered a new phase with the fall of France. In August and September 1940, the early attacks on shipping in the Channel gave way to raids on RAF Fighter Command bases, the all-important radar stations, and aircraft plants. While the young heroes of Fighter Command held their own, the losses mounted. By mid-August the number of Spitfires and Hurricanes lost exceeded the number of available replacement aircraft for the first time, and the Luftwaffe held the better position to win a war of attrition than the RAF.

In an effort to draw the maximum numbers of defending fighters into the air, the Luftwaffe mounted its first serious raid on London on August 24–25, 1940. Thanks to the British ability to read documents transmitted in the German cipher, the RAF saw the raid coming and prepared to strike back with a raid on Berlin the following night. Hitler and Goering now decided to redirect their campaign into unrestricted air attacks on the capital and other British cities.

The Blitz started by the end of the first week in September. The attacks gathered momentum, reaching a crescendo in late December 1940, when the city was in flames, from the historic core around St. Paul's to the East End. Because of bad weather, the attacks eased until March 1941, when the Luftwaffe launched a series of "Baedeker Raids" against other English towns. The last major attack hit London on May 10, 1941.

The bombing was brought to an end not so much by the RAF as by the redeployment of German air units from France to the east in preparation for the attack on Russia. Londoners and other Britons would suffer other air attacks during the war, but nothing, not even the terror campaign of 1944–1945 involving V-1 and V-2 aerial weapons, could match the raids of 1940–1941. A total of sixty thousand English men, women, and children lost their lives to air attacks during the war. Two-thirds of them died during the Blitz.

In lifting their own prohibition against unrestricted air attacks on cities, the Nazi leadership had sown the seeds of their own destruction. Like their counterparts in America, the leaders of the RAF had dreamed of the day when they would carry the war to the enemy heartland. With cities like London and Coventry in flames, RAF leaders had few qualms about unleashing a campaign of unrestricted bombing against German cities.

Vengeance was not the only motivation for the strategic air campaign. Britain stood alone fighting defensive battles in North Africa, on the Atlantic, and in the Mediterranean. Bombing offered the only opportunity to strike an offensive blow against Germany. Prime Minister Churchill emphasized the bombing campaign in his discussions with Stalin, who demanded Allied action against Nazi-occupied Europe in order to relieve pressure on the Soviet Union. In practical terms, the bombers represented a "second front" long before the Allies were ready to invade the continent.

In addition, the leadership of both the RAF and the USAAF were convinced that strategic bombing offered the surest and least painful path to victory. They had spent more than a decade planning for such a campaign and had no difficulty recruiting the president, the prime minister, and other political leaders as enthusiastic supporters.

Bomber Command struggled through 1941 under the command of Air Marshall Charles Portal. That August, Lord Cherwell, Churchill's scientific advisor, ordered a study of bombing accuracy, which revealed that only one-third of all bombers had dropped their loads within five miles of the target.

The big change came in February 1942, when Arthur Travers Harris took the helm of Bomber Command. A member of a family filled with colonels and Colonial Office civil servants, he had earned a reputation in the RAF for his acerbic comments on military life. An outspoken realist, his primary goal was to send the maximum number of airplanes carrying the maximum number of bombs to the maximum number of German cities at the earliest possible moment.

Convinced of the critical importance of the task, and recognizing the limitations of technology, Harris launched the first night incendiary raids against Lübeck and Rostock in the spring of 1942. In May he called up training units and every aircraft that could struggle into the air and launched the first of his "thousand plane raids" on Cologne. Sheer destruction was his goal. He set out to pound Germany's cities into the ground. He destroyed transportation networks, killed thousands of workers and "dehoused" hundreds of thousands of others, spread terror, and tried to break the German will.

By 1943, an incredible variety of electronic beams, waves, and pulses filled the night skies of Europe. Radar waves emanated from Britain's Chain Home stations and Germany's Kammhuber line. Named for Josef Kammhuber, who directed the air defense of the Reich, the line consisted of radar stations, searchlights, and gun emplacements stretching across Germany. Defenses circled all the major cities, particularly the industrial centers of the Ruhr. As the war progressed, all Germany would be divided into boxes, and radar operators would guide the fighter assigned to each box to a target.

Then there were the Knickebein radio beams that guided German bombers to their targets and signaled them when to drop their bombs. During the course of the war the Germans continued to introduce even more sophisticated navigation and bombing systems.

The RAF introduced its GEE radio navigation system in 1942, and the OBOE radar navigation and bombing system by the end of the year. In addition, English scientists, notably physicist R. V. Jones, focused their attention on developing countermeasures that would render the German systems useless. The strategic air campaign would be remembered as a battle of the beams.

In Germany, Britain, and the United States, specialists developed ever more effective radars. Ground-based systems helped to locate enemy aircraft and aim antiaircraft guns. By the end of the war, onboard radar sets enabled bombardiers to locate their targets at night or through clouds and enabled night fighters to locate their prey.

Things grew more complex after the discovery that a night fighter could follow the electronic signal emitted by a bomber right back to its target. RAF crews were instructed to switch on their very useful H2S sets for only short periods. For the first time in the history of aviation, the electronic gizmos stuffed aboard an aircraft contributed to its ability to complete its mission as much as the engines and propellers.

BY MID-1943, the RAF was no longer fighting alone. The USAAF had established the Eighth Air Force in England and the Fifteenth Air Force in Italy. From the outset, the Americans were determined to conduct precision attacks on carefully selected targets. Beginning in August 1942, B-17s and B-24s began gaining experience with attacks on areas where they could be protected by fighter cover. In spite of differences of opinion between U.S. and British air commanders, President Roosevelt and Prime Minister Churchill, meeting at Casablanca in January 1943, approved a combined bomber offensive that would result in around-the-clock attacks on Germany.

The Eighth Air Force supported the RAF with daylight attacks on Hamburg during July 24–28, 1943. The success of these attacks demonstrated the extent to which Bomber Command was warming to its task. On the night of July 27–28, 786 RAF bombers dropped twelve hundred tons of incendiaries on the city, igniting the first great firestorm of the war. At the center of the conflagration, temperatures approached 1,000 degrees Celsius, and winds blew at 150 mph. The bombings destroyed thirteen square miles of the city, killing over forty-two thousand people, with thousands more simply listed as missing.

The attackers also paid a price. In early August, 147 B-24s operating from bases in North Africa struck the oil fields around Ploeşti, Rumania. Fifty-four of them, an incredible 36 percent, failed to return. That fall (October 9–14, 1943) the Eighth Air Force suffered through "Black Week." American airmen flew four missions deep into Germany without fighter cover over the targets. On the last of those missions, 291 bombers attacked the ball bearing plant at Schweinfurt. Sixty B-17s, 16 percent of the total, were downed. All told, 148 bombers were lost on the four missions. They were the last USAAF missions deep into Germany for the rest of the year. For the moment, the Luftwaffe still controlled the daytime skies over the Reich.

The men of Bomber Command also had a difficult time fighting the Battle of Berlin (November 18, 1943–March 31, 1944). In an effort to keep the Germans off balance, Harris launched sixteen major attacks on the German capital, as well as twenty-nine attacks on other cities in Germany and France. The RAF flew 29,459 sorties during this period, with a total loss of 1,117 aircraft (3.8 percent). Over 1,600 additional aircraft made it home but never flew again.

These statistics are a bit misleading. While the average number lost was not out of line with what had come before, the percentage climbed over time, reaching 7 and 8 percent by December. A raid on Nuremburg in March resulted in the loss of 11.2 percent of the bombers involved, the highest rate for any RAF raid of the war.

Worse, individual units that found themselves in the wrong place at the wrong time lost 20 to 30 percent of their aircraft. The real impact of losing over 2,700 aircraft from a force with fewer than 900 bombers at any one time during this five-month period is obvious. Harris turned from attacks on Berlin to support for the coming invasion of Europe, granting a little breathing space for his crews.[8]

The proponents of strategic bombing argued that this approach would provide an escape from the meat grinder of the trenches. The fear that no government would ever again persuade its young men to take up arms in a repeat of the Western Front had been a significant factor in British enthusiasm for an aerial alternative. In truth, the air war simply proved to be a substitute for a war of attrition on the ground.

For the USAAF, the turning point came with the development of fuel drop tanks that enabled the P-51 Mustangs to accompany the B-17s and B-24s all the way to Berlin and fight when they got there. From January 1945 on, the air war over Europe served a new purpose. As the raids deep into Germany resumed with fighter cover, additional Luftwaffe units withdrew back to the Reich to participate in home defense. Now, the bombers destroyed targets on the ground, while the Mustangs began the process of destroying the German fighter force.

Things started looking up for Bomber Command as well. In 1943, the combined bomber offensive delivered 400,056 tons of bombs

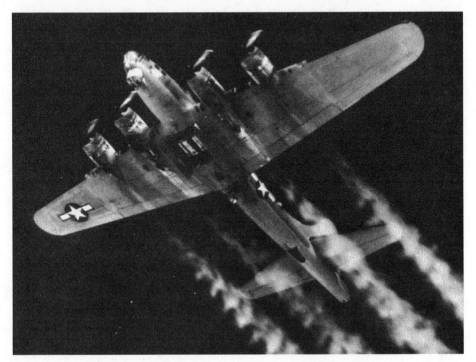

Boeing B-17F Flying Fortress of the 452nd Bomb Group

(259,989 tons by the RAF, 140,067 tons by the USAAF). The following year the RAF and USAAF dropped four times that weight of bombs, 1,592,108 tons (1,203,025 by the RAF, 389,083 by the USAAF).[9]

Just as the presence of fighter escorts began to overwhelm the German fighter units coming up to meet the USAAF bombers, so resistance to night attacks seemed to be diminishing by the fall of 1944. The number of sorties and the weight of bombs delivered remained near the peak, while the loss rate fell. In January 1944, the worst month of the war for the RAF, the loss rate approached 6 percent. By December of that year, it had fallen to just over 1 percent, where it remained for the rest of the war.

It was a very different kind of war for the young airmen who left the relative safety and comfort of air bases in England to do battle around-the-clock thirty thousand feet over Germany. Temperatures dropped to -30 degrees Celsius in the unpressurized B-17s and B-24s. The 150-mph slipstream rushed through the open windows where waist gunners stood watch for enemy fighters. Unprotected skin froze to the metal interior of the airplane. Gunners wore layers of clothing, including electrically heated flying suits, but breaks in the thin wires running through the fabric could cause serious burns or even set the garment on fire.

Only in the event of direst need did a crew member make a trip to the "tin can with a lid on it" serving as a latrine in a B-17. At least the "facility" in a B-24 came complete with wax-paper liners that could be chucked out an open window. Relief tubes almost always froze at altitude, causing urine to flood the floor of the airplane, only to freeze on contact and then melt on the way home. "As a result," one veteran commented, "there was no smell like the smell that greeted the ground crew when a combat crew came back from a particularly long and harrowing mission."[10]

Above all, of course, there was the terror of combat. You could shoot back, however ineffectually, at oncoming fighters, but the feeling of helplessness experienced by a bomber crew flying through a barrage of antiaircraft flack could never adequately be described. You had to have been there.

Serving with the bombers was a very dangerous pursuit. Early in

1944, the worst time for the USAAF, heavy-bomber groups suffered 88 percent casualties over a six-month period. During the same period, fighter units averaged a loss rate of 52 percent, while medium-bomber groups lost 33 percent of their aircrew.[11] Some 125,000 aircrew from seventeen nations served with RAF Bomber Command during 1939–1945. A full 44 percent of them died in combat or in training. Sixty percent of those who served with Bomber Command became casualties.

RAF LEADERS disagreed as to how to conduct the final phases of the bombing war. Sir Charles Portal, chief of the Air Staff, favored attacking petroleum facilities and other industrial targets using the precision tactics developed by Group Capt. Guy Gibson for the famous attacks on the Ruhr Dams in May 1943. Harris preferred to increase night attacks on German urban centers. For the most part, he had his way.

The strategic air campaign now gathered terrible momentum. Between July 1944 and May 1945, fifty German towns went up in smoke. By the end of the war, the RAF revisited places that had been reduced to rubble months before. Periodically, under perfect conditions, the bombing ignited firestorms of the sort that devastated Hamburg. More than fifty thousand people lost their lives on the night of February 13–14, 1945, when Bomber Command struck Dresden.

No longer able to launch effective bombing attacks on England, the Germans attempted to strike back with "wonder weapons," the V-2 rocket and pulse jet–propelled V-1 that were launched from land. While the V-weapons caused much concern, they proved to be a very poor investment for the Germans. The total cost of the German guided-missile program has been estimated at roughly half a million U.S. dollars at the time of World War II, one-fourth the price of the Manhattan Project, which produced the atomic bomb. The combined Vengeance weapon campaign against England, France, and Belgium took 12,685 lives and injured another 26,400. As noted, single air raids of this period took two to four times as many lives in a single night.

The introduction of the jet-powered Me 262 represented a more important contribution to the German war effort, although there was never any danger that it would recapture control of the air over the Reich. In the end, the Allied nations benefitted the most from the enormous wartime German investment in research and development.

The Eight Air Force had also begun to move away from its insistence on precision bombing. While this approach had taken a toll on German industry, it had become apparent that the average bomb dropped from thirty thousand feet on an operational mission would fall five miles from its target. By the end of 1944, 80 percent of Eighth Air Force missions involved blind bombing using radar. Raids like that on Berlin in May 1945, which took as many as twenty-five thousand lives, were indistinguishable from a Bomber Command area raid. In the air war against Japan, the USAAF would completely abandon its commitment to precision bombing and undertake the most devastating area raids of all time.

THE B-29 AND THE STRATEGIC AIR CAMPAIGN AGAINST JAPAN

For most of the Pacific war, the Japanese home islands lay far beyond the range of American aircraft. Only once, in April 1942, did Col. James "Jimmy" Doolittle lead a flight of sixteen North American B-25 bombers on a raid against Tokyo and Yokohama. Forced to take off from the aircraft carrier *Hornet* at a greater distance from Japan than planned, every crew completed its mission, but none succeeded in landing safely on the designated airfields in China.

Far from being a disaster, however, the raid boosted morale in America and earned Doolittle a medal of honor. It also created considerable concern in Japan. Admiral Yamamoto's decision to attack Midway Island grew out of the pressure generated by the Doolittle raid. That attack caused little physical damage, but had required an extraordinary effort. Over two years would pass before the next American airplane appeared in the skies over the Japanese homeland.

•   •   •

AIR CORPS PLANNERS had long recognized the need for a very-long-range (VLR) bomber capable of flying much farther, faster, and higher than the new B-17. The Flying Fortresses flew into combat at thirty thousand feet with their windows open. The new VLR aircraft would be pressurized, so that the crew could fly above the weather in shirt-sleeve comfort, and feature tricycle landing gear to increase its mobility on the ground. In 1937, the staff at Wright Field invited manufacturers to submit their thoughts on the design of such an aircraft.

In an era of fixed-priced contracts, a company had to invest its own funds in the design, development, and manufacture of a new aircraft in the hope of earning a profit when the government placed an order for production models. In 1937, aircraft companies thought themselves lucky to be squeaking by on the sale of current design or production for export. They were reluctant to invest substantial sums of their own money in the design of a "dream" aircraft that might never be funded. The government had purchased so few B-17s to date that Boeing initially did not want to put too much time and energy into the VLR project. Even Douglas, the most prosperous of the major manufacturers, was not willing to submit anything more imaginative than a modification of the DC-4E.

Three years later, after Congress funded the project and the Air Corps issued a call for formal proposals, Boeing and Consolidated were awarded contracts to develop their design for a VLR bomber. Consolidated produced the XB-32, a development of its B-24. Boeing submitted its Model 345, which Air Corps officials promptly identified as the XB-29. By 1941, enthusiasm for the VLR ran so high that even longer-term contracts were given to Consolidated, for what would become the B-36, and to Northrop for development of the XB-35 flying wing.

With a promise of the sale of two airplanes, Boeing obtained bank loans to fund production. In fact, the company received an early cost-plus-fixed-fee contract for the XB-29s, marking a new era in the relationship between government and industry. At the end of the project, Boeing would add up all of its costs, down to the last dime, everything from salaries and raw materials to the depreciation of equipment. The government would pay all of those costs, after some careful checking, and Boeing would repay the banks. In addition, the government would pay the company 6 percent of total costs as a fee for managing the project. If the costs were less than expected, the company would receive a bonus. The management fee and any bonus money represented corporate profits. The arrangement began a new and much brighter day for aircraft companies.

The XB-29 was designed for ease of construction and efficiency in the air. With its long, thin wing, tubular fuselage, and countersunk rivets, it was so streamlined that the simple act of dropping the landing gear doubled the drag of the airplane. When extended for take-off and landing, big electrically operated Fowler flaps increased the wing area by 20 percent.

Test flights began in September 1942. Tragedy struck. Boeing chief test pilot Eddie Allen and his crew died on February 18, 1943, when an engine fire brought their airplane down in a Seattle neighborhood. Overheating and fires with the huge, eighteen-cylinder Pratt & Whitney R-3350 engines and a host of other technical problems plagued the program for months to come.

By December 1942, as much as $3 billion had already been invested in the new airplane. The B-29 program would cost even more than the most potent weapon it would carry—the atomic bomb. As the pressure built in 1942 to begin B-29 production, the government agreed to assist Boeing in transforming a B-17 factory already under construction in Wichita, Kansas, into a B-29 plant. In addition, North American and Fisher Body also signed on to build B-29s under license. Bell Aircraft was awarded a contract for final assembly at a new plant to be built near Atlanta. Yet another huge plant devoted to B-29 production would go up in Omaha, Nebraska. And that represented only the tip of the iceberg. A host of subcontractors across the nation would supply parts and subassemblies for the big birds.

The business of producing the B-29 Superfortress and getting it into combat proved as complex as the airplane itself. A B-29 liaison committee headed by Wright Field's Gen. Kenneth B. Wolfe managed the effort. As the test program continued, a steady stream of orders for changes began making their way through the complex system designed to produce B-29s. By early 1944 the situation had reached crisis proportions, endangering the program as a whole. That February, the officer commanding the Twentieth Air Force, which would fly the airplanes into combat, complained that "not a single B-29 complete and ready for war had been delivered."[12] General Hap Arnold demanded action, and General Wolfe fought the Battle of Wichita, ordering that production move forward with minimum changes. He established a modification center, where airplanes were flown for the required changes before delivery to operating units.

THE USAAF FINALLY RETURNED to Japan on June 15, 1944, when fifty B-29s flew from Chengdu, China, to bomb the steel mills at Yawata, Japan. Even for the B-29s, such missions stretched the limits of the possible. The crews first had to fly their aircraft some twelve hundred miles from a safe haven in India, over the "Hump" of the Himalayas to Chengdu, where they landed for refueling with gas that had been flown in separately from India. It was estimated that as many as twelve gallons of gas were consumed to get one gallon to Chengdu.

From Chengdu to the target and back might be as far as thirty-two hundred miles, so that a single mission might involve up to three thousand miles of flying and twenty hours in the air. From June 1944 until March 1945, the XX Bomber Command flew forty-five missions from China, most of them directed at targets in China or Manchuria. The nine attacks on the home islands succeeded in delivering only eight hundred tons of bombs. It was not the sort of record that General Arnold had hoped for.

U.S. Marines stormed the beaches of Saipan on the very day the first raid took off from China. On October 12, 1944, the first Superfortress landed on the mile-and-a-half-long runway on Saipan's Isley Field. The islands of Tinian and Guam also were transformed into major B-29 airfields.

A new organization, the XXI Bomber Command of the Twentieth Air Force, commanded by Gen. Haywood S. Hansell Jr., operated outside the normal chain of command, reporting directly to General Arnold in Washington. The leaders of the USAAF had a weapon and a set of targets that might, at long last, enable them to demonstrate that the airplane could win the war. They were determined not to allow this opportunity to slip through their fingers.

Hansell, who had helped to shape Air Corps doctrine during the years before World War II, saw an opportunity to provide unmistakable proof of the power of precision bombing. Daunting problems had to be overcome first, though. The distances were enormous, three thousand miles from Saipan to central Japan and back without refueling. Until the capture of Iwo Jima, the midpoint of that trip, no safety net existed for crews who found themselves in trouble on the way home. The fact that enemy opposition was much weaker than over Germany (losses in the B-29 force did not rise above 2 percent) remained small consolation to a crew battling their way through flack and fighters over southern Japan.

Weather continued to be a problem, obscuring targets and scattering bombs dropped from over thirty thousand feet. Then there was the jet stream, a band of strong, steady winds blowing at speeds of up to 230 to 250 knots per hour across Japan. A B-29 encountering such a wind might be swept along too rapidly for an accurate bomb run, or held motionless and helpless over the target by a powerful headwind.

Through the fall and winter of 1944, the XXI Bomber Command conducted high-altitude raids against important industrial targets on the home islands. Not only did conditions prevent the ideal demonstration of precision bombing that Hansell had hoped for, but the weather made it difficult to obtain regular reconnaissance photography of target areas. Arnold ordered a reluctant Hansell to conduct an area raid on Nagoya on January 3, 1945, dropping a mix of high-explosive bombs and the new, lightweight M60 incendiaries.

Less than three weeks later, Hansell was replaced by Gen. Curtiss Emerson LeMay, a veteran of the Eighth Air Force who had been heading XX Bomber Command in China. LeMay, who had developed the combat box formation for B-17s and B-24s attacking Germany, continued the precision bombing attacks for a time, interspersed with occasional high-altitude incendiary attacks, as on February 25, when 150 B-29s burned out one square mile of Tokyo.

The new commander, certain that the Japanese could not offer much opposition to a massive night attack, decided to strip most of the

Boeing B-29 Superfortresses

armament from his B-29s and send them over Japanese cities, low and in the dark. The tactic had a number of advantages. The destruction of a city would mean that the small factories embedded in the neighborhoods would go up in flames along with everything else. By killing workers, or driving them from their homes, LeMay would strike another blow at Japanese production. Finally, there was the old hope of breaking the enemy's will.

The results were breathtaking. On the night of March 9–10, 1945, a total of 334 B-29s flew across Tokyo at altitudes from five to nine thousand feet, scattering two thousand tons of bombs, most of them incendiaries. One-fourth of the city was transformed into a sea of flames that pushed waves of superheated air in front of it. Flame and debris climbed several thousand feet into the air, while columns of smoke rose to fifteen thousand feet, high above the airplanes. The official death toll was fixed at 83,793, although unofficial estimates of up to 100,000 dead may be closer to the truth. In any case, more humans died at the hand of their fellows on the night of March 9–10, 1945, than in any other twenty-four-hour period in history.

The incineration of urban Japan was carefully choreographed. During April, May, and June, the bombers continued to strike the major cities: Tokyo, Nagoya, Yokohama, Kobe, Osaka, Kawasaki. Daylight raids drew Japanese fighters into the air where they could be destroyed. Japanese authorities grounded their fighters in June to preserve them for the final battle that would come with the invasion of Japan. Incendiary attacks on smaller towns began soon, along with high-altitude strikes centering on the petroleum industry. During the entire period, B-29s also mined Japanese home waters, cutting the nation off from food, supplies, and troop transfers from China and Manchuria.

By the end of July, the B-29s had run out of targets. Japan was isolated, her industry in shambles. The transportation network no longer operated. Hundreds of thousands of men, women, and children lay dead or injured. Famine and disease spread across a nation containing 8.5 million homeless people. While the devastation led some Japanese officials to argue for an end to the conflict, army leaders insisted that the entire nation should fight the invading Americans to the death.

In the end, the bombers prevailed, with a new weapon of unimaginable power and almost unlimited capacity for development. The atomic bomb was designed and built at Los Alamos, New Mexico, with assistance from laboratories in California, Illinois, and Massachusetts, using fissionable material produced by factories at Oak Ridge, Tennessee, and Hanford, Washington. The first plutonium bomb was tested at a remote site in New Mexico on July 16, 1945. The first uranium bomb was tested at Hiroshima, Japan, on August 6, 1945. A second plutonium bomb destroyed the Urakami district of Nagasaki on August 9.

Within .02 of a second, the temperature within the expanding fireball reached 7,700 degrees Celsius (13,900 degrees Fahrenheit), vaporizing humans, melting steel beams, etching shadows on walls. Within two-miles of the hypocenter, virtually everything was leveled. In Hiroshima, a firestorm fed by broken gas lines raised temperatures back to the point where houses burst into spontaneous flame two to three hours after the blast.

During the American Civil War, the Union Army lost 110,010 men to injuries suffered in combat. The best estimate for Hiroshima suggests that by the end of November 1945, some 130,000 people lost their lives as a direct result of the bomb. The total number of dead for Nagasaki, where the effects of the blast were somewhat contained because the bomb exploded over a valley two miles from the intended target area in the center of the town, reached 60,000 to 70,000. The tally in both cities would continue to climb for decades, as additional people fell victim to cancer resulting from exposure to the radiation.

The destruction of Hiroshima and Nagasaki, coupled with the entry of the Soviet Union into the war against Japan on August 8, stunned Emperor Hirohito and the more rational members of the government into suing for peace. The bomb seared itself into American memory as well. The prospect of the terrible losses that would be suffered in an invasion of Japan suddenly vanished. A generation of Americans, grateful that the dying was finished, and unwilling to seriously face the loss of life in the two cities, echoed the words of author and veteran Paul Fussell: "Thank God for the Atomic Bomb."[13]

The atomic bombing of Japan can only be understood in the context of 1945. The tempo built slowly over time, progressing from tentative raids and tactical strikes to thousand-plane attacks that burned the core of centuries-old cities. In the end, the no-holds-barred incendiary and atomic bomb attacks on Japan marked the removal of all moral restraint. Total war had come at last, with no mercy, no quarter, and no limit to the capacity for destruction.

All of that is undeniable. And yet the awesome destruction of the bombing war was a critically important factor in the defeat of unspeakable tyranny. The men, women, and children who died in Hamburg, Berlin, Tokyo, Hiroshima, and Nagasaki were the citizens of nations that had sent six million innocent souls to their deaths in concentration camps, taken countless civilian lives on the steppes of Russia, and butchered additional millions in China and Southeast Asia.

Strategic bombing had not broken the will of any nation, nor had it proved to be either as cheap or as decisive as its proponents had hoped. Along with success on the Eastern Front, the Battle of the Atlantic, and the reality of American productivity, however, the bombing campaigns played a central role in achieving victory.

The strategic air offensive permitted the Allies to strike back at the enemy at a time when they could otherwise only nibble at the edges of the Axis empire. Albert Speer, Hitler's minister of Production, admitted that the bombing campaign had "meant the end of German armaments production."[14]

If the RAF and USAAF had broken the back of the German economy, the B-29s of the XX Bomber Command had burned urban Japan to the ground and much of Japanese industry along with it. Last but not least, by forcing the enemy to seek battle in the skies over his homeland, the USAAF was able to fight and win a war of attrition against the German and Japanese air forces. And that victory made everything else possible.

The destruction wrought by the strategic air campaigns was to some degree intentional. The desire to punish the enemy, to bring him to his knees, was very real. Ultimately, however, the technology of the day simply could not deliver the degree of bombing accuracy sought by prewar air planners. Unable to strike the industrial heart of the enemy with surgical precision, the temptation to bludgeon him to death proved simply irresistible.

Those caught in the maelstrom on the ground, and the young airmen who rained destruction on them, paid a fearful price for the bombing war. Did the end justify the means? Did the defeat of tyranny require the abandonment of all restraint? Small wonder that the air campaigns against Germany and Japan continue to spark impassioned and often bitter debate.

FORGING THE ARSENAL OF DEMOCRACY

No aspect of World War II would have a greater impact on the future, however, than the transformation of the relatively small prewar community of airframe and engine builders into a huge aerospace and defense industrial complex that would reshape the postwar world. Some notion of the enormous growth of the global aviation industry during the war years can be found in the raw number of aircraft produced by four of the five leading belligerents.

Number of Military Aircraft Produced, 1938–1944 (in thousands)[15]

Year	Germany	Japan	Great Britain	United States
1938	5.6	3.2	2.8	1.8
1939	8.3	4.5	7.0	2.1
1940	10.8	4.8	15.0	6.1
1941	11.8	5.1	20.1	29.4
1942	15.6	8.9	23.7	47.8
1943	25.5	16.7	26.3	85.9
1944	39.8	28.2	26.5	96.3

Reliable statistics are harder to obtain for the fifth great power. Best estimates, however, suggest that Soviet production grew from 10,000 aircraft in 1940 to 40,000 four years later. The numbers in the table are misleading to some extent. Much of the huge increase in German and Japanese aircraft came in the form of the single-engine fighters desperately needed for the home defense of both nations. In the case of Germany, the proportion of fighters to total output climbed from 24 percent in 1940 to 65 percent in 1944.[16]

As the table indicates, aircraft production in the United States expanded greatly. The 1930s had been a golden age for the aviation industry. American airplanes were the envy of the world, but they were the product of a very small enterprise. In 1939, aviation ranked forty-first among American industries. Roughly forty manufacturers employed as many as 50,000 workers and produced 5,865 airplanes. Most (3,555 machines) were business aircraft or light airplanes. Only 159 were commercial airliners. The bulk of the production (2,141 machines) represented military types, only 560 of which were delivered to the Air Corps.

Those figures suggest the complexities of a fluid market. The number of light aircraft produced had more than doubled from the 1938 figure (1,745) as a result of purchases by flying schools contracting with the U.S. government to train pilots under the new Civilian Pilot Training Program. While this number seems impressive, it is important to keep it in perspective. The average price of a one- to five-place airplane in 1938 was $3,500. All other aircraft cost an average of $63,000.[17] Clearly, the money was in larger machines.

Before the stockmarket crash of 1929, investors and manufacturers had dreamed of the rich profits they would reap in commercial aviation. Indeed, by the end of the decade, the United States boasted the finest commercial aviation system in the world. Some firms made their mark producing civil aircraft. The various incarnations of the Lockheed Company sold a grand total of 578 airplanes during 1919–1938, almost all of which had gone to civilian customers. One of the most famous aviation companies in the world, Lockheed was also one of the smallest of the top-six U.S. aircraft manufacturers in the years 1929–1939, employing only 332 people at the peak of its fame in 1934.

Throughout the years 1931–1939, however, total military expenditures amounting to $380 million ($219 million for the army, $161 million for the navy) remained the most important source of income for airframe manufacturers. Douglas emerged as the largest and most successful of these firms (which included Boeing, Consolidated, Curtiss-Wright, Douglas, Lockheed, and Martin) by 1936.

State of the U.S. Aviation Industry, 1936 (in thousands)[18]

Company	Plant Area	Employees	1936 Sales	Unfilled Orders
Douglas	869	7.0	$7,948	$28,545
Martin	600	1.5	$6,220	$12,500
Consolidated	462	4.0	$4,218	$20,000
Boeing	400	1.9	$2,293	$8,900

Douglas was not only larger than Lockheed but also more typical of the industry. By 1937, the company was certainly the best-known and most successful producer of commercial aircraft in the world. Yet, since 1931, over 70 percent of corporate income had come from military contracts. For all the high hopes for commercial profits, aviation in the

United States, as elsewhere in the world, survived on military sales. In 1937, for example, U.S. manufacturers had earned $19 million on the sale of 2,281 civil aircraft and $37 million, almost twice as much, for 949 military airplanes.

THE UNITED STATES had exported very few aircraft in the immediate years after World War I. In 1922, American industry sold only 37 aircraft and 147 engines abroad. European nations preferred to spend their scarce defense dollars in support of their own aviation manufacturers. By the mid-1920s, however, export sales of military aircraft to Asia were on the rise. Between 1925 and 1939, China, the largest export market for U.S. aircraft, purchased 19,392 machines.[19]

Latin American sales were also climbing. In 1929, for example, U.S. manufacturers sold 12 aircraft in Europe and 196 in South America, where a considerable air war was just getting underway. The airmen of Paraguay and Bolivia were battling one another with American, British, French, and Italian aircraft in the skies over prospective oil fields of the desolate Gran Chaco region. By time of the cease-fire in 1935, the two nations had lost tens of thousands of men and totally exhausted themselves. The oil failed to materialize.

By 1938, with war looming on the European horizon, the situation abruptly changed. Daunted by the apparent strength of the Luftwaffe, England and France exchanged the Sudeten region of Czechoslovakia for some breathing space. With their own aviation industries operating at full capacity, the beleaguered nations turned to America.

In November 1938, in the immediate wake of the Munich conference, President Roosevelt established a preparedness program that included an air force of 10,000 aircraft. A year and a half later, in May 1940, the president called for a total annual production of 50,000 aircraft. By 1941, the White House was asking for 60,000 airplanes a year, a number that more than doubled within a year. In an effort to solve looming production problems, the federal government created a National Defense Commission, headed by William S. Knudsen, a dollar-a-year man on leave from his position as president of General Motors.

But export sales, not government purchases, would fund the initial expansion of the U.S. aviation industry. A combination of neutrality laws and security regulations in place since 1917 restricted the export of aircraft to the trainers and machines that were approaching obsolescence. By 1938, President Roosevelt was stretching the bounds of neutrality in favor of the French and British at every opportunity. He arranged for the Chinese government to receive a $25 million loan from the Import-Export Bank, and pressured army officials to allow the members of the Anglo-French Purchasing Commission to inspect and even fly American military aircraft.

Isolationist congressmen took a dim view of the White House initiatives. In January 1939, Capt. Paul Chemidlin, a member of the Anglo-French Purchasing Commission, was injured in the crash of an experimental Douglas bomber. When the story became public, Senators Bennett Champ Clarke and Gerald Prentice Nye immediately scheduled hearings.

For Roosevelt, the outcome could not have been better. The controversy revealed that the effort to support Britain and France was entirely within his prerogatives. More important, the policy proved to be far more popular than administration officials could have hoped. While the isolationists provided considerable opposition, most newspaper commentators recognized that the Roosevelt policy was in the best interest of the nation.

The barriers were falling. In February 1939, the British committed $25 million for the purchase of 650 frontline military aircraft from American industry. The French followed suit with contracts for 615 airplanes from Curtiss, Douglas, Martin, and North American at a total cost of $60 million. By the early spring of 1940, the British and French had contracted to purchase 6,000 aircraft. After the fall of France, Britain picked up the French options and increased her own purchases to a total of over $1.5 billion worth of aircraft. Australia, Belgium, Canada, Norway, and Iraq also purchased large numbers of American aircraft.[20]

THE SUDDEN INFLUX of money from both U.S. and foreign governments transformed the American aviation industry. The impact on

Lockheed was typical. Before 1938, the company had never produced more than 148 aircraft of a single type. Beginning that year, they produced the first of what would become 2,941 twin-engine Hudson bombers. Over half (1,602) of those aircraft were exported. Between July 1, 1940, and August 31, 1945, the company would produce 19,077 airplanes. Even at that, Lockheed production amounted to only 6.6 percent of the U.S. total.

Employment in the industry grew to a peak of 94,329 in mid-1943. Forty percent of those workers in the Los Angeles area were women. Lockheed factory-floor space increased from 550,000 square feet in 1939 to 7,700,000 square feet in 1943. In addition to its two major assembly facilities, the company acquired ten feeder plants and two modification facilities in the United States, as well as parts depots and reassembly centers in Great Britain and Australia.

The Douglas Company, less than twenty years old in 1939, would deliver 30,980 aircraft (twenty-two distinct types) by the end of August 1945. That year, the company that had captured the world market for airliners would earn military profits that dwarfed its commercial sales. Military exports constituted 59.7 percent of total industry sales in 1939, with sales to the War and Navy Department amounting to another 34.6 percent. Domestic and foreign commercial sales accounted for only 7.5 percent of the total.

The Douglas war record was exemplary. Measured in terms of airframe weight (306,573,000 pounds), 15.3 percent of the U.S. total, the company could claim honors as the nation's largest aircraft manufacturer.

Airframe Tonnage [21]

Manufacturer	Percentage of Total
Douglas	15.3
Consolidated	14.6
Boeing	11.3
Lockheed	9.0
Curtiss	6.9
Martin	6.3

Ford	6.2
Republic	3.9
Grumman	3.7
Bell	2.7
Chance Vought	1.4
Goodyear	0.7
All others	6.5

In terms of the number of actual airplanes rolled through the factory doors, however, Douglas ranked third behind North American and Consolidated, the industry leaders.

Number of Aircraft Accepted [22]

Manufacturer	Army	Navy
North American	41,839	0
Consolidated	27,634	3,296
Douglas	25,569	5,411
Curtiss	19,703	6,934
Boeing	17,231	291
Lockheed	17,148	1,929
Republic	15,663	0
Bell	12,941	1
Martin	7,711	1,272
Beech	7,430	0
Fairchild	6,080	300
Cessna	5,359	0
Piper	5,611	330
Taylor	1,940	0

THE NEED TO EXPAND factory-floor space was a critical problem. Douglas, for example, continued to operate its Santa Monica and El Segundo (Northrop) plants at full capacity and created a new organization, the Western Land Improvement Company, to acquire land and build a new plant adjacent to the Long Beach Municipal Airport.

However, no corporation could afford to buy acres of land and spend millions on building and equipping factories that might stand empty after the war. As a result, the government created the Emergency Plant Facilities program, which reimbursed companies for construction costs over a five-year period, with the government agreeing to take possession of the space when peace returned and orders were reduced.

When the Emergency Plant Facilities program failed to meet the need, the Reconstruction Finance Corporation (RFC) created a new subsidiary, the Defense Plant Corporation (DPC), which acquired land and built factories that were then leased to manufacturers. Douglas, for example, leased space from the RFC in Chicago, Tulsa, and Oklahoma City. By 1945, the DPC had created over a thousand facilities at a cost of $7 billion. Over one-half of that additional floor space went to aircraft manufacturers. The federal government funded over 90 percent of the wartime plant expansion of the aircraft industry.

Some of the new plants were incredibly large. A single Dodge engine plant in Chicago offered 6.5 million square feet of floor space, half as much as had been available in the entire industry in 1940. By mid-1945, the U.S. aircraft industry boasted a total of 160 million square feet of space. The DPC built a 1.4-million-square-foot facility in Long Beach to accommodate the final assembly of Douglas aircraft.

SURELY THE FORD plant at Willow Run, near Ypsilanti, Michigan, was the best-known industrial facility in the nation. "Will it run?" was the question being asked when Henry Ford and his son Edsel opened the enormous single-story structure that had been built for only one purpose—to turn out B-24 bombers. The building measured 3,200 by 1,280 feet. Ninety football fields could have been laid out on the 2.5-million-square-foot floor. This single plant boasted more floor space for aircraft construction than what Boeing, Douglas, and Consolidated had combined. Charles Lindbergh described the building as "the Grand Canyon of the mechanical world."[23]

Albert Kahn (1869–1942), chief architect of the age of the automobile and the airplane, designed Willow Run. A native of Rhaunen,

Germany, Kahn had immigrated to the United States in 1880. His career began with his brother Joseph's development of a patented process for reinforced concrete construction. The new approach enabled the architect to design buildings with fewer internal supports, maximum open floor space, and walls with windows. The pair made their early reputations with two concrete buildings: Packard Shop Number 10 (1903) and a single-story, top-lit modular factory building for the George N. Pierce Company (1906).

For Kahn, architecture did not involve the creation of an aesthetically pleasing external shell. Rather, the function of the building should drive design. His next building, the new Highland Park, Michigan, factory (1913) in which Henry Ford operated his assembly-line production of the Model T, exemplified exactly what he had in mind. A perfectly functional building in which assembly began on the roof and an endless stream of the most famous automobiles in America flowed out onto the street, it immediately became the best-known factory in the nation.

Kahn and Ford broke their own mold in 1917, when they began work on the single-story River Rouge plant near Detroit. Originally designed to produce small naval vessels under contract, the factory was located close to a canal, railroad, and highways. Featuring two thousand acres of floor space when first constructed, the plant would become Ford's major auto plant after 1918 and continue to grow for the next two decades, by which time it contained thirteen square miles of shop and assembly space. By the 1930s it was famed as the plant where iron ore entered one end of the building and automobiles exited the other.

Like his friend and employer Henry Ford, Kahn became heavily involved with the industrialization of the Soviet Union. Credited with the design of the famous Ford tractor factory at Stalingrad, the architect once commented that he had designed five hundred industrial buildings in the United States and as many in the Soviet Union.

Kahn also designed the buildings in which American aviation would grow to maturity. His aeronautical structures were as functional, practical, and flexible as his auto plants. In 1917, U.S. Army officials named him architect in chief of the Army Signal Corps. In that capacity he was responsible for site planning and architectural design for two permanent Air Service facilities (Langley Field, Virginia, and

Rockwell Field, California) and a series of temporary flying fields (Brooks and Kelly Fields, Texas; Bolling Field, Washington, D.C.; March Field, California; Chanute Field, Illinois; Maxwell Field, Alabama; McCook and Wilbur Wright Fields, Ohio).

A typical facility consisted of fifty-four buildings to house 100 airplanes and 150 students and instructors. Kahn paid special attention to site plans for the leading U.S. aeronautical research facilities at Langley Field and the Air Service Engineering Division headquarters at McCook Field. When McCook Field grew too small and the citizens of Dayton contributed the land for a new facility, Kahn was a major influence on the site planning and architecture for Wright Field, which was built in 1925. In addition, the architect designed the Tudor-style military housing units found on air bases across the nation.

By the 1930s, Kahn also earned a reputation as a designer of efficient aircraft manufacturing plants. His most famous project involved the expansion of the Glenn L. Martin plant at Middle River, Maryland, in 1931. Martin had given much thought to factory design. His new plant, he explained to the members of the Royal Aeronautical Society in 1931, embodied "all the lessons learned from years gone by, and which could successfully cope with all conditions that might arise in the future."

Martin had selected the suburban-rural Middle River site rather than the location the city officials preferred, much closer to the heart of Baltimore. He based the decision on the opportunity to acquire sufficient land for future expansion. The layout of the new factory itself carefully reflected the most efficient flow of work. During the early years of the decade, the Middle River plant became almost universally recognized as the ideal aircraft manufacturing facility.[24]

By 1937, however, increasing orders and the need to produce larger aircraft, notably the M-130 Clippers, led Martin to hire Kahn to plan an expansion program. In addition to increased factory-floor space, the architect developed a "garden city" stretching along the banks of the Chesapeake Bay to house the workers to whom Martin had given so much thought. A community of ten thousand people would rise along the shores of the bay, with apartments, single-family homes, shopping centers, schools, churches, and other amenities.

Construction began on Kahn's community in 1939. It would continue to grow throughout the war, although it would never function in the utopian fashion that Martin had envisioned. As the master of the manor had noted, aircraft workers tended to be relatively underpaid. Engineers and junior executives could afford to rent or buy in "Martinville"; assembly workers, for the most part, could not.[25]

Kahn's ultimate factory was Willow Run. The project began in January 1941, when members of the Advisory Council for National Defense asked Ford executives to visit the Consolidated plant in San Diego, where final assembly took place out of doors, and consider becoming involved in expanding B-24 production. Edsel Ford and Charles "Cast Iron" Sorenson, Ford's production chief, were singularly unimpressed with Consolidated's approach.

Remarking that Consolidated built "custom-made" airplanes the way a tailor "cut and fit a suit of clothes," Sorenson developed the notion of a plant in which a hundred thousand workers could turn out a finished airplane every hour. But airplanes were not automobiles. Each B-24 consisted of 1,225,000 parts held together with four thousand rivets. Was it possible to build something as complex and unforgiving as an airplane in the same way that you built an automobile? Time would tell.[26]

Kahn referred to Willow Run as "the biggest room in the world."[27] He applied everything that he had learned about the design of production facilities to the new plant. Where Consolidated had relied on skilled workers using expensive tools to custom fit each airplane, Ford planners invested in punches, presses, and dies based on their experience with mass production. The secret to success involved the coordinated movement of parts and subassemblies to precisely the right place on the line at precisely the right moment. Kahn and the Ford engineers considered every aspect of production and realized savings and efficiencies that would have been impossible in a smaller operation.

Ford workmen set to work clearing the site in March 1941. Production began nine months later, but it would be another ten months after that before the first B-24 rolled off the line. The numbers climbed very slowly, and Willow Run remained the object of finger-pointing and humor for a considerable time. Finally, by March 1944, the plant came close to matching Sorenson's expectations, turning out 453 airplanes in 463 hours. Will it run? Indeed it did.

THEORY INTO PRACTICE: THE CASE OF THE P-51

Thirty-nine-year-old James Howard "Dutch" Kindelberger resigned his position as vice president of engineering at Douglas and moved east to Dundalk, Maryland, in 1934, where he took command of the General Aviation Corporation, the principal manufacturing arm of the now-defunct North American holding company. Assisted by two other Douglas veterans, John Leland "Lee" Atwood and J.M. Smithson, Kindelberger kept the company afloat with a contract to supply floats to the navy, followed by the sale of trainers and observation aircraft to the army.

Longing for the clear skies and open-shop policies of southern California by 1935, Kindelberger transplanted the company, including all of the tools and equipment and the seventy-five employees willing to move, into a 159,000-square-foot factory on a twenty-acre site adjoining the Los Angeles Municipal Airport in Inglewood. The rent was $600 per month.

The NA-16 (1935), a low-wing trainer with fixed landing gear, was the first North American airplane to leave the ground. As the government allowed the export of trainers under the neutrality laws, Kindelberger negotiated sales to France, England, Peru, Argentina, Brazil, and Chile as well as the U.S. military. That first design evolved into the AT-6/SNJ, an advanced trainer that would operate with Allied air forces around the globe.

Given its existing relationship with the RAF and experience with the production of high-performance single-engine trainers, it was only natural that the Manhattan-based Anglo-French Purchasing Commission turned to North American Aviation early in 1940, when Curtiss-Wright was unable to meet their need for P-40s. Kindelberger and Atwood, however, had little interest in paying a licensing fee to produce obsolete airplanes designed by someone else.

Colonel Oliver Patton Echols, the ever-vigilant head of procurement at Wright Field, saw an opportunity to obtain yet another new fighter at European expense. He arranged federal permission for North American to develop an entirely new design for the Purchasing Commission, made some key Air Corps research reports available to the company, and encouraged Kindelberger to purchase from Curtiss-Wright some interesting wind tunnel data on placement of the radiator and air intake. In May 1940, the Europeans signed a contract to purchase four hundred of the yet-to-be-designed airplanes that North American identified as the NA-73.

It would be Edgar Schmued's first assignment as chief engineer. An Austrian mechanical engineer who would never lose his thick German accent, Schmued had emigrated to Brazil in 1925 to take a job with General Motors. When GM helped create North American Aviation in 1929, Schmued transferred to the United States to take a job with the Fokker Aircraft Corporation, which North American quickly folded into the General Aviation Corporation.

Accommodating his wife's wishes, Schmued did not transfer to California with the rest of North American. After a few weeks with Bellanca, however, he loaded his wife and son into the family car and drove to California to rejoin Kindelberger and Atwood. East of Los Angeles they suffered an auto accident that took Mrs. Schmued's life and kept him from work until early 1936. Thereafter he continued to ascend the corporate ladder, achieving the role of chief engineer in 1940.

The success of the P-51 Mustang, the airplane that would emerge from the North American drawing boards as a replacement for the P-40, rested on several basic design decisions. The notion of locating the large radiator and air intake on the underside of the fuselage behind the cockpit was critically important, as it streamlined the exterior of the aircraft. The design also provided the space for a series of expanding and contracting ducts that directed a steady flow of air through the radiator to an exhaust point halfway back along the tail cone. The system ensured efficient cooling and provided a bit of increased thrust.

The P-51 sported a revolutionary wing, an example of the critically important role that NACA played in American aeronautics. The story begins in 1935, when engineer Eastman N. Jacobs, the brilliant supervisor of the variable-density wind tunnel group at NACA Langley

Laboratory, attended the Fifth Volta Conference on High-Speed Aeronautics in Rome. While in Europe he visited with B. Melville Jones, a senior professor of aeronautics at Cambridge University. A pioneer aerodynamicist and an authority on streamlining, Jones told his visitor that he had achieved laminar flow over the forward sections of very smooth wings by decreasing the pressure between the leading and trailing edges.

Eastman Jacobs became intrigued. Laminar flow occurs when the air moves smoothly over the top surface of the wing in even, compressed layers, producing maximum lift and minimum drag. In the real world, flow invariably becomes detached from the wing, creating turbulence and increased drag. Jacobs launched a cooperative venture between his own wind tunnel group and their more theoretical colleagues, the goal of which was to develop an airfoil that would feature decreasing air pressure from the leading edge toward the rear, a condition that would tend to produce laminar flow.

Jacobs succeeded, with the assistance of his close friend Robert T. Jones. Already well on his way to becoming a legendary figure, Jones had been "discovered" by a congressional leader who was surprised to find his elevator operator reading calculus textbooks to pass the time. The congressman helped Jones find more suitable employment with NACA. Together, Jones and Jacobs, H. Julian "Harvey" Allen, and other members of the variable-density wind tunnel team developed an airfoil design of considerable promise.

The Langley group issued a classified report of their work in 1939. Edward J. Horkey, the aerodynamicist working with Ed Schmued, took immediate note and contacted the group at Langley. The North American engineers produced a model wing and conducted their own extensive wind tunnel tests at Caltech and the University of Washington. Their airfoil produced the lowest drag coefficient of any wing tested to date.

The P-51 became the first military airplane to feature a "laminar flow" airfoil. In practice, however, preventing the onset of turbulence depended on much more than airfoil design. The wing surface had to be absolutely smooth. While Ed Schmued, a perfectionist of the first order, produced the "cleanest" design of its generation, it was not good enough to maintain genuine laminar flow. The surface scuffs and scratches that the wing inevitably developed in operational service further reduced the advantage. Half a century later, engineers would still be attempting to realize the practical benefits of laminar flow.

The reputation of the Mustang as the finest piston-engine fighter of its generation resulted entirely from good engineering. Schmued and his team not only produced an airplane with minimum drag, but also designed it for production. Their extensive wind tunnel tests revealed only a minimum aerodynamic penalty for neatly clipped wing tips that would make production easier. Whenever possible, the engineers employed existing components and in several instances, they incorporated several features of the AT-6 trainer into the design of the P-51.

The gestation of the P-51 illuminates the complex nature of the American aeronautical community in the years immediately before the nation was swept into war. Even during an era when American commercial airplanes dominated the world's airlines, military sales paid the bills. Even in the case of export sales, American military procurement officers remained very much a part of the process.

North American P-51D Mustang, "Tika V,"
Lt. Vernon L. Richards at the controls

Finally, the P-51 exemplified the central role that the public-private research establishment created in the 1920s and 1930s played in the triumph of American aviation. From advice on new materials to practical suggestions for airfoil design and streamlining, to the development of new theoretical insights, NACA had been a full partner in the success of the industry. Wright Field and the various navy flight research facilities had made important contributions as well, in areas ranging from the development of modern propellers to the introduction of the pressurized cabin. The Guggenheim aeronautical laboratories created at universities scattered from coast to coast had not only fed a steady stream of graduates into industry, but also provided sophisticated and expensive testing facilities where engineers could gather information on their latest designs.

Yet the ultimate success of this proud product of the arsenal of democracy represented an international achievement. The finest American fighter of the war had, after all, been developed with European funds. Moreover, its original 1,150-horsepower Allison engine was less than satisfactory. Powered by the Packard version of the 1,650 horsepower Rolls-Royce Merlin power plant, fitted with a two-stage supercharger, the P-51B became the fastest piston-engine fighter in mass production, with superb altitude performance.

The first NA-73 (the initial designation for the P-51) rolled out of the factory at Inglewood only 102 days after the Europeans signed the purchase contract. Ultimately, North American would produce 15,486 P-51s in thirty-nine variants. That does not count the F-6 reconnaissance versions or the foreign-built Mustangs. North American would construct a second factory in Dallas, Texas, just for P-51 production. The attention to quality control required that engineers be stationed on the production line. Once the operation began, a Mustang rolled off the line every twenty-one minutes.

The P-51 represented the ultimate in piston-engine, propeller-driven fighters. Just ask a man who flew one. Louis R. Purnell, for example, one of the legendary Tuskeegee Airmen, flew Mustangs with the all-black 99th Fighter Squadron of the 332nd Pursuit Group.

> If that plane had been a girl, I'd have married it right on the spot. Damn right! It was like dancing with a good partner. You could

almost think left turn and the damn plane was right with you. Good response on the controls, good stability. It was a miracle to get in and fly with all that horsepower at your fingertips. Speed, maneuverability, climb rate, reliability? We had it in the P-51. Anyone who has flown a P-51 will agree with me. And those who haven't wish they had.[28]

The P-51 and its naval counterpart, the Chance Vought F4U Corsair, would continue to serve as frontline combat aircraft well into the postwar years. However, they represented the end of a long line of fighters that had been pulled, or sometimes pushed, through the air by propellers. As they battled their enemies to defeat in the skies over Europe and the Pacific, the smooth, throaty roar of their powerful in-line and rotary engines was already being drowned out by the high-pitched shriek of a new kind of power plant that would give its name to a new age in aviation.

19

TOWARD NEW HORIZONS

THE LEGACY OF TYRANNY

Allied leaders expected that the troops racing across Germany in the final weeks of the war would discover a wealth of technical information on the wonder weapons of the Third Reich. They were not disappointed. Infantry and armor units captured examples of the German operational jets: the Me 262 and He 162 fighters, the Arado 234 bomber, and the rocket-propelled Me 163 interceptor.

On April 11, 1945, forward elements of the Third U.S. Armored Division and the 104th Infantry reached Dora, a slave labor camp near Nordhausen, in Thuringia, where they found over four hundred living skeletons and piles of corpses near the crematoria. They were the last of the tens of thousands of slave laborers who had assembled the V-2 rockets, pulse jet–powered V-1 flying bombs, and Junkers Jumo 004 jet engines under unimaginably hellish conditions in an elaborate network of tunnels driven into the heart of Kohnstein Mountain.

In addition to what had been expected, there were a series of stunning surprises. A company of U.S. infantry discovered the secret Messerschmitt plant at Oberammergau, Germany, and its fantastic contents on April 30, 1945. Eight days later, Bob Wood, chief engineer and cofounder of Bell Aircraft, arrived to view the prize: the P 1101, a small aircraft with a stubby fuselage setting on top of a Heinkel-Hirth 011 turbojet engine, with wings and horizontal and vertical stabilizers swept back at a forty-five-degree angle. It was not quite complete and had never been flown. Investigation revealed that the sweep of the wings could be altered to meet varying flight conditions. Wood, who had designed the XP-59, the first American jet, had never seen anything like this. Six years later he would supervise the design, development, and testing of the Bell X-5, a version of the P 1101 intended to provide information on variable-sweep wings.

Later that month, Allied troops found the far more radical Horton Ho IX V3 (Gotha Go 229 V3), a twin jet–powered flying wing, at Friedrichsroda. Only partially complete, it was a follow-on to the Ho IX V2, which had attained a speed of 497 mph before being destroyed in a landing accident.

In addition to the piloted jets and rockets, the advancing Allied troops recovered strange new surface-to-surface, surface-to-air, and air-to-air missiles; a treasure trove of aerodynamic data on supersonic and hypersonic flight; and information on propulsion, electronic systems, missile guidance, and a dozen other topics that would become critically important over the next decade. They found the world's most advanced high-speed wind tunnel facility in the Hartz Mountains. Perhaps most important, they found the scientists and engineers who had created these wonders.

It is fair to ask how Germany, collapsing in defeat, facing invading armies to the east and west, suffering under the weight of Allied bombing, could have produced a series of high-technology weapons that were a full decade ahead of the rest of the world. Simply put, they chose to do so. As the military situation grew worse, the possibility that an incredible wonder weapon might reverse the course of the war became an article of faith in the upper echelons of the Third Reich.

The strong German university tradition of excellence in applied science and technology also helps to explain the penchant for operating at the cutting edge. During the First World War, Ludwig Prandtl and others had pioneered theoretical aerodynamics at Göttingen and Aachen Universities, while well-trained engineers like Junkers,

Dornier, and Rohrbach had bridged the gap between university theory and industrial practice. A generation later, Jacob Ackeret, Adolf Busemann, Alexander Lippisch, Woldemar Voigt, Hans von Ohain, Wernher von Braun, and others like them continued the tradition.

Some scholars have argued that the Nazis managed their technologies poorly, pointing to the dismal planning failures of Hermann Goering and Ernst Udet, as well as the Goering and Hitler directives of 1940–1941 canceling work on weapons that would not reach the front within a year.[1] The truth is more complicated. In the labyrinthine bureaucracy of the Third Reich, pronouncements from on high did not always shape policy.

As early as 1936, John Jay Ide, NACA's man in Europe, noted that the Reichsluftfahrtministerium (RLM), the Reich Air Ministry, was supporting major aeronautical research efforts at Aachen, Göttingen, Stuttgart, and Braunschweig. Moreover, the Deutsche Versuchsanstalt für Luftfahrt (DVL), the quasi-official German central aeronautical research facility dating to 1911, remained an international center for work in fields ranging from high-speed flight to radar. Proof of the RLM/DVL commitment to high-technology weaponry is found in the proliferation of advanced aircraft and missile programs still underway at the end of the war.

The success of those programs is not evidence of good judgment, however. With few exceptions, the wonder weapons represented a very poor investment for the Reich. General Adolf Galland, the last commander of the Luftwaffe, would have much preferred to buy more Me 262s, rather than spend money on wildly experimental ventures like the P 1101. Poor decisions with regard to the allocation of scarce resources had directly contributed to the collapse of the Third Reich. And the Allies would reap the benefit.

THE JET AGE

The engineers who uncovered the secrets of Nazi technology might have been surprised to learn that the new age of high-speed aeronautics actually began in America in the fall of 1918. Airplanes of the day had a top speed of less than 125 mph, but the tips of their propellers were moving at close to 650 mph. High-speed wind tunnel tests of propeller airfoil sections undertaken by Frank Caldwell, the MIT graduate who headed propeller research at McCook Field, revealed a sudden increase in drag and loss of lift at speeds around 450 mph. The air moving over the top of the small blade sections was approaching supersonic speed and detaching from the airfoil. Researchers Hugh Dryden and Lyman Briggs of the U.S. National Bureau of Standards subsequently confirmed Caldwell's findings.

At relatively low speeds, air behaves like an incompressible fluid. Approaching the speed of sound, however, the atmosphere begins to compress in front of an aircraft, creating a shock wave sweeping back from the nose in a great cone shape. When the shock wave crosses the wings, the lift-drag ratio plummets, and the mixed flow causes the air to detach from the surface. The pressure on the wing rises to the point where the pilot cannot operate the controls. With high-speed aircraft passing the 400-mph mark in 1930, the problem no longer remained theoretical.

Jacob Ackeret completed the world's first Mach 2 (a *Mach*, named for physicist Ernst Mach, is the ratio of the speed of an object to the speed of sound) wind tunnel at a research facility in Zurich, Switzerland. As early as 1933, O. Walchner and Adolf Busemann, a brilliant young aerodynamicist from Lübeck, published a paper discussing the compressibility problem. At the Volta conference on high-speed flight held at Rome in 1935, Busemann suggested that swept wings, or a delta-shaped form in which the wing would remain inside the shock cone, would enable an airplane to escape compressibility effects.

IF THE FUNDAMENTALS of high-speed aerodynamics were falling into place, however, the limitations of traditional aeronautical propulsion loomed large on the horizon. The drag penalty of the propeller, coupled with the increasing complexity of the internal combustion engine, seemed to bar the way to the future.

The propulsion industry responded by developing larger and more powerful piston engines. It became apparent to a handful of perceptive outsiders, however, that the normal pattern of achieving increases in performance by pushing the limits of the existing technology would no longer suffice. Those perceptive enough to read the signs recognized that the time was ripe for a paradigm shift, the introduction of a radically different type of power plant capable of leapfrogging over the difficulties of the old technology.

A reaction propulsion system seemed the only logical candidate. By the mid-1930s, German army and air force officials had sponsored several rocket-propelled aircraft and missile programs. The research department of the RLM, in cooperation with the DVL, was studying pulse-jet/ram-jet power plants; supporting the research of the Austrian Eugen Sanger, whose dreams ranged from a supersonic interceptor to a hypersonic craft that would skip across the top of the atmosphere; and funding the development of two rocket-powered airplanes. One of them, the tiny Heinkel He 176, flew for the first time on June 15, 1939. The second project, headed by Alexander M. Lippisch (1894–1976), proved far more interesting.

A Heidelberg engineer, Lippisch worked for Zeppelin during World War I and then developed a radical tailless design for the German Institute for Gliding before turning his attention to high-speed flight. By the summer of 1941, his rocket-powered, swept-wing Me 163 Komet, the design reflecting the work of Busemann, had carried its pilot to speeds of over 500 mph, well into the range of compressibility and faster than anyone had flown before. Lippisch's masterpiece, the first operational rocket plane, was lucky to remain in the air for ten minutes at a time, however, and proved almost as dangerous to its pilots as it was to Allied aircrews. The rocket would not soon replace the piston engine as a standard means of propelling airplanes.

INITIALLY, THE POSSIBILITY of a gas turbojet engine seemed far less promising than the rocket. The story begins with Benoît Fourneyron, a nineteenth-century French engineer who combined applied fluid dynamic theory with the best technology of the period to produce the first high-speed water turbine in 1827. Over the next few decades, James Francis, Lester Pelton, James Leffel, and other innovators transformed the water turbine into a major source of industrial power.

The English engineer Charles Parsons introduced the modern steam turbine and launched a new age in marine propulsion with his revolutionary vessel *Turbinia* (1897). By the early years of the twentieth century, new theoretical insights, improved design, and advances in metallurgy had produced high-speed water and steam turbines that were at the very cutting edge of technology.

Auguste Rateau, a French engineer with the Lorraine Dietrich Company, employed turbine technology to effect a major improvement in the performance of aircraft engines. His turbosupercharger, introduced in 1917, compressed the air before it entered the cylinders, increasing the power of the engine and enabling it to operate efficiently at high altitude.

William F. Durand, a Stanford University engineering professor who was chairing NACA, asked the General Electric Company, with its long experience in turbine design and production, to develop an American supercharger. The program, headed by GE's Sanford Moss, laid the foundation for the complex turbosupercharger systems that enabled the American airmen of World War II to fly and fight in the substratosphere.

As early as 1912, the Rumanian Henri M. Coanda had constructed an aircraft powered by a piston engine driving a turbine, or ducted fan, housed in a nacelle. The aircraft refused to leave the ground, but the basic idea refused to die. In 1940, the Italians flew the Caproni-Campini N1, powered by a piston engine driving a compressor that forced air into a combustion chamber. The hot gases exiting the engine propelled the plane into the air, but the system proved wildly inefficient.

Established engine manufacturers, with their heavy investment in the normal piston engine and propeller technology, resisted attempts to develop radically new propulsion systems. Nor did the great American and English research organizations, NACA and the National Physical Laboratory, devote much effort to exploring alternative power plants. As a result, fundamental change would inevitably come from outside the establishment.

It remained for two such outsiders to apply a sophisticated understanding of aerodynamics, thermodynamics, and turbine technology to the design of a continuous-flow gas turbojet reaction engine. In such a power plant, the air enters at the front, becomes compressed, is mixed with fuel, and then burns. The hot propelling gases roaring out of the tailpipe pass through turbines that operate the compressors at the front of the engine. This elegant notion would prove very difficult to achieve.

FRANK WHITTLE (1907–1996), the son of a machinist, entered the RAF aviation mechanics apprentice course in 1923 and was selected as one of five flying officer-engineer cadets to enter the RAF college at Cranwell in 1926. Noting the need for improved propulsion in his senior thesis on high-speed flight, he considered and rejected as too inefficient both the rocket and the possibility of a gas turbine driving a propeller. By late 1929 he had completely abandoned traditional aeronautical propulsion in favor of a pure turbojet.

Posted to the Central Flying School (CFS) as an instructor, Whittle took his idea to a colleague who had worked as a patent lawyer. The commandant of the CFS forwarded the idea to the Air Ministry, which promptly rejected it as impractical. Having obtained a patent and conducted an unsuccessful search for a company willing to pursue his idea, Flying Officer Whittle earned an engineering degree at Cambridge University during 1932–1936. With the assistance of professors, businessmen, and local bankers, he finally organized Power Jets, in 1936, to begin development of his engine.

Hans Joachim Pabst von Ohain (1911–1998), a native of Dessau, earned his doctorate in physics and aerodynamics from Göttingen University in 1935. Recognizing the aerodynamic advantages to be realized through high-speed flight, he conceived the notion of a turbojet engine quite independently from Whittle and remained at the university for an additional year to refine his design, obtain a patent, and build a working model. Like Whittle, he was unable to interest engine manufacturers in his ideas. Ernst Heinkel, always interested in speed and already involved with the DVL rocket program, offered von Ohain a contract.

Whittle, after signing over a substantial portion of his shares in Power Jets to the Air Ministry, was allowed to devote a portion of his official RAF time to the company. The first Whittle jet engine was tested in April 1937. Von Ohain's He-S.1 had been tested with hydrogen fuel, to guarantee the smoothest combustion, at least a month earlier. The He 178, the first airplane to fly with a pure jet engine, took off on August 27, 1939. The Gloster E.28/39, powered by the Whittle W.1, made its first flight on May 15, 1941.

Both the Whittle and von Ohain engines were radial, or centrifugal-flow designs, in which an impeller forces air into diffusing chambers, where it is compressed and then redirected into the combustion chambers. This simple, rugged design is still employed for smaller gas turbo-jet engines. Centrifugal-flow engines also feature a relatively large frontal area and are not particularly fuel efficient.

In 1939, Anselm Franz, an Austrian engineer working for the Junkers Company, developed the first axial-flow jet engine, in which the air flows straight through the engine, from the intake, through compression, into the combustion chamber, through the turbines, and out the nozzle. Not only was the engine thinner and far more fuel efficient than the centrifugal-flow design, but also compression could be increased by adding additional turbine stages.

Following a lengthy series of bureaucratic battles as to the role of the first operational jet, the Me 262, powered by Anselm Franz's Junkers Jumo 004, reached operational units in April 1944. The twin-engine Gloster Meteor, the first operational British jet, and the Me 163, the first operational rocket airplane, both entered service in July 1944. While a handful of the little jet-propelled Heinkel He 162 Volksjager reached operational units, there is no evidence that they ever saw combat. The Arado 234, a twin-engine jet bomber, entered service as a Luftwaffe reconnaissance aircraft in September 1944.

Frank Whittle remained a leading developer of jet engines until 1946, when the government that had reluctantly taken an interest in his work finally merged all but one division of the already nationalized Power Jets into a National Gas Turbine Establishment, which would benefit all British jet builders, including traditional engine manufacturers like Rolls-Royce. Knighted for his services, Whittle worked as a consultant, eventually emigrating to the United States. Hans von Ohain accepted a position with the U.S. Air Force in 1947 and ended his career as the chief scientist of the Air Force Propulsion Laboratory at Wright-Patterson Air Force Base.

THE JET ENGINE came as an unpleasant surprise to General Hap Arnold, chief of the Air Corps. U.S. government researchers had consistently rejected the notion of a pure jet engine. As early as 1923, Edgar Buckingham, of the National Bureau of Standards, had declared that any such approach to aircraft propulsion was "practically impossible."[2] While aerodynamicists were developing very successful multistage compressors for superchargers, engine specialists at both NACA Langley Laboratory and Wright Field remained wedded to normal piston-engine technology. NACA officials rejected out of hand at least one proposal for research on a pure jet engine.

In January 1941 the National Academy of Sciences reported gas turbines as impractical for aircraft propulsion but urged industry to begin work on improved turbine systems for powering ships. GE, Allis-Chalmers, and Westinghouse, the nation's most-experienced turbine builders, accepted the challenge. That February, uncertain about the academy's recommendations and generally aware that the British were conducting some work in the area of reaction propulsion, General Arnold asked Vannevar Bush, chairman of NACA and head of the Office of Scientific Research and Development, to establish a special committee on jet propulsion, to be headed by William Durand, who had set Sanford Moss to work on the supercharger a generation before.

Touring England that April, General Arnold was stunned to discover that not only did the English disagree with the judgment of the National Academy of Sciences, but also they had a jet engine in hand and were preparing to fly a jet airplane. He returned to the states with one thought in mind: the time had come for some reverse lend-lease. Arnold assembled a team that included Gen. Franklin O. Carroll, head of the Air Corps Engineering Division at Wright Field; Oliver Patton Echols, now assigned to the Air Staff in Washington; and officials of the GE and Bell companies who would produce copies of the Whittle engine and the airplane that it would propel.

The Navy Bureau of Aeronautics contracted with Westinghouse, the other large-scale U.S. producer of turbines, for a jet engine of its own. The resulting Westinghouse 9XB-2B would eventually power the McDonnell FH-1 Phantom, the first U.S. jet to operate from an aircraft carrier.

On October 1, 1941, a B-24 took off from Prestwick, Scotland, bound for the United States, with a Whittle W.1X safely tucked away

Bell XP-59A Airacomet

in the bomb bay, along with a set of drawings for the next-generation Power Jets W.2B. The RAF was sending the very engine that Arnold had seen mounted on the E.28/39 during the April taxi tests. Exactly one year after that take-off, the Bell XP-59, the first American jet, took to the air for the first time.

The British would continue to dominate turbojet technology for some time to come. The Lockheed P-80, the first genuinely successful operational U.S. jet, was powered by a GE J-33, a variant of the De

Havilland Goblin engine produced by GE and eventually manufactured by the Allison Division of General Motors. The Grumman F9F Panther flew with a Pratt & Whitney J-42, based on the very successful Rolls-Royce Nene. Later Grumman models were powered by the Pratt & Whitney J-48 version of the Rolls-Royce Tay.

The United States was not the only nation to profit from the considerable British lead in jet-engine technology. The earliest Soviet jet power plants were based on the Rolls-Royce Atar. Visiting Britain in 1946, three Soviet aviation design bureau heads, including Artem Mikoyan, saw the Rolls-Royce Nene and Derwent V engines in operation and received assurances that they could buy examples of these most up-to-date power plants.

By the end of 1947, the Soviets had purchased twenty-five Nene and thirty Derwent V engines. Overjoyed, Soviet manufacturers reconfigured their fighter and bomber designs for the new power plants, which they reproduced without paying any license fees to the British firm. The Lavochkin La-168, the Tupolev Tu-73 and Tu-77, and the legendary MiG 15 all flew into the Cold War with copies of Rolls-Royce power plants. The Soviets stole the secrets of the atomic bomb. Acquiring modern jet engine technology proved considerably simpler.

By the early 1950s, the enormous U.S. investment in research and development enabled American companies to pull ahead of the Brits. At the end of the decade, Pratt & Whitney and GE shared leadership of the Western market for large turbojet engines with Rolls-Royce.

THE PURE TURBOJET engine operates most efficiently at relatively high altitudes and speeds. At low altitudes, as on take-off and landing, it becomes much less efficient. For aircraft that fly shorter distances at slower speeds and lower altitudes, turboprop engines offer a more efficient alternative. Simply put, a turboprop is a turbojet engine in which the exiting gases turn the compressors and a turbine, which drives the propeller. Most of the power of the engine gets transferred to the propeller, and the reaction effect is much reduced. Rolls-Royce put the first turboprop on a Gloster Meteor in 1945.

Immediately following World War II, it was generally assumed that the turboprop would propel the next generation of airliners. It offers greater speed and performance than the piston engine, yet is more efficient than the turbojet at the speeds, altitudes, and distances involved. In fact, the turboprop became and remains the power plant of choice for many short- and medium-range airliners, business aircraft, and transports.

In a turboshaft engine, the hot gases drive a shaft rather than a propeller gearbox. Since the 1960s, small gas turboshaft engines produced by U.S. companies like Williams International, Teledyne, Lycoming, Pratt & Whitney Canada, Garrett, and Allison have propelled helicopters, tanks, and boats. Small gas turbojet engines produced by the same firms power pilotless aircraft and small airplanes.

If the turboprop is at the bottom of the speed and altitude continuum, and turbojets are at the top, low- and high-bypass turbofan engines close the gap between the two. In both cases, special multiblade propellers, driven by the turbine, force small or large amounts of air through a carefully designed nacelle surrounding the head of the engine. The cold bypassing air generates most of its thrust, with some coming from the exhausting gases.

Pratt & Whitney pioneered the turbofan with the JT3D in the early 1960s. High-bypass engines are nearly as fuel efficient as turboprops and low-bypass engines are still more fuel efficient than pure jets. With many blades turning inside a nacelle, a turbofan operates at higher speeds with greater efficiency than a propeller. By the end of the century, turbofans had become the preferred power plants for aircraft operating at speeds from 350 to 650 mph, including most large airliners and a number of high-performance subsonic military aircraft.

TESTING TIME

NACA and the Engineering Division of the U.S. Air Force Materiel Command had missed the opportunity to ride the crest of the turbojet revolution, but they had by no means ignored the possibility of high-speed flight. As early as 1928, University of California–trained Eastman

N. Jacobs and John Stack, a young engineer fresh from MIT, had created a small, high-speed wind tunnel in which they could explore compressibility effects, and had even photographed shock waves on airfoils using the Schlierin system developed by Ernst Mach himself. Jacobs began the process of developing high-speed airfoils, while Stack (1934) published a conjectural drawing of a propeller-driven, 500-mph research airplane.

The research continued in 1935, when Jacobs, on his own and in direct violation of a NACA rule against supersonic research, assigned another newcomer, Columbia University graduate Arthur Kantrowitz, to design Langley's first true supersonic wind tunnel. Some notion of Jacobs's penchant for striking out on his own can be seen in the fact that he and Kantrowitz launched their own experiments with nuclear fusion in 1938. They operated their apparatus with a huge electric motor normally used to drive a wind tunnel. If his superiors discovered the project, Jacobs planned to claim that they were investigating the possibility of nuclear propulsion! George Lewis, the NACA chief of research, did discover the project and brought it to an immediate conclusion.[3]

Atomic energy aside, John Stack had a good reason for suggesting a new type of airplane, the sole purpose of which was to gather information on aerodynamic conditions close to the speed of sound. From the time of Frank Caldwell to that of John Stack and Eastman Jacobs, researchers had used wind tunnels to probe compressibility effects in the high subsonic region. European and NACA researchers had developed tunnels producing conditions well in excess of the speed of sound. At transonic speeds, from Mach 0.7 to Mach 1.3, however, the shock waves streaming off the test items reverberated off the walls of the tunnel, choking the airflow. The answer to the problem, John Stack believed, was to build an airplane that could fly faster than sound, and see what happened.

Captain Walter S. Diehl, who represented the U.S. Navy Bureau of Aeronautics at NACA Langley, agreed. So did Ezra Kotcher, an instructor at Wright Field's Air Corps Engineering School, who had advocated a transonic flight research program as early as 1939. The problem moved from abstract theory to life-and-death reality with the appearance of the twin-engine Lockheed P-38 Lightning. The shock waves forming on the wing of a Lightning in a steep dive could result in a loss of control and structural failure. A Lockheed test pilot died just that way in December 1942. Dive flaps alleviated the problem with the P-38 and other high-speed fighters of the era, but it was clear that serious problems lay just ahead.

By the spring of 1944, at the urging of George Lewis, Langley engineers were detailed to the Navy Bureau of Aeronautics to assist in the preliminary design of a transonic airplane. That May, Kotcher traveled to Langley with a proposal for a "Mach 0.999 airplane." The Navy/Marine Corps and NACA preferred a conservative approach, using a turbojet-powered aircraft. Air force officials at Wright Field opted for a rocket-propelled research vehicle.

Bell Aircraft, with its reputation for innovative design and the experience of the XP-59 under its belt, won the contract for the air force project. Reaction Motors of Pompano Plains, New Jersey, would provide a six-thousand-pound, liquid-propellant, four-chamber rocket engine. The airplane was originally identified as the XS-1, Experimental Sonic One.

Given the absence of hard knowledge, the team based the shape of the fuselage on a fifty-caliber bullet, which remained stable while traveling faster than the speed of sound. It would have straight wings, as well, even though Robert T. Jones had explained the advantages of swept wings to Kotcher and Jean Roche, Wright Field's liaison to Langley.

Already something of a legend, Jones had taught himself fluid dynamics while working as a mechanic for a flying circus. Unable to break into engineering, he ran an elevator in a congressional office building until a legislator arranged a Work Projects Administration appointment with NACA. One day in the middle of the war, a small balsa model of a delta-wing airplane arrived on his desk. It was the work of Michael Gluhareff, a Russian émigré and Igor Sikorsky's chief designer, who proposed the design as a means of delaying the onset of compressibility in a high-speed interceptor, a la Busemann, Lippisch, and Sanger.

In spite of Jones's enthusiasm, the decision makers ruled that a straight wing would provide information of greater value for the design of the Lockheed P-80, which would have a traditional wing. The compressibility problems experienced by the P-38 and other aircraft inspired one major innovation, however. At relatively low speeds, the pilot of the XS-1 would employ the elevator for pitch control. At high speeds, he would be able swivel the entire horizontal stabilizer.

With the support of NACA personnel, the Navy Bureau of Aeronautics began to develop specifications for a turbojet-powered high-speed research airplane in the spring of 1944. The Douglas Company won the contract for the D-558-1, which would fly at subsonic speeds and provide data for the designers of next-generation naval aircraft. They also suggested a second rocket-powered research airplane, the D-558-2, that would fly at perhaps twice the speed of sound.

The dangers were apparent. In February 1946, Sir Benjamin Lockspeiser, director-general of Scientific Air Research of the Ministry of Supply, announced that Britain was abandoning piloted attempts to fly faster than sound. "We have not the heart," he noted, "to ask pilots to fly the high speed models, so we shall make them radio-controlled."[4]

To this point, Britain had led the United States in high-speed-flight research. Work had been underway on jet- and rocket-powered versions of the Miles M.52 since 1943. That very advanced aircraft, now almost complete, would never fly. As though to confirm Lockspeiser's grim words, test pilot Geoffrey De Havilland, son of Sir Geoffrey De Havilland, died in the crash of a D.H. 108 Swallow on September 27, 1946. The small, subsonic research airplane with swept wings and a swept tail broke up in the air as a result of compressibility effects.

The rival American programs forged ahead. Bell test pilot Jack Woolams manned the controls of the Bell XS-1 when it was dropped from the belly of a specially configured B-29 on its first glide test over Pinecastle, Florida, in January 1946. The operation shifted across the continent that fall to Muroc Army Air Field, in the high desert of California.

IN 1910 the Corum family established a small settlement where the Santa Fe tracks crossed the edge of Rodriguez Dry Lake. With a church, school, and grocery store going up, they petitioned for a post office. When officials pointed out that there was already a Coram in California, the town fathers opted for "Muroc" and changed the name of the dry lake as well. Commanding March Field near Los Angeles in 1932, General Hap Arnold settled on the dry lake as an isolated area where his airmen could practice gunnery and bombing. In 1942, Wright Field designated the area the Materiel Center Flight Test Site. Initial flight testing of the XP-59 began in great secrecy here.

Bell conducted the early glide and power tests of the XS-1. The men of Wright Field's Flight Test Division, commanded by Col. Albert Boyd, arrived in California to take over the program one day after President Truman signed the Armed Forces Unification Act creating the United States Air Force. Langley's Walter Williams led the NACA team that would work with the Bell and Douglas programs. On the morning of October 14, 1947, Capt. Charles E. "Chuck" Yeager, who had chalked up eleven victories over occupied Europe, flew the XS-1 faster than sound and into history.

The air force did its best to keep the flight secret. When *Aviation Week* broke the story in December, the Justice Department considered prosecution. The air force and NACA finally admitted the truth in June 1948, when Yeager was awarded the Mackay Trophy and another oak-leaf cluster to his wartime Distinguished Flying Cross. That December, Yeager, John Stack, and Lawrence Bell were awarded the Collier Trophy for conceiving, building, and flying an airplane faster than sound.

Whereas Charles Lindbergh had instantly captured the public's imagination, Chuck Yeager took hold a bit more slowly. In the immediate postwar years, the test pilots who were pushing back the boundaries of a new frontier in the sky replaced the fighter pilots of World War I and the speed and distance flyers of the 1920s and 1930s as the ultimate heroes of the air. Some great names of postwar aviation were veterans of the various X-1 and D-558-1 and -2 programs of 1946–1958: A. Scott Crossfield, William Bridgeman, Robert Hoover, Howard Lilly, Alra "Tex" Johnson, Marion Carl, Frank "Pete" Everest Jr., Joseph Walker, Neil Armstrong, Arthur "Kit" Murray.

There could be no doubt as to who was the king of that hill, how-

Lawrence Bell, Charles E. "Chuck" Yeager, and Hoyt S. Vandenberg standing in front of the Bell X-1

ever. Chuck Yeager personified the cool confidence and supreme competence of the men who went higher and faster than anyone had gone before. He had already influenced a generation of pilots when author Tom Wolfe catapulted him to cultural superstardom as the hero with *The Right Stuff*.[5]

The golden age of the high-speed, high-altitude research airplane lasted for twenty-one years, from the appearance of the XS-1 at Muroc in 1947 to the final flight of the X-15 in October 1968. By that time, Muroc Army Air Field had been transformed into sprawling Edwards Air Force Base, named for Capt. Glen Edwards, who died here in the crash of the Northrop YB-49 Flying Wing in June 1948. The facility that Walt Williams and his team had established as the NACA High-

Speed Flight Research Center would be renamed the Hugh L. Dryden Flight Research Center in 1976. Since the flight test of the XP-59, this shared space is also where NACA/NASA (National Aeronautics and Space Administration), the military services, and aircraft manufacturers have come to analyze the flying characteristics of their latest prototypes.

Many of the research airplanes that took to the skies over Edwards/Dryden did not fly all that high or fast. The Northrop X-4 (1948–1954) gathered information on a swept-wing aircraft with no vertical stabilizer, whereas the Bell X-5 (1951–1953), based on the Messerschmitt P 1101, enabled engineers to study the use of variably swept wings.

Some test vehicles, like the Lunar Landing Research Vehicle, a flying simulator designed to provide experience for the astronauts who would land a lunar module on the moon, did not even have wings. Neither did the lifting bodies, the HL-10, M2-F2/3, and X-24 (1963–1975). Wingless shapes that generated lift by the flow of air around their bodies, these strange craft shed light on the aerodynamic problems of spacecraft reentering Earth's atmosphere.

The XV-3 (1958) and the XV-15 (1981) demonstrated the tilt-rotor concept, in which twin rotors mounted on the end of short wings are positioned vertically to permit a helicopter-like take-off and landing, and swiveled to the horizontal for normal flight. The Grumman X-29 (1989), with its forward-swept wing, forward elevator (canard), and electrical (fly-by-wire) controls, tested systems and design features planned for future military aircraft. The North American Rockwell HiMAT (1979), a subscale research airplane flown from the ground, demonstrated the potential of remotely piloted test vehicles.

IDEAS WERE TESTED, as well as machines. The area rule and the supercritical wing, two of the most important concepts to emerge in postwar aerodynamics, were first demonstrated over the high desert of California. Both represented the work of a young aerodynamicist named Richard T. Whitcomb, a graduate of the Worcester Polytechnic Institute who had reported to work at NACA Langley in 1943 and quickly turned his attention to the problem of increased drag at transonic speeds.

John Stack had become interested in the "slotted-wall" wind tunnel design suggested by engineer Ray Walker in 1946 as a means of gathering accurate transonic data. By 1950, an existing eight-foot high-speed tunnel had been converted to the new design, and an additional transonic tunnel was under construction. Once again, John Stack and his team were rewarded with the Collier Trophy for their efforts.

Experimenting with the converted tunnel, Richard Whitcomb realized that the sharp rise in drag near the speed of sound was not the result of shock waves generated by the nose of an aircraft, but by those formed behind the trailing edge of the wings. It occurred to him that creating a "wasp-waisted" fuselage, pinched in where the wings met the body of the aircraft, would produce a total cross-sectional area of fuselage, wings, and tail that represented an ideal streamlined body. Dubbed the "area rule," it seemed counterintuitive, but repeated wind tunnel tests suggested that it was true.

Richard T. Whitcomb

In 1952, the Convair XF-102 faced serious problems. Powered by the new Pratt & Whitney J-35, the delta-winged interceptor was designed to slice through Mach 1, but wind tunnel tests revealed unexpected shock waves on the wings that would limit the performance of the airplane. Whitcomb and his colleagues described their findings to the Convair engineers, who returned to Langley in 1953 with a model of the now wasp-waisted YF-102. The success of the NACA flight tests of the prototype airplane at Muroc in 1953–1954 provided a final demonstration of an important concept.

Whitcomb launched another era of change in 1966, when he announced the design of a "supercritical wing." Intended to drastically reduce the drag on a wing approaching the speed of sound, the airfoil that emerged from the Langley wind tunnels was so oddly shaped, Whitcomb realized, "that nobody's going to touch it with a ten foot pole without somebody going out and flying it."[6] That is just what they did, mounting the first full-scale supercritical wing on a Chance Vought F8 that was flown at the Dryden Research Center.

In the end, however, it was the record-setting research airplanes and test pilots who pushed the limits of speed and altitude that captured the public's imagination. A. Scott Crossfield, a veteran naval aviator turned engineering test pilot, replaced Chuck Yeager as the fastest human alive when he flew the Douglas D-558-2 Skyrocket to Mach 2 on November 20, 1953. The Bell X-2 flew three times the speed of sound in level flight on September 27, 1956.

ON THE FAR SIDE of the sound barrier no problem loomed larger than aerodynamic heating. At three times the speed of sound, skin friction raised temperatures to a level where standard light alloys began to lose their strength and resistance to deformation. Designed to probe this "thermal thicket," the Bell X-2 was constructed of a heat-resistant nickel alloy called K-Monel and stainless steel, presenting little danger that extreme heat would soak through the skin to the vital structure of an experimental airplane flying faster than sound for only a few minutes. There would be very real problems, however, for the next-generation airplanes operating at supersonic speeds.

The North American X-15, constructed of a nickel steel alloy known as Inconal-X, was the ultimate airplane. Designed to explore flight at hypersonic speeds and to reach altitudes where the atmosphere stopped and space began, the first of three X-15s constructed took to the air on September 17, 1959. Over the next nine years of the program, these aircraft reached speeds of up to 6.72 Mach and altitudes of 354,200 feet. It would be difficult to define anything that flew higher or faster as an aircraft. In fact, eight pilots earned their astronaut wings flying the X-15.

Wartime German research still inspired U.S. Air Force and NACA thinking as late as 1957, when planning began for the X-20 Dynasoar, a follow-on to the X-15. Based on the "dynamic soaring" notion of Eugen Sanger, Dynasoar would be launched into space atop a Titan rocket and glide back to a runway landing. Secretary of Defense Robert McNamara canceled the project in 1963, in favor of the less ambitious Manned Orbiting Laboratory military program, which was dropped in 1969.

Dynasoar was only one of a series of cutting-edge technological projects abandoned during the 1960s and early 1970s. The period began and ended with the cancelation of both North American supersonic bomber projects, the XB-70 (1959) and the B-58 (1970). Secretary of Defense Robert McNamara defied the will of Congress in 1966, halting development of the Lockheed YF-12, an interceptor version of the SR-71 reconnaissance aircraft. The House of Representatives closed the books on the American supersonic transport in 1971, when it refused to continue the funding on which the program depended.

Progress in the air would no longer be defined solely by who flew higher and faster. Stealth technology proved more valuable to military aircraft than higher speeds. Supersonic airliners proved less economical than very large subsonic transports.

In the early years of the twenty-first century, staff members of the high-tech center where the hottest flying machines ever built had taken to the sky took special pride in the record flight of Helios. A solar-powered, remotely controlled flying wing with a span longer than that of a Boeing 747, the environmentally friendly craft reached an altitude of 96,500 feet, a record for non-rocket-propelled winged airplanes. It was but one example of the extent to which the ability to fly cleaner, quieter, and more fuel efficiently now balanced the need to fly higher and faster.

STRAIGHT UP!

The helicopter was another technical marvel to emerge from the crucible of war. The invention of the airplane had been a fairly clear-cut business. The Wright brothers had achieved a considerable feat well in advance of any other experimenters, clearly earning the distinction of having invented the airplane. The helicopter was a very different matter. In this case, so many individuals were involved, and the contributions so complex, that identifying the inventor of the helicopter, or even the first helicopter, is a pointless exercise.

The idea of rising straight up into the air was not new. French experimenter Louis Breguet's Gyrocopter No. 1 was the first rotary-wing machine to leave the ground with a pilot on board (1907), although four men with poles had to balance the aircraft as it hovered just a foot off the ground. Paul Cornu made the first free flights (1907–1908) with a helicopter, although his aircraft was clearly very far from practical. The engineers from a variety of nations who continued the work on the problem over the next two decades—Igor Sikorsky (1910), Jacob C. Ellehammer (1912), Henry Berliner (1922), Raul Pescara (1923), George de Bothezat (1921–1924)—fared little better.

It remained for a Spanish engineer, Juan de la Cierva (1896–1936), to adopt a compromise approach to vertical flight. The son of a former cabinet minister, Cierva earned a degree in civil engineering and served in Spain's national legislature. Fascinated by flight since childhood, he had been involved in several less-than-successful fixed-wing projects before turning his attention to the rotary wing.

Recognizing the technical difficulties that stood in the way of developing a true helicopter, Cierva conceived a brilliant half-measure, the autogiro. Rather than powering a rotary wing, he would set a free-wheeling rotor at a positive angle on top of a machine fitted with a conventional engine and a propeller mounted on the nose. The forward motion of the craft would turn the rotor, lifting the machine into the air. The pilot would operate standard airplane controls: ailerons mounted on a pair of stubby wings, a rudder, and an elevator. Cierva's C.4 took to the air for the first time in January 1923, once the inventor had developed a hinge that enabled flexible blades to change angles naturally as they rotated. With the engine shut off, the craft would "autorotate" safely to the ground. While the autogiro did not take off straight up, it required a very short take-off run.

The flying windmill, an apt description, drew immediate international interest. Harold Frederick Pitcairn (1897–1960), a Pennsylvania aircraft manufacturer, bought the American rights to the autogiro and did his best to convince the public that his PA-18 tandem autogiro, with its $5,000 price tag, deserved a spot in the average garage. He placed lush-color advertisements in national magazines and hired famous pilots like Amelia Earhart to demonstrate his wares. Pitcairn's machines sported some of the most-famous corporate liveries in American advertising: Beech-Nut, Coca Cola, Champion Spark Plugs, Pep Boys, Standard Oil of New Jersey.

Pitcairn also licensed other U.S. producers of autogiros. The Buhl Aircraft Company of Marysville, Michigan, produced the first pusher autogiro. The Kellett Aircraft Company, a Philadelphia firm founded in 1920 by W. Wallace Kellett, his brother Rodney, and the airline-building Luddington brothers, C. Townsend and Nicholas, also obtained a license from Pitcairn. Ultimately Kellett would rival the mother company, selling autogiros to the military and sending one of their products to the Antarctic base "Little America" with Adm. Richard Byrd.

The original autogiros could be downright dangerous to land, because slow speed and the lack of airflow made the aerodynamic control surfaces next to useless. Cierva realized that the only real solution involved exercising direct control by changing the angle of the rotors. By March 1932 he was flying an autogiro without wings, ailerons, or elevators. Pitcairn and his associate James Ray flew these machines in England that summer and built their own direct-control machine in 1933. Strangely, Kellett did not introduce the first American-produced direct-control autogiro until 1941. Pitcairn spent considerable time and energy developing and publicizing smaller autogiros, some of which were roadable. With the approach of war, both firms marketed autogyros to the army, navy, and RAF.

THE APPEARANCE OF the first practical helicopters before and during World War II brought the era of the autogiro to an end. Still, Cierva, who had pioneered autorotation, the blade-and-hinge design, and the principles of direct control, deserves recognition as one of the great innovators in the history of rotary-wing flight. Largely as a result of his efforts, a number of engineers who had experimented with helicopters in the early years of the century returned to the problem of rotary-wing flight in the mid-1930s, along with some newcomers.

Corradino d'Ascanio, an Italian experimenter, set Fédération Aéronautique Internationale helicopter records for distance, altitude, and endurance (1930), but was unable to transform his twin-rotor design into a practical machine. Aviation pioneer Louis Breguet, who had built his first experimental rotary-wing machine in 1908, won a 1936 prize from the French government for the development of a helicopter that covered twenty-seven miles and hovered for ten minutes, but it vibrated so badly that it was still not regarded as practical when the war brought an end to the project.

Dr. Heinrich Karl Johann Focke, a World War I veteran who had founded the Focke-Wulf Company with Georg Wulf and Werner Naumann in 1924, was forced out of the firm in 1933 as a result of his anti-Nazi views. On the basis of his experience with Cierva autogiros, however, Focke was permitted to fund a series of wind tunnel tests and experiments with a full-scale model of a true helicopter.

He unveiled the Fa-61 in a series of record-breaking flights in 1936–1937. Featuring twin-powered rotors mounted on outriggers on either side of the fuselage, the machine had standard controls. A movement of the stick to the front or rear tilted the rotors fore or aft to bring the nose up or down. By moving the stick to the right or left, the pilot increased lift on one side and reduced it on the other, for roll control. The rudder pedals tilted the rotors differentially, turning the nose to the right or left.

In February 1938, Nazi heroine Hanna Reitsch captured the attention of the nation when she demonstrated the machine inside a Berlin sports hall. Recognizing the potential of the machine, the German government allowed Focke to partner with pilot Gerd Achgelis. The result was the Focke-Achgelis Fa-223 Drache (Dragon). Originally designed as a transport helicopter for Deutsche Lufthansa, the Fa-223 first flew in 1939, and was ordered into production following acceptance trials in 1942. As a result of Allied bombing, however, only three of the machines entered service.

One Fa-223, flown to a flying field in southern England at the end of the war, became the first helicopter to fly the English Channel. Another, rebuilt in France by SNCA (Societé Nationale de Constructiones Aéronautiques) Sud-Est with the assistance of Heinrich Focke, was important in launching the helicopter industry in France. Fa-223 technology also played a key role in initiating rotary-wing production in Czechoslovakia.

Like Focke, Anton Flettner moved from autogiros to helicopters. He flew his Fl-265, featuring counterrotating, intermeshing twin rotors, in 1939. The follow-on Fl-282 Kolibri (Hummingbird) entered service in 1942 and was employed as an observation craft operating from ships at sea. Much smaller and lighter than the Fa-223, the Kolibri could fly at almost 90 mph and reach altitudes of up to ten thousand feet. Flettner did not invent the helicopter, but he had produced the first practical model that saw active military service.

Friedrich von Doblhoff and the brothers A. Stephan and Theodor Laufer built and flew the first helicopter using blade-tip jets. Their WNF-342, first flown in 1943, saw limited use aboard U-boats. At the end of the war, Doblhoff went to work for McDonnell Aircraft, while the Laufer brothers played key roles in the helicopter programs underway at Fairey in Britain and Sud-Est in France.

IN THE UNITED STATES, no name is more closely associated with the development of the helicopter than Igor Ivan Sikorsky (1889–1972), one of the most extraordinary individuals in the history of flight. The son of a pioneer psychologist, Sikorsky combined the sensibilities of a

Russian Orthodox mystic with the hard-nosed logic and determined spirit of an innovator and engineer.

A graduate of the Imperial Naval Academy, he studied engineering in both Paris and St. Petersburg, conducted early and unsuccessful experiments with a helicopter, pioneered a native aircraft industry in Russia, and produced the world's first four-engine transport aircraft, which he transformed into the world's first four-engine bomber during World War I. Having fled from Russia during the revolution, he spent time in France before immigrating to New York in 1919. He lectured on aeronautics and taught mathematics to keep body and soul together until 1923, when he convinced a substantial number of fellow émigrés to invest in the Sikorsky Aero Engineering Corporation, established on a Long Island chicken farm owned by a fellow Russian.

The new company produced a large transport aircraft thought capable of flying the Atlantic and introduced the classic A-38 amphibian in 1939. Reorganized as the Sikorsky Aviation Corporation under the umbrella of the United Aircraft and Transport Corporation in 1929, and transferred to Stratford, Connecticut, the firm emerged as a major producer of large flying boats.

By 1938, with flying-boat contracts going to Martin and Boeing, the powers-that-be at United Aircraft informed Sikorsky that they were closing his division, although he would be allowed to continue work on any research project that he thought promising. He convinced corporate officials to allow him and the key members of his engineering team to begin serious work on his old dream of vertical flight.

Sikorsky made a quick trip to Europe to meet Heinrich Focke and Louis Breguet and then set to work. Mindful of corporate budgetary restraints, the little crew incorporated an automobile transmission and motorcycle parts in the early test vehicles. They finished work on the original version of the VS-300, the first Sikorsky helicopter, in September 1939. Considerable work and rebuilding were required before the first free flight in May 1940. Still, Sikorsky continued to struggle with control problems. When Capt. H. Franklin "Frank" Gregory, Wright Field's rotary-wing project officer, tried to fly the machine, it behaved "like a bucking bronco." It was, he noted, "ornery."[7]

As if the technical problems were not enough, the Sikorsky team had competition. W. Laurence LePage, a Pitcairn veteran, and Havilland H. Platt, had formed the Platt-LePage Aircraft Company, won a $300,000 army contract, and set out to produce the XR-1, their own version of the Fa-61. With the firm making slow, steady progress, Frank Gregory decided to hedge his bet by offering a $30,000 contract to Sikorsky for continued work toward an operational helicopter that would be known as the XR-4 (the XR-2 and XR-3 were Kellett autogiros).

Sikorsky made rapid progress. His move from multiple tail rotors on outriggers to a single rotor counteracting the torque of the main rotor was a major step toward the development of a practical helicopter. He also adapted Anton Flettner's means of maintaining lateral

Igor Ivan Sikorsky aboard an early version of the Sikorsky VS-300

and longitudinal control by increasing the angle of the blades at one point and decreasing it on the opposite side. The pilot moved a "collective" lever up and down with the left hand, and manipulated the hand-grip throttle, to control climb and descent. His right hand operated a "cyclic" control to tilt the machine in any direction. Rudder pedals controlled the tail rotor and pointed the nose to the right or left.

By the end of 1941, the almost constant stream of changes had transformed the VS-300 into a complete success. The XR-4 made its first test flight on January 14, 1942. That May, Sikorsky and test pilot Charles Morris flew the helicopter from Stratford to Wright Field in five days. Contracts for the production model, YR-4, and later models soon followed. Sikorsky had saved his company, and his career, through the development of an entirely new machine.

A BURST OF ENTHUSIASM for vertical flight swept over the American home front. The notion of the helicopter as the personal transport of tomorrow had great popular appeal. Industry pioneer Grover Loening quickly branded that sort of thinking as wildly optimistic. "Any notion . . . that everybody is going to fly helicopters right after the war is nonsense," he remarked in 1943. "[The] . . . amount of skill required to fly these machines . . . is even greater than is now required of an airplane, and . . . very much greater than is needed to drive a car."[8]

Clearly, however, a machine that could rise straight up into the air and hover over one spot served some functions. In addition to its military utility, the helicopter could play a major role in urban and regional transportation. New names and faces and new kinds of helicopters appeared on the scene.

Frank Piasecki, born in 1919 to a Polish tailor, had worked for Kellett before earning a mechanical engineering degree from the University of Pennsylvania and a degree in aeronautical engineering from New York University. The new graduate worked at Platt-LePage for a time, then began to develop his own helicopter design, the PV-1, with a group of UPenn engineering students. The follow-on PV-2 flew well when demonstrated to the military in 1943.

Piasecki quickly moved on to what would become his signature tandem-rotor design, however, reasoning that the poor power and lift characteristics of first-generation helicopters could be overcome with two rotors, one at the front and one at the rear. The XHRP-1, the original "flying banana," developed under a U.S. Coast Guard–U.S. Navy contract, first flew in February 1945. Piasecki moved forward, focusing on the development of large tandems with much greater carrying capacity than other models.

The first Bell helicopter also took to the air in 1943. Arthur Young had sold Lawrence Bell on the helicopter during a meeting in a Washington hotel in the fall of 1941. Young, a wealthy Princeton graduate, had traveled to the nation's capital in 1928 to study patent applications covering ideas that appealed to him: wire recording, television, color and three-dimensional motion pictures. He decided to pursue the helicopter and spent considerable time and effort over the next decade developing a small model featuring an all-important stabilizer bar that controlled the angle of the individual rotor blades while maintaining the position of the rotor disk.

Wright Field's Frank Gregory, intrigued by the somewhat eccentric Young, sent him to Lawrence Bell, who agreed to fund the development of a full-scale helicopter. The resulting Model 30 flew in June 1943 and led to the Model 47, the bubble-nosed classic that became the first helicopter certified by the Civil Aviation Administration (CAA) for civil operations.

Stanley Hiller Jr., a University of California dropout, organized the Hiller Aircraft Company in 1942 and flew a coaxial double-rotor helicopter in 1944. By 1947, he had abandoned that design in favor of a two-bladed main rotor with a stabilizer bar and a single tail rotor, the Model 360. His company built eleven hundred for the army and navy.

Newcomers swarmed into the field—Frederick Landgraff, Charles Siebel, Kelvinator, Kaiser Fleetwings, Bendix, McDonnell—and left just as quickly. Some of the more familiar names came to stay. The Hughes Aircraft Company, a smallish arm of the Hughes Tool Company that had been little more than Howard Hughes's hobby shop, acquired a Kellett contract for a large transport helicopter in 1949. Rolled out in 1952, the Hughes XH-17 was powered by two GE J-35 turbojets that exhausted their gases through nozzles on the tip of the twin blades. Boeing was a serious competitor as well, building its Vertol Division around Piasecki's company, which it acquired in 1960.

Charles H. Kaman (pronounced "command" without the "d") took an enormous step forward when he brought the helicopter into the jet age. He had set out in 1945 to develop a Flettner-style helicopter with intermeshing rotors and achieved that goal with the introduction of the K-225 (1949). Test pilot William Murray impressed observers in March 1950 when he flew the first intentional helicopter loop with one of those machines at the Patuxent River Naval Air Station. Sales were so disappointing, however, that Kaman resorted to leasing his whirly-birds to crop dusters, who were intrigued by the new technology but unwilling to invest in it. The sale of thirty HTK-1 and HOK-1 military variants barely kept the company afloat.

Kaman was floundering when several of his navy contacts suggested that jet propulsion might solve some of the problems retarding the growth of vertical flight. Piston engines were heavy, difficult to maintain, and seldom provided sufficient power to enable a helicopter to do much more than hold itself in the air. Carrying capacity remained severely limited and vibration a constant problem.

Kaman rejected Hiller's blade-tip ram-jets, and the Hughes approach of exhausting the hot jet gases through the rotor tips, in favor of a turboshaft engine driving the rotors through a transmission. A K-225 powered by a 175-horsepower Boeing marine gas turbine flew for the first time on December 11, 1951. A spectacular success, it set the stage for the introduction of light and increasingly powerful turboshaft engines like the Allison 250, the AVCO Lycoming T-53, and the GE T-58. The appearance of the first turboshaft-propelled helicopter provided a revolutionary jump in performance and marked the single most important turning point in the history of rotary-wing flight.

By 1960 the American helicopter industry was maturing. Some 7,200 rotary-wing craft had been built in the United States since 1943. Total sales were estimated at $2.5 billion, only $500 million of which had been for civil aircraft. The military services had purchased 6,300 machines. Some 235 commercial operators and 50 civilian flight schools accounted for roughly 900 helicopters.[9]

THE ADVENT OF jet-powered helicopters had a profound impact on military operations. Since World War II, a variety of nations had employed helicopters for search-and-rescue and medical evacuation duties. Film and photos of Bell H-13s (Model 47s) and Sikorsky S-55s flying wounded men into a field hospital were among the most familiar images of the Korean War. Valerie André, a woman physician, pilot, and parachutist, who commanded a medical evacuation squadron operating Hiller helicopters near Hanoi, became one of the great French heroes of the Indochina War.

The U.S. Marines experimented with the use of Piasecki helicopters to drop soldiers into battle. In the fall of 1951 Marine helicopters lifted a full battalion, a thousand fully equipped men, into the combat zone over a period of six hours. With the U.S. Air Force apparently unwilling to commit to the task of ferrying troops into the battle zone, army planners simply ignored regulations that limited them to operating aircraft weighing less than two tons and began to build their own troop-carrying capacity. Air mobility was one of the most important notions to come out of the Korean War.

With the Vietnam War gathering momentum, the army carried the idea to a new level. Before the end of 1961, twin-rotor Vertol CH-21 Shawnees, the descendants of Frank Piasecki's original "flying banana," were dropping assault troops directly onto enemy positions. The next-generation jet-propelled CH-47 Chinook, the workhorse of the Vietnam War, would carry forty-four troops over a distance of 110 miles.

This was a war without front lines. The enemy struck and disappeared at will. Fixed emplacements established at strategic points across South Vietnam had to be supplied and supported. Mobility became the key to success, and the helicopter the key to mobility.

The First Air Cavalry Division, a unit designed to take full advantage of the helicopter, arrived in Vietnam in 1965. Equipped with far fewer wheeled vehicles than a standard division, and light on artillery, they would move by air and count on the gunships to pound the enemy. From the earliest aerial assaults in 1961 to the final evacuation of Saigon in April 1975, this was a helicopter war.

While everyone who served in Southeast Asia knew of the Chinook, the Bell HU-1 (Helicopter Utility-1) would become the very symbol of the war. Officially known as the Iroquois, the men whose lives depended on it dubbed it the "Huey," and so it would remain. Huey "slicks," free of protruding armament mounts, flew men into combat. Huey gunships hovered over the battlefield, laying down fire on the enemy. Hueys lifted the wounded out, and pulled everyone out when the job was done or the going got too tough. For an entire generation, the rhythmic "wop, wop, wop" of a Huey symbolized that tragic war.

A Boeing-Vertol CH-47 Chinook, Republic of Vietnam, April 2, 1966

Then there were the big "Jolly Green Giants." The Sikorsky S-61R, the heavy-lifting transport chopper, came to get downed airmen and bring them home. Sikorsky's CH-54 Skycrane carried enormous loads everywhere in Southeast Asia. The Bell AH-1 Huey Cobra, a revolutionary new weapon, performed the ground-attack/battlefield-support role previously assigned to the airplane. A Cobra could roar into action at 220 mph, carrying a ton and a half of munitions.

As NOTED, French and English manufacturers played a strong role in the development of the helicopter. The French first marketed a tur-boshaft-powered helicopter in large numbers, the Sud Aviation S.E.

3130 Alouette II (1955). Westland supplied civil and military helicopters for half a century and pioneered the rotodyne, a machine featuring both a powered rotor and a tractor propeller. In 1952, Agusta, an Italian motorcycle manufacturer, acquired the right to build and sell the Bell 47G in Europe. The company grew to become the largest Western producer of rotary-wing aircraft outside the United States. While much of the company's success came through the licensed production of American designs, Agusta marketed its own models as well.

Soviet helicopter development began at the Central Aerodynamic and Hydrodynamic Institute in 1928, when engineers under the command of Boris Yuriev began work on the I-EA, a true helicopter that actually rose to an altitude of 1,985 feet in 1932. Control problems and poor power plants brought this project to an end. The war put an end to a second effort, inspired by the success of the revolutionary Fa 61.

The helicopter enthusiasts at the institute set out in pursuit of the Americans following World War II. Mikhail Leontyevich Mil (1909–1970), placed in command of his own design bureau in 1947, produced the Mi-1, the first Soviet helicopter to enter production. Aleksandir Yakovlev, one of the Soviet Union's best-known designers, produced the Yak-24, a larger transport helicopter that entered production in 1954. Nikolai Kamov, who had designed and built autogyros for the institute during the 1930s, launched his own design bureau with the development of small helicopters dubbed "flying motorcycles." His first production machine, the Ka-15 (1952), inaugurated a long line of rotary-wing craft.

By the end of the century, both Mil and Kamov had taken their place among the world's leading producers of rotary-wing aircraft. Mil had sold some thirty thousand helicopters since 1947. The company claimed to have built every third helicopter in the world and boasted that the total payload-lifting capacity of Mil helicopters was greater than that of all other rotary-wing machines combined.

Mil became best known for the Mi-24 Hind, twenty-six hundred of which were built after 1970. Available as both an eight-man transport and a formidable gunship, it was exported to twenty nations and participated in thirty conflicts. The Hind was as familiar to veterans of the Afghan conflict as the Huey had been to combatants in Vietnam. Mil also took understandable pride in having produced the giant Mi-12, capable of carrying a 16,081-pound payload for 800 miles at a speed of 420 mph.

ROTARY-WING FLIGHT represents a significant component of the international aerospace industry. Twenty-five major companies worldwide delivered 846 new helicopters in 2001, with a total value of $6.7 billion. Civil deliveries were valued at $1.2 billion, only 17 percent of the military sales.[10]

In the United States, nine firms produced twenty-six helicopter models (ten military, sixteen civil) in 1997. Rotary-wing aircraft accounted for 11 percent of total airframe production. American manufacturers rolled 405 helicopters out of their factory doors that year. Military procurement officials paid almost $2 billion for 59 aircraft, while domestic (87) and foreign (259) buyers paid $231 million for 346 machines.[11]

THE RESEARCH ESTABLISHMENT

World War II produced a series of stunning new technologies: nuclear weapons, jet aircraft, guided missiles, long-range rockets, and an array of electronic systems. From these dazzling achievements of directed research, governments harnessed the forces of science and industry to produce wonder weapons scarcely imagined a decade before. Those programs offered powerful lessons that altered the pattern of basic research in the United States, and fundamentally transformed the nation and the world in the process.

Before 1940, federal agencies, from the Department of Agriculture to NACA, pursued in-house research, as did the industrial laboratories maintained by corporations like Bell, GE, and DuPont. Efforts to create a national research fund to support academic science had failed during the Great Depression. As a result, the majority of American scientists pursued their own work with relatively small grants from their universities or from one of a handful of private foundations or institutions.

"By the time the bombs fell on Hiroshima and Nagasaki," historian A. Hunter Dupree noted, "the entire country was aware that science was a political, economic, and social force of the first magnitude."[12] The National Defense Research Committee (NDRC), started in 1940 and intended to focus the power of American science on the development of new weapons, resulted from meetings between President Roosevelt and four leading American scientists, including Vannevar Bush, president of the Carnegie Institution of Washington and chairman of NACA.

From the outset, the leaders of the NDRC decided to pursue a new course. Having collected projects and ideas from the military services, the new organization contracted with American universities and companies for the required research. When the emphasis on weapons research proved too narrow, the president issued an executive order in 1941 subordinating the NDRC to a new Office of Scientific Research and Development (OSRD). OSRD was empowered to marshall the scientific resources of the nation for the war effort, and to coordinate all of the basic research undertaken by the federal government.

Bush and the other leaders of OSRD rejected the time-honored committee system, borrowed from NACA, as too cumbersome and bureaucratic to meet the needs of a national emergency. The OSRD presided over the creation of a new partnership between military customers, the creativity of academic science, and the productive capacity of American industry.

During the course of the war, two hundred universities won a quarter of a billion dollars in research grants. The major share of the funds went to a handful of prestigious research institutions. The University of California at Berkeley and the University of Chicago became integral parts of the Manhattan Project. Engineers at Caltech emerged as leading pioneers of rocketry. The radiation and servo-mechanism laboratories of MIT contributed radar and fire-control systems. The wartime links forged between American science and industry proved critical to victory and would shape the future of the nation.

THE OSRD was a wartime expedient. After 1945, responsibility for research and development passed back to the military services. No one was more aware of the need to enlist the forces of science and technology to meet the challenges of the postwar world than the commanding general of the U.S. Army Air Forces. Frustrated by the inertia and red tape of the prewar aeronautical research establishment, General Hap Arnold became determined to chart a very different course for the future.

Arnold had trained as an engineer at West Point, but he was not especially mechanically inclined. His failure to include brakes on his children's donkey cart led to a near disaster that became a legend in the Arnold family. What he did have was a crystal clear vision of the importance of science and technology to the future of the air force, and a rock solid determination to learn from the lessons of the past.

The appearance of the turbojet marked one of the most important turning points in the history of aviation. It opened the way to new speeds and altitudes and changed our very notion of what an airplane looks and sounds like. Why, Arnold wondered, did the NACA and Wright Field organizations, which made other critically important contributions to the Allied victory, overlook the possibility of a fundamental shift in technology?

Both organizations were relatively conservative and traditionally focused on well-defined and relatively short-term problems. They followed a course that had served the nation and the aircraft industry well. Unlike Germany, after all, the United States had invested in technology that would prove useful in *this* war. It was not, however, an attitude calculated to encourage thinking "outside the box" of existing technology.

One NACA official explained to Arnold that the organization did not pursue turbojet propulsion with greater vigor because the general did not ask them to do so. In the end, Arnold did not inform NACA of the jet engine project or of the existence of the XP-59, with the exception of long-time committee member William F. Durand, who he swore to secrecy.

Nor was Arnold a particular admirer of Vannevar Bush, the prewar chair of NACA and head of both the NDRC and the OSRD. Bush had once remarked that he could not understand how a serious engineer or scientist could take an interest in rockets, one of Arnold's prewar enthusiasms. In a November 1945 report to the secretary of war, Arnold predicted the advent of nuclear-tipped ballistic missiles and suggested that the nations of the world would one day build "space ships capable of operating outside the atmosphere." Bush countered with a public comment that a rocket capable of delivering a nuclear payload over a distance of three thousand miles would be "impossible for many years to come."[13]

Exasperated, Arnold turned to a more visionary advisor. His relationship with Theodor von Kármán (1881–1963) had begun in the late 1930s, when the Caltech professor had advised the Air Corps on a high-speed wind tunnel for Wright Field. Kármán had originally requested funding for such a tunnel from NACA. Bush responded by asking, "Is this the best thing you can do for your country?" Kármán brushed the rebuke off, assuming that Bush was "a good man of limited vision." When Arnold approached the professor for just such a wind tunnel, the two men made an immediate connection.[14]

Theodor von Kármán

Born in Budapest, Hungary, Kármán arrived at Göttingen with a degree in mechanical engineering, earned a doctorate in fluid dynamics (1908), taught at Aachen, and served in the First World War. By the early 1920s, he rivaled his major professor, Ludwig Prandtl, as the intellectual leader of theoretical aerodynamics.

In 1926 Kármán accepted Robert Millikan's invitation to lecture at the California Institute of Technology, and returned to stay three years later when he assumed directorship of Caltech's Guggenheim Aeronautical Laboratory (GALCIT). Over the next decade, thanks in large measure to his efforts, GALCIT emerged as an international center for the study of aeronautics. Aircraft companies in southern California drew on both the research facilities and the pool of faculty and student talent.

In 1938, General Arnold asked Kármán to sit on a National Academy of Sciences advisory board and to accept one of a series of experimental research contracts from the U.S. Army Air Corps. MIT officials agreed to pursue the development of a windscreen defrosting system. Kármán signed up to develop a rocket propulsion system designed to lift a heavily laden airplane off the runway.

The Air Corps contract drew on the experience of a GALCIT solid/liquid-propellant rocket program that had begun a few years before as a dissertation project supervised by Kármán. The federal funding produced the rocket-assisted take-off (RATO) system and prepared the way for the establishment of the Aerojet General Corporation, one of the nation's two pioneering rocket companies.

Compared to the bureaucratic conservatism of NACA, the Air Corps Engineering Division, and OSRD, Arnold found Kármán's operation to be efficient and refreshingly free of red tape. In the fall of 1944, with the approval of Robert Millikan, Arnold asked Kármán to serve as scientific advisor to the chief of the Army Air Forces, and to Gen. Frank Carroll, commander of the Materiel Division at Wright Field.

As his first assignment, Kármán agreed to organize a committee of civilian experts from government, academe, and industry whose task was to consider how developments in science and technology would shape future air wars. The Army Air Forces Scientific Advisory Group

(SAG) was soon established in the Pentagon, with NACA's Hugh Dryden serving as Kármán's scientific deputy and a staff of bright young scientists and engineers drawn primarily from universities.

In order to better understand wartime advancements, Kármán and eight colleagues left in April 1945 on a sixty-day fact-finding tour that would carry them from English factories and laboratories to inspections of German facilities and interviews with the men who created the Nazi wonder weapons. They were part of a larger Army Air Forces program known as Operation Lusty (Luftwaffe Secret Technology), which included the collection of German aviation hardware. While in Europe, Kármán also traveled to the Soviet Union, where he met with Joseph Stalin and visited some technical facilities.

Six weeks after his return, Kármán offered his initial thoughts on the state of the art and provided some very prescient observations on the future of air war, in an interim report entitled *Where We Stand*. Aircraft, he noted, would soon be moving faster than the speed of sound. Improvements in aerodynamics, propulsion, and electronics would enable guided missiles to strike targets thousands of miles away. "Small amounts" of explosive would be able to destroy several square miles of target area. "Target-seeking" missiles would provide an air defense effective against all but the fastest aircraft. Ground-to-air communications would be perfected, and aerial operations would be undertaken without regard to visibility or weather.

Kármán's observations were based on wartime German achievements, a knowledge of the U.S. Manhattan Project, and three decades of experience in aeronautical research. His vision of the future, however, is what most impressed Hap Arnold and his colleagues. By the end of 1945, *Where We Stand*, the first of what would become twelve volumes of the full study, *Toward New Horizons*, landed on Arnold's desk. Offering detailed analyses of the research that would be required in areas ranging from aerodynamics and propulsion to missiles, electronics, weather, and aviation medicine, the complete report was one of the most important documents in the history of American air power.

The professor suggested that the air force should track developments in science with a view to their applications to air power, recommended the creation of an organization dedicated to research and development, and suggested that as much as one-third of the postwar air force budget should be devoted to research. His message shaped thinking at the highest levels of the air force. While research would never dominate the budget, there would be a new Air Research and Development Command (ARDC).[15]

Now reporting to the chief of the Research and Development Directorate (later the ARDC), Kármán and his organization (now the Scientific Advisory Board, or SAB) continued to perform important services, including planning for a world-class wind tunnel research complex to be known as the Arnold Engineering Development Center, at Tullahoma, Tennessee.

The SAB was not Hap Arnold's only means of obtaining advice on scientific and technical planning. On October 1, 1945, he flew to Hamilton Field, California, for a meeting with Edward Bowles (an MIT consultant to the secretary of war), Donald Douglas, and Douglas engineers Arthur Raymond and Franklin Collbohm.

During the war, Collbohm and Raymond, who had headed the DC-3 project, stepped away from the drawing board and undertook operational analyses aimed at improving the performance of B-29s. Now Arnold asked Douglas to create a new division within his company, to be headed by Collbohm, that would analyze a range of scientific and technical questions and advise the Army Air Forces. The new consulting organization, known as Project RAND (research *and* development), was open for business in December 1945 and delivered its first report in March 1946, an analysis of the design and potential impact of an earth satellite.

A decade later, the notion of a government official paying a major supplier for advice on policy and potential procurement issues would surely have caught the attention of a congressional investigating committee. From Arnold's point of view, he was simply contracting for insight and expertise from people and a firm whom he trusted. RAND separated from the Douglas Aircraft Company in the spring of 1948 and broadened its scope to conduct studies of a wide range of scientific, technical, social, and economic problems.

General Carl M. "Tooey" Spaatz, who began his career as a combat pilot during World War I and concluded it by serving as the first commander of the independent U.S. Air Force, shared Arnold's commitment to basic research. "Science is in the saddle," he remarked. "Science is the dictator, whether we like it or not. Science runs ahead of both politics and military affairs. Science evolves new conditions to which institutions must be adopted. Let us keep our science dry."[16]

A new generation of officers would direct the U.S. Air Force research and development effort. Brigadier General Donald L. Putt was appointed head of the Research and Development Directorate in 1948 and took command of the ARDC four years later. An electrical engineer who had earned a master's degree in aeronautical engineering at Caltech, Putt took full advantage of the captured German scientific, technical, and human resources and continued the business of establishing research and development as the very heart of the newly created U.S. Air Force. General Bernard A. Schriever began his association with ARDC in 1954, before establishing the air force ballistic missile program.

THE NAVY HAD a longstanding research tradition. On the advice of Thomas Edison, the secretary of the navy had established a Naval Research Laboratory in 1916. During the two decades between the wars, the laboratory pioneered communications equipment, direction-finding sets, sonar gear, and the first successful American radar.

During World War II, it grew from 396 to 4,400 employees. Research projects ranged from the development of dye packets to mark the position of pilots downed at sea, to some the world's most advanced radar systems, to a thermal diffusion process that produced some of the uranium isotope used in the atomic bomb. The Naval Research Laboratory would continue to play a major role in the postwar world, managing the early sounding rocket programs and upper-atmosphere studies, culminating in Project Vanguard, the nation's first official earth satellite program.

On the basis of the OSRD experience, the navy created a new Office of Naval Research (ONR) in 1946. Unlike the navy's research lab, the ONR would assess the future needs of the navy and issue research contracts to universities and industry. Over half a century,

ONR projects would produce fifty Nobel prizes and result in new technologies ranging from the laser to the global positioning satellite system, the single most important development in the entire history of navigation.

The ONR pioneered "operations research" as well, a new term applied to the analysis of technical and social systems. The field was rooted in wartime British attempts to study and improve the performance of human and machine systems in areas like air defense and antisubmarine warfare. The ONR contracted with MIT to advise an operations evaluations group, which would study radar, antisubmarine warfare, missiles, and atomic weaponry. RAND conducted operations research under contract for the air force. The National Research Council also created an operations research committee.

NACA, THE NATION'S most visible flight research organization, underwent a radical change during the postwar years. Initially, the organization had advised Congress on national aeronautical policy. Following the establishment of the Langley Research Center in 1917, NACA emerged as one of the world's leading aeronautical research organizations.

The Committee established a West Coast aeronautical laboratory at Moffet Field in California in December 1939. Two years later, the new facility was named for Joseph Sweetman Ames, a founding member of NACA who chaired the organization from 1924 to 1937. A third laboratory, the Lewis Research Center, was established adjacent to the Cleveland airport in 1941. Named in honor of George W. Lewis, the NACA director of research from 1924–1947, the center focused on propulsion.

While flight research was deeply rooted at NACA, the advent of X-airplanes in 1947 marked a new era for the organization. The high-altitude rocket launches undertaken at Wallops Island off the Virginia coast, and the flight test program culminating in the flights of the X-15, demonstrated a shifting of the organization's vision to the future of flight beyond the atmosphere.

Most Americans reacted to the Soviet launch of the world's first artificial earth satellite in 1957 as a technological Pearl Harbor. President Dwight Eisenhower was determined to separate ballistic missile and military space efforts aimed at developing reconnaissance satellites, from a strong civilian space program that would pursue sound scientific objectives and perhaps persuade the Soviets to accept an open-skies policy. The National Aeronautics and Space Act of 1958 brought the history of the venerable NACA to a close, and launched the National Aeronautics and Space Administration (NASA) in its place.

In addition to continuing the NACA tradition of in-house aerospace research, NASA would operate the nation's civil space program. The new organization would conduct research, acquire hardware, and launch payloads into space. As the American standard-bearer in the "space race" with the Soviets, NASA immediately catapulted into the international spotlight as one of the best-known and most visible federal agencies.

The organization immediately began to grow. Eight new centers were established in the first decade. In five short years, the agency budget soared over 1,000 percent from $523.6 million in 1960 to a record $5.25 billion in 1965. An official of the Office of Management and Budget remarked admiringly that NASA administrator James Webb was a man "who knew what a billion dollars was."[17]

The U.S. Air Force, U.S. Navy, and NASA maintained their own laboratories, but they also managed billions of dollars in research grants and development contracts held by universities and corporations. Before 1940, the military services spent less than 10 percent of their combined annual budget on research, and that was almost entirely for the support of in-house activity. Between 1960 and 1974, the Department of Defense alone allocated from 26 to 37 percent of its annual budget for research, development, and testing. Defense Department research grants and contracts increased by an order of magnitude from 1951 ($758 million) to 1967 ($7.75 billion). Seen from another view, the department doled out as much as 80 percent of the federal research budget during the 1950s.[18]

NASA did its share to bring boom times to the aerospace industry, distributing billions of dollars to contractors and subcontractors scattered across the nation. At the peak of the Apollo moon program in the 1960s, the space agency supported an estimated half a million Americans. In July 1967, NASA paid $7.3 million in overtime alone.

THE POSTWAR ERA of contract research literally redirected the course of basic scientific and engineering, privileging some areas of inquiry while ignoring others. It transformed aerospace corporations as well. North American Aviation, for example, manufactured aircraft, spacecraft, and rocket engines, yet corporate strategy focused on maximizing profits from research contracts, as evidenced by its workforce. In 1961, 22,000 of the 88,000 company employees were engineers or scientists.[19]

"Big Science" defined the Cold War national security states, east and west. The era was marked by a permanent war economy that supported great national scientific and technological projects aimed at the creation of advanced weapons systems.

The process led to a spiraling arms race, the creation of ever growing stockpiles of assorted nuclear and thermonuclear weapons, and the development of aircraft and missile systems to deliver them. Deterrence remained the order of the day, as the two most powerful nations in history sought to prevent nuclear war by threatening mutual destruction on an unimaginable scale.

Intercontinental early-warning and defense systems became a requirement. These intricately woven, technical and social webs employing computers and sophisticated communications networks to link electronic detectors of various sorts stretched across the top of the continent to decision makers and the counterstrike weapons, interceptors, and antiaircraft missiles that they controlled.

Nor could conventional weapons development be abandoned in an era of perpetual tension and frequent regional conflicts. Finally, there was that most expensive spin-off of weapons development, the space race. The ultimate result, of course, was a restructuring of government, the economy, and society. What had begun as a wartime partnership between government, science, and industry became a central feature of American life.

13

FROM AVIATION TO AEROSPACE,
1945–2003

THE CONJUNCTION

"Remember that the seed comes first," General Hap Arnold remarked to those attending the Western Aviation Planning Conference in the fall of 1937.

> [If] you are to reap a harvest of aeronautical development, you must plant the seed called *experimental research*. Install aeronautical branches in your universities; encourage your young men to take up aeronautical engineering. It is a new field but it is likely to prove a very productive one indeed. Spend all the funds you can possibly make available on experimentation and research. Next, do not visualize aviation merely as a collection of airplanes. It is broad and far reaching. It combines manufacture, schools, transportation, airdrome, building and management, air munitions and armaments, metallurgy, mills and mines, finance and banking, and finally, public security-national defense.[1]

Could Hap Arnold have imagined the extent to which his advice would transform the nation and the world? Just twenty-two years later, President Dwight D. Eisenhower warned his fellow Americans of the "economic, political, even spiritual" consequences of the "conjunction of an immense military establishment and a large arms industry." While he recognized "the imperative need for this development," he also believed that the democratic process, "the very structure of our society," was at risk. "In the councils of government, we must guard against the acquisition of unwarranted influence, whether sought or unsought, by the military-industrial complex. The potential for the disastrous rise of misplaced power exists and will persist."[2]

MUSTERING OUT

In the two decades separating Hap Arnold's prescription for American strength in the air from President Eisenhower's warning of corporate power and influence, aircraft manufacturers went through constant changes. The American industry had come of age during World War II. Relative small fry in 1937, aircraft and engine builders took their place among the ranks of the industrial giants by 1945.

Curtiss-Wright, the product of a merger between the two firms founded by the great rivals of early aviation, was second only to General Motors as the nation's leading defense contractor. Consolidated-Vultee followed Ford as the fourth largest government contractor. Douglas captured fifth place, followed by United Aircraft in sixth, ahead of both Chrysler and General Electric. Excluding the manufacturers of light planes and companies like Ryan that produced only trainers, fourteen aircraft builders appeared on the list of the top-fifty defense contractors, thirteen of them in the top half of the list.[3]

The industry produced five times more airplanes (324,750) from 1939 to 1945 than the total number (50,031) manufactured during the years 1911–1938. Factory floor space dedicated to aeronautical production grew from 9.5 million square feet in January 1939 to 175 million square feet by the end of 1943. More Americans were employed in building airplanes than in any U.S. manufacturing enterprise at any time in the past, or so the Aircraft Industries Association claimed.[4]

U.S. Aircraft Manufacturers, 1945[5]

Companies	Percentage of Total Federal Contracts
Curtiss-Wright Corporation	4.1
Consolidated-Vultee Aircraft Corporation	2.8
Douglas Aircraft Company	2.5
United Aircraft Corporation (including Chance Vought and Sikorsky)	2.2
Lockheed Aircraft Company	1.9
North American Aviation	1.6
Boeing Airplane Company	1.5
Glenn L. Martin Company	1.3
Grumman Aircraft Engineering Company	0.8
Republic Aviation Corporation	0.7
Bell Aircraft Corporation	0.7
Fairchild Airplane and Engine Company	0.2
Northrop Aircraft	0.1
McDonnell Aircraft Corporation	*Not Available*

As expected, peace brought an end to the wartime boom. In 1945, military expenditures totaled $80,537,000, a whopping 82 percent of the total federal budget. By 1950, that figure had fallen to $13,440,000, only 35 percent of the total budget. The cancelation of over $21 billion in wartime contracts inflicted a serious blow to the industry.

In addition, war-surplus aircraft flooded the civilian market. Douglas, for example, competed for aircraft sales against veteran C-47 and C-54 transports. The company released ninety-nine thousand employees by the end of 1945, closed plants in Tulsa, Chicago, and Oklahoma City, and still reported a $2 million loss in 1948.

Things were no better at Consolidated-Vultee, which closed plants in Tucson, San Diego, Elizabeth City, Louisville, and New Orleans and laid off 12,822 workers A series of cost overruns on new designs resulted in a loss of $36 million for the company in 1947, a year in which North American also went into the red.

Boeing suffered a $5 million loss in 1946 and would not show a profit until 1948. "Nowhere in the nation is the problem of reconversion being worked out as painfully and from the ground up as in Seattle," a *New York Herald* reporter noted.[6] Aircraft manufacturers across the nation supplemented their aeronautical earnings by producing buses, kitchen ranges, prefabricated homes, home freezers, and automobile and marine engines.

THEN THERE WERE the labor problems. Historically, the relationship between aviation manufacturers and their workers had been difficult at best. In this industry the cost of labor often represented the difference between profit and loss. When the aviation bubble burst in 1929, aircraft builders cut wages by 40 percent across the board and braced themselves for the wave of strikes that followed in 1930–1933. An International Association of Machinists (IAM) strike against Wright Aeronautical, a company with a generally good reputation as an employer, ended in defeat for the union. The independent Buffalo Aeronautical Workers Union enjoyed greater success in 1933 strikes against Consolidated and Curtiss.

Glenn Martin, who claimed to have made "a profound study of aircraft employment sociology," thought that he understood his workmen. The average aircraft worker, he noted, was several years younger than the typical factory laborer. He kept "abreast or a little ahead of the times, and [was] something of a pioneer." Such a man took special pride in his involvement with aviation. "The type of workman who is interested in aircraft work," Martin explained, "is willing to make sacrifices for the sake of his calling."[7]

Martin was just the man to demand those sacrifices. Most of his employees earned fifty cents an hour, 20 percent under the national average. In order to meet his schedule for B-10 bomber production in 1933, he instituted a mandatory twelve-hour day. He had a reputation for firing workers who wasted time in conversation on the factory floor, and he resisted every attempt to organize his workers. When the IAM, an American Federation of Labor (AFL) skilled craft union, attempted to recruit at Middle River, Martin fired those who signed up. Employees petitioned the National Recovery Administration (NRA), a

New Deal agency designed to protect the rights of labor in companies with federal contracts, for permission to organize a federal labor union. Such a company-wide bargaining unit could then affiliate with the Congress of Industrial Organizations (CIO). Martin promptly fired the organizing committee. General Hugh Johnson, head of the NRA, admitted that there was nothing he could do, as Martin's contract with the army predated the authority of the NRA.[8]

Martin's virulent antiunion attitude set the industry standard. Southern California was open-shop country. Harry Chandler, owner of the *Los Angeles Times*, together with the notorious Los Angeles Merchants and Manufacturers Association, had worked hard to see that it remained so. Donald Douglas, one of the bright stars in Los Angeles's industrial firmament, ruled over his employees like a "feudal baron." He paid considerably less than the going industrial wage in Los Angeles, demanded long hours and weekend work without overtime pay, and dismissed workers "for the least slander or remark." Whatever the New Deal regulations, he cut wages at will and fired employees who undertook union activity.[9] Neither the IAM nor the United Auto Workers (UAW) enjoyed much success in *Los Angeles Times* country. Lockheed was the only major southern California firm to unionize before the war.

In contrast, the IAM established a West Coast beachhead in Seattle, where Boeing was far friendlier to labor than the southern Californians. By 1936, Aeronautical Mechanics lodge No. 751 of the IAM had signed 70 percent of the eligible Boeing workers to the first major union contract in the aviation industry.

The war drew a flood of new and less-skilled workers into the industry. Union membership at Lockheed jumped from 400 in 1939 to more than 37,000 by 1943. Wages skyrocketed from an average of $1.10 an hour at the beginning of the war to $1.90 in 1945. While there were a few wildcat strikes, including a half-day walkout at Boeing in 1943, both the AFL and the CIO pledged no labor actions for the duration.[10]

The real change occurred in the immediate postwar years, as both management and labor faced postwar demobilization and an uncertain future. A wave of labor unrest began to sweep the nation in January 1946, with a walkout by 200,000 Chicago meatpackers. Later that month 800,000 steel workers went on strike. Ford and General Electric workers took to the picket lines. General Motors employees set an industry record with a 113-day strike.

With patriotic enthusiasm ebbing, a new generation of aircraft workers organized to ensure that labor would no longer be manipulated to corporate advantage. In addition to its other problems, Consolidated-Vultee suffered through a 101-day strike in 1946. Boeing, which had a prewar reputation for good labor relations, faced four bitter years of strikes and labor problems, from 1946 to 1950.

As is so often the case during periods of retrenchment and shrinking markets, industry leaders considered reorganization and corporate mergers as a possible solution to their problems. Vultee had acquired Consolidated in March 1943. The nickname of the new firm, Convair, became official in 1954. Postwar financial problems led AVCO, which owned 26 percent of Consolidated-Vultee stock, to sell to Floyd B. Odlum, president of the Atlas Company, an investment firm.

Boeing was also under new management. Corporate attorney William M. Allen replaced Phillip Johnson, who had died in 1944. Allen considered, then rejected, the prospect of a merger with Curtiss-Wright. Government antitrust concerns prevented the merger of either Lockheed or North American with Consolidated-Vultee. Jack Northrop claimed that Secretary of the Air Force Stuart Symington had pressured him to merge his company with Consolidated-Vultee in the summer of 1948, when the two firms were contending for a U.S. Air Force bomber contract.

The navy persuaded Chance Vought to relocate from its historic home in Connecticut to new quarters in Texas to take advantage of better production facilities and good flying weather. A decade later (in 1961), the company merged with two Dallas neighbors to form Ling-Temco-Vought.

Ironically, Curtiss-Wright, the industry giant, gradually withdrew from aircraft production. The story illustrates the importance of good government relations during the postwar era. Structurally, Curtiss-Wright and United Aircraft remained the last of the integrated aviation companies. In 1945, Curtiss-Wright was made up of divisions that produced airframes (Curtiss Airplane Division), engines (Wright Aeronautical Division), and propellers (Curtiss Propeller Division).

All three divisions entered the postwar era with some disadvantages. Curtiss Airplane had spent the war years producing dated types, including its own P-40 fighter and C-46 transport. The government had not allowed Wright Aeronautical to enter the emerging jet-engine business because of the importance of its piston-engine production. While the propeller division did well, the future of the technology was clearly limited. Still, the company seemed committed to overcoming its problems. Curtiss-Wright entered the U.S. Air Force competition for an all-weather jet fighter, designed a new military transport and civil airliner, produced jet engines under a British license, and developed a rocket engine. One after another, government procurement officials selected competing projects. As a result, the company's role shrank to that of a relatively small subcontractor by the end of the 1950s.

Why did the company fail? While an emphasis on paying stock dividends rather than reinvesting profits seems to have been a factor, analyst Eugene Gholz argues that poor corporate relationships with the principle military procurement offices was perhaps the critical factor. "Lockheed," he notes, "accepted a high degree of financial risk—the very opposite of Curtiss-Wright's frequent insistence on subsidized development and production contracts."[11]

Government concern about the condition of the aircraft industry grew ever more acute as problems with the Soviets loomed on the horizon. On July 16, 1947, President Harry S. Truman appointed attorney Thomas K. Finletter to head a commission to study federal air policy. The commission report, *Survival in the Air Age*, issued that December, underscored the special problems of aircraft manufacture.

The industry had one major customer—the government. Demand fluctuated, making it hard to maintain continuous production and retain an experienced workforce. Aircraft builders remained captives of a constantly advancing technology that required a considerable investment in research and long development times. Wise government policy should support the industry as a national asset, for the defense of the nation. "It may even be desirable," the report noted, "to keep a few marginal manufacturers in business who might be forced out if the normal laws of supply and demand were allowed to operate."[12]

POSTWAR PRODUCTION, 1945–1950

For all of the postwar economic uncertainty, aviation manufacturers faced the future with genuine optimism. Tax carryovers based on wartime profits eased the losses of the immediate postwar years. By 1948, most companies once again posted profits. Moreover, while the development of new military aircraft had slowed, it had by no means stopped.

The Lockheed XP-80 Shooting Star—the first U.S. operational jet fighter, the first U.S. airplane to fly 500 mph, and the first U.S. jet to see combat—flew for the first time in 1944. It was also the first product of "Kelly" Johnson's "Skunk Works." Clarence Leonard Johnson (1910–1990), a native of Ishpeming, Michigan, earned bachelor and master of arts degrees in aeronautical engineering at the University of Michigan. He went to work for Lockheed in 1933 and rose to the position of chief research engineer in five years. He led the teams that developed the Electra, Hudson, Constellation, and P-38 Lightning.

In June 1943, Kelly Johnson and a team of 123 handpicked engineers and technicians set out to design a U.S. jet fighter to be powered by an English jet engine. The XP-80 was complete just 143 days later. Originally housed in a temporary building constructed of packing crates and a rented circus tent, Johnson and his cohorts dubbed themselves the "Skunk Works," in honor of the area where the characters in Al Capp's "L'il Abner" comic strip brewed their "Kickapoo Joy Juice" out of old shoes and dead skunks. Over the years, the Skunk Works would turn out one remarkable airplane after another.

Other companies were producing their own first-generation jets. The Republic F-84 left the ground for the first time in February 1946. The classic North American F-86 made its first flight at Muroc dry lake in October 1947. The Convair XF-92 and Northop F-89 were unveiled in 1948, while the Lockheed F-94 took to the air for the first time the following year. The first two U.S. operational jet bombers, the North American B-45 and the Boeing B-47, flew in 1947.

The Navy had entered the jet age as well. Vought, Grumman, and Douglas all had carrier-based jet fighters in service before 1950. But a new manufacturer had beat all of them into the air. First flown on July 21, 1946, the McDonnell FH-1 Phantom was the first U.S. Navy operational jet, the first naval aircraft to fly 500 mph, and the first to take off and land from an American carrier.

James Smith McDonnell (1899–1980) had deep roots in aviation. A graduate of both Princeton and MIT, he had learned to fly in 1923 and played a major role in the design of the Ford Tri-motor. McDonnell worked for Huff-Daland and several other companies before rising to the position of chief engineer with the Martin Company. The last of the great aeronautical entrepreneurs to matriculate with the Glenn Luther Martin school of management, he incorporated his own firm in St. Louis in 1939.

McDonnell Aircraft began with fifteen employees and a contract to

James Smith McDonnell stands in front of the
five-thousandth McDonnell F4-E Phantom II

supply Stinson Aircraft with parts. By the end of the war, the company had produced seven million pounds of parts, invested in the Platt-LePage helicopter project, and produced one experimental fighter, the XP-67. It was the only propeller-driven fighter that McDonnell would ever build.

McDonnell built the FH-1 and the F2D Banshee (1947), a larger and more powerful version of the Phantom. Over the next three decades, the company became a leading manufacturer of jet fighters for the U.S. Air Force, Navy, and Marine Corps, built commercial airliners, and produced the Mercury and Gemini spacecraft that carried the first Americans into orbit.

IN ADDITION TO producing military jets, Douglas, Lockheed, and Boeing reasserted their dominance over international civil aviation with the four-engine airliners that they had developed since 1939. Larger than their predecessors, with higher wing loading and twice the number of powerful engines burning superior fuels, the airliners of 1945–1955 could carry up to a hundred passengers and crew at top speeds of 340 mph, twice as fast as a DC-3. They had a range of forty-three hundred miles and cruised at thirty-five thousand feet. The end of a developmental line dating to 1932, they laid the foundation for mass air travel and the first generation of jet airlines.

In 1935, the nation's five largest airlines (American, Eastern, Pan American, TWA, and United) offered Douglas $100,000 apiece to develop an airliner capable of bridging the continent with only one refueling stop, instead of the three required by the DC-3. Both the company and NACA invested considerable time, energy, and money in the resulting DC-4E. The final product, a technological marvel featuring tricycle landing gear, flush riveting, and boosted controls, was large, complex, and experimental. When the company prepared to begin production in 1939, the airplane attracted only six orders.

Donald Douglas lowered his sights and produced the four-engine DC-4 in 1942. The new aircraft offered many of the features of the DC-4E in a smaller package that was a natural step beyond the DC-3. Pressed into service as the C-54, a military transport, the DC-4 played as important a role in winning the war as the B-29 or P-51.

Boeing moved in a different direction, combining elements of its successful bomber designs with its own cabin-pressurization valve to produce the Model 307 Stratoliner in 1939. While only ten of these aircraft entered airline service, they were economical to operate and demonstrated Boeing's determination to remain a power in air transportation.

Lockheed offered the most radical entry in the prewar airliner derby. The development of the L-049 Constellation began shortly before World War II, when the legendary Howard Hughes became a major investor in TWA. Hughes had supported acquisition of the Boeing 307 but was convinced of the need for a new airliner that would carry air travelers farther, higher, and faster than ever before. Robert Gross, Kelly Johnson, and Hal Hibbard of Lockheed accepted the challenge, and Howard Hughes's admonition that the project had to remain absolutely secret.

Lockheed engineers chose the eighteen-cylinder Curtiss-Wright R-3350 power plant, then under development for the Boeing B-29. At Hughes's insistence, they hired Raymond Loewy to design the passenger area, as he had for the DC-3 sleepers. The airplane would feature a unique, streamlined fuselage set on high landing gear struts to allow clearance for the fifteen-foot propellers.

The nose of the thin fuselage pointed slightly down to reduce the height of the nose gear. The large tail surface, too tall to fit into many hangars, was redesigned into the classic triple-tail configuration that became the signature of the airplane. The finished product could fly coast to coast nonstop with a standard load of fifty-four passengers.

The veil of secrecy was lifted a few months before Pearl Harbor. Once the war began, TWA assigned the first forty L-049s to the military. The L-049/C-61 joined the DC-4/C-54, DC-3/C-47, and the Curtiss C-46 Commando in shuttling people and supplies over a complex web of air routes linking the arsenal of democracy to supply depots and battlefields scattered around the globe. By the end of the war, transatlantic flights were an everyday occurrence for Allied airmen.[13]

A new generation of airliners had proved themselves in the crucible of war. Douglas continued to market the DC-4 generation (DC-6,

Douglas DC-4

DC-6A, DC-6B, DC-7, DC-7B, and the DC-7C "Seven Seas") of airplanes into the early years of the jet age. Lockheed followed the same
pattern, developing the Constellation into the L-1049 Super
Constellation, so familiar to air travelers of the 1950s.

American aircraft manufacturers maintained their hold on the
international market for airlines during the immediate postwar years.
At the end of 1953, the world's airliners, excluding those in the USSR,
operated a grand total of 2,441 aircraft, 2,065 (84.5 percent) of which
were the products of American industry. Of the remaining airliners,
11.6 percent were British operating for British or Commonwealth airlines. Almost twenty years after the introduction of the DC series, over
31 percent of the world's airliners, more than twice the number for any
other model, were DC-3s. For the remainder of the piston-engine era,
the American aircraft industry continued to provide at least 75 percent
of the free world's airliners. That did not mean, however, that U.S. aircraft manufacturers were growing rich on their profits.[14]

Take the case of the Boeing 377 Stratocruiser, introduced in 1947. The company combined its experience with the Model 307 Stratoliner (1939) and the B-29 to produce a double-deck airliner offering an unprecedented degree of comfort. As historian Roger Bilstein points out, however, the Stratocruiser demonstrated just how difficult it was to keep the corporate body and soul together while building airliners. In this case, Boeing actually lost money on the initial sale of each aircraft.

It required ten years of selling spare parts to the airlines for the company to post a tiny profit from sales of the Model 377. In fact, sales of the C-97 Stratofreighter/KC-97 Stratotanker, the military versions of the Stratocruiser, enabled the company to make money on the design long before that. The value of developing a basic design that could serve as the basis for both military and civilian aircraft was a lesson that Boeing officials would not soon forget.[15]

GENERAL AVIATION

In addition to recapturing the international market for airliners, many industry leaders were confident that they could tap a mass market for private aircraft. Eugene Vidal's dream of an airplane in every garage was alive and well. Between 1937 and 1945 aeronautical journals and popular magazines featured stories suggesting that "foolproof" airplanes, autogiros, helicopters, and "roadable" flying machines might rival the automobile as family transportation in the near future. A 1944 *Collier's* survey of the postwar market for private aircraft revealed that 65 percent of the civilians who hoped to purchase airplanes after the war preferred roadable or helicopter types.

William A. M. Burden, a Department of Commerce official, informed Congress that private plane sales represented the most logical field for postwar expansion of the aeronautical industry and suggested that as many as 450,000 aircraft might be in the air within five or ten years after the war. Charles Stanton, administrator of the Civil Aviation Administration (CAA), and Andrew Kucher, director of research for the Bendix Corporation, both predicted the sale of up to 300,000 light airplanes by 1950.[16]

Magazine articles with titles like "Your Family Plane of Tomorrow," "Wings for the Average Man," and "Planes for All" abounded. Surveys by *Collier's* and *Ladies' Home Journal* indicated that thousands of returning flyers would be unwilling to give up their wings, while other veterans would use funds from the GI Bill to learn to fly. Civilian war workers also indicated a desire to own a personal plane.

Indeed, the number of licensed pilots in the United States jumped from 31,264 in 1940 to 400,061 in 1947. Much of that increase came as a result of the CAA's offer of a commercial license to returning military aviators. The Aircraft Owners and Pilots Association (AOPA), founded in 1939, billed itself as the "voice" of private flying and grew from 10,000 members before the war to 30,000 members enrolled in twenty-seven local chapters in the United States and Canada in 1946.

The market seemed so promising that major aeronautical firms with no previous interest in light aircraft entered the field. Republic Aviation offered the amphibious Sea Bee, while North American introduced the four-place Navion. Douglas unveiled the Cloudster, a low-wing monoplane seating five, with the propeller mounted on the tail. Fairchild offered the more conventional, gull-winged Model 24.

Indeed, the sale of light aircraft rose from 7,700 in 1941 to a record high of 33,254 in 1946. This level could not be sustained, however. The predicted postwar boom collapsed in 1947, as production fell to 15,593. By 1951 the annual production of general-aviation aircraft had hit bottom, at 2,302. As late as 1963, production continued to lag behind the 1941 level. By 1964, 40 percent of the active general-aviation aircraft were fifteen years old or older, most of them remnants of the 1946–1947 peak output.

North American, Douglas, Republic, and Fairchild left the field as quickly as they had come. Some of the old-timers folded as well. Waco, which spent the war years building combat and training gliders, tried and failed to reenter the civilian market with its Aristocraft. Piper gobbled up what was left of Stinson. Luscombe disappeared in 1952. Production at Aeronca fell from 7,555 aircraft in 1946 to 34 in 1951, when production ceased for a time.

The Ercoupe, designed by NACA veteran and Collier Trophy winner Fred E. Weick, was one of the most visible casualties. The

Engineering and Research Corporation (Erco), founded in Riverdale, Maryland, in 1930, had manufactured aircraft parts until 1940, when it introduced the Ercoupe, an all-metal monoplane with seating for a pilot and passenger. A direct descendant of Weick's 1934 W-1A, the Ercoupe was a two-control airplane with tricycle landing gear. Touted as an airplane that was almost as easy to fly as an automobile was to drive, the Ercoupe featured linked aileron and rudder control, and no pesky and confusing rudder pedals.

By early 1946, Ercoupes were rolling off the line at a rate of ten a day. Production doubled with the addition of a second shift, and orders still piled up. Late that spring the factory turned out thirty-five airplanes a day, and plans were underway to expand production to fifty a day. Suddenly, in the fall of 1946, Weick noticed that the number of airplanes tied down on the field waiting delivery had jumped from one hundred to three hundred.

It was the beginning of the end. "By the summer of 1946," Weick explained, "the boom had . . . peaked; the pent-up demand for small airplanes like the Ercoupe had been mostly satisfied, and demand for further production would be at a greatly reduced rate." Erco ceased production in 1951, having produced 5,081 airplanes.[17]

When the dust settled, the big three—Piper, Beech, and Cessna—were still standing. Piper came close to collapse when the traditional J-3 Cub, a two-place, wood-and-fabric airplane, failed to attract postwar customers. The introduction of the four-place Piper Pacer (1949) and Tri-Pacer (1951), with its user-friendly tricycle landing gear, saved the day. Cessna entered the market with the all-metal Model 140, then quickly moved on to the four-place 170/172 models with tricycle landing gear (1948). Beech followed suit with the single-engine, four-place, fully equipped V-tailed Model 35 Bonanza. These sturdy, top-of-the-line metal airplanes with well-equipped cockpits were suitable for use as light business aircraft.

Beech reintroduced its twin-engine D-18 and followed up with the Model B50 Twin Bonanza (in 1949). Piper countered with the Apache (1952) and Cessna with its five-place, twin-engine Model 310. North American attempted to capture the high end of the business market with the twin-engine Aero Commander (1954).

The Beech Bonanza and all of the twin-engine business models featured retractable landing gear and improved engines. The most important changes, however, occurred in the cockpit. Companies like Bendix, Collins, RCA, and Sperry brought the avionics revolution to private flying. The new generation of general-aviation aircraft came fitted with radios, improved instruments, and navigational aids.

The leaders of the aviation industry, however, no longer dreamed of a mass market. Even small airplanes cost far more than the average automobile, and the market was relatively inelastic. The operators of flying schools and fixed-base operations tended to take good care of their airplanes and invested in new equipment only when they were sure the investment would pay off. The struggle to hold down the relatively high cost of private flying also limited the technological development of light aircraft. While there were some improvements in power plants and avionics, and only marginal improvements in safety, comfort, and performance, single-engine general-aviation aircraft in service at the end of the century looked much like those introduced fifty years before.

And there was worse to come for private flying. By the mid-1980s, the threat of product liability suits had forced manufacturers to substantially increase the purchase price of small airplanes, causing the large-scale manufacture of light aircraft to virtually cease in the United States. M. Stuart Millar, hailed as the "savior" of Piper Aircraft when he took over the company in 1987, filed for bankruptcy protection in 1991. Cessna, purchased by General Dynamics in January 1992 and sold to Textron three months later, had ceased production of single-engine airplanes. Like Cessna and Piper, Beech Aircraft was concentrating on the stable and lucrative corporate market for twin-engine aircraft, turboprops, and turbojets. The Mooney Aircraft Corporation, which continued to produce traditional light aircraft, was controlled by French interests.[18]

Congressional action limited the liability of general-aviation manufacturers in the summer of 1994, leading Cessna and other firms to announce plans for the resumption of single-engine aircraft production. The old problems remained, however. In addition, the costs of flight instruction, fuel, hangar space, and maintenance were very high. The need to develop competence in the use of the latest communications gear and avionics packages had become an absolute requirement, particularly for pilots who operated in the neighborhood of busy commercial airports. Finally, enthusiasm had waned. "Unlike 40 or even 20 years ago," one industry observer noted, "young people today are rarely seen climbing the airport fence for a closer look at aviation, and the kid who begs to wash aircraft in return for a flight is as extinct as a dinosaur."[19]

As a result of all this, private flying turned to a new direction: home-built aircraft. The construction of airplanes and gliders in home workshops was not a new phenomena in the United States, but during the war years it had subsided. After 1945, however, the movement gathered momentum once again, representing the single biggest shift in postwar private flying. The founding of the Experimental Aircraft Association (EAA) by Paul H. Poberezny in January 1953 served the needs of a new generation of home-built-aircraft enthusiasts. Less than fifty airplanes showed up in September 1953 for the first EAA "fly-in" convention at Milwaukee's Curtiss-Wright Field. As the organization continued to grow, the annual event shifted to the municipal airport in Rockford, Illinois, in 1959 and to Oshkosh, Wisconsin, in 1970. By 2001, the EAA boasted 170,000 members in a thousand chapters. Attendance at the week-long fly-in reached 800,000. The urge to build and fly one's own airplane, and the fascination with people who achieved that goal, had become a very important social movement inside the aeronautical community.

By the end of the century, home-built airplanes were providing the model for an entirely new generation of general-aviation aircraft. Burt Rutan pioneered the use of composite structures in the design of innovative home-built machines. His accomplishments range from the design and fabrication of the *Voyager* (1986), in which his brother Dick and Jeanna Yaeger completed the first unrefueled, nonstop flight around the world, to service as a corporate official of Beech Aircraft and the development of the Beech Starship corporate aircraft.

IF THE MANUFACTURERS of recreational aircraft struggled from time to time in the postwar decades, business aviation flourished. By 1960, business flying accounted for 37 percent of total general-aviation air mileage. Flying service operators represented an additional 40 percent, leaving only 23 percent for all personal flying. In 1998, while only 33 percent of general-aviation aircraft were used primarily for business purposes, business/corporate and instructional flying accounted for 82 percent of general-aviation hours in the air.[20]

Thanks to business and corporate flying, general-aviation sales doubled between 1959 and 1963. While the dollar value seldom amounted to 3 percent of the industry total, an estimated 90 percent of the world's general-aviation aircraft flying in the mid-1960s were made in America.[21]

Unlike the private pilot whose insistence on a moderate price tag discouraged rapid technical advance, the businessman was willing to pay for increased speed, comfort, and prestige. The first generation of postwar twin-engine business models gave way to high-performance multiengine aircraft, turboprops, and turbojets. The Grumman Gulfstream G-159 (later the G-1), introduced in 1959, was the first twin-engine turboprop aircraft specifically aimed at the corporate market. The six- to nine-place Beech King Air, first flown in 1964, remained the most popular of the medium-range business twin-engine turboprops for a quarter of a century.

The best known of the business jets, and one of the most recognizable of all U.S. postwar aircraft, derived from the fertile brain of William P. Lear (1902–1978). A talented innovator, Lear had developed the first practical automobile radio (1922), introduced the aeronautical radio compass, perfected an automatic pilot system, and demonstrated the first automatic landing system, for which he was awarded the Collier Trophy in 1950.

Anxious to move on to a new challenge, he sold all of his stock in Lear, Incorporated, and used the funds to begin work on a relatively small business jet that would outperform almost any nonmilitary airplane in the sky. The result, the Learjet, made its first flight on October 2, 1963. By the end of the century, some eighteen hundred Learjets of various types had been sold.

The turbofan-powered Gulfstream II (1968) was the ultimate business aircraft of its generation and the first capable of a nonstop flight across the country. Foreign manufacturers also entered the field. Beech marketed the Moraine-Saulnier M.S. 760 (1960), while Fairchild offered the Fokker F-27 as an early turboprop suitable for corporate use. De Havilland and Hawker Siddeley both offered swept-wing business jets. The Dassault Falcon fan-jets sold well internationally. Mitsubishi, Piaggio, Dornier, Canadair, and Bombardier are among the modern leaders in the field.

By 1968 a total of 1,833 turbine-powered airplanes were at work in general aviation, almost three-fourths of them serving as business transports. By 1969, all of the top-ten firms on *Fortune*'s 500 list maintained fleets of these aircraft. For all of the success, however, the last decade of the century brought substantial change to the industry. The original Piper Company folded in the mid-1990s. The name of Beech disappeared when the company became a subsidiary of Raytheon (1981). Bombardier acquired Learjet. General Dynamics purchased Gulfstream, acquired Cessna in the fall of 1985, and sold the company to Textron seven years later.

BETTER DAYS, 1950–1970

The postwar retrenchment was short-lived. With the Korean War underway in 1950–1951, defense spending skyrocketed. By 1954, the Cold War was in full swing, and with it the constant threat of a nuclear confrontation. For the first time in U.S. history, a large standing military presence was a reality of American life. Previous generations could afford to rebuild military strength during the early months or even years of a military conflict. This generation had to be prepared to fight a nuclear war that might be won or lost in a day. The Cold War, sociologist C. Wright Mills remarked, produced a "great structural shift of American capitalism toward a permanent war economy."[22]

During the decade 1952–1962, military expenditures constituted over 50 percent of the total federal budget. Between 1962 and 1971, the years of the Great Society and the Vietnam War, over 40 percent of federal spending went to defense. Between 1946 and 1970, the U.S. government spent $1.1 trillion on defense, a sum greater that the total value of all business and residential structures in the United States in 1967.

That level of spending fueled the phenomenal growth of a postwar defense industry dominated by aircraft manufacturers. By 1959, the U.S. Bureau of Labor Statistics ranked the aviation industry as the largest employer in the manufacturing sector.[23] In 1967, after eight years of trading first and second place with motor vehicles and equipment, aviation once again led the nation with 1,484,000 employees. Aerospace had the second-best sales record in the industrial sector, having sold $27 billion worth of products in 1967.[24]

New technologies transformed the industry. Sikorsky and Bell abandoned the airplane in favor of the helicopter. Rotary-wing flight drew some brilliant innovators into the field, men like Stanley Hiller, Frank Piasecki, Arthur Young, and Charles Kaman.

It was the jet age. Newcomers like General Electric and Westinghouse, having acquired a mastery of turbojet technology at government expense, drove Curtiss-Wright from the field and left Pratt & Whitney running to catch up. The turbojet not only revolutionized the performance of military aircraft, it gave birth to the era of mass commercial air travel. Overnight, it seemed, jetliners had made transcontinental trains and ocean liners obsolete.

The dawn of a new era is evident in the postwar market statistics. During the years 1946–1958, the dollar value of civil aircraft production never rose above 20 percent of total industry sales. By 1972, the value of civil aircraft manufactured in the United States was still only half that military production. The value of commercial sales surpassed that of military production for the first time in 1992. For the rest of the century, the value of civil and military production remained in rough balance. The years during which military sales absolutely dominated the aviation industry were at an end.

Before World War II, the performance of airframes and engines had been the yardstick of aeronautical progress. By the last quarter of the century, the cutting edge of flight technology had often become defined by the performance of the electronic systems that a flying machine carried aloft. Housed in nondescript "black boxes," electronic packages took responsibility for guidance and control, navigation, communications, and detecting everything from the location of a distant enemy to the nature of terrain shrouded by darkness or cloud cover.

The control cables and hydraulic lines of earlier generations gave way to "fly-by-wire" arrangements in which the "joystick" sensed the pressure of the pilot's hand and sent electrons streaming to the appropriate control circuit. The instrument panel was replaced by the "heads-up" display of critically important information on the cockpit windows. Satellite-based global positioning systems (GPSs) replaced the use of sextants and radio navigation devices.

Aviation, once a word that inspired visions of up-to-the-minute technology, suddenly sounded archaic. By the mid-1950s, anxious to stake a claim on the future, Air Force Chief of Staff Thomas D. White described air and space as "an indivisible field of operations."[25] The leaders of the Aircraft Industries Association renamed their organization the Aerospace Industries Association in 1959, the year in which the term *aerospace* ("an operationally indivisible medium consisting of the total expanse beyond the earth's surface") found a place in the official U.S. Air Force lexicon.[26]

"As readily as missiles become operationally suitable," an air force source commented in 1957, "they will be placed into units either to completely or partially substitute for manned aircraft."[27] There were those who wondered about the future of an industry that had always depended on the sale of winged vehicles. "What has put it in jeopardy is the change that missiles have brought to the industry," *Time* magazine reported. "They not only promise the end of the manned military bombers and fighters, but have brought such other lightning changes that huge projects, calling for hundreds of millions of dollars, can be obsolete overnight. To meet the challenge, the plane and engine makers are well aware that their industry must undergo the fastest and most radical change in its history—or die."[28]

The most dramatic change in the century-long history of the industry, the shift from aviation to aerospace, occurred in a single extraordinary decade, 1954–1964. In 1954, missile production amounted to only 9 percent of total industry sales. A decade later, the dollar value of missile and space production stood at 49 percent of the

industry total! The mid-1960s marked the peak spending years for
both the Apollo lunar program and the development of new families of
nuclear-tipped, land-based and submarine-launched guided missiles.
By the 1970s and 1980s, missile and space production stabilized at 25 to
35 percent of total industry sales.

At the end of 1960, officials of the Glenn L. Martin Company, the
oldest surviving U.S. aircraft manufacturer, announced their departure
from the airplane business. Following the 1961 merger of Martin with
the American-Marietta Corporation, a chemical firm, Martin Marietta
built an enviable reputation as a manufacturer of missiles, launch vehicles, and electronic systems.

Other veteran firms, including Boeing, Lockheed, General Dynamics, McDonnell, Fairchild, and North American, were soon earning a
significant portion of their income from the production of missiles and
spacecraft. A host of new companies swarmed into the field: Aerospace
Corporation, TRW, LTV Corporation, Space Technology Laboratories.
Electronics firms like Raytheon, Hughes, and Sperry were not only critical to the effort but also often prime contractors.

Structural changes occurred as well. Before World War II, aircraft
companies normally produced the entire airframe, purchasing the
engines, propellers, radio, instruments, and other odds and ends from
specialist suppliers. All of that changed during World War II, when
manufacturers had to subcontract the construction of sections of the
airframe in order to meet the extraordinary wartime need.

While industry leaders dropped the practice for a time after 1945,
subcontracting returned within a decade to become a cornerstone of
the modern aerospace-defense industry. No longer the small and well-
defined collection of airframe and engine manufacturers and parts suppliers centered in a few locations, the aerospace enterprise relied on
hundreds of subcontractors in every corner of the nation.

Take the Vanguard satellite launch vehicle (1958), for example.
The Navy Research Laboratory managed the project, with the army,
navy, and air force contributing to the program in important ways. The
Glenn L. Martin Company was the prime contractor, while General
Electric, Aerojet General, the Grand Central Rocket Company, the
Hercules Powder Company, and Atlantic Research Corporation pro-

vided the various rocket motors that propelled and controlled the craft. The major subcontractors included

- Air Associates—accelerometers
- Bendix Radio—Minitrack system for satellite tracking
- Benson-Lehner Company—data reduction equipment
- Brooks & Perkins Company—satellite shell
- Connecticut Telephone & Electric Company—transistorized decoder
- Derby Steel Company—test stands and related tools
- Designers for Industry—programmers
- Dian Laboratory—computational services
- Elsin Electronics—telemetry ground stations
- Empire Devices Corporation—noise intensity meter
- Hoover Electronics Company—frequency converters
- Henry O. Berman—control equipment
- IBM—orbital computations
- Loewy Hydropress—static firing and launching structure
- Ludwig Henald Manufacturing Company—special trucks for ground handling data
- Minneapolis-Honeywell Company—gyroscopic reference system
- Polarad Electronics—ground handling test equipment
- Radiation—data recording and reduction equipment
- Raymond Engineering Company—satellite separation mechanism
- Reeves Instrument—onboard computers
- University of Maryland—wind tunnel testing
- William T. Lyons Company—test stand for vertical assembly

Other firms—Fruehof, General Radio, Hazelton Electronics, Hewlett-Packard, Melpar, New Mexico College, Tektronix—supplied an array of miscellaneous items. Project Vanguard, which began with one of the most newsworthy explosions in American aerospace history and ended with the launch of several basketball-size satellites, cost a little over $111 million. Relatively inexpensive compared to the projects that followed, it demonstrated the extent to which aerospace dollars rippled through the economy by the mid-1950s.[29]

Subcontracting became the rule in the production of aircraft as well. As much as 40 percent of the last generation of piston engine–powered airliners was the work of subcontractors. By the time Boeing introduced the 747 in 1969, subcontractors produced perhaps 70 percent of the airplane. Building the General Dynamics F-111, first flown in December 1964, involved 18 major contractors and 6,703 sub-contractors and suppliers. It was, one wag suggested, the perfect weapons system, with one contractor in every congressional district.

Managing the development of a complex weapons system was an enormously difficult and confusing business. The U.S. Air Force hired TRW to advise on the management of projects for which it was not producing hardware. Founded in 1958, when the Ramo Wooldridge Company merged with Thompson Products, a traditional parts sup-plier, TRW also served as a prime contractor for satellites. Just as Hap Arnold had presided at the birth of the RAND Corporation, the Department of Defense engineered the creation of the nonprofit Aerospace Corporation in 1960, to advise on the management of com-plex space ventures.

New tools and techniques were developed to manage complex aerospace projects. U.S. Navy officials introduced the Program Evaluation Review Technique (PERT) during the 1950s as a means of maintaining control of the Polaris submarine-based missile program. The centerpiece of the process was the PERT chart, a management tool used to schedule, organize, and coordinate tasks within a project. By the end of the century, the techniques developed and pioneered in aero-space project management had revolutionized the approach to solving difficult problems in business, government, and society.

Aerospace funding had a major impact on government and the economy. It steered the course of scientific research in postwar America, drove the advance of a broad range of critically important technologies, and laid the foundation for new industries that would shape the future of the nation and the world. Take the computer, for example.

COMPUTERS AND AEROSPACE

Postwar research and development spending had far-reaching social, political, and economic consequences. In the beginning, airplanes were relatively simple machines of wood and fabric, built one at a time by skilled craftsmen in garages and woodworking shops and powered by engines designed to propel motorcycles and automobiles. Just four decades later, flying machines had evolved to complex metal structures, the product of vast industrial networks that drew on the resources of the entire nation.

Airplanes were now embedded in larger technological systems. The thousands of airplanes that contested the night skies over Europe rode invisible electronic beams to their targets and back. They dropped their bombs where and when instructed to do so by signals from a black box, or on the basis of the ghostly green images on their radar screens. Night fighters found their targets by detecting the beams emanating from enemy aircraft. With the return of peace, pilots flew airlines along predetermined routes, linked to the ground by radio, their progress observed by radar, and were able to navigate and even operate in bad weather owing to a rapidly evolving host of ground-based and airborne electronic systems.

Aeronautical progress once rested on a fairly narrow research agenda aimed at improvements in aerodynamics, structures, and propulsion. Postwar defense spending on aerospace weaponry would change that, producing unexpected technological consequences. The complex relationship between flight and the computer is a case in point.

THE STORY BEGINS in the 1930s, when faster aircraft encountered increased stress and unpredictable problems. Flutter, an aerodynamically induced vibration in the wing or tail surface, could break an airplane apart in midair. Theory provided a means of calculating the degree of stiffness and other design factors that would reduce the potential for flutter, but the equations were so complex that aircraft firms had to employ large numbers of "computers," humans who calculated.

The DVL, the leading German aviation research organization, took an interest in this problem, just as it had the issues of reaction propulsion and radar. Beginning in 1941, the DVL supported the work of engineer Konrad Zuse on an experimental computer employed during the design of the Henschel HS-293, a radio-controlled glide bomb launched from bombers against Allied shipping.

Data reduction remained a major bottleneck for the postwar aircraft industry. Groups of "gypsy engineers" moved from company to company, project to project, performing the detailed stress calculations for new aircraft. During World War II, engineers from Consolidated, Lockheed, Douglas, and Caltech began to attack the problem with IBM punch-card tabulators. Aviation types dominated the annual IBM Research Forums of 1948–1951, where participants discussed the requirements of "scientific computation." Southern California aeronautical firms purchased some of the earliest Remington Rand UNIVAC (Universal Automatic Computer) machines. Aircraft manufacturers or government agencies dealing with aeronautical problems purchased ten of the first nineteen IBM 701 general-purpose computers.[30]

The power of the computer gave birth to computational fluid dynamics. Wind tunnels would still supply essential data, but the computer would manipulate that information, transforming incredibly complex mathematical equations into accurate visual representations of fluid flow.

THE NEW TECHNOLOGY completely reshaped the way in which airplanes were designed as well. Traditionally, designers communicated through drawings. A project began with conceptual drawings and ended with hundreds of sheets of blueprints detailing every feature of the machine. At the appropriate point in the process, a company would hire dozens of additional draftsmen to produce the multiple sets of drawings that would go to the shop floor. Preparing and checking those drawings, and ensuring that they were updated to reflect the thousands of changes made to a design over the course of the project, was an overwhelming job.

Then there was the business of lofting. The term comes from ship-building. To ensure that the lines of the hull were just right, ship builders prepared full-scale drawings in a large loft, where sheets of vellum could be laid flat and connected to one another. Aeronautical engineers employed the same process to reproduce the complex, sweeping curves that made up the exterior of an airplane with the precision that only a full-scale representation could provide.

Even when the basic shape was rendered accurately, no set of drawings could fully describe the complexity of a modern aircraft with a precision that would actually enable the crew on the factory floor to build one. "You have five thousand engineers designing the airplane," a Boeing engineer explained. "It's very difficult for those engineers to coordinate with two-dimensional pieces of paper, or for the designer who is designing an air-conditioning duct to walk over to somebody who is in structures and say, 'Now here's my duct, does it match up with your structure?' Very difficult with two-dimensional drawings."[31]

The difficulties of designing so complicated a machine necessitated the use of a two-stage mock-up before production began. An initial wooden mock-up provided a check against the drawings to ensure that the pieces fit. With the addition of metal pieces, the mock-up enabled engineers to determine the way in which wiring bundles, cables, hydraulic lines, and other essential elements would be threaded through the aircraft. In most cases, such items would be fitted to the mock-up, then removed and measured in order to determine the size required for the finished airplane.

This time-honored, labor-intensive system of designing airplanes began to change in 1961, when an MIT doctoral student set to work on a software program capable of advanced graphics processing. Within two years, computer terminals began replacing drafting boards in one industry after another. Automobile manufacturers and architects explored computer-aided design at a fairly early date. Not until the early 1980s, however, did improved software and high-resolution screens lead to the introduction of the revolutionary CAD/CAM (computer-assisted design/computer-assisted manufacturing) programs that offered the precision required by the aerospace industry.[32]

The CAD program brought an end to a host of industry traditions, from the long hours spent at a drawing board, to the periodic arrival and departure of hordes of temporary draftsmen and engineers, the production of endless reams of drawings, and the arcane business of lofting. Henceforth, drawing would be done on the computer, where complex curves based on conic sections could be created with what was quite literally mathematical precision.

The machine would also perform all of the necessary calculations. Details, like the hundreds of thousands of rivets holding a large airplane together, could be added with a few key strokes. The computer could create an accurate, three-dimensional image of any part, enabling the engineer to view his handiwork from any angle. Single drawings, or entire sets, could be sent anywhere, any time, at the touch of a finger. A change of any sort would send any resulting alterations cascading through all of the appropriate drawings. By 1990, Boeing engineers were realizing the full benefits of the system as they moved forward with the design of their model 777 airliner, which they touted as the first "paperless airplane."

FINALLY, THE COMPUTER, together with the aerospace research dollars pouring into the coffers of American universities and corporations, changed the way in which airplanes, and a great many other things, were manufactured. While the introduction of both general and specialized machine tools had been an important feature of the shift from wood to metal construction in the 1930s, the aircraft industry had flourished on the basis of highly skilled labor performing a considerable amount of work by hand. Under the pressures of war the business of building airplanes grew from small-scale batch production undertaken by craftsmen, to a mass production industry in which special-purpose machines enabled semiskilled workers to send a steady stream of war planes out the factory doors in record time.

Since the emergence of the all-metal airplane, aircraft workers had identified themselves as "tin benders," workers who were employed in "cutting metal." Those were apt phrases for an industry that dealt in very thin sheets of metal, bent and riveted to internal supports fabricated by bending additional thin sheets into channels and other rigid forms. Workers literally fabricated the airplane on the factory floor. Weight savings was the single most important factor in aircraft design and production. Even with the higher speeds and wing loadings of wartime aircraft, this process produced the lightest final product.

There was a price to be paid, however. Assembling those sheets of metal, the most difficult part of the process, required a great many specialized jigs and fixtures to position them while workers riveted or welded them into place. The relatively flimsy nature of the materials separated aircraft manufacture from automobile assembly. Because weight was less important than speed of assembly, automobiles were built of rigid, generally interchangeable, forged or pressed elements.

With the advent of the jet age and extended operations at high subsonic speeds, increased strength became essential. At twice the speed of sound, aerodynamic heating began to reduce the strength of aluminum. "The heavier gauges [of metal], more critical tolerances and specialized forms of modern aircraft," an industry leader explained, "imposed . . . the need for larger and more complicated machine tools . . . special-purpose milling machines, large stretch-forming machines, giant hydraulic presses and other costly high-performance machinery not economically practical for use on small peacetime orders."[33] The new machines shaped metal into larger and more rigid forms. Now airplanes were assembled from structural elements, a process that required fewer skilled workers than the prewar approach of actually fabricating the machine on the floor of the factory. In addition, weight savings now required the use of lightweight materials capable of withstanding the extreme temperatures inside a jet engine and the heat generated by flight beyond the speed of sound. The North American F-100, the first U.S. Air Force fighter to achieve supersonic speed in level flight, contained six times more titanium than its predecessor, the F-86 Sabre Jet. The supersonic North American XB-70 was constructed of titanium and special, high-strength stainless-steel alloys. By the mid-1950s, North American purchased 80 percent of the titanium used by American industry.[34]

Aerospace manufacturers produced light-alloy forgings of

unprecedented size. In order to reduce weight and increase strength, relatively complex elements of the airframe were now machined as single pieces. Integrally stiffened skins replaced the old system of thin skins fastened to rigid formers. Where possible, new bonding methods replaced rivets to create a smoother skin.

Large sections of both the XB-70 and the delta-wing, supersonic Convair B-58 were constructed of a brazed stainless-steel honeycomb structure. The honeycomb cores were machined and then brazed to top and bottom sheets of stainless steel. That piece was then machined to the contour of the section of the aircraft where it would be located. Small wonder that the structure cost $200 to $600 per square foot in 1950s dollars. The larger XB-70 contained even more of a structure so expensive it was almost worth its weight in gold. Later high-speed aircraft, notably the Mach 3 A-11/SR-71, were built almost entirely of titanium.

The SR-71 exemplified the problems with the new materials. Developed by Lockheed's Kelly Johnson at the request of the Central Intelligence Agency's Richard Bissell, the Blackbird, as it would become known, replaced the U-2 as the nation's leading strategic reconnaissance aircraft. It bore little resemblance to its predecessor, however. The SR-71 operated at eighty-five thousand feet and cruised at Mach 3.2. A titanium skin could withstand surface temperatures of over 600 degrees Fahrenheit. Tough as stainless steel with half the density, titanium cracked when it was dropped, yet wore out standard drill bits in a remarkably short time. It had to be handled with extraordinary care. The ink of a pen, the thin layer of protective cadmium on a worker's tool, or the faint trace of chlorine in the water used to wash a finished part would destroy the strength of the material.

The construction of the most-advanced military aircraft was now a labor-intensive business involving complex structures and lightweight, difficult-to-handle materials. Electronic packages had to be closely packed into the airframe and guided weapons produced for use with the new generations of aircraft. Costs skyrocketed. By 1988, the price of a single B-2 bomber had reached $2.3 billion.

Missiles, which would fly only once, were fabricated by attaching thin metal sheets to a light internal structure, much as airplanes had been. The structure of Convair's Atlas intercontinental ballistic missile was so fragile that it would collapse of its own weight unless pressurized. With the cost of military aircraft rising, and defense budgets declining, relatively inexpensive missiles were seen as a means of filling the gap.

THE NEW APPROACH to aircraft construction required radically new machine tools. As early 1948, the air force began subsidizing the development of very heavy-duty presses required to produce larger forgings. Structural elements that would once have been assembled from sheets of aluminum were now produced as integral units. The desire to automate the production of those structural elements drove the development of new machine tools. The computer was the key.

Traditional machine tools were controlled by the skilled hands of the operator. Historian David Noble argues that some defense planners saw skilled machining as both a production bottleneck and a critically important area that might be disrupted by labor problems. Following World War II, he contends, air force officials set out to create an automated machining system that would increase efficiency and shift control of production from skilled workers on the factory floor to the engineering offices controlled by management.

In 1949, the Manufacturing Methods Branch at Wright-Patterson Air Force Base offered tool builder John T. Parsons a $200,000 contract for work on a contour cutting machine controlled by the IBM punch-card system. By the mid-1950s, working with the Servomechanisms Laboratory at MIT, Parsons had produced a programmable, or numerically controlled (NC), milling machine in which punch cards or tapes replaced the skilled hands of the operator, just as the player piano roll once replaced the fingers of the pianist.

Within a few years, numerically controlled technology was giving way to computer numerically controlled (CNC) machine tools, in which a computer supplies a stream of digital information that controls the cutting and shaping process. The air force continued to fund MIT work in this area until 1959, with the Air Materiel Command planners at Wright-Patterson Air Force Base spending another $180 million in contracts for advanced machine tools and new processes.

High-strength materials and exotic metals required even more sophisticated machining techniques. A machine shaping steel or titanium required six times the cutting capacity in order to match a machine operating on softer aluminum. Eventually, new methods, including electrical discharge machining (EDM), in which an electrical current passing through a "hot wire" does the cutting, helped to revolutionize the business of shaping metal.

The impact of a single decade of the U.S. Air Force's investment on the development of new productive machinery was extraordinary. By 1957, the U.S. government owned more machine tools of all types than anyone else in the nation, roughly 15% of the total number in use, most of which were assigned to aircraft plants.[35]

Military research and development funding aimed at improving the way in which airplanes were manufactured in the later half of the twentieth century had profound social consequences. Developments since the 1980s offer the potential for a return to decentralized and less authoritarian systems that would restore a sense of autonomy and participation to the worker on the shop floor. Still, the case of NC and CNC machine tools demonstrates the extent to which the planners who distribute research funding have the power to shape the way in which we live and work.

Computers provided a new tool for aeronautical research and changed the way in which aircraft were designed and built. The drive was also on to develop lightweight, onboard computers to operate guidance and navigation and other systems. For one last time, Jack Northrop led the pack.

NORTHROP HAD SOLD his interest in the Northrop Company to Douglas Aircraft in 1938 and founded Northrop Aviation, where he remained as president and chief engineer until his retirement in 1952. The firm prospered during the war, producing subassemblies for Consolidated, selling Northrop-designed N-3PB aircraft to the Norwegians, manufacturing Vultee Vengeance dive-bombers, and developing the very successful Northrop P-61 Black Widow night fighter.

The company entered the jet age with the development of the F-89 Scorpion, a twin-engine, all-weather interceptor first flown in 1948. Northrop's personal interest, however, focused on the development of aerodynamically efficient flying wing aircraft. Calculating the performance of such an aircraft represented a genuine challenge without a capacity for high-speed computing.

Northrop's involvement in the uncharted field of missile development also drew the company into electronic computing. Responding to a wartime U.S. Army Air Forces request for a winged cruise missile, the company set to work on a subsonic, turbojet-powered aircraft capable of carrying a two-thousand-pound payload 1,500 to 5,000 miles. When the project fell victim to postwar budget cuts, Northrop appealed to Gen. Carl M. Spaatz, promising to solve the daunting problems during the course of a two-and-one-half-year development effort. Spaatz gave him a reprieve but Northrop missed the deadline.

The missile, the B-62 Snark (named after a Lewis Carroll nonsense poem), went through a decade of problems before being declared operational. While Snark had its defenders, it was also an object of ridicule. So many test missiles were lost that air force wags began to speak of "the Snark-filled waters" of the Atlantic.

By the time Snark became operational in 1959, the advent of ballistic missiles had rendered it obsolete. The missile may have failed, but the attempt to create an onboard guidance system had carried Northrop engineers deep into the new field of computing. The company originally contracted with Electronic Control Company (ECC) for a guidance system. John Mauchly, the president of ECC, and his University of Pennsylvania colleague J. Prosper Eckert, had developed ENIAC (Electronic Numerical Integrator and Computer), an early computer used to perform ballistic calculations. ECC was never able to meet Northrop's need, but the missile contract paid for the development of UNIVAC, which launched the commercial computer industry in the United States.

Discouraged, Northrop turned the guidance problem over to the Hewlett-Packard Company in 1949. The result was MADDIDA (Magnetic Drum Differential Analyzer). While the system was still too large and heavy for use aboard Snark, the members of the Northrop team involved in the development of MADDIDA argued that the company should manufacture the machines for sale.

Northrop rejected the suggestion in the spring of 1950, and a dozen or so key employees left the company to form the Computer Research Corporation, which succeeded in marketing MADDIDA to other aerospace firms. Although not general-purpose computers, these machines served as the heart of subsequent guidance systems for missiles like Polaris. Historian Paul Ceruzzi notes that no fewer than fourteen computer firms can trace their roots to the Northrop group. For all of its contributions to the foundations of the computer industry, Snark ultimately flew with an unsatisfactory analog system.[36]

COMPUTERS WERE ALSO applied to the solution of a series of ground-based aerospace problems, from simulating reality to protecting the nation from nuclear attack. The earliest of these systems derived from the wartime work of Capt. (later Admiral) Luis de Florez (1889–1962).

A 1911 graduate of MIT, the flamboyant de Florez returned to alumni gatherings in a flying boat that he landed on the Charles River. He developed antiaircraft gun sights, a mechanical system for cracking petroleum, industrial furnaces, and over thirty aeronautical devices for the U.S. Navy during World War I. Half a century later, he served as the chairman of research for the Central Intelligence Agency.

Carrying a reputation as an aviator with a talent for invention, de Florez was named commander of the U.S. Navy Bureau of Aeronautics Special Devices Division (SDD), which developed training aids for naval aviation during World War II. The group turned out everything from wooden aircraft identification models and ingenious target kites designed to hone the shooting skills of shipboard antiaircraft gunners, to the most sophisticated electrical-mechanical simulators for pilot training.

In the postwar era, de Florez broke entirely new ground by combining his wartime experience with the developing power of the computer to create ground-based aircraft- and missile-tracking systems (Project Hurricane) and a means of simulating both the flight of a missile (Project Cyclone) and the track of an antiaircraft missile intercepting a target (Project Typhoon). His most ambitious effort involved creating a simulator capable of predicting the flight characteristics of an airplane that had yet to be built and of training the pilots to fly it (Project Whirlwind).

Project Whirlwind grew out of a 1944 SDD contract with the MIT Servomechanisms Laboratory for a universal pilot trainer that could be "programmed" to simulate the flight characteristics of different aircraft types. When the effort continued after 1945, Jay W. Forrester, the MIT project director, set his team to work on a general-purpose digital computer capable of driving the simulator and performing any number of other tasks for the navy.

Threatened with cancelation in 1950, Project Whirlwind received a new lease on life when the air force continued its funding. The computer was worth waiting for. What had begun as an analog device to control a simulator became the first electronic digital computer with a magnetic core–stored memory to speed operation over the slower computers made with vacuum tubes. The modern computer had come of age.

The air force had something bigger than flight training in mind for Whirlwind. In 1952, with memories of Pearl Harbor still fresh in the minds of most Americans, the U.S. Air Force and MIT contractors set out to create an effective electronic air defense system for the entire continent. A decade before, Britain had created a small-scale system by linking radar and ground observers to central plotting stations that guided fighter pilots to their targets. Humans served as the integrating factors. This time a vast array of ground-based, airborne, and ship-based detectors, including a distant early warning (DEW) line of radar stations stretching across the roof of the continent, would feed information to linked computers that would provide an integrated view of the total situation to decision makers.

Creating a system to manage that sort of complexity would be the job of the MITRE Corporation. This independent, not-for-profit organization was created in 1959 by 489 employees of the MIT Lincoln Laboratory, the navy and air force contractor for Whirlwind. While accounts vary, the name was apparently meant to honor the MIT heritage and suggest a well-designed joint. The first product of the organization was SAGE, an acronym for a euphemism that said nothing about the purpose of the system: semiautomatic ground environment.

SAGE, up and running by 1963, remained in service until 1983. Fortunately, its effectiveness never met the ultimate test of an enemy attack. As the very first large-scale, electronic command-and-control system, however, SAGE introduced the world to the power of what MIT mathematician Norbert Wiener called *cybernetics*, the systems through which humans are linked to machines.

Defense spending also produced new technologies that had a direct impact on daily life. During the 1960s, for example, the Autonetics Division of North American Rockwell won the contract to produce the guidance and navigation system for the Minuteman II missile. Each system contained some two thousand integrated circuit chips, developed by Texas Instruments to replace earlier and bulkier components. At peak production, 20 percent of all the integrated circuits produced in the United States went into Minuteman II missiles. The program reduced the cost of chips to the point where the producers of electronic consumer goods could begin to take advantage of the new technology, thereby launching the age of the microchip.

GLOBALIZATION, 1965–2000

The U.S. Department of Commerce reported some 1,828 companies as being involved in aerospace manufacturing in 1997. Over half of the establishments were small contractors employing less than fifty workers. At the same time, 70 percent of all aerospace employees worked in less than 4 percent of the aerospace firms (16 percent in the case of missile producers) that employed more than a thousand workers.[37]

By the end of the century, the aerospace enterprise remained among the top-five American manufacturing sectors in terms of the value of shipments and the number of employees. In the year 2000, total industry sales amounted to $144 billion. Just over 40 percent of the sales were to the U.S. government. Another 18 percent involved domestic civilian sales. The largest portion, a full 41 percent of the total, represented export sales. While motor vehicles posted the worst trade balance in the American economy, transportation equipment, including aerospace manufacturing, had the best record.

American manufacturers had dominated the international market for airliners since the introduction of the Boeing 247 and Douglas DC-3 in the mid-1930s. The United States had recaptured the market following World War II and held off the early threat of British jetliners. As a result, American manufacturers supplied 87 percent of the jet transports flown by the world's airlines during the years 1958–1985.[38]

The exports were not restricted to civil airliners. Throughout the Cold War, the sale of military aircraft to friendly nations in Latin America, Europe, Asia, and Africa remained a major source of income for American manufacturers. The air forces of Great Britain, Iran, Israel, Korea, Australia, West Germany, Japan, Greece, Turkey, and Egypt, for example, used the McDonnell F4 Phantom II (first flown in 1961). For some companies, and some aircraft, foreign air forces were better customers than the U.S. armed forces.

The critical importance of the export market, combined with the growing reliance on subcontracting, drew the U.S. aerospace industry into the era of globalization. In 1953, the Allied powers (excluding the USSR) decided to allow Japan to develop a limited capacity for self-defense. Two years later, Mitsubishi Heavy Industries, eager to rebuild a capacity for high-technology manufacturing, signed an agreement with North American Aviation allowing the Japanese firm to assemble all of the F-86F fighters that would be flown by the Koku Jietai (Japan Air Self Defense Force).

The next step came in 1960, when the Japanese government announced that a consortium of companies led by Mitsubishi would manufacture a special F-104J version of the Lockheed Starfighter intended for the air defense force. The process began with the assembly of a few Starfighters sent from the United States, after which the Japanese firms manufactured 178 aircraft powered by jet engines made in Japan. Beginning in 1981, a new generation of Mitsubishi-assembled F-15J aircraft entered service with the Koku Jietai.

The relationship between the two nations entered a new phase in the early 1960s, when a Japanese firm won the contract to produce gear boxes for the Boeing 707. When the Boeing 727 took to the sky in 1964, it flew with gear boxes, galleys, lavatories, and structural elements made in Japan. Additional contracts and coproduction agreements funded the rise of a Japanese machine-tool industry and the purchase of the most advanced American machining technology. Japanese firms built elements of the Douglas DC-10, the Boeing 767, and some models of the 747. Soon Japanese industry adopted the American pattern of subcontracting. Mitsubishi produced major sections of the P-3C Orion, which Kawanishi was building under a coproduction agreement with Lockheed.

"Offsets," or favorable coproduction agreements designed to attract foreign customers, became an important feature of the industry during the 1970s. General Dynamics, for example, recruited a consortium of European nations to participate in the production of the F-16. Under the terms of the agreement, European manufacturers would produce over one-third of the initial run, including 10 percent of the airplanes that would go to the U.S. Air Force and over 40 percent of those intended for other air forces. General Dynamics had created a market large enough to generate a profit on their airplane. In turn, the European partners received access to cutting-edge manufacturing and electronic technology, support for their own aerospace industries, and twenty-five thousand new jobs.

The process worked the other way as well. The Dutch-built Fokker 100, a mid-size airliner, sported systems and parts supplied by Goodyear, Grumman, Garrett, and Teledyne. In 1984, Airbus Industrie, the European consortium that had emerged as Boeing's only significant competition in the international market for large airliners, pointed out that their latest transport incorporated parts from five hundred American companies in thirty-five states.[39]

Douglas managers introduced the notion of cost and risk sharing in 1965–1966, when they enlisted a number of domestic and foreign partners who agreed to produce major portions of the DC-9 jetliner, earning a profit or suffering a loss right along with the prime contractor. Aeritalia, headquartered in Naples, Italy, became a leading participant in such ventures, contributing sections of the DC-9 fuselage, the design and construction of the DC-10 vertical stabilizer, and a 15 percent share in the production of the Boeing 767.

Globalization and coproduction were applied to the design and manufacture of engines as well. GE launched a 1971 effort with the French firm SNECMA to develop a new turbofan engine, the CFM56. The project illustrated one of the critical problems involved in any partnership with a foreign company—the protection of key defense technologies. In this case, the Department of Defense barred GE from the use of some core technology that had been employed in the engine that powered the B-1 bomber. The CFM56 also illustrated the complexity of international corporate relationships. While the French government controlled 80 percent of SNECMA stock, Pratt & Whitney owned 10 percent. GE was making money for its most important competitor.

But the potential for shared profits was balanced by the possibility of mutual disaster. Lockheed developed its L-1011 Tristar during the late 1960s in tandem with the light, quiet, and fuel-efficient Rolls-Royce RB.211 turbofan engine. The airplane flew for the first time in 1970, but the engines continued to have problems. The development of the C-5A military transport had sapped Lockheed's financial strength, and the failure to deliver the L-1011 on schedule might send the company into a death spiral, and Rolls-Royce with it.

Neither the United States nor Great Britain could afford to risk the cornerstones of their defense industries. The government of Prime Minister Edward Heath refinanced Rolls-Royce, while the Nixon administration arranged a famous "bailout," a guaranteed loan of $250 million for Lockheed. The company would pay the loan back, but the episode underscored the critical importance of export sales in an age of global commerce. Those circumstances set the stage for a series of scandals that rocked the aerospace industry.

THE MARKETEERS AT Lockheed had a well-earned reputation for doing whatever it took to close a foreign sale. That often meant a major payoff at some point in the process. The company's relationship with Prince Bernhard of the Netherlands began in the 1950s, when the board of KLM, on which the prince served, voted to equip the royal Dutch airline with the triple-tailed Lockheed Super Constellation. By

1960 Lockheed had funneled as much as a million dollars to the prince through Swiss banks at a time when the Dutch Air Force was deciding to purchase Lockheed's F-104 Starfighters. The sale of the F-104 to Germany and other partners in the North Atlantic Treaty Organization (NATO) also raised questions in the minds of some industry watchers.[40]

Suspicions were raised in Japan and elsewhere in 1972, when ANA (All-Nipon Airways), which had apparently been preparing to purchase a fleet of McDonnell Douglas DC-10s, suddenly decided in favor of the Lockheed L-1011. It was later alleged that both U.S. and British officials pressured the Japanese government to favor the troubled airplane in which both nations now had a significant investment.

Daniel J. Haughton, Lockheed's chairman of the board, preferred a more direct approach, dispatching Corporate President A. Carl Kotchian to take charge of the "sales" effort in Japan. In the end, Lockheed paid as much as $14 million in bribes to an apparently endless string of Japanese officials. The ensuing scandal brought down the government of Prime Minister Kakuei Tanaka. Chairman Haughton explained that the sale was of vital importance to his company and that bribes paid to officials of a foreign government had been perfectly legal at the time.[41]

That was only the very visible tip of the iceberg. In all, Lockheed managers admitted to distributing $200 million in improper payments to officials in Turkey, Indonesia, Saudi Arabia, Italy, Japan, and West Germany. Northrop had greased foreign palms to the extent of $30 million during the course of marketing their fighter aircraft abroad. Grumman had spent $28 million on "commissions" to individuals close to the Shah of Iran, who not only equipped his air force with F-14s but also offered loans to assist the Long Island–based company. Boeing, General Dynamics, and McDonnell Douglas also engaged in questionable sales tactics.[42]

The passage of the Foreign Corrupt Practices Act, which President Jimmy Carter signed into law in December 1977, was intended to end an unsavory era in the history of the American aerospace industry. The absolute need for American aerospace firms to tap foreign markets remained, however, along with the problems of offsets, technology transfer, the loss of American jobs, and unethical business dealings, not to mention the use of U.S. technology in foreign conflicts.

As President Eisenhower had feared, corruption and the attempts of the aerospace industry to buy political influence were not limited to foreign governments. Even before the European and Asian scandals hit the front pages, the industry had exercised influence over the procurement process. Investigators questioned the tactics used to "sell" weapons systems to procurement officials and Congress, and the role that U.S. government officials had played in marketing American weapons abroad. Business leaders moved back and forth between the corporate boardroom and high-level government positions. The ease with which military procurement officers found well-paid employment in the aerospace industry after retirement was well known.

Aerospace corporations arranged "junkets" for influential officials and politicians, entertained lavishly, and contributed heavily to campaign war chests. The Watergate investigations of 1972 revealed the extent to which corporate America had sought to obtain political influence. Northrop, convicted of having made at least $476,000 in illegal contributions to the Nixon campaign, led the pack. Although the conviction forced Thomas Jones to resign the presidency of the corporation, he remained as chief executive.

Americans have never been quite sure how they feel about big business. On the one hand, free enterprise is the cornerstone of national prosperity. On the other, we have a long tradition of opposition to the corrupt and undemocratic business practices of railroads, banks, mines, and oil companies. Corporations that abused workers, took advantage of the public, and restrained trade inspired the birth of populism, labor unions, and the progressive movement. The most successful turn-of-the-century businessmen were dubbed the "Robber Barons." John D. Rockefeller, the richest man in America, was as reviled as any criminal.

Before 1939, the aviation industry was occasionally accused of shady dealing, as during the aircraft production scandal of 1918 or the airmail crisis of 1933. For the most part, however, aircraft manufacturers projected a positive, even heroic, image. While by no means opposed to making money, they were determined to do it building airplanes. They struggled to survive in a business that universally favored the customer, so that they could push the limits of a new and exciting technology.

That era ended in the last quarter of the century. As the scale, power, and wealth of the aerospace industry grew, it became impossible to maintain the pure public enthusiasm for aviation that had been the hallmark of an earlier and more naïve age. Greed and the lust for power and influence stained the industry whose motto had once been "higher, faster, farther."

The political and ethical traps that ensnared the industry in 1950–1980 resulted, in part at least, from endemic problems. The industry had difficulty diversifying. After decades of trying, aerospace corporations had failed to develop any more successful long-term ancillary products than canoes, house trailers, or lawn furniture. The critically important technologies that had been rooted in aerospace, like the computer, had spun off into separate industries.

The aerospace industry continued to sell its wares in a limited and highly competitive marketplace. Moreover, as the cost of aerospace projects skyrocketed, the leaders of even the most successful and well-financed corporations might have little choice but to bet the future of the company on one or two designs. Moreover, international competition was on the rise.

THE EUROPEAN PHOENIX

Great Britain had emerged from World War II with a very strong aircraft industry operating at peak efficiency. Disastrous government policies, poor business decisions, a limited domestic market, and plain bad luck limited Britain's ability to compete with the United States. By 1960, the twenty-seven or so healthy companies of 1945 had dwindled to two super corporations: the British Aircraft Corporation (BAC) and Hawker Siddeley. Like Sikorsky and Bell, Westland had abandoned the airplane for the helicopter. Some of the most historic names in the industry—De Havilland, Avro, Bristol, Gloster, Fairey, Saunder-Roe, and Vickers—had closed their doors or vanished into one of the two aerospace giants.

French industry had been badly battered by the war. Four of the companies that had been nationalized in 1936 were still in operation in 1945. They were joined by reestablished firms bearing some of the greatest names in French aviation, including both Breguet and Morane-Saulnier. Marcel Bloch (1892–1986), another prewar leader of the industry, had returned with a new name.

Trained as an electrical engineer, Bloch redesigned the Caudron G-3 and developed new and more efficient propellers. Following World War I, he emerged as a leading manufacturer, producing a successful line of Bloch civil and military aircraft until the fall of France in 1940. Jewish and a member of the Resistance, Bloch was captured by the Gestapo in 1944 and sent to the Buchenwald concentration camp. He survived, but contracted diphtheria, the effects of which would plague him for the rest of his life.

Reentering aviation, he insisted on being known as Marcel Dassault, the code name that his brother Paul had used in the Resistance. He produced the Ouragan, an early European jet; the supersonic Mystere; the Mach 2 Mirage series; and the Falcon executive jets. His work contributed to the reemergence of France as a military and technological powerhouse. He helped to build an air force for the new state of Israel and served as an important political supporter of Charles de Gaulle, winning election to the French legislature in 1950 and serving as a senator into the 1980s.

Germany and Italy were not permitted to build airplanes until 1950. The aging Claudius Dornier and the still relatively young Willy Messerschmitt both set up shop in Spain. In 1951, when the construction of gliders and light aircraft was permitted, Focke-Wulf reestablished itself with two hundred employees in a workshop at the Bremen airport. As late as 1955–1956, *Jane's All the World's Airplanes* did not list any German firms.

Back in Germany in the mid-1950s, Messerschmitt manufactured motorcycles and cooperated with Junkers and Heinkel to produce French and Italian jet trainers under license. By the early 1970s, German industry had coalesced into three large firms: Dornier, Messerschmitt-Bölkow-Blohm (MBB), and VFW-Fokker. Dornier and Fokker both developed executive aircraft and small airliners. Italy, Sweden, and Switzerland became aircraft producers as well.

WITH THE EXCEPTION of Marcel Dassault, and a handful of European aircraft companies that filled an empty niche here and there, foreign manufacturers had no luck challenging American mastery of the international aerospace marketplace. With relatively small domestic markets, they did not have the competitive advantages that enabled American companies to operate on an international scale. Beginning in 1960, however, the Europeans moved in a new and promising direction.

That year, the British Air Ministry set out to find international partners to cooperate in the development of a supersonic airliner. German leaders responded that they were not ready to undertake so bold a venture, but the French were very interested. Formal agreements between the two governments were supplemented by contracts between BAC and Sud-Aviation, the principal contractors. The resulting Anglo-French Concorde first took to the air in December 1967.

Great Britain, West Germany, and Italy launched a second European consortium in 1965, when they agreed to the joint development of a multimission strike aircraft to enter service in 1975. A new, jointly held company, Panavia coordinated the work of the primary contractors: BAC and Turbo Union in England, MBB in Germany, and the Italian firm of Aeritalia. The Netherlands, Belgium, and Canada joined the effort for a time but then dropped out.

First flown on August 14, 1974, the consortium's product, the Tornado, featured a swing wing and twin turbofan engines that could propel it to speeds of up to Mach 2.2 at altitude. Developing the prototype into a practical weapons system that met the needs of all three air forces required considerable time and effort. By 1979, however, the consortium had established a joint training facility for the Tornado at the Royal Air Force (RAF) base at Cottesmere. The RAF and the Royal Saudi Air Force used them during the Desert Shield and Desert Storm operations against Iraq.

The Concorde project and Panavia helped to lay the foundation for Airbus Industrie, the enterprise that would finally challenge American hegemony. The project began with Henri Ziegler and Roger Bétallie, of the French firm Sub-Aviation, who had analyzed the market and identified a niche for a true air bus, a short- to medium-range twin-engine airliner with a capacity for 250 to 300 passengers. By the fall of 1967, recognizing that they could not undertake this project on their own, Sud-Aviation enlisted aerospace manufacturers in Germany and Britain. When the formal agreement was finalized in 1970, the Netherlands, Spain, and Belgium had also signed up with Airbus

Airbus A 300-600

Industries. The first product of the new joint venture, the A 300, was the first twin-aisle, twin-engine jetliner to provide wide-body seating capacity with the ability to accommodate industry-standard cargo containers under the passenger deck. It first flew in October 1972.

The product was first rate, and the manufacturers were prepared to provide the full range of parts and service demanded by the airlines. For the first time, a foreign manufacturer began selling large transport aircraft to organizations other than their national airlines. By the end of the decade, Airbus Industrie was offering a range of jetliners to air carriers around the globe. Along with Dassault on the military side,

Airbus represented a great success story for the European aerospace industry.

CENTURY'S END

Survival in the postwar aerospace industry required adaptability to the technological changes and shifting market conditions. By 1960, Republic Aviation was struggling. The company had prospered for thirty years by producing three generations of fighter, bomber, and ground-attack aircraft developed by Alexander Kartveli and his team of engineers. Secretary of Defense Robert McNamara's decision to replace several aircraft types with a single multipurpose joint-service airplane created problems for the small and narrowly focused company. By 1965, Republic was reduced to producing subassemblies for other companies, and losing money at that.

Fairchild, which had recently purchased Hiller Helicopters, bought Republic in 1965 and transferred operations to its Hagerstown, Maryland, plant. Fairchild would continue to produce a diverse product line that included U.S. Air Force transports, short-haul airliners, the A-10 ground-attack machine (a product of the Republic Division), helicopters, and spacecraft. By 1987, however, a series of mergers and business shifts essentially removed Fairchild from aircraft manufacture. At century's end, a small-scale business aircraft manufacturer kept the historic name alive.

Ironically, Douglas aircraft suffered from too much success. Donald Douglas, the grand old man of the industry, became chairman of the board in 1957 and turned over daily operations to his son. The company had two successful jetliners in production and a string of military and space contracts in hand, but Donald Douglas Jr. had a difficult time managing prosperity. Poor planning led to rising costs and the threat of missed delivery dates. Sensing trouble on the horizon, investment bankers hesitated to help solve cash flow problems.

Much smaller than Douglas, McDonnell Aircraft was very well managed and boasted rock-solid credit. James McDonnell recognized that a merger with Douglas would create a much stronger company offering a healthy and diverse mix of civil, military, and space products that would guarantee stability and steady profits. With the approval of the Justice Department, and a $300 million revolving credit account provided by ten banks, the McDonnell Douglas Corporation began operations in 1967.

In similar fashion, Lee Atwood, president and CEO of North American Aviation, pursued a 1967 merger with the Rockwell Standard Company of Pittsburgh as a means of escaping the boom-and-bust character of the aerospace industry. Rockwell, which produced truck axles, would act as a flywheel, offering steady sales that would smooth out North American's cyclical fluctuations.

But the junior partners, Willard F. Rockwell and his son, Willard F. "Al" Rockwell Jr., proved more than a match for Lee Atwood, the quiet engineer-manager. Aghast at the $25 million that Atwood had spent in preparing to bid on a contract that he lost, the Rockwells tried to prevent a bid on the B-1 contract, which North American Rockwell won. When Atwood reached the mandatory retirement age a short while later, Al Rockwell replaced him with Robert Anderson, a Chrysler executive who eased the corporation away from airframe manufacture. By 1991, the company that had produced the P-51, F-86, XB-70, X-15, and the Apollo spacecraft was no longer building flying machines.

The three decades following the mergers of the 1960s presented great difficulties for the American aerospace industry. The cost of modern military aircraft, expensive structures built of exotic materials and filled with complex electronic systems, skyrocketed. That fact, combined with the development of new generations of accurate surface-to-surface guided missiles and "smart" weaponry that enabled an aircraft to "stand off" at a distance and still hit its target, limited the number of aircraft that the military required or could afford.

Confronted with a shrinking U.S. military market, manufacturers counted on commercial sales and exports to maintain profits. As early as 1993, military sales amounted to only 20 percent of Boeing's annual business. Two years later, 88 percent of Boeing's airliner sales were to overseas carriers. By the middle of the decade, however, American manufacturers faced serious competition in a market that they had long regarded as their own. While Boeing manufactured 70 percent of the airliners seating over eighty persons sold in 1997, Airbus had already captured 30 percent of that market. General Electric and Pratt & Whitney tied for control of the world market for jet engines, but Rolls-Royce ran a strong third.[43]

As *Aviation Week and Space Technology* reported, aerospace manufacturers were engaged in "a Darwinian struggle for survival" during the last decade of the century. Once again, the time seemed ripe for corporate mergers. Combining two or more businesses offered the possibility of expanding production capacity, infusing new blood into management, diversifying the product line, reducing the competition, and enjoying economies of scale.[44]

Between 1985 and 2000, seventy-six defense contractors, from large airframe manufacturers to small software providers, merged into five giant aerospace corporations: Lockheed Martin, Northrop Grumman, Boeing, Raytheon, and General Dynamics. Douglas, Ryan, North American, Vought, McDonnell—some of the most distinguished names in American aviation—vanished from the scene.

Successful as it was, the F-14 Tomcat would be the last in a long line of carrier-based navy fighters to emerge from what became affectionately known, in testimony to the solidity of its products, as the Grumman Iron Works. With no similar contracts in the offing, company officials reoriented the firm to the production of defense electronics and systems integration. Grumman began to look like a very appealing acquisition for an airframe manufacturer. Northrop bought the company for $2.4 billion in May 1994. Over the next six years, Northrop Grumman would continue to gobble up smaller companies, from Newport News Shipbuilding to Comsat, the U.S. telecommunications satellite company.

Even more stunning was the August 1994 announcement that Lockheed and Martin Marietta would integrate their various businesses through a $10 billion exchange of stock. The world's largest defense and aerospace company, Lockheed Martin would employ 170,000 workers in facilities scattered throughout the nation. Daniel M. Tellep, the first chairman and CEO of the new firm, and Norman Augustine, who followed him, took critical steps to streamline corporate bureaucracy and eliminate duplicate functions.

"The saving will not be trivial," noted Augustine, who emerged as one of the best-known management gurus of the 1990s. Indeed, by 1997, Lockheed Martin revenues approached $27 billion. The mega-corporation soon prowled for other targets, going so far as to eye Northrop Grumman until the Federal Trade Commission ruled that the combination would be in violation of antitrust laws.[45]

Boeing proved to be even more acquisitive, gobbling up Rockwell International's aerospace and defense holdings for $3.1 billion late in 1996 and acquiring McDonnell Douglas at a cost of $14 billion in August 1997. The Federal Trade Commission ruled in favor of this merger. McDonnell Douglas was no longer an active manufacturer of airliners, so the acquisition could be regarded as Boeing's attempt to diversify. While Lockheed Martin might fairly be regarded as the world's largest end-of-the-century weapons builder, Boeing was a much larger corporation, employing a workforce of 225,000 and posting 1997 sales totaling $48 billion.

Raytheon also grew in the mid-1990s. Rather than diversifying, however, the company preferred to build on its existing strengths in electronic systems and missile production.

Astronaut William A. Anders, named chairman of General Dynamics in 1989, stunned the aerospace community by divesting the company of its principal aerospace assets. When attempts to acquire other firms that would strengthen the company's position as a producer of military aircraft failed, Anders sold the historic Fort Worth Division, with its lucrative contracts for the F-16 fighter, to Lockheed Martin. After parting with what had traditionally been regarded General Dynamic's flagship operation, Anders sold Cessna to Textron and parted with the Space Systems Division as well. The company turned its back on aerospace in favor of naval shipbuilding, ground combat systems, and electronics.

Such an example of sudden corporate downsizing is rare in American business history. Sales fell from $10 billion in 1992 to $3.5 billion when the dust settled. The sudden influx of cash certainly pleased shareholders, and the strategy seemed to play well on Wall Street, but defense industry insiders wondered if General Dynamics would not be gobbled up or simply disappear.

The company survived, ending the century as the leading supplier of combat vessels to the U.S. Navy. Following Ander's retirement in 1996, the new management of General Dynamics even returned to aerospace through the acquisition of Gulfstream, becoming an immediate powerhouse as a producer of executive jets. Rueben Fleet, who had founded Consolidated, the core company, would surely have been pleased.

14

COLD WAR, HOT WAR

STRATEGIC THINKING

The greatest war in history was over, but real peace remained elusive. By the spring of 1946, the Soviet Union had emerged as an ideological and military threat to the West. One after another, Stalinist puppet regimes took control of the nations overrun by the Red Army. For a time it appeared that Greece might fall into the Soviet sphere of influence. In an appearance at Missouri's Westminster College on March 5, 1946, Prime Minister Winston Churchill warned that the "iron curtain" of Communism was descending across the face of Europe.

Like their rivals in the West, the Soviets were exploring new military technologies introduced during the war. The first two Soviet jet fighters, the I-300(F) (later the MiG-9), designed by Artem Mikoyan and Mikhail Gurevich, and Aleksandir Yakovlev's Yak-15, both took to the air for the first time on April 24, 1946.

Joseph Stalin unveiled yet another surprise in August 1947, when three Tu-4 bombers participated in an Aviation Day flyover witnessed by foreign observers. The four-engine Tu-4 appeared to be an exact copy of the Boeing B-29, the most advanced American bomber of the day. As if to prove that these airplanes were not the three B-29s forced down in Russia during World War II, they were accompanied by a Tu-70, a unique Soviet transport version of the airplane.

The details of the incredible story of the Tu-4 would remain a secret to the West for half a century. Recognizing the important role of strategic bombing in the war against Germany and Japan, and impressed by the B-29, Stalin ended work on Soviet-designed four-engine bombers in 1944. Instead, he ordered Andrei Tupolev, who had spent the war in a *sharaga*, a prison for scientists and engineers, to copy the B-29.

Tupolev disassembled one of the interned airplanes, piece by piece, and turned meticulous drawings over to those who would build the machines. Copying anything as complex as a modern airplane proved incredibly difficult, but the quality of the work was beyond reproach. The Tu-4 was so accurate that Tupolev included the patched bullet holes present in the American original. He did not want to have to explain any discrepancies if Lavrentii Beria, head of the KGB, should inquire. Stalin now commanded a small fleet of intercontinental bombers capable of attacking the cities of Europe, or even undertaking one-way bombing attacks on the American continent. The prospect became even more frightening in August 1949, when the Soviets stunned the West with their first atomic bomb test. The United States no longer had a monopoly on nuclear weapons or the means of delivering them.

AMERICANS SPENT the months following the end of World War II demobilizing the air force that fought the last war and acquiring the new technology with which to fight the next. The number of aircraft in the U.S. Army Air Forces (USAAF) inventory dropped from a wartime high of 79,000 to a postwar low of 29,000 in 1947, with only 18 percent of them considered combat ready. The number of U.S. military airfields fell from the 783 in 1943 to 177 at the end of 1946. Personnel fell from the wartime peak of 2,253,000 in August 1945 to 304,000 by May 1947. During this same period, revolutionary new aircraft, from the North American F-86 to the Grumman F9F Panther and the Boeing B-47, appeared on the horizon.[1]

With Communist forces on the move across the globe, from Eastern Europe to China, North Korea, and Southeast Asia, President Harry Truman was determined to counter the Soviet-backed expansionism. One of the most important steps in that direction came in June 1947, when Secretary of State George C. Marshall unveiled a plan to provide unprecedented economic assistance in support of European recovery.

In another important step, the Truman administration increased defense funding and reorganized the U.S. military establishment to modernize the Pentagon bureaucracy. The National Security Act of 1947 created a unified Department of Defense and an independent air force. James Vincent Forrestal, a World War I naval aviator who had served as secretary of the navy, was sworn in as the first secretary of defense. W. Stuart Symington, the last assistant secretary of war for air, became the first secretary of the air force.

Suffering from heart problems, Hap Arnold had retired in June 1946. The man who learned to fly at the Wright brothers' flying school, stood beside Billy Mitchell when the struggle for independence began, and commanded the greatest air armada in history died at his California home on January 15, 1950. The honor of serving as the first commander of the U.S. Air Force went to Gen. Carl M. "Tooey" Spaatz.

Not everyone expressed enthusiasm about the new arrangement. Naval leaders opposed unification, arguing that they were in a better position to judge the needs of their service than a joint staff committee. They saw threats on every side. Small wonder, since General Spaatz was suggesting that his service should take responsibility for all land-based air power, including naval reconnaissance, antisubmarine warfare, and convoy protection. "It is not whether the Navy and Navy advocates are sincere in their expressed beliefs," Gen. Jimmy Doolittle remarked. "It is that they are wrong."[2]

The airmen had been the masters of public relations since the days of Billy Mitchell. During World War II, USAAF leaders had cooperated with writers and filmmakers to shape an informal media campaign aimed at generating public enthusiasm and congressional support for "air power." Some of the publicity efforts, notably Alexander de

Seversky's best-seller, *Victory through Air Power* (1942), the 1943 Walt Disney feature film of the same title, and William Bradford Huie's book *The Case against the Admirals* (1946), were so anti-navy that air force leaders distanced themselves from those projects.

The Aircraft Industries Association (AIA) organized a formal campaign to underscore the importance of aviation as a bulwark of freedom and a means of protecting the safety and security of the nation. The collective voice of the industry since 1917, the AIA had been founded as the Aircraft Manufacturers Association (the original patent pool), renamed the Aeronautical Chamber of Commerce in 1922, and finally reorganized as the AIA in 1945. Headed by two major figures in wartime procurement, the U.S. Army's Oliver Patton Echols (1947–1949) and Adm. Dewitt Clinton Ramsey (1949–1956), the AIA filled a critically important role for the industry during the years following World War II.

As early as 1943, the AIA had hired the New York public relations firm Hill & Knowlton (H & K) to "sell" the American public on the critical importance of air power. With an annual budget of $300,000 devoted to the project, and access to much larger amounts from the public relations and advertising budgets of member corporations, Hill & Knowlton prepared print advertisements, pamphlets, radio programming, and a host of other materials pointing out that aviation, the key to victory on every front, would shape the future.

The organization redirected the campaign after World War II to generate grassroots support for something new to most Americans, a very large postwar air force that would maintain the peace in the face of challenges from a Cold War enemy. "Air Power," the Hill & Knowlton slogan insisted, "is Peace Power."

The program was a great success, laying a foundation for an expanded postwar military establishment. As historian Karen Miller comments, "H & K had not fooled or forced anyone to accept a military-industrial-complex." By marshalling public support for air power deterrence as an essential feature of national defense, however, the agency had "created a climate in which such a partnership was acceptable."[3]

Prohibited from lobbying Congress, Hap Arnold and other air

force leaders orchestrated the creation of the Air Force Association (AFA) in 1946. A civilian lobbying organization that could generate both public and official support, the AFA operated something like an "alumni association" for the 2.4 million men who had served in the wartime USAAF ("Let's Keep the Old Gang Together!"). It would not function as a veterans organization, however, nor would it have official ties to the air force. Serving officers would be eligible for membership, but they could not vote.

As James Straubel, executive director of the organization in the years 1948–1980, explained, "A new Air Force would have to be forged in the face of the public apathy, if not public opposition, that is common to anything military in a postwar period. And despite the wartime accomplishments of the Air Force, the Navy Department, at least, would continue to oppose a unified land, sea and air establishment."[4] With retired Gen. Jimmy Doolittle as its first president, and movie star and war hero Jimmy Stewart as vice president, the AFA took its message of preparedness in the air directly to the public, assisted by such well-known USAAF veterans as Hollywood mogul Jack Warner and movie star Ronald Reagan. Off to a strong start, the AFA would remain an aggressive, even strident, voice on behalf of U.S. Air Force leadership and policy.

A crisis in Berlin provided the first opportunity for the independent U.S. Air Force to prove itself. In April 1948, just weeks after a Communist regime had taken control of Czechoslovakia, the Soviets refused to allow supplies intended for Allied troops occupying West Berlin to move on the East German roads leading into the city. Since the narrow, established air lanes through which Allied aircraft flew to and from the city remained open, Gen. Curtis Emerson LeMay, commanding the U.S. Air Force in Europe, resupplied the garrison by air for ten days, until the Soviets reopened the highways.

On June 18, the Soviets closed the roads again, this time refusing to allow any supplies into the city. They intended to force the Allies out of Berlin without provoking a war. President Truman ordered an airlift that would supply the necessities of life to the two million people living in the western sector of the city. General Hoyt S. Vandenberg, a nephew of Senator Arthur Vandenberg and the new commander of the U.S. Air Force, created a joint aerial task force composed of U.S. Air Force and Royal Air Force elements along with a small contingent from the U.S. Navy.

Commanded by Gen. William H. Tunner, the men and aircraft of the Berlin Airlift delivered 2.3 million tons of supplies to the beleaguered city in fifteen months. Recognizing that the blockade was counterproductive, and unwilling to risk closing the air lanes, the Soviets agreed to reopen the highways in May 1949. The airlift continued to operate for a few months, building up a stockpile of supplies for use if new problems arose.

GENERAL VANDENBERG ordered General LeMay home from Europe in October 1948, once the Berlin Airlift was well underway. His new job was to forge the less-than-adequate Strategic Air Command (SAC) into the sharp nuclear point of the American spear. The air force initially treated the atomic bomb as a very powerful conventional weapon. A series of war plans—Makefast, Pincher, Broiler, Halfmoon, and Harrow—called for an "atomic blitz," strategic nuclear attacks on enemy cities and key economic and industrial targets, as the only means of countering the enormous Soviet advantage in manpower and proximity to the presumed combat areas in Central Europe.

Bernard Brodie, a professor at Yale's Institute for International Relations, was appalled by the thought that the strategic bombing doctrine might be extended into the nuclear age, with one airplane carrying one bomb standing in for the thousand bombers of a wartime raid. With a doctorate from the University of Chicago, Brodie became an authority on the impact of technology on naval warfare. In an influential book, *The Absolute Weapon* (1946), the young professor argued that the atomic bomb represented "a change not merely in the degree of destructiveness of modern war but in its basic character."[5] Historically, the business of the military was to win wars. "From now on," he argued, "its chief purpose must be to avert them. It can have almost no other useful purpose."[6]

The young scholar suggested a policy of deterrence. The threat of certain and overwhelming nuclear retaliation, he believed, provided the best safeguard against an attack. Invited to join the Air Targeting Division of Air Force Intelligence in 1950, he found that Generals Vandenberg, LeMay, and Charles Cabell, head of Air Intelligence, agreed on one thing—people would be the ultimate target of a nuclear strike.

Brodie stood Giulio Douhet on his head. In an atomic age, morality and good sense suggested that it would be more effective to hold *all* valuable targets hostage, rather than destroy them. The power of the nuclear bomb resided in the threat of its use. To attack a heavily populated area would be to initiate a nuclear exchange, a catastrophic failure of policy. He made scarcely a dent in air force thinking and took a job with the Washington Office of the RAND Corporation in 1951.

Herman Kahn (1922–1983), a colleague of Brodie's at RAND, took a very different view. Applying game theory and systems analysis to diplomacy and military affairs, Kahn argued that nuclear war was not only thinkable but also winnable. The advent of thermonuclear weapons, he believed, had "sort of swamped Brodie."[7]

Indeed, Brodie did lose confidence in deterrence for a time. The possibility of threatening another nation with a thermonuclear weapon seemed unthinkable. Surely, such weapons were as dangerous to the nation that held them as to the nation being threatened. His views no longer seemed as clear or as consistent as they had been early in his career. During the 1950s he alienated antinuclear colleagues at RAND by urging the use of tactical nuclear weapons in a last-ditch effort to avoid a thermonuclear exchange. He ultimately abandoned that position, admitting that the use of theater weapons would inevitably lead to Armageddon—a thermonuclear exchange.

Brodie did not stand alone in fearing the dangers of deterrence in a thermonuclear age. "We may anticipate a state of affairs in which two Great Powers will each be in a position to put an end to the civilization and life of the other, though not without risking its own," J. Robert Oppenheimer remarked in 1953. "We may be likened to two scorpions in a bottle, each capable of killing the other, but only at the risk of his own life."[8]

Frightening as that prospect was, many saw deterrence as the only reasonable alternative between complete disarmament and nuclear

war. It became official U.S. policy beginning with the Truman administration. Was the collapse of the Soviet Union a vindication of deterrence? Did half a century of defense spending on arms stockpiles and
delivery systems break the back of the Soviet economy? If true, at least
some of the credit for charting a course that avoided disaster during the
Cold War belongs to the largely forgotten figure of Bernard Brodie.

Brodie was fascinated by the air force's point of view, so different
from his own, and considered writing a book-length psychological
study of Curtis LeMay.[9] There is no evidence that LeMay gave much
thought to Brodie, or to Herman Kahn, for that matter. He had no
need for anyone's advice when it came to the defense of his nation.

CURTIS EMERSON LEMAY (1906–1990) was the oldest of seven children born to Erving and Arizona LeMay of Columbus, Ohio. An engineering major who reserved his real enthusiasm for the Reserve
Officers Training Corps (ROTC), he put himself through Ohio State
working in a foundry. After entering the air corps as a flying cadet in
1928, he served as a fighter pilot until 1933, when he turned his atten-

*Curtis Emerson LeMay stands in front of the dispatch board
at Tempelhof Air Base, Berlin, Germany, October 13, 1948*

tion to the training of navigators for the long-range bombers just entering service. He first came to public attention during the 1930s, as lead navigator on several well-publicized long-distance flights designed to demonstrate the potential of the B-17.

His prewar career was solid enough, but it hardly suggested that he would emerge from World War II as the most successful tactician, strategist, and commander of bombers in the USAAF. From his development of the combat box formation employed in the air war against Germany, to his introduction of the night incendiary raids that burned Japanese cities to the ground, he got the job done. The most visible public figure in the postwar history of the U.S. Air Force, LeMay capped his stellar career with service as air force chief of staff, but would be best remembered as commander of SAC (1948–1957).

Through sheer force of will and instinctive management skills, he transformed the weak organization that he inherited into a fearsome instrument of American power and policy. "Peace is our Profession," was the motto he chose for a command that was constantly prepared to launch a nuclear attack. He demanded total commitment from the men and women of SAC. At the same time, he fought for better pay and conditions for those who devoted their lives to the service of their nation.

It would be difficult to imagine a more intimidating military figure than the barrel-chested general with a cigar clamped in his square jaw and a steely glint in his eye. His ideas were as stern as his appearance. He rejected any notion of restraint, arguing that the business of SAC was to prepare for a single mission during which it would deliver all of the weapons available as quickly as possible. His contribution to the 1949 Joint Chiefs of Staff war plan called for dropping 133 atomic bombs on seventy-seven Soviet cities, taking 2.7 million lives and causing another 4 million casualties.[10]

Over the years, nothing would change but the scale of the destruction. By 1955, LeMay and his planners were prepared to destroy 118 cities in thermonuclear attacks that would take as many as 77 million lives.[11] "The final impression," reported an appalled naval officer who attended a 1954 SAC briefing, "was that virtually all of Russia would be nothing but a smoking, radiating ruin at the end of two hours."[12]

LeMay was the ultimate cold warrior, a commander who joked about the potential for reconnaissance flights over the Soviet Union (which the president had authorized) to ignite World War III. "If I see that the Russians are amassing their planes for an attack," he remarked to Robert Sprague, president of General Electric, "I'm going to knock the shit out of them before they can even take off the ground." Stunned, Sprague protested that such action ran counter to American policy. "I don't care," came the response. "It's my policy. That's what I am going to do."[13]

Can that really have been the view of the man entrusted with command of American air power? He was all too easy to caricature as "Bombs Away" LeMay, the inspiration for the crazed Gen. Jack D. Ripper in Stanley Kubrick's 1964 black-comic masterpiece, *Dr. Strangelove; or, How I Learned to Stop Worrying and Love the Bomb*. Even in retirement, his assurances that the impact of thermonuclear testing on Pacific islands was not all that bad embarrassed George Wallace, the right-wing independent who had selected LeMay as his vice presidential running mate in 1968.

Yet those closest to him suggest that LeMay carefully calculated his most outrageous comments for effect. Whatever he actually believed, however dangerous his personal views, it is entirely reasonable to suppose that he served a genuine purpose. In a world where fear maintained the balance of world peace, it may have been very useful indeed for the Soviets to recognize that they faced an adversary whose resolution was beyond question.

THE REVOLT OF THE ADMIRALS

When LeMay took command of SAC in 1948, he faced the problem of whipping the organization into shape and acquiring a new bomber that had some hope of actually dropping nuclear weapons on the enemy. That process began in April 1941, when the army announced its need for a very large bomber capable of flying from the U.S. to Europe and back in the event that English air bases were not available. Six months later, General Hap Arnold approved the procurement of two Consolidated XB-36 aircraft, but the project had low priority until the end of World War II. Developmental problems prevented a first flight until August 8, 1946.

Initial reaction to the airplane was less than enthusiastic. General George Kenney, LeMay's predecessor at SAC, complained that the B-50, the updated "super" B-29, exceeded the new airplane in every respect except range. The XB-36 could fly four thousand miles with an eighty-thousand-pound payload.

Just a month after setting the B-36 project in motion, the air force signed a contract with Jack Northrop for another very different high-altitude, long-range heavy bomber. Northrop had long regarded a flying wing as the ideal airplane, offering maximum lift with minimum drag. He had taken his first step in that direction in 1929 with a small aircraft featuring twin tail booms. He returned to the idea a decade later with the N1M (1940), followed by the N9M (1942), the immediate predecessors of the XB-35, the piston-engine flying wing bomber first flown on June 25, 1946. The new design, plagued by propulsion and stability problems, gave way to the YB-49, a jet-propelled version of the XB-35 first flown on October 21, 1947.

It was a stunning sight, a perfect flying wing, with the exception of four small vertical surfaces on the trailing edge. Flight testing revealed stability problems that made the airplane an unsuitable bombing platform, however. The YB-49 also had a bomb bay too small for the largest nuclear weapons then in use. The loss of Capt. Glen W. Edwards and a five-man crew in the crash of the second YB-49 on June 5, 1948, made headlines. Given the problems of the prototypes and the drive to reduce military spending, the air force canceled the YB-49 in 1949.

Northrop proposed a reconnaissance version, the YRB-49, which promised a 400-mph cruise speed at 35,000 feet. When the airplane proved to be slower than the Boeing B-47, the air force canceled the project and transferred the remaining funds to the B-36 account. Rumors swirled about that the secretary of the air force, Stuart Symington, tried to force Northrop to merge with Consolidated-Vultee as the price of keeping the flying-wing project alive. Northrop denied the story during congressional hearings, but suggested many years later that it was in fact true.

• • •

THE NAVY HAD its doubts about the B-36 and the air force's plan for nuclear war. Given SAC's early reliance on bases in Great Britain (1947–1949), navy planners argued that a carrier-based, long-range atomic attack capability might be useful. They also argued against the air force's goal of maximum destruction and in favor of precision nuclear attacks on industrial and economic targets. Naval officers prepared draft war plans complete with maps showing that carriers operating in the Norwegian, Arabian, Mediterranean, and Yellow Seas could reach targets deep in the Soviet Union. Admiral Daniel Gallery, assistant commanding naval officer for guided missiles in 1947, argued that the navy could deliver nuclear weapons "more effectively than the Air Force can." Two years later, naval aviators lifted a P2V-3C Neptune off the deck of the USS *Coral Sea* and flew a four-thousand-mile mission that involved dropping a dummy bomb the size and weight of a standard nuclear weapon.[14]

By 1948 navy officials had developed an integrated plan for the design and construction of a new generation of very large flush-deck carriers to support the operation of relatively large and heavy attack

Consolidated RB-36D, with six turning and four burning engines

aircraft capable of delivering nuclear weapons within a combat radius of two thousand miles. The first of those ships, the USS *United States* (CVA-58), would displace eighty thousand tons, almost twice that of a standard World War II carrier. Three members of the Joint Chiefs of Staff approved the navy plan on May 26, 1948. Air Force Chief of Staff Hoyt Vandenberg refused, arguing that such an expenditure should be considered within the framework of a national plan for atomic war. Nevertheless, Congress appropriated the funds for the carrier that June, and President Truman authorized construction in July.

At the same time, Secretary Symington decided to fund improvements to transform the unsatisfactory XB-36 into a bomber that the air force could sell to the public and to Congress. The addition of four GE J-47 turbojets (developed to power the Boeing B-47) to the six reciprocating engines ("six turning and four burning") significantly increased performance. The hope that the aircraft could avoid interception by operating at forty thousand feet proved an important selling point. It was the first airplane capable of reaching probable targets from the continental United States. Until something better came along, the air force would take it into combat—against the navy, if not the Russians.

Secretary of Defense James Forrestal, a supporter of the USS *United States*, but not a political friend of the president, turned the Pentagon over to a new secretary, Louis A. Johnson, in March 1949, and shortly thereafter ended his life by leaping from a Bethesda, Maryland, hospital window. Johnson, a World War I veteran who had been a founder of the American Legion, assistant secretary of war from 1937 to 1940, and a director of Consolidated-Vultee/Convair since 1942, was an air force supporter.

Less than three weeks after taking office, the new secretary asked the Joint Chiefs of Staff for a new memorandum of advice on the matter of the supercarrier. This time, General Omar N. Bradley, the army chief of staff, reversed his earlier position and supported General Vandenberg. Secretary Johnson circulated a press release canceling work on the USS *United States* less than half an hour after receiving the memo. Secretary of the Navy John Sullivan resigned.

The air power campaign was in full swing. In the nuclear age, air force spokesmen pointed out, a single bomb could destroy a fleet as easily as a city. The notion of equality among the services was all well and good, General Vandenberg argued, as long as the air force, the nation's primary striking force, was seen as first among equals.

Eager for a hearing, navy officials circulated press reports underscoring the deficiencies of the B-36 and "irregularities" connected to its procurement. On June 9, 1949, Carl Vinson (D-Georgia), chairman of the House Armed Services Committee, announced hearings on the B-36. After one round of hearings, the committee announced the B-36 as the best airplane available and reported no evidence of fraud or corruption in its acquisition.

Running against the political tide, senior naval officers testifying at a second round of hearings continued to attack the air force in general and the B-36 in particular. Reacting to this "revolt of the admirals," Secretary Johnson and the new secretary of the navy, who were attempting to calm the waters, insisted on the resignation of Adm. Louis E. Denfield, chief of naval operations.

The navy lost the *United States*, but the future of naval aviation was not as dark as it seemed. Less than a year after the hearings, Communist troops invaded South Korea. Once again in combat, carriers demonstrated their value beyond any question. At the end of the century, the aircraft carrier remained a standard means of projecting American power to trouble spots around the globe.

The B-36 Peacemaker, conceived before Pearl Harbor, was obsolete when it entered service in 1948. The air force had bent the truth in an effort to sell the monster plane to Congress and the public. Public relations officials did their best to talk Capt. Charles Yeager, their hero of the hour, into testifying that the B-36 was difficult to intercept. He refused.

For all of its faults, the Peacemaker was the only airplane in the world capable of carrying the big thermonuclear weapons of the era over intercontinental distances. Moreover, it was physically impressive to someone standing on the ground while it passed low overhead, with its 230-foot wingspan and six slightly-out-of-synch engines throbbing away. By 1953, some 238 of the airplanes served with the SAC until something better came along.

KOREA, 1950–1953

The ultimate strategic mission belonged to the air force, free and clear. Whatever their additional duties, the airmen were prepared to shower atomic bombs on the enemy. Hap Arnold, their wartime commander, taught that success lay in an alliance with the forces of research and industry. His heirs expected that approach to produce new generations of bombers that flew higher, faster, and farther. There would be a need for interceptors as well, airplanes stuffed with electronic gear that could find and destroy enemy bombers who dared to invade American air space. With their eyes firmly focused on nuclear missions, U.S. Air Force officials combined tactical aviation and air defense into the single Continental Air Command.

There was dissent. Lieutenant General Elwood R. "Pete" Quesada (1904–1993), the voice of experience on tactical aviation, had led the IX Tactical Air Command, providing air cover for American troops from the spring of 1944 until the end of the war, and was named head of the Third Air Force in 1946. He retired in 1951, in part because he believed that air force leadership had broken a 1945 promise to General Eisenhower that an independent air arm would put a high priority on close air support.[15]

THE KOREAN WAR struck like a thunderbolt when Communist troops poured across the thirty-eighth parallel early on the morning of June 25, 1950. A costly war of attrition, the fighting in Korea seemed to drag on forever, and set the pattern for half a century of regional conflict. It was not the war for which either the air force or the navy had prepared.

This was a ground war. The most important job of air power, from start to finish, entailed supporting the troops and striking key targets on the ground. As Pete Quesada warned, the air force was neither trained nor well equipped for that task. There had been no joint force exercises to hone the skills of pilots or air controllers. Most of the aircraft dedicated to the task during the initial phase of the war were veterans of World War II: F-51s, F4Us, B-26s. The B-29 served as the standard heavy bomber of the war. An oddball like the F-82 Twin Mustang played the role of a night fighter, along with the Northrop P-63 Black Widow, which was seeing duty in its second war. The F-80, the standard operational air force fighter in 1950, had short legs, was not well suited to low-level attacks, and was outclassed when the swept-wing MiG-15 appeared on the scene. The F-84, the workhorse ground-attack aircraft for the air force, had a difficult time operating without air cover.

Following the demise of the USS *United States* and the debacle of the revolt of the admirals, Korea marked a positive turning point for naval aviation. Rear Admiral Forrest P. Sherman, who followed Admiral Denfield as chief of naval operations, began to turn things around. He won substantial budget increases for fleet modernization, argued for a nuclear submarine, and incredibly, won approval for a new class of aircraft carrier, the first of which, appropriately enough, would be called the USS *Forrestal* (CVA-59).

When the Korean War began, naval aviation was a force in transition. World War II veterans like the F4U were giving way to newer attack aircraft, including the heavy-weight Lockheed P2V-3C Neptune and North American AJ-1 Savage, both of which could carry nuclear weapons. The jets were coming aboard as well. The Grumman F9F-2 Panther, the McDonnell F2H-1 Banshee, and the Douglas AD Skyraider, with its reciprocating engine, would see the most active service as ground-attack aircraft.

If the war underscored shortcomings in the way in which the U.S. Air Force had conceptualized its mission, it inaugurated a new and very positive era for naval aviation. During the Second World War, the aircraft carrier served as an instrument of sea power, a weapon that enabled the navy to reach over the horizon to attack an enemy fleet. Korea would demonstrate the importance of the carrier as a floating airfield that could carry U.S. air power into areas where land bases were not available. During the Korean War a single carrier, the USS *Princeton*, delivered 26,402 tons of ordnance in combat, almost half of the total tonnage (57,154 tons) delivered by all naval aviators during World War II.[16]

The novelist can sometimes capture the essential truth of a time and place more effectively than the historian. No book offers a clearer vision of the air war over Korea than James Michener's *The Bridges at Toko-Ri*.[17] This tale of a retread World War II carrier pilot who dies in a muddy Korean ditch captures the experience of the brave men who came in low against well-defended targets on the ground, and the air rescue helicopter crews who did their best to pull them out of danger.

What James Michener did for naval aviation, James Salter did for the men who jousted in "MiG Alley." In his novel *The Hunters*, Salter, who had flown the F-86 Sabre in Korea, offered readers a gritty and realistic portrait of the life of a fighter pilot who, like James Michener's hero, would not be coming home.

LIKE THE SPITFIRE and the Bf 109, spinning delicate contrails over the English countryside in the summer of 1940, the MiG and the Sabre are forever linked in our imaginations, chasing one another through the thin, cold air high over the Yalu River. Since 1915, the fighter pilot had been the ultimate military hero, the man who carried his nation's flag into solitary combat, where life or death depended on his senses and skills. Fighters would take on one another in the future, but the Korean war the last time that single-seat airplanes designed to do nothing more than shoot one another down with machine guns or cannons would go head to head in large numbers on a regular basis.

The North American F-86 Sabre took shape on the drawing boards late in World War II. The design began as a straight-wing jet fighter for the navy—the FJ-1 Fury. Captured German aerodynamic data, coupled with some NACA thinking on the matter, convinced the engineers at North American to design a swept wing and tail for the airplane. The result was one of the most stunning fighters ever to take to the sky.

George "Wheaties" Welch, a North American test pilot who had been one of the few U.S. airmen to score victories over the Japanese aircraft attacking Pearl Harbor, lifted the first F-86 off the runway at

Muroc for the first time on October 1, 1947. The North American crew shared the base with Bell Aircraft's X-1 team. Chuck Yeager was still two weeks from breaking the sound barrier. Welch and the F-86 team reminded their friends from Bell and the U.S. Air Force that the Sabre could take off from the ground, remain aloft for an extended period, exceed the speed of sound in a dive, and shoot down the enemy. Yeager actually took the X-1 off from a runway once, just to prove that he could do it.

The MiG-15, developed by the Soviet design bureau headed by Artem Mikoyan and Mikhail Gurevich, first flew on December 30, 1947, three months after the Sabre. With its swept wing and tail based on the same German aerodynamic data, the MiG was powered by a copy of the Rolls-Royce Nene. The Soviets had purchased the engines from Britain and copied them with the same attention to detail that had produced the Tu-4. Stubby in contrast to the lovely lines of the Sabre, the MiG nevertheless proved to be a worthy adversary.

The West first caught sight of the new fighter at a 1948 air show near Moscow. Its appearance in combat on November 1, 1950, however, came as a nasty surprise. After MiGs destroyed one B-29 and shot up another so badly that it crashed on landing, commanders halted

North American F-86A Sabre

unescorted bombing raids near the Yalu River. The MiG outclassed the straight-winged F-80, F-84, and F9F Panthers, although a few American pilots brought down some unwary and inexperienced Soviet pilots before the Sabres appeared on the scene in December.

Both the MiG and the Sabre had relatively short legs and sported less-than-adequate armament. The Sabre carried only machine guns. The MiG flew with two slow-firing cannons, perfect for shooting down B-29s but too slow for taking on a modern jet. Lighter than its adversary, the MiG had a better rate of climb and could turn inside anything in the sky above thirty-five thousand feet. The F-86 was faster, could barrel past a MiG in a dive, and had better low-altitude and high-speed performance.

Americans tend to forget that the leading aces of the Korean War were Soviet pilots. Nikolaj Sutyagin scored twenty-one victories in Korea. Polkovnik Pepelyev, commander of the 196th Fighter Air Regiment in Korea, shot down nineteen allied aircraft, including four-teen Sabres.[18]

Nevertheless, the Americans had the overall advantage. The U.S. Air Force lost seventy-eight Sabres in aerial combat. The Soviets, who flew the MiGs almost exclusively until the spring of 1953, admitted to the loss of 345 aircraft in air-to-air action. The actual total of downed MiGs may be close to 380, for a Sabre-to-MiG victory ratio of 4.8 to 1.[19]

The biggest single difference seems to have been the experience of the pilots. The Soviets saw Korea as an opportunity to provide the maximum number of pilots with combat experience. Shorter periods of time in action and rotation by unit, rather than by individual, made it difficult to share valuable experience with new arrivals. Moreover, the fear that a Soviet pilot might be captured kept the MiGs north of the Yalu River.

To a greater extent than in World War I or II, U.S. Air Force lead-ers in Korea sought to identify "tigers" and put them in a position to score. Only 4.8 percent of U.S. pilots in Korea became aces, but they accounted for 38 percent of all kills. Some high-scoring pilots, like Capt. James Jabara (15 victories), the first U.S. jet ace and the second-highest-scoring U.S. airman of the war, were veterans of World War II. Colonel Francis Gabreski, who had scored 28 kills in Europe, added another 6.5 enemy aircraft to his score in Korea. William Whisner, Bud Mahurin, and Glen Eagleston, also World War II aces, repeated their success in Korea. Not all of the aces were veteran pilots, however. Captain Joseph McConnell (16 kills), the top U.S. scorer, had been a navigator in World War II.[20]

Major (later Major General) Frederick C. "Boots" Blesse (10 victories) drew on his Korean experience to prepare a primer for novice pilots, an internal air force document entitled *No Guts, No Glory*. Blesse noted that "situational awareness" remained the key to success for the fighter pilot. The aviator who prevailed was the fellow who could visualize his own position and that of his friends and adversaries and grasp the energy state of the various airplanes and the maneuvers available to each.

THE KOREAN WAR gave naval aviation an opportunity to recover from the disasters of the immediate postwar period. The USS *Forrestal*, launched in December 1954, was the first of a new class of postwar carrier, three more of which would be completed by 1959. The new ship featured three important innovations borrowed from the British. The deck was angled, which allowed an aircraft that missed a wire on landing to add power and "go around," rather than run into aircraft parked on the end of the deck, as had occurred during a tragic incident off the coast of Korea. The old hydraulic catapult in use on the largest World War II carriers gave way to the much more powerful steam catapult, which could shoot the heavier jets into the air. Finally, a new landing system employing lights and mirrors proved far more effective with the heavier, faster aircraft coming into service.

The next major step came in 1961 with the installation of eight nuclear reactors aboard the USS *Enterprise* (CVN-65). Nuclear propulsion enabled the ship to steam for long periods of time without refueling, did away with smoke, and provided constant and unlimited steam for the catapults. The Nimitz-class carriers, the first of which (USS *Nimitz* [CVN-68]) was launched in 1972, required only two of the new and more powerful reactors. Costs, nevertheless, skyrocketed. The *Enterprise* had cost $450 million. Just a decade later, the cost of the

Nimitz jumped to $1,881 million. Personnel costs also soared, as the crew and air group of the *Nimitz* totaled 5,758 people![21]

PEACE IS OUR PROFESSION

Ignoring the lessons of the Korea War, the U.S. Air Force continued to focus on the strategic nuclear mission. The search began for a long-range bomber to replace the B-36. The first generation of U.S. jet bombers (the Douglas XB-43, Convair XB-46, Martin XB-48, and the Northrop YB-49) left much to be desired. The North American B-45, the first U.S. jet bomber to enter production, looked like a World War II medium bomber fitted with a bubble canopy and jet engines. The Boeing XB-47 medium bomber, first flown on December 17, 1947, was quite another matter.

The design of the B-47, the foundation for half a century of pros-

Boeing B-47 Stratojet

perity at Boeing, benefitted from German aerodynamic data and the company's new wind tunnel. It was a collaborative effort of the legendary Ed Wells (of B-17 and B-29 fame) and younger colleagues, including George Schairer, George Martin, and Robert Jewett. The new airplane, with its clean lines and pod-mounted engines slung beneath thin, radically swept wings, inspired a generation of military and civil aircraft.

The difficulty of refueling the B-47, with its high stall speed, from the lumbering, propeller-driven Boeing KC-97 tanker led to the Boeing KC-135 jet tanker and Boeing 707 jetliner. The remarkably low-drag characteristics of the B-47 suggested the possibility of a heavy bomber with more powerful engines suspended beneath a clean swept wing.

The air force had requested proposals for a next-generation heavy bomber in the spring of 1946, even before the B-36 had flown. Eager to recapture the niche that it had filled with the B-17, B-29, and B-50, Boeing proposed a conventional aircraft powered by turboprop engines. Wells, Schairer, and several colleagues flew to Dayton in October 1948 to discuss their evolving design. Wright Field's Col. Henry E. "Pete" Warden suggested that they take a bigger step into the future and consider using the powerful new Pratt & Whitney J-57 turbojet.

The engineers went to work that weekend at Dayton's Van Cleve Hotel, placing a good many long-distance calls to Seattle. They returned to Warden's office the next week, armed with three-view drawings, rough performance figures, and a hand-carved wooden model of what would become the B-52 Stratofortress. Warden was suitably impressed.

Lieutenant Colonel Guy Townsend, the Wright Field engineer-pilot who shepherded both the B-47 and B-52 through development and testing, and Alvin M. "Tex" Johnson, who had flown the X-1 for Lawrence Bell before signing on as Boeing's chief test pilot, flew the YB-52 from Seattle to the company test facility at Moses Lake, Washington, on April 15, 1952. A total of 744 aircraft, models A through H, were produced by the time the last B-52 was delivered to the U.S. Air Force on October 26, 1962.

Fifty years after that first flight, the B-52 remains the standard heavy bomber of the U.S. Air Force. No other airplane, civil or military, has maintained its position as the very best of its kind for so long a period, and its career is far from over. If the air force's estimates are correct, the B-52 will still be flying as a frontline bomber in the year 2045. At that point, some of the airplanes will be an astonishing *ninety-one years old*!

Of course, these B-52s are not the same airplanes that rolled out of the factory in the 1950s and 1960s. They have new engines and updated structural elements. If the outside of the B-52 looks much the same, the inside is constantly evolving as old pieces of electronic equipment are replaced by new black boxes. Even so, what other land, sea, or air vehicle remains the best of its kind for nine decades?

Officially, it is called the Stratofortress. For decades, however, the

Boeing B-52 Stratofortress

crews referred to it as the "BUFF," the "Big Ugly Fat Fellow," at least in polite company. It requires a crew of five or six, has a wingspan of 185 feet, and can carry seventy thousand pounds of ordinance on unrefueled flights of up to 8,800 miles. It travels at speeds of 650 mph (Mach 0.85) nine miles (50,000 feet) up in the sky. The B-52 not only is the primary nuclear bomber in the air force's inventory, but also served as a conventional bomber in Vietnam, Iraq, and Afghanistan. As it flies on during the twenty-first century, it deserves to be recognized as the most successful design in the history of military aviation.

ONLY TWO OTHER nations developed long-range strategic bombers following the Second World War. Great Britain produced the twin-engine English Electric Canbera, a tactical bomber and reconnaissance aircraft that served the Commonwealth Air Forces with distinction. As the Martin B-57, it was a favorite with the U.S. Air Force through Vietnam. The British also developed three nuclear bombers. The Vickers Valiant and Handley Page Victor were high-speed, high-altitude bombers in a class with the B-47. The larger and more versatile Avro Vulcan, a graceful delta-wing plane with flowing lines, remained in service through the Falklands War (1982). By the end of the century, Britain, the home of the Handley Page V/1400 and

A Soviet Bison-C with a McDonnell F-4 Phantom II off the wing tip, 1964

the Lancaster, no longer had a strategic bomber in the air.

The earliest Soviet jet bombers roughly mirrored their American counterparts. The classic Cold War intermediate- and long-range bombers—swept-wing, turboprop- and turbojet-powered airplanes like the Tu-14 Bison, Tu-16 Badger, and the Tu-95H, a contemporary of the B-52—not only were capable of delivering nuclear weapons but also saw duty as long-range reconnaissance, maritime patrol, antisubmarine, electronic surveillance, and command-and-control aircraft.

IN TRUTH, by 1955, no bomber in the world could touch the B-52. Its longevity was totally unintended. Air force planners assumed that it would be replaced by new generations of bombers flying so high and fast that enemy interceptors would be unable to stop them. Establishing future requirements and assisting contractors to meet them was now the job of the Air Research and Development Command (ARDC), established at Wright-Patterson Air Force Base in the spring of 1951.

North American B-58 Hustler

That fall, eager to push the limits of technology, the leaders of ARDC asked for a next-generation B-47, a small bomber with a range of twenty-three hundred miles and the ability both to fly low-altitude subsonic missions and to make high-altitude supersonic dashes into the target. Three years later, in October 1954, they asked for a B-52 replacement with a seven-thousand-mile range and a speed of Mach 2 over the target. Five months later, they split that requirement in two, asking for one aircraft that would be powered by kerosene and another propelled by both jets and a nuclear power plant. The latter would loiter aloft for days on nuclear power, then make a jet-propelled dash into the target.

The response to the first request, the Convair B-58 Hustler, first flown in November 1956, was a radical wasp-waisted delta-wing craft that carried a nuclear weapon and virtually all of its fuel in a large external pod. Resembling its little brother, the Convair F-102 delta-wing fighter, the Hustler required two huge air-conditioning units to cool the vacuum tube–era electronics that were jam packed into the airframe. The structure of the B-58 demonstrated what could be achieved with new materials and innovative design.

A very impressive airplane, the Hustler broke twelve world speed records and won the Bendix, Harmon, Thompson, and Blériot Trophies. Twice it won the McKay Trophy for air force achievement.

None of that had come cheap. The Hustler cost three times as much as a B-52. In a State of the Union address on January 9, 1959, President Eisenhower noted that the B-58 literally cost its weight in gold.[22] The airplane may have fulfilled a pilot's dream, but it was a maintenance nightmare. Moreover, while it had the high-end performance required of it, it lacked versatility and performed poorly at lower speeds and altitudes. The airplane was far more popular with ARDC, which conceived it, than with the leadership of SAC, which flew it.

Even the enthusiasts admitted that the nuclear-powered bomber, the second request, was a distant dream, or nightmare. North American won what should have been the big prize, a contract for the XB-70 Valkyrie, the conventionally fueled replacement for the B-52. The B-70 looked as if it had just flown in from the future, with its twin

North American XB-70A Valkyrie

tails, a cockpit stretching out in front and above the aircraft, and the huge delta wing sitting on top of an enormous box housing six GE YJ-93 engines. The airplane flew in the fall of 1964 and achieved Mach 3 just a year later. An advanced aircraft, filled with the latest in electronic systems and built of stainless-steel honeycomb panels and titanium, the Valkyrie's price tag dwarfed that of the B-58.

The situation changed at 1:53 A.M. Washington time, on May 1, 1960, when Francis Gary Powers, a pilot flying a Lockheed U-2 reconnaissance aircraft for the Central Intelligence Agency (CIA) at sixty thousand feet over the Soviet city of Sverdlovsk, heard a dull thump, as an orange light filled the cockpit. He had been struck by an SA-2 Guideline antiaircraft missile. The Soviets had demonstrated their capacity to bring down the highest-flying airplanes in the American inventory.

Just as the antiaircraft missile threatened the high-flying, high-speed bomber, the intercontinental ballistic missile offered an entirely new approach to the delivery of nuclear weapons. Missiles flew much faster than airplanes, reducing the warning that an enemy would have of an attack from hours to minutes. Training was safe, simple, and cost little more than the time of the crews. Maintaining an air force full of experienced pilots, on the other hand, required constant flying, a dangerous and expensive activity.

Missiles were used only once, as the relatively fragile shell of the launch vehicle is discarded and the warhead dropped onto its target in a simple ablative shield. Such a vehicle cost much less than a B-70. As the weight of ever more powerful thermonuclear weapons decreased, and the power and reliability of the intercontinental ballistic missile increased, land-based and submarine-launched missiles inherited the ultimate strategic role.

THE U.S. AIR FORCE purchased 116 B-58 Hustlers. In 1965, only three years after the last airplane was delivered, Secretary of Defense Robert McNamara announced that the B-58 would be phased out of service by 1970. Only two XB-70s, which had a huge radar signature, were built. One B-70 was destroyed in a June 1966 midair collision. The other gathered information on the behavior of large supersonic aircraft before being retired to the U.S. Air Force Museum at Dayton, Ohio.

Still, the search for a bomber to replace the B-52 continued. Two days after McNamara ended the B-58 program, he announced that SAC would purchase 263 FB-111s, the bomber version of a multipurpose joint-service aircraft that comprised the centerpiece of the secretary's scheme to realize savings in weapons acquisition.

The navy and air force had enjoyed some success operating variants of the same aircraft: the North American B-66/AJ3, for example, and the McDonnell Douglas F4, the leading U.S. Navy and U.S. Air Force fighter bomber during the Vietnam era. Now McNamara rejected a navy proposal for a new fighter and persuaded the U.S. Air Force to cut production of the Republic F-105 short so that both could participate in a fixed-price-contract acquisition of a multipurpose fighter bomber, the Tactical Fighter Experimental (TFX). Such a contract specified a total cost, which included a negotiated profit. The contractor who came in under budget or inside the deadline earned a bonus.

In the fall of 1962, Secretary McNamara awarded the contract for the TFX, now the F-111, to General Dynamics. The airplane, featuring a variably swept wing, was designed to have an air-to-air capability, as well as the ability to deliver either conventional or nuclear bombs on enemy targets. The navy version, hopelessly overweight and far too complicated for carrier service, was never built. The U.S. Air Force F-111A faced design problems that prevented it from entering service until 1967. Over the next two decades, thanks to refueling, F-111Fs and EF-111s proved themselves in combat, from long-range bombing attacks on Libya (1986) to participation in Desert Storm (1990). The B-52, however, remained the air force's primary heavy bomber.

Another candidate, the Rockwell B-1, proved as controversial as the B-36. Originally intended to reach Mach 2 at high altitude and 600 mph on ground-hugging low-level missions, the B-1A suffered from cost cutting that trimmed critical performance. President Jimmy Carter canceled the B-1A in 1977.

The Reagan administration brought the project back to life in the fall of 1981, when the U.S. Air Force placed an order for one hundred of the redesigned and now almost entirely subsonic Rockwell B-1Bs. The plan called for the B-52 to remain in service as an airborne launch platform for cruise missiles, while the new airplane would come in low under Soviet radar. The continued success of the B-52, difficulties with the complex electronics of the B-1B, and the advent of an entirely new technology limited the role of the B-1B to that of an aircraft supplementing older and newer bombers.

SHOOTING WARS, 1953–1971

The air force's emphasis on its ability to mount an intercontinental nuclear strike blinded some leaders to the practical lessons of the Korean War. Historian Richard Hallion notes that the Tactical Air Command (TAC) was "SACumcized" as early as 1957, when it sought to participate in the all-important nuclear mission. Two years later, General LeMay suggested folding the two units into a single Air Offensive Command, with long-range strategic aviation very much the senior party.[23]

The Century Series of aircraft dominated the post-Korean air force: the F-100, F-101, F-102, F-104, F-105, and F-106. Of these, only the F-100 and F-105 offered the sort of multirole performance that the great World War II fighters—the P-47, P-51, and F4U—had provided. The rest were designed to intercept enemy bombers at high altitudes and supersonic speeds. From the F-102 on, most of them were wasp-waisted members of the area-rule generation. Powered by new generations of jet engines, they sported advanced electronics, complete with onboard computers to enhance stability and ever more sophisticated search radars.

A new generation of aircraft operated from the angled decks of the U.S. Navy's new carriers. The Douglas AD (A-1) Skyraider flew for the first time six months before the end of World War II. It must have seemed that the big propeller-driven "Able Dog" would have a short service life in a jet-propelled navy. In fact, the last "Spad," as the design was affectionately known, did not leave squadron service until the end of 1971.

Powered by the Wright R-3350 Cyclone, one of the ultimate piston engines, the Skyraider could barrel in low to avoid radar detection and strike targets on the ground. It was considered for roles ranging from nuclear attack, using a hair-raising over-the-shoulder "bomb-tossing" technique, to the transportation of cargo and personnel. The AD/A-5 version could carry twelve passengers, four stretchers, or two thousand pounds of cargo. The navy had also acquired jet-propelled ground-attack aircraft ranging from the small Douglas A4D (A-4) Skyhawk ("Heinemann's Hotrod") to the Grumman A-6 Intruder, first flown in 1960, and all of its variants.

The inability of navy fighters to hold their own against the MiG-15 resulted in the creation of two of the finest multirole supersonic fighters of the Vietnam era. The Vought F8U Crusader first flew in 1955, five years before the McDonnell F-4 Phantom II. The first navy aircraft capable of sustained supersonic flight, the Crusader was sometimes referred to as the last gunfighter. The Phantom II was intended to be armed with air-to-air missiles.

◆   ◆   ◆

THE ARRIVAL OF supersonic fighters seemed to signal the end of an era in aircraft armament. During a high-speed firing test with the Grumman F11F Tiger, cannon shells sucked into the engine caused a flameout and a forced landing. The day when an airplane would out-run its own bullets and shoot itself down seemed to be just around the corner. In any case, the appearance of lightweight, transistorized search radars capable of seeing over the horizon suggested the need for an air-to-air weapon that could hit targets far beyond the range of machine guns or cannons.

Unguided high-velocity aircraft rockets (HVARs) were used against ground targets in both Europe and the Pacific. First-generation postwar jet interceptors often used radar to bring them close to a target, where they functioned as aerial shotguns, discharging a barrage of unguided air-to-air rockets in the direction of the enemy. The Northrop F-89D Scorpion was armed with 104 rockets mounted in wing-tip pods. The F-86D, the "Dog Sabre," could unload 24 Mighty Mouse folding fin rockets (FFARs) at an oncoming Soviet bomber.

At the far end of the scale lay the Douglas MB-1 Genie, an unguided air-to-air nuclear missile that could also be carried by the F-89. An intrepid interceptor pilot would unleash the Genie fairly close to its bomber target, then pull away in a sharp turn that might enable him to escape the subsequent blast. Understandably, there was only one live test of the missile.

By the mid-1950s, most officials viewed guided air-to-air rockets as the wave of the future. Missiles, it was generally assumed, would replace guns and cannons. William Burdett McLean, the head of the Aviation Ordnance Division at the Naval Ordnance Test Station, China Lake, California, began working on such a weapon in 1946. Onboard radar systems were very large and heavy, while contemporary infrared detectors designed to sense heat emissions were the size of a dime. McLean set out to develop a heat-seeking missile.

Others opted for larger and more complicated radar-guided missiles that could track a target through clouds that might blind a heat-seeker. Hughes Aircraft, for example, established the Electronics and Guided Missile Department in 1949, under the leadership of Simon Ramo and Dean Wooldridge. In 1956, the Hughes GAR-1D Falcon (later the AIM) became the first guided air-to-air missile to enter operational service. Ramo and Wooldridge formed their own company (which became TRW) in 1953.

The U.S. Navy Bureau of Aeronautics had contracted with the Sperry Company for a radar-guided missile in 1947. In spite of continuing technical problems, the resulting Sparrow II missile was introduced to fleet aircraft in 1952–1954. Raytheon continued to develop improved radar systems that would be employed in the Sparrow III (AIM-7).

It was Bill McLean's little heat-seeker that would triumph, however. The engineer met and mastered the technical problems, all the while keeping costs down. By the end of 1953, his Sidewinder (AIM-9) was regularly knocking drones out of the sky. In 1955, the air force requested a "fly-off" competition between the Falcon and Sidewinder. McLean's rocket not only hit the targets consistently but proved much more rugged, maintenance free, and less temperamental than the complicated, radar-guided Falcon.[24]

Nationalist Chinese pilots flying F-86Ds armed with Sidewinders initiated a new era in aerial combat in the fall of 1958, when they downed four Communist Chinese MiGs during a single confrontation. Improved versions of the Sidewinder and Sparrow remained in service for decades. By the 1980s, however, new systems, notably the Hughes AIM-120 Advanced Medium-Range Air-to-Air Missile (AMRAAM), had arrived on the scene. The new missile received its baptism of fire in December 1992, when an F-16 pilot downed a MiG-25 over southern Iraq with an AIM-120.

DURING THE YEARS after Korea, air forces around the world equipped themselves with the products of American industry. The Lockheed F-104 sold well from Germany to Japan. The Douglas A4D (A-4) Skyhawk, a light attack bomber served the navy and marines as well as the armed forces of Argentina, Australia, Israel, Kuwait, Singapore, Indonesia, Malaysia, and New Zealand. Israeli A-4s played a critical role in the Yom Kippur War of 1973, striking targets in the Sinai and the Golan Heights and even chalking up a few aerial victories.

Skyhawks were still in service with several air forces at the end of the century.

America did not dominate the market for military aircraft to the extent that it did for large commercial airliners, however. A nation as pacific as Sweden, with its small population and limited defense budget, equipped its own air force with the Mach 2 Saab J35 Drakken (1954), sold the airplane to Austria, and continued to produce new generations of fighter bombers, including the J37 Viggin and JAS-39A Gripen, which could stand up to any adversary in the world. The British equipped the RAF and Royal Naval Air Force with the products of their own industry, and supplied other nations with De Havilland Vampires, Hawker Hunters, Gloster Javelins, and English Electric Lightnings.

Marcel Dassault was the most successful manufacturer of military aircraft in postwar Europe. The long line of versatile Dassault fighter bombers began with the MD450 Ouragan (1949), which saw active service with the air forces of both Israel and India. The next-generation Mystere IIC and IVA were marketed in the mid-1950s, followed by the Mirage series. Israel acquired the Mirage III, a very advanced aircraft, during the 1960s. Their success in the 1967 Six Day War was so impres-

Dassault Mystere IV

sive that Dassualt sold the Mirage to twenty foreign air forces.

These airplanes, and the generations of MiG-15s, -17s, -19s, -21s, -23s, -25s, and -27s that the Soviets supplied to their client states, participated in the long series of regional conflicts that followed the Korean War. In the colonial wars of the 1950s, from Indochina to Malaya, Kenya, and Algeria, geography and other factors placed distinct limits on the application of air power. There were innovations, however, including the use of helicopter gunships in Algeria.

Air combat played a larger role in the Arab-Israeli conflicts of the past half-century. During the Suez Crisis of 1956, Israeli pilots flying Oragans and Vampires, downed six Egyptian MiG-15s. At the beginning of the 1967 Six Day War, the badly outnumbered Israeli Air Force seized the initiative at the outset, destroying over 450 Egyptian and Syrian aircraft on the ground. During the fourteen-month War of Attrition from 1969 to 1970, Israeli pilots flying the A-4 Skyhawk, F-4 Phantom II, and Mirage took on the MiG-21E. For the first time, Egyptian surface-to-air missiles played a considerable role, forcing air leaders around the globe to rethink plans for high-speed penetrating nuclear bombers that would sweep into their targets in spite of any countermeasures.

The India-Pakistan border was another hot spot that burst into occasional flame. Twice, in 1965 and again in 1971, a mix of American, European, Soviet, and even Chinese aircraft met in combat over the desolate border region that remained very much in dispute at the end of the century.

VIETNAM, 1965–1973

French attempts to reestablish control over Indochina after 1945 met strenuous resistance from the Communist Viet Minh guerilla force, led by Ho Chi Minh, who had been struggling for national independence since 1919. In spite of massive American assistance, estimated at one-third the equipment employed in the conflict, the French could not restore order. By 1952, as the Korean War wound down, the U.S. Far East Air Forces increased the level of support, flying cargo into the combat zone and providing transports, bombers, and maintenance and logistical detachments to the French.

The possibility of B-29 attacks or naval air strikes from carriers in support of the Foreign Legionnaires clinging to the besieged garrison at Dien Bien Phu was considered and rejected. In the face of U.S. opposition, the French signed the Geneva Accords in July 1954, dividing Vietnam into a northern region under the control of Ho Chi Minh and a southern area led by Ngo Dinh Diem. The hope that the nation would be united within two years on the basis of democratic elections proved futile.

America returned to Southeast Asia in 1961, when the army and air force sent advisors to assist the government of South Vietnam. The last U.S. serviceman left Vietnam on March 28, 1973. It was America's longest war and, with the exception of the Civil War, our most divisive. It cut short a presidency that had brought social justice to millions, sent hundreds of thousands of people into the street in protest, and inaugurated an era during which millions of Americans would lose faith in their government. The lessons of the war in Southeast Asia, understood or misunderstood, became the benchmark against which future American decisions to intervene would be measured. Would this lead to another Vietnam? How would the public respond? Would the level of casualties rival those suffered in Southeast Asia?

From the mid-1950s, Army Chief of Staff Maxwell D. Taylor had advocated a "new look" for the American defense establishment. Preparations for the conventional regional conflicts that had marked the postwar era, he argued, should receive as much support as strategic nuclear forces. The air force resisted the policy, confident that no third-world guerilla force could stand up to vastly superior technology. There would be a cruel awakening in the rice paddies and jungles of Vietnam.

FROM THE OUTSET, Americans applied treasure and technology to the problem. It was the American way of war. As early as 1961–1962, while the North Vietnamese walked into battle, the United States flew their South Vietnamese allies into action aboard helicopters. If the enemy hid in the jungle, we would launch a defoliation campaign, using Agent Orange and other toxic chemicals to remove the foliage.

Eager to devastate relatively small areas, the air force sent AC-47 gunships into action for the first time in December 1964. Known as Puff, Spooky, or the dragon ship, each of these aircraft was equipped with three GE 7.62-millimeter "Gatling guns," each of which fired six thousand rounds a minute. Three years later, the first of twenty-eight AC-130 gunships was combat tested in South Vietnam. Then came the army with its helicopter gunships.

Political leaders in Washington employed strategic bombing, not to destroy the enemy's industry and resolve, but as a tool to force the North Vietnamese to the bargaining table. Rolling Thunder, the first systematic bombing campaign of the war, began in March 1965 with attacks on the demilitarized zone separating North and South Vietnam. From the beginning to the end, targets were carefully selected to avoid antagonizing the Chinese or Soviets. Because of the need for precision, U.S. Air Force and Navy fighter bombers—the F-105 Thunderchief, F-4 Phantom II, F-8U Crusader, and A-6 Intruder—carried out the attacks. The only heavy bomber in the theater, the B-52, initially supported tactical operations in the south, dropping tons of bombs on supply lines and targets hidden beneath the jungle canopy.

President Lyndon B. Johnson ordered bombing halts in May and December 1965. Paradoxically, in view of the intent of the bombing, the halts were also designed to bring the North Vietnamese to peace talks. When they did not respond, the bombing proceeded. By 1966–1967, the attacks included key targets around the North Vietnamese capital of Hanoi. As the campaign moved north, American losses grew. The first loss to a Soviet-built surface-to-air-missile (SAM) came in July 1965. The detection and destruction of SAM sites had a high priority for the rest of the war.

By the fall of 1966, the North Vietnamese regularly sent MiG-21s, armed with heat-seeking Atoll missiles, up to do battle with the American attackers. Before 1972, the American victory-to-loss ratio for aerial combat was only 2.45 to 1 (U.S. Air Force, 2.15; U.S. Navy, 2.75), much less than the ratio achieved in Korea. Air force pilots were credited with a total of 136 aerial victories during the Vietnam War. The Sparrow III, the standard weapon for the F-4, accounted for 49 of those kills, almost 37 percent of the total; guns and Sparrows, for 2 additional victories; guns alone, for 37 aircraft; Sidewinders, which had a much better reputation with pilots than the Sparrow, for 35 victories. The Falcon was credited with only 5 kills.[25]

Only two U.S. pilots, Randall Cunningham (U.S. Navy, 5 victories) and Steve Ritchie (U.S. Air Force, 5 victories), emerged as aces. Because of the importance of a rear-seat weapons officer in the F-4 Phantom, they were also credited with kills. Three back-seaters— Charles B. DeBellevue (U.S. Air Force, 6 victories), William Driscoll (U.S. Navy, 5 victories), and Jeffery Feinstein (U.S. Air Force, 6 victories)—qualified as aces. Robin Olds (U.S. Air Force), one of the best-known fighter pilots of the war, added 4 victories to the twelve kills that he had piled up in World War II. North Vietnam boasted two aces: Nguyen Dinh Ton (14 victories) and Nguyen Van Coc (9 victories).

On October 31, 1968, President Johnson ordered a bombing halt north of the twentieth parallel. With the exception of occasional attacks on specific SAM sites that had fired on U.S. reconnaissance aircraft, no more bombs would fall on North Vietnam for the next three and a half years. A North Vietnamese offensive in the spring of 1972 led President Richard M. Nixon to withdraw from ongoing peace talks and resume the bombing of North Vietnam in an operation known as Linebacker. Following a bombing halt in October to allow the North Vietnamese to reopen negotiations, Nixon ordered Linebacker II (December 18–29, 1972) into effect. In the heaviest bombing attacks of the war, B-52s and attack aircraft pounded targets in and around Hanoi and Haiphong. Eleven days later, the North Vietnamese agreed to return to the peace talks. A nine-point cease-fire agreement was signed in Paris on January 23, 1973.

NOT ALL OF the airmen who flew and fought in Southeast Asia went to war in high-performance jets. There were no braver men in that war than the crews who manned the helicopters of the U.S. Air Force's

Aerospace Rescue and Recovery Service. They risked and sometimes lost their lives while plucking downed airmen out of danger. It is worth noting that six of the thirteen Medals of Honor awarded to air force personnel during the Vietnam War went to crew members of search-and-rescue helicopters or to forward air controllers (FACs).

FACs flew light airplanes such as the Cessna O-1 and U-17. They served as a liaison between troops on the ground and the airmen who supported them, assisted in the rescue of downed airmen, performed close-in reconnaissance, and identified targets of opportunity. A special group of FACs, known as the Ravens, operated with Laotian forces opposing the incursion of North Vietnamese troops. Like their compatriots operating in Vietnam, the Ravens flew light aircraft for the most part, armed with nothing more than smoke rockets to mark targets. A few Ravens were fortunate enough to fly the T-28, the standard air force trainer, which was large and heavy enough to be armed with napalm, rockets, and light machine guns.

ACTS OF COURAGE and examples of pure heroism took place every day in Vietnam. That did not change the outcome of the conflict. In Korea, UN policy had succeeded in establishing a stable regime, capable, with assistance, of holding the Communists at bay on the thirty-eighth parallel. In Vietnam, complete Communist victory occurred in the immediate aftermath of American withdrawal. It was impossible to escape the fact that we had lost the war in Southeast Asia. As to what had gone wrong, there was no agreement.

Had Pentagon and White House control of the bombing campaigns and individual air strikes made victory impossible? Was the great care taken to avoid provoking China warranted? There can be no doubt that the air war in Vietnam was conducted on a tight leash. But those who argue that an unrestrained air campaign would have produced victory ignore the determination of the North Vietnamese.

They were an extraordinarily courageous and determined enemy, willing to fight the most powerful nation in the world with weapons ranging from sharp sticks to sophisticated Soviet aircraft and missile systems. The North Vietnamese had fought for their independence since the Japanese arrived in 1940. They had not simply worn the French down. They had defeated them. They were united in their purpose and would accept nothing other than victory or death.

In May 1964, Curtis LeMay suggested that we tell the North Vietnamese to "pull in their horns" or face the prospect of being "bombed back to the stone age." That is what it would have taken. The simple and fortunate truth remains that Americans were unwilling to visit that level of destruction on this enemy.

K.I.S.S.

The U.S. Air Force had largely ignored the lessons of Korea. Vietnam got their attention. The low victory ratio was a special concern. Early in 1968, the Naval Air Systems Command developed a special program to teach air combat maneuvering to F-4 pilots. The improvement was so stunning that the navy formalized the program in the Top Gun Fighter Weapons School at California's Miramar Naval Air Station in 1972.

The air force followed suit with its Red Flag aggressor program at the U.S. Air Force Fighter Weapons School, at Nellis Air Force Base near Las Vegas, Nevada. Instruction involved a mix of theory and practice. Classroom topics ranged from energy management in aerial maneuvering to the lessons provided by the fighter pilots of earlier generations. Once in the air, students at Top Gun and Red Flag faced instructors who flew lighter-weight aircraft that mimicked the characteristics of MiG and Sukhoi fighter planes. By the early 1980s, both the navy and the air force were home to a new generation of very confident and well-trained aerial warriors.[26]

IF THERE WAS ROOM for improvement in pilot training, the need for superior aircraft was even more obvious. A considerable shock reverberated through the air force in 1965, when a pair of obsolete MiG-17s downed two F-105 Thunderchiefs during a single mission. The Thunderchief scored only seven kills during the entire Southeast Asia war. It could handle ground-attack duties but had a tough time defending itself.

U.S. Air Force pilots scored 129 air-to-air victories with the F-4 Phantom. Even that airplane rubbed some pilots the wrong way, however. The legendary Col. Robin Olds talked about "turning off" the more distracting systems of his Phantom II as he approached a combat area. Even so, Olds, who had shot down twelve aircraft and destroyed another eleven on the ground during World War II, achieved only four missile kills in 152 combat missions during the Vietnam War. He missed several others either because he was too close or because of missile failures. "A fighter without a gun," he noted, "is like an airplane without a wing."[27]

Major John Boyd of the air force certainly agreed. A trained engineer, a veteran of aerial combat in Korea and Vietnam, and a Red Flag instructor with a legendary reputation, Boyd combined the mind of an engineer and the skills of an airman to develop the notion of "energy maneuverability" as a way of teaching air combat and comparing the suitability of various combat aircraft. Along with a small group of like-minded officers who constituted a "fighter mafia," Boyd lobbied effectively for the need to step away from multimission aircraft like the F-4 and F-105 and focus on developing a basic air superiority fighter.[28]

The Soviets unveiled some very advanced and versatile aircraft in 1967: the prototype MiG-23 Flogger, the variable-sweep Sukhoi-7 Fitter, and the MiG-25 Foxbat, capable of speed in excess of Mach 3. What next-generation aircraft would the United States send against such adversaries? Costs were skyrocketing. A World War I fighter cost some $5,000. By the 1970s, a top-of-the-line fighter had a price tag of over $20 million. At those prices, the military could no longer afford the luxury of investing in multiple designs to perform the same task, as had been the case during World War II. Moreover, a modern military airplane was expected to remain in service for decades. Clearly, procurement decisions had grown complex and critically important.[29]

The McDonnell Douglas F-15 Eagle, flown in 1972, represented a compromise between the desire of John Boyd and his colleagues for an air superiority fighter and the wisdom of program managers who demanded substantial versatility. The Eagle, powered by twin Pratt &

Whitney engines, could climb straight up. It had low wing loading and great maneuverability. Armed with rapid-firing Gatling guns, cannons, and missiles, it offered "heads-up" displays and systems that met a basic criterion of the "fighter mafia"—K.I.S.S., "keep it simple, stupid."

The F-15 scored most of the air force's aerial victories in the Gulf War and remained its most successful all-around fighter airplane at the end of the century. It was produced in a variety of specialized models, including two-seat aircraft and even a ground-attack version, the F-15 Strike Eagle. Relatively expensive, averaging $38 million a piece, it sold well to affluent foreign nations, including Japan, Saudi Arabia, and Israel.

While the fighter gurus took pride in the Eagle, they believed that flexibility meant rising costs, complexity, and increased weight. They still saw the need for a relatively simple, lightweight, air superiority fighter. Once again, air force planners moved in that direction. The result, the General Dynamics F-16A Fighting Falcon, first took to the air in December 1976. Like the F-15, wise project managers transformed the Falcon into something of a multirole aircraft. The price remained relatively low, however, averaging between $14 and $18 million by the end of the century.

General Dynamics produced the F-16 through an international consortium involving the United States, Belgium, Denmark, the Netherlands, and Norway. It was to be the NATO airplane. By the end of 2000, the U.S. Air Force had purchased 2,206 F-16s of all models. At the same time, the service was operating 1,100 F-15s of all variants, 713 Fairchild A-10 ground-attack aircraft, and 59 Lockheed F-117 Nighthawks.[30]

In addition, seventeen nations around the globe, from Bahrain to Venezuela, purchased a total of 1,797 F-16s. Into the new century, the F-16 was still being produced in several countries under the coproduction and joint-venture agreements that had been so important to the program from the outset.[31]

Grumman engineers and navy officials shared a vision of the next-generation carrier-based fighter as a very heavy, twin-engine, two-place air superiority machine, armed with both missiles and guns. The resulting swing-wing F-14 Tomcat, delivered to the navy in 1972, offered a remarkable performance and few causes for complaint, except for the sticker shock: $38 million each. Congress questioned the cost of replacing the F-4 Phantom and A-7 Corsair II force with F-14s. Over the objections of some in Naval Air Systems Command, officials decided to supplement a smaller F-14 with a lighter-weight multirole U.S. Navy–Marine Corps aircraft, the McDonnell Douglas F-18 Hornet.

The services also acquired specialized aircraft that would carry them to the end of the century. The air force's Fairchild A-10, designed to provide close ground support, was the product of the Alexander Kartveli and Republic Aviation team acquired by Fairchild. Far from the sleek and streamlined appearance of other single-seat aircraft, the A-10 was dubbed the Warthog.

THE EXPERIENCE in Vietnam had underscored the need for a U.S. Marine Corps aircraft that could operate from unimproved airstrips. Some saw the answer in a return to the vertical take-off and landing (VTOL) experiments of the 1950s. Convair (XFY-1), Lockheed (XFV-1), and Ryan (X-13) had produced a trio of aircraft that took off and landed sitting on their tails, but that were less than satisfactory. Bell (X-14) experimented with vectoring the thrust of jet engines. Both the French and the British tried their hands at VTOL designs.

Real success finally appeared with the Hawker 1127, which made its first vertical take-off in 1960. The prototype led to the FGA Mk. 1 Kestrel. When the hot jet thrust and cold bypass air were exhausted straight down through swiveling nozzles on the sides of the fuselage, the airplane rose straight into the air. When the Kestrel hovered, gas jets like those of a spacecraft provided control. As the nozzles swiveled to the rear, the airplane moved forward.

Pilots from the United States, Britain, and Germany flight-tested the Kestrel. The Harrier, as the production aircraft became known, entered squadron service with the RAF in July 1969. The Royal Navy developed special aircraft carriers, far less expensive than standard carriers, to operate Harriers.

Both the U.S. Air Force and Navy studied and rejected the Harrier, but the U.S. Marine Corps expressed an interest in the airplane even before it entered RAF service. In an arrangement typical of the final decades of the century, Hawker Siddeley (later British Aerospace), Rolls-Royce, and McDonnell Douglas began work on an improved version, the AV-8B Harrier II, which entered service with the RAF, U.S. Marine Corps, and the navies of Spain and Italy. It would see its share of combat, and then some.

SMART AND STEALTHY

One of the great turning points in the history of air warfare occurred on April 27, 1972, as four F-4s approached the Thanh Hoa Bridge over the Song Mai River, seventy miles south of Hanoi. Since 1966, American fighter bombers had launched 871 attacks on this target, losing eleven aircraft in the process. So far, the bridge had not been scratched. This morning would be different. As each airplane swept in to drop a Paveway I bomb, the back-seater in another aircraft "painted" the target with a laser beam. A sensor on the nose of the bomb locked onto the laser and guided the weapon to the target. When the smoke cleared, the bridge was gone.

Since the beginning of the air age, bombing accuracy had always been a major factor limiting the effective application of air power. A wartime British study revealed that only one-third of RAF bomber crews who reported hitting their targets had come within five miles of the aiming point. The circular error of probability (the radius around the target within which 50 percent of aimed bombs would land) for the vaunted Norden bombsight was over three miles. The horrific saturation bombing attacks of World War II primarily resulted from an inability to hit critically important targets with any precision. That failure produced the first attempts to create "smart" weapons that would be guided directly to their target by internal or external systems.

On May 12, 1943, an RAF bomber damaged the submarine U-456 with an Mk 24 acoustic homing torpedo. On September 9, 1943, a Dornier Do 217 sank the Italian battleship *Roma* with a radio-guided Fritz-X glide bomb. German fighters were experimentally armed with the wire-guided X-4 antiaircraft missile. USAAF crews destroyed fourteen bridges in the China-Burma-India theater using the VB-1 Azon radio-guided bomb. During the Korean War, B-29 crews knocked out fifteen hard-to-reach North Korean bridges using the VB-3 Razon version of the guided bomb. The AGM-62 Walleye II television-guided bomb, developed by Naval Weapons Center in China Lake, California, demonstrated promise when tested in Vietnam.

The modern effort began in 1964, when Martin Marietta engineers demonstrated to Col. Joe Davis Jr., an aerial veteran of World War II and the Korean War, that they could "paint" a moving target with a laser beam. Davis, a representative of the U.S. Air Force's ARDC, immediately recognized the value of the new technology for guiding a weapon onto a target. During the following months, the ARDC offered contracts to both Texas Instruments and North American Aviation for sensors and bolt-on tail fins that would transform a normal iron bomb into a precision guided weapon. Eight years later, the Thanh Hoa Bridge was destroyed. By the end of the war in 1975, U.S. forces had dropped twenty-eight thousand precision guided Paveways on Southeast Asian targets.[32]

Military planners saw precision munitions technology as a revolutionary alternative to the use of theater nuclear weapons. The Texas Instruments BOLT-117 was the first operational laser-guided bomb, while China Lake's AGM-83 Bulldog, the first laser-guided air-to-ground missile, led to later weapons like the AGM-114 Hellfire. The AGM-65 Maverick typified the infrared air-to-ground missiles available in the final decades of the century. Specialized smart weapons like the Texas Instruments AGM-88 HARM were designed to target ground radar sites.

The spectacular surface-to-surface and air-to-surface smart bombs and missiles derived from breakthroughs in electronics during the 1970s. Those breakthroughs also created a revolution in cruise missiles, winged flying bombs launched at a distance from their target. The earliest such weapons, like the German V-1, were launched in the general direction of the target and kept flying straight and level by gyroscopes. A preset timer sent the craft diving to earth when it had been aloft long enough to have carried it over the target.

Advances in electronics, from terrain-following radars to satellite navigation, made it possible to create cruise missiles capable of breathtaking accuracy. The Egyptians captured the world's attention in 1967 when they sank the Israeli destroyer *Eliat* with a Soviet Styx (SS-N-2C) missile. The United States countered with antiship weapons like the McDonnell Douglas AGM-84 Harpoon, which entered operational service in 1977. Other cruise missiles included the General Dynamics BGM-109 Tomahawk, a ship-launched weapon intended for use against land targets. B-52s began carrying the Boeing AGM-86B air-launched cruise missile in 1982. Most early cruise missile navigation systems compared terrain maps implanted in their computer memories with the results of terrain-following radar. Later missiles achieved genuine accuracy when researchers coupled inertial guidance systems, which employed gyroscopic sensors to keep track of current location, with the space-based global positioning system (GPS), which enabled a missile to check its position.

THE RISE OF precision guided weaponry was as important to the development of military aviation as the invention of the jet engine. When combined with another unexpected set of technologies that would enable an aircraft to evade detection by radar, the revolution became complete.

"The most valuable characteristic for air-to-air combat" Charles E. Myers Jr. opined, "is the degree of invisibility." Myers, a test pilot and air combat veteran, was the first to use the word *stealth* to describe an airplane that could avoid detection by radar or infrared detectors. He began to advocate the development of such a "surprise" machine in 1973, soon signing on with the Pentagon's Office of Defense Research and Engineering.[33]

The need for such a craft was obvious. The American experience in Vietnam had underscored the effectiveness of Soviet radar-guided SAMs. During Linebacker II (December 1972), the heaviest bombing campaign of the war, North Vietnamese fighters shot down two B-52s, while SAM crews downed eighteen aircraft, including fifteen B-52s.

In the first four days of the 1973 Egyptian war, Soviet SAMs brought down sixty Israeli aircraft, roughly 19 percent of the nation's prewar combat aircraft inventory. The situation became so serious that the Israeli army had to overrun SA-6 launch sites before obtaining air support. During nineteen days of combat, the Israelis lost 109 aircraft, 35 percent of their total air strength at the beginning of the war.[34]

SINCE THE LOSS of Francis Gary Powers in 1960, engineers had been attempting to reduce the radar signature of reconnaissance aircraft. The Lockheed A-12, a Mach 3 replacement for the U-2, was coated with radar-absorbing materials, featured structures that "trapped" radar signals, and burned a fuel designed to reduce infrared visibility. The lessons learned were applied to the design of the Lockheed SR-71 Blackbird, the ultimate reconnaissance airplane of the century, which had the radar signature of a Piper Cub.

Lockheed built fifteen single-seat A-12s; three YF-12s, a potential combat version; and thirty-one SR-71s. One of the great successes of American postwar aviation, the SR-71 was the highest-flying, fastest aircraft in the operational inventory of any nation. It provided decision makers at the highest level with up-to-the-minute imagery of trouble spots around the globe. Improvements in satellite reconnaissance led to the retirement of the SR-71 in 1995.

As stealthy as the SR-71 was, further reducing the radar image of an airplane became too complex a problem to be solved empirically. Russian mathematician Pyotr Ufimtsev launched a quiet revolution in 1966 when he published a technical paper entitled "Method of Edge Waves in the Physical Theory of Diffraction." Building on the work of the nineteenth-century Scottish physicist James Clerk Maxwell, Ufimtsev developed equations that could be used to calculate the radar signature of any design.

The calculations were so complex, however, that this approach remained impractical until the rise of a new generation of powerful computers. In any case, computer-operated fly-by-wire systems would be absolutely required to control the otherwise unflyable shapes that would be invisible to radar. Finally, ground-based and onboard computers capable of planning the optimum route to and from a target and operating the navigation, targeting, and other systems would be key to the success of a stealth airplane.

In 1975, Denys Overholser, a thirty-six-year-old radar specialist at Skunk Works, now officially known as the Lockheed Advanced Technology Division, read a copy of Ufimtsev's paper that had been translated and distributed by the air force. With the assistance of William Schroeder, a retired colleague who had been Kelly Johnson's authority on mathematical analysis, Overholser and his team developed a computer program, ECHO 1, that could predict the radar cross section of a given design. A model of the resulting optimum shape, a flat faceted object that engineers took to calling the "Hopeless Diamond," was tested in an indoor radar chamber. As other members of the preliminary design group entered the process, the elements of a test aircraft with the code name "Have Blue" took shape.

In the spring of 1966, the U.S. Air Force authorized Lockheed to build two experimental aircraft, the first of which flew on December 1, 1977. With a new contract in hand, Skunk Works set to work on the first operational Senior Trend aircraft, which would be designated the F-117. Operational units began to receive the aircraft in 1982.

Lockheed F-117

The F-117, the long-awaited "surprise" aircraft, could penetrate enemy air space without detection. Although designated a fighter, it was never intended to engage in combat with other aircraft. Rather, the "black jet" would deliver precision attacks on ground targets.

THE 1969 APPEARANCE of the Soviet Tu-22M Backfire, a bomber with a variable-sweep wing and an external resemblance to the B-1, helped to keep U.S. bomber development programs alive. In addition to the resurrection of the B-1 in the fall of 1981, President Ronald Reagan announced a contract with Northrop for an advanced technology bomber.

Cloaked in tight security during its development, the Northrop B-2 was unveiled on November 22, 1988, eight months before its first flight on July 17, 1989. A range of new technologies had converged to enable engineers to realize Jack Northrop's old dream of a flying wing. The Lockheed F-117 was a wedge, all planes and facets designed to reflect radar energy anywhere but back to the receiver. Northrop engineers, using more advanced programs, took a more sophisticated approach.

Just thirty years before, engineers had still been "lofting" the external lines of their airplanes in full scale, using special drawing instruments to create precise curves. Now they produced conic sections on the screens of computers, which could calculate the way in which sweeping, graceful curves would reflect radar signals. The B-2 is an airplane without a seam, crease, or angle. One curve blends imperceptibly into another. The result is something that looks more like a piece of modern sculpture than an airplane designed to carry destruction to an enemy.

The B-2 program was controversial. Its price tag, $2.2 billion a copy, put all other expensive military aircraft programs in perspective. Moreover, the airplane required 24.6 hours of maintenance for every hour of flight time. During the Kosovo campaign (1999–2000) much was made of the fact that B-2s took off from bases in the United States, flew their missions in the Balkans, and returned home without landing. In fact, there had been little choice. The airplanes have to be kept in climate-controlled hangars to preserve the radar-absorbing coating on the leading edges of the wings.

The impressive B-2 can carry up to sixteen nuclear weapons or a very large load of conventional armament for distances up to six thousand miles without refueling. It played a role in the Balkans and in Afghanistan. At the same time, it has not become the backbone of the U.S. Air Force strike force. The age of the long-range strategic bomber is actually over. Ground-based and submarine-launched intercontinental ballistic missiles and advanced cruise missiles are the primary carriers of nuclear weapons.

FIN DE SIÈCLE

Most Americans watched the tragedy of Vietnam unfold on the evening news. They watched Desert Storm live on the Cable News Network (CNN). Correspondents began breaking into the regular programming just before 7 P.M. on the evening of January 16, 1991. The early reports did little more than describe the incredible show of antiaircraft fire over Baghdad. Then, suddenly, the voice of the newsmen vanished, replaced by static. A cheer went up in the Pentagon and in American headquarters in Saudi Arabia. The loss of signal was unmistakable proof that an F-117 had hit its target, a major communications center through which all telephone traffic was routed. Baghdad, literally and figuratively, was off the air.

Immediately after taking office as president of Iraq in 1979, Saddam Hussein demonstrated his penchant for destabilizing the region. He attacked his neighbor, Iran. What was intended to be a short war lasted for eight years and took tens of thousands of lives in both nations. Following the cease-fire, the Iraqi leader sought to raise oil prices to speed recovery. In August 1990, when Kuwait refused to cooperate, Saddam Hussein invaded. The United Nations authorized military action. The first Bush administration instituted economic sanctions, dispatched troops to Saudi Arabia, and persuaded twenty-six nations to join a military coalition against Iraq.

The Vietnam experience had left ground commanders with doubts as to the ability of air power to shape a campaign. "Colin Powell and I understood very early on that a strategic bombing campaign in and of itself had never won a war and had never forced anyone to do anything if they wanted to sit it out," Gen. Norman Schwarzkopf explained.[35]

Colonel John A. Warden III, the chief planner of the Desert Storm air campaign, changed their mind. While a student at the National War College, Warden had focused on the nature and structure of air war. Air power, he argued, could strike every level of society simultaneously. He briefed General Schwarzkopf on the air plan in August 1990. The airmen would begin with precision strikes at the center, knocking out command-and-control centers, military headquarters, and communication and power networks. Exercising absolute air control, they would then strike the Iraqi army in the field, picking the enemy military machine apart. Schwarzkopf was impressed, as were Gen. Colin Powell and Pentagon officials. The airmen would have the opportunity to show what they could do.

The hammer fell on the night of January 18, 1991. B-52s, their bellies full of iron bombs, flew nonstop from Louisiana, England, and Diego Garcia, off the African coast. One hundred and sixty tankers hovered in the air that night, on station outside the range of Iraqi radar. Eight AGM-86B U.S. Air Force cruise missiles, their nuclear tips replaced with high-explosive warheads, were targeted to strike key communications and electrical power centers. One hundred and six Tomahawk cruise missiles started toward their targets before dawn.

F-117 Nighthawks, laser-guided bombs safely stowed in their bomb bays, headed for downtown Baghdad. Because of the heavy concentration of antiaircraft fire, the cruise missiles and the black jets would have the heart of the city all to themselves. Elsewhere, F-14s, F-15Es, F-16s, F-18s, EF-111s, F4-G Wild Weasels, A6-E Intruders, Tornadoes, Jaguars, and Apache helicopters, 668 airplanes in all, were striking the carefully selected targets assigned to them.[36]

And so it went for the forty-three days of the Gulf War. The combined orders describing the missions to be flown on any one day equaled the size of a city telephone directory. The airmen dropped 88,500 tons of ordnance. The air force alone delivered 69 percent of that total, dropping a monthly average of 40,416 tons on Iraq and occupied Kuwait, fully 85 percent of the monthly average that the service had dropped *worldwide* during World War II.

The air operations came with a price tag. The coalition lost 39 aircraft, 16 in the first three days of combat. Especially at high risk were the airmen who provided close air support for ground forces and flew low-level missions. They could neither take advantage of stealth technology nor deliver death from a distance. The RAF and Royal Saudi Air Force lost 9 Tornadoes; the U.S. Air Force, 7 A-10As and an OV-10; and the U.S. Navy and Marine Corps, 3 Harriers and an OV-10— all close to the ground.

For the millions who watched the grainy footage of smart weapons registering one direct hit after another on Iraqi targets, precision seemed to be the rule in Desert Storm, but the situation was not that clear-cut. Fully one-third of the aerial weapons used during Desert Storm were iron bombs dropped from forty-year-old B-52s on Iraqi armored divisions. Precision weapons accounted for less than 9 percent of the total. They are estimated to have caused 75 percent of the damage to Iraqi strategic targets, however.

Still, some of the wonder weapons proved more than a little disappointing. The Navy launched 307 Tomahawk cruise missiles ($1.3 million each) during the early days of the war. The Defense Intelligence Agency estimated that only half of those hit their targets. Without GPS, the terrain-following systems of the early missiles became confused by the featureless Iraqi landscape. It was, one defense official remarked, "a fiasco."[37]

Nevertheless, the air campaign had clearly broken the back of Iraqi resistance. The land campaign, while by no means a walkover, lasted only four days, from February 23 to February 27. "Air power is the decisive arm so far," U.S. Chief of Staff Gen. Colin Powell remarked, "and I expect it will be the decisive arm into the end of the campaign."[38]

This style of campaign, with variations, characterized the UN effort to halt the depredations of Yugoslavian dictator Slobodon Milosevic (1999) and the U.S. fight to defeat the Taliban rulers of Afghanistan (2001–2002). However, it became apparent that American air power operated much more effectively in conjunction with troops on the ground. In Afghanistan, for example, a few hundred highly trained members of the U.S. Army special forces operating with Afghan rebels were able to call in devastating air strikes that defeated Taliban military forces and lay the foundation for a new government.

Weaponry had improved during the decade since Desert Storm. Smart weapons were easier to aim. Cruise missiles now sported auxiliary GPS that enabled navigation with greater reliability. Boeing developed the GBU-31/32, the joint direct attack munitions (JDAMs)—tail units that transformed iron bombs into smart weapons, with satellite-directed targeting and inertial navigation replacing the laser systems. A JDAM is preprogrammed with the precise coordinates of a target and guided to precisely that point by GPS satellite signals. Air force officials estimated that 95 percent of the JDAMs dropped in Afghanistan fell within thirty feet of their targets. Improvements in unmanned aerial vehicles (UAVs) occurred as well.

Israelis developed and used the first UAVs as small reconnaissance aircraft in the 1980s. Intrigued, the U.S. Navy acquired experimental models of the Pioneer from Israel Aircraft Industries and the Maryland-based AAI Corporation in 1985. Relatively simple, with only a fourteen-foot wingspan, the Pioneer was fraught with technical problems. Nevertheless its use during Desert Storm by U.S. forces demonstrated the potential of a UAV. It gave ground units a chance to see what lay ahead, and navy units to spot offshore gunnery. The Iraqis learned that when one of the little twin-tailed UAVs came buzzing overhead, a crushing artillery barrage was likely to follow. One of the classic stories of Desert Storm involved Iraqi soldiers wildly signaling their willingness to surrender to a Pioneer flying low overhead.

The experience with the Pioneer led to the development of more sophisticated UAVs. Boeing and Lockheed Martin teamed up in 1994 to produce the stealthy, turbofan-powered DarkStar. With a wingspan of sixty-nine feet, it could reach altitudes of forty-five thousand feet and remain aloft for eight hours. The project was canceled in 1999, in favor of the Predator, a General Atomics Aeronautical Systems design.

Smaller than the ambitious DarkStar, the Predator had an operational ceiling of twenty-six thousand feet but could remain aloft for up to forty hours. Controlled by a pilot on the ground, it offered optical vision, as well as an infrared and a radar system that could see at night and through clouds. Quiet, relatively small, and painted entirely white, it was very difficult to see from the ground.

U.S. forces began using the Predator in Yugoslavia in 1995. Long before the UN launched Operation Allied Force in March 1999, Predators observed borders, military units and installations, and urban demonstrations. When Pope John Paul II toured Bosnia in 1997, a U.S. Predator monitored activity along his route. Once air strikes began, Predators surveyed each target before an attack. Between 1995 and early 2001, Predators flew over six hundred missions in support of U.S. and UN forces.

Both the U.S. Air Force and the CIA began to use Predators as weapons carriers during the Afghan campaign. The notion of replacing one of the cameras with a Hellfire missile and laser designator came up during operations in Bosnia, and officials conducted the first highly publicized test in February 2001. CIA operators were the first to fly combat missions with the UAVs, targeting convoys, buildings, and, on at least one occasion, groups of humans. One Pentagon official reported a nearly "100 percent record of hits" during "several dozen attacks."[39]

THE CLOSING AIR campaigns of the century marked the final realization of the American way of war. The minimum number of highly trained combatants, operating sophisticated machines, delivered maximum destruction with a precision undreamed of only a quarter of a century before. The horrific destruction produced by the area bombing of urban centers as a matter of national policy became a thing of the past. The Cold War was over as well, and with it the terrifying prospect of mutually assured destruction. Redefined by new technology, air power became the principal weapon of choice for maintaining stability in trouble spots around the globe.

John Keegan, a distinguished military historian, spoke for many analysts who were taken aback by the results of the air campaigns of the late 1990s.

There are certain dates in the history of warfare that mark real turning points. . . . Now there is a new turning point to fix on the calendar: June 3, 1999, when the capitulation of President Milosevic proved that a war can be won by air power alone. . . . The air forces have won a triumph, are entitled to every plaudit they will receive and can look forward to enjoying a transformed status in the strategic community, one they have earned by their single-handed efforts. All this can be said without reservation, and should be conceded by the doubters, of whom I was one, with generosity. Already some of the critics of the war are indulging in ungracious revisionism, suggesting that we have not witnessed a strategic revolution and that Milosevic was humbled by the threat to deploy ground troops or by the processes of traditional diplomacy. . . . The revisionists are wrong. This was a victory through air power.[40]

Obviously, the new technology did not solve all of the old problems. Improved weaponry enable airmen to achieve precision bombing, but B-52s still drop World War II–era iron bombs on enemy troops. Even when air power is most effective, ground troops are still required to take and hold the ground. And while smart weapons have reduced civilian casualties by many orders of magnitude, there is no such thing as perfection. The smartest weapons aimed at a military headquarters will occasionally hit schools or hospitals. Moreover, bad intelligence can lead to hitting the wrong target with extraordinary precision.

For all of that, precision weapons technology has returned the United States to a position of world dominance equal to that which it held in the few months after World War II when it had a monopoly on the atomic bomb. Such power carries with it a great responsibility, however, and is no guarantee of national safety. The events of September 11, 2001, proved that. The destruction of the World Trade Center and the attack on the Pentagon demonstrated the ease with which a relatively small band of well-financed terrorists can turn our most advanced technology against us. It is worth recalling the words of historian Melvin Kranzberg quoted at the beginning of this book: "Technology is neither good nor bad; nor is it neutral." Those who expect that technology will be employed only to achieve good and righteous ends are doomed to disappointment.[41]

Finally, if there is a lesson to be gleaned from the history of air warfare, it is that new measures inevitably inspire countermeasures. As President George W. Bush threatened Saddam Hussein with war in the summer of 2002, newspapers reported that surfers on the Internet could purchase a device capable of jamming GPS signals for only $39.35. Would it disrupt smart weapons? Probably. Research will solve the problem in good order, but the round of measures and countermeasures will continue.

Take a step back from all of that and consider the big picture. The airplane was the most important military technology since the invention of gunpowder. It added an entirely new dimension to warfare. It revolutionized the way to project force over distance and raised troubling moral questions in the process. Air power evolved from a blunt and imprecise instrument most effectively employed to smash entire cities to a means of striking targets with breathtaking precision.

Samuel Johnson, the eighteenth-century writer and lexicographer, once remarked, "If men were all virtuous . . . I should with alacrity teach them all to fly. But what would be the security of the good, if the bad could at pleasure invade them from the sky?" It would be interesting to know what he would say about such matters at the beginning of the twenty-first century.[42]

15

A WORLD IN THE AIR,
1945-2003

TRANSCONTINENTAL FLIGHT

The trip did not begin well. "The airlines have taken little thought of their patrons on the ground," Bernard DeVoto grumbled while waiting to board a DC-6 at Washington National Airport on an afternoon in late April 1952. "Once in the air you are surrounded with luxury above your station and treated with a deference elsewhere reserved for movie stars." But it was raining in the nation's capital, "which meant that departures were delayed while homing planes felt their way in. This meant in turn the restless, frustrated strolling that is the lot of passengers at an airport."[1]

Things didn't improve after take-off. Passengers received information over a "squawk box." Lunch was cold and unappetizing. Seated in a pressurized tube, looking out the window at the cloud-shrouded landscape, it seemed to DeVoto that "flying was the dullest mode of travel."

Travel was something he knew a great deal about, having chronicled the overland journey of Lewis and Clark, the travels of the Rocky Mountain trappers, and the long trek of the immigrants who crossed the plains and mountains in everything from handcarts to covered wagons. A westerner who had come east, DeVoto had earned a reputation as a leading authority on the generations of nineteenth-century Americans who had crossed the continent in the other direction.

Clearing skies over Illinois brought an improvement in his mood. Few Americans could match his knowledge of the landscape, or his delight in seeing it from eleven thousand feet. The impact of the Land Ordinance of 1785, and its system of neatly surveyed townships and ranges, still remained visible in the crisply drawn checkerboard pattern of the Midwest landscape. The history of the westward movement unrolled beneath him: the Mississippi River, the Missouri, Council Bluffs, the sandhills of Nebraska, Long's Peak, Pike's Peak. He did not resent the short layover in the new Denver airport, commenting that he "would have been content to stay for hours watching the blue mountains darken toward night." Then they were off again, past the lights of Cheyenne, Butte, and Reno.

Above Nevada, clusters of light, smaller and farther apart, broke the silky blackness of earth and sky. This was the west he had left so many years before, and he wondered if the "people in the occasional ranch house whose light glimmers for a second have lain awake to hear the plane pass, as in the high plains they wait to hear the whistle of the night train, then turn out the light, secure and warm because of that momentary contact with other lives."

"An airliner at night is one of the most beautiful, most peaceful, most comfortable of places," DeVoto mused. "Only the focused cones of light break the darkness; one sinks deep into oneself. The dark has brought a sense of the plane's speed and power that cannot be felt in daylight; it is a sense too of serenity." A large aircraft, he decided, offered the smoothest and most relaxing way to travel, and it was far quieter than the "badly orchestrated tone poem of groans, creaks, squeals, and kettledrum pounding of any train."

The airplane came alive again as it descended toward San Francisco. The landing gear dropped down and locked into place. The flaps extended. Eleven hours and twenty minutes after leaving Washington, the DC-6 touched down in the City by the Bay. The speed and convenience of air travel, and the view from two miles up, had won him over. "Logic dissolves away," he realized, "when you summon up the other schedules." The trip that he had just completed in half a day had required six months by covered wagon, eight days by steamboat and stagecoach, and two days by train. DeVoto, who had always loved driving cross-country, had to admit, "There is no answer to the speed of a plane." Still, enough was enough. "I hope," he concluded, "they never compress it further with jets."

It was already to late. On May 2, 1952, just a few days after DeVoto flew to California, a sleek De Havilland Comet, with four jets buried in its swept wings, took off from the London Airport. It was bound for Johannesburg, South Africa, via Rome, Beirut, Khartoum, Entebbe, and Livingstone. Yesterday, the journey had taken 40 hours. The Comet would do it in 23.5 hours.

Pan American and TWA had inaugurated a bold experiment of their own on May 1, offering coach-class service across the Atlantic. Since the beginning, all airlines had offered only one class of service. For the first time, passengers could pay a reduced fare ($270) to cross the Atlantic in a more densely packed area of the airplane. The following year, Pan American introduced mixed-class transatlantic service. TWA introduced nonstop coast-to-coast service in the fall of 1953. Domestic mixed-class service followed in September 1955.

A month later, American World Airlines inaugurated a jet "buying spree" when it ordered twenty Boeing 707s and twenty-five Douglas DC-8s, neither of which was yet in service. Pan American inaugurated its jet service on October 26, 1958, when it flew 111 passengers from New York to Paris aboard a Boeing 707. The rush was on. Between 1958 and 1961 the airlines of the world purchased some five hundred Boeing 707s, Douglas DC-8s, and Convair CV-880s.[2]

The age of mass air transit was dawning. The number of domestic intercity passengers traveling by air exceeded the number of bus passengers for the first time in 1956. That year, more people flew over the Atlantic than crossed it by ship. By 1958, four times as many Americans traveled overseas by plane than by ship. Air travelers exceeded train passengers for the first time early the following year. In a few short years, transcontinental rail travel and transatlantic ocean liners became relics of the past. If it was too far to drive, Americans flew. By 1963, airplanes carried over 85 percent of our total sea-air traffic with the rest of the world.[3]

"What the air age has done," cultural critic Max Lerner commented in 1957, "has been to make the far away vacation possible for the boss's secretary as well as the boss." Vacations were the least of it. The democratization of air travel enabled families scattered across the nation to come together on holidays and special occasions. Business travel had limited appeal when a train trip to California required two days and an ocean voyage to Europe almost a week. Overnight, it seemed, business travelers became the economic mainstay of the airlines. Sports teams and fans alike jetted across continents and oceans. International tourism developed into a boom industry.[4]

As Bernard DeVoto had feared, there was a price to be paid for all of this. Historian Daniel J. Boorstin boarded an airplane at New York's Idlewild Airport at 6:30 P.M. on an evening in 1960 and arrived in Amsterdam at 11:30 the next morning. He had flown at twenty-three thousand feet, far above the weather and everything else of interest. "My only problem en route," he noted, "was to pass the time." It occurred to him that a weekend automobile trip with the family, or a train ride from his suburban home to the university, provided far more entertainment than a flight over the Atlantic. "The airplane," he noted, "had robbed me of the landscape." It had also robbed him of time. Having flown east, he had lost six hours somewhere. "I had not flown through space," he remarked, "but through time."[5]

The airlines introduced amenities to help passengers like Boorstin pass the time. European and American carriers had experimented with in-flight movies in the 1920s. It was not until 1961, however, that TWA began offering films as a means of luring passengers into first-class seats on transcontinental Super Jet flights. The innovation caught on. Airlines added in-flight magazines, shopping catalogues, and many channels of musical entertainment to beguile the long-distance flyer.

Then there were the flight attendants, who still referred to themselves as stewardesses. Boeing Air Transport introduced the notion of cabin attendants when it hired eight young nurses in 1930. Two years later, a pioneer stewardess explained her function in the scheme of things. "By taking our home-making skills into the cabins of the commercial airliners, we can lend familiar aspects to which travelers may cling."[6]

The stewardess idea spread to airlines around the globe. By 1958,

U.S. flag carriers employed eighty-two hundred young women. They were no longer selected and trained to project the image of a nurse and mother figure. One reporter noted that the job qualifications required a woman between the ages of twenty-one and twenty-six, "unmarried, reasonably pretty and slender, especially around the hips, which will be at eye level for the passengers." Eye level indeed. In 1965, Continental Airlines issued a new poster, the central feature of which was the skirt-clad posterior of a stewardess, complete with lovely long legs terminating in spike heels. "Our first run movies are so interesting," the caption read, "we hope you're not missing the other attractions on board."[7]

As AIR TRAVEL blossomed in the 1950s, American commercial culture began to spread around the globe. Conrad Hilton, recognizing the rosy glow of international tourism on the horizon, established Hilton Hotels International at the end of World War II. By 1961, twenty-nine Hiltons, either open or under construction, circled the globe. The corporate flag flew on every continent except Antarctica. "Each of our hotels," he announced at the 1955 opening of the Istanbul Hilton, "is a little America."[8]

During the decades that followed, soft drinks, food products, fast-food restaurants, and a host of other products colonized overseas markets. It seemed to Boorstin that the advent of mass air travel and the spread of American commercial enterprise made international travel less "vivid" than it had once been. Staying in American-style accommodations in a foreign land, he remarked, gives visitors "the comforting feeling of not really being there." Charles Lindbergh agreed. "I never feel more keenly the separation of tourist from native life than when I stay in an 'American hotel' abroad."[9]

Those trends increased over the last half of the century, as more people traveled by air. Bernard DeVoto had been one of 25,019,700 passengers who took a domestic flight in 1952. Eight years later, that number had more than doubled to 58 million. In 1969, U.S. airlines carried 159 million passengers. The world's airlines flew 106 million people, including Daniel Boorstin, in 1960. That number had more than tripled to 311 million in 1970. By 2000, over 538 million citizens of the world would travel by air.[10]

Airliners grew larger and more crowded. The Boeing 707-120, the original production model that entered service in 1958, sat a minimum of 118 passengers, 20 percent more than the De Havilland Comet. The 707-320 intercontinental model normally offered seating for 147 passengers in two classes. Later models of the aircraft carried up to 181 passengers. The Boeing 747, introduced by Pan Am in 1970, initially designed to carry up to 407 persons, would eventually grow to seat 500. Airliners on the drawing board at the turn of the century would seat up to 800. The magic number of 1,000 passengers per flight loomed on the horizon.

Boorstin and Lindbergh were correct in noting that international air travel would alter cultures around the globe in complex ways, both positive and negative. Moreover, the personal experience of air travel grew less pleasant over time. When all is said and done, however, we do not fly for the pleasure of the trip, but to reach distant places in a relatively short time. Automobiles and trains may have the advantage over the short haul. For traveling long distances, however, or shorter distances when time is of the essence, there was, as Bernard DeVoto had discovered, "no answer to the speed of a plane." In the second half of the twentieth century, time became the most important measure of distance. The jetliner had literally shrunk the globe.

REGULATING AIR TRAVEL

The American approach to airway regulation evolved over time. The Air Mail Act of 1925 gave the Post Office Department initial responsibility for overseeing the business aspects of commercial aviation, establishing routes, setting rates, and regulating airmail contractors. The Air Commerce Act of 1926 charged the Department of Commerce with licensing pilots, certifying the airworthiness of aircraft, and otherwise working to ensure safety.

A decade later, the Roosevelt administration attempted to stabilize civil aviation following the airmail debacle with the passage of the Air

Mail Act of 1934. The Bureau of Air Commerce and the Post Office would continue their customary functions, while the new Interstate Commerce Commission (ICC) would control the rates paid to airmail carriers.

Chaos ensued. The ICC lowered the rates, creating an economic crisis for the already hard-pressed airmail carriers. Regulations barring airlines from carrying passengers on a route to which they did not hold the airmail contract made the situation worse. By 1938, the nation's air carriers were drained of capital and, in the words of one authority, "in a state akin to insolvency." American airlines were flying toward bankruptcy in airplanes that were the envy of the world.[11]

Government support proved as important to air commerce as technological change. Recognizing the critical value of civil aviation to a healthy aircraft industry and a strong nation in a world drifting toward war, the Roosevelt administration took radical action. The Civil Aeronautics Act of 1938 removed the Post Office, the Department of Commerce, and the ICC from the aviation business. An independent organization, the Civil Aeronautics Authority (CAA), inherited the power both to license and regulate air safety and to set fares and distribute routes.

In 1940, the Roosevelt administration split the new agency in two. The CAA, now the Civil Aviation Administration, would exercise the duties of the old Bureau of Air Commerce: certifying aircraft and aviators, operating the air traffic control system, and promoting air safety and the improvement of airways. A Civil Aeronautics Board (CAB) would set rules and standards, investigate accidents, establish fares, and regulate the economic aspects of the industry.

Earlier regulatory agencies protected consumers from the monopolistic tendencies of public utilities and rapacious businesses. The CAB protected business from the rigors of competition. Government, from local jurisdictions to federal agencies, provided the required infrastructure: airports, airways, aides to navigation, air traffic control, weather forecasting, and research that would lead to future improvements. Now the CAB would provide an economic safety net, distributing routes so as to reduce competition and establishing fares that would enable a prudent operator to make a profit.

•   •   •

AT THE END of World War II, U.S. airlines were eager to begin overseas operations. The problems of international air commerce had been under discussion since 1910. The International Air Convention, adopted in 1919, established a nation's right to sovereignty over its own airspace; called for international standards for aircraft registration, air worthiness, and the licensing of aviators; and created an International Commission for Air Navigation (ICAN). The ICAN, headquartered in Paris, shared information on technical advances, coordinated efforts to achieve air safety, and distributed forecasts based on weather reports from airports across Europe.

Economic matters, however, remained the province of the airlines. Before 1940, Juan Terry Trippe, the head of Pan American and brother-in-law of Undersecretary of State Edward Stettinius, had negotiated with foreign governments for the right to fly overseas air routes, taking unofficial responsibility for aviation aspects of American foreign policy. That came to a halt in 1939–1940, when the British government ruled that transatlantic air routes were a matter of vital national interest and would only be approved when both nations could offer parallel service.

Given the importance of overseas air commerce to postwar power and prestige, both the CAB and the U.S. Department of State decided, in the fall of 1943, that matters relating to international air travel would be negotiated between governments. Underscoring the new role of the federal government, and forecasting a future that would be very different from the past, Lloyd Welch Pogue, head of the CAB, announced postwar plans for a web of twenty air routes that would link the U.S. continent to Europe, Asia, Africa, and Australia.[12]

The International Air Conference, organized by the State Department in Chicago between November 1 and December 7, 1944, laid a foundation for postwar air commerce. One thousand delegates, consultants, and advisors attended. Some hoped for a future that would be radically different from the past. Australians and New Zealanders argued for the creation of a single "global airline," to be jointly owned and staffed by the participating nations. Such an international corporation would have the sole right to operate on international air routes. When that proposal was dismissed, Lord Swinton, the head of the British delegation, suggested the creation of a global CAA/CAB, an international agency that would control both the safety and the economics of international air commerce. The U.S. delegates defeated the proposal, with considerable effort.

The conference eventually established an International Civil Aeronautics Organization (ICAO) to replace the prewar ICAN. Seventy-two of the nations attending the conference accepted the Air Services Transit Agreement, which gave signatories the right to transit one another's airspace on regular air routes. Most rejected an international air transport treaty that would have opened the way for bilateral agreements, however. The United States, they feared, would dominate the international airways while they were still recovering from the war. By January 1946, however, Britain, feeling renewed confidence, invited U.S. officials to a Bermuda conference, where they negotiated a route agreement. The conference inaugurated the era of postwar international air commerce.

AMERICAN AIRCRAFT dominated the postwar airways, and U.S. airlines prospered at home and abroad. The system that had been in place since 1937 was modified once, by the Federal Aviation Act of 1958. Prompted by a series of accidents and the headlong rush of commercial aviation into the jet age, a new Federal Aviation Agency (later Federal Aviation Administration, or FAA) replaced the CAA and assumed some of the CAB's functions, including the establishment of safety rules. The changes were not fundamental, however.

The basic regulatory structure governing U.S. air commerce remained essentially unchanged for forty years. It worked well. With government assistance, the airline industry enjoyed decades of growth and prosperity. Following World War II, U.S. airlines developed the finest air transport system in the free world, thanks to a very large domestic market, the best transport aircraft in the world, and government planning and protection. CAB officials claimed that as late as 1960, European fares, calculated per seat mile, were much higher than American domestic fares.[13]

The federal agencies had established standardized fares that were related to costs. They banned economic discrimination and unfair competition. Having enabled a well-run airline to earn a reasonable profit, the government insisted on good aircraft maintenance. Unable to offer lower fares than the other fellow, the airlines competed by offering amenities and improved service. Ultimately, federal officials had found a way to stand behind all U.S. airlines without resorting to government operation or the direct subsidies that other nations used to support a single-flag carrier.

Problems occurred, however. As early as 1962, in an effort to help the airlines keep up with rising costs that came with increased traffic, the CAB mandated a 3 percent fare increase. The airlines had hoped for 7 percent. To calculate a fare that would cover real costs and include a reasonable profit was, the chairman of the CAB remarked, "an exercise in futility."[14]

Airline executives were not amused. With economic problems looming on the horizon, the winds of change started blowing in a very different direction. New Deal enthusiasm for government regulation seemed wildly inefficient to a group of economists and political philosophers who urged that the forces of competition be unleashed.

DEREGULATING THE AIRWAYS

The FAA/CAB system represented the ideals of an older America in which government intervention seemed a reasonable means of protecting consumers and encouraging industry. During the New Deal years of the Roosevelt administration, the theories of the English economist John Maynard Keynes provided intellectual support for such federal involvement.

By the mid-1970s, however, free-market thinkers had begun to reject Keynesian economics as hopelessly outmoded and inefficient. Alfred Kahn, a graduate of New York University with a doctorate from Yale, taught economics at both Ripon College and Cornell University. In 1974, Governor Malcolm Wilson of New York appointed him chairman of the Public Service Commission, which regulated electric, gas, water, and telephone companies under a series of laws passed during the Great Depression. During a period of double-digit inflation, the commissioners were bombarded with requests for rate increases. Kahn became convinced that if they removed the regulations, free competition would stabilize the public utilities and lower rates. This enormously complex task provided Kahn with an opportunity to learn important lessons. His two-volume study, *The Economics of Deregulation*, became the bible of a new economic doctrine.

Kahn saw the airlines as prime candidates for deregulation. Although the industry and the unions supported the idea of government protection, both parties had to admit that profits were growing very thin. Since fares were fixed and they could not fly new routes, the airlines began to offer additional flights. The convenience of more frequent flights may have sold more tickets, but this inefficient approach resulted in a great many half-empty airplanes pulling away from the gate. The problem grew worse in the 1960s and early 1970s, as the airlines equipped themselves with the first generation of larger, faster jets. Skyrocketing fuel costs completed the picture.

Airline executives and policy analysts noted that lively competition and lower fares characterized the handful of markets free of CAB control, notably the north-south California routes. During the Ford administration, the CAB experimented with liberalization, allowing the first discount fares. The Air Cargo Deregulation Act of 1976 freed one segment of the industry from federal economic regulation. The pace of change increased in 1977, when President Jimmy Carter named Alfred Kahn to head the CAB, and Senator Ted Kennedy defined deregulation as a consumer issue and held hearings on the matter. The CAB struggled along for a few more years, then went out of business on January 1, 1985.

The Airline Deregulation Act of 1978 led to a complete restructuring of the airlines. Competition and efficiency became the order of the day. The first wave of change produced a major shift from point-to-point service to a hub-and-spoke system, which Delta Airlines had pioneered at Atlanta's Hartsfield Airport before deregulation. Instead of offering flights directly connecting cities, the airlines now flew passengers from a number of areas to hubs, where they were redistributed to create full flights to their final destinations.

In an effort to achieve a new level of efficiency and cost savings, the airlines began to reequip themselves with smaller aircraft that would make more frequent flights filled to capacity. Douglas DC-10s replaced Boeing 747s on transcontinental routes. Later, Boeing 767s and 757s replaced those airplanes. Boeing 737s and Douglas DC-9s flew up and down the spokes, while commuter airlines, often contracting to the major airlines, served the smaller markets with smaller jets like the BAC 111.

The new approach allowed prudent operators to make more efficient use of their equipment, but strained the overburdened airports and the air traffic control system. As congestion at the hubs grew, operators like Southwest Airlines broke the newly established mold by offering inexpensive, no-frills, point-to-point service linking underserved communities and secondary airports in large cities. Southwest climbed onto the list of the nation's top-ten airlines. Other newcomers like Alaska and Midwest Express followed that pattern. By the 1990s, commuter airlines and contract carriers were flying the spokes and offering point-to-point service with regional jets seating from 20 to 70 persons, often from foreign manufacturers like Bombardier, Canadair, Brazil's Embraer, and Fairchild Dornier, and twin turboprops such as the Fokker/Fairchild F-27. The revolutionary, layered restructuring of the American airline system was complete.

DISENTANGLING THE complex legacy of deregulation is no easy task. A 1996 General Accounting Office (GAO) study found that the average fare per passenger mile had fallen by 9 percent between 1978 and 1994. In 1977, U.S. air carriers had carried 221,713,000 passengers on domestic flights and 18,044,000 to and from overseas destinations. By the year 2000, those numbers had increased to 608,036,000 domestic passengers and 55,309,000 foreign travelers. A Gallup poll indicated that as many as 80 percent of adult Americans had flown at least once by the end of the century. The combination of lower fares, more frequent flights, and the arrival of entire families of jetliners brought on the age of mass air transit at long last.[15]

But if fares were lower, they also varied wildly. While the price of flying to hubs and other primary centers generally dropped, the cost of

travel to some mid-sized markets soared. Airlines offered special dis-
counts and employed complex formulas to set ticket prices, so that two
individuals seated next to one another on a flight might have paid very
different prices for their tickets. "My wife and I happened to be attending the same conference in Philadelphia," reporter Robert Kuttner
explains. "Her round trip fare from Boston was $257.50. Mine was
$645.50. Imagine, $645 to fly to Philadelphia!" Why does an airline get
to charge so much, he asked. "Because it's a monopoly silly, and they
stopped regulating air fares in 1978."[16]

The old stability that had been the goal of the CAB simply vanished. The number of U.S. airlines in 1978 (forty-three) had doubled by
the end of 2001. The competition was fierce. Between 1978 and the end
of the century, nine major carriers and as many as a hundred smaller
airlines declared bankruptcy.

One after another, the great names in the history of American civil
aviation vanished from the scene. Braniff collapsed in 1982, struggled
along for a few more years, and went bankrupt in 1989. Pan American,
for decades the leading U.S. international carrier, now faced competition from upstart discount airlines such as Laker and Donald Burr's
People Express. By 1991, Juan Trippe's "chosen instrument" of
American aeronautical policy had faded into history. Mismanaged and
unable to stand up to the competition, TWA declared bankruptcy in
1992. Any hope of resuscitating the company died in 2001, when
American folded the remaining TWA assets into its own organization.
Long before that, both Laker and People Express had been forced out
of business by older operations that could undercut *their* fares and provide better service.

Eastern and Continental Airlines fell victim to a schemer named
Frank Lorenzo. Continental, which Robert F. Six had built into an
industry powerhouse during the early 1970s, began to lose steam after
deregulation and Six's retirement in 1982. Lorenzo, whose Texas
International Airlines prospered under deregulation, had a reputation
for ruthless cost cutting and tough dealing with labor unions. After
taking over Continental in the mid-1980s, he cut jobs, slashed pay and
benefits, and reduced the destinations served by the airline. Lorenzo
took over ailing Eastern Airlines in 1986. The sudden expansion

caught up with him in 1990. Escalating labor problems and mounting debts led to such drastic measures as the sale of all the company's East Coast routes. Lorenzo sold out that year. Eastern suspended operations and was liquidated in 1991.

By 1992, three remaining traditional major airlines—American, United, and Delta—controlled fully one-half of the domestic market. As in the case of the aircraft industry during these years, airlines faced the prospect of either gobbling up smaller companies in order to grow or being gobbled up in turn. On that basis, U.S. Air, heir to Allegheny Airlines, worked its way into the top ten in the 1990s.

If the airlines struggled to survive in an environment of unre-strained competition, things did not get any better for the flying public. Before World War II, someone who had flown across the country could dine out on the story. Travelers fortunate enough to travel across the Pacific on one of Pan American's famed Clippers, or who crossed the Atlantic on the airships *Graf Zeppelin* or the *Hindenburg*, could expect a level of service that surpassed that of an ocean liner. Unable to compete with lower fares, the airlines offered other incentives. After 1978, prices dropped and the amenities vanished. The quality of the food service suffered. Reasonable seat space and leg room disappeared in an effort to fit more people onto a flight. The notion of flying to Japan, trapped in a middle seat of the middle aisle of a 747, was enough to give any passenger nightmares. Airliners grew larger, but not much faster than when the jetliners were introduced.

Deregulation lowered average fares and forced airlines to operate more efficiently or fail. Twenty years after deregulation, however, problems remain. Fares are uneven and sometimes inequitable. Some small communities remain underserved or are served by a single car-rier. Overcrowded airports and air traffic control systems produce flight delays and cancelations. Small carriers often have a difficult time getting started in a competitive environment. Customer service has suffered.

There are those who argue that the solution to these problems lay in a return to partial regulation. "The finest airline system in the world . . . built up over forty years with magnificent effort and financial back-ing, is gone," Welch Pogue complained in 1991. "Airline casualties litter the deregulation arena. Almost all of the once promising and eager newcomers, and many of the old timers, are now a part of that litter. Even the six giant airlines, surviving from the days before deregulation, are running scared; they are mostly losing vast amounts of money; they are staggering with too much debt, with overextension, overcapacity, with old aircraft, and with hordes of furloughed employees."[17]

Others argued for more deregulation. While the airlines are now subject to competition, they explain, the infrastructure, including airports and the air traffic control system, remain in the hands of intransigent governments. "Today's real challenge," they claim, "should be to remove the remaining government interventions in aviation infrastructure that restrict competition and hinder the growth of new forms of airline service."[18]

Any hope that airports or the air traffic control system might be deregulated vanished with the terrorist attack on the World Trade Center on September 11, 2001. Increased security at airports placed even greater pressure on both the airlines and the government. Lines grew longer and passenger frustration mounted. Through it all, the debate over the impact of deregulation continues.

TAKING OFF, LANDING, AND STAYING IN TOUCH

In 1920, the nation had 145 municipally owned airports, marginal places unfamiliar to most Americans. As late as 1926 the nation's scheduled airlines operated a total of twenty-six airplanes. If all of them had been in the air at once, filled to capacity, they would have carried 112 passengers.

Through the war years, railroad stations served as the urban centerpieces of large cities and small towns across the nation. They were the splendid portals through which people entered the great cities of the land. Their grand concourses, with their great arched ceilings and light streaming in through tall windows, were the great public spaces of the era. New York's Penn and Grand Central Stations, perhaps the grandest of them all, were the real stars of such films as *The Clock* (1945) and Alfred Hitchcock's classic *North by Northwest* (1959).

Airports, on the other hand, were located on the outskirts of the city. Instead of vaulted ceilings and breathtaking architecture, they offered a handful of unimpressive hangars running along two sides of the grassy square where airplanes took off and landed. The hustle and bustle, the swirling crowds of travelers coming and going, was entirely absent. This was the habitat of daredevils, grease monkeys, and the wealthy risk takers who could afford to fly.

Things had changed by 1940. Airports had become romantic places from which the great aviators of the age departed and to which they returned. The rows of weather-beaten hangars had been replaced by stunning new terminals, familiar sights in American newspapers and on the silver screen. More important, American airports had been linked into a cohesive national system.

THE PROCESS of connecting the nation's airports began when the U.S. Air Mail Service installed lighting on the airports from which they operated, and created marked air routes linking flying fields from coast to coast. Airports had always been the business of local municipalities. Hopes that the federal government might accept responsibility for flying fields were dashed when the Air Commerce Act of 1926 forbade Bureau of Air Commerce support for airport construction.

The Roosevelt administration found a way to reverse that policy by approving the expenditure of relief dollars on airport projects. Both the Public Works Administration (PWA) and the Civil Works Administration (CWA) began work on airports in 1933. The government provided the workmen, while the local governments supplied the land, equipment, and most of the material. By mid-1934, construction had started on some eight hundred flying fields. Sixty percent of that work involved the creation of new airports or the reopening of old landing fields. Federal relief funds continued to support American airport construction until 1938, when the Civil Aeronautics Act allowed the CAA to become involved in airport support and construction.

The advent of the Boeing 247 and Douglas DC-3 called the modern airport into being. Hard-surface runways were now a necessity. The years of the New Deal and World War II had opened the great era for the establishment of U.S. airports. Only a relative handful of major American airports were founded after 1950: Washington Dulles, Dallas–Fort Worth, Kansas City International, and Denver International.

Washington National typified the new airports, offering everything from impressive terminal buildings to multiple paved runways and taxiways and modern maintenance facilities. National replaced an older field, Hoover Airport. The story begins with Thomas Mitten, head of Philadelphia Rapid Transit Company, which held the contract to carry mail from Philadelphia to Washington, D.C. In 1926, with the assistance of Secretary of Commerce Herbert Hoover, Mitten began work on a major airport for the nation's capital. The site, next to a dump on the Virginia side of the Potomac, was less than ideal. Power lines ran along one side of the field, and a smoke stack rose right in the middle of the approach. Worse, Hoover's main runway ran across a major highway. A flagman had to stop traffic when an aircraft was taking off or landing. The nation's capital deserved better.

The new facility rose from the mudflats of Gravelly Point, on the Virginia side of the Potomac, where Captain John Alexander had built Abingdon plantation in 1746. This would be the first federal airport. A variety of agencies were involved, including the CAA and CAB, the Work Projects Administration, the Army Corps of Engineers, and the National Park Service. When work began, the site was underwater. The first step involved constructing a dike around the perimeter of the airfield. Next, construction workers used hydraulic dredges to remove eleven feet of silt from the runway area, and then pumped in twenty million yards of sand and gravel to provide a solid foundation for runways, twenty feet above the level of the river.

National Airport opened in 1941 with six hangars and four runways, the longest of which measured 6,855 feet. Both American and Eastern Airlines were based at the airport. Short-sighted critics complained about the large size of the neoclassical terminal. They were wrong. Over 344,250 passengers passed through the facility in the first year. The one-millionth passenger arrived in 1946.

The terminal was extended in 1950. Five years later, a second addition added almost ten thousand square feet of new passenger-loading gates. Airport officials opened a new north terminal in 1958. Three years later the two terminals were linked by an enclosed passageway. Community pressure led to a nighttime noise-limitation policy in 1982. Washington Dulles airport opened in the Virginia suburbs in 1962. With a terminal designed by famed architect Ero Saarinen, Dulles would handle long-distance and overseas traffic. In 1987, the federal government turned control of both Washington National and Dulles Airports over to a new Metropolitan Washington Airports Authority.

The most significant round of changes in the history of National Airport began in 1989, when an older hangar became an interim terminal. Officials dedicated their first parking garage in 1991, broke ground for a structure that would more than double the size of the airport in 1993, and opened a new terminal in 1997. Congress renamed the entire facility Reagan Washington National Airport on February 6, 1998. From the 1980s into the early years of the new century, a time when I sometimes felt that National Airport was my second home, 16 million people passed through the terminal each year.

The story of National Airport echoed in cities across the nation. In 1975, Chicago's O'Hare Airport handled two hundred take-offs and landings a day. That year, 37 million passengers boarded airplanes at O'Hare, the nation's busiest airport. A quarter of a century later, 683 million passengers boarded airplanes at 422 major American airports.

Americans were now far more familiar with their local airport than the railroad station, if their town still had one. Federal assistance had funded this transformation. From the time of its creation in 1946, until its expiration in 1969, the Federal Aid for Airports Program (FAAP) distributed $1.2 billion to airports. Even that level of spending did not enable airports to keep pace with the explosive growth of air travel and the advent of much larger and heavier aircraft.

The Airport and Airway Development Act (ADAP) of 1970, which replaced the FAAP, distributed $1.3 billion in just five years. The money paid for eighty-five new airports and more than a thousand improvement projects. Partially funded by taxes and surcharges on domestic and overseas airfares and aviation gasoline, the ADAP spent $4.1 billion on the national airport system during the years 1971–1980. The Airport and Airway Improvement Act of 1982 (AIP) continued the trust fund expenditures, distributing over $22 billion during 1982–1998 to the 3,344 existing and 217 proposed airports eligible for federal support.

LIKE THE RAILROAD stations before them, modern airports are embedded in several technological systems. Airport administrators speak of the "air side" and the "land side" of their operation. On the land side, the airport comprises one part of a surface-transportation web enabling passengers to continue their journeys by highway, light rail, or subway. On the air side, the airport is a node in an intricate network of international airways.

The control tower is the most distinguishing feature of an airport. The world's first "purpose-built" control tower came into use at London's Croydon Airport in 1928. An all-glass structure on stilts, known as the "chart house," the first tower had a wide walkway where a radio operator, spotters, and the officer in charge kept track of airplanes on the ground and in the air, and communicated through hand signals, flags, disks, chalkboards, highly focused Aldis lamps, and radio.

Radio communications started linking ground stations and aircraft in flight in 1920, when the Marconi Company established an experimental radio telephone station at Croydon Airport. As the weight of equipment decreased in the mid-1920s, more and more European airliners carried radios.

In the United States, the Bureau of Standards began operating an experimental air-to-ground radio station at College Park, Maryland, in 1927. Within two years, the Department of Commerce took over seventeen aeronautical radio stations established by the Post Office Department and was hard at work expanding the system.

Cleveland Municipal Airport put the first radio-equipped control tower in the United States into service in 1930. Within ten years, virtually all airliners were equipped for voice communication with ground stations. By 1935, some twenty radio control towers operated in the U.S.

That year, a consortium of airlines opened the first air traffic control center in Newark, New Jersey. The idea was to manage air traffic between airports. Unable to contact airplanes in flight, the controllers relayed messages to pilots in the air through airline dispatchers. The Bureau of Air Commerce took over the Newark center and two similar facilities in Chicago and Cleveland in 1936. By the end of World War II, twenty-seven regional air traffic control centers had been established.

FOR THE MOMENT, a pilot aloft in bad weather had to rely on his own resources for navigation. Fortunately, those resources were improving. The light beacons leading from one airfield to the next had been unnecessary in good weather and unusable when visibility was poor. An electronic beacon provided the solution to the problem. However, Europeans and Americans adopted very different strategies.

Europe kept responsibility for aerial navigation firmly on the ground. In order to ascertain his position, a pilot radioed a ground station for a fix, followed by a long dash in Morse code. Three ground stations would triangulate on the signal. The position could then be calculated and radioed back to the pilot, who would know where he had been—ten minutes before.

Americans preferred to place responsibility in the cockpit. Early Post Office and U.S. Navy experiments aimed to develop an onboard radio direction finding (RDF) system in which the pilot manipulated an antenna loop to determine the direction to a broadcast antenna. When the Harding administration cut Post Office funds supporting work on a more sophisticated radio range system, the U.S. Army Air Service and the U.S. Bureau of Standards picked up the ball. By 1925, the army had developed the elements of a system that would remain the standard navigational aid through the 1930s and beyond.

A pilot "riding the beam" from one point to another would hear a continuously broadcast letter "T," or dash, in Morse code. If he strayed to the right or left, the signal would switch to either an "N" or an "A." By 1932, a pilot was required to master instrument flying and the use of radio navigation aids to earn a commercial license. By the spring of 1939, the United States boasted twenty-five thousand miles of airways equipped with radio aids to navigation.

During World War II, the CAA tested a very-high-frequency (VHF) omnidirectional radio range (VOR), a static-free system that enabled a pilot to navigate using cockpit instruments rather than having to listen for signals. By 1952, the federal government had established forty-five thousand miles of VHF and VOR air routes. In 1947, the CAA established Skyway One, a pair of paths leading from Washington, D.C., to Los Angeles. The next year, Skyway Two provided an electronic aerial path from Boston to Seattle. By 1950, low-frequency signals broadcast from a series of three-hundred-foot towers helped airliners navigate their way across the Atlantic and Pacific.

The global positioning system (GPS) represents the most significant revolution in the history of navigation. It began with the launch of the first earth satellite in 1957. Satellites were originally envisioned as eyes in the sky, the ultimate means of looking down on the enemy. It occurred to some, however, that signals from space could be used for pinpoint navigation. The earliest experiments aimed at providing precise targeting for ballistic missiles. By 1978, the first-generation GPS satellites were in orbit, with use of the system restricted to the military.

In 1983, a Soviet pilot shot down a Korean airliner that had strayed off course. The incident led officials to consider making GPS technology available to civilians. A decade later, the federal government did precisely that. The old problems of navigation—for hikers, sailors, or pilots of the largest airliners—were history.

NAVIGATING THE SKIES was one thing; landing at night or in low visibility presented quite another challenge. The earliest experiments involved lighting systems that enabled a pilot to find an airport and then led him to a landing. Low-frequency radio beams comprised the next step. A pilot would pick up a broad audio signal at some distance from the airport and fly down an electronic "funnel" to the end of the runway.

Beginning with Jimmy Doolittle's famous 1929 "blind flight" for the Guggenheim Fund, however, the Bureau of Standards developed the elements of what would become the standard U.S. instrument landing system (ILS), which relied on special instruments rather than audio signals. Cockpit instruments indicated if the plane was to the right or to the left of the runway's centerline, above or below the glide slope, and informed the pilot of his distance to the landing field. With refinements, the system continued in use after World War II. Since the 1980s, microwave landing systems (MLSs), which enable airmen to land from a number of directions, have replaced ILS in Europe. The FAA continued to explore alternative systems, including the use of the GPS and MLS.

Technological change revolutionized the air traffic control system. Radar represented the first breakthrough. Now controllers on the ground could pierce fog, cloud, and dark of night to identify aircraft and guide them home. Beginning in 1960, the FAA required that aircraft be equipped with a radar transponder that would identify the flight on air traffic control screens. Computers, introduced into the system in 1956, altered the air traffic control system as thoroughly as it did so many aspects of aviation.

Technology did not ease the stress of the job, however. When an air traffic controller makes a mistake, people might die. In response to job demands, members of the Professional Air Traffic Controllers Organization (PATCO) began negotiating with the government for higher wages, a shorter workweek, and better retirement benefits. When there was no meeting of the minds, PATCO leadership threatened to break their pledge as federal employees not to strike. On August 30, 1981, 13,000 of 17,500 members of the union walked off the job. President Reagan announced that any member of PATCO who did not return to work within forty-eight hours would be terminated. That is precisely what happened to the more than 12,000 controllers who ignored the ultimatum. FAA supervisors, military controllers, and other employees pitched in to keep the air traffic system up and running. The FAA training program worked overtime to refill the ranks.

The air traffic control system entered the twenty-first century with aging equipment and gridlock on the horizon. As in the past, new technology eventually will keep the system above water. New computer systems will come on line, and there is the promise of new satellite navigation equipment that would literally control the airplane, preventing collisions and making it impossible for terrorists to crash an airplane into a building.

HAULING FREIGHT

The notion of shipping freight by air is as old as the airplane. The flight of ten bolts of silk aboard a Wright airplane from Dayton to Columbus in 1910 generated extraordinary excitement. The serious history of the air freight industry begins in 1925, when the Ford Motor Company began scheduled service between corporate facilities in Dearborn and Chicago. Intended to meet company needs, the service continued to operate until 1932, when Ford withdrew from the field.

In 1925, American Railway Express entered the air freight business by contracting with four airlines that agreed to carry the cargo while Railway Express handled promotion, processing, pick up, and delivery. After the company's expenses were covered, they would all split the revenues, with 75 percent going to the airlines. Following a 1929 reorganization and the creation of Railway Express Agency (REA), the air freight operation expanded to include ten airlines serving eighty-two cities. In order to attract customers, REA priced its service below that of airmail and above that of railway carriage.

A 1929 drop in the airmail rate undercut REA. Airlines that had once cooperated with the service now partnered with Western Union, Postal Telegraph, Greyhound, and other ground operations to provide air cargo service of their own. REA's market share fell from 75 percent in 1929 to 13 percent in 1931.

An even more serious blow fell in 1934, when seven airlines, including some former REA partners, combined to form General Air Express. Managed by a committee of participating airlines, the new firm launched a price war that continued until 1935, when all of the General Air Express carriers except TWA surrendered and signed contracts with REA. By 1939, REA once again controlled a whopping 98.4 percent of the air freight business.

As business boomed during World War II, the airlines chaffed under the arrangement with REA. In March 1941, four airlines broke away once again to form Air Cargo. Other airlines tested the postwar waters with their own air freight services. Two specialist cargo airlines appeared on the scene: Slick Airways, founded by Earl Slick in 1945, and Flying Tigers, established the following year by U.S. Army Air Force veteran Robert Prescott. Smaller operations including U.S. Airlines, Airnews, and Airlift International came and went. Slick, unable to compete with the airline freight services, temporarily ceased operations in 1958 and folded for good in 1965. Flying Tiger survived into the 1980s, when it fell victim to a bright young man with a unique approach to the air freight business.

As a Yale undergraduate, Frederick W. Smith wrote a term paper revealing the inefficiency of operating an air cargo service over passenger air routes. He suggested a new system specifically designed to handle high-value, time-sensitive shipments. Following his discharge from the military in 1971, Smith entered business and immediately encountered problems with existing air freight services. Recalling his term paper, he analyzed the difficulties of air freight operations and pinpointed the problem as poor systems management. Federal Express began operations at Memphis International Airport with fourteen small aircraft on April 17, 1973.

The idea was simple. Packages from across the nation would be flown into a central hub, sorted, and flown back out to their destinations. At Federal Express, time was money, and overnight delivery the goal. The initial going was tough though. Smith occasionally urged his drivers to take the company trucks home for the night so that they would not be seized by creditors. Federal Express did not earn a profit until its third year. A good idea, however, combined with savvy advertising became the ticket for prosperity. The company posted $1 billion in revenues for 1983, the first American company to achieve that goal within ten years of its founding. FedEx, as it would be known after 1994, acquired Flying Tiger in 1989, becoming the world's largest dedicated air freight service.

The scent of profits drew some experienced competition into the market. United Parcel Service began in 1907 as a private messenger and delivery business founded by James E. Casey, a young Seattle man. Within a decade the firm grew to a citywide package delivery service serving leading department stores. Packages came together at a central point and were then dispersed to the neighborhoods.

Expanding down the coast to California, the company partnered with United Air Lines in 1929 to establish United Air Express. The experiment ended eight months later, a victim of hard times and a technology that was all too fallible. United Parcel took to the air a second time in 1953 as United Blue Label Air, which shipped parcels with scheduled airlines. Rising demand, the deregulation of air cargo operations in 1974, and the success of FedEx led to the creation of the largest fleet of aircraft in the business. By the end of the century, UPS was delivering 11.5 million packages to one million customers in 185 nations each day. The convergence of high-speed airliners, computers, and advanced systems management had given the air cargo industry an entirely new dimension.

JETLINERS

The British aircraft industry entered the postwar world with some significant strengths and weaknesses. The industry operated at peak efficiency, producing some of the most advanced aircraft and the finest jet engines in the world, but it was overpopulated. An August 1945 supplement to *Jane's All the World's Aircraft* listed thirty-two manufacturers actively producing aircraft in Great Britain, not one of which had built a production airliner in almost six years. British leaders, anxious to assist the industry in transitioning back to civil production, created two wartime committees headed by Lord Brabazon of Tara to establish postwar policy for airliner development.

John Theodore Cuthbert Moore-Brabazon (1884–1964), whom Gabriel Voisin had taught to fly in Paris in 1908, was the first licensed British pilot and the winner of a 1910 *Daily Mail* prize for a flight from England to Belgium. A member of Parliament, he spent his life close to the heart of British aviation, climaxing his long career by serving as minister of aircraft production during World War II. Certain that postwar transatlantic air travelers would not face their twelve-hour journey without significant comforts, he emphasized the need for very large and luxurious airliners.

If American manufacturers were able to reenter the commercial market with four-engine airliners that had proved themselves in wartime service, British manufacturers were eager to introduce brand new four-engine designs that had been incubating during the war years. Armstrong Whitworth offered the A.W.27A Ensign, while A. V. Roe unveiled the AVRO 688 Tudor I and Handley Page the H.P 81 Hermes 4A. Both Bristol (V.C. 1 Viking) and De Havilland (D.H. 104 Dove) were preparing to introduce twin-engine airliners. Saunders-Roe announced plans for the Princess (S.R. 45), a huge, ten-engine, double-deck, transatlantic flying boat. Bristol's entry into the transatlantic field, the Type 167 Brabazon I, an eight-engine, seventy-two- to eighty-seat airliner, was the most ambitious of the postwar projects.

The British dream of capturing the Atlantic from the Americans failed spectacularly. First flown in 1949, the Brabazon I was broken up in 1953, having logged only four hundred hours in the air. The Saunders-Roe Princess, only one of which ever flew, never crossed the Atlantic and became obsolete before its completion. Limited performance and a crash that took the life of designer Roy Chadwick (who had also designed the Lancaster) limited the success of the Tudor. The first Hermes crashed on its first take-off. Later models served as troop carriers and were operated by British Overseas Airways Corporation (BOAC) and smaller airlines in Africa and elsewhere.

There were some successes. The Vickers Viscount, designed to fill the Brabazon committee's call for a short- to medium-range airliner and first flown as Model 630 in 1948, was the first turboprop airliner to enter passenger service. Offering smooth, vibration-free, high-altitude air travel, it demonstrated the advantages of turbojet propulsion. The follow-on Viscount 700 sold well in Europe and, entering service with Capital Airlines, became the first British design to do well in the American market.

Determined to take full advantage of the British lead in jet-engine technology, the Brabazon committee also called for a pure turbojet airliner to operate on midlength routes. The engineers at De Havilland saw jet technology as the answer to long-distance travel and the means of capturing the international market from the Americans. Their original tailless design (1945) gave way to the sleek, mildly swept-wing D.H. 106 Comet 1, first flown in July 1949. The Comet became the first jet airliner to enter service in May 1952, when it began flying the BOAC route from London to Johannesburg.

Over the following months, the Comet's routes extended across Asia to Tokyo. That fall, Pan American, Air France, and Canadian Pacific airlines all signed up for later-model, longer-range Comets. This airplane carried forty-four passengers a distance of 1,750 miles at 490 mph. It cruised at forty thousand feet, far above bad weather and

De Havilland D.H. 106 Comet

all other airliners. It appeared that Britain would, after all, rival the Americans as a producer of transport aircraft. Then, on January 10, 1954, a BOAC Comet broke up in the air after take-off from Rome.

The Comet had had earlier problems. It had a reputation for being touchy on landing and take-off, and an earlier Comet had broken up in a tropical storm. Following the disaster at Rome, all of the aircraft were taken out of service for a time and inspected. On April 8, 1954, just two weeks after the Comets resumed service, a South African Airways jet plunged into the Mediterranean near Sicily. Salvaged pieces of the Comet that crashed in Rome were shipped to the Royal Aircraft Establishment in Farnborough, where engineers discovered that repeated pressurization cycles had led to metal fatigue in the sharp corners of the cabin windows.

De Havilland had broken new ground. No one had experience with pressurized airplanes flying at forty thousand feet. After discovery of the problem, the company spent two years designing an improved and lengthened Comet 4, which enjoyed a long career as an airliner, a military transport, and a long-range search aircraft. The overseas sales had vanished, however, and with them the opportunity to capture the top end of the world airliner market, as Douglas had a generation before.

A second jetliner, the Tupolev Tu-104, landed at a London airport in March 1956. Andrei Tupolev built his first airplane in 1921. As noted earlier, he spent the worst years of Stalinist terror and wartime loss as the head of a *sharaga*, an intellectual prison where engineers developed the weapons with which to save the Motherland while living and working under armed guard.

During the years after World War II, the Yak, Lavochkin, Sukhoi, and Mikoyan and Gurevich (MiG) design bureaus focused on the development of fighters that would enable Soviet pilots to go head-to-head with their Western counterparts, while the Tupolev and Ilyushin design bureaus produced competing first-generation jet bombers. Tupolev developed what became the standard Soviet medium bomber of the era, the Tu-16 Badger, first flown in 1952.

The Badger served as the foundation for the design of the twin-engine Tu-104, the first Soviet jetliner. Initially seating seventy passengers, the Tu-104A would become the most widely used of the early midrange Soviet jetliners, remaining in service until the 1970s. The Tu-110 was a four-engine version of the same design. While very different airplanes, the Tu-124 and Tu-134 followed the same tradition.

In similar fashion, the large turbojet-powered Tu-95 Bear led to the Tu-114D, the largest airliner in the world at the time of its introduction in 1956. Powered by four turboprops, the swept-wing Bear was perhaps most successful of all Soviet strategic bombers, developed in a wide range of variants. The Tu-114, which employed a low wing, as opposed to the midwing of the Tu-95, could carry much higher loads at speeds almost equal to that of the new pure jets just entering service.

•   •   •

LIKE TUPOLEV, Boeing maintained its reputation as the leading American producer of bombers into the postwar era. In the area of heavy bombers, the B-29 gave way to the more powerful Boeing B-50 and the Convair B-36, the later models of which were propelled by six piston engines and four turbojets. The original American turbojet medium bombers—the Douglas XB-42, Martin XB-43, Northrop YB-49, Martin B-51, and North American B-45—left much to be desired.

Boeing reestablished its hegemony with the B-47 medium bomber, first flown at Wichita, Kansas, on April 26, 1951. The company would produce 1,373 of the aircraft, with Douglas and Lockheed manufacturing an additional 659. Boeing followed that success with the B-52, which first took to the air on April 15, 1952. Boeing managers ceased production of the KC-97G, their last propeller-driven tanker, and began to plan for a new jet aircraft that could serve as the basis for both a military tanker/transport and an airliner. Their own experience in the design and production of two very successful jet bombers, and the early excitement over the Comet, led them to consider the pattern of a swept-wing jet.

It was a big year for Boeing. The first production B-52 emerged from Seattle plant No. 2 in March 1954. The one-thousandth B-47 was completed at the Wichita plant that October. In terms of the future of the company, however, May 14 may have been the most important date. A local high school band played the air force song as the yellow and brown Boeing Model 367-80 rolled through the big doors of the factory in Renton, Washington. Eight thousand workers just coming off a shift joined seventy-two-year-old William Boeing, the founder of the company, as his wife Bertha christened the machine on which corporate hopes rode.

Boeing paid for this airplane out of its own pockets. The Dash 80, as it was called, cost $16 million, four times the total profits that the company had earned since 1945. No airline had as yet ordered the commercial version of the airplane. The air force had not expressed interest in a jet tanker. Undeterred, company president William Allen approved funding to purchase tooling and begin preparations to manufacture the new aircraft. He was betting the company on the project.

Legendary Boeing test pilot Tex Johnson flew the Dash 80 for the first time on July 15, 1954. In August 1955, he slowly rolled the airplane during a demonstration pass over the crowd attending the Gold Cup hydroplane races. The air force placed its first order for what was to

Boeing Model 707-321C

become the KC-135 jet tanker in early August 1954, and agreed to allow the company to simultaneously build and sell the Boeing 707 civil version to the airlines.

With the DC-7 still selling well, Douglas was slower to take an interest in a commercial jets. At the same time, company officials grew as anxious as Boeing managers to maintain their long-time leadership in airline production. Always ready to realize a savings by encouraging competition, Juan Trippe of Pan American persuaded Douglas to develop the DC-8 jetliner.

While the 707-120, the first production version, would beat the competition into the air by a year or more, the DC-8 would be larger, faster, and capable of crossing the Atlantic nonstop. Pan American, which had already signed up for twenty 707s, now ordered twenty-five of the Douglas jets. United Air Lines followed suit with an order for thirty DC-8s. With American preparing to sign up with Douglas as well, Boeing engineers announced the 707-320, featuring larger wings, additional seating, and Pratt & Whitney JT3C-6 engines that enabled it to cruise faster than the DC-8.

Ultimately, in terms of sales, the 707 far surpassed the DC-8. Douglas sold 556 of its original jetliners, which remained in production until 1972, whereas Boeing sold 725 of its 707s to the world's airlines between 1957 and 1978. Boeing built the airplane in a great many variants to meet the needs of its customers. An additional 130 military versions of the 707-300 were manufactured by 1992, when production finally ceased. The 707 was not the first commercial jet, but it won the competition for industry dominance.

Convair announced its entrance into the jetliner competition in April 1956. The Convair 880, a medium-range airliner first flown in January 1959, cruised at Mach .87, much faster than any other airliner of the time. It hit the market late, however, after the major airlines had already invested in new aircraft. As a result, Convair built only sixty-five of the airplanes and only thirty-seven of the follow-on Convair 990. While both Boeing and Douglas spent very large sums developing their aircraft, they ultimately made money. Convair, on the other hand, lost an estimated $425 million attempting to market a commercial jet.

THE REDESIGNED COMET 4 made the first jet passenger flights across the Atlantic in the fall of 1958, three weeks before the first transatlantic flight of a passenger-carrying 707. It was a small moment though. Boeing had already captured the field. As had been the case in the past, a head-to-head competition between manufacturers, arranged by the airlines, produced the most successful commercial airplane of its generation. Moreover, 707 fuselage sections would form the basis for new families of Boeing aircraft in the decades to come, including the 727 and 737. Boeing had finally replaced Douglas as the free world's leading producer of airliners.

Other new aircraft soon began to fill the route niches of the world's airliners. European turboprop aircraft like the Vickers Viscount and the Fokker F-27 Friendship did well on shorter routes with regional carriers. Lockheed entered the field with its L-188 Electra II, delivering the first of these twin turboprops to American Airlines in December 1958. Like the Comet, however, the Electra suffered a fatal flaw, the potential to develop a harmonic vibration that could literally tear a wing off, and periodically did just that. As in the case of the Comet, engineers solved the problem, but not before sales had plummeted. Lockheed did profit from the design, however, using it as the basis for the very successful P-3 Orion, which saw yeoman service with the U.S. Navy.

The turboprops did well enough on the very short, low-traffic city-to-city routes. New families of smaller turbojets forced them off even slightly longer routes, however. Like the Viscount and the Comet, the French Caravelle, a midrange airliner, introduced a new concept in aircraft design to the world market. First flown in May 1955, the Caravelle was produced by Sud-Aviation, the name applied to the firm created by the 1957 merger of two of the old nationalized companies, Sud-Est and Sud-Ouest. The new airplane featured twin Rolls-Royce jet engines mounted on the rear fuselage, allowing for an extraordinarily clean and efficient wing.

The Hawker Siddeley Trident, first flown in 1962, offered three engines mounted at the rear of the aircraft, a configuration that appealed to airline executives. Boeing responded with the 727, while Douglas countered with the DC-9 powered by twin-engines mounted on the fuselage. Both planes were extraordinarily successful. Boeing built 1,831 of the midrange aircraft between 1964 and 1983. Douglas sold 2,100 DC-9s until 1983, when McDonnell Douglas introduced the MD-80/MD-90 series.

The success of the DC-9 and the British Aircraft Corporation's BAC-111 prompted Boeing to introduce the 737. The 727 had introduced passengers to a system of high lift devices so complex that it almost seemed that the wing was disassembling itself on landing. The 737 provided even better low-speed characteristics, and a capacity to operate from short or even unimproved runways. With its six-across seating arrangement, the little jet would never be a favorite with passengers, but it offered a seat cost per mile that was hard to beat. Still, a CAB ruling that the airplane required a three-person crew in the cockpit, as opposed to the two-person crew of the DC-9, raised the cost of operation and limited its appeal to the airlines.

Deregulation and changes to the crew requirement, coupled with the addition of new and more powerful engines, changed the situation completely. By 1993, when Boeing had sold 3,100 of the aircraft, company public relations people were touting the 737 as "the most ordered" airplane in the history of commercial aviation.

BIGGER AND FASTER

The relentless beeping of *Sputnik* as it passed overhead in the fall of 1957 heralded the coming of a new age, or so it seemed. Just as the military was developing supersonic bombers, many assumed that civilians would soon travel faster than sound across the Atlantic and around the world. The price that the services had to pay for supersonic warplanes, however, made it clear that no company could borrow enough money to develop such an airliner, nor could any consortium of airlines afford such a project. Government support would be required.

Undeterred by the Comet setback, British leaders continued to dream of producing a superior aircraft that would take back the skies from the Americans. The Royal Aviation Establishment in Farnborough created a Supersonic Transport Aircraft Committee in 1956. By 1960, the engineers at Bristol, now merged into British Aircraft, proposed a slender delta-wing configuration powered by six turbojets capable of flying 130 passengers across the Atlantic. The project, however, proved larger than Britain could handle alone.

France and Britain were growing accustomed to cooperation on aerospace projects. The Caravelle, built in France and powered by British engines, had sold well, even in the United States. In 1962, eager to continue challenging American hegemony in commercial aviation, the French agreed to collaborate with the British in developing a supersonic transport. Everything would be shared: costs, the opportunities to develop advanced technology, jobs, and profits. Work on the airframe would be split 60-40, with the lion's share going to France. Britain and France would also share in the production of the Olympus 593 engines. The British referred to the aircraft as the "223," the Bristol design number, or the "Supersonic Transport (SST)." The French used the designation "TTS" (for *transport supersonique*), or the "Super Caravelle," to which the British objected. The name "Concorde" emerged from a joint meeting in January 1963.

During the Eisenhower administration, FAA Administrator Elwood "Pete" Quesada argued unsuccessfully for a government-supported supersonic transport program. Juan Trippe of Pan American stirred the pot once again, announcing that while he would prefer to purchase an American supersonic jet, he was depositing earnest money on six Concordes. President John F. Kennedy decided to accept the European challenge and expanded the role of the FAA to include the development of an American supersonic transport. Early in 1961, Najeeb E. Halaby, the new administrator, received an $11 million appropriation to support preliminary design studies. President Kennedy asked Congress for another $750 million and promised that the contractors would put up 25 percent of the cost.

When the heads of North American, Lockheed, and Boeing proved less than enthusiastic, the president responded by appointing a study commission headed by bankers and business executives. The report recommended that the government fund 90 percent of the program and suggested that the FAA was not the most appropriate agency to manage things. Lyndon Johnson, the new president, ruled that the supersonic transport would be funded through the FAA but managed by a committee headed by Secretary of Defense Robert McNamara. With McNamara in charge, it was likely that the program would rise or fall on the basis of economic analysis.

With the costs of the Concorde rising, Harold Wilson, the new prime minister of England, sought to withdraw from the Concorde agreement. Charles de Gaulle, who had blackballed Britain from entry into the European Common Market, threatened to resort to international law. Wilson returned to the fold.

The Soviet Union was also in the running. While some analysts have suggested that work on a Soviet supersonic transport began in an effort to keep up with the West, other indications are that the success of the Tu-104 over long-distance Soviet routes revealed the potential of such a jet. Soviet leaders, flush with space-age confidence in the early 1960s, decided to build their own supersonic passenger jet. Andrei Tupolev, the longest lived and most experienced of Russian designers, exhibited a model of the aircraft at the 1965 Paris Air Show.

Some wags referred to the Tu-144 as "Konkordski," because of its resemblance to the Concorde. Soviet espionage did penetrate the Concorde project and may have made use of Anglo-French data, but the Russian product was by no means a clone. All supersonic transports designed in the early 1960s looked something alike. In fact, Tupolev would have done well to copy the Concorde as closely as he had the B-29, because the Soviet design contained several flaws, notably the placement of the engines and air intakes. Nevertheless, the Tu-144 took to the skies in December 1968, two months before the Concorde. It flew faster than sound for the first time on June 5, 1969, and became the first civil aircraft to reach Mach 2 on May 26, 1970.

The 1973 Paris Air Show was to be the showcase for both the Concorde and the Tu-144. A crew of six took to the air in the pride of Soviet aviation, following a sterling performance by the Concorde. With twenty thousand spectators looking on, the Tu-144 performed a series of maneuvers, then, after attempting to avoid a collision with a French Mirage photographing the performance, returned to earth out of control. The crew and eight people on the ground died. The remaining fleet of sixteen Tu-144s proved uneconomical. In 1997, one of the remaining aircraft was refurbished and used to fly tests related to a U.S. hypersonic research effort.

In all, twenty Concordes were built. A Concorde flew the Atlantic for the first time in September 1973. The high price of a ticket, and the refusal of the U.S. government to allow supersonic flights over land, meant that the airplane could only demonstrate its full capabilities on flights to and from Europe. It soon became apparent that the Concorde would be an economic failure. Passenger service never broke even. The British and French governments were satisfied, however, with the enormous prestige of offering luxury service that cut transatlantic

Concorde

travel time in half. Moreover, the project demonstrated the real value of cross-Channel cooperation in high-technology endeavors.

The Americans kept their eyes focused on the bottom line. It was assumed that the supersonic transport would enter service in the early 1970s and come to dominate overseas routes. From the outset, however, officials expressed concerns. Studies indicated that people would react against frequent sonic booms. The air force reported that B-58 operations invariably provoked a steady stream of complaints from farmers, homeowners, and light sleepers. Talk of a supersonic passenger jet sparked the creation of antisonic boom groups. Robert McNamara's coordinating committee realized that supersonic flights over land would not be allowed.

Boeing won the contract for two prototypes in January 1967. As the competitors pointed out, these would be the first airplanes built in Seattle to fly faster than sound. Boeing was delighted, but corporate attention focused on another new project.

●　　　　●　　　　●

IN THE MID-1960s, Pan American's Juan Trippe noted that passenger traffic was increasing from 10 to 12 percent a year, airports were growing more congested, and the air traffic control system was stretched thin. Trippe thought that an aircraft capable of carrying large numbers of people over long distances could significantly address these issues and at the same time reduce the seat cost per mile. In an effort to extend the utility of such an airplane, Trippe insisted on an air freight version. The size of two standard freight containers, side by side, set the "wide-body" shape of the new airplane.

Lockheed had won the contract for the C-5A, a military transport that was too large and too slow to serve as the basis for the airliner. Boeing, having lost the contract to Lockheed was hungry. Trippe had lured Boeing's William Allen into taking a major risk once before, and they had both won big as a result, with the Boeing 707. Now they were making history with the American supersonic transport. The new airplane, the 747, would cement the hold of the airline and the manufacturer on the future of air transportation.

Once again, Allen bet the company on the new product. The cost of design, tooling, and facility construction would be $500 million, a sum that would double as a result of labor, material, and certification expenses leading up to its first flight. The new airplane, 225 feet long with a tail six stories tall, would be assembled in a new plant constructed at Everett, Washington. With forty acres of floor space, it had a larger volume than any other building.

Problems popped up in short order. Pratt & Whitney was slow to deliver the JT-9D turbofan engines. When they did arrive, William Allen recalled, "they didn't work."[19] Components actually stretched out of shape and had to be reinforced. After an initial round of sales, the prospects dried up. In 1970, air passenger traffic reached a plateau, and equipment purchases decreased. John Steiner, Boeing's vice president, noted that "at the bottom, we did not sell a single commercial airplane to a U.S. trunk carrier for a period of seventeen months."[20]

The clouds over Seattle grew thicker than usual. Boeing instituted a series of layoffs that rippled through the local economy. Unemployment reached an unprecedented 13 percent in the metropolitan area. Auto sales, housing rentals, and motel occupancy plummeted. Moving-van rentals increased, however. The local media reported on the exodus of ex-Boeing employees from Seattle. Two laid-off workers sponsored a billboard on the way to the airport. It read

> Will the last person
> Leaving SEATTLE—
> Turn out the lights.[21]

It was at this moment that the Boeing supersonic project began to spiral toward extinction. Boeing had been pleased to win the contract but could scarcely imagine the problems that lay ahead. Some were technical. Engineers, for example, had to abandon the swing wing at the core of their original design because it was too heavy.

The real difficulties, however, were political and cultural. The environmental movement began to attract widespread public support. One group, the Citizens League Against the Sonic Boom, organized by William Shurcliff, took the early lead in opposing the supersonic jet. Concern also mounted that the high-flying airplane would damage the upper atmosphere. By 1970, a coalition of powerful voices—the Sierra Club, the Wilderness Society, the National Wildlife Federation—joined hands to stop the project. The Federation of American Scientists joined the opposition.

No voice proved more damaging than Juan Trippe's old friend, Charles Lindbergh. "The regular operation of SST's in their present state of development will be disadvantageous both to aviation and to the peoples of the world," he remarked in a *New York Times* op-ed piece. "I believe we should prohibit their scheduled operation on or above United States territory as long as their effect on our over-all environment remains unsatisfactory."[22]

The cost of the program raised eyebrows. The Nixon plan called for Congress to provide the FAA with $1.3 billion to cover the cost of two supersonic transports to be used as technology demonstrators. Boeing would repay the money once it began to market the aircraft. Key U.S. senators, William Proxmire and Gaylord Nelson, questioned the expenditure of so many taxpayer dollars on an airplane that would offer a service affordable only by elite travelers. A dozen leading economists, including a former chair of the president's Council of Economic Advisors, questioned the economics of such a service.

By 1971, polls indicated that 85 percent of Americans opposed the plane. The Senate voted against funding the project late in 1970. The House of Representatives followed suit in 1974. Americans, speaking with a remarkably unified voice, had rejected it. They preferred an efficient, clean, quiet operation and sound economics to an increase in speed. The military also had turned away from high speed and high altitude for bombers in favor of stealth and precision. The definition of progress was growing more complex.

STRUGGLING WITH the 747 problems, and having lost the contract for the supersonic jet, Boeing now faced increased competition. Frank Kolk, an American Airlines executive, decided that Trippe and Boeing had gone too far. With the assistance and advice of other airline leaders, he invited bids for a wide-body airliner, powered by three turbofan engines, that would be midway between the first-generation jetliners and the 747.

James McDonnell, head of the newly merged McDonnell Douglas firm, was eager to enter the market with a midrange wide-body product on the basis of the Douglas experience. The result was the DC-10.

Like Bill Allen, Daniel Haughton would bet the future of *his* company on a third wide-body design, the Lockheed L-1011. Across the Atlantic, Rolls-Royce would sink or swim on the sale of the RB-211, which would power the L-1011. Forced into receivership by existing business problems, the historic firm saw the Lockheed contract as its salvation. Lockheed, faced with the prospect of building "the world's biggest glider," in the words of one worried official, had problems of its own. Recognizing the importance of his firm to the United States and Rolls-Royce to Great Britain, Haughton persuaded federal officials to underwrite $250 million in bank loans, which Lockheed could not otherwise obtain. The famous "bailout" kept both companies afloat. Lockheed did repay the loans, but the sale of the 250 L-1011s did not cover costs.

As it had in the past, Boeing emerged as the big winner in the battle of the wide bodies. The first 747, the 747-100, rolled out of the Seattle works on September 30, 1968, and flew on February 9, 1969. Pan Am introduced the airplane on the New York-London route in January 1970. After a difficult decade when few airlines could afford the 747, the market finally caught up with the big airplane. By 1993, the one-thousandth 747 entered airline service. The 747-400 was made to order for the longest routes across the Pacific. In Japan, 747s filled to capacity shuttled between Tokyo and Osaka. The wide body sold so well at a hefty $177 million that Boeing could afford to discount smaller and slower-selling aircraft.

Boeing 747SP "Clipper Constitution"

By the end of the century, merger and consolidation left Boeing as the only American maker of large transport aircraft. For the first time since the early 1930s, a European manufacturer, enjoying the benefit of subsidies from participating governments, emerged as a significant rival. In 1990, Airbus Industrie surpassed Boeing in its sales of every class of airplane smaller than the 747. By 1994, Airbus sold more airplanes than the Americans, a significant number of them in North America.[23]

In the early years of the new century, the European and American rivals started moving toward the future in different directions. This time it was Airbus that announced plans for a new class of very large airliner that would seat eight hundred persons, with the potential for a thousand-passenger craft in the foreseeable future. Boeing countered with a plan for a supersonic transport aircraft. What impact would the midafternoon arrival of a dozen huge airliners from Europe have on an American airport? Could a high-speed Boeing airliner make a profit where the Concorde had failed? Only time will tell which direction represents the wave of the future.

CONCLUSION

9/11

At 8:51 A.M. on September 11, 2001, television news anchor Paula Zahn announced that there had been an explosion at the World Trade Center in Lower Manhattan. In fact, a hijacked Boeing 767, American Airlines flight 11 from Boston's Logan Airport, had crashed into One World Trade Center just three minutes before. At 9:03 A.M., television cameras focused on the plume of acrid smoke billowing out of the north tower recorded a second Boeing 767, United flight 175, as it plunged into Two World Trade Center.

There seemed no end to the horrors unfolding that morning. An American Airlines Boeing 757 smashed into the Pentagon at 9:43 A.M. The south tower of the World Trade Center gave way at 9:59 A.M., as millions of television viewers watched. One minute later, a second hijacked 757, United Airlines flight 93, crashed into a field near Somerset, Pennsylvania. With flame and smoke pouring out of the nation's military nerve center, a section of the Pentagon collapsed at 10:10 A.M. One World Trade Center, where it had all begun just one hour and forty minutes before, collapsed at 10:28 A.M.

A year after the tragedy, the official death count stood at 2,999. But the damage done that morning was not limited to the loss of life and property. "Not least among the grave injuries the world suffered on September 11," the editors of *Air & Space Smithsonian* magazine suggested, "was the desecration of the airliners." The actions of a handful of terrorists had repudiated "every advancement ever made in aviation—every piece of precision engineering, every tweak in performance and safety, all the world-wide, decades-long efforts made to improve air travel."[1]

PROBLEMS

The attack sent airlines reeling. By the end of 2001, business travel had fallen by 40 percent. U.S. airlines reported losses of $12 billion in 2001 and were on line to lose $5 billion in 2002. Domestic passenger miles were down 20 percent. Things were even worse on the international scene, where traffic was down 37 percent. Labor organizations estimated that two hundred thousand people lost their jobs in the wake of 9/11. American and United Air Lines cut forty thousand workers between them. The bad news continued. National Airlines folded. US Airways filed for bankruptcy.

Congress created the Air Transportation Stabilization Board following the terrorist attacks to extend loan guarantees to troubled airlines. Some corporations were too far gone to be helped. In December 2002 the board approved loans to five carriers, but rejected an appeal from United, the nation's second largest airline, for a $1.8 billion guarantee. Unable to control costs, United executives failed to convince the board that they could return the corporation to profitability by 2004–2005. Bankruptcy loomed on the horizon.

The problem, aviation pundits declared, was overcapacity. Too many airlines with too many airplanes. Desperate executives all too often plunged into fare wars. As prices fall, so do profits. The Air Transportation Association estimates that the cumulative profit of the industry from 1947 to 2002 totals $1.5 billion, less than the full amount of United's loan request. "Friends don't let friends invest in airlines," one wag commented. "Let's face it," an airline executive remarked, "the industry is flat on its back."[2]

The problems trickled down to aircraft manufacturers. Boeing officials approved thirty thousand layoffs by October 2002 and warned that more were coming. Production plummeted. If these trends continue, a company official reported, sales of 767, 757, and 747 aircraft would soon fall to one a month. "The industry isn't getting any better," Boeing spokesman Craig Martin warned, "and airplane orders aren't picking up all that much." With the passage of time, even carefully laid plans for the future were collapsing. In December 2002, for example, Boeing announced cancellation of its highly touted supersonic airliner, the Sonic Cruiser.[3]

Analysts pointed to deeper problems. For one, the industry was aging. *USA Today* noted that most of the aerospace luminaries attending the World Space Congress in Houston in October 2002 had gray hair. The Bureau of Labor Statistics reported that 54 percent of American aerospace workers were over forty-five years old. The government estimated that six million jobs vital to the economy and national security would open up by 2010. At the same time, the number of degrees awarded to U.S. citizens in aerospace engineering dropped by half between 1991 and the end of the century. The industry faced fierce competition from abroad. At the end of the century, U.S. Air Force satellites were being launched by Russian rocket engines, because U.S. industry was unable to meet the need. What would Curtis LeMay have said?[4]

Would the American aerospace industry go the way of steel, shipbuilding, automobiles, and textiles? At the very least, Congressman Robert Walker suggested, it was "riding on fumes." In August 2001, President George W. Bush appointed Walker chairman of the twelve-person Commission on the Future of the United States Aerospace Industry. The group issued three interim reports by the fall of 2002. They called for educational initiatives to prepare students for aerospace careers; support for industry, from research and development to global marketing; and a complete transformation of the air transportation system.[5]

LOOKING AHEAD

What does the future hold? At the beginning of the twentieth century, even the inventors of the airplane found it impossible to predict the future of their technology. "No airship will ever fly from New York to Paris," Wilbur Wright remarked in 1909. "No engine can run . . . for four days without stopping." Nor did he hold out much hope for large aircraft. "The airship will always be a special messenger," he predicted, "never a load-carrier."[6] His brother Orville did not "believe that the airplane will ever take the place of trains or steamships for the carrying of passengers."[7]

Why were the Wrights unable to see even a few years into the future of their invention? Flight technology was new and immature. Simple improvements resulted in great leaps in performance. The U.S. Army bought its first airplane from the Wright brothers in 1909. Just two years later, officials judged it to be obsolete and gave it to the Smithsonian. Under such conditions, change is rapid, and its consequences difficult for even the most knowledgeable practitioner to predict.

In 1953, aerospace leaders celebrating the fiftieth anniversary of the airplane pondered what might be achieved in flight by the centennial year of 2003. This time, some of the most experienced individuals proved to be wildly optimistic. Rocket pioneer Wernher von Braun believed that atomic-powered aircraft would dominate future skies. Donald Douglas, president of Douglas Aircraft, and C. R. Smith, the head of American Airlines, agreed.

Ralph S. Damon, president of Trans World Airlines, and Alex Dawydoff, an industry journalist, were certain the convertiplane, a combination helicopter and airplane that could lift straight up into the air, would serve as the airliner of the future. Von Braun envisioned "helicopters all over the place." There would be roadable helicopters in every garage. These aerial runabouts of the future would be operated at low altitudes, to avoid crowding the upper airspace reserved for passenger airliners and military aircraft. "Helicopter house trailers" would enable vacationers to escape by air to the beach or the mountains, taking their accommodations with them.[8]

Others took a much more conservative view. Igor Sikorsky, who had helped to launch the air age and pioneered the practical helicopter, predicted that jetliners, traveling above the weather, "will bring any point of the globe to within a few hours comfortable travel of any other point." He foresaw the birth of the space age and argued that even a lunar landing was "by no means impossible."[9]

None of the prognosticators of 1953 came closer to the mark than Boeing's vice president for engineering, Ed Wells. Within ten years, he thought, jet transports would be "almost universally accepted on the airline routes of the world." As a practical engineer with a lifetime of experience behind him, he dismissed the notion of nuclear-propelled aircraft. Guided missiles, he predicted, were the wave of the future.

If experienced engineers and industrialists like Ed Wells and Igor Sikorsky found it easier to peer into the future than the inventors of the airplane had, it was because flight technology was approaching maturity. The pace of change was generally slower and more predictable. Airplanes cost more and remained in service longer. A typical World War I fighter cost about $5,000 and had a useful life of a year or less. The classic U.S. military aircraft introduced in the middle of World War II—the P-51 Mustang or F4U Corsair—had a price tag of $50,000 and served the nation in two wars. The trend would continue. The F-15 of the 1970s cost $40 million and remained the top-of-the-line U.S. Air Force fighter a quarter of a century after it first took to the air. If things go as planned, the Boeing B-52, a classic product of mature technology, will remain in service for eighty years.

Not even Ed Wells had a perfectly clear view of things to come, however. He scoffed at "loose talk" about "so-called mechanical and electronic 'brains,'" and suggested that it was "impossible to design a mechanical device with 'intelligence.'"[10] As late as 1953, the most perceptive industry leaders still failed to recognize the revolutionary potential of the computer. Those, like Wernher von Braun, who offered a far too optimistic vision of the future were blinded by their unbridled enthusiasm for new technology. That is something to keep in mind when considering the next fifty years of flight from our vantage point at the beginning of the second century of flight.

Is the dream of a hypersonic airliner capable of flying from the United States to Japan in an hour or two the present-day equivalent of the nuclear airplane of 1953? For the next fifty years, it seems far more likely that the current trend toward ever larger subsonic "air buses" will continue. The airplanes now on the drawing board will still be flying a half-century from now, and with the collapse of the Boeing Sonic Cruiser in 2002, the hypersonic passenger transport has receded into the more distant future. Will there ever be a flying machine in every garage? That seems no more likely today than it did in 1933, or 1953.

It is perhaps easier to look fifty years into the future of military aviation. The F-22 Raptor, first flown in 1997, is scheduled to enter service in 2005, with production stretching to 2013. There is every reason to think that the Raptor will still be flying in 2040, and perhaps beyond. A joint product of Lockheed Martin, Boeing, and Pratt & Whitney, the F-22 also offers a view of the future of aircraft manufacturing as a more cooperative venture designed to preserve the health of several corporations.

The Joint Strike Fighter, the F-35, illustrates the continuation of other trends. Lockheed Martin will lead an international coalition producing the stealthy, high-tech aircraft in three variants. There will be a standard air force version, a navy carrier airplane, and a short take-off and landing version for the U.S. Marines and the Royal Navy. So far, seven additional nations have signed up for the airplane. If all goes well, the first F-35 will enter service in 2008.

That will carry us close to the midcentury, and it is indeed difficult to see beyond that point. Some things will not change, however. Government investment will continue to fuel new technologies that transform the way in which we fly. Technology will revolutionize air transportation, transferring a measure of control from the cockpit to computerized systems in the air and on the ground. Inevitably, technology will also replace pilots in an increasing number of military cockpits. Will the F-35 be the last in a long line of single-seat fighters stretching back to the Fokker E.III?

There seems little doubt that the United States will remain the world's leading airpower for the foreseeable future. Will the European consortium dominate the world market for large airliners in the decades to come? If the airlines continue to struggle, will the government re-regulate the industry? Will new technology lead to the realization of other old dreams? All of that, and a great deal more, remains to be seen.

Whatever the future holds, it is unlikely that we will lose our sense of wonder at our ability to fly. Even in an age when air travel to the other side of the world is commonplace, and humans have established a permanent foothold in space, flight continues to inspire much the same sense of awe and power that it did when the airplane was new. Aviation, that most hard-edged of technologies, has somehow retained an element of magic. We can explain the physical mechanisms of flight in the cold, hard language of the scientist and engineer, but *miracle* and *dream* are still the words that come most readily to mind at the sight of an airplane tracing a contrail across the sky. Orville Wright summed the matter up in a letter to his friend George Spratt. "Isn't it astonishing that all these secrets have been preserved for so many years just so that we could discover them!!"[11]

GLOSSARY

Aerodrome the name Samuel Pierpont Langley applied to his models and full-scale aircraft; more appropriately, an English term for a flying field.

aerodynamics the branch of fluid dynamics that deals with the flow of air around a solid body.

aeronaut the operator of a lighter-than-air craft.

aeronautics the design and operation of any aircraft.

aerostation the achievement of flight by buoyant means, by filling an envelop with hot air or a lightweight gas.

ailerons movable surfaces, usually on the trailing edge of the wing, used to control the motion of the aircraft in the roll axis.

airfoil a specially shaped solid surface generating a lifting force, such as a wing or propeller.

airframe the structure of a flying machine.

airship a dirigible, or powered, lighter-than-air craft.

altimeter an instrument indicating the altitude of the aircraft.

amphibian an aircraft equipped to take off from either land or water.

angle of attack the angle between the chord of the wing and undisturbed airflow; also known as the angle of incidence. The angle of attack can be described as high or low.

arc of a circle airfoil an airfoil in which the peak of the arch is at the midpoint of the chord.

aspect ratio the ratio of wingspan to wing chord. A wing with a high aspect ratio is relatively long and narrow.

autogiro the name applied by inventor Juan de la Cierva to describe a gyroplane; a machine in which the forward motion of a conventionally powered aircraft turns an otherwise unpowered rotary wing.

aviation the entire field of artificial flight.

axial flow a turbojet design in which air flows through the center of the engine.

axis an imaginary line passing through a body, and around which that body is free to rotate. See *lateral*, *pitch*, and *yaw control*.

biplane an aircraft with an upper and lower wing carefully trussed together to provide a strong structure.

boundary layer a thin layer of fluid next to a solid surface that plays a critically important role in the circulation of fluid about a body.

box kite a tailless kite design consisting of two or more open-ended "boxes," or cells. It was invented by the Australian experimenter Lawrence Hargrave.

camber the curve of an airfoil, from the leading to the trailing edge.

canard an aircraft in which the elevator is placed at the front of the craft. The word means "duck" in French, and was apparently applied to describe the look of such a machine in the air.

cantilever a structure, including a wing, supported at one end only with no external bracing.

center of gravity the point at which the combined weight forces are located on an aircraft.

center of lift the point at which an aircraft in equilibrium is supported.

center of pressure the point on an airfoil where the resultant of all pressure forces acts.

centrifugal-flow engine a type of turbojet engine in which the flow of air is diverted into mixing chambers surrounding the centerline of the engine.

circulation theory of lift the oldest and most complex theory developed to explain aerodynamic lift. The total flow over and under the wing is the result of "net" circulation. The air passing over the wing adds to the overall speed of the flow; that moving beneath the wing reduces it. Lift is the result of the differential pressure caused by differential flow.

coefficient of enlargement a coefficient required to transform wind tunnel data gathered using models to full-scale designs.

collective-pitch control a control in which the pitch of the blades of a helicopter rotor is increased or decreased to ascend or descend.

computer numerically controlled (CNC) machining a technology that uses a computer which supplies a stream of digital information to instruct a machine tool that cuts raw material into a finished product.

contra-rotating propellers twin propellers that rotate in opposite directions to offset the torque of a single propeller.

constant-speed propeller a propeller that automatically changes pitch to meet varying conditions of flight.

cowl flaps small flaps at the rear of the engine cowling that can be opened to increase the flow of cooling air.

cyclic-pitch control a control in which the angle of attack of the helicopter rotor disk is changed to direct the motion of the machine.

dead stick landing a landing without power.

delta wing a design in which the wing is in the form of a triangle, with the trailing edge serving as the base.

dihedral a situation in which the wing tips are higher than the point where the wings meet the fuselage.

dirigible an airship, or any powered lighter-than-air craft.

dive brake a surface extended from the wing or fuselage to slow the speed of a dive.

drag the force resisting the forward motion of a body immersed in a fluid.

elevator a horizontal surface that controls an aircraft in pitch.

elevon a control surface combining the function of the elevator and ailerons, as on a delta-wing craft or a flying wing.

empennage the control surfaces on the tail of an aircraft.

engine the power plant of an aircraft.

escadrille a French military flying unit.

fairing a streamlined housing, as, for example, to reduce the drag on fixed landing gear.

fillet a fairing to streamline the area in which two surfaces, such as a wing and fuselage, meet.

fixed-base operator an air service located at an airport that services aircraft and frequently offers flying instruction and a range of other services.

fixed landing gear landing gear that does not retract out of the air stream.

Flap a control surface that is extended, usually out and down from the trailing edge of the wing (a Fowler flap), to increase lift at the critical moments of take-off and landing.

floatplane a seaplane that takes off and lands on floats.

flutter an aerodynamically induced vibrating force operating on the wing or tail of an airplane.

flying boat a seaplane that takes off and lands on its hull.

flying speed the speed at which an aircraft will take off and remain in the air.

flying tail a horizontal stabilizer, the angle of attack of which can be altered in flight.

flying wing an aircraft built entirely, or almost entirely, in the shape of an airfoil. The passengers and crew are entirely housed in the wing.

gap the distance between the wings of a biplane or multiplane.

heavier-than-air machine an aircraft that is heavier than the volume of air it displaces.

high-wing monoplane an aircraft in which the wing is attached to the top of the fuselage.

inherent stability the capacity of an aircraft to continue in straight and level flight until the pilot intervenes to change altitude or direction.

inertial navigation a self-contained navigation system that keeps constant track of the position of a craft with regard to an initial reference point.

in-line engine an internal combustion engine in which one row of cylinders or more are arranged in straight lines.

laminar flow a condition in which layers of air flow smoothly from the leading edge to the trailing edge of a wing.

lateral control the control of an airplane around the roll axis, which passes from the nose through the tail of an aircraft.

leading edge the forward edge of the wing.

lighter-than-air machine a craft operating on the principles of buoyancy.

low-wing monoplane an aircraft in which the wing is attached to the bottom of the fuselage.

Mach the ratio of the airspeed of an aircraft to the speed of sound.

mid-wing monoplane an aircraft in which the wings attach at the mid-point of the fuselage.

monocoque construction single-shell construction, in which the fuselage of an aircraft supports itself without elaborate internal supports.

monoplane an airplane with a single wing.

multiplane machine an aircraft with more than three wings.

nacelle a streamlined housing, usually for engines.

numerically controlled (NC) machining a technology developed with U.S. Air Force funding during the late 1940s and early 1950s that uses paper tapes with holes punched in them to control the cutting tools. The system functions something like an old-fashioned player piano roll.

ornithopter a machine in which beating wings provide both lift and propulsion.

parasol wing a monoplane wing elevated above the fuselage on struts.

pitch control the control of an airplane around the pitch axis, which passes through the span of a wing, from tip to tip.

pusher a propeller that pushes, rather than pulls, the aircraft.

radial engine an engine in which the cylinders are arranged in a circle around the crankshaft.

reversible-pitch propeller a propeller in which the pitch of the blades can be reversed to stop forward motion of the airplane on the runway.

roll control see *lateral control*.

rudder a vertical surface that controls the yaw of an aircraft.

slot (also slat) a surface located slightly forward of the leading edge of the wing, and separated from it by a small gap. The purpose is to "hold" the airflow to the surface of the wing.

supercharger a turbine-powered device that increases the flow of air into an internal combustion engine, enabling it to function efficiently at very high altitudes.

tractor a propeller that pulls, rather than pushes, an airplane through the air.

trim tabs small movable surfaces that enable a pilot to balance controls to meet changing flight conditions.

triplane an aircraft with three wings.

variable-pitch propeller a propeller in which the angle of the blades can be changed to operate efficiently at take-off and during cruise.

whirling arm an engineering instrument in which test surfaces are mounted on a rotating arm, together with a means of measuring the resulting forces.

wind tunnel a hollow tubular structure that allows one to move air over a surface, rather than propelling a surface through air, so that the resulting forces can be measured.

wing loading the gross weight of an airplane divided by the wing area.

wingspan the length of the wing from tip to tip.

wing-warping inducing an even, helical twist across the span of a wing, so that the angle of attack, and the lift, are increased on one side and decreased on the other. This causes one tip to rise and the other to drop.

yaw control control of an aircraft about the yaw axis, which passes vertically through the fuselage.

NOTES

PROLOGUE

1 All Borglum quotes are from Gutzon Borglum to Ned, September 10, 1908, Gutzon Borglum Papers, Box 52, Manuscript Division, Library of Congress, Washington, D.C.; the identity of Ned is not clear. The assumption that the recipient was Gutzon's brother Solon, and that he may have been nicknamed Ned, is based on evidence internal to the letter. My deepest thanks to my friend and colleague of many years Leonard Bruno, of the Manuscript Division, Library of Congress, for introducing me to Borglum's account of his first encounter with a flying machine.

2 Gutzon Borglum quoted in Rex Alan Smith, *The Carving of Mount Rushmore* (New York: Abbeville, 1985), 54.

3 *Le figaro*, August 11, 1908.

4 *Times* (London), August 14, 1908.

5 Augustus Post to G., morning of September 9, 1908, copy in a memorial book prepared by the Aero Club of America to commemorate the tenth anniversary of the first flight, Aero Club of America Collection, Accession No. xxxx-0627, National Air and Space Museum Archives, Washington, D.C.

6 Ibid.

7 Fred Kelly, "They Wouldn't Believe the Wrights Had Flown," *Harpers*, August 1940, 30.

8 Charles K. Field, "On the Wings of Today," *Sunset*, March 1910, 249.

9 Wilbur Wright quoted in "Airship Safe: Air Motoring No More Dangerous Than Land Motoring," *Cairo (Illinois) Bulletin*, March 25, 1909; Orville

Wright quoted in "Catherine [*sic*] Wright Going Abroad to Witness Brother's Triumph," *Dayton Herald*, January 2, 1909.

[10] Luke E. Wright quoted in "New World's Aeroplane Records Established," *Journal of Commerce* (New York) September 10, 1908.

[11] H. G. Wells, *The War in the Air, and Particularly How Mr. Bert Smallways Faired While It Lasted* (London, 1908), 246; see also I. F. Clarke, *Voices Prophesying War: Future Wars 1763–3749* (Oxford: Oxford University Press, 1992).

[12] Orville Wright to C. H. Hancock, June 21, 1917, in Fred C. Kelly, ed., *Miracle at Kitty Hawk: The Letters of Wilbur and Orville Wright* (New York: Farrar, Straus and Giroux, 1951), 405.

[13] Orville Wright quoted in "What Is Ahead in Aviation: America's Foremost Leaders in Many Branches of Flying Give Remarkable Forecasts of the Future," *Popular Science*, June 1929, 124–129.

[14] Both the newspaper and the museum are controlled by the Gannett Corp. On the morning when the story appeared, I immediately called the museum in question and pointed out the logical inconsistency. Available at: http://www.newseum.org/century/about.htm. Accessed May 6, 2001. For the response, see Bob Thompson, "The Museum of the American Century," *Washington Post Magazine*, September 17, 2000, 10.

[15] Melvin Kranzberg, "Technology and History: 'Kranzberg's Laws,'" *Technology and Culture* 27, no. 3 (July 1986): 544–560.

[16] Mme. Chiang Kai-shek, "Wings over China," *Shanghai Evening Post*, March 12, 1937.

[17] Charles A. Lindbergh, "Aviation, Geography, and Race," *Reader's Digest*, November 1939, 64–67.

[18] Thanks to my colleague of many years, R. E. G. Davies, for suggesting the connection to religion.

[19] Carl M. Spaatz quoted in Phillip S. Meillinger, *10 Propositions regarding Air Power* (Washington, D.C.: Air Force History and Museum Program, 1995), 95.

[20] Charles A. Lindbergh to G. Edward Pendray, December 2, 1966, G. Edward Pendray Papers, Manuscript Division, Department of Rare Books and Special Collections, Princeton University Library, Princeton N.J. Copy in the author's collection.

[21] Charles Augustus Lindbergh, *Autobiography of Values* (New York: Harcourt Brace Jovanovich, 1976), 41.

[22] Orville Wright quoted in Fred Kelly, "Orville Wright Looks Back on Forty Years since First Flight," *St. Louis Post Dispatch*, November 7, 1943, 1D, 4D.

[23] Richard Potts, "Flying Machines," in Jonathan Brockman, ed., *The Greatest Inventions of the Past 2000 Years* (New York: Simon and Schuster, 2000), 37–39.

[24] Walter McDougall, ". . . *The Heavens and the Earth": A Political History of the Space Age* (New York: Basic Books, 1985).

CHAPTER 1

1 Cayley notebook, in C. H. Gibbs-Smith, *Sir George Cayley's Aeronautics, 1796–1855* (London: HMSO, 1962), 18.

2 Richard Bach, "Egyptians Are One Day Going to Fly," in *A Gift of Wings* (New York: Dell, 1974), 273–275.

3 For more information on the *Condor* project, see Jim Woodward, *Nazca: Journey to the Sun* (New York: Pocket Books, 1977).

4 Joseph Montgolfier quoted in ibid., 17.

5 B. Franklin to J. Banks, August 30, 1783, in A. L. Rotch, *Benjamin Franklin and the First Balloons* (Worcester, Mass.: American Antiquarian Society, 1907), 5.

6 Clive Hart, *Kites: An Historical Survey* (New York: Praeger, 1967), provides the best introduction to the early history of the kite.

7 Lynn White Jr., *Medieval Technology and Social Change* (London: Oxford University Press, 1962), provides a first-rate introduction to the early history of the windmill.

8 For additional details of the *moulinet à vent et à noix,* see C. H. Gibbs-Smith, *Aviation: An Historical Survey from Its Origins to the End of World War II* (London: HMSO, 1970), 4–6; Clive Hart, *The Dream of Flight: Aeronautics from Classical Times to the Renaissance* (New York: Winchester Press, 1972), 116–117.

9 For complete technical history of the helicopter toy from 1784 to 1870, see Octave Chanute, *Progress in Flying Machines* (New York: American Engineer and Railroad Journal, 1894).

10 Gibbs-Smith, *Sir George Cayley's Aeronautics*, 1.

11 Chanute, *Progress in Flying Machines*, 55.

12 Wright brothers quoted in Grace Boston, "Wright Boys Interested in Aviation When They Were School Boys in This City," *Cedar Rapids Evening Gazette*, September 19, 1928.

13 Wilbur Wright to the Smithsonian Institution, May 30, 1899, in Marvin W. McFarland, ed., *The Papers of Wilbur and Orville Wright* (New York: McGraw-Hill, 1953), 1: 4.

14 "Remarks by Milton Wright," in Ivonette Wright Miller, *Wright Reminiscences* (Dayton, Ohio: n.p., 1978), 68.

15 Benjamin Robbins quoted in John Anderson, *A History of Aerodynamics and Its Impact on Flying Machines* (New York: Cambridge University Press, 1997), 55.

16 John Smeaton quoted in Anderson, *History of Aerodynamics and Its Impact*, 58; see also J. L. Pritchard, "The Dawn of Aerodynamics," *Journal of the Royal Aeronautical Society* 61 (March 1957): 149–180.

17 Anderson, *History of Aerodynamics and Its Impact*, 55.

18 J. Laurence Pritchard, *Sir George Cayley: The Inventor of the Aeroplane* (New York: Horizon Press, 1962), 6.

19 C. H. Gibbs-Smith, *Sir George Cayley's Aeronautics*, 11.

20 George Cayley, "On Aerial Navigation," *A Journal of Natural Philosophy,*

Chemistry and the Arts, published by W. Nicholson (New Series) in London, November 1809 (vol. 24: 164–174), February 1810 (vol. 25: 81–87), March 1810 (25: 161–169), in Gibbs-Smith, *Sir George Cayley's Aeronautics*, 213–214.

[21] Cayley, "On Aerial Navigation," in Gibbs-Smith, *Sir George Cayley's Aeronautics*, 217.

[22] Ibid., 42.

[23] Quotes from Francis Paget Hett, ed., *The Memoirs of Susan Sibbald (1783–1812)* (London: John Lane, 1926), 284–285.

[24] George Cayley quoted in Gibbs-Smith, *Sir George Cayley*, 16.

[25] Mrs. George Thompson quoted in Gibbs-Smith, *Cayley's Aeronautics*, 177.

[26] Orville Wright to Henry Woodhouse, December 9, 1912, in Fred C. Kelly, *Miracle at Kitty Hawk: The Letters of Wilbur and Orville Wright* (New York: Farrar, Straus and Giroux, 1951), 395.

[27] Orville Wright to William Enyart, June 22, 1944, in the Papers of Wilbur and Orville Wright, Correspondence with Lester Gardiner, Box 26, Manuscript Division, Library of Congress, Washington, D.C.

[28] For information on Frederick Brearey, see J. Laurence Pritchard, "Francis Herbert Wenham, Honorary Member, 1824–1908: An Appreciation of the First Lecturer to the Aeronautical Society," *Journal of the Royal Aeronautical Society* 62 (August 1958): 572; J. Laurence Pritchard, "A Century of British Aeronautics: The Royal Aeronautical Society, 1866–1966," *Journal of the Royal Aeronautical Society* 70 (January 1966): 6; Royal Aeronautical Society, *The Royal Aeronautical Society, 1866-1966: A Short History* (London: Royal Aeronautical Society, 1967); "The Pioneers: Saluting the Men and Women of Aviation History," available at www.ctie.monash.edu.au/hargrave/brearey.html. Accessed February 20, 2003.

[29] Francis Herbert Wenham quoted in Pritchard, "Francis Herbert Wenham," 572.

[30] Ibid., 580.

[31] The first eleven wind tunnels were built in the following years by the following people: 1871—F. H. Wenham, England; 1884—H. Phillips, England; 1893—Ludwig Mach, Austria; 1894—Johan Irminger and H. C. Vogt, Denmark; 1896—Col. Charles Renard, France; 1896—Massachusetts Institute of Technology, United States; 1896—Sir Hiram Maxim, England; 1897—Paul La Cour, Denmark; 1899—Etienne Marey, France; 1901—A. F. Zahm, United States; 1901—Wright brothers, United States.

[32] Hiram Maxim quoted in John Leinhard, "Hiram Maxim," available at www.uh.edu/engines/epi694.htm. Accessed February 19, 2003. See also, Hiram Maxim, *My Life* (London: Metheun, 1915).

[33] Wilbur Wright, "Some Aeronautical Experiments," in Marvin W. McFarland, ed., *The Papers of Wilbur and Orville Wright* (New York: McGraw-Hill, 1953), 1: 103.

[34] Louis Mouillard quoted in Chanute, *Progress in Flying Machines*, 150.

35 S. P. Langley, "The Story of Experiments in Mechanical Flight," *Aeronautical Annual* (Boston, 1897): 13.

36 S. P. Langley, *Experiments in Aerodynamics* (Washington, D.C.: Smithsonian Institution, 1891), 107.

37 Otto Lilienthal, "Practical Experiments for the Development of Human Flight," *Report for the Board of Regents of the Smithsonian Institution for 1893* (Washington, D.C., 1894), 199.

38 Otto Lilienthal quote from the following Web site: http://invention.psychol ogy.msstate.edu/. Accessed February 25, 2003.

39 While Felts's attempt to glide down Pikes Peak actually dates to 1897, the incident underscores the confidence inspired by the Lilienthal design, even after the death of the German engineer. James McChristal, *Pikes Peak: Legends of America's Mountain* (Colorado Springs: Sierra Grande Press, 1999), 84.

40 Wright, "Some Aeronautical Experiments," 1: 103.

CHAPTER 2

1 Orville Wright to Milton Wright, April 1, 1881, in Fred C. Kelly, ed., *Miracle at Kitty Hawk: The Letters of Wilbur and Orville Wright* (New York: Farrar, Straus and Giroux, 1951), 3.

2 Orville Write quoted in Fred C. Kelly, *The Wright Brothers: A Biography Authorized by Orville Wright* (New York: Harcourt Brace, 1943), 15.

3 Wilbur Wright, April 3, 1912, in Marvin W. McFarland, ed., *The Papers of Wilbur and Orville Wright* (New York: McGraw-Hill, 1953), v.

4 Charles H. Bauer, "Ed Sines: Pal of the Wrights," *Popular Aviation* (June 1938): 40.

5 Robert Frost, "Kitty Hawk," in *In the Clearing* (New York: Holt, Rinehart and Winston, 1962).

6 Orville Wright's deposition, United States District Court, Southern District of Ohio, Western Division, *Charles H. Lamson vs. The Wright Company*, in Equity No. 6,611, p. 78, Defendant's Copy, in the Papers of Wilbur and Orville Wright, Box 63, Manuscript Division, Library of Congress, Washington, D.C.

7 Wilbur Wright's testimony, *Wright Company vs. Herring-Curtiss Co. and Glenn H. Curtiss*, in McFarland, *Papers*, 1: 474.

8 Wilbur Wright to Smithsonian Institution, May 30, 1899, in McFarland, *Papers*, 1: 4–5.

9 Wilbur Wright's testimony, *Wright Company vs. Herring-Curtiss Co. and Glenn H. Curtiss*, in McFarland, *Papers*, 1: 478.

10 *Binghamton (New York) Republican*, June 4, 1896.

11 James Means, "Wheeling and Flying," *Aeronautical Annual* (Boston, 1896): 25.

12 Otto Lilienthal to James Means, April 17, 1896, James Howard Means

Collection, Accession No. xxxx-0106, Box 2, National Air and Space Museum Archives, Washington, D.C.

[13] Wilbur Wright to Octave Chanute, May 13, 1900, in McFarland, *Papers*, 1: 15.

[14] William J. Tate to Wilbur Wright, August 18, 1900, in Kelly, *Miracle at Kitty Hawk*, 27.

[15] Wilbur Wright, "Some Aeronautical Experiments," in McFarland, *Papers*, 1: 105.

[16] Wilbur Wright, "Brief and Digest of the Evidence for the Complainant on Final Hearing," *Wright Company vs. Herring-Curtiss Company and Glenn H. Curtiss*, in Equity No. 400, pp. 4–25, National Archives and Record Administration, Washington, D.C.

[17] Octave Chanute quoted in C. H. Gibbs-Smith, *Aviation: An Historical Survey from Its Origins to the End of World War II* (London: HMSO, 1970), 98.

[18] Orville Wright, "How We Invented the Airplane," *Flying* (December 1913).

[19] *Washington Post*, October 8, 1903.

[20] Orville Wright, "Wright Tells of Airplane by Wireless," *Dayton Journal*, December 17, 1923.

[21] Wright brothers to Milton Wright, December 17, 1903, in McFarland, *Papers*, 1: 397.

[22] Percy B. Walker, *Early Aviation at Farnborough: The First Aeroplanes* (London: Macdonald, 1974), 19.

[23] Alberto Santos-Dumont quoted in Douglas Botting, *The Giant Airships* (Arlington, Va.: Time-Life Books, 1980), 29.

[24] Wilbur Wright, "The Angle of Incidence," *Aeronautical Journal* (July 1901): 47–49; Wilbur Wright, "Die wagereche Lage während des Gleitfluges," *Illustrierte Aeronautische Mitteilungen* (July 1901): 108–109.

[25] J. Laurence Pritchard, "The Wright Brothers and the Royal Aeronautical Society: A Survey and a Tribute," *Journal of the Royal Aeronautical Society* 57 (December 1953): 766.

[26] Comte de la Vaulx, *La triomphe de la navigation Aerienne aéroplanes, dirigeables, spheriques* (Paris: J. Tallandier, 1911), 274.

[27] Ernest Archdeacon, "M. Chanute en Paris," *La locomotion* (April 11, 1903): 225–227.

[28] Amos I. Root, "Our Homes," *Gleanings in Bee Culture* 33 (January 1, 1905): 38.

CHAPTER 3

[1] Gabriel Voisin, *Men, Women and Ten Thousand Kites* (London: Putnam, 1962).

[2] Robert Esnault-Pelterie quoted in C. H. Gibbs-Smith, *The Rebirth of European Aviation, 1902–1908* (London: HMSO, 1974), 152.

[3] Ferdinand Ferber quoted in Gibbs-Smith, *Rebirth*, 221.

[4] E. Archdeacon quoted in Gibbs-Smith, *Rebirth*, 223.

5 "The Startling Achievement of Santos-Dumont—First Real Flying Machine," *New York American*, November 8, 1906.

6 Alexander Graham Bell quoted in "Air Conquered by This Machine, Alexander Graham Bells Tells Scientific Men That Practical Flyer Has Been Invented," *Boston Herald*, November 22, 1906.

7 E. Archdeacon quoted in Gibbs-Smith, *Rebirth*, 245.

8 Alexander Graham Bell quoted in J. H. Parkin, *Bell and Baldwin: Their Development of the Aerodrome and Hydrodromes at Baddeck, Nova Scotia* (Toronto: University of Toronto, 1964), 92.

9 Glenn Curtiss quoted in C. Roseberry, *Glenn Curtiss: Pioneer of Flight* (Garden City, N.Y.: Doubleday, 1972), 49–53.

10 Arnold Kruckman, "The Sport of Kings—Ballooning," *Aeronautics* 1 (July 1907), 10–11.

11 Orville Wright to Glenn Curtiss, July 20, 1908, in Marvin W. McFarland, ed., *The Papers of Wilbur and Orville Wright* (New York: McGraw-Hill, 1953), 2: 907.

12 Wilbur Wright to Orville Wright, June 3, 1908, in McFarland, *Papers*, 2: 886–887.

13 François Peyrey quoted in *Times* (London), August 14, 1908.

14 Franz Reichel quoted in *Le Figaro*, August 11, 1908.

15 *L'Aérophile*, August 15, 1908.

16 Réné Gasnier quoted in *New York Herald*, August 9, 1908, cited in Gibbs-Smith, *Rebirth*, 286–287.

17 Paul Zens quoted in Gibbs-Smith, *Rebirth*, 287.

18 M. Surcouf quoted in Gibbs-Smith, *Rebirth*, 287.

19 Delagrange quoted in Gibbs-Smith, *Rebirth*, 288.

20 Henry Farman quoted in *Le matin*, August 26, 1908.

21 Louis Blériot quoted in Gibbs-Smith, *Rebirth*, 288.

22 Charles and Gabriel Voisin, letter to editor, *Le matin*, September 5, 1908.

23 Louis Blériot quoted in Gibbs-Smith, *Rebirth*, 286.

24 Ross Browne, interview with Kenneth Leish, transcript, p. 17, Columbia University Oral History Collection, New York, N.Y.

25 Ibid.

26 Ferdinand Collin, *Parmi les prècurseurs du ciel* (Paris: J. Peyronnet, 1943), 50.

27 Quote from "Prizes for Flight," *Flight* (April 7, 1909): 216.

28 Hubert Latham quoted in Tom D. Crouch, *The Bleriot XI: The Story of a Classic Airplane* (Washington, D.C.: Smithsonian Institution Press, 1982), 33.

29 Léon Levavaseur quoted in "Continental News," *Aero*, July 27, 1909, 156.

30 "Channel Flight," *Daily Mail* (London), July 22, 1909.

31 *Daily Mail* (London), July 26, 1909.

32 *Pall Mall Gazette*, July 27, 1909.

33 Allan Cobham quoted in C. H. Gibbs-Smith, "The Man Who Came by Air," *Shell Aviation News* (June 1959): 6.

[34] H. G. Wells quoted in Gibbs-Smith, "The Man Who Came by Air," 6.

[35] H. Massac Bist, "The Flying Races at Rheims," *Flight* (September 11, 1909): 555.

[36] Ibid., 557.

CHAPTER 4

[1] Claude Grahame-White, *The Aeroplane: Past, Present and Future* (London: T.W. Laurie, 1911), 48.

[2] Franz Kafka, "Die Aeroplane in Brescia," in Robert Wohl, *A Passion for Wings: Aviation and the Western Imagination, 1908–1918* (New Haven, Conn.: Yale University Press, 1994), 112. Wohl's wonderful volume is the source of information in this unit.

[3] Gabriele D'Annunzio quoted in Wohl, *Passion for Wings*, 116.

[4] Filippo Tommaso Marinetti quoted in Wohl, *Passion*, 139.

[5] Vasily Vasilyevich Kamensky quoted in Wohl, *Passion*, 151.

[6] John Anderson, *A History of Aerodynamics and Its Impact on Flying Machines* (Cambridge: Cambridge University Press, 1997), 252.

[7] Emmanuel Chadeau, *De Blériot à Dassault: historie de l'industrie aéronautique en France, 1900–1950* (Paris: Fayard, 1987), 435.

[8] C. Faroux and G. Bonnet, *Aéro-manuel: répertoire sportif technique et commerciale de aeronautique* (Paris: H. Dunod et E. Pinat, 1914), 427.

[9] Earl Ovington, "Diary," in Adelaide Ovington, *An Aviator's Wife* (New York: Dodi, Meade, 1920), 20–21.

[10] Faroux and Bonnet, *Aéro-manuel*, 427.

[11] The authoritative estimates of Gnôme production are provided in Lauren S. McCready, *The Invention and Development of the Gnôme Rotary Engine*, master's thesis, Polytechnic Institute of Brooklyn, 1973.

[12] Chadeau, *Blériot à Dassault*, 435.

[13] John Morrow, *The Great War in the Air: Military Aviation from 1909–1921* (Washington, D.C.: Smithsonian Institution, 1993), 33.

[14] Faroux and Bonnet, *Aéro-manuel*, 186–197.

[15] Granville E. Bradshaw, "Aeroplanes as Mechanical Constructions," *Flight*, (June 29, 1912): 593.

[16] House Committee on Military Affairs, *Aeronautics in the Army: Hearing before the Committee on Military Affairs*, 63rd Congress, 1st sess., 1913.

[17] Ibid.

[18] Harold Penrose, *British Aviation: The Pioneer Years, 1903–1914* (London: Putnam, 1967), 98. For general information on flight research in Europe prior to 1914, see A. F. Zahm, "Eiffel's Aerodynamic Laboratory and Studies," *Aero Club of America Bulletin* 1, no. 7 (August 1912): 3–4; A. Lawrence Rotch,

"Aerial Engineering," *Aero Club of America Bulletin* 1, no. 7 (August 1912): 9–10; J. C. Hunsaker, "Europe's Facilities for Aeronautical Research," *Flying* 3, no. 3 (April 1914): 75, 93; J. C. Hunsaker, "Europe's Facilities for Aeronautical Research, II," *Flying* 3, no. 4 (May 1914): 108–109.

19 Walter T. Bonney, *The Heritage of Kitty Hawk* (New York: W. W. Norton, 1962), 155.

20 Ibid., 156.

21 Penrose, *British Aviation*, 98–99.

22 Ibid., 167.

23 Richard Hallion, *Test Pilots: The Frontiersmen of Flight* (Garden City, N.Y.: Doubleday, 1981), 48–49.

24 Von Hardesty, "Early Flight in Russia," in Robin Higham, John T. Greenwood, and Von Hardesty, eds., *Russian Aviation and Air Power in the Twentieth Century* (London: Frank Cass, 1998), 18–36.

25 Ibid., 16.

26 *L'Aérophile*, 6 (March 15, 1914): 124–127.

27 Lee Kennett, *The First Air War, 1914–1918* (New York: Free Press, 1991), 8.

28 For information on the Zeppelin company, see Henry Cord Myer, *Airshipmen, Businessmen and Politics, 1890–1940* (Washington, D.C.: Smithsonian Institution Press, 1991); Peter W. Brooks, *Zeppelin: Rigid Airships, 1893–1940* (Washington, D.C.: Smithsonian Institution Press, 1992); Douglas Robinson, *Giants in the Sky: A History of the Rigid Airship* (Seattle: University of Washington Press, 1973).

29 For information on prewar British aviation policy, see Alfred Gollin, *The Impact of Air Power on the British People and Their Government, 1909–1914* (Stanford, Calif.: Stanford University Press, 1989).

30 Von Hardesty, "Early Flight in Russia."

31 Quote from John W. Taylor, Michael J. W. Taylor, and David Mondey, *Air Facts and Feats* (Toronto: Bantam Books, 1977), 49–50.

32 Charles B. Hayward, *Practical Aeronautics: An Understandable Presentation of Interesting and Essential Facts in Aeronautical Science* (Chicago: American Technical Society, 1917), 505.

33 *Aerial Age* (New York), 1, no. 10 (May 24, 1915): 221; *Aeronautics* (New York), 9, no. 1 (July 1911): 25; Alden Hatch, *Glenn Curtiss: Pioneer of Naval Aviation* (New York: Julian Messner, 1942), 253.

34 James C. Fahey, *U.S. Army Aircraft (Heavier-Than-Air), 1908–1946* (New York: Ships and Aircraft, 1946), 6.

35 Ibid.

36 Precise statistics on early U.S. military aircraft purchases are difficult to find. The best sources include Fahey, *U.S. Army Aircraft*; Robert B. Casari, *U.S. Army Serial Numbers and Orders, 1908–1922 Reconstructed* (Chillicothe, Ohio: Military Aircraft Publications, 1995); *United States Naval Aviation, 1910–1980* (Washington, D.C.: Naval Air Systems Command, 1981), appendices 4 and 8;

William T. Larkins, *U.S. Naval Aircraft, 1921–1941* (New York: Orion Books, 1988), 344–348.

37 Quote from Kennett, *First Air War*, 17.
38 Giulio Douhet quoted in Kennett, *First Air War*, 18.

CHAPTER 5

1 Ferdinand Foch quoted in John Morrow, *The Great War in the Air* (Washington, D.C.: Smithsonian Institution Press, 1993), 35.
2 Pierre August Roques quoted in Morrow, *Great War in the Air*, 15.
3 Sir John French quoted in "Editorial Comment," *Flight* (December 4, 1914): 8.
4 James McCudden, *Flying Fury: Five Years in the Royal Flying Corps* (New York: Ace Books, 1968), 73.
5 E. M. Roberts quoted in Dominick Pisano, Thomas J. Dietz, Joanne Gernstein, and Karl Schniede, *Legend, Memory and the Great War in the Air* (Seattle: University of Washington Press, 1992), 75.
6 *Flight* (August 14, 1914): 849.
7 Alphonse Pegoud quoted in Aaron Norman, *The Great Air War: The Men, the Planes, the Saga of Military Aviation, 1914–1918* (New York: Macmillan, 1968), 119.
8 Ibid., 120.
9 Oswald Boelcke quoted in Norman, *Great Air War*, 177.
10 Georges Clemenceau quoted in Norman, *Great Air War*, 113.
11 Morrow, *Great War in the Air*, 367.
12 Lee Kennett, *The First Air War, 1914–1918* (New York: Free Press, 1991), 121.
13 Quoted in James Norman Hall, *High Adventure* (New York: Houghton Mifflin, 1918), 32–33.
14 René Fonck, *Ace of Aces* (Garden City, N.Y.: Doubleday, 1967), 3–6.
15 Cecil Lewis, *Sagittarius Rising* (Harrisburg, Penn.: Stackpole Books, 1963), 11–15.
16 Leonard Bridgeman, *The Clouds Remember* (London: Gale & Polden, 1938), 8.
17 Willy Coppens, *Flying in Flanders* (New York: Ace Books, 1971), 32.
18 William Bishop, *Winged Warfare* (New York: Ace Books, 1967), 21.
19 Lewis, *Sagittarius Rising*, 40.
20 Morrow, *Great War in the Air*, 367, suggests an alternative figure of 4,333 (23 percent) for the number of French who died in the air war.
21 All figures are drawn from Charles Christienne and Pierre Lissarague, *A History of French Military Aviation* (Washington, D.C.: Smithsonian Institution Press, 1986), 130–133; Morrow, *Great War in the Air*, 366–367.
22 Christienne and Lissarague, *History of French Military Aviation*, 132.
23 Ibid.

24 Quoted from Bridgeman, *Clouds Remember*, 19.

25 Lewis, *Sagittarius Rising*, 137.

26 Morrow, *Great War in the Air*, 173.

27 Thomas O. M. Sopwith quoted in Kennett, *First Air War*, 95.

28 Quoted from James J. Hudson, *Hostile Skies: A History of the American Air Service in World War I* (Syracuse, N.Y.: Syracuse University Press, 1968), 202.

29 My gratitude to Howard Wolko, a friend and colleague for two decades, who taught me what I know of aluminum and a great deal more.

30 Much of the discussion of the early history of metal aircraft construction is drawn from Eric Schatzberg, *Wings of Wood, Wings of Metal: Culture and Technical Choice in American Airplane Materials, 1914–1945* (Princeton: Princeton University Press, 1999).

31 All figures are based on Christenne and Lissarague, *History of French Military Aviation*, 155.

32 *Daily Mail* (London), July 11, 1908.

33 Quote from *Daily Mail* (London), October 9, 1908.

34 Albert Robida, *The Electric Life* (1883) and *The War of the Twentieth Century* (1887); Emile Driant, *L'aviateur du pacifique* (1909) and *Au-dessus du continent noir* (1911); George Griffiths, *Angel of the Revolution* (1893) and *Olga Romaoff* (1894); Rudolph Martin, *Berlin-Bagdad* (1907).

35 H. G. Wells, *The War in the Air, and Particularly How Mr. Bert Smallways Faired While It Lasted* (London: G. Bell, 1908).

36 Stewart L. Murray, "Internal Conditions of Britain during a War," *Journal of the Royal United Services Institution*, 57, no. 430 (December 1913), in Tammi Davis Biddle, "Strategic Air Warfare: An Analysis," unpublished paper in the author's collection.

37 Jacques Mortane, "Aerial Warfare," in *Aeronautics in the Army*, Hearings before the Committee on Military Affairs, House of Representatives, Sixty-third Congress, First Session, in Connection with H.R. 5304 (Washington, D.C.: U.S. Government Printing Office, 1913), 273.

38 Ernst Lehman quoted in Norman, *Great Air War*, 51.

39 Raymond Fredette, *The Sky on Fire: The First Battle of Britain* (New York: Holt, Rinehart and Winston, 1966), 231.

40 Donald Wills Douglas quoted in Wayne Biddle, *Barons of the Sky* (New York: Simon and Schuster, 1991), 82–83.

41 Ibid., 83.

42 Washington Irving Chambers quoted in Alex Roland, *Model Research: The National Advisory Committee for Aeronautics, 1915–1958* (Washington, D.C.: U.S. Government Printing Office, 1985), 7.

43 Quote from Roland, *Model Research*, 22.

44 Ibid.

45 James C. Fahey, *U.S. Army Aircraft (Heavier-Than-Air), 1908–1946* (New York: Ships and Aircraft, 1946), 4.

[46] Grover Loening, *Our Wings Grow Faster* (New York: Doubleday, Doran, 1935), 43.

[47] Elsbeth E. Freudenthal, *The Aviation Business: From Kitty Hawk to Wall Street* (New York: Vanguard Press, 1940), 31.

[48] Ibid., 35.

[49] *New York Times*, November 22, 1937.

[50] Freudenthal, *Aviation Business*, 35.

[51] Quentin Roosevelt quoted in Norman, *Great Air War*, 7.

[52] Eddie Rickenbacker quoted in Biddle, *Barons of the Sky*, 113.

CHAPTER 6

[1] For more on Soviet aviation from 1917 to 1930, see John T. Greenwood, "The Aviation Industry, 1917–1997," in Robin Higham, John T. Greenwood, and Von Hardesty, eds., *Russian Aviation and Air Power in the Twentieth Century* (London: Frank Cass, 1998), 126–167, and John T. Greenwood, "The Designers: Their Design Bureaux and Aircraft," in Higham, *Russian Aviation*, 162–190; on the roots of Soviet space exploration, see Asif Siddiqi, *Challenge to Apollo: The Soviet Union and the Space Race, 1945–1974* (Washington, D.C.: NASA, 2000).

[2] John Rae, *Climb to Greatness: The American Aircraft Industry, 1920–1960* (Cambridge: MIT Press, 1968), 3–5; Roger Bilstein, *The American Aerospace Industry: From Workshop to Global Enterprise* (New York: Twayne, 1996), 20–22; Elsbeth E. Freudenthal, *The Aviation Business: From Kitty Hawk to Wall Street* (New York: Vanguard Press, 1940), 62–65.

[3] Quote from E. M. Maitland, *The Air Log of H.M.A. R 34: Journey to American and Back* (London: Hodder and Stoughton, 1921), 84.

[4] Rudyard Kipling to E. M. Maitland, November 26, 1920, in Maitland, *Air Log*, v.

[5] R. E. G. Davies, *A History of the World's Airlines* (London: Oxford University Press, 1964), 11.

[6] League of Nations, *Inquiries into the Economic Administration and Legal Situation of International Aerial Navigation* (Geneva: League of Nations, 1930), 8; Ronald Miller and David Sawer, *The Technical Development of Modern Aviation* (London: Routledge and Kegan Paul, 1968) 13.

[7] *Parliamentary Debates*, Commons, 123 (col. 138), December 15, 1919; Miller and Sawer, *Technical Development of Modern Aviation*, 13.

[8] Antoine de Saint-Exupéry, *Wind, Sand and Stars*, in *Airman's Odyssey* (New York: Harcourt, Brace, 1939), 21.

[9] Saint-Exupéry, *Wind, Sand and Stars*, 22.

[10] Saint-Exupéry, *Wind, Sand and Stars*, 22–23.

[11] The best coverage of Aéropostale and Marcel Bouilloux-Lafont is to be found

in R. E. G. Davies, *Rebels and Reformers of the Airways* (Washington, D.C.: Smithsonian Institution Press, 1987), 283–297.

[12] Henri Bouchet, *Economics of Air Transportation* (Hague: League of Nations, 1933), 23.

[13] Lester Durand Gardner, "Passenger Exhibition Flying," *Aviation* (October 1919): 255.

[14] Charles Augustus Lindbergh, *Autobiography of Values* (New York: Harcourt Brace Jovanovich, 1976), 74.

[15] Ibid., 9.

[16] Doris Rich, *Queen Bess: Daredevil Aviator* (Washington, D.C.: Smithsonian Institution Press, 1993).

[17] Aeronautical Chamber of Commerce, *The Aircraft Yearbook* (New York: Aeronautical Chamber of Commerce, see text for the year).

[18] C. G. Grey, *Bombers* (London: Faber and Faber, 1941), 65.

[19] Quote from David Nevin, *The Architects of Air Power* (Alexandria, Va.: Time-Life Books, 1981), 33.

[20] Hugh Trenchard quoted in Lee Kennett, *A History of Strategic Bombing* (New York: Charles Scribner's Sons, 1982), 69.

[21] Grey, *Bombers*, 67–68.

[22] Sir Maurice Dean, *The Royal Air Force and Two World Wars* (London: Cassell, 1979), 77.

[23] Grey, *Bombers*, 65.

[24] Burke Davis, *The Billy Mitchell Affair* (New York: Random House, 1967), 18.

[25] Lester Maitland, *Knights of the Air* (Garden City, N.Y.: Doubleday, Doran, 1929), 278.

[26] Giolio Douhet, *Command of the Air*, transl. Dino Ferrari (Washington, D.C.: Office of Air Force History, 1983).

[27] Douhet, *Command of the Air*, 164.

[28] Douhet quoted in Kennett, *History of Strategic Bombing*, 54.

[29] Ibid., 55; on the first English translation of Douhet, see James L. Cate, "Development of United States Air Doctrine, 1917–1941," in Eugene Emme, ed., *The Impact of Air Power: National Security and World Politics* (Princeton, N.J.: Van Norstrand, 1959), 186–191.

[30] William Mitchell, *Skyways: A Book on Modern Aeronautics* (Philadelphia: J. B. Lippincott, 1930), 255.

[31] Admiral Charles Benson quoted in Nevin, *Architects of Air Power*, 58.

[32] Admiral William Fullam quoted in Nevin, *Architects of Air Power*, 59.

[33] Admiral William S. Simms quoted in Nevin, *Architects of Air Power*, 59.

[34] Bascom Slemp quoted in Nevin, *Architects of Air Power*, 59.

[35] William Mitchell quoted in Nevin, *Architects of Air Power*, 69.

[36] Quote from Nick Komons, *Bonfires to Beacons: Federal Civil Aviation Policy under the Air Commerce Act, 1926–1938* (Washington, D.C.: U.S. Department of Transportation, 1978), 29.

37 "Memorandum on the Organization and Operation of Air Mail Service," January 22, 1925, Clement Keys Papers, Accession No. xxxx-0091, Archive Division, National Air and Space Museum, Washington, D.C. For a full discussion on the subject, see William Leary, *Aerial Pioneers: The U.S. Air Mail Service, 1918–1927* (Washington, D.C.: Smithsonian Institution Press, 1985).

38 The best treatment of the Daniel Guggenheim Fund for the Promotion of Aeronautics, and one of the best studies of the institutional history of American aviation, is Richard Hallion, *Legacy of Flight: The Guggenheim Contribution to American Aviation* (Seattle: University of Washington Press, 1977).

39 Daniel Guggenheim quoted in C. V. Glines, "The Guggenheims: Aviation Visionaries," *Aviation History* 6 (November 1996).

CHAPTER 7

1 C. G. Grey quoted in Nick Komons, *Bonfires to Beacons: Federal Civil Aviation Policy under the Air Commerce Act, 1926–1938* (Washington, D.C.: U.S. Department of Transportation, 1978), 66.

2 Corliss C. Moseley quoted in Sydney J. Albright, "Fred W. Kelly Story, Part 1," *American Aviation Historical Society Journal* 13, no. 3 (1968): 193.

3 Rudolph Schroeder quoted in David Weiss, *The Saga of the Tin Goose* (New York: Crown, 1971), 115.

4 Ernest K. Gann, *Ernest K. Gann's Flying Circus* (New York: Macmillan, 1974), 114.

5 Will Rogers quoted in Komons, *Bonfires to Beacons*, 67.

6 Quote from Richard Hallion, *Legacy of Flight: The Guggenheim Contribution to American Aviation* (Seattle: University of Washington Press, 1977), 97.

7 Margery Brown, "What Aviation Means to Women," *Popular Aviation* 3 (September 1928): 32.

8 The information on Lindbergh songs is drawn from the following Web site: www.americancomposers.org/lindberghmusic.htm. Accessed June 1, 2001.

9 Jack Northrop quoted in Ted Coleman, *Jack Northrop and the Flying Wing* (New York: Paragon House, 1988), 15.

10 Jack Northrop quoted in Coleman, *Jack Northrop*, 37.

11 Frank Tallman, *Flying the Old Planes* (Garden City, N.Y.: Doubleday, 1973), 173–175.

12 Charles A. Lindbergh, "Aviation, Geography, and Race," *Reader's Digest*, November 1939, 64.

13 Quotes from Charles Augustus Lindbergh, *Autobiography of Values* (New York: Harcourt Brace Jovanovich, 1976), 400–401.

14 Elsbeth Freudenthal, *The Aviation Business: From Kitty Hawk to Wall Street* (New York: Vanguard Press, 1940), 86.

[15] Dutch Kindelberger quoted in John B. Rae, *Climb to Greatness: The American Aircraft Industry, 1920–1960* (Cambridge, Mass.: MIT Press, 1968), 40.

[16] Freudenthal, *Aviation Business*, 128.

[17] Rae, *Climb to Greatness*, 49.

[18] C. R. Roseberry, *The Challenging Skies* (New York: Doubleday, 1966), 390.

[19] Walter Brown quoted in Freudenthal, *Aviation Business*, 109.

[20] Paul Henderson quoted in Freudenthal, *Aviation Business*, 113.

[21] Benjamin Foulois quoted in Maurer Maurer, *Aviation in the U.S. Army, 1919–1934* (Washington, D.C.: Office of Air Force History, 1987), 303.

[22] Quotes from Komons, *Bonfires to Beacons*, 264.

[23] Cy Caldwell quoted in Komons, *Bonfires to Beacons*, 296.

CHAPTER 8

[1] Lady Lacy Houston quoted in Paul O'Neill, *Barnstormers & Speed Kings* (Alexandria, Va.: Time-Life Books, 1981), 98.

[2] Aeronautical Chamber of Commerce, *The Aircraft Yearbook* (New York: Aeronautical Chamber of Commerce, see text for the year).

[3] Aeronautical Chamber of Commerce, *Aircraft Yearbook* (1923).

[4] "Portrait of a Prospect for a Private Plane," *Sportsman Pilot* 11, no. 3 (October 1929): 11.

[5] John H. Geisse, *Report to W. A. M. Burden on Postwar Outlook for Private Flying* (Washington, D.C.: n.p., 1944), 80.

[6] Le Corbusier, *Aircraft* (1935; reprint, New York: Universe Books, 1988).

[7] Robert Atwan, *Edsels, Luckies, and Frigidairies* (New York: Dell, 1979).

[8] Margery Brown, "What Aviation Means to Women," *Popular Aviation* 3 (September 1928): 32.

[9] Claude Graham-White quoted in Valerie Moolman, *Women Aloft* (Alexandria Va.: Time-Life Books, 1981), 9.

[10] Louise Thaden quoted in Joseph Corn, *The Winged Gospel: America's Romance with Aviation, 1900–1950* (New York: Oxford University Press, 1983), 75.

[11] Quote from ibid., 77.

[12] William J. Powell quoted in Von Hardesty, "William J. Powell and the Story of Black Wings," in William J. Powell, *Black Aviator* (Washington, D.C.: Smithsonian Institution Press, 1994), xii.

[13] Ibid.

[14] I owe a very considerable debt to Von Hardesty, a colleague and friend of many years, for material on black aviation in America.

[15] James Doolittle with C. V. Glines, *I Could Never Be So Lucky Again: An Autobiography* (New York: Bantam Books, 1991).

[16] William Randolph Hearst quoted in Corn, *Winged Gospel*, 116.

[17] Quote from *America's Youth and Aviation* (n.p., n.d.), Air Youth of America organization file, Accession No. xxxx-0209, National Air and Space Museum archives, Washington, D.C.

CHAPTER 9

[1] Bill Gunston, *Fedden: The Life of Sir Roy Fedden*, Historical Series no. 26 (Bristol, U.K.: Rolls-Royce Heritage Trust, 1988), 273.

[2] Richard K. Smith, "The Rise and Fall of the Baldwin Bomber and the Myth of Douhet," unpublished manuscript dated January 13, 1985, p. 13. Copy in the author's collection. My thanks to Richard Smith for calling attention to the Roy Fedden story.

[3] Richard Saunders Allen, *Revolution in the Sky: The Fabulous Lockheeds and Pilots Who Flew Them* (Brattleboro, Vt.: Stephen Greene Press, 1967), is the guide to all things Lockheed during the golden age.

[4] Eric Schatzberg, *Wings of Wood, Wings of Metal: Culture and Technical Choice in American Airplane Materials* (Princeton: Princeton University Press, 1999).

[5] Glenn L. Martin, *The Development of Aircraft Manufacture* (London: Royal Aeronautical Society, 1931), 12–13.

[6] As in the case of virtually all of my commentaries on metal aircraft structures, I owe an enormous debt to Howard Wolko, friend, colleague, and authority on aircraft structures. See also Walter Vincenti, "Technological knowledge without Science: The Innovation of Flush Riveting in American Airplanes, ca. 1930–ca. 1950," *Technology and Culture* 25 (July 1984): 540–576.

[7] Walter Vincenti, "The Retractable Airplane Landing Gear and the Northrop 'Anomaly': Variation-Selection and the Shaping of Technology," *Technology and Culture* 35 (January 1994): 1–33.

[8] My account of Frank Caldwell and the development of the modern propeller is entirely based on the work of my colleague Jeremy Kinney, "Frank Caldwell and the Development of the Variable Pitch Propeller, 1918–1938," a paper delivered to the thirty-sixth AIAA/ASME/ASEE Joint Propulsion Conference, AIAA 2000-3151; Jeremy Kinney, "The Propeller That Took Lindbergh Across: America's Development of the Metal Ground-Adjustable Propeller, 1917–1927," a paper presented at the ninth biennial meeting of the Conference of Historic Aviation Writers, St. Louis, Missouri, 22–24, 1999. Copies of both papers in the author's collection.

[9] C. N. Montieth quoted in Robert van der Linden, *The Boeing 247: The First Modern Airliner* (Seattle: University of Washington Press, 1991), 91.

[10] *London Morning Post*, October 24, 1934.

[11] Roger E. Bilstein, *The American Aerospace Industry: From Workshop to Global Enterprise* (New York: Twayne, 1996), 59.

[12] Lord Kelvin quoted in Richard K. Smith, *The Weight Envelope: An Airplane's Fourth Dimension* (self-published, 1985). Copy in the author's collection.

[13] John D. Anderson Jr., *Introduction to Flight* (Boston: McGraw-Hill, 2000), 458. For another measure, see Laurence K. Loftin, *The Quest for Performance: The Evolution of Modern Aircraft*, special publication 468 (Washington, D.C.: National Aeronautics and Space Administration, 1985).

[14] My comments on the professionalization in the airlines are drawn directly from Roger Bilstein, *Flight in America, 1900–1983* (Baltimore: Johns Hopkins University, 1984), 98–108.

[15] For a masterful analysis of the great flying boats, see Richard K. Smith, "The Intercontinental Airliner and the Essence of Airplane Performance, 1929-1939," *Technology and Culture* 24, no. 3 (July 1983), 428–449. The best single-volume treatment of the subject is Robert L. Gandt, *China Clipper: The Age of the Great Flying Boats* (Annapolis, Md.: Naval Institute Press, 1991). Gandt has been my guide to the subject of flying boats.

[16] Antoine de Saint-Exupéry, *Wind, Sand and Stars*, in *Airman's Odyssey* (New York: Harcourt, Brace, 1939), 24.

[17] Gandt, *China Clipper*, 36.

[18] On the character of Glenn Martin, here and elsewhere in the book, see Wayne Biddle, *Barons of the Sky* (New York: Simon and Schuster, 1991), 191–192.

[19] Quote from Smith, "Intercontinental Airliner," 438.

[20] Eddie Allen quoted in Anonymous, *Year by Year: 75 Years of Boeing History, 1916–1991* (Seattle: Boeing Historical Archive, 1991), 42.

[21] Loftin, *Quest for Performance*, Figure 8.2.7.

CHAPTER 10

[1] Stanley Baldwin quoted in Sir Maurice Dean, *The Royal Air Force in Two World Wars* (London: Cassell, 1979), 59.

[2] All quotations are from Clive Hart, *A Prehistory of Flight* (Berkeley: University of California Press, 1985), 116–119.

[3] Samuel Johnson, *The History of Rasselas, Prince of Abissinia* (London: Oxford University Press, 1971), 17.

[4] "Editorial Comment," *Flight* (January 8, 1932): 1.

[5] Winston Churchill, *The World Crisis* (New York: Charles Scribner's Sons, 1931).

[6] "Japan-China," *Time*, February 2, 1932, 19.

[7] British War Office records quoted in Meirion and Susie Harris, *Soldiers of the Sun: The Rise and Fall of the Imperial Japanese Army* (New York: Random House, 1991), 160.

[8] "Japan-China," *Time*, February 2, 1932, 19.

9 Hallett Abend, "Planes Terrorize City," *New York Times*, January 29, 1932, 1–2.

10 Stanley Baldwin quoted in "Japan-China," *Time*, February 2, 1932, 19.

11 Quote from Clark G. Reynolds, *The Carrier War* (Alexandria, Va.: Time-Life Books, 1982), 35.

12 Jiro Horikoshi, *Eagles of Mitsubishi: The Story of the Zero Fighter* (Seattle: University of Washington Press, 1970), 9.

13 George L. Steer, "The Tragedy of Guernica," *Times* (London), April 28, 1937.

14 David Nevin, *The Architects of Air Power* (Alexandria, Va.: Time-Life Books, 1981), 160; David Irving, letter to the editor, *Daily Telegraph*, April 25, 1987.

15 My treatment of France for 1929–1939 is based on Charles Christienne and Pierre Lissarrague, *A History of French Military Aviation* (Washington, D.C.: Smithsonian Institution Press, 1986); Emmanuel Chadeau, *De Blériot à Dassault: histoire de l'industrie aéronautique en France, 1900–1950* (Paris: Fayard, 1987).

16 John Terraine, *A Time for Courage: The Royal Air Force in the European War, 1939–1945* (New York: Macmillan, 1985), 6.

17 The list of achievements for Ellington's years is courtesy of Terraine, *A Time for Courage*, 16–17.

18 Robert T. Finney, *History of the Air Corps Tactical School, 1920–1940* (Washington, D.C.: Center for Air Force History, 1992), 55.

19 Quoted from Wesley Frank Craven and James Lea Cate, *Men and Planes* (Chicago: University of Chicago Press, 1955), 3.

20 Benjamin Kelsey, *The Dragon's Teeth? The Creation of United States Air Power in World War II* (Washington, D.C.: Smithsonian Institution Press, 1982), Dedication.

21 Oscar Westover quote from Stephen L. McFarland, "Fueling Aircraft Engines since 1903: Government as Catalyst," *Conference Proceedings: The Meaning of Flight in the 20th Century* (Dayton, Ohio: Wright State University, 1999), 210.

22 Stephen McFarland, "Higher, Faster, Farther: Fueling the Aeronautical Revolution, 1919–1945," in Roger Launius, ed., *Innovation and the Development of Flight* (College Station: Texas A&M University Press, 1999), 100.

23 A British thermal unit is the quantity of heat required to raise 1 pound of water 1 degree Fahrenheit.

24 For information on the Norden bombsight, see Stephen L. McFarland, *America's Pursuit of Precision Bombing, 1910–1945* (Washington, D.C.: Smithsonian Institution Press, 1995).

CHAPTER 11

1 Quotes from Paul Joseph Travers, *Eyewitness to Infamy: An Oral History of Pearl Harbor* (Lankham, Md.: Madison Books, 1991), 2.

2 This account of Pearl Harbor draws from Travers, *Eyewitness to Infamy*. The best account of all phases of the attack remains Gordon Prang, *At Dawn We slept: The Untold Story of Pearl Harbor* (New York: McGraw-Hill, 1981).

3 Gerhard Weinberg, *A World at Arms: A Global History of World War II* (Cambridge: Cambridge University Press, 1994), 894–895.

4 Comment made to the author at the opening of an exhibition on the P-47, National Air and Space Museum, Washington, D.C.

5 Franklin Roosevelt quoted in Ronald Schaffer, *Wings of Judgment: American Bombing in World War II* (New York: Oxford University Press, 1985), 31–32.

6 Winston Churchill quoted in John Terraine, *A Time For Courage: The Royal Air Force in the European War, 1939–1945* (New York: Macmillan, 1985), 259.

7 Sir Charles Webster and Noble Frankland, *The Strategic Air Offensive against Germany, 1939–1945* (London: HMSO, 1961), 2.

8 The statistics covering the RAF campaign are drawn from Martin Middlebrook and Chris Everitt, *The Bomber Command War Diaries* (London: Penguin Books, 1990).

9 Richard Overy, "Strategic Air Offensives: Against Germany," in I. C. B Dear, ed., *The Oxford Companion to World War II* (New York: Oxford University Press, 1995), 1066.

10 Quote from John C. McManus, *Deadly Skies: The American Combat Airman in World War II* (Novato, Calif.: Presidio Press, 2000), 177.

11 McManus, *Deadly Skies*, 338.

12 Quote from Jacob Vander Meulen, *Building the B-29* (Washington, D.C.: Smithsonian Institution Press, 1995), 35.

13 Paul Fussell, *Thank God for the Atomic Bomb and Other Essays* (New York: Summit Books, 1985).

14 Albert Speer quoted in Bernard C. Nalty, John F. Shiner, and George Watson, *With Courage: The U.S. Army Air Forces in World War II* (Washington, D.C.: Air Force History and Museums Program, 1994), 257.

15 Denis Richards, "Air Power," in I. C. B. Dear, ed., *The Oxford Companion to World War II* (New York: Oxford University Press, 1995).

16 Richards, "Air Power," 22.

17 I. B. Holley, *Buying Aircraft: Materiél Procurement for the Army Air Forces* (Washington, D.C.: Office of the Chief of Military History, 1966), 10–11.

18 Douglas Aircraft Company, Annual Report for 1937, in the Archives of the Institute of Aeronautical Sciences in the American Institute of Aeronautics and Astronautics Historical Collection, unmarked folder, Box 145, Manuscript Division, Library of Congress, Washington, D.C.

19 All production and sales figures are drawn from Holley, *Buying Aircraft*, 1–21.

20 Export figures are from Holley, *Buying Aircraft*, 201; Roger Bilstein, *The American Aerospace Industry: From Workshop to Global Industry* (New York: Twayne, 1996), 68.

21 Holley, *Buying Aircraft*, 561.

[22] Ibid.

[23] Charles Lindbergh quoted in Don Sherman, "Willow Run," *Air & Space Smithsonian* (August/September 1992): 79.

[24] Quotes from Glenn L. Martin, *The Development of Aircraft Manufacture* (London: Royal Aeronautical Society, 1931), 11.

[25] See Jack R. Breihan, "Glenn Martin and the Air City," in Tom D. Crouch and Janet Bednarek, eds., *The Meaning of Flight in the 20th Century: Proceedings of the 1998 National Aerospace Conference* (Dayton, Ohio: Wright State University, 2000), i431–437.

[26] Charles Sorenson quoted in Sherman, "Willow Run," 76.

[27] Albert Kahn quoted in Sherman, "Willow Run," 78.

[28] Louis R. Purnell quoted in McManus, *Deadly Skies*, 51.

CHAPTER 12

[1] See, for example, Horst Boog, "The Luftwaffe and Technology," *Aerospace Historian* (Fall 1983): 200–206. For the opposing view, see Michael Neufeld, "Rocket Aircraft and the Turbojet Revolution," in Roger Launius, ed., *Innovation and the Development of Flight* (College Station: Texas A&M University Press, 1999), 207–234.

[2] Edgar Buckingham quoted in James R. Hansen, *Engineer in Charge: A History of the Langley Aeronautical Laboratory, 1917–1958* (Washington, D.C.: National Aeronautics and Space Administration, 1987), 224–225. We are indeed fortunate to have both Hansen's masterful study of Langley lab and Alex Roland's *Model Research: The National Advisory Committee for Aeronautics, 1915–1958* (Washington D.C.: U.S. Government Printing Office, 1985).

[3] James Hanson, "Secretly Going Nuclear," *American Heritage of Invention and Technology* (Spring 1992): 60–64.

[4] Benjamin Lockspeiser quoted in Richard P. Hallion, *Supersonic Flight: Breaking the Sound Barrier and Beyond* (New York: Macmillan, 1972), 1.

[5] Tom Wolfe, *The Right Stuff* (New York: Farrar, Straus and Giroux, 1979).

[6] Richard Whitcomb quoted in Michael H. Gorn, *Expanding the Envelope: Flight Research at NACA and NASA* (Lexington: University of Kentucky Press, 2001), 332.

[7] H. Franklin Gregory quoted in Warren R. Young, *The Helicopters* (Alexandria, Va.: Time-Life Books, 1982), 81.

[8] Grover Loening, "The Helicopter's Limited Future," a lecture to the Brooklyn Institute of Arts and Sciences, December 3, 1943. Copy in the author's collection. My thanks to colleague Roger Conner for calling this paper to my attention.

[9] Ralph Alex, "How Are You Fixed for Blades?" in Walter J. Boyne and Donald S. Lopez, eds., *The Age of the Helicopter: Vertical Flight* (Washington, D.C.: Smithsonian Institution Press, 1984), 43–44.

[10] "Rotorcraft Market Growth Continues," *Aviation Week and Space Technology* (January 14, 2002): 75.

[11] *Aerospace Facts and Figures* (Washington, D.C.: Aerospace Industries Association, 1998–1999).

[12] A. Hunter Dupree, *Science in the Federal Government: A History of Policies and Activities to 1940* (Cambridge, Mass.: Harvard University Press, 1957), 369.

[13] United States Army Air Forces, *Third Report of the Commanding General of the Army Air Forces to the Secretary of War*, General Henry H. Arnold, November 12, 1945, 68, quoted, along with Vannevar Bush, in R. Cargill Hall, "The Origins of U.S. Space Policy," in John Logsdon, ed., *Exploring the Unknown: Selected Documents in the History of the U.S. Space Program* (Washington, D.C.: National Aeronautics and Space Administration, 1995), 213–215.

[14] Vannevar Bush quoted in Dik Daso, *Architects of American Air Supremacy: General Hap Arnold and Dr. Theodor von Kármán* (Maxwell Air Force Base, Ala.: Air University Press, 1997), 118.

[15] For a full account of the Scientific Advisory Group and Scientific Advisory Board and technology forecasting in the U.S. Air Force, see Michael Gorn, *Harnessing the Genie: Science and Technology Forecasting for the Air Force, 1944–1986* (Washington, D.C.: Office of Air Force History, 1988); Michael Gorn, *Prophecy Fulfilled: "Toward New Horizons" and Its Legacy* (Washington, D.C.: Air Force History and Museum Program, 1994).

[16] Carl M. Spaatz quoted in Phillip S. Meillinger, *10 Propositions regarding Air Power* (n.p.: Air Force History and Museum Program, 1995), 95.

[17] Quote from Wayne Biddle, "A Great New Enterprise," *Air & Space Smithsonian* 4, no. 7 (June/July 1989): 32.

[18] All budget figures are drawn from a variety of tables in *Aerospace Facts and Figures* (Washington, D.C.: Aerospace Industries Association, 1953–2001).

[19] Charles D. Bright, *The Jet Makers: The Aerospace Industry from 1945 to 1972* (Lawrence: Regents Press of Kansas, 1978), 114.

CHAPTER 13

[1] Hap Arnold quoted in Dik Daso, *Architects of American Air Supremacy: General Hap Arnold and Dr. Theodor von Kármán* (Maxwell Air Force Base, Ala.: Air University Press, 1997), 57.

[2] *Public Papers of the Presidents, Dwight D. Eisenhower* (Washington, D.C.: U.S. Government Printing Office, 1960), 1035–1040.

[3] *Aviation Facts and Figures, 1953* (Washington, D.C.: Aircraft Industries Association, 1954), 19.

[4] Ibid., 44.

[5] Ibid., 19.

[6] Quote from Anonymous, *Year by Year: 75 Years of Boeing History, 1916–1991* (Seattle: Boeing Historical Archives, 1991), 59.

[7] Glenn L. Martin, *The Development of Aircraft Manufacture* (London: Royal Aeronautical Society, 1931), 11.

[8] Jacob Vander Meulen, *The Politics of Aircraft: Building an American Military Industry* (Manhattan: University of Kansas Press, 1991), 163.

[9] Vander Meulen, *Politics of Aircraft*, 165–166.

[10] The information on unionization in the aircraft industry is drawn from Robert G. Rodden, *The Fighting Machinists: A Century of Struggle* (Washington, D.C.: Kelly Press, 1984).

[11] Eugene Gholz, "The Curtiss-Wright Corporation and Cold War-Era Defense Procurement," *Journal of Cold War Studies* 2, no. 1 (Winter 2000): 75.

[12] Quote from John Rae, *Climb to Greatness: The American Aircraft Industry, 1920–1960* (Cambridge, Mass.: MIT Press, 1968), 193–194.

[13] Richard P. Hallion, "Commercial Aviation: From the Benoist Air Boat to the SST," in Eugene Emme, ed., *Two Hundred Years of Flight in America: A Bicentennial Survey* (San Diego: American Astronautical Society, 1977), 165.

[14] *Aviation Facts and Figures, 1954* (Washington, D.C.: Aircraft Industries Association, 1955), 68.

[15] Roger Bilstein, *The American Aviation Industry: From Workshop to Global Enterprise* (New York: Twayne, 1996), 138–139.

[16] Aviation Research Associates, *Aviation Predictions* (New York: Aviation Research Associates, 1944), 2.

[17] Fred Weick and James Hanson, *From the Ground Up: The Autobiography of an Aeronautical Engineer* (Washington D.C.: Smithsonian Institution Press, 1988), 226.

[18] "Obsolete Designs, Shrinking Customer Bass Spell Doom for U.S. Light-Aircraft Industry," *Aviation Week and Space Technology* (December 24, 1990): 68–69; "Piper Seeks Bankruptcy Protection, Ceases Operations Pending Reorganization," *Aviation Week and Space Technology* (July 8, 1991): 24; "Who Will Build New Light Airplanes," *Flying* (April 1991): 44; "Textron Buys Cessna from General Dynamics," *Flying* (April 1992): 24.

[19] Quote from "Obsolete Designs," 68.

[20] First Equity Group, *Aviation and Aerospace Almanac, 2002* (New York: McGraw-Hill, 2002), General Aviation tables.

[21] Bilstein, *American Aerospace Industry*, 83; G. R. Simonson, ed., *The History of the American Aviation Industry: An Anthology* (Cambridge, Mass.: MIT Press, 1968), 227.

[22] C. Wright Mills quoted in David Noble, *Forces of Production: A Social History of Industrial Automation* (New York: Alfred A. Knopf, 1984), 21.

[23] Data from Simonson, *History of the American Aircraft Industry*, 248–249.

[24] *Aerospace Facts and Figures, 1967* (Washington, D.C.: Aircraft Industries Association, 1968), 8.

[25] Thomas D. White quoted in Frank W. Jennings, "Genesis of the Aerospace Concept," *Air Power History* (Spring 2001): 48.

[26] *"Interim Aerospace Terminology Reference,"* Air Force pamphlet no. 111-1-4, October 30, 1959, in Jennings, "Genesis of Aerospace," 48.

[27] Quote from "The Guided Missile," *Air Force Reservist* (December 1957), in Simonson, *History of the American Aircraft Industry*, 229.

[28] "Aviation," *Time*, September 14, 1959, 92, quoted in Simonson, *History of the American Aircraft Industry*, 229.

[29] Leonard S. Silk, "Outer Space: The Impact on the American Economy," in Simonson, *History of the American Aircraft Industry*, 248–249.

[30] Paul Ceruzzi, *Beyond the Limits: Flight Enters the Computer Age* (Cambridge, Mass.: MIT Press, 1989), 46.

[31] Quote from Karl Sabbagh, *Twentieth-Century Jet: The Making and Marketing of the Boeing 777* (New York: Charles Scribner's Sons, 1996), 59.

[32] Ceruzzi, *Beyond the Limits*, 121.

[33] Quote from *Aerospace Facts and Figures, 1953*, 7.

[34] Bilstein, *American Aerospace Industry*, 95.

[35] Noble, *Forces of Production*, is the source for all of the commentary on U.S. Air Force machine-tool programs.

[36] Ceruzzi, *Beyond the Limits*, 46.

[37] Data from the *1997 Economic Census, Manufacturing Industry Series, Aircraft Manufacturing,* U.S. Census Bureau, available at census Web site: www.census.gov/eped/prod/ec97/97m364a.pdf.

[38] Bilstein, *American Aviation Industry*, 188.

[39] Ibid., 194.

[40] Donald M. Pattillo, *Pushing the Envelope: The American Aircraft Industry* (Ann Arbor: University of Michigan Press, 1998), 298.

[41] Pattillo, *Pushing the Envelope*, 298; Anthony Newhouse, *The Sporty Game: The High Risk Competitive Business of Making and Selling Commercial Airliners* (New York: Alfred A. Knopf, 1983), 132; Anthony Sampson, *The Arms Bazaar* (New York: Viking, 1977), 216.

[42] William D. Hartung, *And Weapons for All* (New York: HarperPerennial, 1994), 35–41.

[43] William Gordon, "Japan's Aerospace Industry," November 1997, available at William Gordon's Web site: http://wgordon.web.wesleyan.edu/papersaerosp.htm. Accessed March 3, 2002.

[44] "Megamerger Points to Industry's Future," *Aviation Week and Space Technology* (September 5, 1994): 37.

[45] Norman Augustine quoted in "Aerospace Consolidation Accelerates," *Aviation Week and Space Technology* (September 5, 1994): 38.

CHAPTER 14

[1] Bernard C. Nalty, ed., *Winged Shield, Winged Sword: A History of the United States Air Force* (Washington, D.C.: Air Force History and Museums Program, 1997), 378.

[2] James Doolittle quoted in James Straubel, *Crusade for Air Power: The Story of the Air Force Association* (Washington, D.C.: Aerospace Education Foundation, 1982), 36.

[3] Karen Miller, "Air Power Is Peace Power: The Aircraft Industry's Campaign for Public and Political Support, 1943–1949," *Business History Review* 70 (1996): 297.

[4] Straubel, *Crusade for Air Power*, 30–31.

[5] Bernard Brodie quoted in Gregg Herken, *Counsels of War* (New York: Alfred A. Knopf, 1985), 8.

[6] Ibid., 9–10.

[7] Herman Kahn quoted in Herken, *Counsels of War*, 35.

[8] J. Robert Oppenheimer quoted in Richard Rhodes, *Dark Star: The Making of the Hydrogen Bomb* (New York: Simon and Schuster, 1995), 567.

[9] Brodie's wife, Fawn, was the author of well-known and controversial biographies of Joseph Smith, the Mormon prophet, and Thomas Jefferson.

[10] Rhodes, *Dark Star*, 347.

[11] Herken, *Counsels of War*, 83.

[12] Quote from Rhodes, *Dark Star*, 564.

[13] Curtis LeMay quoted in Rhodes, *Dark Star*, 568.

[14] Daniel Gallery quoted in Richard P. Hallion, *The Naval Air War in Korea* (Annapolis, Md.: Nautical and Aviation Publishing Company of America, 1986), 14–15.

[15] Richard P. Hallion, "A Troubling Past: Air Force Fighter Acquisition since 1945," *Airpower Journal* 9, no. 4 (1990).

[16] *Naval Aviation Combat Statistics—World War II,* OPNAV-P-23V publication no. A129 (Washington, D.C.: Air Branch, Office of Naval Intelligence, Office of the Chief of Naval Operations, June 17, 1946). Information on the USS *Princeton* was supplied by George Schnitzer, in author's collection.

[17] James A. Michener, *The Bridges at Toko-Ri* (New York: Random House, 1953).

[18] Hans D. Deidl, *Stalin's Eagles: An Illustrated Study of the Soviet Aces of World War II and Korea* (Atglen, Penn.: Schiffer Military History, 1998), 243.

[19] Nalty, *Winged Shield, Winged Sword*, 29.

[20] Mike Spick, *The Ace Factor* (New York: Avon Books, 1989), 138–141.

[21] Anthony Preston, *Warships of the World* (London: Jane's, 1980), 16.

[22] R. Cargill Hall, "To Acquire Strategic Bombers: The Case of the B-58 Hustler," *Air University Review* 33, no. 1 (September/October 1980): 44–56.

[23] Richard P. Hallion, *Storm over Iraq: Air Power and the Gulf War* (Washington, D.C.: Smithsonian Institution Press, 1992), 16.

24 Ron Westrum and Howard Wilcox, "Sidewinder," *American Heritage of Invention and Technology* (Fall 1989): 56–63.

25 Mike Spick, *Jet Fighter Performance: Korea to Vietnam* (London: Ian Allen, 1986), 149.

26 Hallion, *Storm over Iraq*, 27–33.

27 Bill Gunston, *F-4 Phantom* (New York: Charles Scribner's Sons, 1977), 66.

28 For an especially laudatory account of Boyd's career, see Grant T. Hammond, *The Mind of War: John Boyd and American Security* (Washington, D.C.: Smithsonian Institution Press, 2001).

29 Robert Futrell, *Ideas, Concepts, Doctrine: Basic Thinking in the United States Air Force, Vol. 2, 1961–1984* (Maxwell Air Force Base, Ala.: Air University Press, 1989), 492.

30 "USAF Almanac 2000: The Air Force in Facts and Figures," *Air Force Magazine* 83, no. 4 (May 2000): 137–141.

31 *Jane's All the World's Aircraft 2000–2001* (Alexandria, Va.: Jane's Information Group, 2000), 207; Hallion, "A Troubling Past," 17.

32 Vernon Loeb, "Bursts of Brilliance," *Washington Post Magazine*, December 15, 2002, 6–11, 23–27.

33 Charles Meyers quoted in James P. Stevenson, *The Pentagon Paradox: The Development of the F-18 Hornet* (Annapolis, Md.: Naval Institute Press, 1993), 34; Herbert Fenster, *The $5 Billion Dollar Misunderstanding* (Annapolis, Md.: Naval Institute Press, 2001), 12, identifies this comment as the first use of the work *stealth* with regard to military aircraft.

34 Chaim Herzog, *The War of Atonement, October 1973* (Boston: Little, Brown, 1975), 256.

35 Norman Schwarzkopf quoted in Hallion, *Storm over Iraq*, 140.

36 My account of the Desert Storm air campaign is based on Hallion, *Storm over Iraq*, 162–196.

37 Quote from Fred Kaplan, "US Bombs Not Much Smarter," *Boston Globe*, February 20, 1998.

38 Colin Powell quoted in Hallion, *Storm over Iraq*, 201.

39 Quote from "Q&A on the Use of Predator in Operation Enduring Freedom," press release from Center for Defense Information, Washington, D.C., February 11, 2002.

40 John Keegan, "Please, Mr. Blair, Never Take Such a Risk Again," *Electronic Telegraph*, available at: www.telegraph.co.uk, issue 1472, June 6, 1999. Accessed July 1, 2002.

41 Melvin Kranzberg, "Technology and History: 'Kranzberg's Laws,'" *Technology and Culture* 27, no. 3 (July 1986): 544–560.

42 Samuel Johnson, *The History of Rasselas* (Berkeley: University of California Press, 1985), 116–119.

CHAPTER 15

1 All quotes attributed to DeVoto are from Bernard DeVoto, "Transcontinental Flight," *Harper's* 205 (July 1952): 47–50. I owe a debt to Roger Bilstein for opening this field. See Roger Bilstein, "Air Travel and the Traveling Public: The American Experience, 1920–1970," in William Trimble, ed., *From Airships to Airbus: The History of Civil and Commercial Aviation, Vol. 2, Pioneers and Operations* (Washington, D.C.: Smithsonian Institution Press, 1995), 91–111.

2 Civil Aeronautics Board, *Handbook of Airline Statistics* (Washington, D.C.: Civil Aeronautics Board, 1965), 452–461.

3 Ibid., 541–542.

4 Max Lerner, *America as Civilization* (New York: Simon and Schuster, 1957), 97.

5 Daniel J. Boorstin, *The Image: A Guide to Pseudo-Events in America* (New York: Vintage Books, 1992), 94–99.

6 Quote from Lee Kolm, "Stewardesses' Psychological Punch: Gender and Commercial Aviation in the United States, 1930–1978," in Trimble, *From Airships to Airbus*, 113.

7 Quotes from Boorstin, *Image*, 96; Kolm, "Stewardesses' Psychological Punch," 122.

8 Conrad Hilton quoted in Boorstin, *Image*, 98.

9 Quotes from Boorstin, *Image*, 98; Charles Augustus Lindbergh, *Autobiography of Values* (New York: Harcourt Brace Jovanovich, 1976), 267.

10 *Aerospace Facts and Figures*, 1954 (Washington, D.C.: Aircraft Industries Association, 1955), 55–68; *Aerospace Facts and Figures* (Washington, D.C.: Aerospace Industries Association, 1965, 1978, 1984, 1996–1997), air transportation sections.

11 L. Welch Pogue, *Airline Deregulation, before and after: What Next?* (Washington, D.C.: National Air and Space Museum, 1991), 3.

12 "Take a Trip to Berlin," *Time*, June 26, 1944.

13 Welch Pogue, *Airline Deregulation*, 4.

14 Quote from Peter Gilchrist, *Boeing 747* (London: Ian Allan, 1985), 17.

15 Anonymous, *Aviation and Aerospace Almanac 2000* (New York: McGraw-Hill, 2002), 91.

16 Robert Kuttner, "Air Fair?" available at the following Web site: www.prospect.org/webfeatures/2002/04/kuttner-r-04-22.html. Accessed July 6, 2002.

17 Welch Pogue, *Airline Deregulation*, 19.

18 Robert W. Poole and Viggo Butler, *Airline Deregulation: The Unfinished Revolution*, Policy Study no. 225 (Los Angeles: Reason Public Policy Institute, 1998), 1.

19 William Allen quoted in John Newhouse, *The Sporty Game: The High Risk Competitive Business of Making and Selling Commercial Airliners* (New York: Alfred A. Knopf, 1983), 166.

[20] John Steiner quoted in T. A. Heppenheimer, *Turbulent Skies: The History of Commercial Aviation* (New York: John A. Wiley & Sons, 1995), 238.

[21] Quote from Heppenheimer, *Turbulent Skies*, 240.

[22] Charles Lindbergh quoted in A. Scott Berg, *Lindbergh* (New York: G. P. Putnam's Sons, 1998), 538.

[23] Heppenheimer, *Turbulent Skies*, 302.

CONCLUSION

[1] Editors, *Air & Space Smithsonian* (December 2001/January 2002): 3.

[2] Quote from Steven Pearlstein, "Airlines Pain a Chronic Condition," *Washington Post*, December 6, 2002, E1. See also Sara Terry, "From the Ground Up," *Christian Science Monitor*, available at: csmonitor.com/2001/1029/p11s1-wmgn.html, accessed November 4, 2002; Mark Tran, "US Airlines Still Reeling after September 11," *Guardian*, available at www.guardian.co.uk/air lines/story/0,1371,775204,00.html, accessed November 4, 2002; U.S. Department of Transportation, "BTS Indicators Report Shows September 11 Impact on Large Airlines," available at: www.dot.gov/affairs/bts0302.htm, accessed November 4, 2002; "One Month Later: Emotional and Economic Recovery Slow," available at: www.cnn.com/2001/fyi/news/10/12/one.month.later, accessed November 4, 2002.

[3] Craig Martin quoted in Helen Jung, "Boeing Expects Cuts on 767 Assembly Line," available at *Fresno Bee* Web site: www.fresnobee.com/24hour/special_ reports/terrorism/economics/story/600976p-4651. Accessed November 2, 2003.

[4] Alcestra Oberg, "U.S. Space Leadership Fades," *USA Today*, October 17, 2003, Opinion/Forum.

[5] Robert Walker quoted in Leonard David, "National Commission to Probe Health of Aerospace Industry," available at a NASA Web site: www.space. com/phpup/promo/starrynight/noad_sn_30e_6y4x_021216php. Accessed February 20, 2003.

[6] Wilbur Wright quoted in "Airship Safe: Air Motoring No More Dangerous Than Land Motoring," *Cairo* (Illinois) *Bulletin*, March 5, 1909.

[7] Orville Wright quoted in "Catherine [sic] Wright, "Going Abroad to Witness Brother's Triumph," *Dayton Herald*, January 2, 1909.

[8] Wernher von Bruan quoted in "A Bold Look at the Next Fifty Years of Flight," *New York Times*, October 11, 1953, 25. This article is the source of all related opinions.

[9] Igor Sikorsky quoted in ibid.

[10] Ed Wells quoted in ibid.

[11] Orville Wright to George Spratt, June 7, 1903, in Marvin W. McFarland, ed., *The Papers of Wilbur and Orville Wright* (New York: McGraw-Hill, 1953), 1: 313.

BIBLIOGRAPHY

MANUSCRIPT COLLECTIONS

Aero Club of America Collection, Archive Division, National Air and Space Museum.

Alexander Graham Bell Scrapbooks, Archive Division, National Air and Space Museum.

American Institute of Aeronautics and Astronautics History Collection, Manuscript Division, Library of Congress.

Clement Keys Papers, Archive Division, National Air and Space Museum.

Gutzon Borglum Papers, Manuscript Division, Library of Congress.

Hanging files, Archive Division, National Air and Space Museum.

Papers of Curtis E. LeMay, Manuscript Division, Library of Congress.

Papers of Glenn L. Martin, Manuscript Division, Library of Congress.

Papers of Robert Gross, Manuscript Division, Library of Congress.

Papers of Wilbur and Orville Wright, Manuscript Division, Library of Congress.

Papers of William Mitchell, Manuscript Division, Library of Congress.

Record Group 237, Federal Aviation Administration Central Office Records, National Archives and Record Service.

Records of the Aeronautics Division, Manuscript Division, Library of Congress.

Records of the Aircraft Industries Association, Microform set, Archive Division, National Air and Space Museum.

Samuel Pierpont Langley Scrapbooks, Archive Division, National Air and Space Museum.

Wright Family Collection, Archives and Special Collections, Dunbar Library, Wright State University, Dayton, Ohio.

ARTICLES AND UNPUBLISHED PAPERS

Albright, Sydney J. "Fred W. Kelly Story, Part 1." *American Aviation Historical Society Journal* 13, no. 3 (1968): 193.

Archdeacon, Ernest. "M. Chanute en Paris." *La locomotion* (April 11, 1903): 225–227.

Biddle, Wayne. "A Great New Enterprise." *Air & Space Smithsonian* 4, no. 7 (June/July 1989).

Bilstein, Roger. "Air Travel and the Traveling Public: The American Experience, 1920-1970," in William Trimble, ed., *From Airships to Airbus: The History of Civil and Commercial Aviation, Volume 2, Pioneers and Operations* (Washington, D.C.: Smithsonian Institution Press, 1995), 91-111.

Boog, Horst. "The Luftwaffe and Technology." *Aerospace Historian* (Fall 1983): 200–206.

Bradshaw, Granville E. "Aeroplanes as Mechanical Constructions." *Flight* (June 29, 1912): 593.

Brown, Margery. "What Aviation Means to Women." *Popular Aviation* 3 (September 1928).

Cayley, George. "On Aerial Navigation." *A Journal of Natural Philosophy, Chemistry and the Arts,* published by W. Nicholson (New Series) in London, November 1809, vol. 24: 164–174; February 1810, vol. 25: 81–87; March 1810, vol. 25: 161–169.

De Voto, Bernard. "Transcontinental Flight." *Harper's* 205 (July 1952): 47–50.

Gardner, Lester Durand. "Passenger Exhibition Flying." *Aviation* (October 1919).

Gholz, Eugene. "The Curtiss-Wright Corporation and Cold War-Era Defense Procurement." *Journal of Cold War Studies* 2, no. 1 (Winter 2000).

Gibbs-Smith, C. H. "The Man Who Came by Air." *Shell Aviation News* (June 1959).

Glines, C. V. "The Guggenheims: Aviation Visionaries." *Aviation History* 6 (November 1996).

Hall, R. Cargill. "To Acquire Strategic Bombers: The Case of the B-58 Hustler." *Air University Review* (September/October 1980).

Hall, R. Cargill. "The Origins of U.S. Space Policy," in John Logsdon ed., *Exploring the Unknown: Selected Documents in the History of the U.S. Space Program* (Washington, D.C.: NASA, 1995)

Hallion, Richard P. "A Troubling Past: Air Force Fighter Acquisition since 1945." *Airpower Journal* 9, no. 4 (1990).

Hanson, James. "Secretly Going Nuclear." *American Heritage of Invention and Technology* (Spring 1992): 60–64.

Hunsaker, J. C. "Europe's Facilities for Aeronautical Research." *Flying* 3, no. 3 (April 1914): 75, 93.

Hunsaker, J. C. "Europe's Facilities for Aeronautical Research, II." *Flying* 3, no. 4 (May 1914): 108–109.

Kinney, Jeremy. "Frank Caldwell and the Development of the Variable Pitch Propeller, 1918–1938." A paper delivered to the thirty-sixth AIAA/ASME/ASEE Joint Propulsion Conference, AIAA 2000-3151.

Kinney, Jeremy. "The Propeller That Took Lindbergh Across: America's Development of the Metal Ground-Adjustable Propeller, 1917–1927." A paper presented at the ninth biennial meeting of the Conference of Historic Aviation Writers, St. Louis, Missouri, 22–24, 1999.

Kolm, Lee. "Stewardesses' Psychological Punch: Gender and Commercial Aviation in the United States, 1930–1978," in William Trimble, ed., *From Airships to Airbus: The History of Civil and Commercial Aviation, Vol. 2, Pioneers and Operations.* (Washington, D.C.: Smithsonian Institution Press, 1995).

Kranzberg, Melvin. "Technology and History: 'Kranzberg's Laws.'" *Technology and Culture* 27, no. 3 (July 1986): 544–560.

Langley, S. P. "The Story of Experiments in Mechanical Flight." *Aeronautical Annual* (Boston, 1897): 13.

Lilienthal, Otto. "Practical Experiments for the Development of Human Flight." *Report for the Board of Regents of the Smithsonian Institution for 1893* (Washington, D.C., 1894).

Lindbergh, Charles A. "Aviation, Geography, and Race." *Reader's Digest* November 1939, 64–67.

Means, James. "Wheeling and Flying." *Aeronautical Annual* (Boston, 1896): 25.

Miller, Karen. "Air Power Is Peace Power: The Aircraft Industry's Campaign for Public and Political Support, 1943–1949." *Business History Review* 70 (1996).

Neufeld, Michael. "Rocket Aircraft and the Turbojet Revolution," in Roger Launius, ed., *Innovation and the Development of Flight* (College Station: Texas A&M University Press, 1999), 207–234.

"Portrait of a Prospect for a Private Plane." *Sportsman Pilot* 11, no. 3 (October 1929): 11.

Richard Potts, "Flying Machines," in Jonathan Brockman, ed., *The Greatest Inventions of the Past 2000 Years* (New York: Simon and Schuster, 2000).

Pritchard, J. L. "The Dawn of Aerodynamics." *Journal of the Royal Aeronautical Society* 61 (March 1957): 149–180.

Pritchard, J. Laurence. "The Wright Brothers and the Royal Aeronautical Society: A Survey and a Tribute." *Journal of the Royal Aeronautical Society* 57 (December 1953): 739–819.

Pritchard, J. Laurence. "Francis Herbert Wenham, Honorary Member, 1824–1908: An Appreciation of the First Lecturer to the Aeronautical Society." *Journal of the Royal Aeronautical Society* 62 (August 1958): 571–596.

Root, Amos I. "Our Homes." *Gleanings in Bee Culture* 33 (January 1, 1905): 38.

Rotch, A. Lawrence. "Aerial Engineering." *Aero Club of America Bulletin* 1, no. 7 (August 1912): 9–10.

Sherman, Don. "Willow Run." *Air & Space Smithsonian* (August/September 1992).

Smith, Richard K. "The Intercontinental Airliner and the Essence of Airplane Performance, 1929–1939." *Technology and Culture* 24, no. 3 (July 1983): 428–449.

Smith, Richard K. "The Rise and Fall of the Baldwin Bomber and the Myth of Douhet." Unpublished manuscript dated January 31, 1985. Copy in the author's collection.

Vincenti, Walter. "Technological Knowledge without Science: The Innovation of Flush Riveting in American Airplanes, ca. 1930–ca. 1950." *Technology and Culture* 25 (July 1984): 540–576.

Vincenti, Walter. "The Retractable Airplane Landing Gear and the Northrop 'Anomaly': Variation-Selection and the Shaping of Technology." *Technology and Culture* 35 (January 1994): 1–33.

Westrum, Ron, and Howard Wilcox. "Sidewinder." *American Heritage of Invention and Technology* (Fall 1989): 56–63.

"What Is Ahead in Aviation: America's Foremost Leaders in Many Branches of Flying Give Remarkable Forecasts of the Future." *Popular Science* (June 1929): 124–129.

Wright, Orville. "How We Invented the Airplane." *Flying* (December 1913).

Wright, Wilbur. "The Angle of Incidence." *Aeronautical Journal* (July 1901).

Wright, Wilbur. "Some Aeronautical Experiments," in Marvin W. McFarland, ed., *The Papers of Wilbur and Orville Wright* (New York: McGraw-Hill, 1953), 1: 103.

Zahm, A. F. "Eiffel's Aerodynamic Laboratory and Studies." *Aero Club of America Bulletin* 1, no. 7 (August 1912): 3–4.

BOOKS, DISSERTATIONS, AND THESES

Aeronautics in the Army, Hearings before the Committee on Military Affairs, House of Representatives, Sixty-third Congress, First Session, In Connection with H. R. 5304 (Washington, D.C.: U.S. Government Printing Office, 1913).

Aerospace Facts and Figures (Washington, D.C.: Aerospace Industries Association, 1953–1999).

Allen, Richard Saunders. *Revolution in the Sky: The Fabulous Lockheeds and Pilots Who Flew Them* (Brattleboro, Vt.: Stephen Greene Press, 1967).

Anderson, John. *A History of Aerodynamics and Its Impact on Flying Machines* (New York: Cambridge University Press, 1997).

Anderson, John D., Jr. *Introduction to Flight* (Boston: McGraw-Hill, 2000).

Anonymous. *Aviation and Aerospace Almanac 2000* (New York: McGraw-Hill, 2002).

Anonymous. *Year by Year: 75 Years of Boeing History, 1916–1991* (Seattle: Boeing Historical Archive, 1991).

Atwan, Robert. *Edsels, Luckies, and Frigidaires* (New York: Dell, 1979).

Aviation Research Associates. *Aviation Predictions* (New York: Aviation Research Associates, 1944).

Babbington-Smith, Constance. *Testing Time: The Story of British Test Pilots and Their Aircraft* (New York: Harper Brothers, 1961).

Bach, Richard. *A Gift of Wings* (New York: Dell, 1974).

Bell, Dana. *The Smithsonian National Air and Space Museum Directory of Airplanes, Their Designers and Manufacturers* (London: Greenhill Books, 2002).

Berg, A. Scott. *Lindbergh* (New York: G.P. Putnam's Sons, 1998).

Biddle, Wayne. *Barons of the Sky* (New York: Simon and Schuster, 1991).

Bilstein, Roger. *Flight Patterns: Trends of Aeronautical Development in the United States, 1918–1929* (Athens: University of Georgia Press, 1983).

Bilstein, Roger. *Flight in America, 1900–1983* (Baltimore: Johns Hopkins University Press, 1984).

Bilstein, Roger. *The American Aerospace Industry: From Workshop to Global Enterprise* (New York: Twayne, 1996).

Bishop, William. *Winged Warfare* (New York: Ace Books, 1967).

Bobbro, Carl, and Von Hardesty, eds. *Igor Sikorsky: The Russian Years* (Washington, D.C.: Smithsonian Institution Press, 1987).

Bonney, Walter T. *The Heritage of Kitty Hawk* (New York: W. W. Norton, 1962).

Boorstin, Daniel J. *The Image: A Guide to Pseudo-Events in America* (New York: Vintage Books, 1992).

Botting, Douglas. *The Giant Airships* (Arlington, Va.: Time-Life Books, 1980).

Bouchet, Henri. *Economics of Air Transportation* (Hague: League of Nations, 1933).

Bowen, Ezra. *Knights of the Air* (Alexandria, Va.: Time-Life Books, 1980).

Bowers, Peter M. *Boeing Aircraft since 1916* (London: Putnam, Aero Publishers, 1966).

Bowers, Peter M. *Curtiss Aircraft, 1907–1947* (London: Putnam, 1979).

Boyne, Walter J., and Donald S. Lopez, eds. *The Jet Age: Forty Years of Jet Aviation* (Washington, D.C.: Smithsonian Institution Press, 1979).

Boyne, Walter J., and Donald Lopez, eds. *The Age of the Helicopter: Vertical Flight* (Washington, D.C.: Smithsonian Institution Press, 1984).

Bridgeman, Leonard. *The Clouds Remember* (London: Gale & Polden, 1938).

Bright, Charles D. *The Jet Makers: The Aerospace Industry from 1945 to 1972* (Lawrence: Regents Press of Kansas, 1978).

Brooks, Peter W. *Zeppelin: Rigid Airships, 1893–1940* (Washington, D.C.: Smithsonian Institution Press, 1992).

Bugos, Glen. *Engineering the F-4 Phantom II: Parts into Systems* (Annapolis, Md.: Naval Institute Press, 1996).

Casari, Robert B. *U.S. Army Serial Numbers and Orders, 1908–1922 Reconstructed* (Chillicothe, Ohio: Military Aircraft Publications, 1995).

Casey, Louis. *Curtiss: The Hammondsport Era, 1907–1914* (New York: Crown Publishers, 1981).

Ceruzzi, Paul. *Beyond the Limits: Flight Enters the Computer Age* (Cambridge, Mass.: MIT Press, 1989).

Chadeau, Emmanuel. *De Blériot à Dassault: histoire de l'industrie aéronautique en France, 1900–1950* (Paris: Fayard, 1987).

Chanute, Octave. *Progress in Flying Machines* (New York: American Engineer and Railroad Journal, 1894).

Christienne, Charles, and Pierre Lissarague. *A History of French Military Aviation* (Washington, D.C.: Smithsonian Institution Press, 1986).

Civil Aeronautics Board. *Handbook of Airline Statistics* (Washington, D.C.: Civil Aeronautics Board, 1965).

Cochrane, Dorothy, Von Hardesty, and Russ Lee. *The Aviation Careers of Igor Sikorsky* (Seattle: University of Washington Press, 1989).

Coleman, Ted. *Jack Northrop and the Flying Wing* (New York: Paragon House, 1988).

Collin, Ferdinand. *Parmi les prècurseurs du ciel* (Paris: J. Peyronnet, 1943).

Constant, Edward W., II. *The Origins of the Turbojet Revolution* (Baltimore: Johns Hopkins University Press, 1980).

Coppens, Willy. *Flying in Flanders* (New York: Ace Books, 1971).

Corn, Joseph. *The Winged Gospel: America's Romance with Aviation, 1900–1950* (New York: Oxford University Press, 1983).

Craven, Wesley Frank, and James Lea Cate. *Men and Planes* (Chicago: University of Chicago Press, 1955).

Crouch, Tom D. *A Dream of Wings: Americans and the Airplane, 1875–1905* (New York: W. W. Norton, 1981).

Crouch, Tom D. *The Blériot XI: Story of a Classic Airplane* (Washington, D.C.: Smithsonian Institution Press, 1982).

Crouch, Tom D. *The Bishop's Boys: A Life of Wilbur and Orville Wright* (New York: W. W. Norton, 1989).

Crouch, Tom D., and Janet Bednarek, eds. *The Meaning of Flight in the 20th Century: Proceedings of the 1998 National Aerospace Conference* (Dayton, Ohio: Wright State University Press, 2000).

Daso, Dik. *Architects of American Air Supremacy: General Hap Arnold and Dr. Theodor von Kármán* (Maxwell Air Force Base, Ala.: Air University Press, 1997).

Davies, R. E. G. *A History of the World's Airlines* (London: Oxford University Press, 1964).

Davies, R. E. G. *Airlines of the United States since 1914* (London: Putnam, 1972).

Davies, R. E. G. *Rebels and Reformers of the Airways* (Washington, D.C.: Smithsonian Institution Press, 1987).

Davies, R. E. G. *Lufthansa: An Airline and Its Aircraft* (New York: Orion Books, 1991).

Davis, Burke. *The Billy Mitchell Affair* (New York: Random House, 1967).

Dean, Sir Maurice. *The Royal Air Force in Two World Wars* (London: Cassell, 1979).

Dear, I. C. B., ed. *The Oxford Companion to World War II* (New York: Oxford University Press, 1995).

Deidl, Hans D. *Stalin's Eagles: An Illustrated Study of the Soviet Aces of World War II and Korea* (Atglen, Penn.: Schiffer Military History, 1998).

Doolittle, James, with C. V. Glines, *I Could Never Be So Lucky Again* (New York: Bantam Books, 1991).

Douhet, Giulio. *Command of the Air*, transl. Dino Ferrari (Washington, D.C.: Office of Air Force History, 1983).

Dupree, A. Hunter. *Science in the Federal Government: A History of Policies and Activities to 1940* (Cambridge, Mass.: Harvard University Press, 1957).

Emme, Eugene, ed. *Two Hundred Years of Flight in America: A Bicentennial Survey* (San Diego: American Astronautical Society, 1977).

Fahey, James C. *U.S. Army Aircraft (Heavier-Than-Air), 1908–1946* (New York: Ships and Aircraft, 1946).

Faroux, C., and G. Bonnet. *Aéro-manuel: répertoire sportif technique et commerciale de aéronautique* (Paris: H. Dunod et E. Pinat, 1914).

Fenster, Herbert. *The $5 Billion Dollar Misunderstanding* (Annapolis, Md.: Naval Institute Press, 2001).

Finney, Robert T. *History of the Air Corps Tactical School, 1920–1940* (Washington, D.C.: Center for Air Force History, 1992).

First Equity Group. *Aviation and Aerospace Almanac, 2002* (New York: McGraw-Hill, 2002).

Fonck, René. *Ace of Aces* (Garden City, N.Y.: Doubleday, 1967).

Foxworth, Thomas G. *The Speed Seekers* (New York: Doubleday, 1974).

Francillon, René J. *Lockheed Aircraft since 1913* (London: Putnam, 1982).

Fredette, Raymond. *The Sky on Fire: The First Battle of Britain* (New York: Holt, Rinehart and Winston, 1966).

Freudenthal, Elsbeth E. *The Aviation Business: From Kitty Hawk to Wall Street* (New York: Vanguard Press, 1940).

Frisbee, John. *Makers of the United States Air Force* (Washington, D.C.: Office of Air Force History, 1987).

Fuller, G. A., J. A. Griffin, and K. M. Molson. *125 Years of Canadian Aeronautics, A Chronology, 1840–1965* (Willowdale, Ontario: Canadian Aviation Historical Society, 1963).

Fussell, Paul. *Thank God for the Atomic Bomb and Other Essays* (New York: Summit Books, 1985).

Futrell, Robert. *Ideas, Concepts, Doctrine: Basic Thinking in the United States Air Force, Vol. 2, 1961–1984* (Maxwell Air Force Base, Ala.: Air University Press, 1989).

Gandt, Robert L. *China Clipper: The Age of the Great Flying Boats* (Annapolis, Md.: Naval Institute Press, 1991).

Gann, Ernest K. *Ernest K. Gann's Flying Circus* (New York: Macmillan, 1974).

Geisse, John H. *Report to W. A. M. Burden on Postwar Outlook for Private Flying* (Washington, D.C.: n.p., 1944).

Gibbs-Smith, C. H. *Sir George Cayley's Aeronautics, 1796–1855* (London: HMSO, 1962).

Gibbs-Smith, C. H. *Aviation: An Historical Survey from Its Origins to the End of World War II* (London: HMSO, 1970).

Gibbs-Smith, C. H. *The Invention of the Airplane (1799–1909)* (London: Faber and Faber, 1965).

Gibbs-Smith, C. H. *The Rebirth of European Aviation* (London: HMSO, 1974).

Gilchrist, Peter. *Boeing 747* (London: Ian Allan, 1985).

Gollin, Alfred. *The Impact of Air Power on the British People and Their Government, 1909–1914* (Stanford, Calif.: Stanford University Press, 1989).

Gollin, Alfred. *No Longer an Island: Britain and the Wright Brothers, 1902–1909* (Stanford: Stanford University Press, 1984).

Gorn, Michael. *Harnessing the Genie: Science and Technology Forecasting for the Air Force, 1944–1986* (Washington, D.C.: Office of Air Force History, 1988).

Gorn, Michael. *Prophecy Fulfilled: "Toward New Horizons" and its Legacy* (Washington, D.C.: Air Force History and Museum Program, 1994).

Gorn, Michael H. *Expanding the Envelope: Flight Research at NACA and NASA* (Lexington: University of Kentucky Press, 2001).

Grahame-White, Claude. *The Aeroplane: Past, Present and Future* (London: T.W. Laurie, 1911).

Green, William. *Warplanes of the Third Reich* (Garden City, N.Y.: Doubleday, 1979).

Grey, C. G. *Bombers* (London: Faber and Faber, 1941).

Gunston, Bill. *Fedden: The Life of Sir Roy Fedden*, Historical Series no. 26 (Bristol, U.K.: Rolls Royce Heritage Trust, 1988).

Gunston, Bill. *F-4 Phantom* (New York: Charles Scribner's Sons, 1977).

Hall, James Norman. *High Adventure* (New York: Houghton Mifflin, 1918).

Hallion, Richard P. *Supersonic Flight: Breaking the Sound Barrier and Beyond* (New York: Macmillan, 1972).

Hallion, Richard P. *Legacy of Flight: The Guggenheim Contribution to American Aviation* (Seattle: University of Washington Press, 1977).

Hallion, Richard. *Test Pilots: The Frontiersmen of Flight* (Garden City, N.Y.: Doubleday, 1981).

Hallion, Richard P. *Designers and Test Pilots* (Alexandra, Va.: Time-Life Books, 1983).

Hallion, Richard P. *The Naval Air War in Korea* (Annapolis, Md.: Nautical and Aviation Publishing Company of America, 1986).

Hallion, Richard P. *Storm over Iraq: Air Power and the Gulf War* (Washington, D.C. Smithsonian Institution Press, 1992).

Hammond, Grant T. *The Mind of War: John Boyd and American Security* (Washington, D.C.: Smithsonian Institution Press, 2001).

Hansen, James R. *Engineer in Charge: A History of the Langley Aeronautical Laboratory, 1917–1958* (Washington, D.C.: National Aeronautics and Space Administration, 1987).

Hart, Clive. *Kites: An Historical Survey* (New York: Praeger, 1967).

Hart, Clive. *The Dream of Flight: Aeronautics from Classical Times to the Renaissance* (New York: Winchester Press, 1972).

Hart, Clive. *A Prehistory of Flight* (Berkeley: University of California Press, 1985).

Hartung, William D. *And Weapons for All* (New York: Harper Perennial, 1994).

Hastings, Max. *Bomber Command: The Myths and Reality of the Strategic Bombing Offensive 1939–1945* (New York: Dial Press, 1979).

Hatch, Alden. *Glenn Curtiss: Pioneer of Naval Aviation* (New York: Julian Messner, 1942).

Hayward, Charles B. *Practical Aeronautics: An Understandable Presentation of Interesting and Essential Facts in Aeronautical Science* (Chicago: American Technical Society, 1917).

Heppenheimer, T. A. *Turbulent Skies: The History of Commercial Aviation* (New York: John A. Wiley & Sons, 1995).

Herken, Gregg. *Counsels of War* (New York: Alfred A. Knopf, 1985).

Herzog, Chaim. *The War of Atonement, October 1973* (Boston: Little, Brown, 1975).

Higham, Robin. *Air Power: A Concise History* (New York: St. Martin's Press, 1972).

Higham, Robin, John T. Greenwood, and Von Hardesty, eds. *Russian Aviation and Air Power in the Twentieth Century* (London: Frank Cass, 1998).

Holley, I. B. *Buying Aircraft: Matériel Procurement for the Army Air Forces* (Washington, D.C.: Office of the Chief of Military History, 1966).

Holley, I. B. *Ideas and Weapons: Exploitation of the Aerial Weapon by the United States during World War I; A Study in the Relationship of Technological Advance, Military Doctrine, and the Development of Weapons* (Hamden, Conn.: Archon Books, 1971).

Horikoshi, Jiro. *Eagles of Mitsubishi: The Story of the Zero Fighter* (Seattle: University of Washington Press, 1970).

Horwitch, Mel. *Clipped Wings: The American SST Conflict* (Cambridge, Mass.: MIT Press, 1982).

Hudson, James J. *Hostile Skies: A History of the American Air Service in World War I* (Syracuse, N.Y.: Syracuse University Press, 1968).

Jablonski, Edward. *Atlantic Fever* (New York: Macmillan, 1972).

Jakab, Peter. *Visions of a Flying Machine: The Wright Brothers and the Process of Invention* (Washington, D.C.: Smithsonian Institution Press, 1990).

Jakab, Peter, and Rick Young. *The Published Writings of Wilbur and Orville Wright* (Washington, D.C.: Smithsonian Institution Press, 2000).

Johnson, Herbert. *Wingless Eagles: U.S. Army Aviation through World War I* (Chapel Hill: University of North Carolina Press, 2002).

Kelly, Fred C. *The Wright Brothers: A Biography Authorized by Orville Wright* (New York: Harcourt Brace, 1943).

Kelly, Fred C., ed., *Miracle at Kitty Hawk: The Letters of Wilbur and Orville Wright* (New York: Farrar, Strauss and Giroux, 1951).

Kelsey, Benjamin. *The Dragon's Teeth? The Creation of United States Air Power in World War II* (Washington, D.C.: Smithsonian Institution Press, 1982).

Kennett, Lee. *A History of Strategic Bombing* (New York: Charles Scribner's Sons (1982).

Kennett, Lee. *The First Air War, 1914–1919* (New York: Free Press, 1991).

Komons, Nick. *The Cutting Air Crash: A Case Study in Early Federal Aviation Policy* (Washington, D.C.: Department of Transportation, 1973).

Komons, Nick. *Bonfires to Beacons: Federal Civil Aviation Policy under the Air Commerce Act, 1926–1938* (Washington, D.C.: U.S. Department of Transportation, 1978).

Langley, S.P. *Experiments in Aerodynamics* (Washington, D.C: Smithsonian Institution, 1891).

Larkins, William T. *U.S. Naval Aircraft, 1921–1941* (New York: Orion Books, 1988).

Launius, Roger, ed. *Innovation and the Development of Flight* (College Station: Texas A&M University Press, 1999).

League of Nations. *Inquiries into the Economic Administration and Legal Situation of International Aerial Navigation* (Geneva: League of Nations, 1930).

Leary, William. *Aerial Pioneers: The U.S. Air Mail Service, 1918–1927* (Washington, D.C.: Smithsonian Institution Press, 1985).

Le Corbusier. *Aircraft* (1935; reprint, New York: Universe Books, 1988).

LeMay, Curtis E. *Mission with LeMay* (New York: Doubleday, 1965).

Lerner, Max. *America as Civilization* (New York: Simon and Schuster, 1957).

Lewis, Cecil. *Sagittarius Rising* (Harrisburg, Penn.: Stackpole Books, 1963).

Lincke, Jack. *Jenny Was No Lady* (New York: W.W. Norton, 1970).

Lindbergh, Charles. *The Spirit of St. Louis* (New York: Charles Scribner's Sons, 1953).

Lindbergh, Charles Augustus. *Autobiography of Values* (New York: Harcourt Brace Jovanovich, 1976).

Loening, Grover. *Our Wings Grow Faster* (New York: Doubleday, Doran, 1935).

Loening, Grover. *Takeoff into Greatness: How American Aviation Grew So Big So Fast* (New York: G. P. Putnam's Sons, 1968).

Loftin, Laurence K. *The Quest for Performance: The Evolution of Modern Aircraft, special publication 468* (Washington, D.C.: National Aeronautics and Space Administration, 1985).

Logsdon, John, ed. *Exploring the Unknown: Selected Documents in the History of the U.S. Space Program* (Washington, D.C.: NASA, 1995).

Maitland, Lester. *Knights of the Air* (Garden City, N.Y.: Doubleday, Doran, 1929).

Maitland, E. M. *The Log of H.M.A. R 34: Journey to America and Back* (London: Hodder and Stoughton, 1920).

Martin, Glenn L. *The Development of Aircraft Manufacture* (London: Royal Aeronautical Society, 1931).

Maurer, Maurer. *Aviation in the U.S. Army, 1919–1934* (Washington, D.C.: Office of Air Force History, 1987).

McCready, Lauren S. *The Invention and Development of the Gnome Rotary Engine.* Master's thesis, Polytechnic Institute of Brooklyn, 1973.

McCudden, James. *Flying Fury: Five Years in the Royal Flying Corps* (New York: Ace Books, 1968).

McDougall, Walter. *". . . The Heavens and the Earth": A Political History of the Space Age* (New York: Basic Books, 1985).

McFarland, Marvin W., ed. *The Papers of Wilbur and Orville Wright* (New York: McGraw-Hill, 1953).

McManus, John C. *Deadly Skies: The American Combat Airman in World War II* (Novato, Calif.: Presidio Press, 2000).

Means, James, ed. *The Aeronautical Annual* (Boston: W. E. Clark, 1895–1897).

Meillinger, Phillip S. *10 Propositions regarding Air Power* (Washington, D.C.: Air Force History and Museum Program, 1995).

Michener, James A. *The Bridges at Toko-Ri* (New York: Random House, 1953).

Middlebrook, Martin, and Chris Everitt. *The Bomber Command War Diaries* (London: Penguin Books, 1990).

Miller, Ivonette Wright. *Wright Reminiscences* (Dayton, Ohio: n.p., 1978).

Miller, Ronald, and David Sawer. *The Technical Development of Modern Aviation* (London: Routledge and Kegan Paul, 1968).

Mingos, Howard. *The Birth of an Industry* (New York: W. B. Conkey, 1930).

Mitchell, William. *Skyways* (Philadelphia: J. B. Lippincott, 1930).

Moolman, Valerie. *Women Aloft* (Alexandria, Va.: Time-Life Books, 1981).

Morrow, John. *The Great War in the Air: Military Aviation from 1909–1921* (Washington, D.C.: Smithsonian Institution, 1993).

Munson, Kenneth W. *Airliners since 1946* (New York: Macmillan, 1967).

Munson, Kenneth W. *Helicopters and Other Rotorcraft since 1907* (New York: Macmillan, 1968).

Munson, Kenneth W. *Flying Boats and Seaplanes since 1910* (New York: Macmillan, 1971).

Myer, Henry Cord. *Airshipmen, Businessmen and Politics, 1890–1940* (Washington, D.C.: Smithsonian Institution Press, 1991).

Nalty, Bernard C., ed. *Winged Shield, Winged Sword: A History of the United States Air Force* (Washington, D.C.: Air Force History and Museums Program, 1997).

Nalty, Bernard C., John F. Shiner, and George Watson, *With Courage: The U.S. Army Air Forces in World War II* (Washington, D.C.: Air Force History and Museums Program, 1994).

Nevin, David. *The Architects of Air Power* (Alexandria, Va.: Time-Life Books, 1981).

Newhouse, Anthony. *The Sporty Game: The High Risk Competitive Business of Making and Selling Commercial Airliners* (New York: Alfred A. Knopf, 1983).

Noble, David. *Forces of Production: A Social History of Industrial Automation* (New York: Alfred A. Knopf, 1984).

Norman, Aaron. *The Great Air War: The Men, the Planes, the Saga of Military Aviation, 1914–1918* (New York: Macmillan, 1968).

O'Neill, Paul. *Barnstormers & Speed Kings* (Alexandria, Va.: Time-Life Books, 1981).

Overy, Richard. *The Air War, 1939–1945* (New York: Stein and Day, 1980).

Ovington, Adelaide. *An Aviator's Wife* (New York: Dodd, Meade, 1920).

Parkin, J. H. *Bell and Baldwin, Their Development of Aerodromes and Hydro-dromes at Baddeck, Nova Scotia* (Toronto: University of Toronto Press, 1964).

Pattillo, Donald M. *Pushing the Envelope: The American Aircraft Industry* (Ann Arbor: University of Michigan Press, 1998).

Penrose, Harold. *British Aviation: The Pioneer Years, 1903–1914* (London: Putnam, 1967).

Penrose, Harold. *British Aviation: The Great War and the Armistice, 1915–1919* (London: Putnam, 1969).

Pisano, Dominick, Thomas J. Dietz, Joanne Gernstein, and Karl Schniede. *Legend, Memory and the Great War in the Air* (Seattle: University of Washington Press, 1992).

Poole, Robert W. and Viggo Butler. *Airline Deregulation: The Unfinished Revolution* (Los Angeles: Reason Public Policy Institute, 1998).

Powell, William J. *Black Aviator* (Washington, D.C.: Smithsonian Institution Press, 1994).

Prang, Gordon. *At Dawn We Slept: The Untold Story of Pearl Harbor* (New York: McGraw-Hill, 1981).

Prendergast, Curtis. *The First Aviators* (Alexandria, Va.: Time-Life Books, 1980).

Preston, Anthony. *Warships of the World* (London: Jane's, 1980).

Pritchard, J. Laurence. *Sir George Cayley: The Inventor of the Aeroplane* (New York: Horizon Press, 1962).

Rae, John. *Climb to Greatness: The American Aircraft Industry, 1920–1960* (Cambridge, Mass.: MIT Press, 1968).

Reynolds, Clark G. *The Carrier War* (Alexandria, Va.: Time-Life Books, 1982).

Rhodes, Richard. *Dark Star: The Making of the Hydrogen Bomb* (New York: Simon and Schuster, 1995).

Rich, Doris. *Queen Bess: Daredevil Aviator* (Washington, D.C.: Smithsonian Institution Press, 1993).

Robinson, Douglas. *Giants in the Sky: A History of the Rigid Airship* (Seattle: University of Washington Press, 1973).

Roland, Alex. *Model Research: The National Advisory Committee for Aeronautics, 1915–1958* (Washington, D.C.: U.S. Government Printing Office, 1985).

Roseberry C. R. *The Challenging Skies* (New York: Doubleday, 1966).

Roseberry, C. R. *Glenn Curtiss: Pioneer of Flight* (Garden City, N.Y.: Doubleday, 1972).

Rotch, A. L. *Benjamin Franklin and the First Balloons* (Worcester, Mass.: American Antiquarian Society, 1907).

Sabbagh, Karl. *Twentieth-Century Jet: The Making and Marketing of the Boeing 777* (New York: Charles Scribner's Sons, 1996).

Saint-Exupéry, Antoine de. *Airman's Odyssey* (New York: Harcourt, Brace, 1939).

Sampson, Anthony. *The Arms Bazaar* (New York: Viking, 1977).

Schaffer, Ronald. *Wings of Judgement: American Bombing in World War II* (New York: Oxford University Press, 1985).

Schatzberg, Eric. *Wings of Wood, Wings of Metal: Culture and Technical Choice in American Airplane Materials, 1914–1945* (Princeton: Princeton University Press, 1999).

Simonson, G. R., ed. *The History of the American Aviation Industry: An Anthology* (Cambridge, Mass.: MIT Press, 1968).

Smith, Richard K. *The Airships Akron and Macon: Flying Aircraft Carriers of the United States Navy* (Annapolis, Md.: Naval Institute Press, 1965).

Smith, Richard K. *First across: U.S. Navy's Transatlantic Flight of 1919* (Annapolis, Md.: Naval Institute Press, 1973).

Smith, Richard K. *The Weight Envelope: An Airplane's Fourth Dimension* (Self-published, 1985). Copy in the author's collection.

Spick, Mike. *Jet Fighter Performance: Korea to Vietnam* (London: Ian Allen, 1986).

Spick, Mike. *The Ace Factor* (New York: Avon Books, 1989).

Stevenson, James P. *The Pentagon Paradox: The Development of the F-18 Hornet* (Annapolis, Md.: Naval Institute Press, 1993).

Straubel, James. *Crusade for Air Power: The Story of the Air Force Association* (Washington, D.C.: Aerospace Education Foundation, 1982).

Swanborough, Gordon, and Peter M. Bowers, *United States Navy Aircraft since 1911* (Annapolis, Md.: Naval Institute Press, 1976).

Tallman, Frank. *Flying the Old Planes* (Garden City, N.Y.: Doubleday, 1973).

Taylor, John W., Michael J. W. Taylor, and David Mondey. *Air Facts and Feats* (Toronto: Bantam Books, 1977).

Terraine, John. *A Time for Courage: The Royal Air Force in the European War, 1939–1945* (New York: Macmillan, 1985).

Tillman, Barrett. *The Dauntless Dive Bomber of World War II* (Annapolis, Md.: Naval Institute Press, 1976).

Tillman, Stephen. *Man Unafraid: The Miracle of Military Aviation* (Washington, D.C.: Army Times, 1958).

Travers, Paul Joseph. *Eyewitness to Infamy: An Oral History of Pearl Harbor* (Lanham, Md.: Madison Books, 1991).

Trimble, William. *Wings for the Navy: A history of the Naval Aircraft Factory, 1917–1956* (Annapolis, Md.: Naval Institute Press, 1990).

Trimble, William. *Admiral William Moffett: Architect of Naval Aviation*

(Washington, D.C.: Smithsonian Institution Press, 1994).

Trimble, William, ed. *From Airships to Airbus: The History of Civil and Commercial Aviation* (Washington, D.C.: Smithsonian Institution Press, 1995).

Trycare, Tre. *The Lore of Flight* (Gothenburg, Sweden: Cagner, 1970).

Vaulx, Comte de la. *La triomphe de la navigation aerienne, aéroplanes, dirigeables, sphériques* (Paris: J. Tallandier, 1911).

Voisin, Gabriel. *Men, Women and Ten Thousand Kites* (London: Putnam, 1962).

United States Naval Aviation, 1910–1980 (Washington, D.C.: Naval Air Systems Command, 1981).

van der Linden, Robert. *The Boeing 247: The First Modern Airliner* (Seattle: University of Washington Press, 1991).

Vander Meulen, Jacob. *The Politics of Aircraft: Building an American Military Industry* (Manhattan: University of Kansas Press, 1991).

Vander Meulen, Jacob. *Building the B-29* (Washington, D.C.: Smithsonian Institution Press, 1995).

Villard, Henry Serrano. *Contact: The Story of the Early Birds* (New York: Bonanza Books, 1968).

Walker, Percy B. *Early Aviation at Farnborough: The First Aeroplanes* (London: Macdonald, 1974).

Wegg, John. *General Dynamics Aircraft and Their Predecessors* (Annapolis, Md.: Naval Institute Press, 1990).

Weick, Fred, and James Hanson. *From the Ground Up: The Autobiography of an Aeronautical Engineer* (Washington, D.C.: Smithsonian Institution Press, 1988).

Weinberg, Gerhard. *A World at Arms: A Global History of World War II* (Cambridge: Cambridge University Press, 1994).

Weiss, David. *The Saga of the Tin Goose* (New York: Crown, 1971).

Welch Pogue, L. *Airline Deregulation, before and after: What Next?* (Washington, D.C.: National Air and Space Museum, 1991).

Wells, H. G. *The War in the Air, and Particularly How Mr. Bert Smallways Faired While It Lasted* (London: G. Bell, 1908).

White, Lynn, Jr. *Medieval Technology and Social Change* (London: Oxford University Press, 1962).

Wohl, Robert. *A Passion for Wings: Aviation and the Western Imagination, 1908–1918* (New Haven, Conn.: Yale University Press, 1994).

Wolfe, Tom. *The Right Stuff* (New York: Farrar, Straus and Giroux, 1979).

Woodward, Jim. *Nazca: Journey to the Sun* (New York: Pocket Books, 1977).

Young, Warren R. *The Helicopters* (Alexandria, Va.: Time-Life Books, 1982).

CREDITS

Space Museum, Smithsonian Institution (SI 86-145). Page 292: National Air and Space Museum, Smithsonian Institution (SI 86-5927). Page 293: National Air and Space Museum, Smithsonian Institution (SI 85-19411). Page 318: courtesy Northrop Grumman Corporation. Page 321: National Air and Space Museum, Smithsonian Institution (SI 89-2215). Page 324: Courtesy Northrop Grumman Corporation. Page 325: National Air and Space Museum, Smithsonian Institution (SI 2000-1224). Page 326: National Air and Space Museum, Smithsonian Institution (SI 83-4050). Page 327: National Air and Space Museum, Smithsonian Institution (SI A-42344-E). Page 335: National Air and Space Museum, Smithsonian Institution (SI 83-9838). Page 349: National Air and Space Museum, Smithsonian Institution (SI 78-5520). Page 354: National Air and Space Museum, Smithsonian Institution (SI A-70013). Page 361: National Air and Space Museum (NASM 00172239), Smithsonian Institution. Page 363: National Air and Space Museum (NASM 00161209), Smithsonian Institution. Page 370: National Air and Space Museum, Smithsonian Institution (SI 76-2425). Page 374: Lufthansa, courtesy National Air and Space Museum, Smithsonian Institution (SI89-4061). Page 375: National Air and Space Museum, Smithsonian Institution (SI A-46938-G). Page 384: National Air and Space Museum, Smithsonian Institution (SI 90-9555). Page 386: U.S. Air Force, courtesy National Air and Space Museum, Smithsonian Institution (SI A-45869-D). Page 387: U.S. Air force, courtesy National Air and Space Museum (NASM 7B02286), Smithsonian Institution. Page 398: U.S. Navy, courtesy National Air and Space Museum (NASM 9A00174), Smithsonian Institution. Page 402: Courtesy DaimlerChrysler Page 407: U.S. Navy, courtesy National Air and Space Museum (85-7285), Smithsonian Institution. Page 415: U.S. Air Force, courtesy National Air and Space Museum, Smithsonian Institution (SI 85-10848). Page 423: U.S. Air Force, courtesy National Air and Space Museum, Smithsonian Institution (SI A-46594-F). Page 440: U.S. Air Force, courtesy National Air and Space Museum, Smithsonian Institution (SI 98-15407). Page 452: U.S. Air Force, courtesy National Air and Space Museum (USAF- B28715AC), Smithsonian Institution. Page 459: Courtesy of Bell Helicopter Textron; National Air and Space Museum (NASM 00008142), Smithsonian Institution. Page 461: National Air and Space Museum, Smithsonian Institution (SI 75-4846). Page 469: National Air and Space Museum, Smithsonian Institution (SI 92-706). Page 474: Photo by Sgt. Howard C. Breedlove (U.S. Army), National Air and Space Museum (9A00325), Smithsonian Institution. Page 479: National Air and Space Museum, Smithsonian Institution (SI81-3105). Page 495: copyright Boeing, used under license. Page 498: National Air and Space Museum, Smithsonian Institution (SI 77-5831). Page 531: Herbert Stephen Desind Collection, National Air and Space Museum (NASM 9A00295), Smithsonian Institution. Page 544: U.S. Air Force, courtesy National Air and Space Museum (USAF-68635AC), Smithsonian Institution. Page 548: U.S. Air Force, courtesy National Air and Space Museum (9A00365), Smithsonian Institution. Page 554: 146th Fighter Bomber Wing, California Air National Guard, courtesy National Air and Space Museum (NASM 00076512), Smithsonian Institution. Page 557: copyright Boeing, used under license. Page 559: copyright Boeing, used under license. Page 560: U.S. Navy, courtesy National Air and Space Museum (NASM 7A34272), Smithsonian Institution. Page 561: U.S. Air Force, courtesy National Air and Space Museum, Smithsonian Institution (SI 81-8673). Page 563: National Air and Space Museum (NASM 00076349), Smithsonian Institution. Page 569: copyright Dassault Aviation. Page 583: Photo by Eric Schulzinger and Denny Lombard, Lockheed Martin Corporation, courtesy Herbert S. Desind Collection, National Air and Space Museum (9A00648), Smithsonian Institution. Page 618: courtesy BAE Systems. Page 621: copyright Boeing, used under license. Page 627: Herbert Stephen Desind Collection, National Air and Space Museum (NASM 9A00360), Smithsonian Institution. Page 631: National Air and Space Museum (NASM 7A07341), Smithsonian Institution.

INDEX

Page numbers in *italics* refer to illustrations.